Considering the Patient in Pediatric Drug Development

How Good Intentions Turned Into Harm

Considering the Patient in Pediatric Drug Development

How Good Intentions Turned Into Harm

Klaus Rose
klausrose Consulting, Pediatric Drug Development and More,
Riehen, Switzerland

ELSEVIER
ACADEMIC PRESS
An imprint of Elsevier

Academic Press is an imprint of Elsevier
125 London Wall, London EC2Y 5AS, United Kingdom
525 B Street, Suite 1650, San Diego, CA 92101, United States
50 Hampshire Street, 5th Floor, Cambridge, MA 02139, United States
The Boulevard, Langford Lane, Kidlington, Oxford OX5 1GB, United Kingdom

Notices
Knowledge and best practice in this field are constantly changing. As new research and experience broaden our understanding, changes in research methods, professional practices, or medical treatment may become necessary.

Practitioners and researchers must always rely on their own experience and knowledge in evaluating and using any information, methods, compounds, or experiments described herein. In using such information or methods they should be mindful of their own safety and the safety of others, including parties for whom they have a professional responsibility.

To the fullest extent of the law, neither the Publisher nor the authors, contributors, or editors, assume any liability for any injury and/or damage to persons or property as a matter of products liability, negligence or otherwise, or from any use or operation of any methods, products, instructions, or ideas contained in the material herein.

British Library Cataloguing-in-Publication Data
A catalogue record for this book is available from the British Library

Library of Congress Cataloging-in-Publication Data
A catalog record for this book is available from the Library of Congress

ISBN: 978-0-12-823888-2

For Information on all Academic Press publications
visit our website at https://www.elsevier.com/books-and-journals

Publisher: Andre Gerhard Wolff
Acquisitions Editor: Erin Hill-Parks
Editorial Project Manager: Pat Gonzalez
Production Project Manager: Niranjan Bhaskaran
Cover Designer: Mark Rogers

Typeset by MPS Limited, Chennai, India

Contents

4.5 Diabetes

4.6 Allergies and allergen-specific immunotherapy (ASIT) in young patients

6.3 Extrapolation

6.4 Daily deceit in "pediatric" studies

6.5 Myths in today's medical world and "pediatric" studies

7. Juvenile animal studies 337

Foreword by Jane M. Grant-Kels

Klaus Rose is supremely well qualified to opine on the controversial issues and ethical quandaries surrounding clinical trials. Not only is he a physician but he has also worked in the pharmaceutical industry, was Global Head of Pediatrics for Novartis from 2001 to 2005 and then of Genentech/Roche from 2005 to 2009. Presently he works as an independent consultant in Riehen, Switzerland.

Clinical trials are obviously pivotal for demonstrating the efficacy and safety of new medications. The better blinded and controlled the study, the more significant the outcomes. However, ethical issues arise regarding the therapy offered to the control group. If the study involves a life threatening or life altering illness, the therapeutic offered the control group should be equal to what they would receive as standard of care.

The issues become even more complex when clinical trials involve children. There are several contentious issues.

1. What is the definition of a child vis-à-vis clinical trials? Obviously, infants and toddlers are not just small adults; they physiologically process and metabolize medications differently than adults. Efficacy, safety, and dosing studies are uniquely appropriate for this age group. However, at what age, metabolically, does a child process a medication the same as an adult? Adolescents, many of whom are physically as large as fully mature adults, do not need either proof of efficacy or safety/dosage studies separate from adults. Nonetheless, many so-called "pediatric" clinical trials accept patients who are in their late 10's or even early 20's. These studies usually have very few if any infants or toddlers. Are these studies a worthwhile and appropriate use of research funding? Do these studies rob patients who are less than 18 years of age of medications that have already been demonstrated to be effective in adults?
2. If a medication has been proven efficacious in adults, do you need proof of efficacy studies to be repeated in children? For very young children you may need safety and dosage studies only. Laws mandating these kinds of studies withhold standard of care medications from the young and result in a wastage of time and money.

Herein Dr. Rose will thoroughly review the complex and convoluted bureaucratic, legal, pharmaceutical, and academic history involved in this arena. More than anyone else, he has a grasp on the historical background and ethical implications of this politically and financially charged topic. This book should be required reading for all medical students, pharmaceutical executives, and health care bureaucrats.

Jane M. Grant-Kels, MD, FAAD
Professor of Dermatology, Pathology and Pediatrics
University of Connecticut Health Center
Founding Chair, Emeritus, UCONN Department of Dermatology
Vice Chair, UCONN Department of Dermatology
Founding Director of the UCONN Cutaneous Oncology Center and Melanoma Program
Founding Director Emeritus of the UCONN Dermatopathology Lab and UCONN Dermatology Residency, Farmington, Connecticut and
Adjunct Professor of Dermatology, Dermatology Dept,
University of Florida, Gainesville, Florida

July 20, 2020

Foreword by David Neubauer

I still remember when and where I first met Klaus Rose. This was at the scientific meeting, organized by professor Bounocore in Siena, Italy, in 2005. At that time Klaus was still quite "orthodoxly" and deeply involved in the phamaceutical industry, taking care of pediatric clinical development at Novartis, and just in that year he joined Roche where he established a focus for excellence in pediatric drug development. At that time I was the president of ethics working group at CESP, which later became the European Academy of Paediatrics (EAP), which is the pediatric section in European Union of Medical Specialists (UEMS), and in this position I was asked to give a talk on The development of European ethical guidance in pediatric research. At the end, Klaus approached me and asked if I would agree to write a chapter in his future book that he was preparing together with professor van den Anker, entitled *Guide to Paediatric Clinical Research*, later published by Karger in 2007. Klaus asked me to write something about the ethical challenges of clinical research in children with some critical view on protection from risks versus access to benefits. In that chapter we (Neubauer, Laitinen-Parkkonen, and Matthys) concluded that "it is in the interest of children to evaluate medicinal products with scientifically proven methods, possibly by pediatric placebo-controlled trials, which should only be justified when their design, enrollment and conduct ensure that they really address the best interests of children-participants with a view to their health and a concern of their dignity." After the book was published, Klaus thanked me for the contribution and for a long time we did not see each other. In October 2017 EAP organized a congress and master course in Ljubljana, Slovenia, and during a coffee break I suddenly saw Klaus sitting there. He approached me and greeted and told me in a few minutes his recent history: now he was independent and had established klausrose consulting. His main preoccupation now is to convince pediatricians and others involved in drug development for children that there are too many unnecessary dogmas in this field that actually harm children as they have to wait, due to the EU pediatric regulations, to accomplish the studies appropriate for their age to get the proper and right treatment (which is, unfortunately for many crtically ill children, too late). And also, he added, the "therapeutic orphans concept" and "children are not small adults" mantras are actually flawed and that they just produce a "blur at the interface of law and medicine," as he vividly described the present situation. I was at first astonished, but soon he completely convinced me, and I had to fully agree with him that this is the time when US and EU pediatric legislation needs a thorough revision and that pediatricians shouldn't stand aside and should establish drug development as a fixed topic at their annual meetings. Since my presidency in the ethics working group at EAP was to finish that year, I asked him to give a talk on this issue in December in Brussels at the ethics working group meeting of EAP, but many of the European pediatricians did not agree with these proposals (not surprisingly, I should comment), and approximately the same happened next year when Klaus had a talk at the Slovenian Paediatric Congress in Portorose, Slovenia. Anyhow, I do support him and try to contribute by raising the awareness of the pediatric community and other healthcare professionals that the time has come to change the mantras, as Klaus has coined them, and to modernize the process of drug development. How to do it is perfectly described in this book in which each chapter is written separately and can be read alone, and every pediatric subspeciality will find enough arguments to change the present opinion on this topic. And I am sure that this will happen undoubtedly some day in the future, and this will really be in the best interests of our children-patients.

Professor David Neubauer, MD, PhD
Department of Child, Adolescent & Developmental Neurology,
University Childrens' Hospital, Ljubljana, Slovenia

Rumpelstiltskin and the miller's daughter

The cover shows an attractive young woman at a spinning wheel. Her father, a miller, has told the king she could spin straw into gold. The king will marry her if she produces gold over three nights. Now she reflects what to do. Suddenly, an imp offers help in exchange for her first child. She agrees; the gold is produced, she marries, and the imp demands her first child. He gives her three days to guess his name, or he will take the baby. In despair she walks around and watches him, unseen, in the forest as he hops around a fire. "The queen will never win the game, for Rumpelstiltskin is my name." When she says his name the next day, the spell is broken. Enraged, he drives a foot into the ground up to his waist, seizes the other foot with both hands, tears himself up, and is gone.

There are two reasons for this cover. We see a young woman. In regulatory logic, she would be a "child" if under 18 years old. But bodily, she is already a young woman. Secondly, the imp's power depends on his secret name. Comparably, "pediatric drug development" sounds reasonable until we ask what the term "child" means. Somebody who is *administratively* still a child but *bodily* mature should receive adult treatment. The justifications of "pediatric drug development" collapse when we ask what the term "child" means. Many "pediatric" studies are performed in *administratively* defined children that are *bodily* already mature. Children do not remain newborn until they come of age.

Conclusion and outlook

Introduction

This book describes an ongoing medical disaster that, worldwide, harms daily thousands of young patients with serious and lethal diseases, denies them effective therapy, and/or exposes them to outdated standard-of-care therapy. It began with the flawed concept of children as "therapeutic orphans" in 1968 [1], that emerged in the wake of the thalidomide disaster [2–4]. The flawed concept of children as "therapeutic orphans" extrapolates real dangers of effective antibiotics in preterm neonates, term neonates, and small babies into alleged dangers of modern medicines in all young persons that are administratively and/or legally defined as "children" [5–8]. It started as a semantic blur at the interface of medicine and law. Once codified for the first time in US law, it led to massive conflicts of interest that keep it alive and ongoing, the more so when the EU adopted and expanded it [5–9].

It is not the first medical disaster in modern history, and it will not be the last one. Evil and smoke share the capability to always find new ways when their old ways are blocked. Evil has banal sides because it is often based on very basic human and humane instincts. In this regard, there are many parallels to other medical disasters in history. But there are also new characteristics of the abuse of young persons in allegedly scientific clinical research.

Some medical disasters occurred in secret. The criminal medical twin studies performed by Mengele in Nazi concentration camps were not openly discussed in the Nazi daily press, and the Nazis knew that their exposure to the public would not withstand the negative feedback from ordinary German persons, and that the free world would condemn them [10]. Also, Japanese unit 731, which performed criminal experiments during World War II, did not publish in the daily press [11]. The Tuskegee study on illiterate African American men that suffered from syphilis was performed in rural Alabama [12]. These patients were left untreated even when the efficacy of antibiotics in the treatment of syphilis had become common knowledge [13]. This study provided staff of the US Public Health Service with the opportunity to participate at the obduction of deceased patients [14]. Employees in the US Public Health Service enjoyed a safe job and a high reputation. The motivation to reject during seven years internal requests for the Tuskegee study to be terminated was unbelievably banal [13]. The study was reported and discussed at annual meetings of the American Medical Association (AMA) [15], but at a time when black physicians were not yet allowed to participate in such meetings [14]. The Tuskegee study was only terminated when it was critically reported in a US newspaper and produced a public uproar [11,16]. The thalidomide disaster simmered below the surface of public perception for three years because nobody, apart from the parents of babies with malformations, could imagine the dimension of this new catastrophe. Only when one courageous physician decided to interview twenty affected mothers, including the inspection of their homes and their medicine chests, concluded that thalidomide caused these malformations, reported this at a conference in Germany, and a major newspaper published a first report nationwide, the sales of thalidomide were terminated and it was removed from all pharmacies in Germany. Eventually, it was withdrawn worldwide [2–4]. Today, it is FDA-approved for multiple myeloma and leprosy [17]. The story of how this occurred is another story; see Chapter 6 on the on-label/off-label framework in adult and young patients.

In contrast to disasters and atrocities of the past, the questionable and harmful "pediatric" studies discussed in this book are performed worldwide in medical institutions that are committed to the highest standards of ethics as codified, for example, in the declaration of Helsinki [18]. They are listed in publicly accessible registries such as www.clinicaltrials.gov, are published in medical and scientific journals that follow the recommendations of the International Committee of Medical Journal Editors [19], are supported by leading experts in developmental pharmacology [20], by representatives of the US and EU regulatory authorities [20–22], are demanded by US and EU laws [9], and are accepted study by study by Institutional Review Boards (IRBs)/ ethics committees (ECs). They are based on a blind spot of today's society, which enjoys the highest level of medical care that has ever existed in history, and has access to the best drugs in the history of medicine and mankind. The general public trust in science and authorities is high.

However, this trust is silently and slowly eroding in regard to clinical studies with young patients. Clinicians from various clinical disciplines report that parents have become less willing to let their loved ones participate in clinical studies [23,24].

FDA- and EMA-demanded "pediatric" studies already now block recruitment of patients into really promising new therapies by demanding studies for existing drugs until 2034. The EU "pediatric investigation plan" (PIP) EMEA-002440-PIP01-18 demands "pediatric" studies with the antiviral baloxavir against human immunodeficiency virus (HIV) until 2029; see Chapter 4-J, Table 4.7. The PIPs EMEA-002191-PIP02-17 [Ivacaftor + tezacaftor + VX-659] and EMEA-002324-PIP01-17 [elexacaftor + tezacaftor + ivacaftor] for cystic fibrosis demand "pediatric" studies until 2029; see Chapter 4-J, Table 4.2. Studies demanded by PIP EMEA-002360-PIP01-18 for tirzepatide in diabetes would have to run until 2030; see Chapter 4-E, Table 4.3. The FDA demands a brodalumab open label single arm safety and efficacy study in patients 6–11 years of age with severe plaque psoriasis to be reported until 2029 [25]; see Chapter 4-I, Table 4.1. The FDA-demanded "pediatric" study for ozanimod against multiple sclerosis would have to run until 2034 [26]; see Chapter 4-H, Table 4.1.

This is probably the most fundamental challenge of medicine in the 21st century (for now), reflecting how in our modern Western society, myths, misunderstandings, and wrong beliefs have silently invaded scientific thinking, official positions of regulatory authorities, and guidelines of industrial drug development. The only ones that hesitate, guided by their gut feeling, are parents and some clinicians that have started to question a concept that demands double-blind randomized regulatory studies in young patients for every single new effective drug [8,23,24,27–30].

Clinical challenge

On the cover of this book is a young woman. The spinning wheel and her clothes indicate that she does not live in modern times. It is the miller's daughter whose father had told the king that she could spin straw into gold. The king promises to marry her if she can deliver gold for three nights. In the days of these fairy tails, women were often married young, and they had little say in whom they wanted to marry. The picture shows her during the first night when she is reflecting how to achieve the impossible. Rumpelstiltskin, a powerful sorcerer, had just entering her room. If she was under 18 years old, she would be still a child in regulatory logic. Should she have a sport injury to her knee, the FDA and the EMA would not want her to be treated surgically with tissue-engineered autologous chondrocyte products, e.g., matrix-applied characterized autologous cultured chondrocytes, because she is not yet an adult [31]. Study NCT03588975 is currently recruiting young persons into a prospective study of matrix-applied characterized autologous cultured chondrocytes against microfracture in symptomatic chondral or osteochondral defects of the knee; see Table 4.2, Chapter 4-C. Several PIPs demand surgical "pediatric" studies in young persons between the closure of the growth plates, which defines the end of the bodily process of puberty [32–35], and their 18th birthday; see Table 4.1, Chapter 4-C. Should the miller's daughter have a pelvic inflammatory disease, she could participate in a "pediatric" moxifloxacin study demanded by PIP EMEA-000492-PIP01-08-M01 in young women aged 12 to 17 years of age. Should she, after the birth of her first child, become depressive, she could participate in the ongoing brexanolone study NCT03665038, a "pediatric" multicenter open label safety, tolerability, and pharmacokinetics study in young women with postpartum depression aged 15 to 17 years; see Chapter 4-B, Table 4.1. Or she might be recruited into a "pediatric" allopregnanolone study demanded by PIP EMEA-002051-PIP02-16 in "postpubertal girls"; see Chapter 4-B, Table 4.4. One demanded allopregnanolone study is a double-blind, randomized, placebo-controlled pharmacokinetics, safety, tolerability, and efficacy study in "postpubertal adolescent girls" with postpartum depression, the other one a modeling and simulation study to support the use of intravenous use of allopregnanolone in "postpubertal adolescent girls" with postpartum depression. Thus, there are several ongoing "pediatric" clinical studies for the miller's daughter, and more studies demanded by PIPs that might be opened in the near future. These allegedly "pediatric" studies would welcome the miller's daughter and any other young woman younger than 18 years of age. But the 18th birthday is a legal and administrative age limit. Medicine should not consider the legal status of a patient, but the physically present patient and his/her body.

The entire movement of "pediatric drug development" is based on the semantic blur that classifies young persons as "children" before their 17th/18th birthday. Drugs are often approved in adults, but not in administratively defined "children." Developmental pharmacology can measure the degree of the matureness of the absorption, distribution, metabolism and excretion (ADME) of food and drugs [36]. But leading representatives of developmental pharmacology have developed a material interest to demand "pediatric" studies despite these learnings, alongside with representatives from the FDA [20]. Comparable demands for "pediatric" studies are expressed by European clinicians alongside with representatives from the EMA [37–41]. Further publications that support "pediatric drug development" are published by representatives of the pharmaceutical industry, some of them alongside with representatives from regulatory authorities [42–45].

The tragedy of "pediatric drug development" is not only that it abuses young patients in mostly senseless "pediatric" studies. For decades, it gives pediatric medical research the wrong focus. This is tragic because most young researchers are enthusiastic and full of good intentions. This enthusiasm could be used much better. We have already many effective antiepileptic drugs. Until recently, the focus of pediatric research was to get "pediatric" approval for more antiepileptic drugs, based on the performance of senseless additional regulatory "pediatric" studies. Epilepsy is the one clinical area where objections from the clinical community have led the FDA to lower the age limit of "extrapolation" of efficacy down to two years for partial onset seizures, the most frequent type of epilepsy [46], and the EMA for the moment to down to four years [47]. The aim to get more "pediatric" labels for more and more antiepileptic drugs is vain. Parents with children that suffer from epilepsy should be helped to raise their children over two and more decades, and to continue this support when they are physically adult. There are initiatives to help these parents, but too few [47]. Instead, resources have been wasted for more "pediatric" labels, in drugs where today the FDA and the EMA accept that they are effective in "children" as well [8,27–30].

Economic damage

The exclusion of young patients from effective medicines is bad enough on its own, as discussed for the miller's daughter and the senseless "pediatric" studies she might be recruited into. The EU and its EMA demand PIPs for old and new tissue-engineered products and for allergen products for allergen specific immunotherapy (ASIT). There are many small- and medium-sized companies in Europe that produce and develop modern three-dimensional chondrocyte neotissue to accelerate surgical repair of knee injuries and other joint injuries, and for other tissue repair including tissue-engineered autologous oral mucosa graft for urethral reconstruction [48–56]. Companies would like to introduce recombinant safer types of allergen products for ASIT. All companies that want to introduce a compound that is classified as a drug, including tissue-engineered products, have to submit a PIP that demands "pediatric" studies that are as senseless as the examples given for the miller's daughter above. In children, there are virtually hundreds of examples where tissue engineering can help to reduce damage by accidents, congenital malformations, and other challenges [48,57,58]. The many "pediatric" studies demanded by the EMA for allergen products for ASIT will probably never start [59]. But the EMA demand for these studies continues. It blocks companies from thinking about the introduction of new allergen products for ASIT, including recombinant products, that might be more efficient and safer. As long as companies are aware that they would have to commit to more questionable "pediatric" studies, they invest their resources into other areas, go bankrupt, or have to merge with the competition. The EMA's "pediatric drug development" is successfully blocking the economic development of many companies. In 2000, EU leaders committed the EU to become by 2010 "the most dynamic and competitive knowledge-based economy in the world capable of sustainable economic growth with more and better jobs and greater social cohesion, and respect for the environment," altogether still known as the "Lisbon strategy" [60]. Unfortunately, the opposite is taking place. The EMA and a flawed concept in drug development have become an obstacle for entire industry branches. They threaten and destroy jobs, block a competitive role of Europe in the worldwide competition for better medical treatment of those patients who can afford to go the best available medical centers, and contribute to further erode the public trust in science and authorities. Many citizens have the gut feeling that something is wrong. They vote for nationalistic and/or populistic parties that promise the blue out of the sky for politics that would make things even worse. To improve things really, we must get politicians and institutions out of their comfort zone into a direction that indeed creates better jobs and brings back the original positive vision and spirit that led to the Lisbon strategy.

Legal challenges

Many young patients are harmed in "pediatric" studies by omission, exposing them to no treatment at all in placebo groups, or to substandard comparison [5–8]. There will never be criminal proceedings for these harms, as the regulatory authorities follow the letter of the law. But the law also forbids to harm patients. When there are contradictory aims in the laws, earlier or later judges will have to decide who has to pay for damages. This is not the criminal law, but civil law. It is a question of time until US-based lawyers will start to sue medical centers, clinical research organizations, and pharmaceutical companies in damage lawsuits for the harm that was and is done to young persons in "pediatric" clinical studies.

Public health

The aim of medical research is not to have as many "pediatric" labels as possible. Instead, it *should* be to help young patients with serious medical challenges. Instead, resources and funds are wasted for questionable regulatory studies. PIPs and FDA "pediatric" demands block recruitment of patients for the next 10 to 15 years from reasonable clinical studies by demanding "pediatric" studies for drugs that exist already today and are already effective today also in young patients. The additional "pediatric" studies do nothing but repeat proof of efficacy in young patients.

Trust in science and authorities

Clinical studies help to differentiate between treatments that help and those that have no effect at all. In this regard, clinical studies go beyond the individual hands-on experiences of individual medical doctors in bedside treatment. But clinical studies have also their limitations. They construct an artificial framework with carefully selected patients to proof drug efficacy for regulatory purposes. While this framework works well in general drug development, most "pediatric" clinical studies lack medical sense because they define the participating patients by artificial inclusion criteria. Pharmaceutical companies have shifted toward often including adults and younger patients into their pivotal clinical studies, which is reasonable and more accepted by the FDA. The pivotal studies for crisaborol, a topical nonsteroidal cream against atopic dermatitis, were performed in patients aged 2 to 79 years of age [61].

Already today, parents are increasingly hesitant to allow participation of their children in "pediatric" studies. This is good on one side, as it shows that the parents have often more and better common sense than the academic researchers. On the other side, Emily Whitehead would today be dead if her parents would not have opted for her participation in a cutting-edge advanced clinical study [62,63].

Leading top level scientific journals have failed to detect the challenge of "pediatric drug development." Instead, they contribute to illusion. An editorial in *The Lancet Child & Adolescent Health* 2018 reported about the International Childhood Cancer Day. It claimed that "adolescents are often treated using off-label drugs, licensed for adults only, without full dosing knowledge" [64]. Bodily, adolescents are already mature. They do not need additional dosing knowledge. Instead, they need access to modern anticancer treatment in adult doses. Separate regulatory studies in adolescents result in roughly 95% of drugs with the same recommended dose as in adults [65]. A study with the same question specifically for modern anticancer therapies came to the same conclusions [66]. However, both papers failed to draw the conclusion that adolescents are bodily mature young humans who do not need separate "pediatric" studies.

The place of children in our heart

Most common diseases in children can today be prevented or treated also with the help of modern medicine. But the old-fashioned family structures are gradually disappearing. Not always are grandparents at hand who have gone through the process of child rearing themselves. Children, their well-being, and their healthcare are one of the few themes that still move our heart. The disappointment about the deception of "pediatric drug development" will be a major challenge and a major chance to correct a machinery that has become a point of self-service for institutions that had high merits in the past but have limited merits today. Young individuals that start working in such institutions begin with the best intentions, but when they make a career within these institution, they gradually adapt to fundamental flawed concepts and eventually follow.

No conspiracy

A conspiracy could be handled easily. At present, investigative journalists are proud when they can reveal hidden activities of wealthy individuals and public officials that are used for illegal purposes, including fraud, tax evasion, and evading international sanctions [67]. Pediatric drug development is a new type of challenge. It is not a conspiracy, although a close look at EMA pediatric reports shows that the wording is so misleading that a decoding is necessary to understand their true meanings. When the EMA claims that drugs are now "available" for "children" it does not literally mean that the drugs are now available. It means that now they have an EU "pediatric" label [68]. Nevertheless, this challenge goes deeper. It cannot be resolved by finding a few scapegoats and chasing them out into the desert [69]. "Pediatric drug development" is a concept that has invaded academic science, regulatory authorities, pharmaceutical industry and commercial clinical trials organizations over more than two decades. To correct wrong ideas in persons' and peoples' heads and hearts is challenging.

Discussion

There have been attempts to challenge the concept of "pediatric drug development" intellectually. Boots et al. noted that pediatric laws only focused on those drugs that were developed for the adult population [70]. Kreeftsmeijer et al. looked for the impact of the EU pediatric regulation on the approval of drugs for rare diseases [71]. Adamson et al. analyzed the unintended consequences of US and EU pediatric legislation [72]. They all identified weak points, but they failed to identify and resolve the core challenges.

Outlook

At the end, the US and EU pediatric laws will have to be changed by the lawmakers. The way toward this change is not clear at present. Civil society has many mechanisms that *would* and *should* be able to act once a danger for patients in clinical research is recognized. The challenge of "pediatric drug development" has remained under the radar of most groups, structures, and mechanisms that *should* protect patients. But apart from the long-term vision to change US and EU pediatric legislation, there are many operational steps that can and should be done.

This book discusses a relevant part of clinical areas, but not all of them. Academic centers *should* now start to verify the analyses outlined in the book and to investigate and analyze in depth more clinical areas. Hopefully, their conclusions will confirm the conclusions outlined here and will not stop where earlier analyses came to incomplete results [70–72].

IRBs and ECs *should* undergo urgent training in regulatory affairs to differentiate between reasonable and unreasonable "pediatric" clinical studies. They *should* suspend ongoing questionable "pediatric" studies and reject newly submitted ones.

The International Committee of Medical Journal Editors (ICMJE) should expand its recommendations for the publication of clinical studies and recommend to carefully analyze the medical sense and/or the lack of medical sense of submitted "pediatric" studies [18].

Leading journals like *Science*, *Nature*, *The Lancet*, the *British Medical Journal*, and others should start to accept critical papers that analyze in-depth questionable "pediatric" studies that have been performed and continue being performed worldwide.

References

[1] Shirkey H. Therapeutic orphans. J Pediatr 1968;72(1):119–20. Available from: https://pdfs.semanticscholar.org/f1cb/acdbac19fa56236b919fb7799eaacaa10c77.pdf.

[2] Vargesson N. Thalidomide-induced teratogenesis: history and mechanisms. Birth Defects Res C Embryo Today 2015;105(2):140–56. Available from: https://www.ncbi.nlm.nih.gov/pmc/articles/PMC4737249/.

[3] Ridings JE. The thalidomide disaster, lessons from the past. Methods Mol Biol 2013;947:575–86.

[4] Thomann KD. Die contergan-katastrophe. DÄ 2007;104(41):A2778–82. Available from: https://www.aerzteblatt.de/pdf.asp?id = 57224.

[5] Rose K, Neubauer D, Grant-Kels JM. Rational use of medicine in children – the conflict of interests story. A review. Rambam Maimonides Med J 2019;10(3):e0018. Available from: https://doi.org/10.5041/RMMJ.10371 Review. https://www.rmmj.org.il/userimages/928/2/PublishFiles/953Article.pdf.

[6] Rose K, Grant-Kels JM. The meanings of "pediatric drug development". A review. Ther Innov Regul Sci 2019;53(6):767–74 Dec.

[7] Rose K. The challenges of pediatric drug development. Curr Ther Res Clin Exp 2019;. Available from: https://doi.org/10.1016/j.curtheres.2019.01.007.

[8] Rose K, Neubauer D, Grant-Kels JM. Ethical issues in pediatric regulatory studies involving placebo treatment. J Pediatr Epilepsy 2020; (in press).

[9] Hirschfeld S, Saint-Raymond A. Pediatric regulatory initiatives. Handb Exp Pharmacol 2011;205:245–68.

[10] Mozes-Kor E. The mengele twins and human experimentation. In: Annas G, Grodin M, editors. The Nazi Doctors and the Nuremberg Code. New York, NY, USA: Oxford University Press; 1992.

[11] Hickey D, Li SS, Morrison C, et al. Unit 731 and moral repair. J Med Ethics 2017;43 (4):270–6.

[12] The Tuskegee Syphilis Study. https://de.wikipedia.org/wiki/Tuskegee-Syphilis-Studie.

[13] Peter Buxtun Wikpediai. https://en.wikipedia.org/wiki/Peter_Buxtun.

[14] Harriet A. Washington. Medical Apartheid: The Dark History of Medical Experimentation on Black Americans from Colonial Times to the Present. New York, USA: Anchor Books; 2008.

[15] American Medical Association. https://www.ama-assn.org/.

[16] Adashi EY, Walters LB, Menikoff JA. The belmont report at 40: reckoning with time. Am J Public Health 2018;108(10):1345–8.

[17] FDA 2014. Thalidomide Label. https://www.accessdata.fda.gov/drugsatfda_docs/label/2014/020785s055lbl.pdf.

[18] World Medical Association (WMA) Declaration of Helsinki – Ethical Principles for Medical Research Involving Human Subjects. Adopted by the 18th WMA General Assembly, Helsinki, Finland, June 1964, and amended by the 64th WMA General Assembly, Fortaleza, Brazil, October 2013. https://www.wma.net/policies-post/wma-declaration-of-helsinki-ethical-principles-for-medical-research-involving-human-subjects/.

[19] International Committee of Medical Journal Editors (ICMJE) Recommendations for the Conduct, Reporting, Editing, and Publication of Scholarly work in Medical Journals. http://www.icmje.org/recommendations/.

[20] Ward RM, Benjamin Jr DK, Davis JM, et al. The need for pediatric drug development. J Pediatr 2018;192:13–21.

[21] Tomasi PA, Egger GF, Pallidis C, et al. Enabling development of paediatric medicines in Europe: 10 years of the EU paediatric regulation. Pediatr Drugs 2017;19:505–13.

[22] Rocchi F, Paolucci P, Ceci A, et al. The European paediatric legislation: benefits and perspectives. Ital J Pediatr 2010;36:56. Available from: https://www.ncbi.nlm.nih.gov/pmc/articles/PMC2933611/pdf/1824-7288-36-56.pdf.

[23] Waubant E, Banwell B, Wassmer E, Sormani MP, Amato MP, Hintzen R, et al. Clinical trials of disease-modifying agents in pediatric MS: opportunities, challenges, and recommendations from the IPMSSG. Neurology. 2019;.

[24] Auvin S, French J, Dlugos D, et al. Novel study design to assess the efficacy and tolerability of antiseizure medications for focal-onset seizures in infants and young children: a consensus document from the regulatory task force and the pediatric commission of the

International League against Epilepsy (ILAE), in collaboration with the Pediatric Epilepsy Research Consortium (PERC). Epilepsia Open 2019;4(4):537–43. Available from: https://www.ncbi.nlm.nih.gov/pmc/articles/PMC6885693/pdf/EPI4-4-0.pdf.

[25] FDA 2017. Brodalumab approval letter. https://www.accessdata.fda.gov/drugsatfda_docs/nda/2017/761032Orig1s000Approv.pdf.

[26] FDA 2020. Ozanimod (zeposia) approval package including approval letter. https://www.accessdata.fda.gov/drugsatfda_docs/nda/2020/209899Orig1s000Approv.pdf.

[27] Pellock JM, Carman WJ, Thyagarajan V, Daniels T, Morris DL, D'Cruz O. Efficacy of antiepileptic drugs in adults predicts efficacy in children: a systematic review. Neurology. 2012;79(14):1482–9. Available from: https://www.ncbi.nlm.nih.gov/pmc/articles/PMC4098824/pdf/znl1482.pdf.

[28] Pellock JM, Arzimanoglu A, D'Cruz O, et al. Extrapolating evidence of antiepileptic drug efficacy in adults to children ≥2 years of age with focal seizures: the case for disease similarity. Epilepsia. 2017;58(10):1686–96. Available from: https://onlinelibrary.wiley.com/doi/epdf/10.1111/epi.13859.

[29] Arzimanoglou A, D'Cruz O, Nordli D, et al. A review of the new antiepileptic drugs for focal-onset seizures in pediatrics: role of extrapolation. Paediatr Drugs 2018;20(3):249–64. Available from: https://doi.org/10.1007/s40272-018-0286-0.

[30] Wadsworth I, Jaki T, Sills GJ, et al. Clinical drug development in epilepsy revisited: a proposal for a new paradigm streamlined using extrapolation. CNS Drugs 2016;30(11):1011–17. Available from: https://www.ncbi.nlm.nih.gov/pmc/articles/PMC5078157/pdf/40263_2016_Article_383.pdf.

[31] FDA 2016. MACI label. https://www.fda.gov/media/101914/download.

[32] Khan L. Puberty: onset and progression. Pediatr Ann 2019;48(4):e141–5.

[33] Abreu AP, Kaiser UB. Pubertal development and regulation. Lancet Diabetes Endocrinol 2016;4(3):254–64.

[34] Snyder CK. Puberty: an overview for pediatric nurses. J Pediatr Nurs 2016;31(6):757–9.

[35] Wood CL, Lane LC, Cheetham T. Puberty: normal physiology (brief overview). Best Pract Res Clin Endocrinol Metab 2019;33(3):101265.

[36] Kearns GL, Abdel-Rahman SM, Alander SW, Blowey DL, Leeder JS, Kauffman RE. Developmental pharmacology - drug disposition, action, and therapy in infants and children. N Engl J Med 2003;349(12):1157–67. Available from: https://pdfs.semanticscholar.org/55f8/1745303e9aaec7f4cb85f0b5921eec14a9c0.pdf.

[37] Kelly LE, Davies EH, Saint-Raymond A, et al. Important issues in the justification of a control treatment in paediatric drug trials. Arch Dis Child 2016;.

[38] van Riet-Nales DA, Römkens EG, Saint-Raymond A, Kozarewicz P, Schobben AF, Egberts TC, et al. Oral medicines for children in the European paediatric investigation plans. PLoS One 2014;9(6):e98348.

[39] Herold R, Saint-Raymond A, Norga K. Too few medicines for children with cancer. JAMA Pediatr 2014;168(6):583.

[40] Ruperto N, Vesely R, Saint-Raymond A, et al. Impact of the European paediatric legislation in paediatric rheumatology: past, present and future. Ann Rheum Dis 2013;72(12):1893–6.

[41] Ruperto N, Eichler I, Herold R, et al. A European Network of Paediatric Research at the European Medicines Agency (Enpr-EMA). Arch Dis Child 2012;97(3):185–8.

[42] McCune S, Portman R. Innovation and opportunities in pediatric therapeutic development. Ther Innov Regul Sci 2019;53(5):564–6.

[43] Mulberg AE, Bucci-Rechtweg C, Giuliano J, et al. Regulatory strategies for rare diseases under current global regulatory statutes: a discussion with stakeholders. Orphanet J Rare Dis 2019;14(1):36. Available from: https://ojrd.biomedcentral.com/track/pdf/10.1186/s13023-019-1017-5.

[44] Bucci-Rechtweg CM, Ward RM. Tiny and forgotten: a call for focused neonatal policy reform. Ther Innov Regul Sci 2019;53(5):615–17. Available from: https://doi.org/10.1177/2168479018821922.

[45] Bucci-Rechtsweg C. Enhancing the pediatric drug development framework to deliver better pediatric therapies tomorrow. Clin Ther 2017;39(10):1920–32.

[46] FDA 2019. Drugs for treatment of partial onset seizures: full extrapolation of efficacy from adults to pediatric patients 2 years of age and olderguidance for industry. https://www.fda.gov/media/130449/download.

[47] EMA 2018. Guideline on clinical investigation of medicinal products in the treatment of epileptic disorders. https://www.ema.europa.eu/en/documents/scientific-guideline/draft-guideline-clinical-investigation-medicinal-products-treatment-epileptic-disorders-revision-3_en.pdf.

[48] Ram-Liebig G, Bednarz J, Stuerzebecher B, et al. Regulatory challenges for autologous tissue engineered products on their way from bench to bedside in Europe. Adv Drug Deliv Rev 2015;82–83:181–91. Available from: https://mukocell.com/wp-content/uploads/2016/08/ADDRRam.pdf.

[49] Harris JD, Siston RA, Pan X, et al. Autologous chondrocyte implantation: a systematic review. J Bone Jt Surg Am 2010;92(12):2220–33. Available from: http://citeseerx.ist.psu.edu/viewdoc/download?doi = 10.1.1.1004.3559&rep = rep1&type = pdf.

[50] Ruano-Ravina A, Jato Diaz M. Autologous chondrocyte implantation: a systematic review. Osteoarthr Cartil 2006;14(1):47–51 https://www.oarsijournal.com/article/S1063-4584(05)00201-3/pdf.

[51] Mistry H, Connock M, Pink J, et al. Autologous chondrocyte implantation in the knee: systematic review and economic evaluation. Health Technol Assess 2017;21(6):1–294 https://www.ncbi.nlm.nih.gov/books/NBK424075/ and https://www.journalslibrary.nihr.ac.uk/hta/hta21060/#/abstract.

[52] Barbagli G, Akbarov I, Heidenreich A, et al. Anterior urethroplasty using a new tissue engineered oral mucosa graft: surgical techniques and outcomes. J Urol 2018;200(2):448–56.

[53] Elsanhoury A, Sanzenbacher R, Reinke P, et al. Accelerating patients' access to advanced therapies in the EU. Mol Ther Methods Clin Dev 2017;7:15–19. Available from: https://www.cell.com/action/showPdf?pii = S2329-0501%2817%2930094-3.

[54] Yano K, Watanabe N, Tsuyuki K, et al. Regulatory approval for autologous human cells and tissue products in the United States, the European Union, and Japan. Regen Ther 2014;1:45–56. Available from: https://reader.elsevier.com/reader/sd/pii/S2352320414000029?token = 3F32C2A7B2A94FC2CDDC41976BF607B1A6E3674B10BFF7C490E8F05064FD7BBD4DA129729B6908125AC4FE7CDB2A075C.

[55] Hunziker EB, Lippuner K, Keel MJ, et al. An educational review of cartilage repair: precepts & practice--myths & misconceptions--progress & prospects. Osteoarthr Cartil 2015;23(3):334–50 https://www.oarsijournal.com/article/S1063-4584(14)01383-1/pdf.

[56] Kwon H, Brown WE, Lee CA, et al. Surgical and tissue engineering strategies for articular cartilage and meniscus repair. Nat Rev Rheumatol 2019;15(9):550–70. Available from: https://www.ncbi.nlm.nih.gov/pmc/articles/PMC7192556/pdf/nihms-1579623.pdf.

[57] Mumme M, Wixmerten A, Miot S, et al. Tissue engineering for paediatric patients. Swiss Med Wkly 2019;149:w20032. Available from: https://smw.ch/article/doi/smw.2019.20032.

[58] Rose K, Neubauer D, et al. Comment on: Mumme M et al. Tissue engineering for paediatric patients. Swiss Med Wkly 2020; (in press).

[59] Rose K, Kopp MV. Pediatric investigation plans for specific immunotherapy: Questionable contributions to childhood health. Pediatr Allergy Immunol 2015;26 (8):695–701.

[60] Facing the challenge. The Lisbon strategy for growth and employment. Report from the High Level Group chaired by Wim Kok November 2004. http://ec.europa.eu/research/evaluations/pdf/archive/fp6-evidence-base/evaluation_studies_and_reports/evaluation_studies_and_reports_2004/the_lisbon_strategy_for_growth_and_employment__report_-from_the_high_level_group.pdf.

[61] FDA 2016. Crisaborole label. https://www.accessdata.fda.gov/drugsatfda_docs/label/2016/207695s000lbl.pdf.

[62] Emily Whitehead: A Young Girl Beats Cancer with Immunotherapy. https://www.cancerresearch.org/immunotherapy/stories/patients/emily-whitehead.

[63] Maude SL, Laetsch TW, Buechner J, et al. Tisagenlecleucel in children and young adults with B-cell lymphoblastic leukemia. N Engl J Med 2018;378:439–48.

[64] Editorial. Cancer in the young: progress and priorities. Lancet Child & Adolesc Health 2018;2(3):157. Available from: https://www.thelancet.com/action/showPdf?pii = S2352-4642%2818%2930041-5.

[65] Momper JD, Mulugeta Y, Green DJ, et al. Adolescent dosing and labeling since the food and drug administration amendments act of 2007. JAMA Pediatr 2013;167(10):926–32 Oct.

[66] Paoletti X, Geoerger B, Doz F, et al. A comparative analysis of paediatric dose-finding trials of molecularly targeted agent with adults' trials. Eur J Cancer 2013;49 (10):2392–402.

[67] Panama Papers. https://en.wikipedia.org/wiki/Panama_Papers.

[68] EMA 2017: 10-year Report to the European Commission. https://ec.europa.eu/health/sites/health/files/files/paediatrics/2016_pc_report_2017/ema_10_year_report_for_consultation.pdf.

[69] Bible, Matthew 7:5.

[70] Boots I, Sukhai RN, Klein RH, et al. Stimulation programs for pediatric drug research - do children really benefit? Eur J Pediatr 2007;166(8):849–55. Available at: https://link.springer.com/content/pdf/10.1007%2Fs00431-006-0381-z.pdf (Accessed 26FEB2019).

[71] Kreeftmeijer-Vegter AR, de Boer A, van der Vlugt-Meijer RH, de Vries PJ. The influence of the European paediatric regulation on marketing authorisation of orphan drugs for children. Orphanet J Rare Dis 2014;9:120.

[72] Adamson PC. Unintended consequences of regulatory initiatives in childhood cancer drug development. JAMA Pediatr 2013;167(10):886–7.

Abbreviations and technical explanations

Throughout this book, abbreviations are introduced in each chapter where they are used for the first time. Only the four following key abbreviations are used throughout the book without separate explanation: EMA = European Medicines Agency [1,2]; EU = European Union; FDA = US Food and Drug Administration [2,3]; US = United States of America.

This book uses a number of internet resources that allow the reader to check the accuracy of the statements made.

The most important sources used here are the US database www.clinicaltrials.gov, which among the public clinical trial registries is the largest and most user-friendly one. Clinical studies in www.clinicaltrials.gov are given by their National Clinical Trial (NCT) number. Any NCT number can be given as is into any internet search engine, and the link to the respective clinical study pops up immediately.

EU pediatric investigation plans (PIPs) are given in most tables with their PIP number. If the PIP number is entered into any internet search engine, the PIP document itself opens up immediately, or an EMA website, which allows direct access to the PIP decision. Sometimes, the internet search engine does not find the respective PIP immediately. In this case, it helps to give in the respective drug's name plus PIP. This will retrieve the respective PIP decision.

All drugs in this book are given by their International Nonproprietary Name (INN). Sometimes, in addition, brand names used in the US and/or in the EU are added as well.

References

[1] EMA Wikipedia https://en.wikipedia.org/wiki/European_Medicines_Agency.

[2] Van Norman GA. Drugs and devices. Comparison of European and U.S. approval processes. JACC Basic Transl Sci 2016;1(5):399–412. Available from: https://www.ncbi.nlm.nih.gov/pmc/articles/PMC6113412/pdf/main.pdf.

[3] FDA Wikipedia https://en.wikipedia.org/wiki/Food_and_Drug_Administration.

Background

When half a century ago the pediatrician Harry Shirkey complained that infants and children were "therapeutic orphans," he ascribed this to a "an odd and unfortunate twist of fate" [1]. Society was transitioning into a new era of broadly available effective drugs. A major change of paradigm had transpired in drug development as a result of the USA's response to the thalidomide catastrophe. The new "pediatric warnings" in drug labels were a *legal* precaution from drug manufacturers because as of 1962 drug developers had to prove efficacy and safety in clinical studies for FDA approval [2]. Furthermore, the FDA now also controlled drug advertising [3]. Drug developers' pediatric warnings reflected potential dangers of modern drugs *in babies* as well as the US litigious legal environment and society's lack of knowledge about the maturation of the liver and the kidneys in young human bodies. The new concept of children as "therapeutic orphans" was a superficial, medical interpretation of the manufacturers' pediatric warnings that oversimplified a new challenge. The concept of children as therapeutic orphans evolved into a blurring of the legal and physiological meanings of the word "child."

Historically childhood death was not an infrequent occurrence. This changed gradually with the prevention of infectious diseases by better housing, nutrition, industrially produced substitution of breast milk, improved hygiene, and vaccinations. Subsequently physicians developed the capacity to successfully treat infectious diseases. The fight against childhood cancer required modern transport and communication, as pediatric cancer is so rare that systemic studies required collaboration of more than one center. Pediatric oncology also required the availability of chemotherapeutic agents, which resulted from their investigation and development as part of the preparation of chemical warfare. The development of pediatric oncology was accompanied by intensive coverage in the lay press, with donations made to affected families, and much more [4]. All this contributed to a now much higher level of discussion about children, by a different view regarding children's personality and an entire new industry of children's clothing [5]. This period coincided with declarations and resolutions of the United Nations on the rights of children [6,7].

Whenever new drugs become available, they were and are enthusiastically used by physicians in both adults and children when appropriate. The "therapeutic orphans" concept ignored the complex legal, medical, cultural and societal background and blurred the difference between legal and medical/biological meanings of the word "child." Shirkey himself complained that most physicians ignored these warnings [1]. But for the vast majority of "children" the warnings were irrelevant. The warnings were relevant for infants. The early publications on medicine toxicities in newborns warned physicians to be cautious. Medical practitioners thereafter would treat a premature newborn after appropriate consultation and caution. However, teenagers requiring antibiotic treatment with adult doses was completely justified. Later claims that children were in danger of toxicities because the antibiotics had not been approved in "children" imposed in hindsight the on/off-label framework of the late 1980s into the 1950s.

The on/off-label framework has been successful in preventing dangerous compounds such as thalidomide from being sold. The term "off-label" emerged in 1988 [8]. However, today thalidomide is FDA-approved for the treatment of multiple myeloma and skin inflammation caused by leprosy that is otherwise recalcitrant. The discussion about the FDA's dislike of off-label prescribing versus the physicians' right to prescribe what they think will help must be balanced and openly discussed.

However, the imposture of the on/off-label framework on the "pediatric" population is a fundamentally different issue. It assumes that without separate "pediatric" approval new drugs are ineffective and unsafe in "children." Pediatricians have used formulas and dosing tables for medication dosing in children. Kearns estimated in 2003 that from eight years of age on these formulas and dosing tables fulfilled their purpose, while in younger children additional information is required in terms of absorption, distribution, metabolism, excretion (ADME) [9]. Herein we will not debate if eight years, two years, or one year are the appropriate lower age before which additional pediatric dose-finding is required. The key point is that the term "children" is used ambiguously to confer an apparently physiological characteristic to a chronological age limit, which in reality does not exist. The concept of children as "therapeutic orphans" is medically flawed and has resulted in today's multitude of "pediatric" clinical studies that in postpubertal young patients are totally senseless and in prepubertal children exaggerated. It has resulted in an entire pseudo-science elegantly called "pediatric drug development" [10], as if "children" were another species.

Before 1962, medical treatment was based on the eminence of renown clinicians, a system with high resistance against fast changes. Ignaz Philipp Semmelweis demonstrated in Vienna that the incidence of childbed fever could be drastically reduced by the use of hand disinfection in obstetrical clinics. In Vienna, medical doctors' wards had three times the mortality of midwives' wards. Semmelweis published a book on Etiology, Concept, and Prophylaxis of Childbed Fever. Although hand washing reduced mortality to $<1\%$, his observations conflicted with the established opinions of his time and were largely rejected. Some physicians were furthermore offended by the suggestion to wash their hands. His reputation developed posthumously.

This cycle was to some degree broken by clinical studies, which required the collective action of multiple researchers that limited individual influence on the study data. The ability to falsify data is possible for individual researchers, which occurred with the alleged beneficial effect of high-dose chemotherapy plus autologous bone marrow transplantation for metastatic breast cancer in the 1980/90s by Werner Bezwoda, professor and chair of the Department of Hematology and Oncology in Witwatersrand, Johannesburg, South Africa [11,12]. In contrast, in multicenter trials the evaluation of the study data is done by a central team, then checked by the regulatory authorities. Falsifications by individual study participants would therefore be detected [11]. Clinical studies in humans have answered questions on new vaccines, drugs, or medical devices. Since World War II, biomedical research and its use in daily life have transformed our life. Medicine has expanded from treating acute diseases to treating and even preventing chronic diseases; together with other innovations risks for the body are gradually reduced [13].

Clinical studies are complex, expensive, and their interpretation is not done by one individual physician, but by central evaluation. Clinical studies are decisive for the approval of individual drugs and have to some degree become the currency needed by clinicians and other researchers for academic careers. Although the individual authors have participated in the respective studies, in reality the study infrastructure represents a machinery of its own, controlled by the authors only to some degree. The term "evidence-based medicine" suggests that studies increasingly can help to determine which treatment is the best [14].

The limitations of clinical studies are their strength and their weakness. To avoid later long listings of side effects, companies compose almost endless lists of inclusion and exclusion criteria. Regulatory studies help to decide if the degree to which a drug works is statistically effective; furthermore, they document that the drug is well tolerated. However, the results of these studies represent only one piece of information that clinical physicians must consider before selecting a specific therapy for their patients. Although drug labels impact what we do, it is also the years of training and practical experience that guide how we select to ultimately treat our patients.

The limitations of clinical studies and the exaggerated enthusiasm they enjoy in the medical world are mocked by a well-known publication that apparently seriously laments that the use of parachutes has never been tested in double-blind, placebo-controlled, randomized clinical trials. The authors conclude that only two options exist: either to accept that, "under exceptional circumstances," common sense might be applied when considering the potential risks and benefits of interventions, or to continue the quest for the holy grail of evidence-based interventions and stop parachute use outside of properly conducted trials. They add that they are sure that fierce advocates of evidence-based medicine will not hesitate to show their commitment by volunteering for a double-blind, randomized, placebo-controlled, crossover parachute trial [15]. This publication was not an in-depth analysis of clinical studies in general. It put in writing the critical gut feeling of two clinicians toward an exaggerated insistence on clinical studies instead of the additional use of common sense to address real-world problems.

The fundamental weakness of separate "pediatric" clinical studies is that the inclusion criteria demanded by the FDA and EMA are administrative and arbitrary. The upper age limit of 17/18 years does not correspond to the body's biological maturation. Other, similarly senseless requirements would be to demand that drugs to treat persons 24 years old should have been investigated exclusively in clinical studies with participants 24 years old; treatment of persons 30-years-old to be based on studies in 30-years-old patients, etc. Even more senseless would be to demand clinical studies for patients whose given name starts with an "R" to have been studied only in patients whose first name started with an "R" as well. In computer science exaggerated formal requirements are characterized by "garbage in, garbage out" (GIGO). There are always exceptional examples where additional demands make sense. Drugs do not always work identically in men and women, in persons of different races or ethnicity, or in persons of very different ages. In most cases, this does not prevent reasonable treatment. Nonetheless, the demand for separate "pediatric" studies has become the justification for a parallel setup of clinical studies to either repeat proof of efficacy and safety of drugs whose efficacy is already well known, or to justify senseless and often harmful "pediatric" studies with new anticancer drugs that will not help the young patients and/or expose the placebo group to lesser or no therapy. A concept born out of good intentions and concerns was translated into laws that resulted in payments of billions of dollars and Euros for "pediatric" studies. We will discuss individual diseases in depth in later chapters. The pseudoscience that justifies these studies has been labeled "pediatric drug development" [10]. Pediatric drug development is a new ethical challenge of 21st century medicine.

It took three years until thalidomide was unveiled as the cause of thousands of birth defects. Dr. Lenz, a German pediatrician, interviewed twenty mothers of affected children. Nobody had a clue of the causes of this birth defects. At that time, the German authorities and "specialists" claimed that there was no increase in birth defects. The atomic bombing of Hiroshima and Nagasaki were tentatively blamed. After his interviews Dr. Lenz concluded that the one common factor was that all mothers had taken thalidomide early in pregnancy. He presented his conclusions at a medical conference. When a major German newspaper published it, thalidomide sales were stopped in Germany (and later worldwide) [16,17].

Peter Buxton tried for seven years to have the Tuskegee study, run by the US Public Health Service (PHS), terminated. This infamous study observed male African Americans known to be infected with syphilis while withholding treatment of them with antibiotics. Peter Buxton worked in another project and risked his job. After seven years he understood that there was no way to stop the study internally. He informed the press. When it was published in a major newspaper, the study was immediately terminated. It took a few more decades until President Bill Clinton apologized to the last survivors [18,19].

How could the employees and manager of the PHS Tuskegee study not terminate this study once they understood what was transpiring? Many PHS employees participated at autopsies of deceased study participants. The reasons are hard to imagine except that the study secured jobs for these employees in a well-recognized institution. The Tuskegee study had even been presented at medical conferences, but during a time period when black physicians were not yet allowed to participate [20].

"Pediatric drug development" was triggered by the children-are-therapeutic-orphans concept. It reached an apex when it was copied, adopted, and augmented by the EU that is now promoting worldwide senseless and potentially harmful clinical studies in young patients. The EMA bureaucrats are convinced that they are contributing to improved children's health worldwide as the Tuskegee study group thought they were advancing the understanding of the course of untreated syphilis.

Critical voices have for many years condemned pharmaceutical companies and not allowed them to promote off-label use of their drugs. Many of the companies were fined billions of dollars by the FDA. However, these same critics ignore that off-label use of antidepressants is a legitimate and important tool in treating depression in young patients [13]. Depression can result in suicide, which is the second high cause of death in young persons, far more frequent than death by malignancies [21].

References

[1] Shirkey H. Therapeutic orphans. J Pediatr 1968;72(1):119–20.

[2] Janssen WM. A historical perspective on off-label medicine: from regulation, promotion, and the first amendment to the next frontiers. In: Levy MC, editor. Food and Drug Law Institute. First Washington, D.C: USA Off-Label Communications; 2008.

[3] Donohue JA. History of drug advertising: The evolving roles of consumers and consumer protection. Milbank Q 2006;84:659–99.

[4] Krueger G. Hope and suffering: children, cancer, and the paradox of experimental medicine. Baltimore, MD, USA: John Hopkins University Press; 2008.

[5] Cook DT. The commodification of childhood: the children's clothing industry and the rise of the child consumer. Durham, NC, USA: Duke University Press; 2004.

[6] Declaration of the rights of the child. Adopted by UN general assembly resolution 1386 (XIV) of 10 December 1959. https://web.archive.org/web/20130926070812/http://www.un.org/cyberschoolbus/humanrights/resources/child.asp.

[7] Convention on the rights of the child. Adopted and opened for signature, ratification and accession by General Assembly resolution 44/25 of 20 November 1989. Entry into force 2 September 1990, in accordance with article 49. http://www.ohchr.org/EN/ProfessionalInterest/Pages/CRC.aspx.

[8] Plate V. The impact of off-label, compassionate and unlicensed use on health care laws in preselected countries. http://hss.ulb.uni-bonn.de/2009/1936/1936.pdf.

[9] Kearns GL, Abdel-Rahman SM, Alander SW, Blowey DL, Leeder JS, Kauffman RE. Developmental pharmacology - drug disposition, action, and therapy in infants and children. N Engl J Med 2003;349(12):1157–67.

[10] Ward RM, Benjamin DK, Davis JM, et al. The need for pediatric drug development. J Pediatr 2018;192:13–21.

[11] George SL, Buyse M. Data fraud in clinical trials. Clin Investig (Lond) 2015;5(2):161–73.

[12] Rettig RA, Jacobson PD, Farquhar CM, Aubry WM. False hope: bone marrow transplantation for breast cancer. New York, NY, USA: Oxford University Press; 2007.

[13] Gabriel JM, Goldberg DS. Big pharma and the problem of disease inflation. Int J Health Serv 2014;44(2):307–22.

[14] Sackett DL. Evidence-based medicine. Seminars Perinatol 1997;21(Feb):3–5.

[15] Smith GC, Pell JP. Parachute use to prevent death and major trauma related to gravitational challenge: systematic review of randomised controlled trials. Brit Med J 2003;327:1459–61.

[16] Vargesson N. Thalidomide-induced teratogenesis: history and mechanisms. Birth Defects Res C Embryo Today 2015;105(2):140–56. Available at: https://www.ncbi.nlm.nih.gov/pmc/articles/PMC4737249/ (Accessed 04 June 2019).

[17] Thomann KD. Die contergan-katastrophe. Die trügerische Sicherheit der "harten" Daten. Deutsches Ärzteblatt 2007;104(41):A2078–82. Available at: https://www.aerzteblatt.de/pdf.asp?id = 57224 (Accessed 04 June 2019).

[18] Adashi EY, Walters LB, Menikoff JA. The belmont report at 40: reckoning with time. Public Health 2018;108(10):1345–8.

[19] Rose CD. Ethical conduct of research in children: pediatricians and their IRB (Part 1 of 2). Pediatrics 2017;139(5).

[20] Washington HA. Medical apartheid: the dark history of medical experimentation on Black Americans from colonial times to the present. New York, NY, USA: Doubleday Publishing Group; 2006.

[21] Rose K, Neubauer D, Grant-Kels JM. Too many avoidable suicides occur worldwide in young patients. A review. Rambam Maimonides Med J 2019; in press.

Introduction

"Pediatric drug development" emerged as a major movement with a US pediatric law in 1997. It has a complex historical background, and is today part of the general process of drug development. Did it advance, and does it continue to advance the healthcare of young patients? This is a controversial question. There are several books [1–10] and plenty of publications in high ranking scientific journals that reassure its positive impact and continuing need [11–13].

This book outlines the intellectual fundamentals of "pediatric drug development" and analyzes the clinical studies that the FDA and the European Medicines Agency (EMA) demand for the "pediatric population": "children" defined by an administrative age limit that does not correspond to a bodily metamorphosis. It examines the medical sense of these "pediatric" studies on the background of our current knowledge of the maturation of the body and how it handles absorption, distribution, metabolism, and excretion of food and medicines from birth to adulthood. The guiding question is which clinical studies in the "pediatric population" make clinical sense, if some or all lack medical sense, and if some or all harm patients. This is a legitimate question.

This book has one major advantage. It addresses issues candidly and unambiguously. It outlines facts and data that every reader with internet access can easily verify on his own. Its conclusions are not identical with those of the main players in "pediatric drug development." In one word: the book is provocative.

This book has also one major disadvantage. It addresses issues candidly and unambiguously and comes to unambiguous conclusions. It is provocative.

Controversies are the life blood of science and democracy, as long as the messenger can expect not to be shot.

Healthcare contributes to increased longevity and quality of life, including diseases that were a death sentence until a few years ago, and others that promised a life of misery. The healthcare system is increasingly expensive, complex, and compartmentalized. It is competitive, and confusing, with contradicting claims, specifically when there are different therapeutic options. In the public arena, there are staunch defenses of modern medicine as well as harsh condemnation of modern unaffordable drugs and the pharmaceutical industry that profits from them; additionally there are those who espouse trust in the healing forces of Bach flowers and herbs, hippotherapy, homeopathy, and traditional natural medicines from various ethnic groups and tribes. US citizens live with television and radio commercial advertising newer medications, while direct-to-consumer advertising is more restricted in other countries. But we all learn, more or less, to filter claims from reality. If the balance between commercial interests and prescription medications becomes lopsided, it can have disastrous consequences. Altogether, today's healthcare system is a huge, colorful theatrical performance with characteristics ranging from ridiculous, comical, to literally deadly serious. Within this healthcare theater, everybody makes choices, and everybody tries to find the best outcome.

Within this chaos, there are some pillars. The regulatory authorities make the official decision if new drugs are effective and safe. Despite their caution they may be deceived by a company that presents data in a clever enough manner to mask important negative consequences. However, this occurs rarely. The last large worldwide medical catastrophe with a new drug occurred 1959–1961 when thalidomide caused misshapen limbs. Although the US was largely spared this particular disaster, the US has decisively given unprecedented authority to the FDA to control drug approval. The medical profession is another pillar. Doctors receive several years of professional training and continue their medical education throughout their career. Medical practitioners are the port of entry for patients to receive treatment for often complex complaints, and clinicians are generally highly trusted by their patients.

The development of new treatments requires brilliant ideas, tremendous amounts of financial resources, and much more. New treatments are first conceived as an idea, then developed in the lab, tested in animals and ultimately in humans, and finally approved. Drug development is competitive, driven by both the market and science. Efficacy and safety of new drugs are proven in clinical studies. Before approval, the regulatory authorities check the study results. If they are deemed acceptable, the drug receives approval for the requested indication: a "label" for the medication is created. Then the drug becomes commercially available and can be prescribed.

The general population is divided into adults and minors. Although minors have all human rights, legally their parents decide for them, including regarding medical treatment and participation at clinical studies. For more than 20 years the US has facilitated pediatric clinical studies, and for over 10 years the European Union (EU) has demanded even more studies in minors. This had led to an unprecedented increase in pediatric studies. Most diseases potentially targeted by modern drugs are rare in children and subsequently there are not enough patients in any single country to adequately perform these pediatric clinical trials. Consequently, most pediatric studies need to recruit worldwide.

Do all studies in children make medical sense? Will they help? Parents ask these questions first themselves, then their own parents, friends, and relatives,

Dr. Google, and earlier or later their trusted healthcare practitioner. Practitioners cannot be both, generalists and specialists in pharmacology, developmental pharmacology, regulatory affairs, pediatrics, history, and more.

The demand for pediatric clinical studies has complex roots in history. Regulatory pediatric studies are officially sanctioned by the FDA and its EU counterpart, the EMA. The FDA and the EMA claim to aim at improving young persons' healthcare, but this book shows that this is not the primary goal of all "pediatric" studies. Instead, they aim at pediatric *labels*. The FDA defines children as anybody under 17 years [14], the EMA as anybody under 18 years of age [13,15]. The justifications of "pediatric" studies rewarded and/or demanded by the regulatory authorities blur the legal and physiological meanings of the word "child" [16–18]. They go back to toxicities observed in neonates and infants over sixty years ago [19–21], and pediatric warnings by pharmaceutical companies [22]. These warnings were intended to prevent damage lawsuits in the legally litigious US [23–27]. If you drive by a restaurant, order a coffee, put it between your legs, drive away, and scald yourself, you are angry at yourself in most countries. In the US, you might sue the restaurant claiming the coffee was too hot. The pediatric warnings added by pharmaceutical companies to drug labels were justified for neonates and infants, but not for all "children." They were a legal precaution.

The observations of toxicities in babies and the legal precautions they triggered occurred when new institutions were defining their place in society. The American Academy of Pediatrics (AAP) demanded studies in "children" [28]. Much less was known in those days about the maturation of children's organs that run absorption, distribution, metabolism, and excretion (ADME) of drugs compared with today [29]. The AAP collaborated closely with the FDA. The FDA defined "children" as persons under 17 years old; [14] later the EU as under 18 years old [13,15]. US and EU regulatory authorities issue separate "pediatric" labels in a population labeled administratively as "pediatric," for which they demand "pediatric" studies. Finally, clinical observations of toxicities in babies were translated by law makers into binding law. The concept of "children" as "therapeutic orphans" was adopted despite the fact that it is physiologically flawed and it opened a modern Pandora's box.

Preterm newborns and newborns are indeed very different from adults. But children mature quickly. The FDA's administrative definition of "children" as anybody under 17 years of age essentially extrapolated the toxicities observed in the 1950s in preterm newborns and newborns into all minors up to 16 years of age. But adolescents are bodily no longer "children." They are *legally* still minors, but their body is sufficiently mature to be treated with adult drug doses. And also minors before they reach puberty are no longer as immature and vulnerable as newborns. Semantically, the definition of "children" by an administrative age limit is a blur between different meanings of the term "child." But behind this semantic blur, there are hidden interests that have continued and maintained this blur until today.

Recently, several "pediatric" studies had to be terminated and more will have to be terminated. They recruited minors to receive outdated treatment for malignant melanoma that physicians increasingly refused to recommend [30,31]. Recruitment waned. Instead of apologizing to the public, the regulatory authorities and the involved clinicians continue to sweep these studies under the carpet. Many more harmful studies continue recruiting worldwide.

Despite all this, there are life-saving, real-life studies in young patients. Probably the best-known young patient is Emily Whitehead, who contracted acute lymphoblastic leukemia (ALL) when she was five years old. After chemotherapy and relapse the parents had to decide between hospice, i.e., accepting death, or cutting-edge experimental treatment. Emily became the youngest patient in a study that reprogrammed her T-cells to attack and destroy ALL cells. She also survived the inevitable cytokine release syndrome (CRS) with the help of tocilizumab, a monoclonal antibody (MAB), then approved for adult rheumatoid arthritis and juvenile idiopathic arthritis, but off-label for CRS. Today, eight years later, Emily is a healthy, cancer-free teenager and young woman [32,33]. Administratively and legally, she is still a "child."

How should parents of an ill child differentiate reasonable from senseless studies? It is difficult even for practitioners. Eventually, a critical discussion of pediatric legislation will hopefully be included in academic training, and medical doctors will be better prepared. The challenge of "pediatric" studies rewarded/demanded by FDA and EMA is a relatively new one. Originated in the US, then copied and augmented by the EU, it has created a new type of industry that in most diseases repeats proof of efficacy and safety of new drugs in "children" aged <17/18 years old as if these young patients were another species. This includes placebo-controlled, randomized, double-blind studies in serious diseases such as multiple sclerosis, depression, schizophrenia, or atopic dermatitis that deny young patients in the placebo group effective treatment. Apart from placebo-control, there are other harmful study designs, including comparison to outdated standard-of-care.

Pediatric oncology evolved during its first decades entirely "off-label," long before the term "off-label" existed at all [16–18,30,31]. The term "off-label" emerged in 1988 [34]. The chemotherapy agents used in pediatric leukemia from the 1960s on had been developed and approved for adult cancer types [35,36]. Since the first US pediatric law, the FDA rewarded "pediatric" studies in "children" with cancer aged up to 21 years that investigated single chemotherapeutics despite the fact that these chemotherapeutics were already known to be effective. They were routinely and successfully used in "cocktails," i.e., combinations of several chemotherapeutics [37]. Pediatric oncology had saved many thousands of lives of young patients. But the new generation of FDA-rewarded "pediatric" cancer studies had a new logic: they aimed at "pediatric" *labels*. They were guided by regulatory dogmatism. They "certified" in hindsight effectivity of cytotoxics in "children" up to 21-

years-old even though the efficacy of these cytotoxics was without doubt and had already been demonstrated in adults and children [30].

This new dogmatic label-focused approach was stepwise expanded. Cancer types that exist in patients of all ages were declared "pediatric," e.g., nasopharyngeal carcinoma (NPC). A large international study investigated the addition of docetaxel to standard chemotherapy in "children and adolescents" with nasopharyngeal carcinoma up to 21 years old [30,38]. However, NPC is not a pediatric disease. It is a complex disease that can affect persons of any age. The "pediatric" nasopharyngeal carcinoma study, like many other studies, offered industry funds for researchers, networking, and publishing. The docetaxel producer received a patent extension which allowed the company to more than recover the study costs. The FDA was lauded because it had supported the fight against "pediatric" cancer. "Pediatric" careers in academia, regulatory authorities, and pharmaceutical industry were all advanced. The only ones that did not profit were the patients [16–18,30].

The EMA has further expanded this quest by demanding "pediatric" cancer studies for modern anticancer drugs and biologics. Modern targeted drugs are not cytotoxics and what worked half a century ago with cytotoxics does not work with MABs, cytokine inhibitors and receptor blockers. The EMA is filling the world with senseless "pediatric" cancer studies that do not help young patients, and deter from therapeutic studies with the potential to save lives. What the EMA is mandating is, however, securing jobs in clinical research organizations, pediatric oncology research, pharmaceutical industry, and regulatory authorities. From 2020 on, the FDA also demands additional "pediatric" cancer studies with modern anticancer drugs. At least the FDA advocates today to include juvenile cancer patients into adult pivotal studies, so the "pediatric" cancer studies will be demanded only for patients up to 11 years old. But many of the cancer types that used to be classified as "pediatric" in the past are today seen differently, including ALL from which Emily Whitehead was healed.

The healthcare system generates considerable wealth and is replete with conflicts of interest that are well known and pragmatically managed. One fully justified concern is that pharmaceutical companies have used their wealth to pay ghostwriters to pen pseudoscientific publications for nonpeer reviewed and some peer reviewed but naive medical journals with the goal to influence physicians to prescribe their respective company's drugs. This scenario has led to stricter regulations and a published recommendation from the International Committee of Medical Journal Editors (ICMJE) that quality biomedical journals should only publish studies that have been listed in a publicly available study database that is listed before study start [39]. Ironically, this step, initiated to prevent fraudulent industry-paid pseudoscientific papers and wrong claims, has turned into a key tool to unveil the dimension of questionable, unethical, and harmful "pediatric" studies. The US database www.clinicaltrials.gov is very user-friendly [40]. In contradistinction, the EU database is, unfortunately, reader-unfriendly and confusing with too many country-specific details [41]. The listing of all studies in a publicly available database now allows to retrieve information on studies that can potentially harm patients; these studies are not triggered by big bad pharma's greed, but by the children-are-therapeutic-orphans concept that received and receives part of its life blood from the conviction that big pharma is bad [42–44], that regulatory authorities are good, and that academic science is neutral and unbiased. Historically, tirades against the pharmaceutical industry were en vogue. After two decades of being bashed, pharmaceutical industry has successfully reinvented itself. Modern treatment saved the life of Emily Whitehead.

The "pediatric" studies rewarded/demanded by FDA/EMA are in a constant state of flux. Since 2019, the FDA has recommended inclusion of adolescent patients into promising adult cancer studies, which has resulted in relinquishing the children-are-therapeutic-orphans concept for melanoma patients 12–17 years old [45]. The FDA has relented in several therapeutic areas where it no longer insists on separate "pediatric" studies [46], while the EMA remains more adamant and dogmatic in its "pediatric" demands. For partial onset seizures (POS), the most frequent form of epilepsy, both the FDA and EMA allow "extrapolation" of efficacy for drugs down to the age of four years [47], and the FDA has in the meantime even gone down to the age of two years [48]. However, neither the FDA nor the EMA have initiated a public discussion about the children-are-therapeutic-orphans concept.

"Pediatric" studies offer industry funds, publications, and networking opportunities to academic researchers. Many "pediatric" careers in academia, industry, and regulatory medicine have been established and built on "pediatric" studies. The moral imperative proclaimed by the AAP "to formally study drugs in children so that they can enjoy equal access to existing as well as new therapeutic agents" is universally applauded without attention to the sequelae of conflicts of interest and flawed pediatric studies [21,49]. This new pseudoscience has the catchy name "pediatric drug development" [11].

Medical laypersons need help to differentiate reasonable studies from those driven by regulatory dogmatism. This is a new challenge for medical practitioners, patients, and their families. Clinicians need experience, independent thinking, common sense, and guidance to deal with the cyclone of studies that threaten an increasing number of young patients in "pediatric" studies performed worldwide. The same cyclone keeps young patients away from truly promising studies, and refuses treatment with modern effective drugs to young patients. The goal of this book is to help to navigate through this storm.

Healthcare practitioners should be aware of this challenge for at least four reasons: (1) They will increasingly be approached by parents who seek advice about a clinical study for their child that was offered to them, and for which the study center needs a signed informed consent. (2) It is a principle of medical ethics to give sound advice. (3) A practitioner's reputation will severely be damaged if he or she recommended participation in a study that later is shown to have harmed patients. (4) Failure to be aware of dangerous studies might result in liabilities.

Several pediatric clinical disciplines have realized that separate "pediatric" placebo-controlled proof-of-concept studies lack medical sense [50–55]. Other disciplines enjoy the comfort zone of "pediatric" studies [56,57]. That the FDA/EMA-rewarded/demanded "pediatric" studies lack often sense and harm patients is an open secret in pharmaceutical industry, but also in industry there are those that have come to terms with these studies and justify these studies [58,59], sometimes alongside with representatives of the regulatory authorities [56].

The data on "pediatric" studies requested/demanded by the FDA and the EMA shown in this book show that these studies altogether are the largest abuse of patients in medical research since the numerous questionable clinical studies unveiled by Beecher in 1966 [60], and the termination of the Tuskegee study in Alabama in 1972, where illiterate African American men with syphilis were told they had "bad blood," were observed for decades, and were not treated with antibiotics when these had become broadly available after World War II [61–63].

That the discussed "pediatric" studies lack sense and often harm patients is already bad enough. The worst element, however, is that the underlying concept is directing research with young patients into a wrong direction. Modern drugs are effective against the most frequent type of epilepsy, POS, in patients of any age, at least down to two years, probably even younger. Enormous resources have been wasted and continue to be wasted for separate "pediatric" approval of antiepileptic drugs and for the thousands of other health challenges young patients can have. For modern drugs, we do not need separate proof of efficacy in young patients. Instead, we need studies how to use these drugs in young patients in our complex society. More and more children are born with diseases whose diagnosis was a death sentence in the past. We are not good yet at organizing the necessary support for their families from diagnosis hopefully before birth, through birth, through childhood, and through their entire life. There are such attempts [64], but still too few. This is not purely regulatory, but a complex, societal, multifactorial and multidisciplinary challenge.

The coming years and decades will show if and to what degree the classical disciplines of medical healthcare, i.e., medicine, pharmacology, pediatrics, developmental pharmacology, and others, will be able to adapt to this challenge. Maybe patient advocacy groups will decide that we need new types of guidance through the labyrinths of healthcare and new types of healthcare professions. Maybe the classical disciplines will adapt.

This book addresses a complex issue that has emerged during the period of "adolescence" of drug development in general. The children-are-therapeutic-orphans and children-are-not small-adults mantras have become official doctrine that is taught in academic education of medical doctors, pharmacists, nurses, and many more healthcare professions. The publications that justify and defend these mantras are almost uncountable. This book focuses on a number of key clinical areas plus a number of medical disciplines that until now have a key role in justifying and maintaining these mantras. Each chapter is written as a read-alone chapter. The reader will find the same key arguments in various chapters.

Modern medicine has already fundamentally changed how we live, how long we live, and who lives. The time has come for the process of drug development and its handling by society to become adult. Science and democracy have managed many challenges in the past. This will certainly not be the last one.

References

[1] Rose K, van den Anker JN, editors. Guide to paediatric clinical research. Switzerland: Karger, Basel; 2007.

[2] Rose K, van den Anker JN (Editors). Guide to paediatric clinical research. Table of contents, contributors, and introduction. https://www.karger.com/Article/Pdf/97766.

[3] Rose K, van den Anker JN, editors. Guide to paediatric drug development and clinical research. Switzerland: Karger, Basel; 2010.

[4] Rose K. van den Anker J.N. (Editors): Guide to paediatric drug development and clinical research: contents, contributors, and introduction. https://www.karger.com/Article/Pdf/315565.

[5] Mulberg AE, Silber SA, van den Anker JN, editors. Pediatric drug development – concepts and applications. Hoboken, NJ, USA: Wiley-Blackwell; 2009.

[6] Mulberg AE, Murphy D, Dunne J, Mathis L, editors. Pediatric drug development. 2nd edition Hoboken NJ, USA: Wiley-Blackwell; 2013.

[7] Mulberg A.E., Murphy D., Dunne J., Mathis L. (Editors) Pediatric drug development, 2nd edition. Contents, contributors and preface: https://onlinelibrary.wiley.com/doi/pdf/10.1002/9781118312087.fmatter.

[8] Addressing the barriers to pediatric drug development: workshop summary. National Academies Press, Washington DC, USA, 2008. https://www.ncbi.nlm.nih.gov/books/NBK3994/.

[9] Byrns CD. Safety efforts in pediatric drug development (pharmacology - research, safety testing and regulation. NY, USA: Nova Science Publishers; 2010.

[10] Johnson F. Drug development & rare pediatric diseases pharmacology-research, safety testing and regulation). NY, USA: Nova Science Editors; 2016.

[11] Ward RM, Benjamin Jr. DK, Davis JM, Gorman RL, Kauffman R, Kearns GL, et al. The need for pediatric drug development. J Pediatr 2018 Jan;192:13–21.

[12] Tomasi PA, Egger GF, Pallidis C, et al. Enabling development of paediatric medicines in europe: 10 years of the EU paediatric regulation. Pediatr Drugs 2017;19:505–13.

[13] Hirschfeld S, Saint-Raymond A. Pediatric regulatory initiatives. Handb Exp Pharmacol 2011;556(205):245–68.

[14] Hirschfeld S. History of pediatric labeling. https://slideplayer.com/slide/8600310/.

[15] Regulation (EC) No 1901/2006 of the European Parliament and of the Council of 12 December 2006 on Medicinal Products for Paediatric Use and Amending Regulation (EEC) No 1768/92, Directive 2001/20/EC, Directive 2001/83/EC and Regulation (EC) No 726/2004. http://ec.europa.eu/health/files/eudralex/vol-1/reg_2006_1901/reg_2006_1901_en.pdf.

[16] Rose K, Neubauer D, Grant-Kels JM. Rational use of medicine in children – the conflict of interests story. A review. Rambam Maimonides Med J 2019;10(3):e0018. Available from: https://doi.org/10.5041/RMMJ.10371 Review. https://www.rmmj.org.il/userimages/928/2/PublishFiles/953Article.pdf.

[17] Rose K. The challenges of pediatric drug development. Curr Ther Res Clin Exp 2019;. Available from: https://doi.org/10.1016/j.curtheres.2019.01.007.

[18] Rose K, Grant-Kels JM. The meanings of "pediatric drug development". A review. Therapeutic Innov Regulatory Sci 2018;. Available from: https://doi.org/10.1177/2168479018812060.

[19] Silverman WA, Andersen DH, Blanc WA, Crozier DN. A difference in mortality rate and incidence of kernicterus among premature infants allotted to two prophylactic antibacterial regimens. Pediatrics. 1956;18:614.

[20] Burns LE, Hodgman JE, Cass AB. Fatal circulatory collapse in premature infants receiving chloramphenicol. N Engl 1 Med 1959;261:1318–21.

[21] AAP. Guidelines for the ethical conduct of studies to evaluate drugs in pediatric populations, committee on drugs. Am Acad Pediatrics, Pediatrics 1995;95(2):286–94.

[22] Shirkey H. Therapeutic orphans. J Pediatrics 1968;72(1):119–20 Reprinted in Pediatrics 1999;104(3) (Suppl), 583-584.

[23] Kritzer HM. Propensity to Sue in England and the United States of America: blaming and claiming in tort cases. J Law Soc 1991;18(4):400–27.

[24] Lochlann Jain SS. Injury: the politics of product design and safety law in the United States. Princeton, NJ, USA: Princeton University Press; 2006.

[25] McGovern F. Punitive damages and class actions. Lousiana Law Rev 2010;70:435–62. Available from: https://scholarship.law.duke.edu/cgi/viewcontent.cgi?article = 2762&context = faculty_scholarship.

[26] Bal BS. An introduction to medical malpractice in the United States. Clin Orthop Relat Res 2009;467(2):339–47. Available from: https://www.ncbi.nlm.nih.gov/pmc/articles/PMC2628513/.

[27] Kass JS, Rose RV. Medical malpractice reform: historical approaches, alternative models, and communication and resolution programs. AMA J Ethics 2016;18(3):299–310. Available from: https://journalofethics.ama-assn.org/sites/journalofethics.ama-assn.org/files/2019-12/pfor6-1603.pdf.

[28] Yaffe S.J., Avery M.E., Gold A.P., et al. American academy of pediatrics. Committe on drugs. Drug testing in children: FDA regulations. https://pediatrics.aappublications.org/content/pediatrics/43/3/463.full.pdf.

[29] Kearns GL, Abdel-Rahman SM, Alander SW, Blowey DL, Leeder JS, Kauffman RE. Developmental pharmacology - drug disposition, action, and therapy in infants and children. N Engl J Med 2003;349(12):1157–67. Available from: https://pdfs.semanticscholar.org/55f8/1745303e9aaec7f4cb85f0b5921eec14a9c0.pdf.

[30] Rose K, Grant-Kels JM. Pediatric melanoma – The whole (conflicts of interest) story. Int J Womens Dermatol 2018;5(2):110–15. Available from: https://doi.org/10.1016/j.ijwd.2018.10.020. Available from: https://www.ncbi.nlm.nih.gov/pmc/articles/PMC6451736/pdf/main.pdf.

[31] Geoerger B, Bergeron C, Gore L, et al. Phase II study of ipilimumab in adolescents with unresectable stage III or IV malignant melanoma. Eur J Cancer 2017;86:358–63.

[32] Emily whitehead: a young girl beats cancer with immunotherapy. https://www.cancerresearch.org/immunotherapy/stories/patients/emily-whitehead.

[33] Maude SL, Laetsch TW, Buechner J, et al. Tisagenlecleucel in children and young adults with B-cell lymphoblastic leukemia. N Engl J Med 2018;378:439–48.

[34] Plate V. The impact of off-label, compassionate and unlicensed use on health care laws in preselected countries. http://hss.ulb.uni-bonn.de/2009/1936/1936.pdf.
[35] Adamson PC. Improving the outcome for children with cancer: development of targeted new agents. CA Cancer J Cli 2015;65(3):212–20.
[36] Norris RE, Adamson PC. Challenges and opportunities in childhood cancer drug development. Nat Rev Cancer 2012;12(11):776–82.
[37] Wharton, et al. Impact of pediatric exclusivity on drug labeling and demonstrations of efficacy. Pediatrics. 2014;134(2):e512–18.
[38] Casanova M, Enis Özyar E, Patte C, Orbach D, Ferrari A, Veyrat-Follet C, et al. International randomized phase 2 study on the addition of docetaxel to the combination of cisplatin and 5- fluorouracil in the induction treatment for nasopharyngeal carcinoma in children and adolescents. Cancer Chemother Pharmacol 2016;77(2):289–98.
[39] International Committee of Medical Journal Editors (ICMJE) Recommendations for the Conduct, Reporting, Editing, and Publication of Scholarly work in Medical Journals. http://www.icmje.org/recommendations/.
[40] US National library of medicine. Clinicaltrials.gov www.clinicaltrials.gov.
[41] EU clinical trials register. https://www.clinicaltrialsregister.eu/.
[42] Goldacre B. Bad pharma: how drug companies mislead doctors and harm patients. London, UK: Harper Collins Publishers; 2012.
[43] Angell M. The truth about the drug companies: how they deceive us and what to do about it. New York, USA: Random House Publishers; 2004.
[44] Gøtzsche P. Deadly medicines and organised crime: how big pharma has corrupted healthcare. London, UK: Routledge; 2013.
[45] FDA 2019. Considerations for the inclusion of adolescent patients in adult oncology clinical trials. Guidance for industry. https://www.fda.gov/media/113499/download.
[46] Sun H, Temeck JW, Chambers W, Perkins G, Bonnel R, Murphy D. Extrapolation of efficacy in pediatric drug development and evidence-based medicine: progress and lessons learned. Ther Innov Regul Sci 2017;2017:1–7. Available from: https://www.ncbi.nlm.nih.gov/pmc/articles/PMC5587157/pdf/nihms901908.pdf.
[47] EMA 2018. Guideline on clinical investigation of medicinal products in the treatment of epileptic disorders. https://www.ema.europa.eu/en/documents/scientific-guideline/draft-guideline-clinical-investigation-medicinal-products-treatment-epileptic-disorders-revision-3_en.pdf.
[48] FDA 2019. Drugs for treatment of partial onset seizures: Full extrapolation of efficacy from adults to pediatric patients 2 years of age and olderguidance for industry. https://www.fda.gov/media/130449/download.
[49] Shaddy RE, Denne SC. Committee on drugs and committee on pediatric research. Clinical report--guidelines for the ethical conduct of studies to evaluate drugs in pediatric populations. Pediatrics 2010;125(4):850–60. Available from: https://pediatrics.aappublications.org/content/pediatrics/125/4/850.full.pdf.
[50] Gören JL. Antidepressants use in pediatric populations. Expert Opin Drug Saf 2008;7(3):223–5.
[51] Waubant E, Banwell B, Wassmer E, Sormani MP, Amato MP, Hintzen R, et al. Clinical trials of disease-modifying agents in pediatric MS: opportunities, challenges, and recommendations from the IPMSSG. Neurology. 2019;.
[52] Pellock JM, Carman WJ, Thyagarajan V, Daniels T, Morris DL, D'Cruz O. Efficacy of antiepileptic drugs in adults predicts efficacy in children: a systematic review. Neurology. 2012;79(14):1482–9. Available from: https://www.ncbi.nlm.nih.gov/pmc/articles/PMC4098824/pdf/znl1482.pdf.

[53] Pellock JM, Arzimanoglu A, D'Cruz O, et al. Extrapolating evidence of antiepileptic drug efficacy in adults to children ≥2 years of age with focal seizures: the case for disease similarity. Epilepsia. 2017;58(10):1686–96. Available from: https://onlinelibrary.wiley.com/doi/epdf/10.1111/epi.13859.

[54] Arzimanoglou A, D'Cruz O, Nordli D, et al. A review of the new antiepileptic drugs for focal-onset seizures in pediatrics: role of extrapolation. Paediatr Drugs 2018;20(3):249–64. Available from: https://doi.org/10.1007/s40272-018-0286-0.

[55] Wadsworth I, Jaki T, Sills GJ, et al. Clinical drug development in epilepsy revisited: a proposal for a new paradigm streamlined using extrapolation. CNS Drugs 2016;30(11):1011–17. Available from: https://www.ncbi.nlm.nih.gov/pmc/articles/PMC5078157/pdf/40263_2016_Article_383.pdf.

[56] Ruperto N, Vesely R, Saint-Raymond A, Martini A, for the Paediatric Rheumatology International Trials Organisation (PRINTO). Impact of the European paediatric legislation in paediatric rheumatology: past, present and future. Ann Rheum Dis 2013;72:1893–6.

[57] Lovell DJ, Ruperto N, Giannini EH, Martini A. Advances from clinical trials in juvenile idiopathic arthritis. Nat Rev Rheumatol 2013;9(9):557–63.

[58] Bucci-Rechtsweg C. Enhancing the pediatric drug development framework to deliver better pediatric therapies tomorrow. Clin Ther 2017;39(10):1920–32.

[59] Barrett JS, Bishai R, Bucci-Rechtweg C, et al. Challenges and opportunities in the development of medical therapies for pediatric populations and the role of extrapolation. Clin Pharmacol Ther 2018;103(3):419–33.

[60] Beecher HK. Ethics and clinical research. N Engl J Med 1966;274(24):1354–60. Available from: https://www.observatoriobioetica.org/wp-content/uploads/2016/09/Beecher_Ethics_and_Clinical_Research_1966.pdf.

[61] Rose CD. Ethical conduct of research in children: pediatricians and their IRB (Part 1 of 2). Pediatrics 2017;139(5). Available from: https://pediatrics.aappublications.org/content/pediatrics/139/5/e20163648.full.pdf.

[62] Adashi EY, Walters LB, Menikoff JA. The belmont report at 40: reckoning with time. Am J Public Health 2018;108(10):1345–8.

[63] Washington HA. Medical apartheid: the dark history of medical experimentation on Black Americans from colonial times to the present. New York, NY, USA: Doubleday Publishing Group; 2006.

[64] Berg AT, Baca CB, Loddenkemper T, et al. Priorities in pediatric epilepsy research: improving children's futures today. Neurology. 2013;81(13):1166–75. Available from: https://www.ncbi.nlm.nih.gov/pmc/articles/PMC3795602/pdf/WNL205431.pdf.

Chapter 1

The process of modern drug development and the challenge of young patients

Drug development is the process how today new medicines go through tests and clinical studies, until they are approved by the respective regulatory authority, can be prescribed as medicines, can be sold in pharmacies, and can be used in hospitals. The origin of a new medicine can be an initial idea, a new molecule or biologic, or a substance that exists already in nature. Technically, drug development runs through initial "preclinical" tests in the laboratory. If, in these preclinical tests, no serious reasons are identified to terminate development, development progresses to testing in animals. Again, if these tests do not result in termination, tests in humans can start. If these studies have positive results, the developer will submit an application for approval with the regulatory authority. In the US this is the Food and Drug Administration (FDA), and in the EU the European Medicines Agency (EMA).

Clinical studies can only start with the approval of the respective local authority, and of an Institutional Review Board (IRB) or ethics committee (EC). An essential part of drug development is the investigation of potential organ damage. Routinely, the heart, lungs, brain, liver, and digestive system are investigated, plus organs with a specific reason, e.g., if a new medication is a topical for skin application, then the skin will be examined more closely.

The technical side of drug development is an important part of the entire process, but only a part. Drug development is a living process in our society that is becoming increasingly complex. Penicillin, the first modern antibiotic, was scientifically described by Alexander Fleming for the first time in an academic research institution. To make it available to all humans, other dimension played a key role. While English chemical companies were not interested, the development of penicillin went ahead during World War II with the support of the US Office of Scientific Research and Development (OSRD), an institution today mostly remembered by the "Manhattan Project" that played a key role in the development of the first nuclear bombs. Further factors were the project management capacities of the involved US chemical companies. Penicillin did not start to play a major role in medicine due to

Considering the Patient in Pediatric Drug Development. DOI: https://doi.org/10.1016/B978-0-12-823888-2.00011-9

scientific publications. It started to play a major role when it was produced industrially. First it was reserved to treat wounded soldiers in World War II, then it became available in all US pharmacies, eventually worldwide [1].

Drugs are a part of our modern, complex society. In an extremely prudish society, a drug against male sexual dysfunction would be barely imaginable. The more so a drug against female sexual dysfunction. Sildenafil (Viagra) is available today already as a generic, as it was approved in 1998. Flibanserin was approved by the FDA in 2015 for female sexual dysfunction and is still patent protected [2]. Would drug development be as easy as learning or teaching Latin or Yoga, it would not have evolved into today's pharmaceutical industry that is now moving toward being called "life sciences."

Project management in drug development must handle competing, medical temporary fashion(s), costs for alternative therapies, societal conventions, marketing, and many further challenges. Drugs are part of today's range of goods, with all the strengths and weaknesses of the market. This may not please academics that live in their traditional ivory tower, either because they dream of being wise healers, because they are really unworldly and only want the best for their patients, or because they envy the financial successes of the pharmaceutical industry but would never admit this openly. Any combination of these three attitudes is possible.

Institutions like pediatric hospitals, representative bodies of professions such as pediatricians, clinical pharmacologists, pediatric clinical pharmacologists, and others have grown over the last decades. They all have two sides. They promote their services to the public, which is legitimate, but they also represent the particular professional interests of their respective group. In official self-descriptions, this second side is less emphasized. Again, this is logical and legitimate, but to assess the different and sometimes divergent interests in child health care, these particular interests need to be taken into consideration as well.

Today's system of drug development and drug approval is based, to a relevant part, on the successful processing of the thalidomide catastrophe by the US. Thalidomide had been developed in Germany and was there from the very beginning sold as an over-the-counter (OTC) medication. When its mutilating effects on the fetus became known in 1961, in Germany it was simply taken off the market. The developing company had earned a lot of money. Not one of the company's employees or managers went to prison; its inventor died as a rich and respected person. The company had not broken any law. Worldwide, the pharmaceutical legislation was not yet up to the challenge to handle modern drug development. In the end, a lame settlement between the thalidomide victims and the responsible company was achieved. In contrast to Germany, the United States reacted fast and determinedly. In 1962, a new law authorized the FDA to only approve drugs whose efficacy and safety had been proven by clinical studies. It took decades for the rest of the world to follow this precedence, but today it is in force worldwide [1,3,4].

Clinical studies replace individual observation of the effect of medicines by collective, organized observation. Usually, studies are performed in many centers (multicenter studies). Once enough patients have been treated, the study leadership examines which treatment worked better. As long as of a specific drug is not known whether it works at all, and if the positive results observed so far are based on true efficacy or only on wishful thinking, examination against placebo is usual. Placebo (Latin for "I will please") is a pill or tablet that by the eye and by its taste cannot be differentiated from the drug under examination. "Randomized" treatment means that neither the patient nor the treating doctor know which medication the respective patient receives. Would a doctor know that blue pills contain the true medication and white pills just placebo, he might be tempted to treat patients he perceives as attractive with blue pills, and other ones with white ones. He would not even have to be aware of this.

The central evaluation of the study data examines if the respective drug worked better than placebo or the chosen comparison in a statistically significant way. This approach is in contrast to common sense that relies on individual experiences. Accepting the results of a clinical study is based on trust in the study management, on trust in the involved institutions, and on trust that no cheating occurred. To be sure, regulatory authorities usually demand efficacy proven in two separate pivotal studies.

During the first decades of drug development, pharmaceutical companies deliberately kept quiet about side effects. The sales force was instructed to openly lie to the medical doctors when they were asked for a specific side effect. The current system, in which side effects are reported openly and companies face draconian penalties if they conceal relevant information, has taken decades to develop [1].

In view of the financial dimensions involved today in the development and the approval of a given new drug, it is easy to imagine the potential degree of temptation of drug developers to get an approval based on falsified data. On the other side, the detection of faked data would jeopardize the entire process of drug development and drug approval. The management of a company that invests billions of $ US or € into the development of a given drug would have to be clinically insane or suicidal to yield to such a temptation. There is no other industry that is as strictly controlled as the pharmaceutical industry, although with recent safety issues that surfaced in the car industry (Volkswagen [VW]'s fraudulent software with diesel engines) [5], or two crashed Boeing planes due to the flawed 737 Max antistall system [6], other industries will in the near future be controlled much more strictly as well. Thus, they will no longer be that far behind the pharmaceutical industry.

Life is full of temptations, wherever a lot of money is involved. VW did not withstand the temptation to cheat with the measurement of the amount of harmful exhaust gases by using fraudulent software. In the end, it was not the formerly famous German engineering that revealed the swindle, but the thoroughness of the US Environmental Protection Agency (EPA) [5].

The classical classification of clinical studies is into phase 1 to phase 4 studies. Phase 1 studies are performed with healthy volunteers to check initial safety in humans. Phase 2 studies investigate efficacy and safety in a relatively low number of patents to get an initial idea of the efficacy of the new medication. Phase 3 studies are the pivotal approval studies. Classically, two pivotal safety and efficacy studies were demanded to prove safety and efficacy of the new drug. These studies are the basis of submitting the application for marketing approval. Phase 4 studies test further questions after approval.

This classic classification system is handled more and more flexibly. In acute lymphoblastic leukemia (ALL), the most frequent malignant disease in young people, until a few years ago almost 90% of young patients could be healed by chemotherapy, bone marrow transplantation, and complementary intensive care. But nobody could predict who would survive and who would not. The diagnosis of ALL was an absolute horror for the entire affected family. The next therapeutic breakthrough occurred by engaging the body's own immune system. Treatment with chimeric antigen receptor (CAR) T cells uses reprogrammed T cells of the patient, that in contrast to naive T cells recognize, attack, and destroy malignant ALL cells. This treatment is rather complex. There are frequent side effects, such as a cytokine storm, which is a derailment of the immune system with high fever where cytokines and immune cells activate each other and rock up the storm. Untreated, a cytokine storm can kill a patient. All patients that participated at the pivotal study of tisagenlecleucel, in which the six-year-old Emily Whitehead participated, had no more chance of survival by classical treatment. To test in such patients, a new treatment against placebo would almost amount to murder. In the pivotal study more than 80% of the patients reacted to tisagenlecleucel treatment. Also the cytokine storms could be handled. The FDA approved this new drug in record time. Today tisagenlecleucel is approved in patients up to 25-years-old. No second efficacy study was requested [7,8]. Accelerated approval of successful new breakthrough therapies is usually done by the FDA, while the EU and its EMA have to deal with complicated internal bureaucratic procedures that delay fast and effective decision processes. Of course, there is also a tisagenlecleucel pediatric investigation plan [9].

To deliver a new drug, a number of further conditions are crucial. To develop a new medication, it must be medically and economically reasonable. Smallpox, a highly infective and very dangerous infectious disease, was in 1980 officially declared eradicated by the World Health Organization (WHO). Today, there are only two places with living smallpox viruses: in the US in Atlanta and in Russia in Kolzowo near Nowosibirsk. Of course, the danger continues that smallpox viruses are used in a war as a weapon of terror. The FDA has approved in 2018 tecovirimat to treat smallpox [10].

We have to assume that for the developing company the sales of this drug stock was financially rewarding.

In two-thirds of drugs against partial onset seizures (POS), treatment today works with existing antiepileptic drugs (AEDs). Many AEDs are today already out of patent. This makes it more demanding and more risky for companies to develop new AEDs. Of course, reimbursement institutions prefer cost-efficient treatment. If only a few patients remain that cannot be treated well with existing drugs, it can happen that the development of a new drug against the same disease is no longer financially rewarding.

This competitive development is one of the reasons that today more and more drugs are developed against rare diseases. For the frequent "classical" diseases such as hypertension, dyslipidemia, gastric ulcers, or esophagitis, there are today already many effective generics on the market. A new development for yet another antihypertensive drug would no longer be financially rewarding. But there are also further reasons for development of drugs for rare diseases, specifically US and EU laws that incentivize the development of new drugs against rare diseases

Do children need separate drug development? There are a few diseases that exist exclusively or predominantly in children. The lungs of preterm newborns do often not have lung surfactant, which is needed to keep the alveoli open and able to provide the blood with fresh oxygen. As long as the baby is in the mother, this job is done by the mother's lungs. In preterm newborns, the lungs do not contain yet enough lung surfactant. Without it, the hulls of the alveoli stick together and the lungs do not work sufficiently. Before lung surfactants were developed, many premature newborns died. Most vaccines protect babies against the bacteria, viruses, and fungi that threaten from the moment the young person enters the world outside of the mother's womb. But lung surfactant and vaccines for newborns are rather exceptions. By and large, drugs work in young patients in the same way as in adults. Of course, small children need other doses than adults. And during the first days, weeks, and months the baby is not yet adapted to life outside of the mother. But babies develop, mature and grow fast. Today we can measure the activity of the body's organs that are responsible for absorption, distribution, metabolism, and excretion of nutrition and drugs. The most fundamental changes occur during the first days and weeks of life. The very latest after a year the organs of infants are comparable with the organs of adults. Of course, infants and their organs are still smaller. And of course, there are exceptions and special cases, such as toxicities of some drugs in newborns, or drugs that can impair growth, such as corticosteroids. But that does not mean that we need separate efficacy studies for steroids in all groups of the "pediatric" population. The side effects of steroids are well known today. They are no longer as popular as they were decades ago, but we know how to handle them [11–14].

There is the concept that characterizes children as "therapeutic orphans" [15–18]. In the early days of drug development, drugs were approved in humans in general. But when the American Academy of Pediatrics (AAP) took up the concept of children as "therapeutic orphans" [19], a close collaboration emerged between the AAP and the FDA. The concept emerged that for minors separate proof-of-efficacy and safety studies and entirely separate drug development are required. The first basis (and the kernel of truth) for this concept emerged in the 1950s, in the early days of modern drug development, when preterm newborns received antibiotics that by today's knowledge had probably been dosed too highly. These toxicities were reported in the scientific press. Without knowing the damage from lawsuits in the US legal system, Europeans could not understand why drug manufacturers have introduced "pediatric warnings" into drug labels since 1962. A clever US lawyer would state for a child whose mother had a car accident that the accident was caused by the drug the child received, and as the drug was not approved by the FDA, the child might have behaved in a way that led to the accident. The case of a woman who scalded herself by hot coffee from McDonald's is famous. In the meantime, McDonald's indeed lowered the temperature of the coffee it serves [20]. The US tradition of damage lawsuits had the effect that companies really do everything imaginable to prevent future damage lawsuits. Thus, the culture of damage lawsuits has its positive sides.

The pediatric warnings in US drug labels since 1962 had a predominantly legal purpose. But the concept of special protection of children, whom the FDA defined as anybody younger than 17 years old, also responded to the pulse of the 1960s. The United Nations (UN) declared in 1959 a declaration about the rights of children [21]. The Soviet Union, who imprisoned and murdered millions of citizens in gulags and showed no mercy for children whose parents ended in a gulag [22,23], agreed with this declaration. The more general and noncommittal declarations are, the easier it is for any government to agree.

The call for separate "pediatric" studies in the US had several further reasons. There was a growing recognition that in very small children the organs responsible for absorption, distribution, metabolism, and excretion of nutrition and drugs are still immature [24–26]. While Europe was still recovering from World War II, research in the developing human body was far advanced in the US. All this supported the demand for separate clinical studies in "children" and separate drug approval. In this enthusiasm, it was overlooked that bodily a young person can be already mature, even if he is legally adult in the US, mostly at 18 or 19 years, depending of the respective state. The official FDA definition that everybody younger than 17 is in regard to drug treatment still a "child" met the pharmaceutical industry during a booming economy. During this boom, young persons started to reach puberty earlier [27,28]. When pharmaceutical companies were offered additional financial rewards in the form of a patent prolongation [29], a coalition of academic researchers, the FDA, and pharmaceutical industry came into existence. They all emphasized the high medical need for additional "pediatric" studies. The semantically flawed equalization of two very different meanings of the word "child" became a movement based on massive conflicts of interests [16–18].

The EU has expanded this definition of "children" to everybody under 18 years of age and has expanded the demand for mandatory separate "pediatric" studies also into areas where the FDA has not the authority to mandate "pediatric" studies. At the end, the massive dogmatic exaggerations of the EMA's "pediatric" demands facilitated the discovery of the fundamental flaws in the demand for separate "pediatric" studies and a separate alleged "pediatric drug development" [16–18].

One further fundamental aspect is that the pharmaceutical industry has become a huge economic sector. Those companies that survive the tough competition and trade rivalry represent economic prosperity, wealth, well-paid jobs, reputation, and more. People get older and older, we survive more and more diseases [30]. Child mortality in developed countries has continuously diminished [31]. This is not only the pharmaceutical industry's merit, but prevention by vaccination and treatment of diseases by modern drugs play a key role.

People project many theories and beliefs on the pharmaceutical industry. They range from factual discussion to open condemnation that perceives the pharmaceutical industry as a club of criminals, comparable only to the mafia and other forms of organized crime [32–34]. Others are deeply convinced that pharmaceutical industry should be directed by the state into a "good" direction as far as possible. Although children have profited at least as much as adults from improved pharmaceutical treatment during the last decades (if not even more), the US enacted pediatric laws to correct alleged discrimination of "children" by rewarding "pediatric" studies [29]. Many details are discussed in the specific chapters on respective disease areas. Here we address a very basic aspect: the belief that an entire economic sector should at least to some degree be put under state control. This belief fell in the EU on even more fertile ground than in the US, which had initiated the movement of "pediatric drug development" in 1997.

By twisting several elementary parts of reality, and using the blur of the different meanings of the word "child," a thought that initially wanted to help infants and children to get better pharmaceutical treatment became a movement that demands the relentless subordination of young people under the desire to perform with them as many separate regulatory clinical drug studies as possible. Of course, always disguised in noble, beautifully sounding words. Without this disguise, the US Congress and the parliament of the EU would not have approved the "pediatric" laws. This movement would have been unthinkable and impossible without the general societal conviction that the state deserves high trust in such an elementary matter like child health. To a certain extent, politics is always based on the art of promising a lot until the promising person is entrusted with executive power. What then follows can correspond to the original promises, or it can be something rather different. In "pediatric drug development," this has resulted in thousands of clinical studies that are medically and clinically unnecessary for all young people who already have a mature body, even if they are legally still minors. Other studies harm by studying individual drugs for respective approval, instead of looking at the patient. In the treatment of many diseases, the combination of medications is routinely used today. But many "child" studies were designed for the approval of individual medications, in the worst case testing against placebo or against traditional treatment standards that are inferior to the new compound [35–37]. The EMA insists on five-year "pediatric" studies in adolescents with hay fever (allergic rhinitis) against placebo. Five-year placebo treatment for allergic rhinitis increases the risk that the young person will develop asthma [38]. Other studies are those that demand recruitment of patients that do not exist in the demanded number. Worldwide, pharmaceutical companies are hunting for such young patients in multicenter studies with dozens, sometimes over 100, study centers [39,40]. If these studies would advance child health, this would be acceptable. But they do not. They are medically either completely senseless or massively exaggerated. In the worst case, they harm by withholding existing effective treatment from young people. They harm by omission.

In its entirety, this movement operates as separate, additional, alleged "pediatric drug development" under headlines such as "Better Medicines for Children" [41]. This sounds nice and convincing, as long as the question is not asked to what degree this is necessary at all. Once this critical question is asked, supporters of "pediatric drug development" give pseudoscientific justifications, which, however, do not withstand closer examination.

Today, all medical studies intended to be published or to be used for regulatory purposes must be listed in a publicly accessible study registry. The first such registry, www.clinicaltrials.gov has a fascinating history. Publicly available registers of all clinical trials had been desired by scientists for decades. Medical literature predominantly reported and reports successful trials. Negative results attract less attention, and scientific journals are less interested in publishing them. Clinical research does not take place in a vacuum. There are often diverse interests behind the funding of a clinical study. The first publicly accessible registry was established due to public pressure from people infected with human immunodeficiency virus (HIV), who demanded better access to study data in order to be informed about the current state of research [42]. Infection with HIV results in acquired immunodeficiency syndrome (AIDS) and leads to death, if left untreated. The result of this pressure was initially a US law in 1988 that led to the development of a database on AIDS studies. This database in turn motivated other interest groups to request something comparable for all diseases. Finally, the 1997 FDA Modernization Act (FDAMA), which included the US pediatric law, led also to the creation of www.clinicaltrials.gov, which was released on the internet in 2000. It is operated by the US National Library of Medicine (NLM) within the US National Health Institutes (NIH). It has become the world's largest clinical trial database and currently contains over 300,000 clinical trials. Initially, it only recorded studies that were paid for by the NIH. Today, it also lists all studies, including those sponsored by universities and those sponsored by pharmaceutical companies.

In 2004, the New York state attorney sued GlaxoSmithKline (GSK) for hiding results of "pediatric" studies in depression, suppressing information that would show that certain antidepressants could be harmful [42]. The questionability of these depression "child" studies is discussed in a separate chapter. But what we can see here from this indictment is the tension in which drug development occurs today. If an ambitious public prosecutor believes that he can raise his level of awareness through an appropriate charge, he will indict.

In 2005 the International Committee Of Medical Journal Editors (ICMJE) declared that only those publications would be published, which are or were registered in a study register. Many studies had previously been published without reliable publicly accessible registration. Because the ICMJE represents the most influential medical journals, this declaration had a resounding impact [43,44].

The Declaration of Helsinki was adopted 1964 by the World Medical Association (WMA). It defines the basic principles of medical research in humans. The Declaration of Helsinki is regularly revised at the General Meetings of the WMA. It was adopted on the basis of the Nuremberg Code, passed in 1947 in the trial of medical doctors who had participated in criminal experiments in the Nazi Third Reich. The basic principles of both the Nuremberg Code and the Helsinki Declaration are voluntary study participation and that the questions to be answered by the studies must be medically reasonable. Senseless repetition of clinical studies in officially defined "children" are neither permitted by the Nuremberg Code nor by the Helsinki Declaration. In the meantime, the Helsinki Declaration also requires that clinical studies must be listed in a publicly accessible study registry [45].

There are now several other national and international study registries. The EU has set up its own study registry [46], as has the WHO [47] and Switzerland [48].

Numerous European universities now offer study projects on children's rights [49–53]. Will these courses contribute to the improvement of children's rights and their health, or do they just confer empty words?

References

[1] Hilts PJ. Protecting America's health: The FDA, business, and one hundred years of regulation. New York: Alfred A Knopf Publishers; 2003.

[2] FDA 2015. Flibanserin label. <https://www.accessdata.fda.gov/drugsatfda_docs/label/2015/022526lbl.pdf>.

[3] Vargesson N. Thalidomide-induced teratogenesis: history and mechanisms. Birth Defects Res C Embryo Today 2015;105(2):140–56.

[4] Rägo L, Santo B. Drug regulation: history, present and future. In: van Boxtel CJ, Santo B, Edwards IR, editors. Drug benefits andrisks: international textbook of clinical pharmacology. Revised 2nd ed.

[5] Phys.org 2018. Five things to know about VW's 'dieselgate' scandal. <https://phys.org/news/2018-06-vw-dieselgate-scandal.html>.

[6] Dominic Gates 2020. Boeing's 737 MAX 'design failures' and FAA's 'grossly insufficient' review slammed. https://www.seattletimes.com/business/boeing-aerospace/u-s-house-preliminary-report-faults-boeing-faa-over-737-max-crashes/

[7] FDA 2017. Tisagenlecleucel prescribing information. <https://www.fda.gov/files/vaccines%2C%20blood%20%26%20biologics/published/Package-Insert---KYMRIAH.pdf>.

[8] Maude SL, Laetsch TW, Buechner J, et al. Tisagenlecleucel in children and young adults with B-cell lymphoblastic leukemia. N Engl J Med 2018;378:439–48.

[9] EMA Tisagenlecleucel PIP EMEA-001654-PIP01-14-M03. <https://www.ema.europa.eu/en/documents/pip-decision/p/0008/2019-ema-decision-3-january-2019-acceptance-modification-agreed-paediatric-investigation-plan_en.pdf>.

[10] FDA 2018. Tecovirimat prescribing information. <https://www.accessdata.fda.gov/drugsatfda_docs/label/2018/208627s000lbl.pdf>.

[11] Skoner JD, Schaffner TJ, Schad CA, et al. Addressing steroid phobia: improving the risk-benefit ratio with new agents. Allergy Asthma Proc 2008;29(4):358–64.

[12] Li AW, Yin ES, Antaya RJ. Topical corticosteroid phobia in atopic dermatitis: a systematic review. JAMA Dermatol 2017;153(10):1036–42.

[13] Hui RWH. Inhaled corticosteroid-phobia and childhood asthma: current understanding and management implications. Paediatr Respir Rev 2020;33:62–6.

[14] Psomadakis CE, Han G. New and emerging topical therapies for psoriasis and atopic dermatitis. J Clin Aesthet Dermatol 2019;12(12):28–34 <https://www.ncbi.nlm.nih.gov/pmc/articles/PMC7002051/pdf/jcad_12_12_28.pdf>.

[15] Shirkey H. Therapeutic orphans. J Pediatrics 1968;72(1):119–20 Reprinted in Pediatrics 1999;104(3) (Suppl), 583-584. <https://pediatrics.aappublications.org/content/pediatrics/104/Supplement_3/583.full.pdf>.

[16] Rose K, Neubauer D, Grant-Kels JM. Rational use of medicine in children – the conflict of interests story. A review. Rambam Maimonides Med J 2019;10(3):e0018. Available from: https://doi.org/10.5041/RMMJ.10371; <https://www.rmmj.org.il/userimages/928/2/PublishFiles/953Article.pdf>.

[17] Rose K. The challenges of pediatric drug development. Curr Ther Res Clin Exp 2019. <https://doi.org/10.1016/j.curtheres.2019.01.007>.

[18] Rose K, Grant-Kels JM. The meanings of "pediatric drug development". A review. Therapeutic Innov Regulatory Sci 2018. <https://doi.org/10.1177/2168479018812060>.

[19] Guidelines for the Ethical Conduct of Studies to Evaluate Drugs in Pediatric Populations, Committee on Drugs. American Academy of Pediatrics, Pediatrics 1995;95(2):286–94.

[20] Scalding by hot coffee. <https://en.wikipedia.org/wiki/Liebeck_v._McDonald%27s_Restaurants>

[21] UN declaration of the rights of the child 1959. <https://www.humanium.org/en/declaration-rights-child-2/>.

[22] <https://www.history.com/topics/russia/gulag>.

[23] Frierson CA, Vilensky SS. Children of the Gulag. New Haven, CT: Yale University Press; 2010.
[24] Kearns GL, Abdel-Rahman SM, Alander SW, Blowey DL, Leeder JS, Kauffman RE. Developmental pharmacology - drug disposition, action, and therapy in infants and children. N Engl J Med 2003;349(12):1157–67.
[25] Crane E, Tutag Lehr V, Mathew M, Aranda JV. Developmental pharmacology and therapeutics. In: Buonocore G, Bracci R, Weindling M, editors. Neonatology. Milan, Italy: Springer Publishers; 2012. p. 364–9.
[26] Blumer JL. Developmental pharmacology: past, present and future. Acta Paediatr Jpn 1996;38(6):555–61.
[27] Cone Jr. TE. Secular acceleration of height and biologic maturation in children during the past century. J Pediatr 1961;59:736–40.
[28] Komlos J, Lauderdale BE. The mysterious trend in American heights in the 20th century. Ann Hum Biol 2007;34(2):206–15.
[29] Hirschfeld S, Saint-Raymond A. Pediatric regulatory initiatives. Handb Exp Pharmacol 2011;205:245–68.
[30] Falah G, Giller A, Gutman D, et al. Breaking the glass ceiling. Gerontology 2020;1–6 Feb 26.
[31] Moller AB, Patten JH, Hanson C, et al. Monitoring maternal and newborn health outcomes globally: a brief history of key events and initiatives. Trop Med Int Health 2019; 24(12):1342–68.
[32] Angell M. The truth about the drug companies: how they deceive us and what to do about it. New York, USA: Random House Publishers; 2004.
[33] Gøtzsche PC. Tödliche Medizin und organisierte Kriminalität: Wie die Pharmaindustrie unser Gesundheitswesen korrumpiert. München: Riva Verlag; 2014.
[34] Goldacre B. Bad Pharma: How drug companies mislead doctors and harm patients. London, UK: HarperCollinsPublishers; 2012.
[35] Rose K, Grant-Kels JM. Pediatric melanoma – the whole (conflicts of interest) story. Int J Womens Dermatol 2018;5(2):110–1115. Available from: https://doi.org/10.1016/j.ijwd.2018.10.020; <https://www.ncbi.nlm.nih.gov/pmc/articles/PMC6451736/pdf/main.pdf>.
[36] Rose K, Walson PD. Are regulatory age limits in pediatric melanoma justified? Curr Ther Res Clin Exp 2019. <https://www.ncbi.nlm.nih.gov/pmc/articles/PMC6677782/pdf/main.pdf>.
[37] Rose K, Walson PD. Do the European Medicines Agency (EMA) decisions hurt pediatric melanoma patients? Clin Therapeutics 2017;39(2):253–65. <https://www.clinicaltherapeutics.com/article/S0149-2918(17)30047-4/pdf>.
[38] Rose K, Kopp MV. Pediatric investigation plans for specific immunotherapy: Questionable contributions to childhood health. Pediatr Allergy Immunol 2015 Dec;26(8): 695–701.
[39] Rose K, Grant-Kels JM. Questionable international pediatric studies in the United States and Russia triggered by regulatory authorities. Asian J Res Med Pharm Sci 2018;3(3) <http://www.journalrepository.org/media/journals/AJRIMPS_63/2018/Apr/Rose332018AJRIMPS40776.pdf>.
[40] Rose K, Grant-Kels JM. Questionable industry-sponsored pediatric studies in China Triggered by United States of America (US) and European Union (EU) Regulatory Authorities. SF Pharma J 2018;1:1. <https://www.scifedpublishers.com/open-access/questionable-industry-sponsored-pediatric-studies-in-china-triggeredby-united-states-of-america-us-and-european-union-eu-regulatoryauthorities.pdf>.
[41] EMA 2015. Better medicines for children. <https://www.ema.europa.eu/en/documents/leaflet/better-medicines-children_en.pdf>.

[42] Rennie. Trial registration. A great idea switches from ignored to irresistible. JAMA 2004;292(11):1359–62 2004 Sep 15.

[43] International Committee of Medical Journal Editors (ICMJE) Recommendations for the Conduct, Reporting, Editing, and Publication of Scholarly work in Medical Journals. <http://www.icmje.org/recommendations/>.

[44] Wikipedia ClinicalTrials.gov. https://en.wikipedia.org/wiki/ClinicalTrials.gov

[45] World Medical Association (WMA) Declaration of Helsinki – Ethical Principles for Medical Research Involving Human Subjects. Adopted by the 18th WMA General Assembly, Helsinki, Finland, June 1964, and amended by the 64th WMA General Assembly, Fortaleza, Brazil, October 2013. <https://www.wma.net/policies-post/wma-declaration-of-helsinki-ethical-principles-for-medical-research-involving-human-subjects/>

[46] EU clinical trials registry. <https://www.clinicaltrialsregister.eu>

[47] WHO clinical trials registry. <https://apps.who.int/trialsearch/>

[48] Swiss clinical trials registry. <https://www.kofam.ch>

[49] Master of Advanced Studies in Children's Rights (MCR) an der Universität Geneve, Schweiz. <https://www.unige.ch/cide/fr/formations/formation-continue/master-advanced-studies-childrens-rights-mcr/>

[50] Master of Laws: Advanced Studies in International Children's Rights (LL.M.) an der Universität Leiden, Niederlande. <https://www.universiteitleiden.nl/en/education/study-programmes/master/international-childrens-rights>.

[51] Master of Arts: Childhood Studies and Children's Rights, University Potsdam, Germany. <https://www.fh-potsdam.de/en/studieren/fachbereiche/sozial-und-bildungswissenschaften/studium/studiengaenge/master/ma-childhood-studies-and-childrens-rights/>

[52] Master of Arts: Childhood Studies and Children's Rights, University Magdeburg, Germany. <https://www.hs-magdeburg.de/en/studies/masters-programmes/childhood-studies-and-childrens-rights.html>.

[53] Children's Rights: Master of Science, Belfast, UK. <https://www.qub.ac.uk/courses/post-graduate-taught/childrens-rights-msc/>

Chapter 2

US and EU pediatric legislation

There are many overviews in the literature over the US and EU pediatric legislation [1–5]. To prevent the reader from being lost, we focus on the essentials. The guiding principle is to describe and analyze the laws themselves, their scientific and conceptual background, their justifications, the medical and scientific sense of the laws themselves, and the medical and scientific sense of the implementation of these laws by the US Food and Drug Administration (FDA) and the European Medicines Agency (EMA).

In 1979, the FDA defined "children" as anyone under the age of 17 years [6], and introduced a pediatric use subsection into the label template [5]. Both decisions were based on the firm belief that "children" are fundamentally different from adults. This administrative definition of "children" had been preceded by a long debate in the US, triggered by pediatric warnings in drug labels and/or prescription information that the respective drug had not been tested in children, that these warnings showed that children were excluded from participation in pharmacological progress, and that hence children were "therapeutic orphans" [7]. But these warnings had primarily the *legal* purpose to protect drug developers from damage lawsuits, a well-known characteristic of the US legal culture [8–12]. The pediatric warnings were intended to protect against claims of alleged injuries of young persons treated by a drug without "pediatric" approval that a resourceful lawyer might turn into a claim for damage compensation.

In 1994, the FDA asked pharmaceutical companies to submit literature and other data with additional information on the use of drugs in "children." If they had such data, they should apply for pediatric approval. If the data were inadequate, the labels/prescription information now had to contain the sentence "safety and effectiveness in pediatric patients have not been established" [3,5,13,14]. This defined a new category of patients by an age limit, regardless of whether they were bodily still children or not. By today's knowledge, this classification lacked sense medically and scientifically. The bodies of premature babies, newborns, and infants absorb, distribute, metabolize, and excrete food and drugs very differently from adults. Absorption, distribution, metabolism, and excretion change mostly during the first months of life [15]. But babies and infants do not remain newborn until they come officially of age. After the first months, the next fundamental change in the human body occurs during the process of puberty [16].

Considering the Patient in Pediatric Drug Development. DOI: https://doi.org/10.1016/B978-0-12-823888-2.00029-6

The FDA decree of 1994 resulted only in a few additional "pediatric" labels. To increase the number of "pediatric" approvals and "pediatric" labels, various stakeholders and the FDA advocated a law to facilitate more "pediatric" labels. Such "pediatric" labels had to be based on separate "pediatric" studies. Pharmaceutical companies were offered six months patent extension for such studies. Back then several drugs sold already at $US billions a year. It was very lucrative for companies to sell their drugs for half a year longer at a patented price [17]. The first "pediatric" law was introduced in 1997 as the Food and Drug Modernization Act (FDAMA) [5]. It was supported by the community of "pediatric" researchers, by the American Academy of Pediatrics (AAP), by pediatric clinical pharmacology [18], and by the pharmaceutical industry. Pharmaceutical companies began to sponsor "pediatric" studies. The representatives of "pediatric" research and "pediatric" clinical pharmacology were enthusiastic [18–22]. Finally, they received the desired public recognition. Nobody made the difference between physical and legal meanings of the term "child" a subject of discussion. The first pediatric pharmaceutical law within FDAMA was reauthorized in 2002 under the title "Best Pharmaceuticals for Children Act" (BPCA). In 2003, the initial "pediatric" law was supplemented by a second law that authorized the FDA to mandate "pediatric" studies also without a reward (Pediatric Research Equity Act, PREA) [1]. Initially, both laws had to be renewed every five years to remain in force. In 2012, both became valid indefinitely as FDA Safety and Innovation Act (FDASIA) [5,23].

Did the "pediatric" studies triggered by US laws massively improve children's health as their proponents had promised and expected? Medically and clinically, these studies achieved little for young patients. They contributed to many additional "pediatric" studies, "pediatric" approvals, "pediatric" labels [2,3,5] and "pediatric" careers in the FDA, clinical academia, and pharmaceutical industry [24]. The intellectual basis of these laws was the concept that everything is different in "children."

For adolescents who have already a mature body but are administratively still "children," these studies were completely pointless. For school-age children, the old rule of giving half the adult dose was adequate with few exceptions, e.g., extremely overweight or extremely underweight children. In school-age children, dose finding is needed, not international multicenter studies. Thus, in school-age children, the majority of regulatory clinical studies were massively exaggerated, because they focused on regulatory approval and not on clinically reasonable questions.

The only group in which separate pediatric studies would have been necessary were premature babies, newborns, and young infants, but only a tiny fraction of all the "pediatric" studies triggered by regulatory requests/demands were neonate studies. Furthermore, school-age children and infants do not need separate regulatory proof of efficacy. Most clinically relevant questions can be answered by "opportunistic" studies [25–27], a concept that in the meantime has also entered FDA recommendations [28].

It could be argued that through these "pediatric" studies many pediatricians and general practitioners got clinical experience in treating young persons with new drugs. But the entire discipline of pediatric evolved in more than the first half of the 20th century by using all available drugs and technologies without separate "pediatric" approval [29]. The clinical discipline of pediatrics emerged and evolved long before the regulatory authorities began to focus on "children." Shirkey himself noted that most clinicians ignored the "pediatric warnings," but did not process this observation intellectually [7].

The FDA reported in two large reports the experiences made with the US "pediatric" laws. The first report from 2001 predicted that the expected "pediatric" studies would measurably lead to improved child health and less absence of parents from work because the children would now be better cared for [30]. These were reasonable and measurable clinical and economic expectations. But the next report, 15 years later, did no longer address these expectations; they were not even mentioned anymore. Instead, the report lists administrative details about the number of new "pediatric" labels and "pediatric" studies [23].

The EU started thinking about its own "pediatric" law in 1997, followed by ten years of deliberations [31]. The EU pediatric regulation was enacted in 2006 and came legally in force in 2007 [1,32]. It was modeled on the US law, but was more ambitious and extensive from the start. There is only one EU pediatric law, compared to the two US ones. All persons under the age of 18 are defined as "children," which is even further away from reality than the US. Persons that are 17-years-old are usually already bodily mature today [33,34], although not yet mentally and not yet legally. But drugs treat the body. While the US law offered rewards for medicines already on the market, the EU requires discussion of "pediatric" studies years before the pivotal studies that later may lead to the respective drug's approval are even initiated. "Pediatric" studies are required for all drugs, including those for which the FDA does not have the authority to mandate separate "pediatric" studies, including drugs that treat rare diseases, biologicals, and vaccines.

A Pediatric Committee was set up within the EMA. For all new medicines and for regulatory changes for drugs already approved, companies must submit a draft pediatric investigation plan (PIP). This draft PIP is negotiated with the EMA in a rigid procedure that in routine cases takes one year [35]. During this negotiation, the EMA gives feedback whether the proposed PIP appears to be acceptable or not. If the applicant does not improve the submitted draft PIP sufficiently, it is rejected and EU approval is blocked until a new PIP is submitted and accepted.

In the EU pediatric regulation, the underlying core ideas are set out in the first sentences of the preamble. All "children" allegedly face side effects from drugs, right up to death, if the respective drug has not been studied in separate "pediatric" studies. "Children" are defined as everybody under the age of 18 years. Pharmaceutical industry has no economic interest in conducting separate "pediatric" studies. Therefore the state has to step in and enforce these studies that are necessary for child health [32].

All this sounds nice and pathetic. Except that there is no scientific sense in it. The justification of the EU pediatric law is based on the semantic blur between different meanings of the word "child." This justification is a bubble that implodes when the needle of one crucial critical question is applied: How long are minors bodily children, and how different is their body from adults?

Behind the children-are-therapeutic-orphans concept is a deep societal trauma from the history of drug development: the shock of the thalidomide disaster that had shown that an apparently harmless small pill can have devastating effects on thousands of patients and their families [36,37].

Behind the children-are-therapeutic-orphans concept are also massive conflicts of interest. Many "pediatric" careers have been made in regulatory authorities, clinical academia, and pharmaceutical industry [24,38].

Official mainstream science supports separate regulatory "pediatric" studies. Operatively, they are demanded by the regulatory authorities [39,40], and by representatives of the pharmaceutical industry who have made careers about these "pediatric" studies [5,41].

It is not the first time in history that ideas that most people believed in turned out to be wrong years later. Gone are the days when everyone believed that switching from winter time to summer time would save energy. It will take a few more years before the EU manages to reverse the change from winter to summer time in spring and back in fall. We will see if the US will follow. In the past, everyone was convinced that the sun rotated around the earth. During a critical period of time, anybody who disagreed was persecuted by the inquisition and in the worst case burned on the stake. For centuries it was believed that women are less intelligent than men. It took hard fights from female individuals (and those men who supported them) until the first female medical doctor was qualified, the first female physicist could write her PhD thesis, and finally until the first female Nobel prize winner was announced. For decades in Western societies, including Canada, Sweden, Finland, and Australia, indigenous people were regarded to have an inferior culture. Their children were taken away to be educated in the language and in the culture of the majority. Similar atrocities were committed toward minorities and toward individuals that lacked societal protection, including Switzerland and Ireland. These abuses stopped only when the general attitude to different cultures had so far changed that such an approach started first to be seen as unacceptable and eventually was classified as abuse. These abuses are now being uncovered in each single country. All these abuses have in common that they reflected general convictions about the inferiority of persons in society. These abuses were performed once these convictions translated into executive power for individuals and/or institutions where those that organized, coordinated, or performed these abuses in person knew that they were immune from criminal prosecution even if the acts they performed were openly criminal [42–46].

The mainstream representatives of pediatric clinical pharmacology have not challenged so far the children-are-therapeutic-orphans concept in general; the American Academy of Clinical Pharmacology has at least already noted that the FDA now accepts "extrapolation" from adults to adolescents in several clinical areas [47]. But the mantra that defines "children" chronologically remains unchallenged. At least, some comparability of adults and adolescents is grudgingly accepted. This is a phenomenon typical before major paradigm shifts in science: well-established mantras are reiterated; the representatives of learned societies repeat that they support these mantras. But on the other side, they try to reconcile obvious inconsistencies between the official theories and observations by common sense. There is no scientific justification why a drug can be off-label in a 17-year-old person and on-label a year, or even only days later, if the respective person is near their 18th birthday.

Tuskegee is a small town in Macon County, Alabama. This area produced largely cotton before the US civil war, dependent on slave labor. When the war was over, many former slaves continued to work on plantations. On one side, illiteracy was high. On the other side, the Tuskegee Normal School was established as a black college by a former slave. This school eventually became today's Tuskegee University. During World War II, the first squadron of black pilots in the US military was trained in Tuskegee for service in that war (the Tuskegee airmen).

When the US Public Health Service (PHS) began a study in 1932 to monitor syphilis in black men, no effective drugs existed yet to treat syphilis. The Tuskegee study is today taught as a standard example of an unethical study. The recruited patients were told they had "bad blood." Even when effective medication for syphilis began to be available, i.e., antibiotics, the study continued. This study offered employment to the study personnel. Staff members were invited to the autopsy of deceased study participants. The study was not carried out in secret. It was presented at annual meetings of the American Medical Association (AMA). But at that time, black doctors were not admitted to these meetings. The study was discontinued when Peter Buxtun, a PHS employee who had nothing to do with the study, first asked internally for seven years that the study should be terminated. Finally, he realized that he would not achieve anything if he continued in this way. He informed a journalist. It was only when she reported on the study in the Washington Evening Star in 1972 and it became front page news in the New York Times that the public outrage was large enough to force the immediate termination of the study. In our context, the study is important because it was scientifically justified by the people involved in day-to-day scientific work [48–51].

Neither the end of segregation between white and black people, nor the end of the infamous Tuskegee trial were achieved through scientific progress alone. Changes of general attitudes play a major role, in combination with individuals that challenge traditional frameworks.

The basic principle of the "pediatric" studies required in PIPs is that, in addition to the studies that lead to approval in humans ("adults"), efficacy and safety must be separately proven also in "children." EMA-demanded studies are mostly double-blind, randomized, multicenter studies, either against placebo or against routine treatment ("standard of care") in 1-to-17-year-olds, 2-to-17-year-old patients, or several studies in individual subgroups [24,52,53].

The EU PIPs have several characteristics that would make them ridiculous were these issues not too serious to be laughed at. They result in the abuse of young people on at least three levels.

First, the EU PIPs often demand studies in patients that do not exist in the required numbers. Statistics are systematically misinterpreted [54]; publications that reveal these errors are ignored [55]; feedback from drug developers that the demanded patients cannot be recruited are rejected with the recommendation to make greater efforts for recruitment. Often the respective PIPs are modified to allow more time for recruitment. At present, the record number of PIP modifications is 14, visible at the very end of the respective PIP number, e.g., the most recent version of the brivaracetam PIP EMEA-000332-PIP01-08-M14 [56]. Fourteen PIP modifications correspond to a total sum of negotiation of roughly seven-and-a-half years: one year to discuss the original PIP, plus 13 times one-half year, respectively, to negotiate each single new modification. Because many of the adolescent patients requested are too rare to be included in a single clinical research center, many EU PIPs demand multicenter studies. Worldwide studies on young patients with depression and other mental illnesses, malignant illnesses, joint inflammation, diabetes, skin illnesses, hay fever, and many more are carried out due to PIP demands [24,57–60]. Thus, new treatment methods are withheld from young patients for many years because they are initially only approved for people >18 years old. For PIP "pediatric" studies that have already started the sponsoring companies and the clinical research organizations commissioned to perform these studies are literally chasing young patients worldwide. The only continent where these studies are not performed is Antarctica, where people currently have no children. The EMA is aware of this problem [61], but this has neither prevented new PIPs nor in termination of questionable studies. In a few cases, PIPs that demand multiple "pediatric" studies are changed into complete waivers, e.g., the retigabine PIP EMEA-000116-PIP01-07-M08, which until its eighth modification demanded 20 "pediatric" studies in epilepsy [62] but was then replaced by a complete waiver with modification no. 9 (EMEA-000116-PIP01-07-M09) [63]. These studies were first demanded in young human beings, then dropped. This is not responsible treatment of young patients, but an attitude that regards human beings as material of administration. The PIP of the antiepileptic drug perampanel is now in its 11th modification (EMEA-000467-PIP01-08-M11) [64], as is the PIP for the anticoagulant rivaroxaban EMEA-000430-PIP01-08-M11 [65].

Second, several demanded "pediatric" studies programs cover eternities that would condemn recruited patients to outdated treatment. The retigabine PIP demanded all "pediatric" studies to be completed until 2035 [62]. PIP EMEA-000910-PIP01-10 still demands "pediatric" allergen studies to be completed until 2031 [66]. We cannot know today how we will treat allergies or epilepsy in 20 years' time.

Third, the diseases that officially do not occur in "children" have been continuously reduced by the EMA since 2008. Many diseases occur frequently in adults and occasionally in young people. In 2007, melanoma was one of the diseases officially declared not to exist in "children." This was "corrected" in 2008, justified by a sufficient number of young people with melanoma in the US for "pediatric" studies [67]. But in young people who are diagnosed with melanoma, the vast majority of cases are immediately surgically removed. This eliminates the melanoma, and if there are no metastases or affected lymph nodes, then there is no need for medication [54]. These objections were published several times, which the EMA consistently ignored. The EMA has continued to issue melanoma PIPs, now twelve in number [68]. Effective drugs for melanoma are now available. But the EU PIPs require "pediatric" studies with single drugs, while standard therapy of melanoma is today to combine two drugs. Two "pediatric" melanoma studies had to be terminated because there were no more doctors willing to include young people in these "child" studies [24,38,69].

Since 2018, companies that develop drugs against liver cancer drugs must commit to separate "pediatric" studies [70]. All studies in rare young patients are logistically very complex. As long as such studies are later published in prestigious medical journals, clinicians will continue to perform them. If the developing company does not sufficiently comply with the EMA demands, the respective new drug against liver cancer will not be approved in the EU. Thus, the EMA has transformed a law that was *intended* to improve medical treatment of young humans into the opposite: companies are threatened. New, innovative life-saving or life-prolonging treatments will not be approved if the company does not commit to sponsor medically senseless or even harmful "pediatric" studies. Parents can prevent young persons who are unlucky enough to develop liver cancer at a young age from participating in such senseless studies. Without the parents' consent study participation is not possible. Institutional Review Boards (IRBs)/ ethics committees (ECs) have the authority to reject questionable "pediatric" studies and/or to suspend ongoing ones. But so far, IRBs/ECs have not recognized the potential harm of "pediatric" studies requested/demanded by the regulatory authorities.

Regarding drug development, the EU has transformed itself from a region that wanted to become the most science-based region of the world 20 years ago [71] to a region that squeezes additional questionable and harmful "pediatric" studies from companies that develop promising new drugs and treatments. Innovative drug development is answered by a stone age concept that is disguised in an elegant envelope of pseudoscience. Almost all "pediatric" studies required by EMA PIPs violate the Declaration of Helsinki, which prohibits medical and scientifically senseless human studies [72].

Let us hope that in the near future what happened in Europe in 1610 happens again: a young man named Galileo Galilei observed through a self-made telescope (lenses, construction material, and the basics how to build optical instruments had started to be broadly available among educated persons) that four moons circle around the planet Jupiter. He published this and other astronomical observations [73]. Today, we know of many more Jupiter moons, but Galileo Galilei saw the four largest ones. Anyone with a telescope could confirm his observation. That moons circle a planet contradicted the world theory of the Catholic Church at that time. The inquisition forced Galileo to publicly withdraw his observations and to confirm that the sun revolves around the earth. This triumph of the church did not last long. Increasingly, persons that trusted their own eyes more than the teachings of the Catholic Church confirmed over the coming years, decades, and centuries that four moons circle around Jupiter. Today we can see their position directly on the Internet without having to own a telescope. We even have a close-up of every single Jupiter moon via satellite. All this has become visible by satellites, space probes, communication technology, and the Internet.

Comparably, everybody can now check PIP decisions and PIP-triggered "pediatric" studies on the Internet. The EMA must publish every single PIP decision. Every single "pediatric" study is entered in a study register that is available to the general public through the Internet. Every parent and every young patient can check what the EMA is demanding in the name of "children's" health. Most documents are in English.

The EMA runs the "European Network of Pediatric Research at the European Medicines Agency" (Enpr-EMA) [74–78]. Enpr-EMA does not directly distribute research funds, but it facilitates networking for academic pediatric researchers, which naturally includes access to funds.

"Pediatric" regulatory studies harm patients where they test effective treatment against placebo, or monotherapy against already available combination treatment, i.e., against outdated treatment [24,38,64,69].

Pediatric pharmaceutical laws are not merely driven by science, although their protagonists usually justify them by alleged science. The US law of 2012, FDASIA, also contained the Advancing Hope Act, which offers companies that get the approval for a drug against a rare pediatric disease a voucher for a priority review of another drug. Such vouchers are transferable, i.e., the receiving company can sell it to another company. Until 2017, 10 drug companies received such a voucher [5,23]. These vouchers are certainly a good incentive to facilitate drug development. On the other side, the RACE for children act is a step back and imitates the EU approach.

References

[1] Hirschfeld S, Saint-Raymond A. Pediatric regulatory initiatives. Handb Exp Pharmacol 2011;205:245–68.

[2] Ward RM, Benjamin DK, Davis JM, et al. The need for pediatric drug development. J Pediatr 2018;192:13–21.

[3] McCune S. 2019. FDA overview of the pediatric legislation. <https://www.fda.gov/media/132890/download>.

[4] McCune S, Portman R. Innovation and opportunities in pediatric therapeutic development. Ther Innov Regul Sci 2019;53(5):564–6.

[5] Bucci-Rechtweg C. Enhancing the pediatric drug development framework to deliver better pediatric therapiestomorrow. Clin Ther 2017;39(10):1920–32 <https://www.clinicaltherapeutics.com/article/S0149-2918(17)30832-9/pdf>.

[6] Hirschfeld S. History of pediatric labeling. <http://bit.ly/2lYCkAJ>.

[7] Shirkey H. Therapeutic orphans. J Pediatr 1968;72(1):119–20 <https://pdfs.semanticscholar.org/f1cb/acdbac19fa56236b919fb7799eaacaa10c77.pdf>.

[8] Kritzer HM. Propensity to Sue in England and the United States of America: blaming and claiming in tort cases. J Law Soc 1991;18(4):400–27.

[9] Lochlann Jain SS. Injury: the politics of product design and safety law in the United States. Princeton, NJ, USA: Princeton University Press; 2006.

[10] McGovern F. Punitive damages and class actions. Lousiana Law Rev 2010;70:435–62 <https://scholarship.law.duke.edu/cgi/viewcontent.cgi?article = 2762&context = faculty_scholarship>.

[11] Bal BS. An introduction to medical malpractice in the United States. Clin Orthop Relat Res 2009;467(2):339–47 <https://www.ncbi.nlm.nih.gov/pmc/articles/PMC2628513/>.

[12] Kass JS, Rose RV. Medical malpractice reform: historical approaches, alternative models, and communication and resolution programs. AMA J Ethics 2016;18(3):299–310 <https://journalofethics.ama-assn.org/sites/journalofethics.ama-assn.org/files/2019-12/pfor6-1603.pdf>.

[13] FDA 1994. Specific requirements on content and format of labeling for human prescription drugs; revision of "pediatric use" subsection in the labeling. <https://www.govinfo.gov/content/pkg/FR-1994-12-13/html/94-30238.htm>.

[14] Addressing the Barriers to Pediatric Drug Development: Workshop Summary. Institute of Medicine (US) Forum on Drug Discovery, Development, and Translation. Washington DC, National Academies Press, USA, 2008. <https://www.ncbi.nlm.nih.gov/books/NBK3997/>.

[15] Kearns GL, Abdel-Rahman SM, Alander SW, et al. Developmental pharmacology - drug disposition, action, and therapy in infants and children. N Engl J Med 2003;349(12):1157–67 <https://pdfs.semanticscholar.org/55f8/1745303e9aaec7f4cb85f0b5921eec14a9c0.pdf>.

[16] Cheng HL, Harris SR, Sritharan M, et al. The tempo of puberty and its relationship to adolescent health and well-being: A systematic review. Acta Paediatr 2019.

[17] Li JS, Eisenstein EL, Grabowski HG, et al. Economic return of clinical trials performed under the pediatric exclusivity program. JAMA 2007;297(5):480–8.

[18] Cohen SN. The Pediatric Pharmacology Research Unit (PPRU) network and its role in meeting pediatric labeling needs. Pediatrics 1999;104(3 Pt 2):644–5 <https://pediatrics.aappublications.org/content/pediatrics/104/Supplement_3/644.full.pdf>.

[19] Wilson JT. An update on the therapeutic orphan. Pediatrics 1999;104(3 Pt 2):585–90 <https://pediatrics.aappublications.org/content/pediatrics/104/Supplement_3/585.full.pdf>.

[20] Blumer JL. Introduction. Pediatrics 1999;104(3 Pt 2):582 <https://pediatrics.aappublications.org/content/pediatrics/104/Supplement_3/582.full.pdf>.

[21] Blumer JL. Off-label uses of drugs in children. Pediatrics 1999;104(3 Pt 2):598–602 <https://pediatrics.aappublications.org/content/pediatrics/104/Supplement_3/598.full.pdf>.

[22] Christensen ML, Helms RA, Chesney RW. Is pediatric labeling really necessary? Pediatrics 1999;104(3 Pt 2):593–7 <https://pediatrics.aappublications.org/content/pediatrics/104/Supplement_3/593.full.pdf>.

[23] FDA 2016. Best pharmaceuticals for children act and pediatric research equity act. Status report to congress. <www.fda.gov/downloads/ScienceResearch/SpecialTopics/PediatricTherapeuticsResearch/UCM509815.pdf>.

[24] Rose K, Neubauer D, Grant-Kels JM. Rational use of medicine in children – The conflict of interests story. A review. Rambam Maimonides Med J 2019;10(3):e0018 <https://www.rmmj.org.il/userimages/928/2/PublishFiles/953Article.pdf>.

[25] Gonzalez D, Melloni C, Yogev R, et al. Use of opportunistic clinical data and a population pharmacokinetic model to support dosing of clindamycin for premature infants to adolescents. Clin Pharmacology Therapeutics 2014;96(4):429–37.

[26] Thakkar N., Gonzalez D., Cohen-Wolkowiez M. An opportunistic study evaluating pharmacokinetics of sildenafil for the treatment of pulmonary hypertension in infants Perinatol. 2016 September; 36(9): 744–747.

[27] Leroux S, Turner MA, Barin-Le Guellec C, et al. Pharmacokinetic studies in neonates: The utility of an opportunistic sampling design. Clin Pharmacokinet 2015;54(12):1273–85.

[28] FDA 2019. General clinical pharmacology considerations for neonatal studies for drugs and biological products. Guidance for industry. <https://www.fda.gov/media/129532/download>.

[29] Colón AR, Colón PA. Nurturing children: a history of pediatrics. Westport, CT: Greenwood Press; 1999.

[30] FDA 2001. The pediatric exclusivity provision. January 2001. Status report to congress. <https://www.fda.gov/downloads/Drugs/DevelopmentApprovalProcess/DevelopmentResources/UCM049915.pdf>.

[31] EMA 2007 The European paediatric initiative: History of the paediatric regulation. <https://www.ema.europa.eu/en/documents/other/european-paediatric-initiative-history-paediatric-regulation_en.pdf>.

[32] Regulation (EC) No 1901/2006 of the European Parliament and of the Council of 12 December 2006 on Medicinal Products for Paediatric Use and Amending Regulation (EEC) No 1768/92, Directive 2001/20/EC, Directive 2001/83/EC and Regulation (EC) No 726/2004. <http://ec.europa.eu/health/files/eudralex/vol-1/reg_2006_1901/reg_2006_1901_en.pdf>.

[33] Cone Jr. TE. Secular acceleration of height and biologic maturation in children during the past century. J Pediatr 1961;59:736–40.

[34] Komlos J, Lauderdale BE. The mysterious trend in American heights in the 20th century. Ann Hum Biol 2007;34(2):206–15.

[35] Rose K. A paediatric investigation plan case study. Pharm Med 2012;26(5):287–95.

[36] Vargesson N. Thalidomide-induced teratogenesis: history and mechanisms. Birth Defects Res C Embryo Today 2015;105(2):140–56 <https://www.ncbi.nlm.nih.gov/pmc/articles/PMC4737249/>.

[37] Thomann KD. Die contergan-katastrophe. Die trügerische Sicherheit der "harten" Daten. Dtsch Ärzteblatt 2007;104(41):A2078–82 <https://www.aerzteblatt.de/pdf.asp?id = 57224>.

[38] Rose K, Grant-Kels JM. Pediatric melanoma – The whole (conflicts of interest) story. Int J Womens Dermatol 2018;5(2):110–15. Available from: https://doi.org/10.1016/j.ijwd.2018.10.020 <https://www.ncbi.nlm.nih.gov/pmc/articles/PMC6451736/pdf/main.pdf>.

[39] Rocchi F., et al. 2011. The european paediatric legislation: benefits and perspectives. <https://www.ncbi.nlm.nih.gov/pmc/articles/PMC2933611/pdf/1824-7288-36-56.pdf>.

[40] Tomasi PA, Egger GF, Pallidis C, et al. Enabling development of paediatric medicines in Europe: 10 years of the EU paediatric regulation. Pediatr Drugs 2017;19:505–13.

[41] Auby P. Pharmaceutical research in paediatric populations and the new EU paediatric legislation: an industry perspective. Child Adolesc Psychiatry Ment Health 2008;2(1):38 <https://www.ncbi.nlm.nih.gov/pmc/articles/PMC2629463/>.

[42] Mäkelä D. Historical child abuse in out-of-home care: Finland disclosing and discussing its past. Master's Thesis in Child Studies 736A31 (first year), 15 ECTS, Linköping University, Department of Thematic Studies – Child Studies. <http://liu.diva-portal.org/smash/get/diva2:844350/FULLTEXT01.pdf>.

[43] Sköld J. The truth about abuse? A comparative approach to inquiry narratives on historical institutional child abuse. History Educ 2016;45(4):492–509.

[44] Daly K. Conceptualising responses to institutional abuse of children. Current issues in criminal justice. <https://www.griffith.edu.au/__data/assets/pdf_file/0018/223317/2014-Daly-Conceptualising-Responses-to-Inst.-Abuse-of-Chldrn-PUBversion.pdf>.

[45] The local 2017. Switzerland's 'contract children': study to examine dark period of Swiss history. <https://www.thelocal.ch/20170222/switzerlands-contract-children-study-to-examine-dark-period-of-swiss-history>.

[46] Swiss Federal Council 2017. Bundesrat lanciert neues Nationales Forschungsprogramm zum Thema "Fürsorge und Zwang". (Swiss Federal Government starts research program about public welfare and coercion") <www.admin.ch/gov/de/start/dokumentation/medien-mitteilungen.msg-id-65747.html>.

[47] Mohamed MF, Rakhmanina N, Hassan HE. Inclusion of adolescents with adults in Phase 3 clinical trials:overview of the current state and a call for action. J Clin Pharmacol 2020;.

[48] Washington HA. Medical apartheid: the dark history of medical experimentation on black Americans from colonial times to the present. New York, NY: Doubleday Publishing Group; 2006.

[49] Adashi EY, Walters LB, Menikoff JA. The Belmont report at 40: Reckoning with time. Am J Public Health 2018;108(10):1345–8.

[50] Rose K. Ethical, regulatory and scientific challenges in paediatric drug development. Pharm Med 2008;22(4):221–34.

[51] Rose CD. Ethical conduct of research in children: pediatricians and their IRB (Part 1 of 2). Pediatrics 2017;139(5).

[52] Rose K. The challenges of pediatric drug development. Curr Ther Res Clin Exp 2019. Available from: https://doi.org/10.1016/j.curtheres.2019.01.007.

[53] Rose K, Grant-Kels JM. The meanings of "pediatric drug development". A review. Ther Innov Regul Sci 2019;53(6):767–74.

[54] Rose K, Senn S. Drug development: EU paediatric legislation, the European medicines agency and its paediatric committee—adolescents' melanoma as a paradigm. Pharm Stat 2014;13(4):211–13.

[55] Rose K. European union pediatric legislation jeopardizes worldwide, timely future advances in the care of children with cancer. Clin Therapeutics 2014;36(2):163–77 <http://www.clinicaltherapeutics.com/article/S0149-2918(14)00018-6/pdf>.

[56] EMA 2019. Brivaracetam PIP PIP EMEA-000332-PIP01-08-M14. <https://www.ema.europa.eu/en/documents/pip-decision/p/0297/2019-ema-decision-12-august-2019-acceptance-modification-agreed-paediatric-investigation-plan_en.pdf>.

[57] Rose K, Grant-Kels JM. Questionable international pediatric studies in the United States and Russia triggered by regulatory authorities. Asian J Res Med Pharm Sci 2018;3(3) <http://www.journalrepository.org/media/journals/AJRIMPS_63/2018/Apr/Rose332018AJRIMPS40776.pdf>.

[58] Rose K, Grant-Kels JM. Questionable industry-sponsored pediatric studies in China triggered by United States of America (US) and European Union (EU) regulatory authorities. SF Pharma J 2018;1:1 <https://www.scifedpublishers.com/open-access/questionable-industry-sponsored-pediatric-studies-in-china-triggeredby-united-states-of-america-us-and-european-union-eu-regulatoryauthorities.pdf>.

[59] Rose K, Grant-Kels JM. Questionable international pediatric studies with Swiss participation. Swiss Med Wkly 2018; <https://smw.ch/fileadmin/content/blog/PDF/Questionable_pediatric_studies_with_Swiss_participation.pdf>.

[60] Rose K, Neubauer D, Grant-Kels JM. Questionable industry-sponsored studies in children and adolescents in Slovenia. Curr Ther Res Clin Exp 2019; <https://doi.org/10.1016/j.curtheres.2019.01.002>.

[61] Hwang TJ, Tomasi PA, Bourgeois FT. Delays in completion and results reporting of clinical trials under the paediatric regulation in the European Union: a cohort study. PLoS Med 2018;15(3):e1002520 <https://journals.plos.org/plosmedicine/article/file?id = 10.1371/journal.pmed.1002520&type = printable>.

[62] EMA 2016. Retigabine PIP EMEA-000116-PIP01-07-M08 <https://www.ema.europa.eu/en/documents/pip-decision/p/0009/2016-ema-decision-29-january-2016-acceptance-modification-agreed-paediatric-investigation-plan_en.pdf>.

[63] EMA 2018. Retigabine PIP EMEA-000116-PIP01-07-M09 <https://www.ema.europa.eu/en/documents/pip-decision/p/0299/2018-ema-decision-12-september-2018-acceptance-modification-agreed-paediatric-investigation-plan_en.pdf>.

[64] EMA 2019. Perampanel PIP EMEA-000467-PIP01-08-M11 <https://www.ema.europa.eu/en/documents/pip-decision/p/0217/2019-ema-decision-12-june-2019-acceptance-modification-agreed-paediatric-investigation-plan_en.pdf>.

[65] EMA 2019. Rivaroxaban PIP EMEA-000430-PIP01-08-M11 <https://www.ema.europa.eu/en/documents/pip-decision/p/0126/2019-ema-decision-17-april-2019-acceptance-modification-agreed-paediatric-investigation-plan_en.pdf>.

[66] EMA 2010. Allergen PIP MEA-000910-PIP01-10. <https://www.ema.europa.eu/en/documents/pip-decision/p/282/2010-ema-decision-3-december-2010-agreement-paediatric-investigation-plan-granting-deferral-granting_en.pdf>.

[67] EMA Decision P/345/2010, 2010. <https://www.ema.europa.eu/en/documents/other/p/63/2010-ema-decision-20-december-2010-class-waiver-conditions_en.pdf>.

[68] Rose K, Walson PD. Are Regulatory Age Limits in Pediatric Melanoma Justified? Curr Ther Res Clin Exp 2019. <https://doi.org/10.1016/j.curtheres.2019.01.003>.

[69] Geoerger B, Bergeron C, Gore L, et al. Phase II study of ipilimumab in adolescents with unresectable stage III or IV malignant melanoma. Eur J Cancer 2017;86:358–63.

[70] EMA 2015. EMA/PDCO Summary Report on the review of the list of granted Class Waivers. <https://www.ema.europa.eu/en/documents/other/ema/pdco-summary-report-review-list-granted-class-waivers_en.pdf>.

[71] Facing the challenge. The Lisbon strategy for growth and employment. Report from the High Level Group chaired by Wim Kok November 2004. <http://ec.europa.eu/research/evaluations/pdf/archive/fp6-evidence-base/evaluation_studies_and_reports/evaluation_studies_and_reports_2004/the_lisbon_strategy_for_growth_and_employment__report_-from_the_high_level_group.pdf>.

[72] World Medical Association (WMA) Declaration of Helsinki – Ethical Principles for Medical Research Involving Human Subjects. Adopted by the 18th WMA General Assembly, Helsinki, Finland, June 1964, and amended by the 64th WMA General Assembly, Fortaleza, Brazil, October 2013. <https://www.wma.net/policies-post/wma-declaration-of-helsinki-ethical-principles-for-medical-research-involving-human-subjects/>.

[73] Galileo Galilei. Sidereus Nuncius (Starry Messenger). Venice, Italy, 1610.

[74] Ruperto N, Eichler I, Herold R, et al. European Network of Paediatric Research at the European Medicines Agency (Enpr-EMA). Arch Dis Child 2012;97(3):185–8.

[75] Enpr-EMA <https://www.ema.europa.eu/en/partners-networks/networks/european-network-paediatric-research-european-medicines-agency-enpr-ema>.

[76] Enpr-EMA mission statement <https://www.ema.europa.eu/en/documents/other/mission-statement-european-network-paediatric-research-european-medicines-agency-enpr-ema_en.pdf>.

[77] Enpr-EMA brochure <https://www.ema.europa.eu/en/documents/leaflet/european-network-paediatric-research-european-medicines-agency_en.pdf>.

[78] Presentation on Enpr-EMA - background information <https://www.ema.europa.eu/en/documents/presentation/european-network-paediatric-research-european-medicines-agency-background-information_en.pdf>.

Chapter 3

A paradigm shift

A paradigm shift

In the narrow sense, science is the consensus of the scientific community; in a broader sense, it is the consensus in society or at least of a majority in society. It is easy to consent on obvious issues, such as that gold is heavier than a feather, unless, of course, a feather is made of gold. The more complex issues are, the more difficult it is to consent. That is what politics are for. Today, there is broad agreement that science is not sent to earth by God as were the Ten Commandments in the biblical narrative [1], but that science is developed by humans and evolves further. Former centuries perceived the history of science as a progressive accumulation of knowledge. Today, we see the development of science also as a shift of paradigms, where new conceptual systems replace outdated ones, because they explain reality better. Often this occurs within a shifting wider matrix of intellectual and cultural views [2,3].

During the early millennia of human civilization, the scientific consensus perceived the earth as the middle of the universe, with the rest of the universe fixed or orbiting somehow around it. This geocentric concept was based on common sense and daily experience. Opposite theories, such as that the earth orbits around the sun, existed already in classical Greek times, but only during the Copernican Revolution the heliocentric concept won gradually worldwide recognition [4]. This replacement of the geocentric by the heliocentric view is a good example of a paradigm shift [3]. It started with a booklet on observations published by Galileo Galilei in 1610, was carried forward by Copernicus, and was completed by Isaac Newton more than a century later [4,5]. It was not only a new astronomic view about the motion of the heavenly bodies, but also replaced an old view of the entire world by a new one that was based on trust in human observation.

"Pediatric drug development" is here discussed on the background of a slow paradigm shift that occurs in parts of the clinical community, parts of regulatory authorities, parts of pharmaceutical companies, in many parents, and in an increasing part of the general public. It is slowly and gradually replacing a paradigm that has dominated the worlds of medicine, medical care, medical science, and pediatric healthcare since the thalidomide disaster and the US governmental reaction to it in 1962 by introducing clinical studies as the basis of drug approval [6,7].

Considering the Patient in Pediatric Drug Development. DOI: https://doi.org/10.1016/B978-0-12-823888-2.00005-3

Already in 1968, when Harry C. Shirkey introduced the concept of children as "therapeutic orphans," he also noted that most physicians simply ignored the new pediatric warnings in the drug labels issued since 1962 [8]. Using their common sense, most physicians did not see modern drugs as dangerous for young patients. The pediatric warnings served primarily the legal purpose to prevent frivolous damage lawsuits that are characteristic for the US legal system [9–13]. The most relevant changes that differentiate the immature and vulnerable body of newborns from adults occur during the first weeks and months of life [14]. When a first government-sponsored conference on "pediatric" epilepsy took place, the clinicians told the regulators that antiepileptic drugs (AEDs) that were effective for partial onset seizures (POS)-type epilepsy in adults could be trusted to work also in minors, a position the regulators did not want to hear, because in their view, medicines to be used in administratively defined "children" needed separate proof-of-efficacy in separate "pediatric" studies [15,16]. In the meantime, the FDA has reversed its position for AEDs in POS epilepsy and accepts "extrapolation" of efficacy from adult studies [17]. This position shift began when specialists in pediatric neurology examined all "pediatric" clinical studies with AEDs for POS and concluded that they showed the efficacy of AEDs in POS epilepsy in children down to the age of two years [18,19]. One group of clinicians even openly challenged the children-are-not-small-adults mantra [16,20]. Parents' decreased willingness to let their child participate in regulatory epilepsy studies is by now well documented [21]. The need to recruit tens of thousands of children and adolescents into placebo-controlled five-year allergen studies has been challenged in the prestigious journal of pediatric allergology and immunology [22], as this would expose the participants in the placebo group to an increased danger to progress from allergic rhinitis to asthma [23]. Also the need to prove the efficacy of disease-modifying agents in young patients with multiple sclerosis in separate "pediatric" studies is now openly challenged by the International Pediatric Multiple Sclerosis Study Group (IPMSSG) [24,25].

The first FDA-rewarded "pediatric" cancer studies recruited young patients up to 21 years with the aim to prove efficacy of individual cytotoxic agents [16,26]. The FDA now recommends to include adolescents into pivotal adult cancer studies [27]. While for relapsed or refractory young patients with the most frequent type of pediatric cancer, acute lymphoblastic leukemia (ALL), there was no more hope in traditional treatment based on chemotherapy, now the engagement of the patients' own immune system through CAR-T cell therapy allows healing in the vast majority of patients aged up to 25 years [28]; for tisagenlecleucel to be approved in this age group the FDA did not insist on separate "pediatric" studies [29]. The FDA has approved topical crisaborole based on pivotal studies in patients aged 2–79 years without separate "pediatric" studies [30], and the FDA accepts now "extrapolation" of efficacy from adults down to the age of 2 years in partial onset seizures (POS)-type epilepsy without separate "pediatric" studies [17].

These are signs that the general consensus that efficacy of drugs in administratively defined "children" needs separate proof-of-efficacy studies in "children," if possible separately in each of the administratively defined "pediatric" age groups [31], is waning. There are also signs of the struggle of an old consensus that blindly applies administrative and regulatory logic to the treatment of young patients with an emerging, more realistic approach that takes into consideration the degree of maturity of the young person's body.

Whenever in history a paradigm shift occurs, representatives of the old paradigm defend their position, often in circular argumentation, while the new paradigm progresses both in public and scientific circles. Compared to theories about the structure of the universe and the question if the sun orbits around the earth or the earth around the sun, medical science reflects to a larger degree also current general, cultural, and political views. This is the case specifically in areas addressed by specific legislation; here, the laws enacted to promote "pediatric drug development."

There are at least two main areas that need to be addressed here. First, how the representatives of the old dogmatic regulatory paradigm defend their position. Some justify the FDA's shifts of position by stating that "evolving science and knowledge have driven the changes in the extrapolation approach" [32]. This is a defensive and understandable argumentation. The EMA instead argues in carefully coded and misleading pseudoscientific documents that try to create the impression that the EMA's regulatory positions are based on solid science. Examples for this pseudoscience is the EMA's claim that off-label use of drugs in children is always dangerous [33], or the EMA's claims of clinical achievements of the EU pediatric regulation, where it claims to have made drugs "available" for young patients in the treatment of rheumatological diseases, cardiovascular diseases, infectious diseases, and cancer [34]. As soon as these claim are translated/decoded into what they really mean, i.e., that drugs in these disease areas have now an EMA label, their scientific semblance collapses like a house of cards. The EMA document that justifies the expansion of "pediatric" studies into more and more rare diseases has a long list of references to give it the semblance of scientific substance. "Pediatric" studies are now EMA-demanded for liver and intrahepatic bile duct carcinoma, kidney, and renal pelvis carcinoma, coronary atherosclerosis, peripheral atherosclerosis, vascular dementia, and vascular cognitive disorder/impairment; nonjuvenile Parkinson's disease, Huntington chorea, and amyotrophic lateral sclerosis (ALS) [35]. It is ridiculous and wrong to claim that ALS is a "pediatric" disease for which separate "pediatric" efficacy studies are needed. Many diseases affect occasionally patients younger than 18 years. This does not make these diseases "pediatric" diseases.

So far, a solid theoretical and intellectual processing and analysis of "pediatric drug development" has not been performed, nor has the used pseudoscience been addressed candidly. On a practical level the children-are-not-small-adults mantra has become weaker, with the FDA clearly having taken the lead, but neither the FDA nor the EMA have so far rejected the underlying flawed assumptions.

The positions of the FDA and the EMA, respectively, also reflect fundamental differences how they interact with the scientific community and with the general public. The FDA's interactions are rather transparent and correspond to the general degree of transparency that characterizes US public administration. In contrast, the EMA was established in 1995 as an umbrella organization above the traditional EU national regulatory authorities. The EMA is an English-speaking organization within the EU where the majority of citizens have other mother languages. Comparable to the rest of the EU administrative machinery, the EMA is much farer away from the pulse of society and modern science. The EMA has direct executive responsibility for the handling of "pediatric drug development" and demonstrates a much higher degree of regulatory dogmatism than the FDA. While the FDA has gradually on a pragmatic level distanced itself from the children-are-therapeutic-orphans mantra, the EMA continues to demand adamantly pediatric investigation plans (PIPs) for the "pediatric" population defined as anybody below 18 years, as if "children" were another species [36]. This EMA's behavior might be compared to the crisis in a patient in the course of a disease when a decisive change is looming [37].

How should we classify the FDA decisions that rewarded "pediatric" cancer studies in patients up to 21 years old since 1997, in the light of current recommendations to include adolescents with cancer into adult pivotal studies? [27] Were the studies performed between 1997 and 2017 based on science? Were they scientifically justified by contemporary standards? By today's standards?

How should we regard all the "pediatric" studies with antiepileptic drugs, although the clinicians told the FDA from the very beginning that "pediatric drug development" and separate "pediatric" studies were superfluous for POS-type epilepsy? [15]

The positions of the National Institutes of Health (NIH) and the FDA reflected scientific consensus of the general pediatric community in the beginning, even if on the level of specific clinical areas, such as POS epilepsy, this general consensus was met with skepticism and open disagreement from clinically experienced physicians. Their clinical concerns were in hindsight correct and appropriate. The changes of requested/mandated "pediatric" studies in the last years show an occurring paradigm shift [17,27,38]. The belief that everything in "children" is fundamentally different from adults is gradually replaced by a more realistic assessment of the maturity of the growing human body until it reaches adult maturity.

The shift from the geocentric to the heliocentric concept occurred not only within a theoretical and scientific discussion. It also reflected the transition of a world where the catholic church had enjoyed highest spiritual authority and had had considerable secular power as well, toward today's concept of the separation of church and state. To grasp what has changed in the world since the US processed the thalidomide disaster administratively in 1962, and what currently helps to maintain the children-are-not-small-adults and children-are-therapeutic-orphans mantras, we have to look at several key factors that have changed in the last six decades.

With the end of the Middle Ages, the number and weight of monasteries began to decrease, while the number and weight of universities began to increase. In the last hundred years, the percentage of young persons with a university degree has continuously increased [39].

Today's reputation and authority of scientific institutions, universities and learned societies is high. But these institutions are no longer the same as they were two hundred or sixty years ago. Today, the FDA regulates more than $US 2 trillion drugs, food, and other consumer goods, about 25% of consumer expenditures in the US [40]. Regulatory authorities, industries, and scientific institutions have undergone fundamental changes, including their sheer size, their economic weight, their administration, and how they are linked to society.

Worldwide, economy is undergoing a transition from the predominant production of goods toward an increasing provision of service. Today's society is characterized by an increased esteem of knowledge, giving universities and research institutions a growing weight. The primary sector of traditional agricultural production was during the industrial revolution complemented by a secondary sector. Today, new sectors offer telecommunication, hospitality, tourism, mass media, healthcare, and Internet-based and other services. The weight of education, educational institutions, and learned societies has grown. Here, a specific aspect of the institutions dedicated to medical education, the approval drugs, the use of drugs in young patients, and research performed in this area needs closer attention and analysis.

"Pediatric drug development" has for decades been supported by mainstream science, by the pharmaceutical industry, and by the regulatory authorities. These three pillars in healthcare do not have identical interests, but they work closely with each other. For decades, FDA, EMA, and clinical academia have used the public trust and the authority they enjoyed to demand additional separate "pediatric" studies. Within pharmaceutical industry, "pediatric" careers have emerged, whose representatives support "pediatric drug development" [41–44].

When www.clinicaltrials.gov is used to search for industry-sponsored "pediatric" studies, only a minority of studies are exclusively performed in chronologically defined "children." Table 3.1 lists 39 studies that currently are recruiting in epilepsy. These studies are shown upon the search term "epilepsy," plus in "advanced search" by clicking "industry-sponsored" and "child" (1–17 years). Of the 39 displayed studies, only 9 are exclusively in young patients aged <17 years. All others include also adults of various ages.

TABLE 3.1 Industry-sponsored epilepsy studies including minors, March 26, 2020.

	NCT#	Age
1	NCT03222349	2–17 y
2	NCT02914314	1–24mo
3	NCT03405714	1mo–16 y
4	NCT03865732	1–17 y
5	NCT02954107	6–12 y
6	NCT03355300	3–17 y
7	NCT03336242	3–17 y
8	NCT03646240	3–26 y
9	NCT02783092	2–18 y
10	NCT04015141	1mo–18y
11	NCT03428360	2–65 y
12	NCT03635073	2–65 y
13	NCT03207685	≥1mo (CAOA)
14	NCT03529045	CAOA
15	NCT02722590	≥12 y (CAOA)
16	NCT03446664	≥12 y (CAOA)
17	NCT03083665	16–80 y (CAOA)
18	NCT03340064	1mo–3y
19	NCT02721069	6–65 y (CAOA)
20	NCT03531008	16–65 y (CAOA)
21	NCT03356769	6–30 y (CA)
22	NCT03685630	≥16 y (CAOA)
23	NCT03489187	CAOA
24	NCT03775694	CAOA
25	NCT02826863	2–18 y (CA)
26	NCT02934854	≥2mo (CAOA)
27	NCT02696044	≥2 y (CAOA)
28	NCT02175173	CAOA
29	NCT02392078	CAOA

(Continued)

TABLE 3.1 (Continued)

	NCT#	Age
30	NCT02520557	CAOA
31	NCT03572933	2–21 y
32	NCT03976076	6–24mo (C)
33	NCT02036853	1–50 y (CA)
34	NCT03355209	2–35 y (CA)
35	NCT03694275	2–55 y (CA)
36	NCT03325439	≤28days (C)
37	NCT04062981	≥2 y (CAOA)
38	NCT03731715	≥2 y (CAOA)
39	NCT02834793	≥2 y (CAOA)

CAOA, Child, adult, older adult; *C*, child; *CA*, child, adult; *mo*, month; *y*, year.

In the pharmaceutical industry, many companies rationalize inclusion criteria for clinical studies. That most FDA/EMA requested/demanded studies have limited or no clinical and/or scientific sense is an open secret in the pharmaceutical industry. However, this view is not shared or less shared by those employees that have reached management status in their respective company in the area of "pediatric drug development." Where FDA or EMA adamantly insist on exclusively "pediatric" studies or even offer a reward for such studies, companies will comply. The two companies that performed the EMA-demanded "pediatric" melanoma studies with ipilimumab [45] and vemurafenib [46] that had to be terminated because recruitment had waned [47–49], sponsored and/or co-sponsored many further melanoma studies that included young patients of various age groups (Tables 3.2 and 3.3). The ipilimumab study had also been requested by the FDA [35].

Pharmaceutical companies must survive in the market. At present, they cannot challenge fundamentally the regulatory authorities. By the nature of their business, they must maintain a nonhostile relationship with their counterparts in the regulatory authorities. But for the entire clinical development program, they can advocate and plan studies with reasonable and rational inclusion criteria, apart from those studies that either are directly rewarded by patent extension, or EMA-mandated with the direct threat to not approve the respective drugs in adults. This threat is the key element of the EU pediatric regulation [40,47,50–52].

The FDA now accepts "extrapolation" of efficacy of AEDs from adults down to two years. This means that the FDA has promoted "pediatric" studies

TABLE 3.2 BMS-sponsored melanoma studies including minors.

	NCT#	Age
1	NCT01696045	12–17 y
2	NCT04196452	≤18 y (CA)
3	NCT03635983	≥12 y (CAOA)
4	NCT02717364	CAOA
5	NCT00289640	≥16 y (CAOA)
6	NCT00623766	≥16 y (CAOA)
7	NCT02388906	≥15 y (CAOA)
8	NCT04099251	≥12 y (CAOA)
9	NCT03470922	≥12 y (CAOA)
10	NCT03068455	≥12 y (CAOA)
11	NCT02492815	≥16 y (CAOA)
12	NCT00357461	≥16 y (CAOA)
13	NCT01673854	CAOA
14	NCT00495066	≥16 y (CAOA)
15	NCT03329846	≥12 y (CAOA)
16	NCT02854488	CAOA
17	NCT02970981	≥16 y (CAOA)
18	NCT01176474	≥16 y (CAOA)
19	NCT01176461	≥16 y (CAOA)
20	NCT03808441	≥16 y (CAOA)
21	NCT03315468	CAOA

BMS, Bristol-Myers Squibb; *CAOA*, child, adult, older adult; *C*, child; *CA*, child, adult; *mo*, month; *y*, year.

for the last two decades that by the FDA's own standards of today were questionable. There is the claim that the FDA's shift of opinion was triggered by progress in the understanding of physiology and mechanisms of diseases [32]. This is a half-hearted attempt to avoid necessary and painful questions. It is also part of the unavoidable transition toward admitting that exaggerations and mistakes were done. The documents on the discussion of "pediatric" epilepsy show that clinicians told the regulators already twenty-five years ago that there is no need for separate proof-of-efficacy for antiepileptic drugs for POS-type epilepsy, the most frequent type of epilepsy in adults and children. The situation

TABLE 3.3 Roche-sponsored melanoma studies including minors.

	NCT#	Age
1	NCT01519323	12–17 y
2	NCT01744860	CAOA
3	NCT01307397	≥16 y (CAOA)
4	NCT01248936	≥16 y (CAOA)
5	NCT03315468	CAOA

CAOA, Child adult older adult; *C*, child; CA, child, adult; mo, month; *y*, year.

is different in each respective clinical area. In some areas, such as juvenile idiopathic arthritis, both US-based and EU-based learned societies have made "pediatric drug development" a successful business model [53]. Representatives of JIA researchers publish together with representatives of other clinical areas that are profiting from pediatric legislation and with EMA representatives [54,55]. Representatives of the EU-based Paediatric Rheumatology International Trials Organisation (PRINTO) and the North America-based Pediatric Rheumatology Collaborative Study Group (PRCSG) praise both the US and the EU pediatric legislation [53–55].

The EMA is still in almost full denial. It accepts "extrapolation" in "children" with POS epilepsy down to the age of four years. It is a question of time until the EMA will follow the FDA and will accept extrapolation down to two years. But this will not resolve parents' growing and legitimate hesitation to give their informed consent for "pediatric" studies [21].

The paradigm shift reflected in recent FDA decisions is not uniform across all clinical areas. In pediatric oncology there are two contradictory movements. The FDA now accepts inclusion of adolescents into adult cancer trials. But it has also "recommended" basket studies in cancer in the "pediatric population" and demands from 2020 on separate regulatory pediatric cancer studies in patients <12 years old based on the RACE for children act [56–58]. This law reflects that pediatric oncology has still a high moral authority and that there is a strong belief in the public that the more industry is forced to perform separate pediatric studies, the more this will advance clinical care in pediatric cancer. Unfortunately, this is not the case. The breakthrough of tisagenlecleucel in relapsed or recurrent ALL was not achieved through pediatric legislation, but by ordinary profit-oriented drug development in combination and cooperation with clinical research with therapeutic intentions [36].

The flawed children-are-therapeutic-orphans and children-are-not-small-adults mantras that have resulted in separate "pediatric" drug approval have created massive conflicts of interest in science of a dimension that by its sheer size is probably new in history. The report of the EU commission of 2017 estimates the research and development costs of each PIP at €18.9 million [59]. In view of now far more than thousand PIPs issued by the EMA, this amounts to more than €20 billion. The majority of these funds have resulted in questionable pseudoscientific publications that prove that various medicines works also in patients younger than 18 years. The "pediatric imperative" published on the conference 2019 website of the ESDPPP is striking [60,61]. Pediatric clinical pharmacologists are happy to perform studies or give advice, for a fee, respectively. Thoughts with good intentions in their beginning have evolved into a self-maintaing machinery that produces careers. The only ones that do not benefit are the young patients.

This is not a systematic conspiracy. The blind belief in the need for separate "pediatric" regulatory drug approval that was characteristic for the first US pediatric legislation is slowly moving toward a more realistic assessment of the young patient's body. The one missing step is the differentiation between the administrative classification of young persons, which any modern society must do on a daily basis, and the acceptance that there is no strict chronological age limit that could differentiate an adult from a "pediatric" body. Chronological age limits are necessary and rational to define the legal and the administrative status of a person. But not the maturity of a body.

In 2017, a paper complained that worldwide there is no binding definition of adulthood and outlines correctly that the definition of adulthood is not only a semantic issue [62]. But the authors miss the decisive point. There are worldwide multiple chronological definitions of childhood and adulthood. The decisive question is the purpose of such a definition. For statistical or for various administrative purposes, we can define adulthood by various age limits. But for drug treatment, we should not.

The flaws in the children-are-therapeutic-orphans and children-are-not-small adults mantras existed from the day that Shirkey pronounced them [8]. A correction of these flaws is unavoidable.

Do we observe a paradigm shift comparable to the shift from the geocentric to the heliocentric world model after 1610, or are we simply observing how mistakes that were made 60 years ago are gradually corrected?

There are elements of both. Already in 2007, a paper discussed critically and in depth one significant flaw in the pediatric legislation: it is focused on those drugs that are broadly used in adult medicine, as drug development is market driven; the drugs for which pediatric studies were promoted by the US pediatric legislation have their main use in adult healthcare [63]. But the authors failed to see several challenges. Firstly, persons classified as "children" are often bodily no longer children, but already young adults. Some of them can develop diseases that become more frequent in the more senior population. The authors addressed a true challenge of the pediatric legislation, but they did not crack the core of the challenge: for medical and pharmaceutical treatment, the prescribing physician must consider the body of the patient, not his legal status. Secondly, not the entire population administratively labeled "pediatric" remains as immature and vulnerable as preterm newborns and, to a lesser degree, term newborns [14], until they become administratively labeled as adults [36]. Thirdly, the authors did not identify truly clinical negative consequences of the pediatric legislation, such as a warning against the use of antidepressants in young persons, which may be helped to reduce worldwide "suicidality" among young persons, but removed one key instrument in the hands of healthcare professionals to deal with the emotionally extremely critical phase of adolescent self-doubts, insecurity, and depression [64,65]. Also other authors critically analyzed some aspects of the pediatric legislation but failed to find its decisive flaws and took too many claims, terms and statements of the regulatory authorities at face value [66]. As long as the coding used by the regulatory authorities is not deciphered, their claims of providing "better medicines for children" [67] cannot be proven to be wrong. Unfortunately, also the European Organisation for Rare Diseases (Eurordis) has so far accepted the EMA's claims at face value [68]. One critical clinical voice complained that pharmaceutical companies' obligation to negotiate PIPs and to commit to performing the clinical studies delays the availability of effective medicines for the general public [69], but it did not reach the core of the PIP challenge.

The challenge of "pediatric drug development" will need a candid assessment of all the damage that it has done to drug development in general, to innumerable individual patients treated in clinical studies that in the comparison group exposed them to placebo or substandard treatment, and the trust that the general public has toward clinical science, regulatory authorities, and companies that develop modern effective drugs. In this regard, we will face a true paradigm shift, indeed comparable to the change from the geocentric toward the heliocentric view of the world and the universe. The unavoidable debate will not leave all key players in their comfort zone. But this is a challenge that Western society, which is based on the right to express an opinion, is much better prepared than societies that punish divergent opinions, comparable to the attempts of the Catholic Church to maintain the authority it enjoyed during the Middle Ages. This debate will help those healthcare professionals that had already some doubts about the sense of separate "pediatric" studies.

In the long term, independent analyses of the statements made in this book will be necessary. Apart from removing some current thought leaders from their comfort zone, it will help to refresh the athmosphere of science.

This debate will not damage the public basic trust in science fundamentally. The silent waning of parents' blind trust in clinical research and their diminished willingness to let their children participate in placebo-controlled studies in pain, epilepsy, multiple sclerosis, and many more diseases, has significantly contributed to an athmospheric change that allows the publication of a general critical view of "pediatric drug development" at all. The same holds true for those clinical researchers that expressed first doubts against the mainstream mantras that demanded participation of young patients in separate regulatory studies.

Galileo's observations of Jupiter's moons and other observations he published in 1610 would not have been possible without access to glass lenses, letterpress printing, the principles of telescope construction floating around in educated circles, and many more technical advancements that had already slowly changed the world. When US lawmakers passed the pediatric laws, they were deeply convinced this would advance child healthcare. Initially, a comparable enthusiasm for "pediatric drug development" existed also in Europe, in Japan, and worldwide. The detection of the flaws of "pediatric drug development" would not have been possible without the general societal learning process described in the individual chapters of this book.

References

[1] The Bible. Exodus 20:1-17 and Deuteronomy 5:4-21.

[2] Wikipedia, the free encyclopedia. Science. Available from: https://en.wikipedia.org/wiki/Science.

[3] Kuhn TS. The structure of scientific revolutions EnlargedInternational encyclopedia of unified science. Second Edition Chicago, IL: The University of Chicago Press; 1970. Available from: https://www.lri.fr/~mbl/Stanford/CS477/papers/Kuhn-SSR-2ndEd.pdf.

[4] Kuhn TS. The copernican revolution: planetary astronomy in the development of western thought. Cambridge, MA: Harvard University Press; 1990.

[5] Wikipedia, the free encyclopedia. Copernican Revolution. Available from: https://en.wikipedia.org/wiki/Copernican_Revolution.

[6] Rägo L, Santo B. Drug regulation: history, present and future In: van Boxtel CJ, Santo B, Edwards IR, editors. Drug benefits and risks: international textbook of clinical pharmacology. revised 2nd edition Uppsala, Sweder: IOS Press & Uppsala Monitoring Centre; 2008; chapter 6. pp. 65–77. Available from: https://www.who.int/medicines/technical_briefing/tbs/Drug_Regulation_History_Present_Future.pdf.

[7] Janssen WM. A historical perspective on off-label medicine: from regulation, promotion, and the first amendment to the next frontiers. Food and drug law institute, Levy MC (Editor). First Washington, D.C., USA *Off-Label Communications* (2008).

[8] Shirkey H. Therapeutic orphans J Pediatr 1968;72(1):119–20 Jan. Available from: https://pdfs.semanticscholar.org/f1cb/acdbac19fa56236b919fb7799eaacaa10c77.pdf.

[9] Kritzer HM. Propensity to Sue in England and the United States of America: blaming and claiming in tort cases. J Law Soc 1991;18(4):400–27.

[10] Lochlann Jain SS. Injury: The politics of product design and safety law in the United States. Princeton, NJ: Princeton University Press; 2006.

[11] McGovern F. Punitive damages and class actions. Lousiana Law Rev 2010;70:435–62. Available from: https://scholarship.law.duke.edu/cgi/viewcontent.cgi?article=2762&context=faculty_scholarship.

[12] Bal BS. An introduction to medical malpractice in the United States Clin Orthop Relat Res 2009;467(2):339–47 Feb. Available from: https://www.ncbi.nlm.nih.gov/pmc/articles/PMC2628513/.

[13] Kass JS, Rose RV. Medical malpractice reform: historical approaches, alternative models, and communication and resolution programs. AMA J Ethics 2016;18(3):299–310. Available from: https://journalofethics.ama-assn.org/sites/journalofethics.ama-assn.org/files/2019-12/pfor6-1603.pdf.

[14] Kearns GL, Abdel-Rahman SM, Alander SW, Blowey DL, Leeder JS, Kauffman RE. Developmental pharmacology-drug disposition, action, and therapy in infants and children. N Engl J Med 2003;349(12):1157–67. Available from: https://pdfs.semanticscholar.org/55f8/1745303e9aaec7f4cb85f0b5921eec14a9c0.pdf.

[15] Sheridan PH, Jacobs MP. The development of antiepileptic drugs for children. Report from the NIH workshop, Bethesda, Maryland, February 17–18, 1994. Epilepsy Res 1996;23(1):87–92.

[16] Rose K, Neubauer D, Grant-Kels JM. Ethical issues in pediatric regulatory studies involving placebo treatment. J Pediatr Epilepsy 2020, in press.

[17] FDA 2019. Drugs for treatment of partial onset seizures: full extrapolation of efficacy from adults to pediatric patients 2 years of age and olderguidance for industry. Available from: https://www.fda.gov/media/130449/download.

[18] Pellock JM, Carman WJ, Thyagarajan V, Daniels T, Morris DL, D'Cruz O. Efficacy of antiepileptic drugs in adults predicts efficacy in children: a systematic review Neurology. 2012;79(14):1482–9 Oct 2. Available from: https://www.ncbi.nlm.nih.gov/pmc/articles/PMC4098824/pdf/znl1482.pdf.

[19] Pellock JM, et al. Extrapolating evidence of antiepileptic drug efficacy in adults to children ≥2 years of age with focal seizures: The case for disease similarity. Epilepsia. 2017;58(10):1686–96. Available from: https://onlinelibrary.wiley.com/doi/epdf/10.1111/epi.13859.

[20] Wadsworth I, Jaki T, Sills GJ, et al. Clinical drug development in epilepsy revisited: a proposal for a new paradigm streamlined using extrapolation. CNS Drugs 2016;30(11):1011–17. Available from: https://www.ncbi.nlm.nih.gov/pmc/articles/PMC5078157/pdf/40263_2016_Article_383.pdf.

[21] Auvin S, French J, Dlugos D, et al. Novel study design to assess the efficacy and tolerability of antiseizure medications for focal-onset seizures in infants and young children: a consensus document from the regulatory task force and the pediatric commission of the International League against Epilepsy (ILAE), in collaboration with the Pediatric Epilepsy Research Consortium (PERC). Epilepsia Open 2019;4(4):537–43. Available from: https://doi.org/10.1002/epi4.12356 eCollection 2019 Dec.

[22] Rose K, Kopp MV. Pediatric investigation plans for specific immunotherapy: questionable contributions to childhood health. Pediatr Allergy Immunol 2015;26(8):695–701.

[23] Morjaria JB, Caruso M, Rosalia E, et al. Preventing progression of allergic rhinitis to asthma. Curr Allergy Asthma Rep 2014;14(2):412.

[24] Waubant E, Banwell B, Wassmer E, et al. Clinical trials of disease-modifying agents in pediatric MS: opportunities, challenges, and recommendations from the IPMSSG. Neurology. 2019;92(22):e2538–49.

[25] Krysko KM, Graves JS, Rensel M, et al. Real-world effectiveness of initial disease-modifying therapies in pediatric MS. Ann Neurol 2020; Apr 8.

[26] Wharton, et al. Impact of pediatric exclusivity on drug labeling and demonstrations of efficacy. Pediatrics. 2014;134(2):e512–18.

[27] FDA. Considerations for the inclusion of adolescent patients in adult oncology clinical trials. Guidance Ind 2019. Available from: https://www.fda.gov/media/113499/download.

[28] Maude SL, Laetsch TW, Buechner J, et al. Tisagenlecleucel in children and young adults with b-cell lymphoblastic leukemia. N Engl J Med 2018;378:439–48.

[29] FDA 2017. Tisagenlecleucel prescribing information. Available from: https://www.fda.gov/media/107296/download.

[30] FDA Crisaborole label. Available from: https://www.accessdata.fda.gov/drugsatfda_docs/nda/2016/207695Orig1s000Lbl.pdf.

[31] FDA 2000. Guidance for Industry. E 11 Clinical Investigation of Medicinal Products in the Pediatric Population. Available from: https://www.fda.gov/media/71355/download.

[32] Sun H, Temeck JW, Chambers W, Perkins G, Bonnel R, Murphy D. Extrapolation of efficacy in pediatric drug development and evidence-based medicine: progress and lessons learned. Ther Innov Regul Sci 2017;2017:1–7. Available from: https://www.ncbi.nlm.nih.gov/pmc/articles/PMC5587157/pdf/nihms901908.pdf.

[33] EMA 2004. Evidence of harm from off-label or unlicensed medicines in children. Available from: https://www.ema.europa.eu/en/documents/other/evidence-harm-label-unlicensed-medicines-children_en.pdf.

[34] EMA 2016. 10-year Report to the European Commission. General report on the experience acquired as a result of the application of the Paediatric Regulation. Available from: https://ec.europa.eu/health/sites/health/files/files/paediatrics/2016_pc_report_2017/ema_10_year_report_for_consultation.pdf.

[35] EMA 2015. European Medicines Agency decisionCW/0001/2015 of 23 July 2015 on class waivers. Available from: https://www.ema.europa.eu/en/documents/other/european-medicines-agency-decision-cw-0001-2015-23-july-2015-class-waivers-accordance-regulation-ec_en.pdf.

[36] Rose K, Neubauer D, Grant-Kels JM. Rational use of medicine in children – The conflict of interests story. A review Rambam Maimonides Med J 2019;10(3):e0018Review. Available from: https://doi.org/10.5041/RMMJ.10371. Available from: https://www.rmmj.org.il/userimages/928/2/PublishFiles/953Article.pdf.

[37] Runciman WB, Merry AF. Crises in clinical care: an approach to management. Qual Saf Health Care 2005;14(3):156–63. Available from: https://www.ncbi.nlm.nih.gov/pmc/articles/PMC1744000/pdf/v014p00156.pdf.

[38] FDA 2019. General Clinical Pharmacology Considerations for Neonatal Studies for Drugs and Biological ProductsGuidance for Industry. Available from: https://www.fda.gov/media/129532/download.

[39] https://ourworldindata.org/tertiary-education.

[40] Wikipedia, the free encyclopedia. Food and Drug Administration. Available from: https://en.wikipedia.org/wiki/Food_and_Drug_Administration.

[41] Severin T, Corriol-Rohou S, Bucci-Rechtweg C, et al. How is the pharmaceutical industry structured to optimize pediatric drug development? Existing pediatric structure models and proposed recommendations for structural enhancement. Ther Innov Regul Sci 2020; Feb 6.

[42] Barrett JS, Bucci-Rechtweg C, Amy Cheung SY, et al. Pediatric extrapolation in type 2 diabetes: Future implications of a workshop. Clin Pharmacol Ther 2020; Feb 4.

[43] Barrett JS, Bishai R, Bucci-Rechtweg C, et al. Challenges and opportunities in the development of medical therapies for pediatric populations and the role of extrapolation. Clin Pharmacol Ther 2018;103(3):419–33.

[44] Bucci-Rechtweg C. Enhancing the pediatric drug development framework to deliver better pediatric therapies tomorrow. Clin Ther 2017;39(10):1920–32.

[45] Phase 2 Study of Ipilimumab in Children and Adolescents (12 to <18 Years) With Previously Treated or Untreated, Unresectable Stage III or Stage IV Malignant Melanoma. Available from: https://clinicaltrials.gov/ct2/show/NCT01696045.

[46] BRIM-P: A Study of Vemurafenib in Pediatric Patients With Stage IIIC or Stage IV Melanoma Harboring BRAFV600 Mutations. Available from: https://clinicaltrials.gov/ct2/show/NCT01519323.

[47] Rose K, Grant-Kels JM. Pediatric melanoma – The whole (conflicts of interest) story. Int J Womens Dermatol 2018;5(2):110–15. Available from: https://doi.org/10.1016/j.ijwd.2018.10.020. Available from: https://www.ncbi.nlm.nih.gov/pmc/articles/PMC6451736/pdf/main.pdf.

[48] Rose K, Walson PD. Do the European Medicines Agency (EMA) decisions hurt pediatric melanoma patients? Clin Therapeutics 2017;39(2):253–65. Available from: https://www.clinicaltherapeutics.com/article/S0149-2918(17)30047-4/pdf.

[49] Rose K, Walson PD, Are Regulatory Age Limits in Pediatric Melanoma Justified?

[50] Rose K. The challenges of pediatric drug development. Curr Ther Res Clin Exp 2019. Available from: https://doi.org/10.1016/j.curtheres.2019.01.007.

[51] Rose K, Grant-Kels JM. The meanings of "pediatric drug development". A review. Ther Innov Regul Sci 2019;53(6):767–74.

[52] Rose K. European union pediatric legislation jeopardizes worldwide, timely future advances in the care of children with cancer. Clin Therapeutics 2014;36(2):163–77. Available from: http://www.clinicaltherapeutics.com/article/S0149-2918(14)00018-6/pdf.

[53] Brunner HI, Rider LG, Kingsbury DJ, Co D, Schneider R, Goldmuntz E, et al. Pediatric rheumatology collaborative study group - over four decades of pivotal clinical drug research in pediatric rheumatology. Pediatr Rheumatol Online J 2018;16(1):45.

[54] Ruperto N, Vesely R, Saint-Raymond A, et al. Impact of the European paediatric legislation in paediatric rheumatology: past, present and future. Ann Rheum Dis 2013;72(12): 1893–6.

[55] Ruperto N, Eichler I, Herold R, et al. A european network of paediatric research at the european medicines agency (Enpr-EMA). Arch Dis Child 2012;97(3):185–8.

[56] Reaman GH. FDARA 2017 and the RACE for children act: implications for pediatric cancer drug development. Available online: https://www.accelerate-platform.eu/wp-content/uploads/sites/4/2018/02/1640-REAMAN.pdf.

[57] FDA 2019. FDARA implementation guidance for pediatric studies of molecularly targeted oncology drugs: amendments to Sec. 505B of the FD&C Act. Guidance for industry. Available from: https://www.fda.gov/media/133440/download.

[58] FDA 2020. Pediatric Study Plans for Oncology Drugs: Transitional Information Until Full Implementation of FDARA Section 504Questions and Answers Guidance for Industry. Available from: https://www.fda.gov/media/134155/download.

[59] State of Paediatric Medicines in the EU. 10 years of the EU Paediatric Regulation. Report from the Commission to the European Parliament and the Council. COM (2017) 626. Available from: https://ec.europa.eu/health/sites/health/files/files/paediatrics/docs/2017_childrensmedicines_report_en.pdf.

[60] European Society of Development, Perinatal and Pediatric Pharmacology. www.esdppp.org.

[61] ESDPPP conference 2019 website: removed from the internet. The search term "paediatric imperative" still results in a google hit (03APR2020) with its first words ("The *Paediatric Imperative*. No matter if a company has no specific portfolio interest in paediatric medicines new EMA and FDA regulatory requirements demand ..."). Archived by Klaus Rose.

[62] Caneo LF, Neirotti R. The importance of the proper definition of adulthood: what is and what is not included in a scientific publication. Braz J Cardiovasc Surg 2017;32(1):60–1. Available from: https://www.ncbi.nlm.nih.gov/pmc/articles/PMC5382900/pdf/rbccv-32-01-0060.pdf.

[63] Boots I, et al. Stimulation programs for pediatric drug research – do children really benefit? Eur J Pediatr 2007;166(8):849–55. Available from: https://www.ncbi.nlm.nih.gov/pmc/articles/PMC1914295/pdf/431_2006_Article_381.pdf.

[64] Gören JL. Antidepressants use in pediatric populations. Expert Opin Drug Saf 2008;7(3): 223–5.

[65] Rose K, Neubauer D, Grant-Kels JM. Too many avoidable suicides occur worldwide in young patients. A review Rambam Maimonides Med J 2019;Sep 18. Available from: https://www.rmmj.org.il/userimages/965/1/PublishFiles/977OnlineFirst.pdf.

[66] Kreeftmeijer-Vegter AR, de Boer A, van der Vlugt-Meijer RH, et al. The influence of the European paediatric regulation on marketing authorisation of orphan drugs for children Orphanet J Rare Dis 2014;9:120Aug 5. Available from: https://ojrd.biomedcentral.com/track/pdf/10.1186/s13023-014-0120-x.

[67] EMA 2015. Better Medicines for Children. https://www.ema.europa.eu/en/documents/leaflet/better-medicines-children_en.pdf.

[68] European Organisation for Rare Diseases (Eurordis) 2012. Paediatric drugs and rare diseases. http://www.eurordis.org/en/content/paediatric-drugs-and-rare-diseases.

[69] Peyvandi F, Rosendaal FR, O'Mahony B, Mannuccio MP. Pediatric requirements in Europe stymie help for hemophilia. Nat Med 2014;20:117. Available from: https://www.nature.com/articles/nm0214-117.pdf.

Chapter 4

Introduction: specific disease areas

This chapter shows for eleven clinical areas how the "pediatric" clinical studies requested/mandated by the FDA and the EMA, supported by leading representatives of clinical academia, by representatives of large pharmaceutical companies and of commercial clinical research organizations (CROs) appear to be reasonable as long as we blindly accept the use of the terms "child" and "pediatric." The blur in the use of these terms is that they speak of "children," but that the affected "children" are *administratively* defined as "children" but are often *bodily* no longer children, but young, mature human beings. Also younger persons of school age are no longer newborns, but are in the transition toward maturity. Medical treatment should treat both, body and soul, but definitely independently of a person's legal or administrative status.

The order of the first three subchapters reflects the seriousness of the involved challenges, reflected in the frequency of death in young persons in developed countries. The most frequent cause of death is accidents. Many can be prevented in traffic, in households, in the school and in sports, and we try hard to do so. But if they occur, surgery is often the only chance for the respective patient. Modern surgery would be impossible without anesthesia, pain medication, antiinfectives, modern suture materials, modern diagnostics, and more. FDA and EMA approve tissue-engineered products such three-dimensional autologous cultured chondrocytes in a first step only in adults. Such products are used to facilitate the repair of knee injuries. The EMA demands for tissue-engineered products a "pediatric investigation plan" (PIP), in which companies must commit to "pediatric" studies in young persons with closed growth plates but younger than 18 years. Closed growth plates show that the slow process of puberty is over and that the body has become mature. If the miller's daughter on the book cover is younger than 18 years and would injure her

Considering the Patient in Pediatric Drug Development. DOI: https://doi.org/10.1016/B978-0-12-823888-2.00021-1

knee in a sports accident, the EMA classifies her as a "child" and she could participate at a PIP-demanded "pediatric" study. PIPs for tissue engineered products (TEPs) are a major reason that delay the approval of modern tissue-engineered products in persons before their 18th birthday. They thus deny them modern treatment and are a reason for blocking an entire branch of industry from developing.

After accidents, suicide is the next frequent cause of death in young people. Often mental disorders are involved, including depression. In its unlimited wisdom, the FDA has inserted a black box warning into antidepressant labels for young patients, claimed that it leads to "suicidality." This warning has been adopted by regulatory authorities worldwide in various forms. It has probably or even certainly produced more damage than prevented harm.

Cancer is after accidents and suicides the next most frequent cause of death in young people. But not every malignancy before the 18th birthday is "pediatric." The FDA now recommends the inclusion of adolescents into promising adult cancer studies but demands from 2020 on inclusion of younger patients into separate "pediatric" studies, following in this regard the EU's precedence. The EMA continues to demand "pediatric" studies in adolescents with malignant melanoma and has declared many more diseases to be "pediatric" because they occasionally occur also before the 18th birthday. The EMA's regulatory "pediatric" anticancer strategy has in over ten years contributed to many "pediatric" clinical studies and many academic publications, but has not advanced pediatric oncology. But patients that evade the grip of PIP-demanded studies can have a chance, such as Emily Whitehead, a six-years-old girl with relapsed acute lymphoblastic leukemia who was snatched away from the deathbed by cutting-edge CAR-T cell therapy.

The following subchapters show how the demand for separate "pediatric" studies in allegedly "pediatric" diseases lack medical sense and often withhold effective modern therapy to young patients.

The subchapter about cystic fibrosis (CF) shows the new successful approach of "venture philanthropy," where parents of CF children invested money into commercial pharmaceutical companies and have fundamentally changed the fate of this disease.

Last but not least, the subchapter on vaccines and antibiotics shows how the demand for pediatric vaccine studies and for separate pediatric proof of efficacy for antibacterial, antiviral, and antifungal drugs lack, at best, medical sense, and at worst, withhold effective therapy and thus do harm by omission.

Altogether the subchapters in Chapter 4 show that unleashed bureaucracies on both sides of the ocean have comparable tendencies. Both demand "pediatric" studies that often would run for the next ten years. The record are studies until 2034. But today's medicine and drug development are changing fast. To block young patients for the next ten to fifteen years for studies that in the authorities' view are needed to prove again that they work before the 18th birthday is medically and scientifically unjustified.

Enjoy reading.

Subchapter 4.1

Tissue-engineered products (TEPs), advanced medicinal products, and surgery in young patients

Tissue-engineered products (TEPs), somatic cell therapy medical products, and gene therapy medical products are high-tech products with high potential to further improve various healthcare challenges of patients of any age. Both the FDA and the EMA claim to advance the development of such products. The EMA classifies these product types as advanced therapy medicinal products (ATMPs). But the EMA's demand for separate "pediatric" studies for autologous chondrocyte implantation (ACI) products to repair cartilage damages in the knee joint are probably the most striking example of the absurdity of the EMA's crusade of "pediatric drug development." ACI pediatric investigation plans (PIPs) demand separate "pediatric" studies in patients from the closure of the growth plates (epiphyses) up to 17 years old, which is an oxymoron because the closure of the growth plates shows that the body has passed puberty and has become mature. Legally, adolescents with closed growth plates are still children, but no longer bodily. The EU demands PIPs for all ATMPs, which is already today a major hurdle against developing cutting-edge advanced medicinal products. Only a handful of ATMPs have so far passed the hurdle of EU-wide regulatory approval, which further threatens and undermines the EU's place in research and development. The EU Lisbon strategy promised "the most dynamic and competitive knowledge-based economy in the world" with sustainable economic growth, more and better jobs, greater social cohesion, and respect for the environment. Slow approval of ATMPs, in general, and specifically of ACI products to repair cartilage damages, shows that the opposite of the Lisbon strategy is taking place.

Introduction

In contrast to the past, infectious diseases are no longer the most frequent cause of death in young persons in developed countries and societies. Among young persons aged between ten and thirty years, today's most frequent cause of death is accidents, followed by suicide [1].

It is best to prevent accidents. But when persons get injured in traffic, during sports, working, or on the playground, sophisticated surgery is available today. Surgery has evolved during the last century in both adults and young people. Specifically in young children, the treatment of congenital malformations of the heart and blood vessels, of the digestive and other organs, and organ transplantation played a major role in addition to the treatment of children that became victims of accidents. Surgery also plays a key role in the removal of benign and malignant tumors. Pediatric surgery has become a recognized subspecialty of surgery [2–4].

As long as they are young, children are smaller and weigh less than adults. They should be treated with high sensitivity, and in the knowledge that the little patient will grow with the sutures that are necessary for repair. This makes careful planning of every operation in a young person even more important. But fundamentally, pediatric surgery is not different from adult surgery. Pediatric surgeons also use a scalpel, surgical sutures, their knowledge of the human anatomy, their experience, the most modern methods of diagnostics, and, today, all modern instruments that allow "keyhole surgery" which means rather smaller openings for viewing through an endoscope, for introducing the necessary instruments, and then to operate upon the organ(s) and structures concerned. The current state of pediatric surgery is connected to the many advances that have been made in anesthesia, intensive care medicine, psychology in dealing with young people, imaging procedures such as X-rays, magnetic resonance imaging, ultrasound, and many further techniques. A grumpy, always bad-tempered surgeon who behaves like the cartoon of a butcher toward parents, nurses, and young patients would not survive in today's medical system for long. It was different in World War II when children had to be operated after bomb attacks. But World War II is history, and the times have changed.

In addition to needles, sutures, and modern imaging, medication also plays a key role in the surgical treatment of young people, including antibiotics, anesthetics during surgery, pain medication, prevention of rejection of transplanted organs by immunosuppressants, and more [5]. Here we discuss an example from orthopedic surgery that shows the absurdity of separate "pediatric" studies particularly well.

Advanced Therapeutic Medicinal Products (ATMPs)

Three groups of advanced products have the potential to revolutionize healthcare for many different diseases for patients of any age: tissue-engineered products (TEPs), somatic cell therapy medical products, and gene therapy medical products. In the US, human cells or tissue intended for implantation, transplantation, infusion, or transfer into a human recipient are regulated as human cell, tissue, and cellular and tissue-based products or HCT/Ps [6]. The FDA has also introduced a guideline for "regenerative medicine advanced therapy" (RMAT) products to expedite the development of new promising therapies to patients with serious conditions [7]. In the EU, these three categorizes are summarized under the umbrella term advanced therapy medicinal products (ATMPs) [8].

Within the EMA, a special committee, the Committee on Advanced Therapies (CAT), is responsible to handle applications for ATMPs. These products represent a new era of research and drug development with potential high impact on the treatment of diseases as diverse as leukemia [8], sport injuries [9–14], reconstruction of mucosa in internal organs, including urology [15,16], and many more [17–20]. Recently, the Committee for Medicinal Products for Human Use (CHMP) together with the EMA developed a stand-alone assessment pathway tool called priority medicines (PRIME), which aims to accelerate the development of medicines targeting unmet medical needs to reach patients within a shortened time. In 2016, the PRIME scheme became effective, offering several advantages to applicants when accepted for the scheme [17]. Nevertheless, all ATMPs have also to go through the "pediatric investigation plan" (PIP) procedure, which includes the commitment to one or several "pediatric" studies in patients younger than 18 years.

In 2007, the EU decided that all ATMPs, including TEPs, should be regulated as drugs. A regulation for ATMP was adopted with definitions for TEPs and engineered cells. Since 2008, a central EMA approval is required for all ATMPs, including TEPs. A transitional period for TEPs that had already been on the market elapsed in 2012 [7,21–23].

In view of the small scale and developmental nature of some intrahospital ATMPs, the EU ATMP regulation includes a "hospital exemption" for products not intended to be marketed. ATMPs applied via hospital exemption must be prepared on a nonroutine basis, nonindustrially, and must be used as a custom made product for individual patients, respectively [18].

The knee is one of the most complicated human joints. Like other joints, the ends of the upper and lower leg bones are covered with cartilage, allowing a low-friction, shock-absorbing function, so that we can move painlessly into old age. The articular cartilage achieves high biomechanical performance by absorbing and supporting peak pressure forces of many 25 times the body weight during fast movements and especially in sports. To achieve this, articular cartilage is no longer supplied with blood after puberty. The disadvantage of this biomechanical excellence is that articular cartilage heals poorly and slowly when injured. The consequences are pain, swollen joints, and blockades of the knee joint, which often significantly reduce the quality of life. These problems mostly remain and worsen over time. Cartilage damage often increases over time. Cartilage damage has the risk of causing joint wear (arthrosis) [24–27].

The concept of autologous chondrocyte implantation (ACI) emerged in the late 1980s and the early 1990s for the treatment of articular cartilage defects in the knee. In a first operation, the joint is inspected through a small hole into which the endoscope is inserted for a look into the interior. If there is a major cartilage injury, cartilage cells (chondrocytes) are removed from a low-stress area of the joint. Then these are grown in a nutrient solution in the laboratory. In a second operation, this neotissue is inserted back into the joint to cover and repair the damaged cartilage area. The first ACI generation used a patch with cultured chondrocytes, followed by a collagen membrane patch (second-generation ACI). Finally, the application of chondrocytes within a three-dimensional matrix (third-generation ACI) was developed to allow for easier implantation to better replicate the normal cartilage architecture and to accelerate healing and recovery. If everything goes well, the cartilage damage is completely compensated. This two-part operation is now a routine procedure in the surgical treatment of knee injuries [14,24].

As a rule, ACI is used in adult persons. We are talking about physically adult people, i.e., persons after the end of puberty. In younger persons before puberty, the cartilage is still supplied with blood so that there is justified hope that conservative treatment, i.e., protection and waiting, might result in disappearance of the joint damage. If major damage has already occurred and conservative treatment has not been successful for a long time, a responsible surgeon will also operate on a younger patient and perform ACI. There is also another type of cartilage damage and bone damage that occurs mostly in young persons, the cause of which is not entirely clear ("idiopathic"). Even without an accident, the cartilage and the underlying bone can be damaged. This damage is called "osteochondrosis dissecans" and often occurs in adolescence. It might be caused by microtrauma, but other causes are possible as well [28].

Autologous chondrocytes grown and amplified in the laboratory tend to dedifferentiate. Products derived from expanded chondrocytes might have inferior biomechanical properties compared to native, healthy tissue. The development of TEPs for repair of knee damages is still ongoing. Further potential avenues might be to harvest chondrocytes from other joints, or even use tissue that does not come from the own body. There are numerous further potential avenues [27]. With increased participation of young persons in sports, also the number of sport injuries is increasing.

In the US, at present two autologous chondrocyte products are FDA-approved: carticel, and MACI, which stands for "matrix-applied characterized autologous cultured chondrocytes" [23,29–31]. Carticel was initially FDA-approved in 1995 as an unregulated cell therapy, then approved in 1997 on the basis of clinical data from Europe, preregulation US registry data, and because the manufacturer committed to a postmarketing approval study [23,29]. Both carticel and MACI are only approved in "adults," and section 8.4 of the labels emphasize that their safety and effectiveness in "pediatric patients" has not been established [30,31], "children" defined as <17 years [32]. But the FDA did not force companies to perform separate "pediatric" TEP studies. Instead, the respective surgeon can decide on medical grounds and on his own if a young patient needs an ACI.

The EU, however, chose another avenue. Before ACI products were classified as ATMPs, a manufacturing license was sufficient for the cultivation of chondrocytes in several European countries, including Germany.

When ACI products were classified as ATMPs, the manufacturing license was no longer sufficient. Now companies had to apply for approval of autologous chondrocytes as drugs. Companies had to submit clinical trial data on safety and efficacy of their product, even if had been successfully used in practice for many years. One can argue whether such additional clinical studies were really necessary, but this question is not the focus of our discussion. Here we focus on the additional element of "pediatric" development.

Comparably to the classification of allergen products for allergen-specific immunotherapy (ASIT), now also tissue-engineered products had on top of adult clinical documentation to submit a PIP, because in 2008 the EU pediatric regulation was already in force [33,34]. Manufacturers of ACI products had to commit to "pediatric" studies, "children" EU-defined as under the age limit of the 18th birthday.

A first autologous cartilage cell product (ChondroCelect) was approved EU-wide as an ATMP in 2009, followed by MACI ("matrix-applied characterized autologous cultured chondrocytes"). In MACI, the harvested and cultured chondrocytes are seeded on a collagen membrane of porcine origin. MACI was approved as an ATMP in 2013. It had been available in a several EU countries before [23]. In the meantime, both MACI and ChondroCelect have been withdrawn from the EU market. Due to commercial reasons, the company that sold MACI closed the European manufacturing site in 2014; the marketing authorization was suspended and expired during the suspension period. ChondroCelect was withdrawn from the EU market in 2016 due to a lack of reimbursement in key European countries [18]. At present, the only EU-wide EMA-approved ACI TEP is spherox. But even spherox is currently not approved in "children" [18,35,36].

Several further companies can at present continue to market their respective product in individual EU member states [18]. The respective company cultivates the cells harvested and sent in by the operating surgeons. The company sends the final product back after cultivation and final completion in its new three-dimensional structure. The preparations of the individual companies differ somewhat. Of course, every single company will claim that its product is the best, as is customary in marketing. Here we do not focus on the question which company's product is the best, but on the separate approval ACI products in "children" and the resulting demand for separate "pediatric" studies.

Separate "pediatric" studies for autologous chondrocyte products demanded in EU PIPs

A person becomes physically mature when the puberty is complete [37–41]. Reaching puberty can be defined in many ways. Secondary sexual characteristics develop: the growth of pubic hair and broken voice in both sexes; beard growth in young men, growth of the breasts in young women. A standard method of defining the end of puberty is to check by X-ray whether the growth plates (epiphyseal plates) have already closed. Once the growth plates are closed, the growth is largely completed. On the other hand, the horizontal growth, i.e., weight gain, can continue. Five companies that manufacture ACI preparations have so far gone through the PIP process and the five PIP decisions they had to commit to are available on the internet. The PIP negotiation is a lengthy, complicated procedure that takes usually roughly one year. PIP modifications take an additional half year of negotiation. PIP modifications are marked at the end of the modified PIP number by the appendix "-M01", "-M02", etc. All ACI PIPs demand clinical ACI studies in young people who have not yet reached the age of 18 but are physically mature. The PIP-demanded "pediatric" studies are listed in Table 4.1.1.

PIPs # 1 and # 5 are still in their original version, PIPs # 3–5 have been modified. In today's version, two ACI PIPs still demand openly studies in young persons *after* the closure of the epiphyses *before* the 18th birthday (Table 4.1.1, PIPs 4 and 5). The original version of PIP # 3 in Table 4.1.1 in 2012 (EMEA-001264-PIP01–12) required a study "in paediatric patients from closure of the epiphyses to less than 18 years of age treated with the product until December 2011" [42]. PIP # 1, Table 4.1.1 requires a study in patients 16–17-year-olds, and PIP # 2, Table 4.1.1 demands studies in "pediatric" patients aged 10–16 years. To demand clinical studies in patients that are *legally* still minors as defined by the EU pediatric regulation [33], but are already bodily mature, defined by the objective measurement of the closure of the epiphyses, is probably the most open documentation of the absurdity of the PIP demands for "pediatric" studies. Almost all PIP-demanded studies are questionable, many of those that proceed from PIP demands into real-world clinical studies harm young patients as far as they compare effective treatment versus placebo or versus standard-of-care treatment that is clinically inferior to the investigated drug [43–45]. But the autologous chondrocyte PIPs have the dubious honor to document in one phrase, respectively, the blur between the legal and the physiological meaning of the term "child." "Paediatric patients from closure of the epiphyses to less than 18 years of age" are physiologically no longer children. But the EU pediatric legislation exposes them to the rapacious demands of a central authority on its crusade for as many "pediatric" studies as possible. Scientifically and medically, these demands are absurd. The surgeon operates the body, not the legal status of a patient. These demands are based on the executive power the EU pediatric regulation has given to the EMA in, and on the carelessness with which these studies are demanded despite their obvious absurdity. The newest ACI PIP was issued in 2019, see Table 4.1.1, study 5.

TABLE 4.1.1 ACI PIPs.

	PIP number	Abbreviated description of demanded clinical studies
1	EMEA-000736-PIP01–09	1. R evaluator-blinded MC S&E study of ACI compared to MF in patients 16–17 years of age.
2	EMEA-000979-PIP01–10-M02	1. Prospective OL concurrent active-controlled, longitudinal, MC study on S&E of MACI in patients 10–16 years of age with symptomatic chondral or osteochondral defects of the knee due to osteochondritis dissecans or acute trauma 2. Extrapolation of E from adult patients of less than 35 years of age treated with MACI in the SUMMIT study to pediatric patients of less than 17 years of age.
3	EMEA-001264-PIP01–12-M02	1. Prospective noninterventional investigation on long-term S and linked E of the three-dimensional ACI product in pediatric patients 15–17 years of age.
4	EMEA-001823-PIP01–15-M01	1. OL R active-controlled trial to evaluate S&E of AC derived CCs compared to MF in children from closure of the epiphyses to 17 years of age with focal articular cartilage defects of the knee. 2. SA prospective study on S&E of AC derived CCs in children from closure of the epiphyses to 17 years of age with full thickness articular cartilage defect of the knee.
5	EMEA-002217-PIP01–17	1. OL UC SA trial on S&A AC derived cultured chondrocytes in children with closed epiphyses aged 14–17 years of age (and adults) with focal cartilage defects of the knee. 2. OL UC Ret SA noninterventional study on S&A of NOVOCART Inject (product including AC derived cultured chondrocytes, similar but not identical to the subject of this PIP) in children with closed epiphyses below 18 years (and adults) with cartilage defects in the knee.

A, Activity; *AC*, autologous cartilage; *ACI*, autologous chondrocyte implantation; *CCs*, cultured chondrocytes; *MACI*, Matrix-applied characterized autologous cultured chondrocytes; *MC*, multicenter; *MF*, microfracture; *OL*, open label; *R*, randomized; *Ret*, retrospective; *S*, safety; *SA*, single arm; *S&A*, safety and activity; *S&E*, safety and efficacy; *UC*, uncontrolled; *y*, year.

PIP # 2 in Table 4.1.1 demands an "extrapolation study" from under-35-year-old adult patients to "pediatric" patients under 17 years old. Both populations are bodily mature adults. They have a different *legal* status.

Two PIPs demand a randomized comparison in "pediatric" patients against microfracture (Table 4.1.1, PIPs 1 and 4). Microfracture is a method of treating injuries of the knee cartilage by drilling numerous small holes through the cartilage into the underlying bone. Blood is supposed to flow into the cartilage through the holes. Blood also contains stem cells, among other things, and the theory of microfracture postulates that this stimulates new, effective cartilage formation. Many publications discuss ACI versus microfracture and come to opposing conclusions, which is often the case in medicine [9–13]. But it does not make medical sense to repeat proof of efficacy in administratively defined "children" for compounds whose efficacy in humans is already documented. The EMA's insistence on microfracture is based on the assumption that for young people under the age of 18 efficacy must be proven again, i.e., that their body is fundamentally different from adult bodies. The bodies of newborns, and more so of preterm newborns differ indeed very much from adult bodies. But not the bodies of adolescents. What changes in the night of the 18th birthday is the legal status of the respective patient, but not his body [43–45].

Table 4.1.2 shows all industry-sponsored studies listed in www.clinicaltrials.gov with the search terms "chondrocytes" and "MACI" when the search is narrowed on "pediatric" studies.

Table 4.1.2 shows that the vast majority of studies include bodily mature patients irrespective of their legal status, which makes sense. There are only two purely "pediatric" studies that would follow the EMA-definition of children: study 7 in patients aged 13–17 years, and study 14 in patients aged 10–17 years. These studies correspond to the PIPs # 2 and 5 in Table 4.1.1. Both studies are recruiting.

Table 4.1.2, study 7 accompanies routine clinical practice in Germany, where the compound is nationally licensed in the treatment of cartilage defects of the knee in "pediatric patients with closed epiphyseal growth plates." The study is investigating efficacy, safety, and health economics [48]. Table 4.1.2, study 14 compares microfracture against ACI in 10–17 year old patients. It is conducted in 10 clinical centers in the United States [49]. Clinically, study 7 is not damaging any patient, while the medical sense of study 14 is questionable. It compares ACI to microfracture in a randomized fashion, i.e., the individual surgeon does not decide which treatment the individual patient receives. Parents should never consent to participate in this study.

If there were really well-founded safety concerns in young patients, a registry observation might have been considered, regardless of the ACI preparation with which the patients were treated. A registry on a specific product is already running for patients of all ages, see study 8, Table 4.1.2. Insisting on a separate clinical trial for each ACI preparation shows several things.

TABLE 4.1.2 Industry-sponsored pediatric clinical studies in joint cartilage repair listed in www.clinicaltrials.gov using the search terms "chondrocytes" and "MACI".

	NCT #	Study	# of ctrs/pts	Age	Status
1	NCT01056900	Retrospective AC study in articular cartilage defects of the knee	?/127	15–65 y	Completed
2	NCT01050816	OL AC study in ankle cartilage defect	?/30	15–65 y	Completed
3	NCT00729716	OL R S&E of ACI vs. microfracture to repair cartilage lesions of the knee [46,47]	8/40	16–60 y	Unknown
4	NCT03319797	Prospective OL MC S&E study of ACI to repair cartilage lesions of the knee	20/100	14–65 y	AnR
5	NCT01656902	Prospective R OL study of ACI vs. MF to repair cartilage lesions of the knee	?/263	14–65 y	AnR
6	NCT02941120	Ret ACI study in the reconstruction of the knee cartilage defects	7/245	14–50 y	Completed
7	NCT04186208	Prospective, non-interventional S&E study of ACI for knee cartilage defects in pediatric patients with closed epiphyses	7/40	13–17 y	Recruiting
8	NCT00140634	ACI cartilage repair registry	?/2,233	C,A,OA	Completed
9	NCT02348697	Prospective non-interventional S&E study of ACI for knee cartilage defects	9/81	14–50 y	Completed
10	NCT02539056	ACI for knee cartilage defects	2/24	> 15 y	Unknown
11	NCT02539069	OL ACI study for knee cartilage defects	1/10	> 15 y	Unknown
12	NCT02524509	Prospective OL study of ACI vs. MF in cartilage defects of the knee	/50	C,A,OA	Unknown
13	NCT02537067	OL S&E study of ACI in cartilage defects of the ankle	2/28	15–65 y	Unknown
14	NCT03588975	Prospective OL R study MACI vs. MF in SCOOC of the knee	10/45	10–17 y	Recruiting

AnR, Active not recruiting, *AC*, autologous chondrocytes; *ACI*, autologous chondrocyte implantation; *C,A,OA*, child, adult, older adult; *CCs*, cultured chondrocytes; *MACI*, Matrix-applied characterized autologous cultured chondrocytes; *MC*, multicenter; *MF*, microfracture; *OL*, open label; *R*, randomized; *Ret*, retrospective; *S*, safety; *SCOOC*, symptomatic chondral or osteochondral defects; *S&E*, safety and efficacy; *y*, year.

Firstly, the inclusion criteria for the studies required differ. There is no consistency within the PIP-requested studies. Secondly, there is a fixation on the individual medication and not on the patient.

The EMA has classified in several "scientific recommendations of advanced therapy medicinal products" several different types of human autologous chondrocytes as ATMPs whose marketing authorization application has to be handled by the CAT [50–55].

ATMPs, ACI, and the Lisbon strategy

In March 2000, European leaders committed the EU to become by 2010 "the most dynamic and competitive knowledge-based economy in the world capable of sustainable economic growth with more and better jobs and greater social cohesion, and respect for the environment." This has come to be known as the "Lisbon strategy" [56].

Autologous chondrocyte products for ACI operations may on an economic level not be the most important issue in today's worlds of surgery and medical care. But the PIPs for ACI products are probably the most striking example to what degree an unchained bureaucracy can go if there is no qualified medical and scientific control of its decisions. These decisions affect EU-wide the lives of young patients. ACI products are not approved in persons before their 18th birthday. Separate "pediatric" studies are demanded. ATMPs represent the potential of many true medical revolutions. Damaged cartilage in the knee joint (and in many other joints) can today already be repaired by ACI in relatively young patients. Eventually, this might become possible also in older patients with further advances in research and development [27]. Instead of having become the most dynamic and competitive knowledge-based economy in the world, the EU has maneuvered itself into a corner where obviously absurd medical decisions are made by a central authority so far insulated from daily life, from the pulse science, research, and medical progress, that the notices about these absurdities have so far failed to reach the mainstream media. The reason for this is banal: the degree of absurdity of these demands is so deep that this is difficult even to imagine.

This goes far beyond banal medical challenges. Child mortality has gone down. Longevity is advancing, with all sorts of diseases and medical problems that come with life. After having been produced in the kidneys, urine flows into the urinary bladder, is stored there for a while, and then excreted. Urethral stricture impairs the outflow of urine. Backflow of urine can, if it continues for a while, result in severe kidney damage. For surgical treatment of urethral stricture, mucosa is needed. The body will not reject mucosa that comes from another part of the body. One surgical strategy was to remove mucosa from the mouth and use it to repair the urethra. Then surgeons had the idea to cultivate oral mucosa for "tissue-engineered oral mucosa graft" (TEOMG) [7,15]. Successful worldwide clinical trials have been performed [15,16,57–59]. This forward-looking idea that is already translated into a technology now meets the Byzantine "pediatric" demands of the EMA. Here, we do not discuss the general requirements of the development of drugs and tissue engineering. These processes are by nature complex. If a patient is later damaged by a faulty product, critical questions will be asked why the responsible central authority did not prevent the damage. But the common denominator we discuss here is that all ATMPs in the EU have to go through the PIP procedure as well. Table 4.1.1 shows this for the autologous chondrocyte products. Two reviews on the regulatory hurdles for ATMPs worldwide do not even mention the additional EU hurdle of "pediatric drug development" [7,23], which results in the demand for allegedly pediatric studies that are often demanded for young persons whose body is already mature. With very few exceptions, all PIP-demanded "pediatric" studies are "only" medically senseless at best, but often harm young patients [43–45].

The EU's Lisbon dream of "the most dynamic and competitive knowledge-based economy in the world capable of sustainable economic growth with more and better jobs and greater social cohesion, and respect for the environment" has become a nightmarish scenery of regulatory demands that are hostile to science, albeit clad in a pseudo-scientific disguise. The EU represents the region from where modern science and technology expanded worldwide. But this rich historical heritage is no guarantee for the EU to remain at the forefront of scientific progress.

Conclusion

The described "pediatric" activism, here exemplified by EMA demands for alleged "pediatric" studies in ACI, documents a fundamental hostility toward scientific and economic progress that has taken place in a relevant structure of the EMA. The absurd regulatory "pediatric" demands for ATMPs are not only a scientific challenge. They hamper EU economic progress in biomedicine, which represents a major market of the future. This world is competitive. The EU *would* need a regulatory framework that advances medical and biomedical progress. Instead, the current regulatory demand for "pediatric drug development" blocks medical progress. Europe used to be a rich region, and is still rich compared to other regions of this planet. However, the current blockade of cutting-edge new products and techniques is a hurdle not only for science, but also for the economy. It prevents the establishment and growth of new innovative companies and of new jobs. Instead, it rewards backward-oriented academic researchers with pseudoscientific "pediatric" projects that have to be sponsored by successful pharmaceutical and biotech companies. At least, a candid discussion of these challenges is not forbidden in the EU.

References

[1] Ten Leading Causes of Death by Age Group, US 2016. <https://www.cdc.gov/injury/images/lc-charts/leading_causes_of_death_age_group_2016_1056w814h.gif>.

[2] Chang JH. Timelines in the history of pediatric surgery. J Pediatr Surg 1986; 21(12):1068–72.

[3] Bruny J, Ziegler MM. Historical development of pediatric surgical quality: the first 100 years. Adv Pediatr 2013;60(1):281–94.

[4] Ziegler MM. Pediatric surgical training: an historic perspective, a formula for change. J Pediatr Surg 2004;39(8):1159–72.

[5] Colón AR. Nurturing childen. A history of pediatrics. Westport, CT: Greenwood Press; 1999.

[6] FDA 2019. Expedited programs for regenerative medicine therapies for serious conditions. Guidance for industry. <https://www.fda.gov/media/120267/download>.

[7] Ram-Liebig G, Bednarz J, Stuerzebecher B, et al. Regulatory challenges for autologous tissue engineered products on their way from bench to bedside in Europe. Adv Drug Deliv Rev 2015;82-83:181–91. <https://mukocell.com/wp-content/uploads/2016/08/ADDRRam.pdf>.

[8] Maude SL, Laetsch TW, Buechner J, Rives S, Boyer M, Bittencourt H. Tisagenlecleucel in children and young adults with B-cell lymphoblastic leukemia. N Engl J Med 2018; 378(5):439–48.

[9] Kraeutler MJ, Belk JW, Purcell JM, et al. Microfracture versus autologous chondrocyte implantation for articular cartilage lesions in the knee: a systematic review of 5-year outcomes. Am J Sports Med 2018;46(4):995–9.

[10] Coughlin RP, Gupta A, Sogbein OA, et al. Cartilage restoration in the adolescent knee: a systematic review. Curr Rev Musculoskelet Med 2019;12(4):486–96. <https://www.ncbi.nlm.nih.gov/pmc/articles/PMC6942099/pdf/12178_2019_Article_9595.pdf>.

[11] Harris JD, Siston RA, Pan X, et al. Autologous chondrocyte implantation: a systematic review. J Bone Jt Surg Am 2010;92(12):2220–33. <http://citeseerx.ist.psu.edu/viewdoc/download?doi = 10.1.1.1004.3559&rep = rep1&type = pdf>.

[12] Ruano-Ravina A, Jato Diaz M. Autologous chondrocyte implantation: a systematic review. Osteoarthr Cartil 2006;14(1):47–51. <https://www.oarsijournal.com/article/S1063-4584(05)00201-3/pdf>.

[13] Mistry H, Connock M, Pink J, et al. Autologous chondrocyte implantation in the knee: systematic review and economic evaluation. Health Technol Assess 2017;21(6):1–294. <https://www.ncbi.nlm.nih.gov/books/NBK424075/> and <https://www.journalslibrary.nihr.ac.uk/hta/hta21060/#/abstract>.

[14] Krill M, Early N, Everhart JS, et al. Autologous chondrocyte implantation (ACI) for knee cartilage defects: a review of indications, technique, and outcomes. JBJS Rev 2018;6(2):e5.

[15] Ram-Liebig G, Barbagli G, Heidenreich A, et al. Results of use of tissue-engineered autologous oral mucosa graft for urethral reconstruction: a multicenter, prospective, observational trial. EBioMedicine. 2017;23:185–92. <https://www.thelancet.com/action/showPdf?pii = S2352-3964%2817%2930331-6>.

[16] Barbagli G, Akbarov I, Heidenreich A, et al. Anterior urethroplasty using a new tissue engineered oral mucosa graft: surgical techniques and outcomes. J Urol 2018; 200(2):448–56.

[17] Elsanhoury A, Sanzenbacher R, Reinke P, et al. Accelerating patients' access to advanced therapies in the EU. Mol Ther Methods Clin Dev 2017;7:15–19. <https://www.cell.com/action/showPdf?pii = S2329-0501%2817%2930094-3>.

[18] Eder C, Wild C. Technology forecast: advanced therapies in late clinical research, EMA approval or clinical application via hospital exemption. J Mark Access Health Policy 2019;7(1):1600939 <https://www.ncbi.nlm.nih.gov/pmc/articles/PMC6493298/pdf/zjma-7-1600939.pdf>.

[19] Ylä-Herttuala S. The need for increased clarity and transparency in the regulatory pathway for gene medicines in the European Union. Mol Ther 2012;20:471–2.

[20] Schneider CK, Salmikangas P, Jilma B, Flamion B, Todorova LR, Paphitou A, et al. Challenges with advanced therapy medicinal products and how to meet them Committee for Advanced Therapies (CAT); CAT Scientific Secretariat Nat Rev Drug Discov 2010;9:195–201.

[21] Regulation (EC) No 1394/2007 of the European Parliament and of 13 November 2007 on advanced therapy medicinal products and amending Directive 2001/83/EC 2004/2004, Off. J. Eur. Union L 324 (10.12.2007) 121–137. <https://eur-lex.europa.eu/LexUriServ/LexUriServ.do?uri = OJ:L:2007:324:0121:0137:en:PDF>.

[22] Commission Directive 2009/120/EC of 14 September 2009 amending Directive 2001/83/EC of the European Parliament and of the Council on the Communitycode relating to medicinal products for human use as regards advanced therapy medicinal products, Off. J. Eur. Union L 242 (3) (September 15 2009). <https://ec.europa.eu/health/sites/health/files/files/eudralex/vol-1/dir_2001_83_consol_2012/dir_2001_83_cons_2012_en.pdf>.

[23] Yano K, Watanabe N, Tsuyuki K, et al. Regulatory approval for autologous human cells and tissue products in the United States, the European Union, and Japan. Regen Ther 2014;1:45–56 <https://reader.elsevier.com/reader/sd/pii/S2352320414000029?token = 3F32C2A7B2A94FC2CDDC41976BF607B1A6E3674B10BFF7C490E8F05064FD7BBD4DA129729B6908125AC4FE7CDB2A075C>.

[24] Hunziker EB, Lippuner K, Keel MJ, et al. An educational review of cartilage repair: precepts & practice—myths & misconceptions—progress & prospects. Osteoarthr Cartil 2015;23(3):334–50 <https://www.oarsijournal.com/article/S1063-4584(14)01383-1/pdf>.

[25] Sophia Fox AJ, Bedi A, Rodeo SA. The basic science of articular cartilage: structure, composition, and function. Sports Health 2009;1(6):461–8 <https://www.ncbi.nlm.nih.gov/pmc/articles/PMC3445147/pdf/10.1177_1941738109350438.pdf>.

[26] Bhosale AM, Richardson JB. Articular cartilage: structure, injuries and review of management. Br Med Bull 2008;87:77–95.

[27] Kwon H, Brown WE, Lee CA, et al. Surgical and tissue engineering strategies for articular cartilage and meniscus repair. Nat Rev Rheumatol 2019;15(9):550–70 <https://www.ncbi.nlm.nih.gov/pmc/articles/PMC7192556/pdf/nihms-1579623.pdf>.

[28] Accadbled F, Vial J, Sales de Gauzy J. Osteochondritis dissecans of the knee. Orthop Traumatol Surg Res 2018;104(1S):S97–105 <https://reader.elsevier.com/reader/sd/pii/S1877056817303341?token = 2542B06156589093E3099910FC9CF632D37DFBAE784586DBEA0C6B69EFEDF59025C729AB91CC701B6361B97EF18B00F1>.

[29] McGowan KB, Stiegman B. Regulatory challenges for cartilage repair technologies. Cartilage. 2013;4(1):4–11.

[30] FDA 2016. MACI label. <https://www.fda.gov/media/101914/download>.

[31] FDA 2015 Carticel package insert <https://www.maci.com/pdf/CarticelPI_2015_22Jun15_FINAL.pdf>.

[32] Hirschfeld S. History of pediatric labeling. <https://slideplayer.com/slide/8600310/>.

[33] Regulation (EC) No 1901/2006 of the European Parliament and of the Council of 12 December 2006 on Medicinal Products for Paediatric Use and Amending Regulation (EEC)

No 1768/92, Directive 2001/20/EC, Directive 2001/83/EC and Regulation (EC) No 726/2004. <http://ec.europa.eu/health/files/eudralex/vol-1/reg_2006_1901/reg_2006_1901_en.pdf>.

[34] Hirschfeld S, Saint-Raymond A. Pediatric regulatory initiatives. Handb Exp Pharmacol 2011;205:245−68.

[35] Mumme M, Wixmerten A, Miot S, et al. Tissue engineering for paediatric patients. Swiss Med Wkly 2019;149:w20032. Available from: https://smw.ch/article/doi/smw.2019.20032.

[36] Rose K, Neubauer D, et al. Comment on: Mumme M et al. Tissue engineering for paediatric patients. Swiss Medical Weekly 2020 (in press).

[37] Vijayakumar N, Op de Macks Z, Shirtcliff EA, et al. Puberty and the human brain: insights into adolescent development.

[38] Khan L. Puberty: onset and progression. Pediatr Ann 2019;48(4):e141−5.

[39] Abreu AP, Kaiser UB. Pubertal development and regulation. Lancet Diabetes Endocrinol 2016;4(3):254−64.

[40] Snyder CK. Puberty: an overview for pediatric nurses. J Pediatr Nurs 2016;31(6):757−9.

[41] Wood CL, Lane LC, Cheetham T. Puberty: normal physiology (brief overview). Best Pract Res Clin Endocrinol Metab 2019;33(3):101265.

[42] EMEA-001264-PIP01-12, Archived by the author.

[43] Rose K The challenges of pediatric drug development. Curr Ther Res Clin Exp. 2019, https://doi.org/10.1016/j.curtheres.2019.01.007

[44] Rose K, Grant-Kels JM. The meanings of "pediatric drug development". A Rev Ther Innov Regul Sci 2018; Dec 9:2168479018812060 <https://journals.sagepub.com/doi/pdf/10.1177/2168479018812060>.

[45] Rose K, Neubauer D, Grant-Kels JM. Rational use of medicine in children—the conflict of interests story. A review. Rambam Maimonides Med J 2019;10(3):e0018. Available from: https://doi.org/10.5041/RMMJ.10371 <https://www.rmmj.org.il/userimages/928/2/PublishFiles/953Article.pdf>.

[46] Nehrer S, Chiari C, Domayer S, et al. Results of chondrocyte implantation with a fibrin-hyaluronan matrix: a preliminary study. Clin Orthop Relat Res 2008;466(8):1849−55 <https://www.ncbi.nlm.nih.gov/pmc/articles/PMC2584266/pdf/11999_2008_Article_322.pdf>.

[47] Domayer SE, Welsch GH, Nehrer S, et al. T2 mapping and dGEMRIC after autologous chondrocyte implantation with a fibrin-based scaffold in the knee: preliminary results. Eur J Radiol 2010;73(3):636−42.

[48] Non-interventional Study With NOVOCART® 3D for the Treatment of Cartilage Defects of the Knee in Pediatric Patients (JUNOVO). <https://clinicaltrials.gov/ct2/show/NCT04186208>.

[49] A Study of MACI in Patients Aged 10 to 17 Years With Symptomatic Chondral or Osteochondral Defects of the Knee (PEAK). <https://clinicaltrials.gov/ct2/show/NCT03588975>.

[50] EMA 2017. Scientific recommendation on classification of advanced therapy medicinal products—human autologous chondrocytes <https://www.ema.europa.eu/en/documents/report/scientific-recommendation-classification-advanced-therapy-medicinal-products-human-autologous_en-1.pdf>.

[51] EMA 2020. Summaries of scientific recommendations on classification of advanced therapy medicinal products. <https://www.ema.europa.eu/en/human-regulatory/marketing-authorisation/advanced-therapies/advanced-therapy-classification/summaries-scientific-recommendations-classification-advanced-therapy-medicinal-products>.

[52] EMA 2017 Scientific recommendation on classification of advanced therapy medicinal products—Viable chondrocytes cultured within a 3D hydrogel. <https://www.ema.europa.

eu/en/documents/report/scientific-recommendation-classification-advanced-therapy-medicinal-products-viable-chondrocytes_en.pdf>.

[53] EMA 2018 Scientific recommendation on classification of advanced therapy medicinal products—In vitro cultured autologous chondrocytes. <https://www.ema.europa.eu/en/documents/report/scientific-recommendation-classification-advanced-therapy-medicinal-products-vitro-cultured_en.pdf>.

[54] EMA 2016 Scientific recommendation on classification of advanced therapy medicinal products—Autologous expanded viable chondrocytes in a cross-linked hydrogel <https://www.ema.europa.eu/en/documents/report/scientific-recommendation-classification-advanced-therapy-medicinal-products-suspension-autologous_en.pdf>.

[55] EMA 2015 Autologous expanded viable chondrocytes combined with a three dimensional structure (biphasic collagen scaffold). <https://www.ema.europa.eu/en/documents/report/scientific-recommendation-classification-advanced-therapy-medicinal-products-autologous-expanded_en-0.pdf>.

[56] Facing the challenge. The Lisbon strategy for growth and employment. Report from the high level group chaired by Wim Kok November 2004. <http://ec.europa.eu/research/evaluations/pdf/archive/fp6-evidence-base/evaluation_studies_and_reports/evaluation_studies_and_reports_2004/the_lisbon_strategy_for_growth_and_employment__report_-from_the_high_level_group.pdf>.

[57] Karapanos L, Zugor V, Akbarov I, et al. Mid-term results of anterior urethroplasty withtissue-engineered oral mucosa graft mukocell. J Urol 2020 2020;203 4S, Supplement, Sunday, May 17, 202 <https://www.auajournals.org/doi/pdf/10.1097/JU.0000000000000929.012>.

[58] MukoCell – TETUS <https://cordis.europa.eu/project/id/823126/de>.

[59] MukoCell Treatment for urethral strictures. <https://www.youtube.com/watch?v = d30TRFURuMQ>

Subchapter 4.2

Suicide, depression, and mental disorders in young persons

Introduction

After accidents, suicide is the leading cause of death among adolescents and young adults in most developed western countries. It is a far more frequent cause of death than cancer and other malignancies in young persons [1,2]. In recent years, the incidence of suicide among young people has again increased worldwide [3].

Babies cry when they are hungry, when they are in pain, or when they feel uncomfortable for other reasons. But babies are not depressed. Nature has arranged for them to cry because they cannot yet speak. The more the brain and the nervous system mature, the more mental challenges that we see relatively often in adults can also affect young persons. Growing up has always been difficult. Puberty is a slow process that takes several years. With the end of puberty, the body becomes *physiologically* mature [4–7]. Depending on the country, it can take more time until the respective person becomes of age also *legally*. Few will deny that our society is becoming ever more complex and complicated. But there are also more effective medicines today than in the past.

Some reasons for suicide are understandable from an outside perspective, for example, reaching an age in which many organs no longer perform well; the end stage of a disease that massively affects quality of life; or simply the desire to end living after a fulfilled life. Legally, the situation is different worldwide country by country. In many countries, organized suicide is forbidden. Switzerland is liberal and allows it. Very old and very sick patients often travel to Switzerland to have a decent, self-determined end to their lives. Many challenges that from the perspective of a battle-hardened adult are the usual challenges of life can be perceived as very serious by young persons that still are learning to understand society, its contradictory rules, and how to find a place in it. Young persons often compare themselves with beauty ideals and role models shown in movies, TV, YouTube, and other media. The general social pressure and even more the pressure from peers is high. Most young women see themselves as too tall or too small, too thick or too thin, their breasts as too large or too small, their nose as too long or too short, and so on. Young men focused in the past on other things such as the size and appearance of their phallus, the size and "coolness" of their car or motorcycle, and others. Hairdressers, cosmetic surgeons, and entire industry branches make a living from young and older women's external appearance and their belief of not being sufficiently beautiful. And in the meantime, men are catching up and also spend more and more money on cloths, cosmetics, jewelry, and hairdressing. As long as the additional desires for their own external appearance, for the job, the car, the gold chains, or whatever is important for a young person's self-confidence are limited, they are just desires. But when the despair becomes overwhelming and makes everyday life more and more difficult, then this feeling can become pathological. The trigger can be real-life tragedies, such as that a sibling or a parent dies. Or things that are just terrible for the respective young person, such as that the boyfriend or girlfriend walks away, failing school, being kicked out of the soccer team or the volleyball team, that the dog has died, or a lot of other issues. Another factor is impulsiveness based on inexperience. Young persons are mentally less prepared than years later. Any person's internal processing of the conflicting, confusing, contradictory, and fascinating influences of life change slowly over the years or fast with a good or bad experience. But not abruptly at a birthday. To be sad becomes pathological when the connection between sadness and the outside world is no longer comprehensible to outsiders, and when normal everyday life in school, at work, in university, in the family, with friends, and more begin to suffer.

In many suicide attempts and accomplished suicides, mental illnesses play a role, primarily depression and major depressive disorder, obsessive-compulsive disorder (OCD), and non-OCD anxiety disorders [3,8]. Additional factors can be the level of anxiety of a person, substance use disorders, neuropsychiatric disorders, head injury, the genes, aggression and impulsivity, hopelessness, history of childhood abuse, adverse life events and psychosocial stressors, insomnia, and many more. Apart from the fact that suicide can occur as a consequence of severe mental illnesses, it can also be caused by improper treatment of the underlying mental illnesses [3,8,9].

Antidepressant medication

Before effective antidepressants were developed, treatment for depression, which in the past was called melancholy, was barely available. The scientific framework to describe, understand, and classify mental illnesses had to develop, including adequate endpoints for clinical studies to test psychiatric drugs. Depression was regarded as a manifestation of internal personality conflicts. A large portion of the psychiatric community assumed that patients should discover, address and resolve the "true" roots of their internal conflicts. Year-long psychoanalysis was a cornerstone of treatment. Other treatments were an expression of helplessness. Patients were treated with insulin coma, with electric shocks, prescribed "sleep therapy," or immobilized with heavy sedatives, including opiates [7]. In the 1950s, a revolution took place with the clinical introduction of the main groups of psychoactive drugs still used today. This introduction has been described as one of the great medical advances of the last century, comparable with the discovery of antibiotics and vaccines [10]. Different types of effective antidepressants emerged gradually [3,10]. Antidepressants help in many of depressed patients, but not in all of them. Work continues to develop new substances and substance groups [11,12].

Part of today's complex world is that there are confusing theories about everything. Almost every year, another new theory tells depressed persons that they should soldier on with their misery rather than get appropriate treatment; antidepressants are condemned either as quackery or as money-making by pharmaceutical companies [9,13].

Antidepressants are like a crutch. It is best not to need them at all. But if a joint or leg is injured and you cannot walk without support, crutches become indispensable. Just by entering a supermarket we can see how many mental crutches the market offers. There is little to be said against dosed escapes from reality. These escapes include legitimate and forbidden drugs, reading good books, movies, radio, soap operas, television, telling of and listening to fairy tales. That is how human society works. Because human society is so complex, mood disorders are so difficult to grasp. Antidepressants and other psychiatric drugs do not perform miracles. They help against depression and major depressive disorder, against OCD, and non-OCD anxiety disorder [8,14], but they are just one therapeutic instrument beside several others that can be helpful. The many theories of depression and that antidepressants help in many, but definitely not in all patients show that depression is a clinically and etiologically heterogeneous disorder [15].

"Pediatric" studies in antidepressants and the FDA black-box warning

Forty years ago, the predominant believe was that depression did not exist in young persons [14]. When science realized gradually that babies are not small adults, the mantra emerged that all administratively defined "children" (US <17 years, EU <18 years) need separate drug approval and separate "pediatric" regulatory studies [16,17]. In the early years of drug development, this was not very relevant for the treatment of depression, as there were no effective drugs for depression until about 60 years ago.

In 1997, the United States authorized the FDA to reward separate "pediatric" studies by patent extension, based on the belief that the approval of medicines in "children" would massively improve their health care. This belief was based on a coalition of the three major players in "children's" healthcare: the American Academy of Pediatrics (AAP) and other associations interested in "pediatric" research; the FDA; and the pharmaceutical industry. They all had a material interest in "pediatric" studies, and the number of "pediatric" careers in academic positions, in regulatory agencies, and in the pharmaceutical industry has since then continuously increased [18–20].

In the meantime, mainstream medicine had accepted that also young persons can be depressed. As in many other areas, the FDA now rewarded "pediatric" studies in psychiatry in the belief that in "children" all diseases are completely different [21,22]. But depression, schizophrenia, and other mental diseases in young persons are not different diseases in comparison to depression, schizophrenia, and other mental diseases in older persons. Young persons are less prepared for the craziness, the beauty or the complexity of today's society, however we choose to describe it, and each person goes its own way until it gradually becomes experienced, "cool," hardened, or anything in between.

For each individual pharmaceutical company, the separate "pediatric" studies offered patent extensions, with which they could sell their respective products six months longer at patent-protected higher prices, before generic companies could offer the same respective compound and product at a significantly lower price. For researchers, these studies provided publications, lectures at conferences, international meetings, and many other networking opportunities; for the regulatory authorities, these studies were another area where they could demonstrate the authorities' will to do something good for the most vulnerable part of our population, the "children". The AAP proclaimed the "moral imperative" to perform separate "pediatric" studies, blurring that the term "child" means two overlapping, but different things: young, vulnerable babies and infants, and the part of the population that is *legally* not yet of age [23,24]. Everyone benefited, with the exception of those persons it was supposed to help; in this context young persons with depression or other mental challenges.

The core challenge of the concept of separate "pediatric drug development" and separate "pediatric" studies is that it blurs different meanings of the word "child." Preterm neonates, term neonates, and young infants are immature and vulnerable. The toxicities that were reported in the 1950s occurred in babies and infants that were treated with antibiotics [17–19,23]. But children grow and mature. As depression and other mental illnesses require a minimal maturity of the brain and the central nervous system, the imposture of an alleged vulnerability of all "children" was a flawed extrapolation of the observed dangers of some modern and effective drugs in very young babies and infants. This extrapolation was inadequate specifically for mental diseases [20].

The "pediatric" depression studies included only patients younger than 17 years. A company had observed that patients in its studies expressed suicidal thoughts more often. Such thinking is called "suicidality," defined as suicidal thinking and behavior [25]. The FDA convened a meeting of well-known specialists to discuss suicidal tendencies in young people and finally published a "black box" warning that antidepressants can cause suicidal tendencies in young people. "Black box" warnings are so named because they are at the very front of the patient information, framed by thick black lines. These warnings are notorious and feared among doctors and the pharmaceutical industry. Any physician who prescribes medication against a black box warning risks to be sued for damages if anything goes wrong that a resourceful lawyer can interpret in connection with alleged disregard for justified warnings. Such warnings are also not beneficial for sales. Black box warnings also have their own psychodynamics. They put involved specialists who are called to FDA meetings for a short time into the spotlight. They can show how important their opinion is, and they can annoy one or several multibillion dollar pharmaceutical companies. If during a specialist meeting convened by the FDA one professor suddenly expresses the idea of issuing a black box warning, it is like in a company meeting when during a good debate someone suddenly suggests a SWOT analysis (Strengths, Weaknesses, Opportunities, and Threats). This can paralyze a good discussion. The person who proposes a SWOT analysis is rarely the brightest and most productive mind in the room. We will never know the details how the black box warning in antidepressants emerged. However, we know that this recommendation was not unanimously supported by the experts [14].

Regulatory agencies worldwide adopted the FDA warnings in various forms in varying degrees [14]. To this date, there are contradicting assessments of the FDA's black box warnings [2,9,26–30]. The studies underlying the black box warning were not designed to measure suicidality [30]. Several authors emphasize that the black box warning was and is interpreted by health care providers in an exaggerated way and may lead to under-treatment of patients [2,9]. Others emphasize that daily treatment in depressed patients is not a clinical trial. If a drug does not work in a specific patient, the physician can change treatment [26].

Adolescent psychiatrists and general practitioners became more hesitant about prescribing antidepressants. Some psychiatric associations protested and warned that this warning would probably do more harm than good [2,8,9,14,26–36]. But the FDA was at its peak of social recognition at the time. It could afford to ignore these protests.

Lawsuit by the Attorney General of the State of New York

The company that had developed the antidepressant paroxetine had been reluctant to admit that in the "pediatric" depression studies efficacy against placebo had not been statistically significant. Researchers now suspected foul play [37]. But they did not challenge how "pediatric" patients were defined. The Attorney General of the State of New York sued the manufacturer for having concealed clinical trial data that showed that paroxetine was ineffective in "pediatric" patients and might trigger suicidal behavior

[38–40]. The company settled in 2004 and agreed to pay $ US 2.5 million [40,41]. Compared to other settlements of pharmaceutical companies, this was a small sum. Indeed, the legal case of the New York Attorney General was weak. But the company had little choice than to settle if we take into consideration the emotional weight of the accusations [40], and that the overall strength of the concept of "pediatric drug development" as unchallenged in these days.

Common sense versus randomized controlled clinical studies

The core of this challenge has so far not been addressed: a clinical study is a mechanism that proves efficacy of a specific treatment against another treatment in an artificial framework. It has the purpose to help the regulatory authority to decide about approval. Physicians trust the correctness of the collected data and the authorities' approval of the interpretation of the data by the involved clinicians and the involved sponsor. However, as a clinical study creates an artificial environment, if essential ingredients are flawed, the overall results are questionable or even worthless as well. We would not accept if an authority would insist to test antidepressive agents only in blond, red-haired or dark-haired individuals, respectively. To decide if a given new drug is effective in humans, randomized clinical studies are a good tool, specifically, if we compare them to the earlier principle of relying on the eminence of persons who recommended this or that treatment. But the imposture of the on-label/off-label framework to an artificially defined "pediatric" population was a historical mistake.

The demand for separate "pediatric" studies with antidepressants (and many other drugs) led to the recruitment of a small sub-population of depressed patients that were all younger than 17 years. Computer science knows the phenomena of "garbage in, garbage out" (GIGO) [42]. The patients recruited into the "pediatric" studies with antidepressants were not representative of young persons with depression. Instead, it was an artificially created subpopulation. The debate about the black box warning against antidepressants will never end until this undefendable weak point of these studies is addressed: they were at least questionable and probably worthless.

EU expansion of "pediatric" studies

The EU progressed further on the path of demanding separate "pediatric" studies. Without PIPs and "pediatric" studies, companies cannot get approval for new drugs. This applies to antidepressants and all drugs unless they are not explicitly on an EMA list of diseases that are not officially available in "children." This list has been revised regularly since 2008, so that even diseases that only occasionally affect young people are now classified as "pediatric" diseases by the EMA, for which the pharmaceutical industry has to organize and sponsor separate "pediatric" studies, including nonjuvenile Parkinson's disease, Huntington chorea, and amyotrophic lateral sclerosis (ALS) [43].

There are currently at least seven antidepressant studies in children worldwide that are sponsored by pharmaceutical industry to meet regulatory requirements. Many test antidepressants against placebo, assuming that the efficacy of antidepressants in young persons needs to be proven in separate "pediatric" studies, the "pediatric" population defined by the 17th/18th birthday. But the body does not react to the 17th or 18th birthday. These birthdays are *administrative*, not *physiological* age limits. Currently recruiting "pediatric" studies in depression are listed in Table 4.2.1.

Probably the most absurd and openly unethical "pediatric" depression study is a study of young mothers aged 15 to 17 years who become depressed after birth (Table 4.2.1, study 3). Depression after childbirth is relatively common. There is no biological difference between 17, 18, 20, or 22 year old mothers with postpartum depression.

Table 4.2.2 lists exemplary ongoing "pediatric" studies demanded in various further psychiatric diseases.

We see in Table 4.2.2 several purely "pediatric" studies in patients aged 13 to 17 years of age. These studies lack medical sense. They reflect regulatory demands but do not aim at therapeutic improvement. But we also see that there are other studies that recruit patients aged 16 to 40 years of age or 13 to 65 years of age, which makes medically sense.

Table 4.2.3 lists all PIPs issued by the EMA for various psychiatric diseases.

Table 4.2.4 lists exemplary "pediatric" studies demanded in PIPs for various psychiatric disorders.

Even the description of the patients in PIP # 3, Table 4.2.3, and in study 4, Table 4.2.4 is inadequate. Young mothers with postpartum depression should not be addressed as "girls." They are young women.

All exemplary studies listed in Table 4.2.4 are unethical. They compare effective drugs against placebo. The authorities, researchers, and sponsoring pharmaceutical companies want these studies. But these studies are not in the interest of young persons who are talked into study participation together with their parents.

Treatment of depression in young persons is a complex challenge

There are no miracle cures to help young people with self-doubt or serious mental health problems. A very important factor is that the parents notice anything at all, that they are willing and able to talk to the young person about it, and that the young person listens to the parents at all. If the predominant form of communication in the family is to beat the young person up

TABLE 4.2.1 Ongoing industry-sponsored "pediatric" drug studies in depression.

	NCT#	Compound	Abbreviated study description	Age	#ctrs/pts	Status
1	NCT03395353	Duloxetine	LT safety study	9–17 y	?/100	AnR
2	NCT02709655	Fluoxetine	R DB PC fixed-dose S&E study in MDD	7–11 y	136/600	recr
3	NCT03665038	Brexanolone	MC OL S, T, PK study in adolescents with PD	15–17 y	17/20	recr
4	NCT03569475	Levomilnacipran	DB PaAC (versus fluoxetin) S&E study in MDD	7–17 y	57/480	AnR
5	NCT02129751	Bupropion HB	DB PC S&E study in MDD	7–17 y	?/200	nyr
6	NCT03185819	IN esketamine	DB PC S&E study of 3 FDs + CSoC in MDD pts at IRoS	12–17 y	63/145	recr
7	NCT02871297	Vortioxetine	OL LT flexible dose ES in MDD	7–18 y	79/850	EbI

AnR, Active not recruiting; *DB*, double blind; *CsoC*, comprehensive standard of care; *E*, efficacy; *EbI*, enrolling by invitation; *ES*, extension study; *FDs*, fixed doses; *HB*, hydrobromide; *IN*, intranasal; *IroS*, imminent risk of suicide; *MC*, multicenter; *MDD*, major depressive disorder; *nyr*, not yet recruiting; *OL*, open label; *PaAC*, placebo and active-controlled; *PC*, placebo controlled; *PD*, postpartum depression; *PK*, pharmacokinetics; *R*, randomized; *recr*, recruiting; *S*, safety; *S&E*, safety and efficacy; *T*, tolerability; *LT*, long term; *y*, year.
Search terms: Major depressive disorder (MDD); child; industry-sponsored; Only drug trials were selected.

TABLE 4.2.2 Exemplary ongoing industry-sponsored "pediatric" drug studies in schizophrenia.

	NCT#	Compound	Abbreviated study description	Age	#ctrs/pts	Status
1	NCT03198078	Bexpiprazole	MC R DB PaAC (vs. aripiprazole) S&E study	13–17 y	?/480	recr
2	NCT03817502	Cariprazin	MC R DB PC S&E study	13–17 y	8/330	recr
3	NCT01908192	NaBen®	MC DB PC study of NaBen® as add-on	13–17 y	23/126	recr
4	NCT03187769	ALKS 3831	Effect ALKS 3831 vs. olanzapine on body weight of pts with schizophrenia, schizophreniform, or BID	16–40 y[a]	45/425	recr
5	NCT03893825	TV46000	MC DB PC S,T,E study in schizophrenia	13–65	?/300	recr

BID, Bipolar I disorder; *DB*, double blind; *E*, efficacy; *ES*, extension study; *MC*, multicenter; *PaAC*, placebo and active-controlled; *PC*, placebo controlled; *R*, randomized; *recr*, recruiting; *S*, safety; *S&E*, safety and efficacy; *T*, tolerability; *TV-4600*, risperidone extended-release injectable suspension for subcutaneous use; *y*, year
Search terms: Major depressive disorder (MDD); child; industry-sponsored; Only drug trials were selected.
[a]*Enrollment US: adolescents > 16 y; EU: > 18 y.*

TABLE 4.2.3 Psychiatry PIPs.

	PIP#	Compound	Until	Age	Indication
1	EMEA-001428-PIP03–15-M01	Esketamine	2026	12–17 y	Major depressive disorder
2	EMEA-000455-PIP02–10-M04	Vortioxetine	2024	7–17 y	Major depressive disorder
3	EMEA-002051-PIP02–16	Allopregnanolone	2021	"pp girls"	Postpartum depression
4	EMEA-002142-PIP01–17	Trazodone	2022	2–17 y	Insomnia
5	EMEA-001181-PIP01–11-M05	Agomelatine	2023	7–17 y	DOAD/MDD
6	EMEA-001115-PIP01–10-M07	Loxapine	2021	13–17	BD/schizophrenia
7	EMEA-001918-PIP01–15-M02	Balovaptan	2029	2–17 y	Autism
8	EMEA-001230-PIP01–11-M05	Lurasidone	2018	13–17 y	Schizophrenia
9	EMEA-001185-PIP01–11-M05	Brexpiprazole	2023	13–17 y	Schizophrenia
10	EMEA-001652-PIP01–14-M02	Cariprazine	2025	13–17 y	Schizophrenia
11	EMEA-000228-PIP01–08-M04	Asenapine	2018	10–17 y	Bipolar I disorder
12	EMEA-001688-PIP03–16	Pimavanserin	2029	13–17 y	Schizophrenia and OPD
13	EMEA-001742-PIP01–14	BI 409306	2022	13–17 y	Schizophrenia
14	EMEA-001506-PIP01–14-M01	Basmisanil	2024	2–17 y	Down syndrome
15	EMEA-000150-PIP02–10	LY2140023	2021	12–17 y	Schizophrenia
16	EMEA-000553-PIP01–09-M04	Lisdexamfetamine	2014	6–17	ADHD
17	EMEA-000745-PIP01–09-M03	Guanfacine	2013	6–17 y	ADHD

18	EMEA-001167-PIP02–11-M02	Atomoxetine	2013	4–17 y	ADHD
19	EMEA-000439-PIP02–11	Bitopertin	2024	13–17 y	Schizophrenia
20	EMEA-000235-PIP02–10-M02	Aripiprazole	2016	10–17 y	Bipolar affective disorder
21	EMEA-000014-PIP01–07-M06	Paliperidone	2012	12–17 y	Schizophrenia
22	EMEA-001034-PIP01–10	Risperidone	2015	5–17 y	Conduct disorder
23	EMEA-000114-PIP01–07	Eplivanserin	2018	2–17 y	Insomnia

ADHD, Attention deficit hyperactivity disorder; *BD*, bipolar disorder; *DOAD*, depressive or anxiety disorder; *MDD*, major depressive disorder; *OPD*, other psychotic disorders; *pp*, postpubertal.

TABLE 4.2.4 Exemplary PIP-demanded "pediatric" studies in psychiatric diseases.

	PIP#	Compound	Abbreviated study description	Age
1	EMEA-000014-PIP01–07-M06	Paliperidone extended-release tables	1. R 6 weeks DB MC PC S&E study in schizophrenia 2. 26 weeks R DB MC AC S&E study in schizophrenia 3. OL LT S study	12–17 y
2	EMEA-001428-PIP03–15-M01	IN esketamine	1. DB DD R DR E&S PC study in MDD pts at imminent risk for suicide, with an initial 8-week PTFU as part of a full 6-month PTFU 2. D DD R PC S&E study in MDD pts at imminent risk for suicide, with an initial 8-week PTFU as part of a full 6-month posttreatment 3. OL S study of repeated doses in pts with MDD at risk for suicide 4. Pop PK M&S study to identify possible covariates after IN administration and to support dose selection for adolescents	12–17 y
3	EMEA-001688-PIP03–16	Pimavanserin	1. PK,S,T study in currently stable schizophrenia pts 13–17 y 2. R DB PC 6-week S&E study in schizophrenia pts 13–17 y with a suboptimal response to aripiprazole 3. 2-year OL S study of adjunctive pimavanserin in schizophrenia pts 13–17 y with a suboptimal response to aripiprazole 4. R DB PC 6-week S&E study in schizophrenia pts 13–17 y 5. 2-year OL S study in schizophrenia pts 13–17 y 6. EP study based on clinical studies + literature to support the maintenance of efficacy of adjunctive pimavanserin in adolescents 7. EP study based on clinical studies + literature to support the maintenance of efficacy of monotherapy in adolescents	13–17 y
4	EMEA-002051-PIP02–16	Allopregnanolone	1. DB R PC PK,S,T,E study in postpubertal adolescent girls with postpartum depression 2. M&S study to support the use of allopregnanolone i.v. in postpubertal adolescent girls with pp depression	"postpubertal girls"

AC, Active-controlled; *DB*, double blind; *DD*, double dummy; *DR*, dose response; *EP*, extrapolation; *ERM*, exposure-response model; *ES*, extension study; *FU*, follow up; *IN*, intranasal; *LT*, long term; *MC*, multicenter; *MD*, multiple dose; *M&S*, modeling and simulation; *OL*, open label; *PC*, placebo controlled; *PG*, parallel group; *PD*, pharmacodynamic(s); *PK*, pharmacokinetic(s); *PK/PD*, pharmacokinetic/pharmacodynamic; *Pop PK*, population pharmacokinetics; *PTFU*, posttreatment follow up; *R*, randomized; *SD*, single dose; *S*, safety; *S&E*, safety and efficacy; *T*, tolerability; *y*, year.

regularly, or, worse, if the mother (or the father) is beaten up as well, then a young person will hardly want to open up to the beating parent. Or when children are sexually abused by one or both parents. Or when a relative sexually abuses a child and the parents pretend that nothing happens and/or that nothing has happened.

There are many ways to get help. These can be the friends of the young person; colleagues of the same age at school or at work; social services; church institutions; the friends in sports, in the sports club, in whatever club the young person is (hopefully) anchored. A rather small part of the apparatus that parents can fall back on are doctors, i.e., the pediatrician, the family doctor, child and adolescent psychiatrist, also psychologists and many other professional groups.

For young people with mental problems, finding the right people and the right help is rarely easy, like everything in life. Antidepressants and antipsychotic medications are not a panacea. A good doctor can be incredibly helpful, but a stupid doctor can do a lot of damage. It is of course not helpful that conventional medicine supports the saga of allegedly necessary "pediatric" studies. Many, if not most, clinicians are not aware of the flawed foundations of "pediatric drug development."

Antidepressants had "pediatric" warnings for over 15 years, and the two major regulatory agencies, the FDA and EMA, have put their reputation in supporting these warnings. This has put them in an awkward position. They cannot just admit in public that their position was flawed. They will need massive help from outside to come to this conclusion.

The official warning that antidepressants can lead to "suicidality" has led doctors to become cautious about prescribing antidepressants in young persons [2,3,8,9,26–28,30–33]. We will never be able to quantify how many unnecessary suicides could have been avoided by these flawed warnings from the regulatory authorities.

A shortcoming of today's medical and academic world is that critical thoughts are often asked only from the perspective of individual disciplines. A publication reports a young depressed woman who had read the warnings, was afraid of the prescribed antidepressant, and had not taken it. Fortunately, the husband was able to hold her when she tried to jump out the window. Repeated detailed discussions then convinced her to take the medication after all [9]. But even these authors accept the danger of alleged "suicidality" as a "fact."

Limitations of academic discussion of the black box warnings and their limitations

Several metaanalyses and reviews address the unresolved riddle of the FDA black box warning of "suicidality" in "children," adolescents and young adults treated with antidepressants [26–29]. These attempts have one element in common: they accept that the studies in discussion were "pediatric" studies. But they were not. They were studies in young patients administratively labeled "children". But many of these patients were bodily no longer children. They were bodily mature young persons. Antidepressants do not treat the legal status of patients, but the patient.

Ardent supporters of the black box warnings invoke randomized controlled trials as the highest standard of evidence [27]. But randomized controlled trials, bibliographic reviews, and metaanalyses do not address the weak point of randomized controlled trials which are only as good as the assumptions on which the respective protocol and analysis is based. The most ardent proponents of randomized controlled trials, literature reviews, and metaanalyses is Cochrane (previously known as the Cochrane Collaboration), a British international organization formed to organize medical research findings to facilitate "evidence-based" choices about health interventions. But "evidence-based" reviews have the common weak point that in computer science is GIGO [44]. The Cochrane network approaches the challenges of an overwhelmingly complex world with a rigid framework of paradigms that claims to produce certainty; but it also demands adherence to its doctrine [42]. Randomized controlled trials are a good tool for drug approval in adults. But they are nor good to justify or reject separate approval in the arbitrarily and artificially defined subpopulation labeled "pediatric" [17–20].

Even strong critics of the black box warning have not cracked the crux of the problem. Fornaro et al. criticize correctly the "over-concern raised by the FDA," but confirm the "fact" that antidepressants increase the risk of suicide in people younger than 18 years [9]. But there are no good data that would support the alleged suicidality in young patients as a consequence of intake of antidepressants. These studies were performed short-term in an artificially defined population. Scientifically, they were questionable and probably to a large degree worthless.

Conclusions

Parents should not let their child participate in any "pediatric" regulatory study on an antidepressant or any other psychopharmacological drug. There is no solid scientific basis for the believe that drugs against depression, schizophrenia, OCD, generalized anxiety, social anxiety, attention deficit disorder, and/or any other mental disorder work differently before versus after the 17th/18th birthday. A definition of youth by an administrative age limit does not make sense. Furthermore, the acceleration of mental and bodily development during the last century makes on some level young persons today more mature than in the past [45,46], which does not prevent them from being true children often also beyond the 21st birthday. The desire that randomized controlled trials should be considered the most powerful avenue to demonstrate cause–effect relationships [27] is understandable, but unfortunately, randomized controlled trials are only as reasonable as their design and their fundamental assumptions. The term GIGO derives from computer science, but describes nicely what happens when we block out our common sense. The challenge of randomized controlled trials and many other issues in daily life is that many observations made with our common sense need to be relativized. You can smoke four packs of cigarettes every day and become a hundred years old. You can drive your car for decades without ever buckling up. But that does not mean the cigarettes do not harm and that buckling up is unnecessary.

Drugs approved for treatment of depression or any other psychiatric disorder work on the same receptors in the brain of patients before and after their 17th/18th birthday, regardless if such persons are classified as "children." If the attending physician thinks that drug treatment is necessary, the parents should insist that an effective drug is prescribed, regardless of whether it is approved before or after the 18th birthday. The legal status of a young person changes overnight, but not the body.

Attempts to commit suicide, and committed suicides, are often based on serious mental illnesses. Just as life altogether is complex, today's challenges of drug treatment in young persons are complex as well. Parents or other responsible persons should not trust blindly to anybody. Blind trust can be dangerous.

Institutional Review Boards (IRBs)/ethics committees (ECs) should no longer accept "pediatric" studies in depression, schizophrenia, or any other psychiatric disease just because they are required by regulatory authorities. They should also suspend ongoing such studies. Effective treatment is available for young patients. To treat young patients with placebo denies effective treatment and exposes these young persons to an increased danger of suicide.

References

[1] Leading causes of death. <https://www.cdc.gov/injury/images/lc-charts/leading_causes_of_death_by_age_group_2017_1100w850h.jpg>.

[2] Asarnow JR, Mehlum L. Practitioner review: treatment for suicidal and self-harming adolescents—advances in suicide prevention care. J Child Psychol Psychiatry 2019;60(10):1046–54 Oct.

[3] Brent DA. Master clinician review: saving holden caulfield: suicide prevention in children and adolescents. J Am Acad Child Adolesc Psychiatry 2019;58(1):25–35 Jan.

[4] Khan L. Puberty: onset and progression. Pediatr Ann 2019;48(4):e141–5 Apr 1.

[5] Abreu AP, Kaiser UB. Pubertal development and regulation. Lancet Diabetes Endocrinol 2016;4(3):254–64 Mar.

[6] Snyder CK. Puberty: an overview for pediatric nurses. J Pediatr Nurs 2016;31(6):757–9 Nov-Dec.

[7] Wood CL, Lane LC, Cheetham T. Puberty: normal physiology (brief overview). Best Pract Res Clin Endocrinol Metab 2019;33(3):101265 Jun.

[8] Bridge JA, Iyengar S, Salary CB, Barbe RP, Birmaher Pincus HA, Ren L, et al. Clinical response and risk for reported suicidal ideation and suicide attempts in pediatric antidepressant treatment: a meta-analysis of randomized controlled trials. JAMA 2007;297:1683–96.
[9] Fornaro M, et al. The FDA "Black Box" warning on antidepressant suicide risk in young adults: more harm than benefits? Front Psychiatry 2019. <https://www.ncbi.nlm.nih.gov/pmc/articles/PMC6510161/pdf/fpsyt-10-00294.pdf>.
[10] López-Muñoz F, Alamo C. Monoaminergic neurotransmission: the history of the discovery of antidepressants from 1950s until today. Curr Pharm Des 2009;15(14):1563–86.
[11] Hillhouse TM, Porter JH. A brief history of the development of antidepressant drugs: from monoamines to glutamate. Exp Clin Psychopharmacol 2015;23(1):1–21. <https://www.ncbi.nlm.nih.gov/pmc/articles/PMC4428540/pdf/nihms667554.pdf>.
[12] Duman RS. Pathophysiology of depression and innovative treatments: remodeling glutamatergic synaptic connections. Dialogues Clin Neurosci 2014;16(1):11–27.
[13] Gøtzsche PC. Deadly Psychiatry and Organised Denial. København, Denmark: People's Press; 2015. Table of contents and introduction <https://www.deadlymedicines.dk/wp-content/uploads/2014/10/G%C3%B8tzsche-Deadly-Psychiatry-chapter-1.pdf>.
[14] Varley CK. Treating depression in children and adolescents: what options now? CNS Drugs 2006;20(1):1–13.
[15] Hasler G. Pathophysiology of depression: do we have any solid evidence of interest to clinicians? World Psychiatry 2010;9(3):155–61 Oct.
[16] Hirschfeld S, Saint-Raymond A. Pediatric regulatory initiatives. Handb Exp Pharmacol 2011;205:245–68.
[17] Rose K, Neubauer D, Grant-Kels JM. Rational use of medicine in children—the conflict of interests story. A Review. Rambam Maimonides Med J 2019. <https://www.ncbi.nlm.nih.gov/pmc/articles/PMC6649781/pdf/rmmj-10-3-e0018.pdf>.
[18] Rose K. The challenges of pediatric drug development. Curr Ther Res Clin Exp 2019. <https://doi.org/10.1016/j.curtheres.2019.01.007>.
[19] Rose K, Grant-Kels JM. The meanings of "pediatric drug development". A review. Therapeutic Innov Regulatory Sci 2018.
[20] Rose K, Neubauer D, Grant-Kels JM. Too many avoidable suicides occur worldwide in young patients. Rambam Maimonides Med J 2019;10(4) Oct 29. <https://www.ncbi.nlm.nih.gov/pmc/articles/PMC6824826/pdf/rmmj-10-4-e0026.pdf>.
[21] Wharton GT, Murphy MD, Avant D, et al. Impact of pediatric exclusivity on drug labeling and demonstrations of efficacy. Pediatrics. 2014;134(2):e512–18.
[22] Rose K, Neubauer D, Grant-Kels JM. Ethical issues in pediatric regulatory studies involving placebo treatment. J Pediatr Epilepsy 2020; in press.
[23] AAP. Guidelines for the ethical conduct of studies to evaluate drugs in pediatric populations, committee on drugs. Am Acad Pediatrics, Pediatrics 1995;95(2):286–94. 1995 Feb. <https://pediatrics.aappublications.org/content/pediatrics/95/2/286.full.pdf>.
[24] Shaddy RE, Denne SC. Committee on drugs and committee on pediatric research. Clinical report—guidelines for the ethical conduct of studies to evaluate drugs in pediatric populations. Pediatrics 2010;125(4):850–60. Apr. <https://pediatrics.aappublications.org/content/pediatrics/125/4/850.full.pdf>.
[25] FDA 2018. Suicidality in children and adolescents being treated with antidepressant medications. <https://www.fda.gov/drugs/postmarket-drug-safety-information-patients-and-providers/suicidality-children-and-adolescents-being-treated-antidepressant-medications>.
[26] Martinez-Aguayo JC, Arancibia M, Concha S, et al. Ten years after the FDA black box warning for antidepressant drugs: a critical narrative review. Arch Clin Psychiatry (São

Paulo) 2016;43(3) May/June <https://www.scielo.br/pdf/rpc/v43n3/0101-6083-rpc-43-3-0060.pdf>.

[27] Spielmans GI, Spence-Sing T, Parry P. Duty to warn: antidepressant black box suicidality warning is empirically justified. Front Psychiatry 2020;11:18 Feb 13 <https://www.ncbi.nlm.nih.gov/pmc/articles/PMC7031767/pdf/fpsyt-11-00018.pdf>.

[28] Gupta S, Gersing KR, Erkanli A, et al. Antidepressant regulatory warnings, prescription patterns, suicidality and other aggressive behaviors in major depressive disorder and anxiety disorders. Psychiatr Q 2016;87(2):329–42. Jun.

[29] Zito JM, Derivan AT, Kratochvil CJ, et al. Off-label psychopharmacologic prescribing for children: history supports close clinical monitoring. Child Adolesc Psychiatry Ment Health 2008;2(1):24 Sep 15 <https://www.ncbi.nlm.nih.gov/pmc/articles/PMC2566553/pdf/1753-2000-2-24.pdf>.

[30] Gören JL. Antidepressants use in pediatric populations. Expert Opin Drug Saf 2008; 7(3):223–5 May.

[31] Noel C. Antidepressants and suicidality: history, the black-box warning, consequences, and current evidence. Ment Health Clinician 2015;5(5):202–11. Available from: https://doi.org/10.9740/mhc.2015.09.202.

[32] Bushnell GA, Stürmer T, Swanson SA, et al. Dosing of selective serotonin reuptake inhibitors among children and adults before and after the FDA black-box warning. Psychiatr Serv 2016;67(3):302–9 Mar <https://www.ncbi.nlm.nih.gov/pmc/articles/PMC5033112/pdf/nihms811212.pdf>.

[33] Lu CY, Zhang F, Lakoma MD, et al. Changes in antidepressant use by young people andsuicidal behavior after FDA warnings and mediacoverage: quasi-experimental study. BMJ 2014;348:g3596 Jun 18 <https://www.bmj.com/content/bmj/348/bmj.g3596.full.pdf>.

[34] Dawson RS. Depression in children and adolescents: the pediatrician at the front lines. Pediatr Ann 2018;47(7):e261–5.

[35] Cipriani A, Zhou X, Del Giovane C, Hetrick SE, Qin B, Whittington C, et al. Comparative efficacy and tolerability of antidepressants for major depressive disorder in children and adolescents: a network meta-analysis. Lancet. 2016;388(10047):881–90. Aug 27.

[36] Ignaszewski MJ, Waslick B. Update on randomized placebo-controlled trials in the past decade for treatment of major depressive disorder in child and adolescent patients: a systematic review. J Child Adolesc Psychopharmacol 2018; Jul 31.

[37] Whittington CJ, Kendall T, Fonagy P, et al. Selective serotonin reuptake inhibitors in childhood depression: systematic review of published versus unpublished data. Lancet. 2004;363(9418):1341–5. Apr 24.

[38] Rennie D. Trial registration. A great idea switches from ignored to irresistible. JAMA 2004;292(11):1359–62. Sep 15.

[39] Dickersin K, Rennie D. The evolution of trial registries and their use to assess the clinical trial enterprise. JAMA 2012;307(17) May 2.

[40] Kagle A (undated). Driven to settle: eliot Spitzer v. GlaxoSmithKline and Undisclosed Clinical Trials Data Regarding Paxil. <https://web.law.columbia.edu/sites/default/files/microsites/career-services/Driven%20to%20Settle.pdf>.

[41] Wikipedia Study 329. <https://en.wikipedia.org/wiki/Study_329>.

[42] Sturmberg JP. Evidence-based medicine-not a panacea for the problems of a complex adaptive world. J Eval Clin Pract 2019;25(5):706–16. Oct.

[43] EMA 2015: Class waiver decision. <http://www.ema.europa.eu/docs/en_GB/document_library/Other/2015/07/WC500190385.pdf>.
[44] Wikipedia 2020. Garbage in, garbage out. https://en.wikipedia.org/wiki/Garbage_in,_garbage_out
[45] Cone TE Secular acceleration and biologic maturation in children during the past century.
[46] Komlos J The mysterious trend in American heights in the 20th century.

Subchapter 4.3

Cancer and malignancies in young patients

Fundamentals

Cancer occurs in humans and animals. Cancer is not a unique disease, but an umbrella term for malignancies. Usually, cells work in coordination with other cells. They originate, do their job in the respective organ, divide, and finally die; the body's immune system then taken care of the remains. This balance does no longer work when cells become malignant. They divide faster than other cells, or they refuse to die. Malignant cells no longer respect the boundaries of their organ of origin, if their origin is solid tissue. They invade adjacent tissues, and eventually spread through the body, establishing local or distant metastases. They can cause local damage by rupturing blood vessels, compressing organs, destroying organs' functionality, and/or overburden the body with debris. When cells have become malignant, the immune system still accepts them as belonging to the body, and does not attack and destroy them. Probably, thousands of times premalignant stages occur, but are detected, recognized and destroyed by the immune system. But at some point sometimes this balance does no longer work. Our view of malignancies is constantly evolving. In the beginnings of oncology visible malignant tumors were regarded as the main problem. Today, we increasingly see malignancies in its interaction with the entire body.

The rapidity of disappearance of visible leukemic cells from the bone marrow is a good prognostic factor. Measurement of minimal residual disease is possible today by quantitative flow cytometry or polymerase chain reaction. Today, minimal residual disease is widely used in risk stratification and provides a validated early measure of treatment response [1].

Malignant cells can have very different origins. Carcinomas develop from epithelial cells that cover the inner or outer surfaces of organs, including internal ducts and tubuli; sarcomas arise from connective tissue within organs; hematopoietic malignancies arise from cells that normally mature into leukocytes or lymph cells, hence, leukemia or lymphoma; germinomas arise from germ cells. Malignancies can also have mixed origins. Malignancies in general develop more frequently in older persons. There are many different factors that facilitate malignancies, including long-term radiation, exposing the body to various types of pleasure, be it smoking (lung cancer and more cancers in many organs), alcohol (liver cancer & more), processed food typical for modern societies (colonic & rectal cancer), sex with many partners, chemical irritants, and many more. But none of these factors does cause cancer on its own. Not everybody in modern societies dies of colonic cancer. Many heavy smokers never get cancer, nor do many persons that enjoy enormous quantities of wine, beer, or spirits; nor do many persons that have worked for decades with asbestos and/or other irritant factors. There are interactions between the outside world, the body, and the body's genome about which we know increasingly many details, but we have not yet identified a magic key factor, and probably we never will.

Furthermore, today's occurrence of malignancies in senior citizens is balanced by diagnostics, surgery, drug treatment, and changes in life style. If conventional malignant melanoma is removed at an early stage, the patient is healed, does not need any further observation, and has the same life expectancy as other persons of the same age. Colonic and rectal cancer used to kill frequently in the western world, but today, thanks to regular colonoscopy from middle age on, most early forms of colonic and rectal cancers are detected and removed before they had a chance to become aggressively malignant. There are many further comparable cancer types upon which a regular check can prevent further death, including the neck of uterus, where regular control prevents today most advanced stages of cervical carcinoma. Changes in life style include ban of smoking in trains, planes and restaurants The diagnosis of many more cancer types today is no longer an automatic death sentence.

Cancer in children

Cancer has been companion to mankind since earliest history. In the past, it was assumed to occur in adults only. But also young people can get cancer. Rarely, but it occurs. Also in young people, cancer is not a uniform disease, but a group of rare and ultra-rare diseases [2]. Factors that contributed to a growing awareness that cancer occurs also in young people included modern society's growing population; better transport and communication; increased awareness of health issues in general; better living conditions, hygiene, nutrition, and clothing; better prevention of infectious diseases by vaccination; and growing capabilities to successfully treat bacterial, viral and fungal infections. Infectious diseases used to kill horrendous numbers of young children. The more infectious diseases lost their horror, the more cancer became gradually one of the main causes of death by disease in children and adolescents. Most children that died of malignant diseases in the past were assumed to have an infectious disease. As there was almost nothing that could be done, a correct diagnosis would not have had any clinical consequences.

Obviously, when young people get cancer, their body did not have the same time of exposure to harmful factors compared to persons that get cancer at an advanced age. The distribution of cancer types in young people is different from the one in adults. Some cancer types occur predominantly or exclusively in young people only; others have two peaks, one in childhood and one in adulthood; others can occur at any age, such as leukemias or lymphomas, although the distribution is different across different age groups. Furthermore, young children have less frequently carcinomas and more often leukemias, sarcomas or germinomas. The most frequent malignancy in childhood is acute lymphoblastic leukemia (ALL), which, however, can also occur at any age as well.

As cancer in children evolves at an early age and furthermore is rare altogether, some of the counter-measures that are used today against adult cancer types are impossible in children. Regular checks of the colon and rectum or of the neck of uterus makes sense in adults. Such preventive measures in children are not possible.

Today, we also see increasingly the interaction between genetic disposition and malignancies. For example, persons with Down syndrome get leukemia much more frequently. This is also the case with many other genetic disorders.

First treatment successes in childhood cancer

The first ward for pediatric cancer opened in the US during the second world war, in 1939. In these days, there was little the medical system could do beyond easing symptoms, comforting the child and its parents, and supporting the family until the inevitable death of the young patient [3]. Pediatric cancer was perceived as the last disease cluster that continued to kill children, left medical doctors helpless, and defied society and science, and thus needed to be defeated [4]. Finally, after many failed initial attempts, chemotherapy became stepwise successful in treating first pediatric leukemias and in the following also pediatric solid tumors, often combined with radiation and surgery. Early successes in cancer treatment resulted in the passage of the US National Cancer Act of 1971 that launched the "war on cancer" [5].

The drugs used in chemotherapy are cytotoxic. As the name indicates, cytotoxins are poisonous for cells. They inhibit cell division of cells. Most cytotoxic agents are applied intravenously, some also orally. In both ways, they reach all organs of the body. There are several different types of chemotherapy agents that act on different levels of the mechanisms of cell division. Most cancer cells divide faster than normal cells. Chemotherapy has acquired a key role in the treatment of cancer. Unless given to ease the tumor burden, chemotherapy is given in the hope to kill enough malignant cells so that the body and its immune system can take care of the few remaining malignant cells.

Chemotherapy was soon complemented by further patient support that reflected the grown armamentarium of modern medicine, including the institution of preventive treatment for opportunistic infections, evaluation and treatment of febrile neutropenia, and further measures such as granulocyte colony-stimulating factor that allowed further intensification of treatment in subgroups [2].

Side effects of drugs have always to be balanced against the clinical benefit that can be expected from the treatment. Under "normal" circumstances, drugs should not have severe side effects. But in cancer treatment there are other rules, as the alternative is to let the patient die without treatment, which was done in children with cancer in the first half of the 20th century. Then, medical science was convinced that nothing could be done for these patients.

The side effects of chemotherapy correspond to their mechanism of action. As they inhibit cell division, they damage those cell types that divide fast, including the hematopoietic system that produces white and red blood cells, the mucosa of the alimentary truct, and those cells that are responsible for the growth of hair. Typical short-term side effects of chemotherapy include anemia, fatigue, vomiting, nausea, diarrhea, fever, chills, abdominal pain and tenderness, loss of hair, easy bruising, and more.

In the 1960s, not even medical oncology in general was a clinical specialty. The overall attitude toward chemotherapy was rather hostile [5]. Chemotherapy was used for all sorts of adult cancers. Slowly and stepwise, successes by chemotherapy in childhood leukemias were reported. Young patients' bodies are more flexible than adults. Children are smaller and less strong than most adults, but they can mobilize more reserves, if they are given that chance by appropriate treatment. Children survived doses that surprised the pioneering oncologists. Furthermore, drug combinations were used, which until then had not been favored by clinicians. The chemotherapy agents that allowed the first successes in childhood leukemia were not developed specifically for children. To the contrary. Initial knowledge had been generated in military research on chemical warfare. In the early days of chemotherapy, the used agents were clinically developed and approved in various adult cancer types [2,6]. Stepwise, appropriate doses and drug combinations were tested in hands-on trial-and-error by the pediatric oncology collaborative groups, until routine treatment protocols were established. Over the next decades, survival rates of childhood leukemia improved, for a while increasing by roughly 10% during each decade [7]. The guiding principles were increasing doses, drug combinations in "cocktails," advances in pediatric intensive care [6], and advances in general drug development [8].

But at the turn of the millennium, in 2000, a plateau in pediatric oncology was reached. Survival of childhood ALL had reached around 90%, and in general about four out of five children with cancer could be expected to be healed [9,10]. However, cancer in young patients has never been a disease like a flu that once you have survived it is just a bad memory. Pediatric oncology saved the lives of hundreds of thousands of young people, but at a high price. Chemotherapy affects short term the quality of life of the patients themselves, of the parents, and of the entire family. Furthermore, many long-term health problems result from chemotherapy, including secondary malignancies many years after the first malignancy has been healed.

Not all children with cancer survive today. Even in ALL, 10% die despite all the progress that has been achieved with chemotherapy plus further therapeutic advances. The diagnosis of ALL in a child is no longer an automatic death sentence, but it still is for the respective family like a declaration of war. It profoundly changes the life of the entire family. Everything is done to save the child. But, like in war, you cannot be sure of the outcome.

Treatment of pediatric cancer was not only a pioneering act of courageous oncologists. That it was. But it was also an endeavor that involved broad parts of society in general. Newspapers and radio stations reported broadly about children with cancer. Money was collected for families that had to fight for the life of their child. Cancer was perceived as the last area of a deadly disease, or more precisely, of a cluster of diseases that now finally and gradually was defeated and became treatable [3].

Cancer in young people is rare. Pediatric oncology did not emerge in single, isolated, local hospitals, but from the beginning by the networking of specialists across large areas, in the US the Children's Cancer Group, the Pediatric Oncology Group, the National Wilms' Tumor Study Group and the Intergroup Rhabdomyosarcoma Study Group which merged in 2000 into the Children's Oncology Group (COG). The COG is supported by the US National Cancer Institute (NCI) and is the world's largest organization of pediatric cancer research. It runs many clinical studies worldwide. Almost all centers that treat young patients with cancer in the US and Canada are part of the COG: more than 200 centers in the US, Canada, and other countries. These centers have teams of physicians, other scientists, nurses, psychologists, pharmacists and others, altogether several thousand experts worldwide. The COG has almost one hundred clinical studies at any given time. More than 90% of young patients diagnosed with cancer in the US are cared for at COG member institutions [11–13].

In Europe, the respective national pediatric oncology and hematology groups work today closely together also on a European and international level. The International Society of Pediatric Oncology (Société Internationale d'Oncologie Pédiatrique, SIOP) was established in 1969 [14].

The origins and the first decades of pediatric oncology were a *clinical* challenge

Pediatric oncology emerged as a *clinical* challenge. The involved clinicians and other healthcare professionals used whatever was available to help the young patients. Their approach was partially trial-and-error, partially elaborate clinical studies. Furthermore, they had to fight against wrong assumptions such as that nothing could be done anyway. In the 1950, 1960s and 1970s, every single medical discipline had this same basic approach. But two fundamental differences between pediatric oncology and the use of drugs in most other areas of pediatrics was firstly that the collaborative networks organized systematic clinical studies across large geographic areas from very early on [12], and secondly that the drugs now used with increasingly better results had already existed considerable time and were approved for other, predominantly adult malignant diseases. Pediatric oncology did not receive a boost by regulatory authorities. Pediatric oncology emerged almost in parallel to the evolving regulatory framework of drug development.

For the multitude of supportive measures, including preventive treatment for opportunistic infections, treatment of febrile neutropenia, granulocyte colony-stimulating factors that allowed further intensification of treatment in subgroups, administration of antiemetics, prophylaxis & treatment of deep vein thrombosis, use of advanced anticoagulants and many more treatments, pediatric oncology did not wait until the respective drug or biologic had a separate pediatric approval. The pediatric oncologists, and all other pediatricians, simply did what they had been taught in medical school and in what they had further been trained in their professional education: they used whatever was available to help. Medical doctors are not an appendix to the regulatory authorities, but a profession with the right and the duty to decide about therapeutic interventions.

In the attempt to intellectually process the reasons for the plateau in treatment success that was reached toward the turn of the millennium, several basic factors were confounded. This also reflected how far the different pillars of medical progress had moved away from each other. Clinicians knew and still know relatively little about drug development, drug approval, and the interaction between the worlds of pharmaceutical industry, regulatory authorities, and the clinical world. In 2004, a paper complained that few new drugs were FDA-approved in pediatric cancer [15], ignoring that pediatric oncology had emerged "off-label" in a period of time when the term "off-label" did not even exist yet [16–18]. But this paper also reflected a dawning recognition that further advances in treating young patients with cancer would need a change of paradigm. Hands-on clinical care of young people with a combination of chemotherapy, radiation and surgery had indeed reached the peak of its potential.

Clinical care versus regulatory approval

The thalidomide catastrophe had shown that a higher degree of state supervision in drug development was unavoidable. When thalidomide was put on the market in 1957 in Germany and then in many other countries, there was no law that would have obliged the developing company to test its efficacy & safety. People could not even imagine the danger of an apparently harmless small pill. Thalidomide caused most damage in those countries where it was sold without prescriptions by medical doctors, such as in Germany.

When reports about children born with malformations were published, the producer ignored these warnings. Finally, the truth was unveiled, and thalidomide was taken off the market [19,20]. The producing company was never convicted in a court—it had done nothing illegal. Reacting to this, the US updated their pharmaceutical law. From 1962 on, the FDA approved drugs on the basis of clinical studies [21]. Furthermore, also the control of drug advertising was transferred from the Federal Trade Commission (FTC) to the FDA that from this point in time took handled this responsibility rather seriously [22]. Today, the principle of clinical studies as the basis for drug approval is recognized and in force worldwide [23].

The influence of administrative procedures and the weight of the historically relatively new regulatory authority FDA as compared to the well-established and very old medical profession and its representative bodies increased continuously in the following years and decades [21]. Among many other issues this was also reflected in the emergence of the new term "off-label" in 1988 [16]. The US legislation of 1962 had prevented new dangerous compounds comparable to thalidomide to be marketed as medicines. However, with the separation of the human population into a general one and a second one labeled "pediatric," many drugs had initially no separate "pediatric" approval. Translated into operative administrative rules, this made use of effective drugs in persons younger than 17 years "off-label." Gradually and slowly, the impression emerged that drugs that are "on-label" are safe, and that they are not safe when they are prescribed "off-label." In general medicine this is a highly disputed issue. But in the administratively created new sub-population of humans, now labeled "pediatric," this had many real-world consequences.

A paradigm shift not yet processed enough intellectually

Pediatric oncology emerged under very special circumstances. The drugs that eventually proved to have a high potential to treat pediatric cancers existed already, but nobody knew how to use them in young patients. The main group of these drugs were chemotherapy agents. They were continuously replenished by further supportive drugs to prevent and fight anemia, to prevent and fight opportunistic infections, to prevent nausea and vomiting, and many more.

The special circumstances of successful treatment by chemotherapy are now fading, while innovative treatments of malignancies emerge. Society has not yet found proper ways to handle this new challenge, and pediatric oncology has not yet processed this paradigm shift sufficiently.

Overviews over the history of pediatric oncology report proudly the treatment successes that occurred over the last decades [2,6]. But they fail to recognize that these advances occurred by hands-on clinical treatment and clinical studies with therapeutic intention, not within the regulatory framework of general drug development.

Pediatric oncology saved the lives of hundreds of thousands of young patients. Before it emerged, little could be done for young patients. But then pediatric oncology collided and is still colliding with the regulatory framework of drug development in general and with the societal framework of medical treatment of young people.

As long as little could be done for the young patients, it was of limited importance if a specific patient was eight, twelve, or twenty-one years old. It may not have been correct to address all these patients as "children," but it mattered little.

Today, with increasing availability of effective treatment, the age and the degree of physical maturation of each patient has become much more relevant. But a concept that blurs the difference between administrative aspects of medical treatment and the question of which medication should be used in young patients has emerged in general drug development and is now impeding proper further development of drugs for malignancies in young patients. The decisive question today should no longer be the legal status of the respective patient, but the biology of the respective malignancy. Pediatric oncology will have to learn to keep these two aspects apart. Administratively, the legal status of a patient is relevant for the decision if he is admitted to a pediatric or an adult ward. However, the treatment the respective patient receives should correspond to his respective disease only, not to his legal status.

Innovative drugs and treatment concepts are developed *today*, instead of having been developed and approved decades earlier, as this had occurred with chemotherapy agents [5,6]. Successful re-purposing of old out-of-patent drugs for new clinical use exists, e.g., thalidomide for leprosis and multiple myeloma. However, such re-purposing has not allowed breakthroughs such as the development of CAR-T cell therapy to successfully treat relapsing-remitting ALL.

To understand the role of these frameworks, we first need to address several of their components separately. The following subchapters explain that claiming a fundamental difference of adults and "children" has become a roadblock both for drug development in general and specifically for pediatric cancer.

The concept of children as "therapeutic orphans"

Since 1968 the concept of children as "therapeutic orphans" emerged, triggered by pediatric warnings that pharmaceutical companies inserted into drug labels that were now controlled by the FDA [24]. These warnings had primarily a *legal* purpose: to prevent frivolous damage lawsuits in the litigious US [18]. These warnings were taken up by the American Academy of Pediatrics (AAP), where Shirkey had a prominent position, were supported by new branches of academic medicine that specialized on clinical research in young people, specifically pediatric clinical pharmacology, and were adopted by the FDA that in 1979 defined "children" as anybody <17 years of age [25]. Finally, this led to a first US pediatric law in 1997 that offered rewards for studies in children that were now officially defined on US federal level as persons <17 years old [26]. From now on, the FDA demanded separate "pediatric" studies for the approval of new drugs in children. The key flaw of this first US pediatric law has remained unchallenged until today: it blurs the different meanings of the term "child." Administratively, the FDA had created a separate human population labeled "pediatric." But bodily, underage persons do not remain as vulnerable and immature as premature or mature newborns until they are officially recognized as of age.

The concept of an administratively labeled "pediatric" population had originated in drug manufacturers' undifferentiated "pediatric" warnings, was then misapprehended by Shirkey, taken up and adopted by the AAP and the FDA, and resulted finally in US law [17,18], which rendered on a formal level all prescriptions of chemotherapy agents to young patients "off-label." Initially, medical practitioners, including pediatric oncologists, simply ignored the "pediatric" warnings, about which even the originator of the concept of children as "therapeutic orphans" complained [24]. In a time when the application of an antibiotic obviously saved the life of patients that otherwise were condemned to die, there was no place for such subtleties. However, this changed slowly with an increasing number of alternative treatments for many diseases thanks to overall successful drug development, and with the further development of the medical system.

When the first US pediatric legislation was introduced in 1997, pediatric oncology had reached a first peak of clinical success which now became a plateau [10,12]. Roughly 90% of children with ALL could be healed, which was much better than forty years earlier. However, the horror of a diagnosis of cancer in a child was by now aware to every single parent. Nobody could predict at the time point of the diagnosis of a leukemia or any other malignancy in a child if the specific patient would survive or not. But despite continuous fine-tuning of chemotherapy, supported by further treatment options, treatment outcome did not go much further than these 90% in ALL.

Drug development had become very successful. Pharmaceutical industry had emancipated itself from the production first of paints, then of chemicals. It had acquired considerable wealth. The public perception of the place of drug treatment in healthcare had fundamentally changed. Mainstream clinicians had forgotten that the successes of pediatrics had occurred by the combination of at least two factors: the availability of new drugs and new technologies on one side, and the courage and determination of involved clinicians and other healthcare professionals on the other side, independently of the regulatory authorities' separate approval of a given drug in children. In a new, slowly emerging framework the belief had formed that the plateau in pediatric oncology was caused through a lack of new drugs. This was understandable, but wrong. Of all clinical pediatric disciplines, pediatric oncology was very exceptional on several levels. It was extraordinarily successful [7,8]. It had emerged from the very beginning through systematic clinical studies performed in large geographical areas in the US and internationally in Europe and in the rest of the world [14]. It had *not* emerged through new drugs [5,6,27]. And most importantly, it had not emerged in the setting of drug approval. The clinical studies performed during the first decades of pediatric oncology were not driven by regulatory approval, but by the desire to help the young patients.

In 2003, more than 100 drugs have been approved by the FDA for the treatment of malignancies. FDA authors complained that only 15 of these drugs had pediatric use information in their labeling, i.e., less than 50% of the drugs commonly used in the treatment of pediatric malignancies [27]. But when Hirschfeld et al. (all authors were FDA employees) wrote this, pediatric oncology had already reached the first peak of its historical advancement. Indeed, the FDA's did not play a major role in the emergence of pediatric oncology.

The FDA rewards "pediatric" cancer studies with individual cytotoxins

For the FDA every "pediatric" prescription without a "pediatric" label was an anathema, including pediatric oncology, despite its undeniable successes. A double argumentation and an almost schizophrenic activism evolved, enhanced by the FDA's firm conviction that cancer in "children" was fundamentally different from adult cancer.

The FDA approach, authorized by the US lawmakers, was not a clinical approach. It did not focus on patients' well-being, or, specifically in pediatric oncology, on patients' survival. Regulatory authorities do not treat patients. Their job is to analyze the data packages submitted by drug developing companies, check if these data have been generated in a correct way, do not contain falsifications, and that the conclusions of the submitting company correspond to current state-of-the-art scientific standards. Regulatory authorities' logic is centered on drugs. In the FDA's view, the drugs applied in pediatric oncology were not properly used. They had saved hundreds of thousands of young patients' life, but from a *regulatory* point of view, this was less important. For a regulatory authority, the most important questions is if a drug that is administered is also *approved* in the respected clinical area, here in cancer.

While the FDA's initial contribution to oncology had been the approval of chemotherapy agents in adults, "pediatric drug development" now demanded separate "pediatric" studies in oncology. FDA-rewarded "pediatric" oncology studies since 1997 were mostly studies in single drugs, investigated now in heavily pretreated relapsed or refractory (R/R) young cancer patients. Sixteen "pediatric exclusivities" were granted until 2012 by the FDA. "Written request" was issued in 2000 for cytarabine, in 2001 for anastrozole and carboplatin, in 2003 for clofarabine, to name just a few [28].

But the patients that participated in these "pediatric" studies had already gone through the standard-of-care treatment, that consisted of "cocktails." For example, the FDA Written Request for pemetrexed requested studies in R/R pediatric malignancies in persons > 1 month old up to adolescents [29]. The rationale of these studies was completely different from those studies that until now had profoundly improved the survival of young patients with cancer or leukemia. They did not aim at patients' survival or well-being, but at "pediatric" drug labels. Most FDA-rewarded "pediatric" oncology studies were performed in terminally ill young patients with various cancer types where previous rounds of chemotherapy had failed [30,31].

The clinical studies performed by the pediatric oncology collaborative groups had saved so many lives that participation in a clinical trial had become state-of-the-art, a well-known and highly appreciated fact which also the FDA used to justify its "pediatric" cancer studies. In such justifications, the FDA pretended that FDA-rewarded studies aiming at pediatric labels had the same aim as therapeutic studies performed by the pediatric oncology collaborative groups [29]. But there were no therapeutic intentions. Instead, these studies aimed at "pediatric" labels, based on an administrative definition of the "pediatric" population, irrespective of the maturity of the respective patient's body [29].

The basis of the FDA policy in pediatric oncology (and all other clinical areas) was the assumption that pediatric labels would result in better healthcare of young patients [32]. This assumption was and is fundamentally flawed.

The first US pediatric law of 1997 was in 2003 complemented by a second law that gave the FDA the authority to mandate "pediatric" studies also without a reward: pediatric research equity act (PREA) [26]. For biologics, rare diseases and vaccinations the FDA, however, is not authorized to mandate "pediatric" studies. However, it can always offer the voluntary reward of 6 months patent extension.

The FDA-rewarded "pediatric" cancer studies have not advanced cancer treatment of young patients. But other interests were advanced by these studies. A coalition had formed of the FDA, pediatric cancer researchers, and pharmaceutical industry. We can only speculate how far companies were aware that these "pediatric" studies were useless. This question itself is of limited usefulness, because in a commercial environment, a company will do whatever is possible to increase its profits, as long this is allowed. This is how commerce works.

Few of the desperate parents who saw their loved one dying were able to decipher the carefully coded pseudo-scientific justifications of the respective study in the informed consent documentation. There may have been a few such parents, but the only alternative they had in these days was to refuse study participation. The alleged need for "pediatric drug development" had received so strong support that the US lawmakers enacted these laws unanimously. It was in these days unimaginable that already these FDA-triggered "pediatric" cancer studies were simply an abuse of young patients.

While most FDA-rewarded "pediatric" oncology studies were studies with individual cytotoxins, one early exception was a randomized "pediatric" study in nasopharyngeal carcinoma that investigated the addition of docetaxel to chemotherapy with cisplatin and 5-fluourouracil in patients up to 21 years of age [33]. In the academic study publication, Casanova et al. allege that nasopharyngeal carcinoma is a malignant disease that occurs in children and adolescents. This is true, in so far as nasopharyngeal carcinoma occurs in humans of all ages [34,35]. But the claim that nasopharyngeal carcinoma is a "pediatric" disease is untrue. Why should the addition of docetaxel to standard chemotherapy work differently in patients below or above the age limit of 21 years? There was nothing "pediatric" in this study, with the exception of the barely disguised interest to get funds for pseudo-scientific alleged "research." This study is an excellent example how the claim of "pediatric drug development" was simply a mechanism to provide funds for pseudo-scientific clinical research, ruthlessly exploiting parents' and patients' desperation. The FDA had issued a written request for docetaxel [36]. The company that produced and sold docetaxel could enjoy half a year longer sales at patent-protected high prices. One further condition for this ruse to work was and is that respected journals accept(ed) such publications. As long as "pediatric" clinical studies are perceived as honorable endeavors, this charade will continue.

Once large institutions have committed to a specific concept, they would lose face if they simply drop it. Many authors and groups complained about the lack of economic incentives to develop innovative drugs for children, including representatives of the FDA [37], the EMA [38], the preamble of the European Union (EU) pediatric legislation [39], and those authors who make a living out of finding pharmaceutical industry guilty for everything bad under the sky [40,41]. Within a logic that thinks that progress in pediatric healthcare is guaranteed by more drugs with a pediatric label, all these opinions would have been correct. But this logic ignored the true contribution of clinicians, and that specifically pediatric oncology had not emerged through more drugs FDA-approved in "children."

Innovative cancer treatment

Chemotherapy is not very subtle. Essentially, it floods the body with cell poison in the hope to kill enough malignant cells, but that the patient survives so his immune system can take care of the few surviving malignant cell. This principle worked better in children than anybody would have expected in the beginnings of pediatric oncology.

In the meantime, our understanding of malignancies has advanced. We know now much more about the internal decision hierarchy within cells. "Precision" and/or "targeted" medicines aim at the customization of medical decisions and treatments to be tailored to the individual patient and targeted specific targets that have been identified to be responsible for beginning and maintenance of the respective malignancy.

High dose interleukin 2 (IL-2) was the first immunotherapy able to achieve long-term and complete responses in patients with advanced melanoma and renal cancer. The FDA-approved high dose IL-2 for renal cancer in 1992 and for melanoma in 1998, establishing immunotherapy as the newest paradigm for the treatment of cancer [42].

Tyrosine kinases are one of many groups of mediators that in the cells signal cascades that decide about growth, differentiation, metabolism, and cell death [43]. Already in 1959, a tiny flaw in the chromosome 22 of patients with leukemia had been observed in Philadelphia, USA, when the chromosomes of these patients were investigated during cell division under the microscope. This chromosomal anomaly had been named "Philadelphia chromosome." The Philadelphia chromosome is a translocation in which parts of the two chromosomes 9 and 22 swap places, resulting in a longer chromosome 9 and a shorter chromosome 22. Chromosomes store the blueprint of protein production by the cellular production mechanisms. The flawed Philadelphia chromosome triggers the production of a defective protein that tells the cell to produce tyrosine kinase without end, resulting in unlimited cell division that eventually becomes malignant, in this case leukemia.

Tyrosine kinase inhibitors (TKIs) began with the idea for a molecule that would fit into the production site of tyrosine kinases to interrupt the constant command to produce tyrosine kinase without limit. Chemical libraries were screened to find a compound that would inhibit the hyperactive protein. A lead compound was identified, then tested and modified, resulting in imatinib. When imatinib was tested in clinical studies, the results were overwhelming. Leukemias with the Philadelphia chromosome, mostly chronic myeloid leukemia (CML), but also other leukemia types, became chronic diseases that could be handled long term by a daily intake of imatinib. Somewhat later it was found that imatinib works also in other cancer types, including gastrointestinal stroma tumor (GIST). Imatinib is taken by mouth. As all drugs, it also has side effects, but compared with the inevitable outcome without treatment, these side effects did not deter its clinical use.

Imatinib opened a new chapter in oncology. A first time a malignancy was not treated by systemic poisoning the patient's body, or by successful removal of a very localized tumor, which is possible in early stages of some malignancies, but by trying to control and downregulate the underlying mechanism of disease. Imatinib does not heal CML, but it converts a fatal malignancy into a manageable chronic condition. As is normal in drug development, the following progress in developing further targeted anticancer drugs was less quick than initially hoped. Malignant cells often bypass effective therapy. They become resistant. They use new metabolic pathways. And so on. Imatinib was soon followed by other more potent and/or are active TKIs, but the major revolution that many had hoped would come soon did not occur.

Over time, in many malignancies driver mutations were identified. Inhibitors that target aberrant signal transduction molecules were developed [44]. But what works well in test tubes or in animal models does not always work equally well in patients. A good example is conventional malignant melanoma, where several compounds against specific driver mutations have been developed. Some of them have shown good clinical efficacy, including vemurafenib and dabrafenib against B-RAF (BRAF). RAF Raf kinases play a role in regulating signaling pathway that affect cell division, differentiation, and secretion. Another strategy is to block cytotoxic T lymphocyte antigen 4 (CTLA4) with monoclonal antibodies, which is done by ipilimumab.

An even more advanced strategy to treat malignancies is to involve the body's own immune system. In general, patients' immune system does not recognize malignant cells as adversarial. Several ways to help the immune system to overcome this "blindness" have been developed [42]. One such approach are "chimeric antigen receptor T-cells" (CAR-T cells). CAR-T cell therapy re-programs T-cells to recognize malignant cells as hostile and attack & destroy them [45]. Several more strategies are in development [45–49].

Innovative cancer treatment in young patients

Targeted therapy works on a molecular level, as far as chemicals are involved, or on the level of cell biology. Atoms, molecules and blood cells have the same size in adults and young people, and there is no natural law that prohibits translocation of the chromosomes 22 and 9, leading to the Philadelphia chromosome. Philadelphia-positive leukemias occur before and after the 17th or 18th birthday.

To this day, clinical oncology, regulatory authorities, and pharmaceutical industry have not properly addressed the difference between administrative classifications of young people as "children," which is necessary in any complex modern society, and an assessment of medical therapy based on the body's degree of maturity.

When imatinib emerged, the FDA accepted at least for CML that this malignancy was not totally different in adults and "children." But instead of abandoning the "children-are-therapeutic-orphans" mantra, the existing coalition of clinical and academic pediatric oncology, FDA, and pharmaceutical industry dropped as much of this mantra as was no longer compatible with the obvious, but held on in principle.

Imatinib was first approved in adults for CML, and soon thereafter in "children" [50]. CML is a relatively rare form of leukemia in young patients and becomes much more frequent with senior age. Based on the encouraging success of imatinib in adults with CML, it was then soon investigated also in young people with Philadelphia-positive (Ph +) ALL. Also Ph + ALL is much rarer in young patients than in adults. The diagnosis of Ph + ALL had been almost a death sentence for young patients [51]. Today, imatinib is successfully used also in "children" in combination with chemotherapy [50]. That ALL exists both in adults and children has been addressed in the literature, resulting in the correct conclusion that age-unrestricted, biology-based treatment should be the standard for all patients [51]. But the blur between an administrative age classification and decisions for drug approval has not been addressed.

For many years, imatinib was the only FDA-approved TKI for first-line therapy in "children" with CML, followed by approval of dasatinib and nilotinib in "children" [9].

Ipilimumab and vemurafenib are now FDA-approved for treatment of adult malignant melanoma [52]. For ipilimumab, the FDA requested in a "written request" four studies in "children": (1) an open label, dose-escalation study in "pediatric" patients aged 1–21 years; (2) a PK and safety study in "pediatric" patients aged 12–17 years with unresectable or metastatic melanoma; (3) a study in various R/R solid tumors other than melanoma in patients aged 1–17 years; (4) efficacy, safety, tolerability and PK in patients aged 1–17 years with specific primary cancer(s) based on study 3 [53]. This "written request" shows the belief that a group of biologically totally different malignancies might be curable by ipilimumab based on the young age of the patients. The first two studies were performed and published [30,54,55]. The second study had to be terminated because the requested treatment corresponded no longer to the current state-of-the-art treatment, which in the meantime had become combination of two targeted anti-melanoma-drugs [55].

Emily Whitehead came down with ALL when she was 5 years old. After chemotherapy had failed, the parents had to choose between accepting her seemingly inevitable death, or enlist her into a new experimental study [56]. In this study, blood was withdrawn, Emily's T-cells were genetically engineered to make a specific cell surface receptor with components from both a T-cell receptor and an antibody against ALL cells, and were re-transferred back to Emily. This worked well with Emily, who was the youngest patient in the pivotal study of this specific CAR-T cell therapy [57]. The FDA approved tisagenlecleucel in 2018 for patients up to 25 years of age. Emily is today a young cancer-free woman, although legally she is still a "child."

The outlined examples show that the concept of "children" as "therapeutic orphans" fits less and less into the evolving drug development that increasingly uses our advanced understanding of intracellular and intercellular communication and coordination to advance cancer therapy. For almost every single new drug, the FDA rewarded/demanded for many years separate "pediatric" studies.

In the literature, there is no consistent age limit to differentiate adult from "pediatric" cancer in general, or adult from "pediatric" leukemias. The efficacy of imatinib in "children and adolescents" up to 18 years of age is described [58]. But patients that are 18 years of age are already adults. The AAP defines the population to be treated by pediatricians as up to 21 years, even older in patients with special medical needs [59]. This is a reasonable administrative age limit for administrative issues. But to use this age limit as a boundary for drug approval and for therapeutic decisions is scientifically, clinically and from the point of view of ordinary common sense not justified. It is a blur that emerged under specific historical circumstances and is now continued because already the US pediatric laws have created new conflicts of interest where clinical academia, FDA, and pharmaceutical industry have established a coalition that, however, did not advance healthcare of young patients with malignancies.

The politization of pediatric oncology

Why did and does the US clinical pediatric community in general and specifically also the pediatric oncology community support US pediatric legislation? [60] Pediatric oncology had successfully emerged entirely "off-label" in the decades before 1997 [5,6,18,27,30], long before the term "off-label" emerged in 1988 [16]. In the COG chairman's opinion, the most notable impact of the US and EU pediatric laws was the increasing engagement of the biopharmaceutical industry with investigators from academia in planning for pediatric drug development [2]. But despite more than twenty years of this engagement in the US and more than ten years in the EU, this has not led to therapeutic breakthroughs in pediatric oncology.

The current official position of organized pediatric oncology shows its deep politization. The COG runs a multitude of pediatric clinical cancer studies throughout the world. The COG is a nonprofit organization that, however, manages the necessary funds for its numerous clinical studies [13,60,61]. All these studies are performed in good will, but the COG has to this day not recognized that the main driver of the successes of pediatric oncology during the second half of the 20th century were not contributions from the FDA. The consequence of this undetected blur is that the undeniable clinical successes of pediatric oncology are used to justify and maintain regulatory policies that are based on wrong assumptions.

When a clinician complained about the low number of FDA-approved new drugs in pediatric cancer, she showed a remarkable lack of understanding of the history of pediatric oncology [15]. But her position also reflected a new element. The initial round of pediatric oncology, i.e., the healing the majority of malignancies in young patients by the combination of chemotherapy, surgery, radiation and supportive measures, had reached a plateau. The next round will not be characterized by further fine-tuning of chemotherapy and further divisions into even more treatment sub-groups, but by breakthrough innovation that will indeed need FDA approval. For R/R ALL, this breakthrough in treatment was achieved not by pediatric legislation. It will be the same with further new treatment principles such as tumor-infiltrating lymphocytes (TILs) [46], further CAR-T cell therapies [45], and more. But as long the development of pediatric oncology is described and perceived as a continuum of new drugs developed and approved in children, the key point is missed: this has nothing to do with specific cancer types being "adult" or "pediatric." Adults can have malignancies that occur predominantly in younger persons. Young people can fall ill with malignancies that we observe predominantly in more senior persons. In oncology, the FDA has moved the age limit of "pediatric" cancer from under 17 to under 12 years of age. But this is just a partial retreat from the children-are-therapeutic-orphans concept that is misleading western pediatric research since half a century. The differentiation between adult and "pediatric" cancer is scientifically misleading. For clinical care, we need different wards for adults and young people. But therapies and drug approval should correspond to the respective patient's needs, not to his legal status. Pediatric oncologists need other psychological skill sets than adults oncologists. But they should administer the same medication to the same type of cancer, provided the dose is correct.

The European Union (EU) and its European Medicines Agency (EMA) step in

The EU had taken notice of the US pediatric legislation. The European Medicines Agency (EMA) had been established in 1995 as an umbrella organization coordinating the National EU regulatory authorities. The EMA corresponds partially to the FDA, but the respective national regulatory authorities continue to exist. Most bureaucratic processes in the EMA are more complicated and take longer than in the FDA. Talks about an own EU approach resulted finally in an own EU pediatric law that came into force in 2007 [26,62]. The EMA resumed central responsibility for "pediatric" issues, including negotiating PIPs with pharmaceutical companies and finally approving or rejecting them [17]. The EU law was more ambitious from the beginning. "Children" were defined as anybody below 18 years old. For each new drug, the EU and its EMA demand a "pediatric investigation plan" (PIP), for which companies have to submit a proposal at the end of phase 1. The only exception are drugs for diseases that are officially declared to not exist in "children." The PIP "proposal" has to contain a list of "pediatric" studies, apart from development proposals for specific pediatric formulations and for studies in young animals. The standard negotiation time for a PIP is roughly one year [17,26].

The EU pediatric legislation consists of one law, in contrast to the two US laws. The EU demands "pediatric" studies to be planned very early in the drug development process, at the end of phase 1 studies. The EU law also offers a reward in form of a patent extension. But there is no uniform EU patent legislation. Each patent extension must be pursued individually in every single EU member state. Large companies have the administrative capacities to do so at least in the larger member states. For smaller companies, the balance between additional administrative efforts is not always favorable. Furthermore, nobody can know at the end of phase 1 which drug will be successful, and which drug will at the end of its patent life still be competitive compared to newer drugs.

While the mandatory US legislation excludes rare diseases, vaccines and biologics, the EU has no such restrictions. In young people that legally are still children but bodily are already mature, the EMA-demanded "pediatric" studies are medically, scientifically and clinically superfluous and lack medical sense. In contrast to adult cancer, pediatric cancer is very rare. As the EMA demands "pediatric" studies for each single new anticancer drug, there are not enough patients for most of these studies in single countries. Companies must recruit for these rare patients worldwide. In view of the sheer number of new anticancer drugs developed continuously, even the current worldwide pool of young cancer patients is not enough. Companies must now compete for "pediatric" cancer patients, defined by an administrative age limit. These studies are superfluous and useless in the best case, but often they harm young patients.

Since 2008, the EMA has continuously reduced the number of diseases officially declared as nonexistent in "children." Originally, melanoma was classified as a disease not occurring in "children." In 2008, the EMA claimed in referring to US statistics that in adolescents there are enough patients with melanoma to allow "pediatric" studies. But the EMA confused several issues. Firstly, the US statistics had only one group of young patients, aged 15–19 years. Of these patients, those already 18 and 19 years old are already adults by EU law. Secondly, roughly 90% of young patients that contract melanoma are healed by complete excision of the melanoma and do not need systemic treatment. Thirdly, conventional melanoma in adolescent and older patients is genetically the same [63]. Fourthly, there are some very rare melanoma types that occur in prepubertal children, but they are so rare that individual caregivers will not see more than a handful in their entire life, even if they work in a specialized center [30,63,64]. Altogether, the EMA has issued until now 12 (in words: twelve) melanoma PIPs, including one for ipilimumab that demanded the same studies as the FDA (see above), and one for vemurafenib [65]. Two "pediatric" melanoma studies with ipilimumab and vemurafenib, respectively, were initiated. Both studies tried to recruit for monotherapy, respectively, a wrong approach comparable to the FDA-rewarded "pediatric" cancer studies in individual chemotherapy agents that had since ages already found their place in the "cocktails" administered by the specialists in pediatric oncology. Both "pediatric" melanoma studies could after initially recruiting some patients not recruit any longer, as in the meantime combination treatment had been shown to be more efficient. Both studies had to be terminated. In the academic publication of the ipilimumab study, the authors remarked that this shows how difficult recruitment is for pediatric studies [55]. The ipilimumab study had also been requested and rewarded by the FDA. No academic researcher and no regulatory authority has so far apologized for these unethical, totally meaningless studies [30]. These studies were described as "pediatric" studies, but they were not. They were studies in young adults that legally were still "children" but bodily were already mature. Altogether, the EMA has issued many melanoma PIPs that would have to recruit adolescents, i.e., young people with melanoma that only *legally* are still children into "pediatric" studies, while ignoring that there are very rare truly pediatric melanoma types. Specifically for melanoma, these flawed EMA decisions are published since years. While the FDA has at least for adolescents revised its approach, the EMA has not done so.

To get EU approval in adults, companies must commit to a PIP. Without an approved PIP, adult approval is blocked in the EU. Most "pediatric" clinical studies are deferred to a later point in time. In theory, companies could first commit to these PIPs and the clinical studies they demand and later forget them, but companies are reluctant to invoke the anger of the EMA, which might result in other problems. Most companies try to comply with the PIPs they agreed upon, although these studies are medically senseless, often harm patients, and often are impossible to recruit because not enough "pediatric" patients exist worldwide. The EMA is aware of this problem [66], but continues with the PIPs that are filling the world with questionable "pediatric" studies [17,18,30,31,67–69].

Another mechanism developed by the EMA is the differentiation between "indication" and "condition" [70]. Many adult anticancer drugs that are successfully developed by pharmaceutical companies treat cancer types that only occur in adults. Supported by pediatric oncologists who want to use these new drugs also in younger patients, the EMA's construct of "indication" vs. "condition" allows the EMA to demand "pediatric" studies in totally different malignant diseases than in adults. In the meantime, several of these "pediatric" studies have been concluded and published [71–74]. None had positive clinical outcomes. They were not based on reasonable scientific considerations. Instead, their demand followed a flawed, pseudo-scientific concept.

The EMA-demanded studies do not advance care of pediatric cancer, but provide funds for "pediatric" cancer research and "pediatric" careers in regulatory authorities, pharmaceutical companies, and academic research. Table 4.3.1 shows international "pediatric" cancer studies listed in www.clinicaltrials.gov that recruit in administratively defined "children." The respective National Clinical Trials (NCT) number is given in column 2, the respective PIP number in column 6. Detailed study descriptions and more can be retrieved from the internet with the NCT or the PIP number.

TABLE 4.3.1 International industry-sponsored EMA-triggered "pediatric" cancer studies, recruiting (February 2020).

	NCT#	Abbreviated study description	Age	P/C	EMA PIP Number
01	NCT03837899	**Durvalumab** vs. D + T in AST + HM	< 17 y	158/20	EMEA-002028-PIP01–16
02	NCT02124772	**Trametinib** in cancer or PN and trametinib + dabrafenib in cancers with V600 mutations	1mo-17y	142/16	EMEA-001177-PIP01–11-M05
03	NCT03579602	**Lenvatinib** + Everolimus in R/R ST and CNS tumors	2–21 y	120/20	EMEA-001119-PIP02–12-M04
04	NCT01677741	**Dabrafenib** in advanced BRAF V600 + ST	12mo-17y	82/27	EMEA-001147-PIP01–11-M06
05	NCT03458728	S,E,T, PK of **copanlisib** in R/R ST or lymphoma	6mo-21y	130/18	EMEA-001757-PIP02–15
06	NCT03451825	**Avelumab** Ph1/2 study in ped cancers	< 18 y	148/11	EMEA-001849-PIP02–15-M02
07	NCT03611595	**Cabozantinib** + 13-cis-Retinoic Acid in R/R ST	2–21	18/1	EMEA-001143-PIP01–11-M01
08	NCT02372006	**Afatinib** in R/R NEDT, RMS and/or other ST	1–18 y	55/31	EMEA-001596-PIP02–17
09	NCT02756845	**Talimogene laherparepvec** in adv Non CNS tumors	2–21 y	18/18	EMEA-001251-PIP01–11-M03
10	NCT02332668	**Pembrolizumab** in AST or lymphoma	6mo-17y	310/27	EMEA-001474-PIP01–13-M01 EMEA-001474-PIP02–16-M01
11	NCT01956669	**Pazopanib** in solid tumors	1–18	154/63	EMEA-000601-PIP01–09-M05
12	NCT02637687	**Larotrectinib** in ASoP CNS Tumors	< 21 y	104/41	EMEA-001971-PIP02–16-M01
13	NCT03245450	**Eribulin** + irinotecan in R/R solid tumors	6mo-17y	111/32	EMEA-001261-PIP01–11-M05
14	NCT03585465	**Nivolumab** + metronomic CT in R/R ST or Lymphoma	4–18 y	102/?	EMEA-001407-PIP02–15-M02
15	NCT03793478	**Quizartinib** in R/R AML with FLT3-ITD mutations	1mo-21y	65/12	EMEA-001821-PIP01–15-M03
16	NCT03204279	**Netupitant** + Palonosetron to prevent NAV in CT	< 17 y	92/17	EMEA-001198-PIP03–17-M01
17	NCT02684058	**Dabrafenib** + trametinib in LGG or R/R HGL	1–17 y	142/59	EMEA-001147-PIP01–11-M06
18	NCT03591510	**Midostaurin** in AML	3mo-17y	50/9	EMEA-000780-PIP01–09-M04

19	NCT03633708	**Etelcalcetide** in SH + CKD on MH	28d-18y	56/18	EMEA-001554-PIP01–13-M02
20	NCT02393859	**Blinatumumab** vs standard CT in HRFRBPALL	<17 y	202/95	EMEA-000574-PIP02–12-M02
21	NCT02724163	**Gemtuzumab Ozogamicin** + Induction CT in AML	<17 y	700/21	EMEA-001733-PIP02–15-M01
22	NCT03878719	**Binimetinib** + encorafenib in melanoma	12–17 y	18/5	EMEA-001454-PIP03–15-M01
23	NCT03860844	**Isatuximab** + CT in R/R ALL or AML	28d-17y	96/4	EMEA-002205-PIP01–17
24	NCT02979522	**Brentuximab** Vedotin + CT in ANDHK	5–17 y	55/25	EMEA-000980-PIP01–10-M05
25	NCT02369653	**Apixaban** vs. no systemic anticoagulant in preventing blood clots during induction CT	1–17 y	500/76	EMEA-000183-PIP01–08-M06
26	NCT03610724	**Tisagenlecleucel** in Non-Hodgkin Lymphoma	<18 y	35/10	EMEA-001654-PIP01–14-M03
27	NCT02723994	**Ruxolitinib** + CT in ALL	1–21 y	170/109	EMEA-000901-PIP03–16
28	NCT02625480	**Axicabtagene ciloleucel** (KTE-C19) in R/R ALL	2–21 y	100/23	EMEA-002010-PIP01–16-M01
29	NCT03441360	**Eribulin** in R/R RMS, NRSTS, EWS	1–18 y	45/41	EMEA-001261-PIP01–11-M05
30	NCT03913559	**Inotuzumab ozogamicin** in MRD + CD22 + LL	<21 y	32/1	EMEA-001429-PIP01–13-M02
31	NCT02840409	VCT vs. VCT + **Bevacizumab** in LGG	6mo-18y	75/1	EMEA-000056-PIP01–07-M02
32	NCT03817320	**Ixazomib** + CT in ALL + lymphoma	1–21 y	31/1	EMEA-001410-PIP02–17-M01
33	NCT01734512	**Everolimus** in recurrent or progressive LGG	3–21 y	65/18	EMEA-000019-PIP02–07-M05

ADV, Advanced; *ALL*, acute lymphablastic leukemia; *AML*, acute myeloid leukemia; *ANDHK*, Advanced Newly Diagnosed Hodgkin Lymphoma; *ASoP*, Advanced solid or primary; *AST*, advanced solid tumors; *CNS*, central nervous system; *CT*, chemotherapy; *Ctrs*, centers; *D + T*, durvalumab + tremelimumab; *EMA*, European Medicines Agency; *FDA*, Food and Drug Administration; *FLT3-ITD*, FMS-like tyrosine kinase-3-internal tandem duplication; *HGL*, high grade glioma; *HM*, hematological malignancies; *HRFRBPALL*, High risk first relapse B-precursor ALL; *LGG*, low grade glioma; *LL*, lymphoblastic lymphoma; *MH*, maintenance hemodialysis; *NAV*, Nausea and Vomiting; *NB*, neuroblastoma; *NEDT*, Neuroectodermal Tumors; *NFT1*, Neurofibromatosis Type-1; *P/C*, number of patients and centers; *Ph1/2*, phase 1/2; *PIP*, pediatric investigation plan; *PN*, plexiform neurofibroma; *POPG*, Progressive Optic Pathway Glioma; *pts*, patients; *RMS*, rhabdomyosarcoma; *R/R*, relapsed or recurrent; *SH*, secondary hyperparathyroidism; *ST*, solid tumors; *VCT*, Vinblastine chemotherapy; *y*, year.

Apart from lacking medical sense, some of these studies directly harm young patients. Why should parents of a young person with cancer agree to a study that investigates apixaban vs. no anticoagulant therapy? Apixaban is an FDA-approved anticoagulant. To compare apixaban vs. no systemic anticoagulant in preventing blood clots during induction chemotherapy is simply unethical. Isatuximab is in clinical development for multiple myeloma and T-cell leukemia. Why should it work in patients with ALL or acute myeloid leukemia (AML) aged 28 days to 17 years? There are many clinical differences between different myeloma and leukemia types in older and younger patients that need to be taken in consideration in clinical practice. Nevertheless, the age limit of 18 or 21 years is administrative, not clinical.

The EU approach to enforce "pediatric" cancer studies originated in the US. The US-born concept was taken up and amplified by the EU and its EMA. The EMA is an English-speaking institution within the EU, where most persons' everyday language is non-English. The EMA is more insulated from exposure to the public than the FDA.

Of course, there is also a PIP that demands "pediatric" studies for tisagenlecleucel [75]. It demands four studies in "children" 1–17 years old and adults—for a medication that is already approved both by the FDA and the EMA for ALL in adults and "children."

There are even efforts to further expand the EU pediatric legislation, see e.g., a resolution of the European Parliament of 2016 [76]. Should this initiative one day be transformed into law, it will trigger even more needless and harmful "pediatric" cancer studies.

Dose-finding with targeted medicines in "pediatric" malignancies

A publication investigates 19 "pediatric" dose-finding studies of 15 molecularly targeted agents with adult data, defined as compounds that aim at other targets than cytotoxins. These 19 studies included 687 "children" aged 1–22 years. For roughly three quarters of the investigated compounds, the recommended phase 2 dose ranged between 90% and 130% of the body-surface-area (BSA)-adjusted FDA-approved adult dose. Most "pediatric" studies reported a maximum tolerated dose comparable to the BSA-adjusted adult dose. For one drug, sunitinib, the recommended phase 2 dose was much lower (56%) of the adult dose due to severe cardiotoxicity. The authors conclude that except for a narrow therapeutic index, early-phase trials evaluating PK, PD and efficacy from adults while controlling for toxicity might be an alternative "to accelerate drug development in pediatric oncology" [77]. The authors give the age range and the median age of each study, but not the exact patient number which would have to be retrieved from the original publications. From the age ranges and the median ages (up to 16 years!) we see that a considerable part of these "pediatric" studies were performed in *physiologically* young adults that, however, were *legally* still children.

In the most frequent type of epilepsy, partial-onset seizures (POS), neurologists concluded that antiepileptic drugs (AEDs) have efficacy both in adults and "children" down to two years [78,79], This has been accepted by the FDA that first accepted "extrapolation" from adults to children down to four [80], then to two years [81]. Even the heretic question was asked if children are little adults regarding AED treatment, with a clearly positive answer [82].

Why did Paoletti et al. not come to conclusions comparable to their colleagues in neurology? [83] One obvious, but heretic answer is that pediatric oncology has at least in Europe become a habitat of "pediatric" researchers that make a living out of "pediatric" studies. Formally, the EMA demands these studies. However, "multi-stakeholder" organizations support the EMA and have built up pressure to maintain and even strengthen the current regulatory framework that forces pharmaceutical companies to sponsor these "pediatric" cancer studies [84,85]. Sponsoring these studies has become an entrance fee for adult drug approval in all clinical areas, including oncology.

US/FDA movements into opposite directions: adolescents' cancer versus the RACE for children act

In 2019, the FDA revised the children-are-therapeutic-orphans concept for adolescents with malignancies: "Cancers in young pediatric patients are often different from those in adult patients and require unique treatment approaches; however, some cancers found in adolescent patients—such as some soft tissue and bone sarcomas, central nervous system tumors, leukemias and lymphomas, and melanoma—are similar in histology and biologic behavior to those found in adults." [81] Although this is a clear step away from the children-are-therapeutic-orphans mantra, it is not sufficient. Emily Whitehead was 5 years old when she fell ill with ALL. The FDA has approved tisagenlecleucel in R/R B-cell precursor ALL in patients up to 25 years of age.

In recent years, the FDA "encouraged" companies to participate in "pediatric" basket studies [83]. From 2020 on, the FDA demands pediatric cancer studies in children younger than 12 years for new anticancer drugs, based on the "Research to Accelerate Cures and Equity" (RACE) Act [84]. The supporters of this law claim that this will further promote research and development of new treatments for children with cancer [85]. "Pediatric" studies will be required if the drug or biological product is intended for the treatment of adult cancer and aims at a molecular target that FDA determines is substantially relevant to the growth or progression of a pediatric cancer. For this, the FDA will publish a list of molecular targets considered to be substantially relevant for pediatric cancer [85].

There is no science in the RACE for children act and the newest FDA decisions. The FDA reluctantly accepts reality regarding adolescents, but does not candidly handle the mistakes that were done in the past twenty years in rewarding "pediatric" cancer studies. The motivation of the more than hundred institutions that supported the RACE for children act is not difficult to understand. These institutions have massively profited and continue to profit from "pediatric" cancer studies financed by pharmaceutical industry (and other sponsors) [86].

The alleged genomic landscape of pediatric cancer

Terms like "precision medicine," "personalized medicine," or "targeted medicine" in pediatric oncology claim to be able to target vulnerabilities in pediatric cancers with modern anticancer drugs [7,77,85,87]. Three papers discuss the "genomic landscape of pediatric cancers" [88–90]. Gröbner et al. discuss 24 cancers that occur in "children." However, they include B-cell ALL, which occurs also in adults. Tisagenlecleucel is approved in R/R B-cell ALL in patients up to 25 years of age; [91] several more of these cancers occur also in adults. Ninety-five percent of the patients were up to 18 years old. The patients are described as "pediatric," which is wrong for all persons aged 18 years. An 18 years old person is legally adult both in the US and in the EU. Furthermore, 5% were younger than 25 years of age. Thus, already the paper's title is misleading. It describes the results of tissues that were probably collected by pediatric oncologists, and then analyzed by many non-pediatric institutions. The authors *assumed* they analyzed pediatric cancer samples, but the paper lacks a reliable definition of "pediatric." Physiologically, many patients were no longer "children," and not all investigated tissue samples were from truly pediatric cancers. These flaws diminish the value of the paper's results. Of the tissues analyzed by Ma et al., 98.5% were from patients up to 20 years old, i.e., 1.5% were from patients older than 20 years. No upper age limit is given for the older patients [92]. Sweet-Cordero describe "pediatric" cancer as occurring in patients up to 14 years old [90]. These three publications praise precision medicine and personalized medicine, but they present data and results based on unreliable definitions. They claim that "pediatric" cancers have few somatic mutations, but a higher prevalence of germline alterations in cancer predisposition genes [92]. This is interesting and may be of academic relevance, but would on its own not have an immediate clinical relevance. But these papers do have high real-world relevance. They justify regulatory "pediatric" cancer studies. Commercial companies must live with the existing reality. When a company develops a drug like tisagenlecleucel in close collaboration with top scientists, it takes economic risks. Nobody can predict which drug development strategy will eventually result in success. Today, the decisive bottleneck for new drugs is their approval by the FDA and the EMA, separately for adults and "children." If an athlete of 15 years is hospitalized, he or she will be treated in a pediatric ward. This is an administrative reality. But the age limit of 18 years does not make sense for drug approval, drug treatment, or as inclusion/exclusion criterion into clinical studies. Bodies do not change at birthdays, but the legal status of persons does. Separate drug approval in "children" that bodily are no longer children is not based on science [17,18,30,31]. Since 2007, the EMA demands "pediatric" studies as condition for *adult* approval for all new drugs. Here we approach the real-world relevance of the papers on the genomic landscape of pediatric cancers.

Gröbner et al. claim that almost half of pediatric malignancies harbor a "potentially druggable event," which they assess as highly relevant for future clinical trials. They refer to Pearson et al. [93], authored on behalf of "ACCELERATE," a self-declared multistakeholder platform [85]. "Potentially druggable events" justify EMA-demanded "pediatric" cancer studies. Until 2019, the FDA "recommended" pediatric basket trials for new anticancer drugs [83]. From 2020 on it demands pediatric studies for new anticancer compounds to be performed in patients younger than 12 years old [24]. The term "potentially druggable events" is vague and not based on solid science. However, the authors represent institutions that do broad, expensive genomic analyses.

Commercial companies would not invest resources on the base of such "potentially druggable events." Most commercial companies' regulatory pivotal studies comprise already young and more senior patients [61]. But the hope (and illusion) that compounds for adult cancer types might be used for "pediatric" cancer types is still rather strong. It roots both in the history of pediatric oncology and today's framework of drug development and drug approval. Pediatric oncology represents today powerful institutions that employ many highly qualified persons plus many other persons with lower qualifications that are needed to maintain complex infrastructures. This maintenance requires a constant flow of funds. Pseudo-scientifically justified "pediatric" oncology studies must be paid today by commercial pharmaceutical companies that successfully develop anticancer treatments. For the approval of innovative life-saving drugs, companies must finance senseless and worse "pediatric" studies. The decision to do so is for commercial companies a business decision. The companies are forced to finance these studies, or they are blocked from selling innovative drugs in adults. These studies lack medical sense and often harm where they test against outdated treatment or placebo. Companies do not finance them because they think they will advance pediatric cancer healthcare, but because they are blackmailed to do so. In the meantime, a number of pediatric oncologists have left the FDA and the EMA and have continued their career in the pharmaceutical industry.

The first sentences of the EU pediatric regulation declare that this regulation is against the forces of the market [39,94]. In the market, parties engage in exchange. The market rewards the production and the sales of goods that are asked for by economic success. The Soviet Union type economy that wanted to abolish the forces of the market was never able to meet the needs of the citizens. The Soviet Union dissolved, while China has on an economic level arranged itself with the forces of the market. In all medical disciplines, including pediatrics, companies deliver services and products for which they want to get paid. Nothing is wrong with this. In "pediatric drug development," an artificially defined service was created by the use of a semantic blur ("children" in the *legal* vs. in the *physiological* sense of the word), for which an alleged high clinical need was declared. This clinical need never existed. In pediatric oncology, it was academic medicine that provided the necessary experiences, studies, and data for clinical treatment of young patients with cancer, as long as there was still potential for improvement by fine-tuning chemotherapy and further supportive treatment. When the fine-tuning of chemotherapy reached its limits, "pediatric drug development" offered a welcome pseudo-solution that seemed to offer a way forward.

The more science-based oncology and drug development advance that use newest understandings of cell communication, decision hierarchies in the body's immune system, and further progress in developing modern biologics, the more the "pediatric" studies enforced by the regulatory authorities show a logic that does not aim at healthcare and patient treatment. Instead, it is based on regulatory formalism. The COG chairman correctly describes this approach as "drug-centric" [2]. Patients want to be healed by a drug, or at least have a good quality of life. Parents want their children to be healed from cancer or their cancer to be transformed into a manageable chronic disease. For patients and parents, it is of secondary value, if at all, if the respective drug is approved. This might become a burden where reimbursement institutions refuse payment for effective treatment because the respective treatment is not approved in "children." But this is not an acceptable justification to perform separate "pediatric" studies. The declaration of Helsinki does in no place accept performance of clinical studies in humans that lack medical sense or even harm patients, just to fulfill dogmatic regulatory demands.

History has shown many times what happens when bureaucrats have the executive power to decide what is good for people instead of the market. The EU pediatric law is another example of this eternal struggle between bureaucrats who want more power, and individuals who take responsibility for their doing.

There are several reasons why academic research so far has failed to critically look at "pediatric drug development." Drug development has become a complex interface between regulatory rules, science, economics and many more dimensions that are invoked in every discussion that affects the life of many persons. There are also hidden conflicts of interest. Pediatric oncology has become a separate academic and clinical sub-discipline with a high reputation that comprises many institutions.

The emotional power of pediatric oncology

Cancer is described since decades as the leading cause of death by disease in children [2]. Pediatric oncology was an endeavor not only of parents, patients and healthcare professionals, but to considerable degree of all society. Cancer, characterized as "child killer," received a level of attention unmatched by many other childhood diseases in the second half of the 20th century [3]. It touched and still today touches everybody.

The US statistics are unambiguous: in persons aged from 1–44 years, unintentional injury is the most frequent cause of death, followed by suicide in persons aged 10–34 years. Thereafter come congenital anomalies, malignant neoplasms and homicide, with different ranking in different age groups [95]. Prevention of child death by child safety seats in trains, airplanes and cars might have saved more lives than pediatric oncology. This is a point we will not discuss further (statisticians might love such a challenge). But it is simply impossible to ignore that death by suicide in 10–24 years old persons is much more frequent than death by malignancy [67,95]. As suicide is often triggered by depression or other mental challenges, it is relevant in this context to note the regulatory warnings against antidepressants in young patients [67].

The business of pediatric oncology

Pediatric oncology has acquired considerable societal recognition and has become an ordinary part of our society. It has become a respected profession, with clearly defined training requirements [96]. The COG performs many pediatric cancer studies worldwide. All these aspects require budgets. Pediatric oncology has long passed the 1950s, when the Pediatric Blood Club began to have scientific meetings during the annual meetings of the American Pediatric Society (APS) and the Society for Pediatric Research (SPR). Then, the "Pediatric Blood Club" had no formal membership and did not keep formal records. The costs of the room and projection equipment were raised by *passing the hat* at the meetings [97].

The desperation of parents who are losing or have lost a loved one is often used to demand more "research," even if this "research" is simply reproducing knowledge that is already existing.

When Peter Buxtun, who worked in the National Health Service, but not in the Tuskegee study [98,99], learned about this study, he tried for seven years through internal channels to have this study terminated. He was stonewalled [100]. The real-world interest to continue this study was unbelievably banal. NHS employees were invited to the autopsies of the men who eventually succumbed to the untreated syphilis. They reported their observations in scientific publications (nobody got a Nobel price). These employees had a real-world interest for the study to be continued: job security in a job that enjoyed a high reputation. The reasons for Buxtun to be stonewalled were not scientific errors, but banal real-world interests. At the end the general social climate had changed enough for the contacted journalist to dare to write about it. Within days, the study was terminated [101].

The future of pediatric oncology

Pediatric oncology is correctly characterized as a modern success story of medical research that began with successful treatment of young patients with ALL [2]. It emerged with helping patients, and it needs to find its way back to the determination it had in these days. Childhood cancer is a collection of rare and ultra-rare diseases [2]. But the framework of research in oncology is changing. Treatment moves toward interfering with the communication between malignant cells and the rest of the body. Communication within cell departments, between signals and receptors, and between cells does not change with a specific birthday.

Historically, the parallel existence of two separate clinical sub-disciplines was justified. For operational and administrative purposes, separate pediatric wards are needed. Pediatric oncology as a description of the treated patients is what it is. But there is no "pediatric" cancer that could be defined by objective criteria. Any given cancer is the same before and after the 18th birthday. At present, the definition of "pediatric" cancer is circular: "pediatric" cancer is what eminent pediatric oncologists describe as "pediatric" cancers. This is not enough.

The classification of malignancies as "pediatric" occurred when oncology itself was very young. Exemplarily, the question of "pediatric" melanoma has been discussed in the literature in depth, with definitions of melanoma ranging from up to 10 to up to 21 years of age [102,103]. Meanwhile, we know more about the genome of melanoma; we need to differentiate between conventional and other melanomas [63]. Most spitzoid melanomas and melanomas arising in a giant nevus occur in childhood, but none of them is "pediatric." To find genomic characteristics of malignancies in young vs. older patients may be possible. At present, these attempts are of very limited scientific value and are disguised justifications for mediocre pseudo-scientific clinical research that will not help young patients. Instead, it will continue and expand the EU/EMA's endeavor to perform "pediatric" studies in all modern anticancer compounds irrespective of the body's physiological maturity. We need science and drug development for all sorts of rare malignancies, but their characterization as "pediatric" blurs scientific, administrative, and legal aspects. Such characterizations reflect real-world issues such as funding through the current coalition of regulatory authorities, parts of the pediatric oncology community, and the regulatory authorities.

In 2018, the FDA granted accelerated approval for larotrectinib for adult and pediatric cancers driven by a tropomyosin receptor kinase fusion, followed in 2019 by the EMA [104]. This is the second FDA approval of a cancer defined by a genetic feature instead of the location in the body where the tumor originated. In its unlimited wisdom, the EMA has also issued a PIP for larotrectinib [105]. Without such a PIP, larotrectinib approval would have been blocked in the EU. There is no scientific, clinical or medical sense in this PIP.

The approval of drugs by the organ of origin is no longer compatible with modern medicine. In a recent report about a *BRAF* mutation in ovarian cancer, successful treatment with dabrafenib and trametinib was delayed by months as these drugs are only approved for melanoma. The treating physicians characterizes the process associated with obtaining permission to use these medications off-label or via expanded access as byzantine [106]. Obviously, the on/off-label framework can also harm adult patients. But in adults, these are rather exceptions, in contrast to the industry of "pediatric" oncology studies.

To further advance cancer care of young patients, the gap (or abyss) between current clinical care and clinical research needs to be overcome. The current flawed concept has undoubtedly provided funds for many studies and other activities and has resulted in more communication between pediatric oncologists and the biopharmaceutical industry [2]. But its main outcome was not therapeutic improvements, but maintenance of current research infrastructures. However, breakthrough improvements such as the treatment of R/R ALL in young patients have occurred despite this abyss. The time has come to overcome the flawed concept of "pediatric" cancer, caused by the children-are-therapeutic-orphans mantra.

The more economic incentives for research into rare diseases, including malignancies, are offered, the more research and drug development into these diseases will be done. Some malignant diseases occur in childhood only, some both in childhood and adulthood. Some have several peaks, one in childhood, and another one in adulthood. So far, oncology has not been able to define unambiguously what "pediatric" malignancies are. Instead, different administrative age limits are used. The solution to this riddle is almost too obvious and too simple. There are no genuine "pediatric" malignancies.

On the other side, incentives must facilitate appropriate research activities. We could invest many more billions of $ US or € into the current EU pediatric oncology research infrastructure. The outcome would be more papers, more "pediatric" careers in regulatory authorities, research, and industry, but not better healthcare for young patients with malignancies.

Already most FDA-rewarded "pediatric" oncology studies were medically senseless and dictated by regulatory dogmatism. Maybe the randomized allegedly "pediatric" study in nasopharyngeal carcinoma was the worst example, maybe worse studies will be identified in future analyses. EU, EMA, and some European pediatric cancer researchers have further amplified the US precedence and have created an ample network of "pediatric" clinical research that essentially has become an industry to distribute funds for questionable and worse clinical studies, paid by pharmaceutical companies. As is usual where billions of € and $ US are around, a vast network of followers has bloomed that hopefully will be fully revealed in the years to come.

In the short term, the alternative for pediatric oncology is to continue with business as usual and to pretend that everything is perfect. In the long term, there is no alternative than to face and address its fundamental challenges. Academic science has barely started to investigate the medical sense of regulatorily rewarded/demanded "pediatric" studies in cancer and other diseases, partially because of the strong emotional power of cancer in children and the conflicts of interests outlined above.

This discussion will not be comfortable for all involved players. But the history of science is full of errors. We could define the history of science as an uphill struggle against wrong concepts that for long periods hinder and have hindered further advances. At the end, necessary reassessments have always occurred and have finally helped to further advance medicine and science. At least today heretic opinions are no longer threatened by the stake.

This is a very controversial issue. We cannot predict who will take first steps. It might be associations of pediatric oncology; of oncology in general; of pharmacology, developmental pharmacology or clinical pharmacology; patient advocacy groups; parent advocacy groups, medical ethicists, or others. Whoever will start and however it starts, an open and candid discussion will hopefully emerge, instead of sweeping issues under the carpet. Since more than twenty years, young patients and their grieving parents have been systematically misled and continue to be misled. With the EU expansion of "pediatric drug development" in oncology this has reached horrifying dimensions. In parallel, true scientific progress has continued as well, giving hope to young and old patient with malignancies whose diagnoses would have been a death sentence a few years earlier. The public will welcome clarification in the currently confusing situation.

On the level of regulatory authorities, the critical discussion will probably come through political channels, resulting inter alia in personnel decisions on middle- and high level management levels.

Within pharmaceutical industry, there are two different streams. Some employees on management level share the FDA's and the EMA's regulatory dogmatism. On the other side, the nonsense of "pediatric" clinical studies in all clinical areas is an open secret within pharmaceutical industry. Every single company will have to address this. No chief executive officer (CEO) will be happy to learn that billions of € and $ US have been virtually thrown out of the window for studies that for the next decade might invite damage lawsuits in US courts, adding punitive damages to the money already wasted.

References

[1] Saletta F, Seng MS, Lau LM. Advances in paediatric cancer treatment. Transl Pediatr 2014;3 (2):156–82 Apr <https://www.ncbi.nlm.nih.gov/pmc/articles/PMC4729100/pdf/tp-03-02-156.pdf>.

[2] Adamson PC. Improving the outcome for children with cancer: development of targeted new agents. CA Cancer J Cli 2015;65(3):212–20 May-Jun.
[3] Nambayan AG Historical overview of pediatric oncology and pediatric oncology nursing. St. Jude's children's research hospital/Cure4kids 2005. <https://www.cure4kids.org/private/courses_documents/m_1/NEM01D02V07.pdf>.
[4] Krueger G. Hope and suffering: children, cancer, and the paradox of experimental medicine. Baltimore, MD, USA: John Hopkins University Press; 2008.
[5] DeVita Jr VT, Chu E. A history of cancer chemotherapy. Cancer Res 2008;68(21):8643–53 Nov 1 <http://cancerres.aacrjournals.org/content/68/21/8643.full-text.pdf>.
[6] Norris RE, Adamson PC. Challenges and opportunities in childhood cancer drug development. Nat Rev Cancer 2012;12(11):776–82 Nov.
[7] Burdach SEG, Westhoff MA, Steinhauser MF, Debatin KM. Precision medicine in pediatric oncology. Mol Cell Pediatr 2018;5(1):6 Aug 31.
[8] Hudson MM, Link MP, Simone JV. Milestones in the curability of pediatric cancers. J Clin Oncol 2014;32(23):2391–7 Aug 10 <https://www.ncbi.nlm.nih.gov/pmc/articles/PMC4876323/pdf/zlj2391.pdf>.
[9] Athale U, Hijiya N, Patterson BC, et al. Management of chronic myeloid leukemia in children and adolescents: recommendations from the children's oncology group CMLworking group. Pediatr Blood Cancer 2019;66(9):e27827 Sep.
[10] Subbiah V. Fast-tracking novel drugs in pediatric oncology. Cell Cycle 2015;14(8):1127–8 <https://www.ncbi.nlm.nih.gov/pmc/articles/PMC4615060/pdf/kccy-14-08-1018049.pdf>.
[11] Children's Oncology Group (COG) <https://www.childrensoncologygroup.org/>.
[12] O'Leary M, Krailo M, Anderson JR, et al. Progress in childhood cancer: 50 years of research collaboration, a report from the Children's Oncology Group. Semin Oncol 2008;35(5):484–93 Oct.
[13] Withycombe JS, Alonzo TA, Wilkins-Sanchez MA, et al. The children's oncology group: organizational structure, membership, and institutional characteristics. J Pediatr Oncol Nurs 2019;36(1):24–34 Jan/Feb.
[14] Perilongo G, Craft A, Jereb B, et al. The SIOP story: an informal history of the international society of pediatric oncology. Pediatric Blood Cancer 2016;.
[15] Boklan J. Little patients, losing patients: pediatric cancer drug development. Mol Cancer Ther 2006;5(8):1905–8 Aug <http://mct.aacrjournals.org/content/5/8/1905.full-text.pdf>.
[16] Plate V. Impact off-label, compassionate unlicensed use health care laws preselected ctries 2020; <http://hss.ulb.uni-bonn.de/2009/1936/1936.pdf>.
[17] Rose K. The challenges of pediatric drug development. Curr Ther Res Clin Exp 2019; <https://doi.org/10.1016/j.curtheres.2019.01.007>.
[18] Rose K, Neubauer D, Grant-Kels JM. Rational use of medicine in children—the conflict of interests story. A review. Rambam Maimonides Med J 2019;10(3):e0018. Available from: https://doi.org/10.5041/RMMJ.10371 Review <https://www.rmmj.org.il/userimages/928/2/PublishFiles/953Article.pdf>.
[19] Vargesson N. Thalidomide-induced teratogenesis: history and mechanisms. Birth Defects Res C Embryo Today 2015;105(2):140–56 Jun <https://www.ncbi.nlm.nih.gov/pmc/articles/PMC4737249/> (Accessed 04 June 2019).
[20] Thomann KD. Die Contergan-Katastrophe. Die trügerische Sicherh der "harten" Daten Dtsch Ärzteblatt 2007;104(41):A2078–82. Available at <https://www.aerzteblatt.de/pdf.asp?id = 57224> (Accessed 04 June 2019).
[21] Janssen WM. A historical perspective on off-label medicine: from regulation, promotion, and the first amendment to the next frontiers. In: Levy MC, editor. Food and Drug Law Institute. First Washington, D.C.: USA Off-Label Communications; 2008.

[22] Donohue JA. History of drug advertising: the evolving roles of consumers and consumer protection. Milbank Q 2006;84:659–99 <https://www.ncbi.nlm.nih.gov/pmc/articles/PMC2690298/pdf/milq0084-0659.pdf>.

[23] Rägo L, Santo B. Drug regulation: history, present and future. In: van Boxtel CJ, Santo B, Edwards IR, editors. Drug benefits and risks: international textbook of clinical pharmacology, revised. 2nd edition Uppsala, Sweder: IOS Press & Uppsala Monitoring Centre; 2008. p. 65–77. chapter 6 <https://www.who.int/medicines/technical_briefing/tbs/Drug_Regulation_History_Present_Future.pdf>.

[24] Shirkey H. Therapeutic orphans. J Pediatr 1968;72(1):119–20 Jan <https://pdfs.semanticscholar.org/f1cb/acdbac19fa56236b919fb7799eaacaa10c77.pdf>.

[25] Hirschfeld S. History pediatric labeling 2012; <https://www.slideserve.com/marlin/history-of-pediatric-labeling>.

[26] Hirschfeld S, Saint-Raymond A. Pediatric regulatory initiatives. Handb Exp Pharmacol 2011;205:245–68 556.

[27] Hirschfeld S, Ho PT, Smith M, Pazdur R. Regulatory approvals of pediatric oncology drugs: previous experience and new initiatives. J Clin Oncol 2003;21(6):1066–73 Mar 15.

[28] <https://www.fda.gov/drugs/development-resources/written-requests-issued>.

[29] FDA Pemetrexed pediatric written request 2001. <https://www.fda.gov/media/80043/download>.

[30] Rose K, Grant-Kels JM. Pediatric melanoma—the whole (conflicts of interest) story. Int J Womens Dermatol 2018;5(2):110–15 <https://doi.org/10.1016/j.ijwd.2018.10.020> Nov 19 <https://www.ncbi.nlm.nih.gov/pmc/articles/PMC6451736/pdf/main.pdf>.

[31] Rose K, Grant-Kels JM. The meanings of "pediatric drug development". A review. Ther Innov Regul Sci 2018; Dec 9:2168479018812060 <https://journals.sagepub.com/doi/pdf/10.1177/2168479018812060>.

[32] FDA 2001. The pediatric exclusivity provision. January 2001. Status report to congress. <https://www.fda.gov/downloads/Drugs/DevelopmentApprovalProcess/DevelopmentResources/UCM049915.pdf>

[33] Casanova M, Enis Özyar E, Patte C, Orbach D, Ferrari A, Veyrat-Follet C, et al. International randomized phase 2 study on the addition of docetaxel to the combination of cisplatin and 5-fluorouracil in the induction treatment for nasopharyngeal carcinoma in children and adolescents. Cancer Chemother Pharmacol 2016;77(2):289–98 Feb.

[34] Kamran SC, Riaz N, Lee N. Nasopharyngeal carcino-ma. Surg Oncol Clin N Am 2015;24:547–61.

[35] Brennan B. Nasopharyngeal carcinoma. Orphanet J Rare Dis 2006;1:23.

[36] <https://www.fda.gov/drugs/development-resources/written-requests-issued>.

[37] Dunne J, Rodriguez WJ, Murphy MD, et al. Extrapolation of adult data and other data in pediatric drug-development programs. Pediatrics. 2011;128:e1242–9.

[38] Tomasi PA, Egger GF, Pallidis C, et al. Enabling development of paediatric medicines in Europe: 10 years of the EU paediatric regulation. Pediatr Drugs 2017;19:505–13.

[39] Regulation (EC) No 1901/2006 of the European parliament and of the council of 12 December 2006 on Medicinal Products for Paediatric Use and Amending Regulation (EEC) No 1768/92, Directive 2001/20/EC, Directive 2001/83/EC and Regulation (EC) No 726/2004. <http://ec.europa.eu/health/files/eudralex/vol-1/reg_2006_1901/reg_2006_1901_en.pdf>

[40] Goldacre B. Bad pharma: how drug companies mislead doctors and harm patients. London, UK: HarperCollinsPublishers; 2012.

[41] Angell M. The truth about the drug companies: how they deceive us and what to do about it. New York, USA: Random House Publishers; 2004.

[42] Koury J, Lucero M, Cato C, et al. Immunotherapies: exploiting the immune system for cancer treatment. J Immunol Res 2018;9585614 2018 Mar 14.

[43] Iqbal N, Iqbal N. Imatinib: a breakthrough of targeted therapy in cancer. Chemother Res Pract 2014;2014:357027.

[44] Tsimberidou AM, Eggermont AM, Schilsky RL. Precision cancer medicine: the future is now, only better. Am Soc Clin Oncol Educ Book 2014;61–9.

[45] Miliotou AN, Papadopoulou LC. CAR T-cell therapy: a new era in cancer immunotherapy. Curr Pharm Biotechnol 2018;19(1):5–18.

[46] Geukes Foppen MH, Donia M, Svane IM, Haanen JB. Tumor-infiltrating lymphocytes for the treatment of metastatic cancer. Mol Oncol 2015;9(10):1918–35 Dec <https://www.ncbi.nlm.nih.gov/pmc/articles/PMC5528735/pdf/MOL2-9-1918.pdf>.

[47] Sharma P, Allison JP. Immune checkpoint targeting in cancer therapy: toward combination strategies with curative potential. Cell. 2015;161(2):205–14 Apr 9.

[48] Papaioannou NE, Beniata OV, Vitsos P, et al. Harnessing the immune system to improve cancer therapy. Ann Transl Med 2016;4(14):261 Jul.

[49] Postow MA, Callahan MK, Wolchok JD. Immune checkpoint blockade in cancer therapy. J Clin Oncol 2015;33(17):1974–82 Jun 10 <https://www.ncbi.nlm.nih.gov/pmc/articles/PMC4980573/pdf/zlj1974.pdf>.

[50] Barr RD. Imatinib mesylate child adolesc cancerpediatr blood cancer 2010;55:18–25.

[51] Sallan SE. Myths and lessons from the adult/pediatric interface in acute lymphoblastic leukemia. Hematol Am Soc Hematol Educ Program 2006;128–32.

[52] Burke MJ. Burke profile of imatinib in pediatric leukemia. Pediatric Health, Med Therapeutics 2014;5:1–7.

[53] FDA 2014. Ipilimumab pediatric written request <https://www.fda.gov/media/106997/download>.

[54] Merchant MS, Wright M, Baird K, et al. Phase 1 trial of Ipilimumab in pediatric patients with advanced solid tumors. Clin Cancer Res 2016;22(6):1364–70 Mar 15.

[55] Geoerger B, Bergeron C, Gore L, et al. Phase II study of ipilimumab in adolescents with unresectable stage III or IV malignant melanoma. Eur J Cancer 2017;86:358–63 Nov.

[56] Emily Whitehead: a young girl beats cancer with immunotherapy. https://www.cancerresearch.org/immunotherapy/stories/patients/emily-whitehead

[57] Maude SL, Laetsch TW, Buechner J, et al. Tisagenlecleucel in children and young adults with b-cell lymphoblastic leukemia. N Engl J Med 2018;378:439–48.

[58] Suttorp M, Schulze P, Glauche I, et al. Front-line imatinib treatment in children and adolescents with chronic myeloid leukemia: results from a phase III trial. Leukemia. 2018;32(7):1657–69 Jul.

[59] Hardin AP, Hackell JM. Committee on practice and ambulatory medicine. Age limit pediatrics Pediatrics 2017;140(3):e20172151 <https://pediatrics.aappublications.org/content/pediatrics/140/3/e20172151.full.pdf>.

[60] <https://www.kidsvcancer.org/race-for-children-act/endorsements-for-race-act/>.

[61] <www.clinicaltrials.gov>.

[62] EMA 2004. Evidence of harm from off-label or unlicensed medicines in children. <https://www.ema.europa.eu/en/documents/other/evidence-harm-label-unlicensed-medicines-children_en.pdf>.

[63] Pappo AS. Pediatric melanoma: the whole (genome) story. Am Soc Clin Oncolology Educ Book 2014;e432–5.

[64] Rose K, Walson PD. Are regulatory age limits in pediatric melanoma justified? Curr Ther Res Clin Exp 2019 <https://www.ncbi.nlm.nih.gov/pmc/articles/PMC6677782/pdf/main.pdf>.

[65] Rose K, Walson PD. Do the European Medicines Agency (EMA) decisions hurt pediatric melanoma patients? Clin Therapeutics 2017;39(2):253–65 <https://www.clinicaltherapeutics.com/article/S0149-2918(17)30047-4/pdf>.

[66] Hwang TJ, Tomasi PA, Bourgeois FT. Delays in completion and results reporting of clinical trials under the paediatric regulation in the European Union: a cohort study. PLoS Med 2018;15(3):e1002520 Mar 1 <https://www.ncbi.nlm.nih.gov/pmc/articles/PMC5832187/pdf/pmed.1002520.pdf>.

[67] Rose K, Neubauer D, Grant-Kels JM. Too many avoidable suicides occur worldwide in young patients. A review. Rambam Maimonides Med J 2019; Sep 18 <https://www.rmmj.org.il/userimages/965/1/PublishFiles/977OnlineFirst.pdf>.

[68] Rose K, Grant-Kels JM. Questionable industry-sponsored pediatric studies in China triggered by United States of America (US) and European Union (EU) regulatory authorities. SF Pharma J 2018;1:1 <https://www.scifedpublishers.com/open-access/questionable-industry-sponsored-pediatric-studies-in-china-triggeredby-united-states-of-america-us-and-european-union-eu-regulatoryauthorities.pdf>.

[69] Rose K, Grant-Kels JM. Questionable international pediatric studies in the United States and Russia triggered by regulatory authorities. Asian J Res Med Pharm Sci 2018;3(3) <http://www.journalrepository.org/media/journals/AJRIMPS_63/2018/Apr/Rose332018AJRIMPS40776.pdf>.

[70] EMA 2012. Policy on the determination of the condition(s) for a paediatric investigation plan/waiver (scope of the PIP/waiver) <https://www.ema.europa.eu/en/documents/other/policy-determination-conditions-paediatric-investigation-plan-pip/waiver-scope-pip/waiver_en.pdf>.

[71] Geoerger B, Bourdeaut F, DuBois SG, et al. A phase I study of the CDK4/6 inhibitor ribociclib (LEE011) in pediatric patients with malignant rhabdoid tumors, neuroblastoma, and other solid tumors. Clin Cancer Res 2017;23(10):2433–41 May 15.

[72] Geoerger B, Kieran MW, Grupp S, et al. Phase II trial of temsirolimus in children with high-grade glioma, neuroblastoma and rhabdomyosarcoma. Eur J Cancer 2012;48(2):253–62 Jan<https://www.ncbi.nlm.nih.gov/pmc/articles/PMC3539305/pdf/nihms430534.pdf>.

[73] Kieran MW, Chisholm J, Casanova M, et al. Phase I study of oral sonidegib (LDE225) in pediatric brain and solid tumors and a phase II study in children and adults with relapsed medulloblastoma. Neuro Oncol 2017;19(11):1542–52 Oct 19 <https://www.ncbi.nlm.nih.gov/pmc/articles/PMC5737275/pdf/nox109.pdf>.

[74] Chisholm JC, Merks JHM, Casanova M, et al. Open-label, multicentre, randomised, phase II study of the EpSSG and the ITCC evaluating the addition of bevacizumab to chemotherapy in childhood and adolescent patients with metastatic soft tissue sarcoma (the BERNIE study). Eur J Cancer 2017;83:177–84 Sep.

[75] Tisagenlecleucel PIP EMEA-001654-PIP01–14-M03 lgt;https://www.ema.europa.eu/en/documents/pip-decision/p/0008/2019-ema-decision-3-january-2019-acceptance-modification-agreed-paediatric-investigation-plan_en.pdf>.

[76] European Parliament resolution of 15 December 2016 on the regulation on paediatric medicines (2016/2902(RSP)) lgt;http://www.europarl.europa.eu/sides/getDoc.do?pubRef = -//EP//TEXT + TA + P8-TA-2016-0511 + 0 + DOC + XML + V0//EN>.

[77] Paoletti X, Geoerger B, Doz F, et al. A comparative analysis of paediatric dose-finding trials of molecularly targeted agent with adults' trials. Eur J Cancer 2013;49(10):2392–402 Jul.

[78] Pellock JM, Carman WJ, Thyagarajan V, Daniels T, Morris DL, D'Cruz O. Efficacy of antiepileptic drugs in adults predicts efficacy in children: a systematic review. Neurology.

2012;79(14):1482–9 Oct 2 <https://www.ncbi.nlm.nih.gov/pmc/articles/PMC4098824/pdf/znl1482.pdf>.

[79] Pellock JM, et al. Extrapolating evidence of antiepileptic drug efficacy in adults to children ≥ 2 years of age with focal seizures: the case for disease similarity. Epilepsia. 2017;58 (10):1686–96 Oct <https://onlinelibrary.wiley.com/doi/epdf/10.1111/epi.13859>.

[80] Sun H, Temeck JW, Chambers W, Perkins G, Bonnel R, Murphy D. Extrapolation of efficacy in pediatric drug development and evidence-based medicine: progress and lessons learned. Ther Innov Regul Sci 2017;2017:1–7 <https://www.ncbi.nlm.nih.gov/pmc/articles/PMC5587157/pdf/nihms901908.pdf>.

[81] FDA. Considerations for the inclusion of adolescent patients in adult oncology clinical trials. Guidance Ind 2019; <https://www.fda.gov/media/113499/download>.

[82] Wadsworth I, Jaki T, Sills GJ, et al. Clinical drug development in epilepsy revisited: a proposal for a new paradigm streamlined using extrapolation. CNS Drugs 2016;30(11):1011–17 Nov <https://www.ncbi.nlm.nih.gov/pmc/articles/PMC5078157/pdf/40263_2016_Article_383.pdf>.

[83] Khan T, Stewart M, Blackman S, Rousseau R, Donoghue M, Cohen K, et al. Accelerating pediatric cancer drug development: challenges and opportunities for pediatric master protocols. Ther Innov Regul Sci 2019;53(2):270–8 Mar.

[84] Reaman GH FDARA 2017 and the RACE for children act: implications for pediatric cancer drug development. Available online: <https://www.accelerate-platform.eu/wp-content/uploads/sites/4/2018/02/1640-REAMAN.pdf>

[85] ACCELERATE. <https://www.accelerate-platform.eu/>.

[86] Endorsements of RACE act. The RACE for children act coalition. <https://www.kidsv-cancer.org/race-for-children-act/endorsements-for-race-act/>.

[87] Forrest SJ, Geoerger B, Janeway KA. Precision medicine in pediatric oncology. Curr Opin Pediatr 2017;29 000–000.

[88] Gröbner SN, Worst BC, Weischenfeldt J, et al. The landscape of genomic alterations across childhood cancers. Nature. 2018;555(7696):321–7 Mar 15.

[89] Ma X, Liu Y, Liu Y, Alexandrov LB, Edmonson MN, et al. Pan-cancer genome and transcriptome analyses of 1,699 paediatric leukaemias and solid tumours. Nature. 2018;555 (7696):371–6 Mar 15.

[90] Sweet-Cordero EA, Biegel JA. The genomic landscape of pediatric cancers: Implications for diagnosis and treatment. Science. 2019;363(6432):1170–5 <https://doi.org/10.1126/science.aaw3535> Mar 15.

[91] FDA 2017. Tisagenlecleucel label <https://www.fda.gov/files/vaccines%2C%20blood%20%26%20biologics/published/Package-Insert---KYMRIAH.pdf>

[92] Goff SL, Dudley MW, Citrin DE, et al. Randomized, prospective evaluation comparing intensity of lymphodepletion before adoptive transfer of tumor-infiltrating lymphocytes for patients with metastatic melanoma. J Clin Oncol 2016;34(20):2389–97 Jul 10 <https://www.ncbi.nlm.nih.gov/pmc/articles/PMC4981979/pdf/JCO667220.pdf>.

[93] Pearson AD, Herold R, Rousseau R, et al. Implementation of mechanism of action biology-driven early drug development for children with cancer. Eur J Cancer 2016;62:124–31 <https://doi.org/10.1016/j.ejca.2016.04.001> Epub 2016 May 31.

[94] Rocchi F, Paolucci P, Ceci A, et al. The european paediatric legislation: benefits and perspectives. Ital J Pediatr 2010;36:56 Aug 17 <https://www.ncbi.nlm.nih.gov/pmc/articles/PMC2933611/pdf/1824-7288-36-56.pdf>.

[95] Ten leading causes of Death by Age Group, United States—2017 <https://www.cdc.gov/injury/images/lc-charts/leading_causes_of_death_by_age_group_2017_1100w850h.jpg>.

[96] Smith EA. The Children's Oncology Group: an opportunity for pediatric radiologists. Pediatric Radiology 2019;49:1382–3.

[97] Pearson HA. History of pediatric hematology oncology. Pediatr Res 2002;52(6):979–92 Dec.

[98] Rose CD. Ethical conduct of research in children: pediatricians and their IRB (Part 1 of 2). Pediatrics 2017;139(5) May <https://pediatrics.aappublications.org/content/pediatrics/139/5/e20163648.full.pdf>.

[99] Adashi EY, Walters LB, Menikoff JA. The belmont report at 40: reckoning with time. Am J Public Health 2018;108(10):1345–8 Oct.

[100] Rose K. Ethical, regulatory and scientific challenges in paediatric drug development. Pharm Med 2008;22(4):221–34.

[101] Washington HA. Medical apartheid: the dark history of medical experimentation on Black Americans from colonial times to the present. New York, NY, USA: Doubleday Publishing Group; 2006.

[102] Wood BA. Paediatric melanoma. Pathology 2016;48(2):155–65 Feb 2016.

[103] Farago AF, Demetri GD. Larotrectinib, a selective tropomyosin receptor kinase inhibitor for adult and pediatric tropomyosin receptor kinase fusion cancers. Future Oncol 2020; <https://doi.org/10.2217/fon-2019-0647> Mar 4.

[104] Rose K, Walson PD. Are regulatory age limits in pediatric melanoma justified? Curr Ther Res Clin Exp 2019; <https://doi.org/10.1016/j.curtheres.2019.01.003>.

[105] EMA 2018. Larotrectinib PIP EMEA-001971-PIP02–16-M01. <https://www.ema.europa.eu/en/documents/pip-decision/p/0182/2018-ema-decision-15-june-2018-acceptance-modification-agreed-paediatric-investigation-plan_en.pdf>.

[106] Mendivil AA, Chad JA, Goldstein BH. Running out of time: facilitating off label approval in cancer treatment. J Clin Pharmacol 2019;59(5):771–2 May.

Subchapter 4.4

Chronic arthritis in young and adult patients, and "Juvenile Idiopathic Arthritis" (JIA)

Introduction

Literally, arthritis is an inflammation of a joint, but the term "arthritis" is used to refer to more than hundred types of diseases and conditions that affect joints, tissues surrounding the joints, and other connective tissues [1]. Here we focus on chronic types of arthrites that are not caused by infective agents (bacteria, viruses, fungi), but by autoimmune inflammatory processes. In adults, the term "rheumatoid arthritis" is commonly used. Rheumatoid arthritis is rather frequent in adults. But also young people can have inflammatory rheumatic diseases. Symptoms are joint stiffness, swelling, pain, and more.

Historically, the terms juvenile rheumatoid arthritis (JRA) and juvenile chronic arthritis were used in accordance with the American College of Rheumatology (ACR) [2], and the European League Against Rheumatism (EULAR) [3], respectively. The term "juvenile idiopathic arthritis" (JIA) was introduced in 1995 by the International League of Associations for Rheumatology (ILAR) [4], trying to unify the ACR and EULAR criteria and to eliminate confusion. The ILAR's criteria have been adopted by pediatric rheumatologists as a clinical diagnostic approach toward children with chronic arthritis [5].

Several different, mutually exclusive types of arthritis can affect young patients. The term JIA was created as an umbrella term for at present seven types of heterogeneous autoimmune inflammatory diseases that begin before the 16th birthday and last more than six weeks: (1) systemic, (2) polyarthritis rheumatoid factor positive, (3) polyarthritis rheumatoid factor negative, (4) oligoarthritis, (5) psoriatic arthritis, (6) enthesitis-related arthritis, and (7) undifferentiated arthritis [1,6]. In adult rheumatoid arthritis, the majority of patients is rheumatoid factor positive.

Chronic inflammatory diseases that begin in childhood do not stop at the 17th or 18th birthday. Rheumatoid arthritis that begins in advanced age, and the several types of chronic inflammatory idiopathic arthritis that start in younger age are simply different diseases. In adults, most types of polyarthritis and spondylarthritis are rheuma-factor positive, while chronic inflammatory idiopathic arthritis in younger patients is rather the exception [5].

There are many reports about patients that today are diagnosed with JIA after having become adults. If these patients are lucky, they find an adult rheumatologist that knows enough about pediatric rheumatology. But often, adult rheumatologist use their adult diagnostics and misclassify patients to have adult-type rheumatoid arthritis, which they do *not* have [7–12]. There is no clearer way to express the key message of a review analysis of the genetics and the classification of arthritis in adults and children: "There is no such thing as juvenile idiopathic arthritis" [10].

Although the term JIA is not appropriate to describe chronic rheumatoid inflammatory diseases and conditions that begin in young age, this term has achieved such a well-established and frequent use in the medical literature that it is also used here. In the mid-term future, hopefully this term will be replaced by a classification of inflammatory diseases based on science and free of conflicts of interest.

Improvements in clinical treatment

The treatment of rheumatoid arthritis [13], as well as of all types of JIA has in the last decades profoundly improved [14–16]. Representatives of the North American "Pediatric Rheumatology Collaborative Study Group" (PRCSG) [17] and the European "Paediatric Rheumatology International Trials Organization" (PRINTO) [18] claim that this is the consequence of US/EU pediatric laws, the existence of their research networks, and of new drugs, in this order [15,19,20]. The European Medicines Agency (EMA) claims that its "pediatric investigation plans" (PIPs) made many drugs "available" for children [21]. In joint publications, representatives of EMA and PRINTO praise the pediatric laws [19,22]. Two decades ago, young patients could be lucky if their parents found a rheumatologist who could treat them; even with the best available therapy, these patients expected a childhood of pain, disability, and external disfigurement, particularly when the joints of the facial muscles were involved [23].

Efficacy and safety of modern antiinflammatory drugs, including tumor necrosis factor (TNF) antagonists, interleukin inhibitors, and monoclonal antibodies (MABs) had already been approved by the FDA and the EMA, based on regulatory clinical studies. Was and is the same proof necessary again in young patients? If not, the studies demanded by FDA and EMA, performed by PRCSG and PRINTO, and paid by pharmaceutical industry would be medically unnecessary and a waste of time, money, and other resources. Furthermore, these studies would have deceived and continue to deceive unsuspecting young patients, their parents, and those physicians and other healthcare professionals that are involved in these studies in the belief they advance science and pediatric healthcare. Then the beneficiaries of these studies would not be young patients, but all other actors involved: academic researchers, regulatory authorities, pharmaceutical companies that are rewarded for these studies, and particularly those employees in pharmaceutical companies that have established a "pediatric" career in industry. This scenario would jeopardize the trust of the public in pediatric rheumatology, in pediatric medicine, and in pediatric clinical research in general.

Justifications of separate JIA efficacy studies

A recent review claims that the JIA research networks helped to approve drugs in rare childhood diseases, thus supporting the aims of worldwide legal pediatric legislation, introduced when it became known that doses and treatment regimes for children were not established. It discusses US and EU pediatric laws and the regulatory studies they triggered. It discusses that most studies were international due to the rarity of the patients and explains that altogether the PRSCG investigated jointly with PRINTO and industry sponsors 25 drugs and biologics, resulting in 13 pediatric FDA/EMA labels, and that these drugs improved the treatment of children with polyarticular and systemic JIA, allowed better growth and improved quality of life, and reduced joint degeneration [24]. Comparably, PRINTO representatives report that in the past two decades new laws, the international research networks, and the availability of new efficient drugs improved JIA treatment [15].

These and further reviews blur two issues. Firstly, treatment of both young and adult patients with autoimmune inflammatory diseases, including JIA, has massively improved. Secondly, this occurred allegedly due to these drugs' separate approval in the "pediatric population" or "children" [14,20,24,25].

An EMA JIA scientific guideline outlines the current EMA position. It lists the JIA definition and categories as per ILAR, key epidemiological data and key issues, including extrapolation of efficacy from adults; PK and dose-finding studies; therapeutic confirmation studies and specifically placebo-controlled withdrawal designs broadly accepted by the authorities. Furthermore, control medication (placebo versus established comparator), combination therapy, study duration, and safety evaluation are discussed. It does not discuss why "children" defined as persons <18 years old require separate approval studies [26]. Such "pediatric" studies are justified in numerous publication from pediatric researchers, representatives of regulatory authorities, and employees of pharmaceutical industry on a general level [19,27–30]. These studies are also justified in paragraph 3 the preamble of the EU pediatric regulation: "Problems resulting from the absence of suitably adapted medicinal products for the paediatric population include inadequate dosage information which leads to increased risks of adverse reactions including death, ineffective treatment through under-dosage, non-availability to the paediatric population of therapeutic advances, suitable formulations and routes of administration, as well as use of magistral or officinal formulations to treat the paediatric population which may be of poor quality" [31]. All these justifications pretend that there is a physiological difference between persons before and after the 17th/18th birthday, which divides the adult from the "pediatric" population. But the 17th/18th birthday is a *legal* and *administrative* age limit. The process of becoming adult is the slow, physiological process of puberty. In advanced western societies, young persons' bodies are mature long before the 17th/18th birthday. And drugs treat the human body, not its legal or administrative status.

JIA and the history of PRCSG and PRINTO

JIA is altogether rare. Including all subcategories, it occurs in roughly one in thousand young patients [5], i.e., too rare to perform clinical studies in just one center [20]. Comparable to many other rare diseases in young persons, chronic inflammations came into the focus of science, clinical research, and clinical care when infectious diseases became gradually prevented by better hygiene, housing, nutrition, vaccinations, and medical care, and ultimately became treatable with the development of antibiotics and other antiinfectives, combined with advances in diagnostic procedures, an increasing understanding of more and more diseases, advances in surgery and intensive care, advances in neonatology, and further advances in pediatrics [32]. Since its synthesis and first manufacture in 1899, acetylsalicylic acid (aspirin) had been considered by the public and by the medical profession as an effective antipyretic and analgesic, with few side effects when taken at standard doses [33]. It was also the mostly prescribed drugs against chronic inflammations in young people [34].

In the US, 1976 is considered as the official beginning of pediatric rheumatology as a subspecialty, when the first American Rheumatism Association Conference on the Rheumatic Diseases of Childhood was held. The US PRCSG had already been established a few years earlier [35].

Clinical studies in JIA began when after aspirin new nonsteroidal antiinflammatory drugs (NSAIDs) had been developed and became available, and when a first group of dedicated investigators started collaboration on a national US basis in the early 1970s [34]. The PRCSG performed the first systematic study to alleviate the symptoms in JIA, comparing tolmetin and aspirin, two NSAIDs, in young patients [7]. Until then, aspirin was almost universally used, despite the "toxic effects of aspirin are numerous and some may be serious" [34].

Initial challenges in clinical studies in JIA included the definition of suitable measurable clinical endpoints, in a time when standardization of endpoints in clinical studies had not yet been broadly established in JIA [20] and most other diseases in young persons. Apart from outcome measures for JIA, the PRCSG also developed outcome measures for systemic lupus erythematosus and for juvenile dermatomyositis, and contributed to novel study designs [24].

The PRCSG already used the new term "juvenile idiopathic arthritis" [34], while the FDA used the more traditional term "juvenile rheumatoid arthritis" until 2008, following the definition of the American College of Rheumatology (see Table 4.4.1, further below). The first PRCSG-performed trial led to the FDA approval of tolmetin for JIA. Over the next decade the PRCSG published findings from trials of six additional new NSAIDs [20], i.e., fenoprofen, ketoprofen, sodium meclofenamate, pirprofen, and proquazone [35].

NSAIDs helped to control the signs and symptoms of arthritis adequately in a considerable part of patients, but not in all of them. When individual NSAIDs failed, multiple NSAIDs were tried for a while, but this approach waned again. Then "second-line" agents, often referred to as slower-acting antirheumatic drugs or disease-modifying antirheumatic drugs (DMARDs), including gold salts, D-penicillamine, hydroxychloroquine, and finally methotrexate, were increasingly tested and used [20,35]. Methotrexate quickly became the second-line agent of choice in JIA [20]. The arrival of corticosteroids was initially hailed as a major medical event, and enthusiasm ran high for several years; but until 1970, the "double-edged sword" of steroid therapy had become apparent [35]. Steroids suppress inflammation effectively, but have multiple side effects, including weight gain, rounder face, mood changes, slower growth, osteoporosis, more body hair, sleep problems, headache, stomach ache, acne, dry and/or thin skin, and more. Serious concerns about the use of steroids and steroid phobia among patients, parents and healthcare providers are to this day not limited to the area of rheumatology, but exist also in many further clinical areas [36–38].

Until the mid-1990s, few controlled studies were conducted with the aim to get marketing authorization for use in young patients. In 1994, the FDA introduced pediatric labeling requirements. Then in 1997 the first US pediatric legislation was introduced that offered rewards for pharmaceutical companies for studies in the "pediatric population," defined by the FDA already in 1979 as anybody younger than 17 years [39].

From the beginning, PRSCG-performed studies used chronological age to define children. The age of the patients in the first study on tolmetin vs. aspirin was 2–16 years (mean age in the tolmetin group 9.4 years, in the aspirin group 9.0 years), the mean height was 132.3 cm (52.1") in the tolmetin group (range 83.8–170.2 cm [33"–67"]) and 130.6 cm (51.4") (range 86.4–167.6 cm [34"–66"]) in the aspirin group. Thus, the largest participants were bodily and physiologically definitely no longer "children." But they were *legally* still minors, and their classification was administrative [34].

Eventually, the PRCSG leadership was involved in the training of the leadership of the European PRINTO [18,24], which was founded in 1996 [20]. In the following decades, modern antiinflammatory drugs were

TABLE 4.4.1 Examples for FDA-demanded studies in "pediatric rheumatoid arthritis"/JIA [45–54].

Drug	Year	Indication	Studies	Reference
Abatacept	2005	pjRA	Study in 2–16 y patients	[33]
	2008	pjRA	Further study in 2–5 y; data in 6–16 y already submitted	[34]
Adalimumab	2002	pJRA	Study in "children" with pJRA	[35]
Anakinra	2001	JRA	S&E in "pediatric patients" with JRA	[36]
Certolizumab	2009	pJIA	PK/PD, dosing, S, T, IG in the "pediatric population" 2–16 y.	[37]
Etanercept	1999	JRA	1. S&E in >500 pts 2. PK/PD in JRA pts 3. Re-analyze PK-data using an FDA-proposed model 4. Study concurrent use etanercept + methotrexate 5. Initiate study in active systemic onset JRA	[38]
Golimumab	2009	pJIA	PK, S, IG & E in "pediatric patients" 2–16 y with active pJIA	[39]
Infliximab	1999	JRA	Clinical study in JRA	[40]
Tocilizumab	2013	RA	Study in "pediatric patients" 2–17 y	[41]
Tofacitinib	2012	JIA	1. MD PK trial in "children" 2–17 y 2. R DB PC E&S WS in "children" 2–17 y	[42]

DB, Double-blind; *E*, efficacy; *IG*, immunogenicity; *JIA*, juvenile idiopathic arthritis; *JRA*, juvenile rheumatic arthritis; *MC*, multicenter; *MN*, multinational; *M&S*, modeling and simulation; *OL*, open label; *PC*, placebo-controlled; *PA*, polyarticular course; *PD*, pharmacodynamics; *pJIA*, polyarticular JIA; *pjRA*, polyarticular juvenile rheumatoid arthritis; *PK*, pharmacokinetic(s); *PK/PD*, pharmacodynamics/pharmacokinetics; *R*, randomized; *S*, safety; *sJIA*, systemic JIA; *SLE*, systemic lupus erythematodes; *T*, tolerability; *w*, with; *WS*, withdrawal study; *y*, year.

developed, and the treatment of young patients with inflammatory diseases improved dramatically.

Drug approval in "children"

In pediatric rheumatology, the dates of 1997 with the first US pediatric legislation, and of 2007, with the EU pediatric legislation coming into force, represent turning points. Pediatric rheumatology is probably the one clinical sub-discipline that has been shaped mostly by the introduction of separate regulatory requirements for the population labeled "pediatric" by the FDA as anybody below 17 years of age, and by the EU labeled "pediatric" as anybody below 18 years of age. The EU followed the US precedence. Since 2007, PIPs are condition for EU drug approval. PIPs must be negotiated with the EMA, or approval is blocked [40–42].

There is no doubt about the merits of both PRCSG and PRINTO in their early days when clinical research in young patients was still in its infancy. In these days the pharmaceutical treatment options at hand were still rather limited by today's standards [20]. Clinicians agree that the introduction of modern biologic therapies has fundamentally changed the treatment of JIA [23]. However, there is a fundamental difference in the narratives about the underlying reasons for these improvements.

Impact of US and EU pediatric legislation on the learned societies in JIA

While clinicians focused on the hands-on clinical treatment of patients emphasize the massive improvement of clinical care [23], representatives of PRCSG and PRINTO describe US and EU pediatric laws, the activity of their networks, and the existence of new drugs as the main causes of improving the treatment of JIA—in this order [24,25]. The European Medicine Agency EMA claims that its PIPs have made many drugs "available" to children [21]. EMA and PRINTO representatives praise the children's laws in common, co-authored publications [19,22].

FDA-demanded studies in juvenile rheumatoid arthritis/JIA

For biologics, the FDA cannot offer patent extension. But since 2003, it can demand "pediatric" studies as "post-marketing" commitment based on the pediatric research equity act (PREA). The FDA approval letters are internet retrievable. Table 4.4.1 lists FDA-demanded JIA studies. Until 2008, the term "juvenile rheumatoid arthritis" was used, then JIA. But not all 2–17 years olds are "children." Adolescents have a mature body vis-a-vis drug metabolism. Also in younger patients international regulatory PK/PD studies are massively exaggerated. PK/PD studies that use additional blood samples obtained in "opportunistic" study situations would clinically be sufficient [43,44].

The FDA-demanded JIA studies asked for separate studies in the "pediatric population", mostly defined by an age of 2 to 16 years, sometimes by an age of 2 to 17 years. The underlying assumption was that adults and "children" are fundamentally different, and that therefore anti-inflammatory treatment that worked in adult patients needed separate "pediatric" studies.

JIA PIPs

Table 4.4.2 shows exemplary JIA PIPs. PIPs are issued for many indications. For canakinumab there are apart from the JIA PIP ("PIP02") three more PIPs for **(1)** "Cryopyrin-Associated Periodic Syndromes" (CAPS), including "Familial Cold Autoinflammatory Syndrome" (FCAS), "Familial Cold Urticaria" (FCU), "Muckle-Wells Syndrome" (MWS), "Neonatal-Onset Multisystem Inflammatory Disease" (NOMID), "Chronic Infantile Neurological Cutaneous Articular Syndrome" (CINCA) (EMEA-000060-PIP01−07-M03); **(2)** familial Mediterranean fever and hyperimmune-globulin D syndrome (EMEA-000060-PIP04−14-M01); **(3)** TNF-associated periodic syndrome (EMEA-000060-PIP05−14-M01). Other MABs have further PIPs for other autoimmune diseases including morbus Crohn, ulcerative colitis, psoriasis, lupus erythematosus, and more.

Canakinumab is a highly selective human MAB against interleukin-1beta (IL-1β), a member of the interleukin 1 family of cytokines that play a role in inflammatory responses and further cellular activities, including cell proliferation, differentiation, and apoptosis (programmed cell death). Canakinumab was first developed for the treatment of rheumatoid arthritis, but the overall clinical response rate was regarded by the developing company as inferior to the already marketed TNF inhibitors. In consequence, its clinical development in rheumatoid arthritis was discontinued due to a lack of commercial viability. Also clinical development in type 2 diabetes mellitus was terminated. Then the clinical team set out to identify indications that are characterized by pathological overproduction of IL-β, and found first CAPS, then systemic Juvenile Idiopathic Arthritis (sJIA), and its adult form, Adult Onset Still's Disease (AOSD). Then it was found that further syndromes, including mevalonate kinase deficiency (MKD), TNF Receptor Associates Periodic Syndrome (TRAPS), and Familial Mediterranean Fever (FMF) are connected to pathologic activating the inflammasome and overproduction of IL-1β, resulting in irregular fever attacks of variable duration and severity. MKD, also described as Hyper IgD Syndrome (HIDS), is an autosomal recessive disease associated with defects in the mevalonate kinase (MVK) gene. In summary, canakinumab is highly effective in clinical syndromes that are

TABLE 4.4.2 Examples for JIA PIPs.

Compound	Indication	PIP Number
Abatacept s.c.	Chronic idiopathic arthritis*	EMEA-000118-PIP01–07-M01
Abatacept	CIA*; JIA	EMEA-000118-PIP02–10-M02
Abatacept	Systemic LE	EMEA-000118-PIP03–15
Anakinra	CAPS, CIA*	EMEA-001212-PIP01–11
Apremilast	Chronic idiopathic arthritis*	EMEA-000715-PIP05–13-M02
Apremilast	Chronic idiopathic arthritis*	EMEA-000715-PIP02–11-M04
Baricitinib	Chronic idiopathic arthritis*	EMEA-001220-PIP01–11-M01
Belimumab	Systemic LE	EMEA-000520-PIP02–13-M02
Belimumab	Systemic LE	EMEA-000520-PIP01–08-M05
Canakinumab	JIA*; CAPS; NOMID; CINCA	EMEA-000060-PIP02–08-M06
Certolizumab pegol	Chronic idiopathic arthritis*	EMEA-001071-PIP02–12-M01
Clazakizumab	Chronic idiopathic arthritis*	EMEA-001371-PIP01–12
Etanercept	JIA*; plaque psoriasis	EMEA-000299-PIP01–08-M03
Givinostat****	pJIA	EMEA-000551-PIP01–09
Golimumab	Chronic idiopathic arthritis*	EMEA-000265-PIP01–08-M04
Ixekizumab	CIA*, psoriasis	EMEA-001050-PIP01–10-M03
Olokizumab	Chronic idiopathic arthritis*	EMEA-001222-PIP01–11

(*Continued*)

TABLE 4.4.2 (Continued)

Compound	Indication	PIP Number
Peficitinib/ JNJ-54781532	Chronic idiopathic arthritis*	EMEA-001530-PIP01–13
Sarilumab	Chronic idiopathic arthritis*	EMEA-001045-PIP01–10-M01
Secukinumab	Psoriasis	EMEA-000380-PIP02–09-M04
Sirukumab	Chronic idiopathic arthritis*	EMEA-001043-PIP01–10-M03
Tabalumab	Multiple sclerosis; CIA*	EMEA-000802-PIP01–09
Tocilizumab	Chronic idiopathic arthritis*	EMEA-000309-PIP01–08-M07
Tofacitinib	Chronic idiopathic arthritis*	EMEA-000576-PIP01–09-M10
Toreforant/ JNJ-38518168	Chronic idiopathic arthritis*	EMEA-001504-PIP01–13
Upadacitinib	Chronic idiopathic arthritis*	EMEA-001741-PIP01–14-M01
Ustekinumab	Chronic idiopathic arthritis*	EMEA-000311-PIP03–11-M02

CAPS, Cryopyrin-associated periodic syndromes; *CIA**, chronic idiopathic arthritis; Chronic idiopathic arthritis* (CIA) includes rheumatoid arthritis, ankylosing spondylitis, psoriatic arthritis and juvenile idiopathic arthritis; *CINCA*, chronic infantile neurological, cutaneous, articular syndrome; *JIA*, juvenile idiopathic arthritis; *MS*, multiple sclerosis; *NOMID*, Neonatal-onset multisystem inflammatory disease; *pJIA*, polyarticular juvenile idiopathic arthritis.

***Explanatory note: Givinostat—discontinued [35].*

caused by or related to pathological overproduction of IL-1β. It failed in two further major clinical indications, and is in development for a further number of rare diseases and one frequent disease [55].

The syndromes caused by overproduction of IL-1β occur partially in young, partially in patients of all ages. There are not two versions of IL-1β, one in humans before the 17th/18th birthday, and another one after the 17th/18th birthday. There is no scientific justification for separate "pediatric" studies with canakinumab in patients before the 17th/18th birthday in diseases that occur at all ages.

A recent publication presents an overview of PIP-triggered JIA studies [15]. Most PIPs demand randomized double-blind efficacy studies plus a mixture of additional studies, e.g., extrapolation studies. To list all JIA PIP-demanded studies would overwhelm this review. Therefore, as examples, Table 4.4.3 lists the PIP-demanded studies for baricitimib, clazakizumab, and peficitinib. PIP decisions are internet retrievable by the PIP number plus the search term "pediatric investigation plan." Until 2017, the search term "PIP" was good, but following a recent EMA website "modernization" the term PIP leads to expired, no longer functional EMA subwebsites.

Academic "pediatric" publications on JIA

Efficacy of canakinumab in patients 2–19 years old with systemic JIA was shown in two randomized double-blind studies. The first one compared canakinumab with placebo, the second one first treated patients for 32 weeks with canakinumab, followed by randomization to canakinumab or placebo ("withdrawal design") [56]. Efficacy and safety of abatacept in 6–17 year old "children" was shown in a double-blind randomized withdrawal design study with 190 patients in 45 centers worldwide [57]. A follow-up study tested long-term efficacy, safety and quality of life in "children" of the same age [58,59]. Efficacy of tocilizumab was shown in a study with 112 "children" 2–17 years old with systemic JIA [60]. PK and safety of tofacitinib was shown in 26 "children" with polyarticular JIA [61]. PK, efficacy and safety of golimumab was shown in patients 2–17 years old with polyarticular JIA [11]. Two doses of celecoxib and one dose of naproxen were tested in a study with "children" 2–16 years of age with polyarticular JIA for noninferiority [62] One paper discusses the regulatory background and study design in "children" with systemic lupus erythematosus [63]. And a further paper confirmed the efficacy of subcutaneous abatacept in treating patients with polyarticular JIA aged 2–17 years [64].

None of these publications addresses the physiological definition of "children" as $<17/<18$ years of age.

TABLE 4.4.3 Examples for PIP-demanded studies for baricitimib, clazakizumab, peficitinib.

Medikament	Studien	Bis
Baricitimib	1. DB R PC WS on S&E in 2–17 y with JIA 2. DB R PC WS on S, E & PK in 1–17 y w/ sJIA 3. DB R PC S T, & E study in 2–17 y w/ active JIA-associated uveitis.	JUN 2023
Clazakizumab	1. R DB MC PC WS on PK, S&E in 2–17ys w/ PA JIA 2. OL study on PK, S & TE in 1–17 y w/ sJIA 3. MC R PC WS on S&E in 2–17ys w/ JIA-a uveitis	AUG 2028
Peficitinib (JNJ-54781532)	1. PK, S&E study in 2–11ys pJIA or sJIA patients 2. OL exploratory SA study on S&E in refractory active anterior uveitis associated with JIA 3. DB MC R S&E WS in 2–17ys w/pJIA ERA and (ERA) including a vaccination response substudy. 4. DB MC R S&E WS in 2–17ys w/ sJIA 5. Extrapolation study to support the use in JIA in 2–17ys via M&S using all relevant clinical data in adults with RA and children with JIA.	MAR 2027
Belimumab	1. MC R PC DB study on S PK & E in 5–17 y w/ ASLE 2. OL MC study on PK, PD & S in 5–17 y with ASLE 3. M&S study to confirm dose tested in PK/PD study (study 2) or determine a revised dose in 5–17 y with ASLE, based on comparison of pediatric exposure with adult SLE Ph3 trial with a population PK/PD model.	May 2023
Olokizumab	1. DB R PC WS study in children 2–17 y with pJIA; followed by long-term extension. 2. R DB PC study in 1–17 y with systemic JIA with OL extension.	June 2023
Sarilumab	1. OL ascending 12-week repeated dose-finding study in children 2–17 y with pJIA 2. DB R PC CB S PK & IG WS in 2–17 ys w/ TR pJIA 3. OL, ascending 12-week repeated dose-finding study in 1–17ys w/ sJIA 4. DB R PC WS on CB, S, PK & IG in 1–17ys sw/ TR sJIA	June 2022

ASLE, Active systemic lupus erythematodes; *CB*, clinical benefit; *DB*, double-blind; *DRF*, dose range finding; *E*, efficacy; *JIA*, juvenile idiopathic arthritis; *MC*, multicenter; *MN*, multinational; *M&S*, modeling and simulation; *OL*, open label; *PC*, placebo-controlled; *PA*, polyarticular course; *PD*, pharmacodynamics; *PK*, pharmacokinetic(s); *PK/PD*, pharmacodynamics/pharmacokinetics; *R*, randomized; *S*, safety; *sJIA*, systemic JIA; *SLE*, systemic lupus erythematodes; *T*, tolerability; *TR*, treatment response; *w*, with; *WS*, withdrawal study; *y*, year.

FDA/EMA-reported achievements in rheumatology in the "pediatric population"

There are two FDA reports to congress on US pediatric legislation. The 2001 report tentatively discusses clinical endpoints to potentially measure the clinical achievements of the pediatric laws; they were replaced in 2016 by regulatory endpoints [65,66].

In an EMA report from 2016 "achievements" of the EU pediatric regulation for rheumatology are discussed: 14 PIPs were completed, resulting in the pediatric approval of new treatment options, including canakinumab, abatacept, etanercept, adalimumab [21]. However, PIP-triggered regulatory studies did not improve clinical treatment. Regulatory studies lead to pediatric labels. Prior to these studies pediatricians had been using these medications off-label which could be administratively and legally an issue, but is no justification to expose young patients to clinical senseless regulatory studies.

Joint papers by EMA representatives and clinicians

In a joint paper EMA employees and key representatives of European pediatric research networks, including PRINTO, describe the EU pediatric regulation and the EMA-coordinated umbrella organization EnprEMA as very successful. They outline further that before the EU pediatric regulation there was no money for academic studies in pediatric rheumatology; industry was not interested due to the limited size of the pediatric market. This changed with the EU pediatric regulation and brought forward pediatric rheumatology. The authors muse that the future will bring expansion of similar studies into further areas of pediatric rheumatology to enable more evidence-based treatments for "children" with rheumatic disorders [22].

Academic publications by EU regulatory employees

In several papers, employees of EMA and national EU regulatory authorities repeat that there is a lack of suitable drugs for children. They claim that off-label treatment of "children" puts them in danger, and that "children" have the same rights for well investigated medicines as adults. The authors conclude, respectively, that the EU pediatric regulation changed pediatric drug development massively in a positive direction [67–70]

Questionable ongoing international "pediatric" JIA studies

Table 4.4.4 shows ongoing international "pediatric" JIA studies.

TABLE 4.4.4 Medically questionable industry-sponsored international "pediatric" JIA studies.

Compound	NCT#	Abbreviated description/pts/centers	Countries
Abatacept	NCT01844518	PK, E, S in **187** 2−17 y pJIA pts;—55 centers	USA, Argentina, Belgium, Brazil, France, Germany, Italy, Mexico, Peru, Russia, South Africa, Spain
Certolizumab Pegol	NCT01550003	MC OL PK, S&E study in **163** 2−17 y pJIA pts. 36 centers	USA, Argentina, Brazil, Canada, Chile, Mexico, Russia
Golimumab	NCT02277444	PK E&S in **130** pJIA pts 2−17y—38 centers	USA, Argentina, Brazil, Canada, Chile, Israel, Mexico, Russia, South Africa
Sarilumab	NCT02991469	OL PK & DF in **72** 1−17 y sJIA pts—30 centers ww	Argentina, Canada, Czechia, Finland, France, Germany, Italy, Russia, Spain, UK
Sarilumab	NCT02776735	OL PK & DF in 100 2−17 y pJIA pts—33 centers	Argentina, Canada, Chile, Czechia, Finland, France, Germany, Italy, Mexico, Netherlands, Poland, Russia, Spain, UK
Secukinumab	NCT03031782	R DB PC E&S in **86** 2−17 y psJIA + ERA pts—41 centers	USA, Belgium, Germany, Italy, Poland, Russia, South Africa, Spain, Turkey, UK
Tocilicumab	NCT02165345	LT E&S ES in **82** 2−18 y pJIA + sJIA pts—31 centers	USA, Argentina, Australia, Brazil, Canada, France, Germany, Italy, Mexico, Russia, Spain, UK
Tofacitinib	NCT02592434	R DB WS in **225** 2−17 y pts,—103 centers—NYR	USA, Argentina, Australia, Belgium, Brazil, Canada, Israel, Mexico, Poland, Russia, Spain, Turkey, Ukraine, UK
Tofacitinib	NCT01500551	LT OL S&T In **340** 2−18 y JIA pts—132 centers	USA, Argentina, Australia, Belgium, Brazil, Canada, Chile, China, Germany, Israel, Mexico, Poland, Russia, Slovakia, South Africa, Spain, Turkey, Ukraine, UK

ANR, Active not recruiting; *DDFS*, decreased dose frequency study; *DF*, dose-finding; *ERA*, Enthesitis-related Arthritis; *E&S*, efficacy and safety; *ES*, extension study; *JpsA*, Juvenile Psoriatic Arthritis; *LT*, long term; *NCT*, national clinical trial number; *NYR*, not yet recruiting; *oJIA*, oligoarticular JIA; *OL*, open label; *pJIA*, polyarticular JIA; *psJIA*, psoriatic JIA; *pts*, patients; *sJIA*, systemic JIA; *S&T*, safety and tolerability; *UK*, United Kingdom.

Extrapolation of efficacy

Infliximab, a monoclonal antibody (MAB) against TNFα was approved in the U.S. and the EU for several immune-mediated inflammatory diseases including plaque psoriasis in dermatology, rheumatoid arthritis, psoriatic arthritis and ankylosing spondylitis in rheumatology, and Crohn's disease and ulcerative colitis in gastroenterology. Extrapolating efficacy from adults was discussed at an FDA Advisory Committee. It concluded that extrapolation of efficacy was appropriate for pediatric ulcerative colitis [29,71,72]. The EMA CMPH came to the same conclusion [73].

Extrapolation from adults for safety assessment in young patients is not accepted.

Regulators have agreed to waive efficacy studies in certain subgroups of children with JIA. Also for Crohn's disease similarity between adults and children is now accepted. There is also global acceptance that partial extrapolation from adults in inflammatory bowel disease acceptable for "pediatric drug development" [29,73,74].

Clinical hands-on treatment of young patients and "pediatric" JIA research

The clinical care of patients of any age with autoimmune inflammatory diseases, including rheumatoic arthritis [13], JIA, and Crohn's disease [29,73,74] has massively improved over the past decades. Different actors and factors claim responsibility. The learned societies PRCSG and PRINTO claim these achievements to have resulted from US and EU pediatric legislation and from the activities of PRCSG/PRINTO. But PRCSG and PRINTO adorn themselves with borrowed plumes. The decisive factor is the availability of effective modern drugs and biologics and their prescription by medical practitioners. Most regulatory "pediatric" studies in JIA and related diseases are superfluous and even harm patients where they expose them to placebo treatment or other comparison below the current standard-of-care. All this is done in the name of the flawed concept "pediatric drug development" [27]. It is allegedly done to advance "pediatric" health care, but the analyzed studies show a different picture. They are not done in the interest of young patients, but in the interest of those that run and maintain a research machinery that has become a self-interest that serves career developments in clinical academic research, in regulatory authorities, in operational for-profit clinical research, and in pharmaceutical companies.

The reasons for this are many-faceted and societal. The broad belief about pharmaceutical industry's alleged shameless greed has made it easy for alleged benefactors to demand executive power over the direction of pharmaceutical research. The demand for separate "pediatric" studies started with the children-are-therapeutic-orphans concept in 1968 [75], was taken up and continued by the American Academy of Pediatrics' (AAP) "moral imperative" in 1995 and 2010 [76,77], and continues until today with the "pediatric imperative" expressed in the ESDPPP 2019 conference [78,79]. There is an entire "industry" with more or less absurd accusations against the manufacturers of modern drugs. But the books referred to here show that enough criticism against the pharmaceutical industry is around [80–82]. Essentially, the justifications for separate "pediatric" studies in the preamble of the EU pediatric regulation swim on the same wave of blanket condemnation of the pharmaceutical industry where it condemns the powers of the market and justifies the need for more directive power of the state [31]. Behind these pleasing wordings are hard hidden interests [40–42,83].

For healthcare of young patients, this should have fundamental consequences. Administrative classification of patients needs to be differentiated from assessing the maturity of a patient's body. If a patient is treated in a pediatric or an adult ward in a hospital is of secondary importance. What is really important is that he receives adequate medication in correct doses. To this aim, the current "culture" of clinical research contributes very little. There is the contradiction that many of those thought leaders who have the best hands-on medical expertise in treating young patients have also high positions in institutions and learned societies that propagate questionable "pediatric" studies since decades [15,16,24]. Once their conflicts of interests are exposed, it will be the job of academia to decide how to handle this challenge and the fate of individuals who have made their careers based on a flawed concept. Trust of the public in the integrity of medical research is an elementary basis for future research.

Is the divide between "pediatric" and adult rheumatology appropriate? And is the term "juvenile idiopathic arthritis" appropriate?

All types of inflammatory arthritis share the same immune system and a common joint target, and hence also common biologic pathways. Environmental exposures such as viral infections, smoking, and periodontitis vary with age, as do anatomy and physiology, as for example endocrine function. In many cases, early onset may also reflect genetic loading. The administrative division of adults and "children" is appropriate for administrative purposes such as deciding into which ward a young patients is admitted, or up to which age he or she may be treated by a pediatrician [84]. However, pharmaceutical treatment should treat the respective person, not its legal or administrative classification.

The term "JIA" has been the direct and indirect consequence of an inappropriate involvement of regulatory authorities into medical practice. It has resulted in a multitude of senseless and often even harmful alleged "pediatric" studies. It has obscured the clinical view of inflammatory diseases in all ages. As outlined earlier, the term "JIA" has achieved for the moment such a broad use in the medical literature that it is used in this book as well.

However, in the future this term should be abandoned and be replaced by a classification of chronic inflammatory diseases based on science, and not on hidden conflicts of interest of some learned societies.

Conclusions

PRCSG, PRINTO, AAP, FDA, and EMA speak of "children," but the patients in JIA studies are no longer babies or infants where newborn-toxicities are to be feared. It is necessary to decipher the carefully coded regulatory authorities' messages. Some drugs are contraindicated in young patients. Chloramphenical causes toxicities in newborns. Tetracyclines cause teeth discoloration in children. Corticosteroids can impact growth. Apart from toxicities in newborns and babies, a population in which JIA does not exist, drugs and modern targeted biologics work the same in patients of all ages, if dosed correctly and if counterindications are respected. This is also the case for targeted antiinflammatory drugs and biologics. Nothing changes in minors' bodies at the 17th/18th birthday. Parents' fears and physicians' and pharmacists' concerns of unexpected side effects have been exploited and continue to be exploited to justify questionable regulatory studies. In adolescents, these studies are clinically senseless, as the patients have mature bodies that need adult doses. In school children, international multicenter regulatory PK/PD studies are exaggerated. Clinically, small studies with limited blood samples obtained in "opportunistic" studies in patients that need treatment anyway are sufficient [43,44].

Companies that develop effective new drugs are forced to organize and sponsor questionable "pediatric" studies that allegedly serve child healthcare. The results of these studies are banal and predictable. TNF antagonists and monoclonal antibodies work in young patients as they do in older ones. Adolescents are legally still underage, but their body is already mature in terms of absorption, distribution, metabolism, and excretion (ADME) [85]. PIPs did not make "available" one single new drug for "children."

The "therapeutic orphans" concept has been taught to many generations of physicians. There are many illusions involved, including that for better treatment of young patients pediatric labels are required; that authorities can and should force pharmaceutical industry to undertake better studies that industry allegedly could not and would not organize on its own; and that regulatory authorities and their employees are free of conflicts of interest.

JIA studies are published in journals of highest academic reputation, including the New England Journal of Medicine [56]. That the medical world endorses "pediatric" studies since more than 20 years in the US and more than 10 years in the EU shows that the thalidomide shock of 1961 is until today conceptually not sufficiently processed. The western world has too long remained blind toward a development that imposed the on-label/off-label construct on "children" not defined physiologically. This has become a true disaster by the expansion of the definition of "children" as anybody younger than 18 years of age by the EU and its EMA.

References

[1] Centers for Disease Control and Prevention (CDC) 2016. Arthritis in general. <https://web.archive.org/web/20160909205959/ http://www.cdc.gov/arthritis/basics/general.htm>.

[2] American College of Rheumatology (ACR) <https://www.rheumatology.org/>.

[3] European League Against Rheumatism (EULAR) <https://www.eular.org/>.

[4] International League of Associations for Rheumatology (ILAR). www.ilar.org

[5] Crayne CB, Beukelman T. Juvenile idiopathic arthritis. Oligoarthritis and polyarthritis. Pediatr Clin North Am 2018;65(4):657–74 Aug.

[6] Centers for Disease Control and Prevention (CDC) 2015. Childhood arthritis. <https://web.archive.org/web/20160909193613/http://www.cdc.gov/arthritis/basics/childhood.htm>.

[7] Feger DM, Longson N, Dodanwala H, et al. Comparison of adults with polyarticular juvenile idiopathic arthritis to adults with rheumatoid arthritis: a cross-sectional analysis of clinical features and medication use. J Clin Rheumatol 2019;25(4):163–70 Jun <https://www.ncbi.nlm.nih.gov/pmc/articles/PMC6240403/pdf/rhu-25-163.pdf>.

[8] Nigrovic P.A. 2013 What adult rheumatologists need to know about juvenile arthritis. <https://www.the-rheumatologist.org/article/what-adult-rheumatologists-need-to-know-about-juvenile-arthritis/?singlepage = 1&theme = print-friendly>.

[9] Nigrovic PA, White PH. Care of the adult with juvenile rheumatoid arthritis. Arthritis Rheum. 2006;55(2):208–16 Apr 15 <https://onlinelibrary.wiley.com/doi/pdf/10.1002/art.21857>.

[10] Nigrovic PA, Raychaudhuri S, Thompson SD. Review: genetics and the classification of arthritis in adults and children. Arthritis Rheumatol. 2018;70(1):7–17 Jan <https://onlinelibrary.wiley.com/doi/epdf/10.1002/art.40350>.

[11] Oliveira-Ramos F, Eusébio M, Martins FM, et al. Juvenile idiopathic arthritis in adulthood: fulfilment of classification criteria for adult rheumatic diseases, long-term outcomes and predictors of inactive disease, functional status and damage. RMD Open 2016;2(2):e000304 Sep 22 <https://rmdopen.bmj.com/content/2/2/e000304>.

[12] Packham JC, Hall MA. Long-term follow-up of 246 adults with juvenile idiopathic arthritis: functional outcome. Rheumatol (Oxf) 2002;41(12):1428–35 Dec.

[13] [No authors listed]. Rheumatoid Arthritis. Nat Rev Dis Primers. 2018 Feb 8;4:18002.

[14] Cimaz R, Marino A, Martini A. How I treat juvenile idiopathic arthritis: a state of the art review. Autoimmun Rev 2017;16(10):1008–15 Oct.

[15] Ruperto N, Martini A. Current and future perspectives in the management of juvenile idiopathic arthritis. Lancet Child Adolesc Health 2018;2(5):360–70 May.

[16] Vanoni F, Minoia F, Malattia C. Biologics in juvenile idiopathic arthritis: a narrative review. Eur J Pediatr 2017;176(9):1147–53 Sep.

[17] Pediatric Rheumatology Collaborative Study Group (PRCSG). www.prcsg.org

[18] Paediatric Rheumatology International Trials Organization (PRINTO). www.printo.it

[19] Ruperto N, Vesely R, Saint-Raymond A, Martini A. For the Paediatric Rheumatology International Trials Organisation (PRINTO). Impact of the European paediatric legislation in paediatric rheumatology: past, present and future. Ann Rheum Dis 2013;72:1893–6.

[20] Lovell DJ, Ruperto N, Giannini EH, Martini A. Advances from clinical trials in juvenile idiopathic arthritis. Nat Rev Rheumatol 2013;9(9):557–63 Sep.

[21] EMA 2016: 10-year Report to the European Commission. <https://ec.europa.eu/health/sites/health/files/files/paediatrics/2016_pc_report_2017/ema_10_year_report_for_consultation.pdf>.

[22] Ruperto N, Eichler I, Herold R, et al. A European network of paediatric research at the European Medicines Agency (Enpr-EMA). Arch Dis Child 2012;97(3):185–8 Mar.

[23] Stoll ML, Cron RQ. Treatment of juvenile idiopathic arthritis: a revolution in care. Pediatr Rheumatol Online J 2014;12:13 Apr 23.

[24] Brunner HI, Rider LG, Kingsbury DJ, Co D, Schneider R, Goldmuntz E, et al. Pediatric rheumatology collaborative study group—over four decades of pivotal clinical drug research in pediatric rheumatology. Pediatr Rheumatol Online J 2018;16(1):45 Jul 11.

[25] Ruperto N, Brunner HI, Lovell DJ, Martini A. Paediatric Rheumatology International Trials Organisation (PRINTO) and the Pediatric Rheumatology Collaborative Study Group (PRCSG). Extrapolation or controlled trials in paediatrics: the current dilemma. Arch Dis Child 2017;102(10):949–51 Oct.

[26] EMA 2015: Guideline on clinical investigation of medicinal products for the treatment of juvenile idiopathic arthritis <https://www.ema.europa.eu/documents/scientific-guideline/guideline-clinical-investigation-medicinal-products-treatment-juvenile-idiopathic-arthritis_en.pdf>.

[27] Ward RM, Benjamin Jr DK, Davis JM, Gorman RL, Kauffman R, Kearns GL, et al. The need for pediatric drug development. J Pediatr 2018;192:13–21 Jan.

[28] van Riet-Nales DA, Römkens EG, Saint-Raymond A, Kozarewicz P, Schobben AF, Egberts TC, et al. Oral medicines for children in the European paediatric investigation plans. PLoS One 2014;9(6):e98348 Jun 4.

[29] Barrett JS, Bishai R, Bucci-Rechtweg C, et al. Challenges and opportunities in the development of medical therapies for pediatric populations and the role of extrapolation. Clin Pharmacol Ther 2018;103(3):419–33 Mar.

[30] Bucci-Rechtsweg C. Enhancing the pediatric drug development framework to deliver better pediatric therapies tomorrow. Clin Ther 2017;39(10):1920–32 Oct.

[31] Regulation (EC) No 1901/2006 of the European Parliament and of the Council of 12 December 2006 on Medicinal Products for Paediatric Use and Amending Regulation (EEC) No 1768/92, Directive 2001/20/EC, Directive 2001/83/EC and Regulation (EC) No 726/2004<http://ec.europa.eu/health/files/eudralex/vol-1/reg_2006_1901/reg_2006_1901_en.pdf>.

[32] Colón AR. Nurturing childen. A history of pediatrics. Westport, CT: Greenwood Press; 1999.

[33] Desborough MJR, Keeling DM. The aspirin story—from willow to wonder drug. Br J Haematol 2017;177(5):674–83 Jun <https://onlinelibrary.wiley.com/doi/epdf/10.1111/bjh.14520>.

[34] Levinson JE, Baum J, Brewer Jr E, et al. Comparison of tolmetin sodium and aspirin in the treatment of juvenile rheumatoid arthritis. J Pediatr 1977;91(5):799–804 Nov.

[35] Giannini EH, Cawkwell GD. Drug treatment in children with juvenile rheumatoid arthritis. Past, present, and future. Pediatr Clin North Am 1995;42(5):1099–125 Oct.

[36] Higgins GC. Complications of treatments for pediatric rheumatic diseases. Pediatr Clin North Am 2018;65(4):827–54 Aug.

[37] Skoner JD, Schaffner TJ, Schad CA, et al. Addressing steroid phobia: improving the risk-benefit ratio with new agents. Allergy Asthma Proc 2008;29(4):358–64 Jul-Aug.

[38] Li AW, Yin ES, Antaya RJ. Topical corticosteroid phobia in atopic dermatitis: a systematic review. JAMA Dermatol 2017;153(10):1036–42 Oct 1.

[39] Hirschfeld S. History of pediatric labeling. <https://www.slideserve.com/marlin/history-of-pediatric-labeling>.

[40] Rose K, Grant-Kels JM. Pediatric melanoma and drug development Child (Basel) 2018;5 (3)Mar 20. Available from: http://www.mdpi.com/2227-9067/5/3/43.

[41] Rose K, Grant-Kels JM. Pediatric melanoma—the whole (conflicts of interest) story. Int J Womens Dermatol 2018;(4)) in press.

[42] Rose K, Grant-Kels JM. The meanings of "pediatric drug development". A review. Therapeutic Innov Regulatory Sci 2019;53(6):767–74 Nov.

[43] Gonzalez D, Melloni C, Yogev R, et al. Use of opportunistic clinical data and a population pharmacokinetic model to support dosing of clindamycin for premature infants to adolescents. Clin Pharmacol Ther 2014;96(4):429–37 Oct.

[44] Laughon MM, Benjamin DK. Mechanisms to provide safe and effective drugs for children. Pediatrics. 2014;134(2):e562–3 Aug.

[45] FDA approval letter infliximab 1999. <https://www.accessdata.fda.gov/drugsatfda_docs/appletter/1999/inflcen111099L.htm>.

[46] FDA approval letter etanercept 1999. <https://www.accessdata.fda.gov/drugsatfda_docs/nda/2003/103795-5102_Enbrel_Approv.pdf>.

[47] FDA approval letter anakinra 2001. <https://www.accessdata.fda.gov/drugsatfda_docs/nda/2001/103950-0_Kineret_Approv.PDF>.

[48] FDA approval letter adalimumab 2002. <https://www.accessdata.fda.gov/drugsatfda_-docs/nda/2002/BLA_125057_S000_HUMIRA_APPROV.PDF>.

[49] FDA approval letter abatacept 2005. <https://www.accessdata.fda.gov/drugsatfda_docs/appletter/2008/125118s045ltr.pdf>.

[50] FDA approval letter abatacept 2008. <https://www.accessdata.fda.gov/drugsatfda_docs/appletter/2008/125118s045ltr.pdf>.

[51] FDA approval letter certolizumab 2009. <https://www.accessdata.fda.gov/drugsatfda_-docs/appletter/2009/125271s000ltr.pdf>.

[52] FDA approval letter golimumab 2009. <https://www.accessdata.fda.gov/drugsatfda_docs/appletter/2009/125289s006ltr.pdf>.

[53] FDA Supplement Approval/ Fulfillment Of Postmarketing Requirement/ New Postmarketing Requirement tocilizumab 2013. <https://www.accessdata.fda.gov/drugsatf-da_docs/appletter/2013/125276Orig1s064ltr.pdf>.

[54] FDA approval letter tofacitinib 2012. <https://www.accessdata.fda.gov/drugsatfda_docs/nda/2012/203214Orig1s000Approv.pdf>.

[55] Gram H. The long and winding road in pharmaceutical development of canakinumab from rare genetic autoinflammatory syndromes to myocardial infarction and cancer. Pharmacol Res 2019; Jan 14. pii: S1043–6618(18) 31983-2 <https://reader.elsevier.com/reader/sd/pii/S1043661818319832?token = A6994A4A9579EFFE8C5E11B4E735A08C61A1D579DEBDF67 9404CD19064C00F22E6A3213D99C400A4D3F1E106DF65EED2>.

[56] Ruperto N, Brunner HI, Quartier P, et al. Two randomized trials of canakinumab in systemic juvenile idiopathic arthritis. N Engl J Med 2012;367(25):2396–406 Dec 20.

[57] Ruperto N, Lovell DJ, Quartier P, Paz E, Rubio-Pérez N, Silva CA, et al. Abatacept in children with juvenile idiopathic arthritis: a randomised, double-blind, placebo-controlled withdrawal trial. Lancet. 2008;372(9636):383–91. Aug 2.

[58] Ruperto N, Lovell DJ, Quartier P, et al. Long-term safety and efficacy of abatacept in children with juvenile idiopathic arthritis. Arthritis Rheum 2010;62(6):1792–802 Jun.

[59] Lovell DJ, Ruperto N, Mouy R, Paz E, Rubio-Pérez N, Silva CA, et al. Long-term safety, efficacy, and quality of life in patients with juvenile idiopathic arthritis treated with intravenous abatacept for up to seven years. Arthritis Rheumatol 2015;67 (10):2759–70 Oct.

[60] De Benedetti F, Brunner HI, Ruperto N, Kenwright A, Wright S, et al. Randomized trial of tocilizumab in systemic juvenile idiopathic arthritis. N Engl J Med 2012;367:2385–95.

[61] Ruperto N, Brunner HI, Zuber Z, et al. Pharmacokinetic and safety profile of tofacitinib in children with polyarticular course juvenile idiopathic arthritis: results of a phase 1, open-label, multicenter study. Pediatr Rheumatol Online J 2017;15(1):86 Dec 28.

[62] Foeldvari I, Szer IS, Zemel LS, Lovell DJ, Giannini EH, Robbins JL, et al. A prospective study comparing celecoxib with naproxen in children with juvenile rheumatoid arthritis. J Rheumatol 2009;36(1):174–82.

[63] Brunner H, Martini A, Lovell DJ, Ruperto N. On behalf of PRINTO and PRCSG. Clinical trials in children and adolescents with systemic lupus erythematosus: methodological aspects, regulatory landscape and future opportunities. Ann Rheum Dis 2018;0:1–9.

[64] Brunner HI, Tzaribachev N, Vega-Cornejo G, et al. Subcutaneous abatacept in patients with polyarticular-course juvenile idiopathic arthritis: results from a phase III open-label study. Arthritis Rheumatol 2018;70(7):1144–54 Jul<https://www.ncbi.nlm.nih.gov/pmc/articles/PMC6032847/pdf/ART-70-1144.pdf>.

[65] FDA 2001. The pediatric exclusivity provision. January 2001. Status report to congress. <https://www.fda.gov/downloads/Drugs/DevelopmentApprovalProcess/DevelopmentResources/UCM049915.pdf>.

[66] FDA 2016. Best pharmaceuticals for children act and pediatric research equity act. July 2016. Status report to congress. Department of health and human services. Food and drug administration. <https://www.fda.gov/downloads/ScienceResearch/SpecialTopics/PediatricTherapeuticsResearch/UCM509815.pdf>.

[67] Tomasi PA, Egger GF, Pallidis C, Saint-Raymond A. Enabling development of paediatric medicines in Europe: 10 years of the EU paediatric regulation. Pediatr Drugs 2017;19(6):505–13 Dec.

[68] Rocchi F, Paolucci P, Ceci A, Rossi P. The european paediatric legislation: benefits and perspectives. Italian J Pediatrics 2010;36:56 Link: <http://www.ncbi.nlm.nih.gov/pmc/articles/PMC2933611/pdf/1824-7288-36-56.pdf>.

[69] Rocchi F, Tomasi P. The development of medicines for children. Pharmacol Res 2011;64:169–75.

[70] Mentzer D. Progress review of the European paediatric regulatory framework after six years of implementation. Int J Pharm 2014;469(2):240–3 Aug 5.

[71] Hyams J, Damaraju L, Blank M, et al. Induction and maintenance therapy with infliximab for children with moderate to severe ulcerative colitis. Clin Gastroenterol Hepatol 2012;10(4):391–9 e1.

[72] FDA 2016. Ulcerative colitis: clinical trial endpoints: guidance for industry. <https://www.fda.gov/downloads/Drugs/GuidanceComplianceRegulatoryInformation/Guidances/UCM515143.pdf>.

[73] EMA 2016. Guideline on the development of new medicinal products for the treatment of Crohn's Disease. <http://www.ema.europa.eu/docs/en_GB/document_library/Scientific_guideline/2016/07/WC500211430.pdf>.

[74] Vesely R, EMA. Extrapolation workshop: extrapolation of dosing, efficacy and safety of biologics in JIA, IBD and psoriasis. EMA history 2016; <http://www.ema.europa.eu/docs/en_GB/document_library/Presentation/2016/05/WC500207583.pdf>.

[75] Shirkey H. Therapeutic orphans. J Pediatr 1968;72(1):119–20 Jan <https://pdfs.semanticscholar.org/f1cb/acdbac19fa56236b919fb7799eaacaa10c77.pdf>.

[76] AAP. Guidelines for the ethical conduct of studies to evaluate drugs in pediatric populations, committee on drugs. Am Acad Pediatrics, Pediatrics 1995;95(2):286–94 1995 Feb.

[77] Shaddy RE, Denne SC. Committee on drugs and committee on pediatric research. Clinical report—guidelines for the ethical conduct of studies to evaluate drugs in pediatric

populations. Pediatrics 2010;125(4):850–60 Apr <https://pediatrics.aappublications.org/content/pediatrics/125/4/850.full.pdf>.

[78] European society of development, perinatal and pediatric pharmacology. www.esdppp.org

[79] ESDPPP conference 2019 website: removed from the internet. The search term "paediatric imperative" still results in a google hit (03APR2020) with its first words ("The Paediatric Imperative. No matter if a company has no specific portfolio interest in paediatric medicines new EMA and FDA regulatory requirements demand ..."). Archived by Klaus Rose.

[80] Goldacre B. Bad pharma: how drug companies mislead doctors and harm patients. London, UK: HarperCollinsPublishers; 2012.

[81] Angell M. The truth about the drug companies: how they deceive Us and what to do about it. New York, USA: Random House Publishers; 2004.

[82] Gøtzsche P. Deadly medicines and organised crime: how big pharma has corrupted healthcare. London, UK: Routledge; 2013.

[83] Rose K. The challenges of pediatric drug development. Curr Ther Res Clin Exp 2019;. Available from: https://doi.org/10.1016/j.curtheres.2019.01.007.

[84] Hardin AP, Hackell JM. Committee on practice and ambulatory medicine. Age limit of pediatrics. Pediatrics 2017;140(3):e20172151 <https://pediatrics.aappublications.org/content/pediatrics/140/3/e20172151.full.pdf>.

[85] Kearns GL, Abdel-Rahman SM, Alander SW, Blowey DL, Leeder JS, Kauffman RE. Developmental pharmacology—drug disposition, action, and therapy in infants and children. N Engl J Med 2003;349(12):1157–67 Sep 18 <https://pdfs.semanticscholar.org/55f8/1745303e9aaec7f4cb85f0b5921eec14a9c0.pdf>.

Subchapter 4.5

Diabetes

Introduction

Diabetes mellitus is characterized by a high level of blood sugar over an extended period of time. It is caused either because the pancreas does not produce enough insulin, or because the cells of the body do no longer respond properly to insulin. There are two major types: type 1 diabetes mellitus (T1DM) because the pancreas does not produce enough insulin, and type 2 diabetes mellitus (T2DM) because the body is becoming or has already become resistant against insulin. Type 1 (T1DM) was previously referred to as "insulin-dependent diabetes mellitus" or "juvenile diabetes mellitus," because it also occurs in young patients. Type 2 (T2DM) was in the past referred to as "adult-onset diabetes," because it was mostly diagnosed in adults. T1DM is caused by autoimmune mechanisms that are complex and so far only partially understood. It results from a complex interplay between genetic predisposition, environmental factors, and the immune system [1]. Before insulin was discovered and produced industrially, T1DM was a lethal disease. Today, millions live with it. It has become a chronic condition with which decades of life are possible. T2DM is mostly caused by too much body weight, combined with too little active use of the body, be it from manual work, exercising, or sport. The vast majority of diabetes patients have T2DM. As the causes of T2DM are to a large degree well known and as it is in principle preventable, it is not only a medical problem, but also and maybe even predominantly a complex societal challenge. Long-term consequences of diabetes mellitus include cardiovascular diseases, stroke, damaged kidneys, foot ulcers, damage to the nerve system, damage to the eyes, and many more.

The individual development of the body over age has changed considerably in industrialized countries. The bodily maturation of young people has accelerated, due to improved nutrition, clothing, hygiene, prevention of infectious disease, and other factors [2,3]. The same factors, however, have also contributed to an increased portion of people who are overweight [4]. Also the public perception of healthy body weight and what is regarded as an ideal weight have changed considerably during the 20th century. Tall and slim people with ideal body weight are presented in movies and commercials as elegant role models. The real bodies in real life are often different. In western societies, the expenses for food have become a relatively small portion of the overall costs of housing, clothing, transport, leisure activities, and more. To eat well is human, and not all humans are resistant to the temptation to eat too much. In former times, considerable weight was equalized with stature and wealth. Today, increasingly well-off people are conscious of their weight, while more people off the less well-off layers of society tend to be overweight. One consequence is that T2DM has started to affect young people also before their 17th or 18th birthday. The dimension of childhood obesity is increasing dramatically. Since the 1990s, T2DM in young people emerged together with the general epidemic of obesity. In young and adult people, affecting disproportionally people with low societal status and income, including minorities [5–7].

Treatment of diabetes

Management of diabetes mellitus aims at keeping the level of blood sugar close to normal. Mostly, this aims at reducing too-high levels of blood sugar. But sometimes, treatment is needed when the level of blood sugar is severely low. People with T1DM often carry a sugar lump with them for such emergencies, to be put into the mouth. In medical practice, for such situations glucagon is used, which can rapidly correct the level of blood sugar.

Lowering too-high levels of blood sugar includes dietary changes, exercise, weight loss, and appropriate drug treatment. With the management of diabetes mellitus an entire industry has emerged that offers to patients with diabetes mellitus drugs, devices and more to considerably improve their quality of life. The predominant treatment of T2DM is insulin or synthetic insulin analogs. Insulin analogs differ from insulin that occurs in nature, but can be used by the human body. There are those that are more readily absorbed from the injection site and act faster than natural insulin, allowing a bolus level of insulin needed at mealtime (prandial insulin); and those that are released slowly over a period of between 8 and 24 hours, intended to supply a basal level of insulin over the day and at night. The FDA classifies today's insulin types into rapid-acting, short-acting, intermediate-acting, long-acting insulins, and premixed combinations [8].

For T2DM, pharmaceutical companies have developed many drugs that help to lower the glucose production in the liver and to improve the body's sensitivity to insulin so that the body can use its insulin more effectively. Generally, metformin is the first medication. Since 2019, also liraglutide is FDA-approved in T2DM in children down to the age of ten years [9]. Next groups of medications that help the body to secrete more insulin include glyburide, glipizide and glimepiride, and many new drugs helpful against T2DM have been developed and many more are in development [10,11].

"Pediatric" development of antidiabetic drugs

When the first US pediatric legislation came into force in 1997, the FDA started to reward a multitude of "pediatric" studies [12]. "Children" were defined as anybody younger than 17 years [13]. But the 17th birthday does not represent a physiological turning point. It is an administrative age limit. The essential assumption of the FDA policy was that the body of "children" is fundamentally different from adults. This approach was also used in both main types of diabetes mellitus.

The FDA issued for insulin aspart and for insulin glargine pediatric written requests, asking for studies to confirm the efficacy and safety of insulin in the "pediatric population" [14]. The insulin aspart written request offered 6 months patent extension for studies in "pediatric" T1DM patients aged 6 through 18 years [15]. Today, insulin glargine is FDA-approved for T1DM in "children" aged 6–15 years, but not for T2DM [16]. Insulin aspart is FDA-approved for T2DM in "children" down to the age of two years, but not in patients younger than two years [17].

Among the early "pediatric" drug development studies in T2DM, the FDA offered for four oral drugs six months of "pediatric exclusivity," i.e., a patent prolongation, respectively, for metformin, glimepiride, rosiglitazone, and metformin plus glyburide. All these drugs were already approved for use in adults. Now the FDA offered patent extensions to investigate these drugs also in "children." Key elements of these studies are outlined in an academic publication that extracted data from FDA medical and clinical pharmacology reviews, product labels, and other published studies that had completed "pediatric drug development" programs through 2013 [18]. In these "pediatric" studies, each drug reduced glycemic parameters, but three failed to reach the FDA-demanded efficacy threshold defined by statistical significance. Only metformin was FDA-approved in "children." Christensen et al. describe "pediatric drug development" correctly as regulatory approval/nonapproval of drugs whose efficacy in humans was already well proven. But the vast majority of the study participants described by the authors were massively overweight [18].

The fundamental flaw in this approach is that the body does not change in the night of the 17th birthday and hence also not the activity of insulin, other intravenous, or oral antidiabetic drugs. The additional flaw specifically in T2DM is that diabetes mellitus does not develop randomly and unpredictably in a small proportion of young people, as this occurs in many other diseases that occasionally affect also young people, such as malignant melanoma, juvenile forms of arthritis, autoimmune inflammatory diseases, and many more. Instead, in T2DM young people first eat too much and engage too little in exercises, sport or other physically exhausting activities. In consequence, they become overweight and develop T2DM. This is not a "pediatric" challenge, but a complex societal challenge for which no easy solution exists. Furthermore, it is a challenge that affects young people before and after their 17th or 18th birthday equally. While the body of a newborn is indeed very different from an adult body, there is physiologically no major difference between 15, 16, 17, or 18 year-old young people [19].

To become adult in modern times includes the development of a personality that is strong enough to withstand the multiple temptations of today's life and to develop a healthy, nondestructive lifestyle [20]. Comparably to the challenges of juvenile delinquency, the epidemic of young overweight people is a complex challenge that cannot be grasped by blindly applying the isolated logic of medicine, police, sports education, school education, or other regimes. But the concept of separate regulatory studies for both major types of diabetes mellitus has for two decades offered a pseudosolution that offers the feeling that "something" is done. This has provided the funds for countless studies for academic researchers in "pediatric" obesity and diabetes with which academic researchers have advanced their career. When "pediatric drug development" began in the US, this concept offered also rewards for pharmaceutical companies in the form of sic months patent extension. And it helped to increase and maintain the reputation of the FDA [21–24]. When a review article on obesity in young people lists as one highlight "clinical trials are urgently needed of medications for obesity that systematically evaluate their risks and benefits in pediatric patients [25]," this is exaggerated and even wrong. Too many senseless and questionable studies have been performed and continue to be performed, but they all describe the challenge as a "pediatric" challenge, which it is not. It is a challenge often seen by general practitioners and pediatricians in young people, but that does neither make obesity nor T2DM in young people "pediatric" challenges.

Also other oral drugs against T2DM were offered an FDA written request, including liraglutide, a long-acting human glucagon-like peptide 1 analog that was approved by the FDA in 2010 as an adjunct to diet and exercise to improve glycemic control in adults with T2DM [26]. The liraglutide written request asked for a "pediatric" study in patients aged 10 to 17 years to establish the superiority of liraglutide in combination with metformin in controlling glycemia versus metformin and liraglutide placebo in patients 10 to 17 years old [27]. There is no reason that insulin or other oral antidiabetic compounds like liraglutide should work differently before or after the 17th birthday. A first report on "off-label" use of liraglutide in a 16-years-old patient was published in 2013 [26]. Placebo treatment in the FDA-rewarded liraglutide study denied young patients in the placebo group effective medication [25,28–30].

A recent paper justifies separate "pediatric" studies in T2DM by outlining that similar PK-PD relationship between adults and pediatrics has been demonstrated for some classes of oral antidiabetics from short-term studies, but that long-term studies showed greater insulin resistance, higher insulin secretion, and more rapid loss of β-cell function and glycemic control in young patients and continues to describe that "pediatric" clinical development plans include two major components: a pharmacokinetic and pharmacodynamic (PK/PD) study or sub-study to support dosing and administration recommendations, and one confirmatory pivotal clinical study to prove safety and efficacy [31].

The EU steps in

The entire "pediatric drug development" concept was expanded and potentiated when the EU pediatric regulation came into force in 2007 [12,32]. The EMA demands for every single new insulin type and for every single oral antidiabetic agent a separate "pediatric" development program in patients young than 18 years in a "pediatric investigation plan" (PIP). This separate development program essentially repeats the key elements of what has already been done in the general clinical development program. But insulin and oral antidiabetic agents do not change their mode of action in the night of the 18th birthday.

Table 4.5.1 lists the 6 PIPs for T1DM.

Table 4.5.2 lists the 6 PIPs both for T1DM and T2DM

Table 4.5.3 lists the 39 PIPs for T2DM

All T2DM PIPs demand a double-blind randomized placebo-controlled superiority study of the respective agent in "children" variably from 6 to 17, 8 to 17, or 10 to 17 years of age. Some PIPs demand a few more "pediatric" studies. Examples for PIP-demanded studies are given in Table 4.5.4.

The efficacy of exenatide in humans with T2DM is already be proven (Table 4.5.4, study 1). A clinical study that tests this drug against placebo withholds effective treatment to the involved patients and is in breach of the Declaration of Helsinki (Table 4.5.4, study 1). It adds no new understanding and

TABLE 4.5.1 T1DM PIPs.

	PIP#	Compound	Comments	Until
1	EMEA-000609-PIP01–09-M01	Recombinant human glutamic acid decarboxylase		2017
2	EMEA-002233-PIP01–17	Dasiglucagon		2023
3	EMEA-001556-PIP01–13	Human recombinant IL-2		2024
4	EMEA-000694-PIP02–14-M02	Dapagliflozin		2023
5	EMEA-000828-PIP04–16-M03	Empagliflozin		2031
6	EMEA-001657-PIP01–14	Glucagon		2026

TABLE 4.5.2 PIPs for both T1DM and T2DM.

	PIP#	Compound	Until
1	EMEA-001097-PIP01–10-M02	Insulin peglispro	2020
2	EMEA-000479-PIP01–08-M03	Insulin degludec, insulin aspart	2014
3	EMEA-000412-PIP01–08-M01	Insulin detemir	2013
4	EMEA-000456-PIP01–08-M02	Insulin degludec	2013
5	EMEA-000387-PIP01–08	Insulin glargine	2011
6	EMEA-000396-PIP01–08	Insulin glargine	2011

TABLE 4.5.3 T2DM PIPs.

	PIP#	Compound	Until
1	EMEA-001441-PIP01–13-M02	Semaglutide	2026
2	EMEA-000783-PIP01–09-M04	Dulaglutide	2022
3	EMEA-001517-PIP02–14-M02	Sotagliflozin	2025
4	EMEA-001533-PIP01–13-M02	Ertugliflozin	2026
5	EMEA-000470-PIP01–008-M11	Sitagliptin	2019
6	EMEA-000200-PIP01–08-M08	Saxagliptin	2021
7	EMEA-001441-PIP02–15-M2	Semaglutide	2028
8	EMEA-000496-PIP01–08-M06	Alogliptin	2013
9	EMEA-000916-PIP01–10-M06	Lixisenatide	2026
10	EMEA-000498-PIP01–08-M08	Linagliptin	2022
11	EMEA-000128-PIP01–07-M08	Liraglutide	2019
12	EMEA-000694-PIP01–09-M07	Dapagliflozin	2019
13	EMEA-000689-PIP01–09-M08	Exenatide	2021
14	EMEA-001841-PIP01–15	Bexagliflozin	2024
15	EMEA-000828-PIP01–09-M07	Empagliflozin	2022
16	EMEA-001755-PIP01–15	Exenatide	2028
17	EMEA-000649-PIP01–09	Taspoglutide	2017
18	EMEA-001030-PIP01–10-M07	Canagliflozin	2022
19	EMEA-000487-PIP01–08	Bromocriptine	2013
20	EMEA-001175-PIP01–11-M04	Albiglutide	2021

(*Continued*)

TABLE 4.5.3 (Continued)

	PIP#	Compound	Until
21	EMEA-001903-PIP01–15	Efpeglenatide	2025
22	EMEA-002360-PIP01–18	Tirzepatide	2030
23	EMEA-001755-PIP01–15	Exenatide	2028
24	EMEA-001527-PIP01–13	LIK066	2029
25	EMEA-001237-PIP01–11	Adomeglivant[a]	2027
26	EMEA-001234-PIP01–11	MK-3102	2022
27	EMEA-000665-PIP01–09	Taspogutide	2017
28	EMEA-000734-PIP01–09	TAK-875	2022
29	EMEA-002287-PIP01–17	MEDIO382	2024
30	EMEA-001623-PIP01–14-M03	Finerenone	2025
31	EMEA-001373-PIP01–12-M03	Naltrexone, bupropion	2024
32	EMEA-001701-PIP01–14-M01	Metreleptin	2020
33	EMEA-000527-PIP04–13-M01	Lucentis, ranibizumab	2018
34	EMEA-000300-PIP01–07-M04	Pitavastatin	2015
35	EMEA-000054-PIP01–07-M04	Pitavastatin	2015
36	EMEA-001180-PIP01–11	Evacetrapib	2025
37	EMEA-000302-PIP01–08-M03	Pitavastatin	2015
38	EMEA-000301-PIP01–08	Pitavastatin	2015
39	EMEA-000120-PIP01–07-M05	Tigecycline	2010

[a] *Adomeglivant PIP name is "3-[[4-[(1 S)-1-[4-(4-tert-butylphenyl)-3,5-dimethyl-phenoxy]-4,4,4-trifluorobutyl]benzoyl]amino]propanoic acid.".*

no new knowledge. It satisfies regulatory dogmatism, and offers funds for the pediatric researchers and the clinical research organization that runs the study.

Empagliflozin is already approved in T1DM. Double-blind placebo-controlled studies to show its efficacy again in patients aged 6–17 and 2–5 years withhold effective treatment and are unethical. To establish the necessary doses in young patients, an opportunistic study approach would be sufficient [33,34].

The third example, evacetrapib is even more intriguing. Evacetrapib is a cholesteryl ester transfer protein (CETP) inhibitor. There was hope that CETP inhibitors might help against cardiovascular diseases by modifying the composition of blood lipids. But the pivotal study of evacetrapib showed no clinical benefit [35], and its further development was

TABLE 4.5.4 Examples for PIP-demanded "pediatric" clinical studies.

	PIP#	Compound	Abbreviated study description	Age
1	EMEA-000689-PIP01–09-M08	Exenatide	1. R, single-blind, dose-escalating, PC CO study on PK, PD, T in adolescents with T2DM 2. DB PC R MC parallel study on S&E twice daily (as monotherapy and adjunctive therapy to oral antidiabetic agents in T2DM) 3. DB PC R MC parallel study on S&E once weekly as monotherapy and adjunctive therapy to oral antidiabetic agents and/or insulin in T2DM 4. M&S study on the treatment of T2DM	10–18 y
2	EMEA-000828-PIP04–16-M03	Empagliflozin	1. Relative bioavailability study in adults to compare selected age appropriate formulation approach(es) with the solid oral dosage form used in adult/adolescent patients 2. OL R SD PG R PK + PD study in 6–17 y comparing 4 dose levels in T1DM 3. DB R PC PG E&S study as adjunct to insulin over 52 weeks in patients 6–17 y with T1DM 4. OL R SD PG PK + PD study in patients 2–5 y with T1DM, comparing different dose levels of empagliflozin 5. R PC CO study on E&S as adjunct to insulin in patients 2–5 y with T1DM 6. ERM of 24 h urinary glucose excretion after a single drug administration in children with T1DM.	2.17 y
3	EMEA-002360-PIP01–18	Tirzepatide	1. R DB parallel arm PC S, E + PK/PD study vs. placebo as add-on to metformin and/or basal insulin in patients 10–17 y, plus an OLSE	10–17 y

(Continued)

TABLE 4.5.4 (Continued)

	PIP#	Compound	Abbreviated study description	Age
4	EMEA-001180-PIP01–11	Evacetrapib	3. OL MD escalation trial on PK, S, T and the effect of two different doses on serum HDL-C, LDL-C, CETP activity and mass; as add-on to best standard of care in patients with familial hypercholesterolemia, diabetes mellitus or solid organ transplantation 4. DB R MC PC trial on S&E as add-on to best standard of care compared to placebo in patients with familial hypercholesterolemia, diabetes mellitus or solid organ transplantation, with ES extension study	6–17 y

CO, Crossover; *DB*, double-blind; *ERM*, exposure-response model; *ES*, extension study; *MC*, multicenter; *MD*, multiple dose; *M&S*, modeling & simulation; *OL*, open label; *OLSE*, open label safety extension; *PC*, placebo controlled; *PG*, parallel group; *PD*, pharmacodynamic(s); *PK*, pharmacokinetic(s); *PK/PD*, pharmacokinetic/pharmacodynamic; *Pop-PK*, population pharmacokinetics; *R*, randomized; *SD*, single dose; *S*, safety; *S&E*, safety and efficacy; *T*, tolerability; *y*, year.

discontinued. That the EMA forced the developing company to commit to a "pediatric" study in patients with familial hypercholesterolemia, diabetes mellitus, or solid organ transplantation shows the degree of dogmatism and fanatism the EMA has reached in the meantime to enforce as many "pediatric" studies as possible (Table 4.4, study 3). Why should parents with a child that has familial hypercholesterolemia, diabetes mellitus, or solid organ transplantation consent to their child's participate in such a questionable study? This study was questionable already when evacetrapib was still under development.

Table 4.5 lists the "pediatric" studies in T1DM that are ongoing (recruiting, not yet recruiting, active not recruiting, recruiting by invitation).

Table 4.6 lists the "pediatric" studies listed in www.clinicaltrial.gov in T2DM that are ongoing (already recruiting or not yet recruiting).

Discussion

It is often claimed that the PIP studies are "proposed" by pharmaceutical companies during the PIP negotiations [5,38–40]. But the PIP

TABLE 4.5.4 Ongoing industry-sponsored "pediatric" drug studies in T1DM.

	NCT#	Abbreviated study description	Age	#ctrs/ pts	Status
1	NCT03875729	DB MC R PC S&E teplizumab study	8–17 y	40/ 300	AnR
2	NCT01996228	OL R study on stem cell educator therapy	6–14 y	1/20	recr
3	NCT03740919	DB MC R LY900014 vs. insulin lispro study	1–17 y	115/ 945	recr
4	NCT02527265	OL S + PK study afrezza study in T1DM	4–17 y	11/46	recr
5	NCT02846545	DB PC golimumab study on arresting β-cell loss in new onset T1DM	6–21	23/84	AnR
6	NCT02691247	S&E of CLBS03 in recent onset T1DM	8–17	15/ 113	AnR
7	NCT03298542	S&T PC DB golimumab study in presymptomatic T1DM	6–21 y	9/15	recr
8	NCT04233034	HCL + verapamil for β-cell preservation in new onset T1DM	7–17 y	6/131	recr
9	NCT02002130	GAD and GABA in T1DM [36,37]	4–18 y	1/101	AnR

AnR, Active not recruiting; *CLBS03*, Autologous Ex Vivo Expanded Polyclonal Regulatory T-cells; *DB*, double-blind; *E*, efficacy; *GABA*, gamma-amino butyric acid; *GAD*, glutamic acid decarboxylase; *HCL*, hybrid closed loop; *MC*, multicenter; *OL*, open label; *PC*, placebo-controlled; *PK*, pharmacokinetics; *R*, randomized; *recr*, recruiting; *S*, safety; *S&E*, safety and efficacy; *T*, tolerability; *y*, year.

negotiations do not occur on eye level. If a company does not "propose" enough, the proposed PIP is rejected and the approval of the respective drug in the EU is blocked until the company has submitted a new draft PIP with enough "proposals" to satisfy the EMA. The PIPs are not voluntary, and the EMA defines the minimum requirements of demanded "pediatric" studies [12,20–24].

Regulatory authorities, pediatric diabetes research specialists, and representatives of the pharmaceutical industry are aware that for the many demanded "pediatric" clinical studies there are simply not enough patients on this planet [5,6,31,38–40]. The separate regulatory "pediatric" studies recruit very slowly, and already in 2016 the "pediatric" studies demanded in the then issued PIPs would have stretched out to 2027 [5]. Today, this time horizon is extended until 2030 (Table 4.3, tirzepatide, study 22). As long as

TABLE 4.5.6 Ongoing industry-sponsored "pediatric" studies in T2DM.

NCT#	Abbreviated study description	Age	# of centers/pts	Status
NCT04029480	DB MC R PC S&E ertugliflozin study	10–17 y	81/150	recr
NCT01258075	DB MC R S&E dose comparison colesevelam study	10–17 y	24/230	AnR
NCT01554618	DB MC R PC S&E exenatide study	10–17 y	29/84	AnR
NCT03170518	DB MC R PC PG S&E canagliflozin study	10–17 y	111/172	recr
NCT03199053	DB MC R PC S&E study of dapagliflozin and Saxagliptin	10–18 y	195/243	recr
NCT02856113	DB MC R PC S&E study of alogliptin	10–17 y	55/200	nyr

AnR, Active not recruiting; *DB*, double-blind; *E*, efficacy; *MC*, multicenter; *NCT*, national clinical trial number; *nyr*, not yet recruiting; *PC*, placebo-controlled; *PG*, parallel group; *pts*, patients; *R*, randomized; *recr*, recruiting; *S*, safety; *y*, year.

the logic of "pediatric drug development" is accepted, it is logic to propose the inclusion criteria for "pediatric" studies up to the age of 21 or even 25 years [5]. However, scientifically and medically this would not make sense.

The solution to the riddle of "pediatric" diabetes requires to challenge the underlying flawed concepts of children-are-therapeutic-orphans and children-are-not-small-adults. This challenge is comparable to the umbrella term "juvenile idiopathic arthritis" (JIA). Indeed, a group of diseases can start at young age. If a young person catches one of them a day before the 16th birthday, he is diagnosed with JIA, but not if the diagnosis is made a day or a month later. Already this is openly ridiculous. Furthermore, the seven different diseases that currently are put under the umbrella term "JIA" do not stop at the 18th or 21st birthday, nor do they change their mechanism of disease. Instead, they are simply different types of rheumatoid arthritis that continue after these birthdays [41,42]. These arthrites are rare, but they exist, and the term JIA is inadequate and misleading [43]. There is also no "pediatric" versus an "adult" diabetes mellitus. The challenges of young people with obesity and resulting T2DM are not "pediatric" challenges, but challenges of young people that grow up in a complex world where some find an apparent escape from the world's complexities by enjoying too much food, and sometimes other "pleasures," including tobacco, alcohol, cannabis, heroin, cocaine, and more. The question how to help these young people is complex, and there will be never a final solution. The challenge of the strategy offered by "pediatric drug development" is that is offers an activism that is clad in pseudoscience. This pseudoscience ignores the blur of ascribing physiological properties to administrative age ranges and calls the resulting studies "pediatric" studies.

It is of fundamental importance to differentiate between two aspects of diabetes in young people. Comparable to many other diseases that occur both in adults and young people, the dynamics of diabetes mellitus in young people are not identical to those in older people [44,45]. But this is a challenge that is not defined by a birthday. It is a clinical challenge most often seen by pediatricians and general practitioners that take care of young patients. Should they treat a patient with different drugs once he crosses the magic age limit of 17 or 18 years? No. The clinical signs that we observe in young patients with diabetes are clinical challenges primarily due to their obesity, not their birthday.

The clinical studies demanded by the regulatory authorities are drug-centric, and not patient-centric. But healthcare should aim at the patient. These studies do not only lack medical sense, but they withhold effective treatment from young patients, as the EMA demands this for all "pediatric" studies in T2DM.

One challenge we observe in the literature is that many authors pretend to care for patients, but have another agenda. Representatives of the FDA, the EMA, and of the clinical pharmacology departments of several pharmaceutical companies participated in a workshop that was part of a preconference at the American Society for Clinical Pharmacology and Therapeutics (ASCPT) [46] in 2018, co-sponsored by the pediatric working group of the International Consortium for Innovation and Quality in Pharmaceutical Development (IQ) [47] and the special population group at the ASCPT [31]. They discussed ways to overcome the obstacles that "pediatric" clinical studies in diabetes are facing, and discussed specifically the potential of extrapolation of efficacy of antiepileptic drugs in adults into the "pediatric" population. Within this approach, the epidemiology of T2DM, underlying mechanisms of disease, and the differences of disease progression in young and old patients were discussed. But one key questions was carefully avoided: does separate approval in adults and "children" make sense? This heretic questions is now openly addressed in several clinical areas, including epilepsy [48,49] allergen-specific immunotherapy [50], rheumatoid diseases [43], and other clinical areas. Mainstream representatives of clinical diabetology have not yet addressed this question. The term "extrapolation" is inadequate. Young, obese people with T2DM are bodily already adults. It does *medically* not make a difference if a young person becomes obese during his 16th, 17th, or 21st year of life. However, there is a fundamental *administrative* difference, because this person is classified as a "child." This, in turn, results the young patient to be seen by a pediatrician. But that does not change the patient's body, which is already mature.

Modern antidiabetic drugs do not change their mode of action in the night of the 17th or 18th birthday. To learn about their use in young people, we do not need elaborate separate regulatory clinical studies. Instead, an "opportunistic" approach is feasible [33,34].

Parents that refuse participation of their child in one of the countless "pediatric" studies in diabetes have the correct gut feeling. Hopefully, this book will contribute to a discussion that will make it even harder to recruit young patients into such senseless and harmful studies.

Harmful studies are in breach of the declaration of Helsinki. Where effective treatment is withheld from a patient, this patient is harmed by omission. Thus, from now on pharmaceutical companies will have to weigh in additional risks. If they are too obedient toward FDA and EMA, they might find themselves in a lawsuit where eager US lawyers ask for billions of $ US as punitive damages. Thousands of such patients have already been recruited into such questionable studies. It is a question of time until first US lawyers will start to search for patients and parents that have been lured into one of these studies under the pretense that they are scientifically robust.

In a white paper, Tamborlane et al. emphasize that they are committed to the idea that appropriate studies should be done to provide the needed evidence needed to use modern antidiabetic drugs in young patients with T2DM rather than to advocate for off-label use [5]. This is the position of a group of leading research experts in diabetes in young patients. But the true alternatives are not to either accept the on-label/off-label in administratively defined "children," or to advocate the use of modern drugs in young patients off-label, as this is done by some (and hopefully many) clinicians [26].

The path proposed here is to candidly address the on-label/off-label framework in administratively labeled "children" as a historic mistake that urgently needs to be corrected. When Shirkey coined the term of children as "therapeutic orphans," he also observed that most clinicians ignored the pediatric warnings in the new labels that followed the 1962 Kefauver Harris Amendment or "Drug Efficacy Amendment" to the US Federal Food, Drug, and Cosmetic Act [51].

The US federal Pure Food and Drugs Act of 1906 invested the FDA's regulatory predecessor (then called the Bureau of Chemistry) with the power to seize adulterated and misbranded drugs. To this day, the US label is not an information intended to be read and understood by patients, but to inform the prescribing physician. The US law of 1906 and following amendments are not medical laws in the narrow sense, but they regulate the interstate transport and commerce of drugs and food [52]. Later development included the approval based on clinical studies. The term "off-label" emerged in 1988 [53], reflecting the grown status of the FDA in healthcare. There will always be tensions between the regulatory authorities that regulate approval of drugs, and the physicians that take care of the individual patients. There are many good reasons to defend the FDA's strict position toward on-label vs. off-label use of drugs in adults, and many good reasons to criticize it. This debate will never end. Most notably, this debate is out of the scope of this book. At present, the pendulum is swinging cautiously toward emphasizing the right of citizens and companies to openly discuss therapeutic uses of modern drugs [52,54–57].

However, the imposture of the on-label/off-label framework on an administratively labeled "pediatric" population was and is fundamentally flawed. Many scientific flaws in the past had to be overcome. The area of "pediatric" research in diabetes has so far expressed less criticism toward the flawed concept of "pediatric drug development," compared to other clinical areas [20–24,49,50,58].

Pediatric clinical researchers, representatives from pharmaceutical industry, and representatives from both the FDA and the EMA admit openly that for the many "pediatric" studies there are not enough young patients on this earth [5,6,38–40].

Why should parents let their children participate in a study that might expose them to placebo, in a time when a multitude of effective drugs against T2DM exist already? These studies lack scientific and medical sense. So far, refusal to let their child participate in a pediatric study is predominantly the decision of parents on their own, although in some clinical areas the reluctance of parents to let their child participate is openly addressed, e.g., in "pediatric" epilepsy studies [59]. The intellectual fundaments of the "pediatric" studies requested/demanded by FDA and EMA need to be challenged both on the level of individual diseases as well as on a general level. So far, patient advocacy groups assume that the regulators' focus on "children" is something positive. The power of the "moral imperative" for separate "pediatric" studies evoked by the AAP has blinded generations of researchers, clinicians, pharmacists, employees of pharmaceutical industry, members of Institutional Review Boards (IRBs)/ethics committees (ECs), and politicians [60,61]. But the deceptive power of the "moral imperative" does not mean that it will be eternal.

Conclusion

The "pediatric drug development" approach in diabetes is maybe the one clinical area that shows most strikingly that this movement does not aim at helping patients, but is guided by a regulatory logic that demands many "pediatric" studies and advances "pediatric" careers in academic research, regulatory authorities and pharmaceutical industry [5,31,38–40]. The conflict of interests this has produced is the same as in other clinical areas. T2DM occurs in young patients, but only in a subgroup of young patients that are very obese. The mode of action of antidiabetic drugs is the same before and after the 17th or 18th birthday.

References

[1] Yeung WC, Rawlinson WD, Craig ME. Enterovirus infection and type 1 diabetes mellitus: systematic review and meta-analysis of observational molecular studies. BMJ 2011;342:d35 Feb 3 <https://www.bmj.com/content/bmj/342/bmj.d35.full.pdf>.

[2] Cone TE. Secular acceleration and biologic maturation in children during the past century. J Pediatrics 1961;59(5):736–40.

[3] Komlos J. The mysterious trend in American heights in the 20th century. Ann Hum Biol 2007;34(2):206–15.

[4] Blüher M. Obesity: global epidemiology and pathogenesis. Nat Rev Endocrinol 2019;15 (5):288–98 May.

[5] Tamborlane WV, Haymond MW, Dunger D, et al. Expanding treatment options for youth with type 2 diabetes: current problems and proposed solutions. A white paper from the NICHD diabetes working group. Diabetes Care Diabetes Care 2016;39:323–9 <https://www.ncbi.nlm.nih.gov/pmc/articles/PMC4764039/pdf/dc151649.pdf>.

[6] Tamborlane WV, Ruedy K, Van Name M, Klingensmith GJ. Can we get it right for youth with type 2 diabetes? Diabetes Res Clin Pract 2014;106:643–4.

[7] Schmidt AM. Highlighting diabetes mellitus: the epidemic continues. Arterioscler Thromb Vasc Biol 2018;38(1):e1–8 Jan <https://www.ncbi.nlm.nih.gov/pmc/articles/PMC5776687/pdf/nihms922546.pdf>.

[8] FDA. Insulin. <https://www.fda.gov/media/119149/download>.

[9] FDA 2019. Liraglutide label. <https://www.accessdata.fda.gov/drugsatfda_docs/label/2019/022341s031lbl.pdf>.

[10] Krentz AJ, Patel MB, Bailey CJ. New drugs for type 2 diabetes mellitus: what is their place in therapy? Drugs 2008;68(15):2131–62.

[11] Vieira R, Souto SB, Sánchez-López E, et al. Sugar-lowering drugs for type 2 diabetes mellitus and metabolic syndrome-review of classical and new compounds: part-I. Pharm (Basel) 2019;12(4) Oct 10 <https://www.ncbi.nlm.nih.gov/pmc/articles/PMC6958392/pdf/pharmaceuticals-12-00152.pdf>.

[12] Hirschfeld S, Saint-Raymond A. Pediatric regulatory initiatives. Handb Exp Pharmacol 2011;205:245–68.

[13] Hirschfeld S. History of pediatric labeling. <https://slideplayer.com/slide/8600310/>.

[14] FDA 2020. List of issued pediatric written requests. <https://www.fda.gov/drugs/development-resources/written-requests-issued>.

[15] FDA 2005. Insulin aspart clinical review. <https://www.fda.gov/media/88899/download>.

[16] FDA 2018. Insulin glargine label. <https://www.accessdata.fda.gov/drugsatfda_docs/label/2019/021081s072lbl.pdf>.

[17] FDA 2000. Insulin aspart label. <https://www.accessdata.fda.gov/drugsatfda_docs/label/2012/020986s057lbl.pdf>.

[18] Christensen ML, Franklin BE, Momper JD, Reed MD. Pediatric drug development programs for type 2 diabetes: a review. J Clin Pharmacol 2015;55(7):731–8 Jul.

[19] Kearns GL, Abdel-Rahman SM, Alander SW, et al. Developmental pharmacology—drug disposition, action, and therapy in infants and children. N Engl J Med 2003;349(12):1157–67. <https://pdfs.semanticscholar.org/55f8/1745303e9aaec7f4cb85f0b5921eec14a9c0.pdf>.

[20] Rose K, Neubauer D, Grant-Kels JM. Too many avoidable suicides occur worldwide in young patients. A review Rambam Maimonides Med J 2019;Sep 18. Available from: https://www.rmmj.org.il/userimages/965/1/PublishFiles/977OnlineFirst.pdf.

[21] Rose K, Grant-Kels JM. The meanings of "pediatric drug development." A review. Therapeutic Innov Regulatory Sci. 2018. Available at <https://journals.sagepub.com/doi/pdf/10.1177/2168479018812060>.

[22] Rose K, Walson PD. Do Pediatric Investigation Plans (PIPs) advance pediatric healthcare? Pediatr Drugs 2017;19(6):515–22.

[23] Rose K, Neubauer D, Grant-Kels JM. Rational use of medicine in children—the conflict of interests story. A review. Rambam Maimonides Med J 2019;10(3):e0018 Jul 18 <https://www.rmmj.org.il/userimages/928/2/PublishFiles/953Article.pdf>.

[24] Rose K. The challenges of pediatric drug development. Curr Ther Res Clin Exp 2019. Available from: https://doi.org/10.1016/j.curtheres.2019.01.007.

[25] Chao AM, Wadden TA, Berkowitz RI. The safety of pharmacologic treatment for pediatric obesity. Expert Opin Drug Saf 2018;17(4):379–85 Apr.

[26] Micale SJ, Kane MP, Hogan E. Off-label use of liraglutide in the management of a pediatric patient with type 2 diabetes mellitus. Case Rep Pediatr 2013;2013:703925 <http://downloads.hindawi.com/journals/cripe/2013/703925.pdf>.

[27] FDA 2015. Liraglutide pediatric written request. https://www.fda.gov/media/125521/download

[28] Tamborlane WV, Barrientos-Pérez M, Fainberg U, et al. Liraglutide in Children and adolescents with type 2 diabetes. N Engl J Med 2019;381(7):637–46 Aug 15 <https://www.nejm.org/doi/pdf/10.1056/NEJMoa1903822?articleTools = true>.

[29] Ladenheim EE. Liraglutide and obesity: a review of the data so far. Drug Des Devel Ther 2015;9:1867–75 <https://www.ncbi.nlm.nih.gov/pmc/articles/PMC4386791/pdf/dddt-9-1867.pdf>.

[30] Danne T, Biester T, Kapitzke K, et al. Liraglutide in an adolescent population with obesity: a randomized, double-blind, placebo-controlled 5-week trial to assess safety, tolerability, and pharmacokinetics of liraglutide in adolescents aged 12–17 years. J Pediatr 2017;181:146–53 e3 <https://www.jpeds.com/article/S0022-3476(16)31210-0/pdf>.

[31] Barrett JS, Bucci-Rechtweg C, Cheung SYA, et al. Pediatric extrapolation in type 2 diabetes: future implications of a workshop. Clin Pharmacol Ther 2020.

[32] Regulation (EC) No 1901/2006 of the European Parliament and of the Council of 12 December 2006 on Medicinal Products for Paediatric Use and Amending Regulation (EEC) No 1768/92, Directive 2001/20/EC, Directive 2001/83/EC and Regulation (EC) No 726/2004. <http://ec.europa.eu/health/files/eudralex/vol-1/reg_2006_1901/reg_2006_1901_en.pdf>.

[33] Gonzalez D, Melloni C, Yogev R, et al. Use of opportunistic clinical data and a population pharmacokinetic model to support dosing of clindamycin for premature infants to adolescents. Clin Pharmacol Ther 2014;96(4):429–37 Oct.

[34] Laughon MM, Benjamin DK. Mechanisms to provide safe and effective drugs for children. Pediatrics. 2014;134(2):e562–3 Aug.

[35] Eyvazian VA, Frishman WH. Evacetrapib: another CETP inhibitor for dyslipidemia with no clinical benefit. Cardiol Rev 2017;25(2):43–52 Mar/Apr.

[36] Ludvigsson J, Faresjö M, Hjorth M, et al. GAD treatment and insulin secretion in recent-onset type 1 diabetes. N Engl J Med 2008;359(18):1909–20 Oct 30<https://www.nejm.org/doi/10.1056/NEJMoa0804328?url_ver = Z39.88-2003&rfr_id = ori%3Arid%3Acrossref.org&rfr_dat = cr_pub%3Dwww.ncbi.nlm.nih.gov>.

[37] Soltani N, Qiu H, Aleksic M, et al. GABA exerts protective and regenerative effects on islet beta cells and reverses diabetes. Proc Natl Acad Sci U S A 2011;108

(28):11692–7 Jul 12 <https://www.ncbi.nlm.nih.gov/pmc/articles/PMC3136292/pdf/pnas.201102715.pdf>.

[38] Karres J, Tomasi P. New medicines for type 2 diabetes in adolescents: many products, few patients. Expert Rev Clin Pharmacol 2013;6(3):227–9 May.

[39] Karres J, Tomasi P, Saint Raymond A. The development of pharmacological treatment of obesity in children. A European regulatory perspective. Bundesgesundheitsblatt Gesundheitsforschung Gesundheitsschutz 2011;54(5):570–6 May.

[40] Karres J, Pratt V, Guettier JM, et al. Joining forces: a call for greater collaboration to study new medicines in children and adolescents with type 2 diabetes. Diabetes Care 2014;37(10):2665–7. Oct <https://care.diabetesjournals.org/content/diacare/37/10/2665.full.pdf> and <https://www.fda.gov/science-research/pediatrics/joining-forces-call-greater-collaboration-study-new-medicines-children-and-adolescents-type-2>.

[41] Oliveira-Ramos F, Eusébio M, Martins FM, et al. Juvenile idiopathic arthritis in adulthood: fulfilment of classification criteria for adult rheumatic diseases, long-term outcomes and predictors of inactive disease, functional status and damage. RMD Open 2016;2(2):e000304 Sep 22 <https://rmdopen.bmj.com/content/2/2/e000304>.

[42] Packham JC, Hall MA. Long-term follow-up of 246 adults with juvenile idiopathic arthritis: functional outcome. Rheumatol (Oxf) 2002;41(12):1428–35 Dec.

[43] Nigrovic PA, Raychaudhuri S, Thompson SD. Review: genetics and the classification of arthritis in adults and children. Arthritis Rheumatol 2018;70(1):7–17 Jan <https://onlinelibrary.wiley.com/doi/epdf/10.1002/art.40350>.

[44] Nadeau KJ, Anderson BJ, Berg EG, et al. Youth-onset type 2 diabetes consensus report: current status, challenges, and priorities. Diabetes Care 2016;39:1635–42.

[45] Barrett T, Jalaludin MY, Turan S, et al. Rapid progression of type 2 diabetes and related complications in children and young people-A literature review. Pediatr Diabetes 2020;21(2):158–72 Mar <https://onlinelibrary.wiley.com/doi/epdf/10.1111/pedi.12953>.

[46] American Society for Clinical Pharmacology and Therapeutics (ASCPT). www.ascpt.org

[47] International Consortium for Innovation and Quality in Pharmaceutical Development (IQ). <https://iqconsortium.org/>.

[48] Wadsworth I, Jaki T, Sills GJ, et al. Clinical drug development in epilepsy revisited: a proposal for a new paradigm streamlined using extrapolation. CNS Drugs 2016;30(11):1011–17 Nov <https://www.ncbi.nlm.nih.gov/pmc/articles/PMC5078157/pdf/40263_2016_Article_383.pdf>.

[49] Rose K, Neubauer D, Grant-Kels JM. Ethical issues in pediatric regulatory studies involving placebo treatment. J Pediatr Epilepsy 2020; (in press).

[50] Rose K, Kopp MV. Pediatric investigation plans for specific immunotherapy: questionable contributions to childhood health. Pediatr Allergy Immunol 2015;26(8):695–701 Dec.

[51] Shirkey H. Therapeutic orphans. J Pediatr 1968;72(1):119–20 Jan.

[52] Janssen WM. A Historical perspective on off-label medicine: from regulation, promotion, and the first amendment to the next frontiers. In: Levy MC, editor. Food and Drug Law Institute. First Washington, D.C.: USA Off-Label Communications; 2008.

[53] Plate V. 2009. The impact of off-label, compassionate and unlicensed use on health care laws in preselected countries. <http://hss.ulb.uni-bonn.de/2009/1936/1936.pdf>.

[54] Mazina N. Recent developments in off-label use and legal implications to physicians. American bar association, health law section, No. 14 Vol. 3, <https://www.americanbar.org/groups/health_law/publications/aba_health_esource/2016-2017/november2017/offlabeluse.html>.

[55] Wittich CM, Burkle CM, Lanier W. Ten common questions (and their answers) about off-label drug use. Mayo Clin Proc 2012;87(10):982–90. Oct <https://www.ncbi.nlm.nih.gov/pmc/articles/PMC3538391/pdf/main.pdf>.

[56] Abott R, Ayres I. Evidence and extrapolation: mechanisms for regulating off-label uses of drugs. Duke Law J 2014;64(3):377–435 <https://scholarship.law.duke.edu/cgi/viewcontent.cgi?referer = https://www.google.com/&httpsredir = 1&article = 3785&context = dlj>.

[57] Stafford RS. Regulating off-label drug use—rethinking the role of the FDA. N Engl J Med 2008;358(14):1427–9 Apr 3.

[58] Rose K, Walson PD. The contributions of the European medicines agency and its pediatric committee to the fight against childhood leukemia. Risk Manag Health Policy 2015;8:185–205. Available at <https://www.dovepress.com/the-contributions-of-the-european-medicines-agency-and-its-pediatric-c-peer-reviewed-fulltext-article-RMHP>.

[59] Auvin S, French J, Dlugos D, et al. Novel study design to assess the efficacy and tolerability of antiseizure medications for focal-onset seizures in infants and young children: a consensus document from the regulatory task force and the pediatric commission of the International League against Epilepsy (ILAE), in collaboration with the Pediatric Epilepsy Research Consortium (PERC). Epilepsia Open 2019;4(4):537–43. Available from: https://doi.org/10.1002/epi4.12356 eCollection 2019 Dec.

[60] AAP. Guidelines for the ethical conduct of studies to evaluate drugs in pediatric populations, committee on drugs. Am Acad Pediatrics, Pediatrics 1995;95(2):286–94 1995 Feb <https://pediatrics.aappublications.org/content/pediatrics/95/2/286.full.pdf>.

[61] Shaddy RE, Denne SC. Committee on drugs and committee on pediatric research. Clinical report—guidelines for the ethical conduct of studies to evaluate drugs in pediatric populations. Pediatrics 2010;125(4):850–60 Apr <https://pediatrics.aappublications.org/content/pediatrics/125/4/850.full.pdf>.

Subchapter 4.6

Allergies and allergen-specific immunotherapy (ASIT) in young patients

Introduction

Allergy is an excessive defensive reaction of the immune system, triggered by external substances that are otherwise mostly harmless. Such external substances can be pollen, dust mites, peanuts, base metals, and/ or many more. Persons can also become allergic to venoms that under usual circumstances are annoying, but not life threatening, mostly bee venom or wasp venom. Hay fever, food allergies and other disease of allergic origins have been described since the first written records in antiquity all over the world [1]. However, only in the 20th century, scientific understanding of allergic reactions began to develop. The term "allergy" itself was used a first time in 1906, and established its place in the scientific vocabulary after initial fierce resistance among the contemporary specialists [2,3]. In 1911, the efficacy of subcutaneous immunotherapy to prevent hay fever in patients allergic to grass pollen was scientifically described a first time. However, the underlying hypothesis was that the pollen were a soluble toxic [4]. During the next hundred years our understanding of the immune system has fundamentally advanced and expanded [5,6]. Initially, the immune system was seen as a mechanism of protection against diseases. Increasingly, we see it both as protection against external harmful factors [3], and its involvement in many pathological processes, including autoimmune and atopic diseases [7].

In industrialized countries, the proportion of children that suffer from allergic diseases such as asthma, allergic rhinitis or atopic dermatitis has increased. It is higher than in traditional cultures based more on agricultural production. One theory assumes that this is caused by the decreasing incidence of infections and by a diminished exposure in childhood to a multitude of microorganisms that in the past protected against allergies by stimulating the development of the immune system (hygiene hypothesis). This lack of exposure might lead to defects in the establishment of immune tolerance. The time period for exposure would begin in utero and end at school age [8].

Also the public awareness of hay fever and other allergic diseases increased during the first decades of the 20th century, including the foundation of patient associations [2].

The concept of the "atopic march" refers to the course of allergic diseases as they develop over the course of infancy and childhood. Classically, the atopic march starts with eczema (atopic dermatitis), the most common pediatric inflammatory skin disorder. This is then followed by food allergy (such as allergies to milk, soy, eggs, and peanuts), asthma, and allergic rhinitis. However, this observation is rather epidemiologic and not a causal explanation; the underlying mechanisms are complex and discussed controversially [9,10]. Also the sequence in which these diseases can emerge is not cast in stone. Not every child with atopic dermatitis will progress through the atopic march. Some will only have atopic dermatitis, followed by asthma or by allergic rhinitis. Others can have asthma or allergic rhinitis only [11]. The atopic march is another sign that the different allergic diseases are based on an overreaction of the immune system. And this, in turn, is another good reason to treat allergic diseases causally and early.

The early decades of allergen-specific immunotherapy (ASIT)

ASIT exposes the patient slowly to the foreign substance or the foreign substances to which he is allergic. It begins with very small doses that are then slowly and cautiously increased. Technological changes to the better improved the injection therapies during the last decades. ASIT was from its beginning the only causal treatment for allergic diseases, including atopic dermatitis, rhinoconjunctivitis, asthma and food allergies.

The pioneers of hyposensitization in the first half of the 20th century learned fast that the key of successful treatment was the selection and preparation of the right allergen, in these days mostly pollen extract. Testing evolved from initial scratch tests to more elaborated prick tests, and more. To this day, allergens are divided for two fundamental different purposes: test allergens, and therapeutic allergens [12,13]. Old textbooks on allergy from the first half of the 20th century show all kinds of treatment modalities for the various allergic diseases. From the 1950s on, ASIT was increasingly used all over the world with different extracts and modalities. Also the first ASIT clinical trials were performed. In the US, individual allergists prepared (and often still do so) individual extracts for the respective patient from a bulk preparation produced by manufacturers, in Europe companies processing and selling allergens and allergen-derived products prepared increasingly more purified and standardized products leading to fixed combinations of various allergen mixtures in one final product, which then had to be registered by the respective national authorities. By chemical modification of allergenic proteins, allergoids were prepared with the same amount of immunogenicity, but less unexpected side reactions. For this, formaldehyde was used more in the US, glutaraldehyde more in Europe. In the early days allergen extracts were mostly used as aqueous solutions, after World War II the use of depot- or semidepot preparations for injection increased. In analogy to classical vaccines, aluminiumhydroxide was used as adjuvant and semi-depot mediator in most allergen preparations. A further development began with the introduction of small carbamylated allergoids that are resistant to digestion by proteolytic enzymes. They are rapidly absorbed via the oral mucosa and are used for sublingual immunotherapy (SLIT) of mite, grass pollen, and tree pollen allergy [14]. Today, SLIT, i.e., administration of the allergen under the tongue, is becoming more and more broadly used [15–18].

ASIT and modern drug development

ASIT was from the beginning the only causal therapy of allergic rhinitis and other allergic diseases. However, the emerging availability of effective modern drugs began to dominate the medical world in the decades after World War II. There is fierce competition in drugs, medical products and medical services. Antihistamines, cromoglycates, β-mimetics, theophyllin and steroids were broadly used to control allergic symptoms [3]. Specifically steroids were increasingly used to control allergic inflammations in asthma, atopic dermatitis, and allergic rhinoconjunctivitis, particularly when they became available for inhalation. The arrival of corticosteroids was initially hailed as a major medical event, and enthusiasm ran high, but eventually the two sides of steroid therapy became apparent [19]. Steroids suppress inflammation effectively, but have many severe side effects. Concerns about the use of steroids and even steroid phobia of patients, parents and healthcare providers emerged in many clinical areas [20–22].

First ASIT publications and treatments were done by clinical academic researchers; pollen used in initial ASIT were collected in the nature [3]. Eventually, ASIT allergen products were increasingly processed industrially. At the beginning, the precise assessment and description of the allergens was done, followed by their purification, and eventually, steps toward their standardization [23]. Standardization of allergens is a complex challenge that essentially has two sides. Firstly, the purity of the allergen, also based on the understanding which parts of the natural allergen are responsible for the allergic reactions. Secondly, allergens act only in interaction with the immune system. Allergens are not on their own more or less potent. Their potency derives from the reaction of the human immune system in different persons. The discussion of standardization of allergen products has a long, complicated history. It is a complex challenge where different logics, interests, and claims meet [23–28].

The subcutaneous injection of allergen extracts was rapidly applied in North America, where ragweed pollen was early recognized as causing allergies. Gradually, subcutaneous allergen injection was expanded to include extracts of other pollen and animal dander also for asthma and rhinoconjunctivitis. The term "immunotherapy" for these treatments became known from 1968 on. The processing of natural allergens, followed by their purification and then standardization, occurred initially apart from mainstream drug development [29].

FDA handling of allergen products for ASIT

Allergen products for ASIT were for a long time regarded and classified as individual patient products, also in the US. The FDA did not register them as drugs, but accepted their use in medicine. Eventually, it pushed for their standardization [24]. For injection with a therapeutic purpose, many injectable allergen extracts are standardized, using a method to determine their potency (or strength) on a lot-by-lot basis. Other injectable allergen extracts do not have a measure of potency and are called "non-standardized." Furthermore, the FDA also recognizes allergen patch tests and injectable allergen skin tests [12].

Allergen products for ASIT can also be FDA-approved as drugs. Such products have to follow the usual drug approval processes, including clinical studies. The first SLIT clinical trial was published in 1986. SLIT became officially accepted in 2009 with the publication of a first position paper by the World Allergy Organization [18].

Four SLIT tablets are today FDA-approved as drugs: grasstek (timothy grass pollen) from >5 years of age on, oral air (grass allergens of Sweet Vernal, Orchard, Perennial Rye, Timothy, Kentucky Blue Grass) from >10 years on; odactra (house mites) and ragwiteck (short ragweed pollen) in 18–65-year-old patients [30–35].

Regulatory handling of ASIT products in the European Union (EU)

Before the establishment of the EU, the different European national regulatory authorities had rather different attitudes toward ASIT, respectively. The Nordic countries had developed a standardization of ASIT products [24,36]. In England, ASIT almost disappeared after several anaphylactic reactions led to patients' deaths and the authorities established barriers including long waiting time after each ASIT session and fully equipped resuscitation equipment [3,18]. Germany became the largest European ASIT market, with the Paul-Ehrlich-Institute (PEI) having the highest competence among European authorities [36]. The major ASIT manufacturers of ASIT products developed their own internal systems for standardization.

Comparable to the treatment of most other diseases in modern times, prevention and treatment of allergic rhinitis began pragmatically by using what was available to the treating physician. But ASIT followed a unique path of development with limited interference from the regulatory authorities for a much longer period of time compared with general drug development. The working principle of ASIT was described several decades ahead of the emerging availability of modern drugs such as antibiotics that were industrially produced a first time only toward the end of world war II. Physicians that administered ASIT, and allergen manufacturers that provided the necessary products remained for decades in a sphere that was rather distinguished from mainstream trends and discussion in medical development.

Good clinical practice (GCP), drug development, and "pediatric drug development"

During the second half of the 20th century, ASIT and allergology encountered several other main developments in medical science and healthcare.

Drug approval became based on regulatory clinical studies following the US handling of the thalidomide disaster by the drug efficacy amendment (Kefauver-Harris amendment) to the US Federal Food, Drugs and Cosmetics Act (FDCA) in 1962 [37,38]. The international framework for performing clinical studies had been heavily influenced by the criminal Nazi experiments in German concentration camps, resulting in criminal convictions of Nazi medical doctors at the Nuremberg trials which, among many other criminals, also convicted a number of medical doctors [39]. Later it was shown that new questionable and highly unethical studies were also performed by academic clinicians in the US [40]. Furthermore, a study run by the National Health Service (NHS) was revealed in 1972. It had documented and followed the life of illiterate African American men with syphilis over many years, but did not treat them with antibiotics when these had become broadly available [41]. The men recruited into the Tuskegee study were told they had "bad blood." Within medical circles this study was known and reported at scientific conferences. But these were times when physicians with dark skin were still banned from participating at general medical conferences [42]. Repeated attempts within the NHS to have the study terminated were stonewalled. Only when the press reported this study nationwide it was finally terminated [43]. This led to the establishment of the Belmont declaration [41].

The International Conference on Harmonization of Technical Requirements for Registration of Pharmaceuticals for Human Use (ICH) was created in 1990. ICH should initially coordinate the regulatory activities of European, Japanese and regulatory authorities in consultation with the pharmaceutical trade associations and agree on the scientific aspects of product registration [44]. One of the results of this collaboration was the creation of the term GCP. codified in the document ICH E 6 [45].

Drug development led to the emergence of the pharmaceutical industry as an entirely new branch of industry. In parallel with the growing role of medicines in healthcare and society, with the growing wealth of the pharmaceutical industry, and with the increasing number and more and more effective modern medicines, also the regulatory authorities assumed a highly respected and powerful position.

In 1997, the US introduced a first pediatric legislation to advance clinical studies in children. It was followed by an EU pediatric legislation that came into force in 2007. The basis for both legislation is the definition of "child" by an administrative age limit that does not correspond to a physiologic change of the body. While the bodies and specifically absorption, distribution, metabolism and excretion in preterm newborns, term newborns, and infants differ considerably from adults, young persons and their bodies mature. The children-are-not-small-adults and the children-are-therapeutic-orphans mantras pretend that the age limit of the 17th or 18th birthday corresponds to a physiological change of the body that requires separate drug approval and separate "pediatric" studies. Scientifically and medically, these mantras are flawed. However, they have resulted in multitudes of separate "pediatric" studies requested/demanded by the FDA and the EMA in all areas of clinical medicine, and specifically in many pediatric studies demanded by the EMA for ASIT.

ASIT and allergen products meet general drug development

In 1989, the EU classified ASIT products as medicines, subjecting them in principle to regulatory framework of general drug development [46,47]. But all operational details remained under the authority of the respective member states. In most countries, things simply carried on as they had been before.

The EU pediatric regulation [48]

This law, modeled after the US pediatric laws, is effective in all EU member states since 2007. Also EU researchers had advocated for more pediatric research and pediatric studies. The limitations that limit the FDA's authority to demand "pediatric" studies were skipped in the EU; PIPs are demanded also for rare diseases, vaccines and biologics. The pharmaceutical industry had welcomed the establishment of the EMA in 1995 as it was an improvement compared to the previous separate registration of each single drug in each singly European country. The classification of ASIT products as drugs and the ensuing regulatory "pediatric" consequences severely impacted ASIT product manufacturers and academic allergy.

ASIT and young patients

Babies are not born immunologically naive. The immune system begins to develop early in pregnancy. In the first weeks and months after birth, the immune system fine-tunes key functions in the face of direct stimulation from environmental signals not previously encountered during fetal life. The response patterns acquired during this period persist into adult life. The immune system gradually matures during infancy. Early protection against many infectious diseases previously experienced by the mother is given by antibodies transferred from the mother through the placenta and in the breast milk. Thereafter, young children become more vulnerable to infections, although their innate and adaptive immune system works already. Today's vaccinations stimulate protective immune responses in the maturing immune system. Children also go through viral, bacterial and parasitic infections. Most are fought off and controlled by immune responses. Once the patient is recovered, the thus stimulated antigens result in an immunological memory, and gradually young persons suffer fewer infections. However, the immune system can also become overreactive, which results in allergic diseases [49,50].

Allergic rhinitis is the most common chronic condition in children. It is an immunologic, IgE-mediated disease that produces nasal symptoms such as sneezing and congestion. When also the eyes' conjunctiva is inflamed, we speak of allergic rhinoconjunctivitis. Allergic rhinitis is most prevalent during school age, affecting up to 15% of young persons aged 6 to 7 years, and 40% of those aged 13–14 years old. Roughly 80% of allergic rhinitis develop before the age of twenty years [51].

The pediatric warnings introduced into drug labels from 1962 on were adequate for preterm newborns, term newborns and small infants. They were based on observed and reported toxicities of antibiotics in preterm newborns in the 1950s [52–55]. As allergic rhinitis and rhinoconjunctivitis develop mostly from school age on, these pediatric warnings were never relevant in the clinical treatment of allergic rhinitis in young patients. Pediatricians were trained to consider correct dosing of medications used to ease the symptoms of allergic rhinitis [56]. Most reviews over treatment modalities of allergic rhinitis do not even mention the separate "pediatric" approval of drugs used to alleviate its symptoms [51,57–59].

The German Therapy Allergen Ordinance (TAO) [Therapieallergene-Verordnung, TAV]

In 2008, Germany introduced an ordinance requiring new registration of ASIT product for allergic rhinoconjunctivitis as medicines based on clinic studies ["Therapieallergene-Verordnung" (TAV)] [60,61]. Without submitting a marketing authorization application, ASIT products would lose marketability after three years (and many did). If a marketing authorization application had been submitted, the PEI could extend the deadline for clinical data submission.

Interaction of the German TAO and the EU pediatric regulation

There was a multitude of ASIT products of very different quality on the German market. Shortly before the German TAO had been introduced, the EU pediatric regulation had come into force. Thus, ASIT products were now confronted with the EMA crusade for "pediatric" studies. EMA and PEI developed jointly a "standard PIP" for ASIT products, which now is in its 4th version [61,62]. This standard PIP mandates (A) a dose-finding study in adults; (B) extrapolation of dose-finding from adults; inclusion of a dose-finding study in the "pediatric population," or its absence, should be justified particularly for studies with SLIT. (C) from each manufacturer for one leading product a double-blind 5-years placebo-controlled "pediatric" efficacy study (three years treatment, two years follow-up), either as separate studies in patients 5–11 and 12–17 years old, or one study in patients 5–17 years old with separate cohorts. Fifty-eight such 5-years double-blind placebo-controlled studies were demanded on the basis of the PIPs issued in 2010, respectively, for the two populations of 5–11 and 12–17-year-old patients [63]. Depending on the number of patients required per study, these 2 × 58 studies would require tens of thousands patients [64,65].

Table 4.6.1 lists all ASIT PIPs listed on the EMA website May 2, 2020.

The Swiss special path

Switzerland allowed simplified retrospective approval of ASIT products with the exception of recombinant allergens [66]. This approach is based on common sense. ASIT became known in a time when double-blind randomized placebo-controlled clinical studies were not yet standard in medicine.

International regulatory conferences on allergen products for ASIT

Since 1985, it became increasingly easy to prepare natural and recombinant allergen molecules and to analyze them down to the submolecular level. Academic international societies (the International Association of Allergy and Clinical Immunology [IAACI] and the International Union of Immunological Society [IUIS]) discussed standardization. The World Health Organization (WHO) approved several allergen extract standards, but they never came into use as no acceptance between manufacturers, the FDA, and the other regulatory authorities was achieved. The CREATE project (development of certified reference materials for allergenic products and validation

TABLE 4.6.1 ASIT PIPs (02 MAY 2020—89 results).

#	PIP #	Product	App
1	EMEA-001481-PIP01-13-M03	Peanut AE	CP
2	EMEA-000924-PIP01-10	Phleum pratense AE	SL
3	EMEA-000919-PIP01-10	BA AE	SL
4	EMEA-000920-PIP01-10	DP pteronyssimus AE	SL
5	EMEA-000319-PIP01-08-M03	HDM AE	SL
6	EMEA-000959-PIP01-10-	Aqueous birch AE	SL
7	EMEA-001258-PIP01-11-M05	DP pteronyssimus, DP farinae AE	SL
8	EMEA-000847-PIP01-10-M01	Allergens from DP pteronyssimus + DP farinae	SC
9	EMEA-00960-PIP01-10	Aquaeous AE of DP pteronyssimus	SL
10	EMEA-000947-PIP01-10	Modified AE of DP farinae	SC
11	EMEA-000949-PIP01-10	Modified AE of DP pteronyssimus	SC
12	EMEA-000933-PIP01-10	Modified AE of DP farinae	SC
13	EMEA-000962-PIP01-10	Aqueous AE of grass pollen	SL
14	EMEA-000957-PIP01-10	Aqueous AE of rye pollen	SC
15	EMEA-000908-PIP01-10	AE of corylus avellana pollen	SL
16	EMEA-000903-PIP01-10	AE of BV pollen	SL
17	EMEA-000910-PIP01-10	AE of secale cereale pollen	SL
18	EMEA-000909-PIP01-10	AE of phleum pratense pollen	SL
19	EMEA-000935-PIP01-10	Modified AE of DP pteronyssimus	SC
20	EMEA-000941-PIP01-10	Modified AE of hazel pollen	SC
21	EMEA-000946-PIP01-10	Modified AE of birch pollen	SC
22	EMEA-000940-PIP01-10	Modified AE of grass pollen	SC
23	EMEA-000955-PIP01-10	Modified AE of hazel pollen	SC
24	EMEA-000943-PIP01-10	Modified AE of rye pollen	SC
25	EMEA-000954-PIP01-10	Modified AE of grass pollen	SC
26	EMEA-000932-PIP01-10	Modified AE of birch pollen	SC
27	EMEA-000906-PIP01-10	AE of alnus glutinosa pollen	SL
28	EMEA-000860-PIP01-10-M01	AEs of DP farinae + DP pteronyssimus	SL
29	EMEA-000888-PIP01-10	Allergens of birch pollen (BV)	SL
30	EMEA-000866-PIP01-10	AEs of DP farinae + DP pteronyssimus	OS

(Continued)

TABLE 4.6.1 (Continued)

#	PIP #	Product	App
31	EMEA-000948-PIP01-10	Modified AE of DP farinae + DP pteronyssimus	SC
32	EMEA-000966-PIP01-10	Aqueous AE of phleum pratense pollen	SL
33	EMEA-000934-PIP01-10	Modified AE of DP farinae + DP pteronyssimus	SC
34	EMEA-000961-PIP01-10	Aqueous AE of DP farinae + DP pteronyssimus	SL
35	EMEA-000951-PIP01-10	Modified AE of grass and cereal pollen	SC
36	EMEA-000945-PIP01-10	Modified AE of birch and hazel pollen	SC
37	EMEA-000942-PIP01-10	Modified AE of phleum pratense pollen	SC
38	EMEA-000950-PIP01-10	Modified AE of grass and birch pollen	SC
39	EMEA-000937-PIP01-10	Modified AE of grass and cereal pollen	SC
40	EMEA-000944-PIP01-10	Modiied AE of birch, alder and hazel pollen	SC
41	EMEA-000953-PIP01-10	Modified AE of grass and rye pollen	SC
42	EMEA-000939-PIP01-10	Modified AE of grass and rye pollen	SC
43	EMEA-000963-PIP01-10	Aqueous AE of grass and birch pollen	SL
44	EMEA-000965-PIP01-10	Aqueous AE of grass and rye pollen	SL
45	EMEA-000956-PIP01-10	Modified AE of phleum pratense pollen	SC
46	EMEA-000938-PIP01-10	Modified AE of grass and rye pollen	SC
47	EMEA-000964-PIP01-10	Aqueous AE of grass and cereal pollen	SL
48	EMEA-000931-PIP01-10	Modified AE of birch and hazel pollen	SC
49	EMEA-000930-PIP01-10	Modified AE of birch, alder and hazel pollen	SC
50	EMEA-000936-PIP01-10	Modified AE of grass and birch pollen	SC

(*Continued*)

TABLE 4.6.1 (Continued)

#	PIP #	Product	App
51	EMEA-000958-PIP01-10	Aqueous AE of birch, alder and hazel pollen	SL
52	EMEA-000929-PIP01-10	Modified AE of grass and mugwort pollen	SC
53	EMEA-000918-PIP01-10	Mixture of birch, alder and hazel AEs	SL
54	EMEA-000926-PIP01-10	Mixture of DP pteronyssinus and DP farinae AEs	SL
55	EMEA-000925-PIP01-10	Mixture of phleum pratense and secale cereale AEs	SL
56	EMEA-000662-PIP01-09	AHADGP AE of birch, alder and hazel pollen (RW)	SC
57	EMEA-001011-PIP01-10-M01	Modified HDM AE (DP pteronyssinus + DP farinae)	SC
58	EMEA-001014-PIP01-10-M01	Modified HDM AE (DP pteronyssinus + DP farinae)	SL
59	EMEA-000662-PIP02-09-M03	AHADGP AE of birch, alder and hazel pollen	SC
60	EMEA-000630-PIP02-09-M03	AHADGP AE of BA pollen	SC
61	EMEA-000837-PIP01-10-M01	AHADGP AE of birch pollen	SC
62	EMEA-000838-PIP01-10-M01	AHADGP AE of birch, alder and hazel pollen	SC
63	EMEA-001015-PIP01-10	Modified HDM AE (DP pteronyssinus + DP farinae)	SL
64	EMEA-000977-PIP01-10	Modified HDM AE (DP pteronyssinus + DP farinae)	SL
65	EMEA-000911-PIP01-10	AE of BV, corlyus avellana, and alnus glutinosa pollen	SL
66	EMEA-000907-PIP01-10	AE of DP pteronyssinus + DP farinae	SL
67	EMEA-000902-PIP01-10	Adsorbed modified AE of DP pteronyssinus + DP farinae	SC
68	EMEA-000904-PIP01-10	AE of LP, PP + POP pollen	SL
69	EMEA-000921-PIP01-10	AEs of PP, DG, festuca elatior, LP + POP	SL
70	EMEA-000839-PIP01-10	AHADGP AE of PP pollen	SC

(*Continued*)

TABLE 4.6.1 (Continued)

#	PIP #	Product	App
71	EMEA-000976-PIP01-10	AE of DG, anthoxanthum odoratum, LP, POP, + PP	SL
72	EMEA-000905-PIP01-10	AE of LP, PP, POP, secale cereale pollen	SL
73	EMEA-000923-PIP01-10	AEs of PP, DG, FE, LP + POP	SL
74	EMEA-000922-PIP01-10	AEs of PP, DG, FE, LP, POP, and secale cereale	SL
75	EMEA-000840-PIP01-10	AHADGP AEs of PP, DG, FE, LP, and POP	SC
76	EMEA-000841-PIP01-10	AHADGP AEs PP, DG, FE, LP, POP, and secale cereale	SC
77	EMEA-000795-PIP01-09-M01	AHADGP AE of PP	SC
78	EMEA-000794-PIP01-09-M01	AHADGP AE of PP, DG, FE, LP, and POP	SC
79	EMEA-000792-PIP01-09-M01	AHADGP AE of PP, DG, FE, LP, POP, and secale cereale	SC
80	EMEA-001054-PIP01-10-M03	Cat-PAD	ID
81	EMEA-000835-PIP01-10	AE of DP pteronyssinus	SC
82	EMEA-000836-PIP01-10	AE of DP pteronyssinus + DP farinae	SC
83	EMEA-000834-PIP01-10	AE of DP farinae	SC
84	EMEA-000742-PIP01-09	Recombinant Bet v 1 folding variant	SC
85	EMEA-000793-PIP01-09	AHADGP AE of PP and secale cereale pollen	SC
86	EMEA-000790-PIP01-09	AHADGP AE of PP, DG, FE, LP, + POP pollen	SC
87	EMEA-000791-PIP01-09	AHADGP AE of mixed grass pollen + secale cereale pollen	SC
88	EMEA-000789-PIP01-09	AHADGP AE of mixed grass pollen + mixed tree pollen	SC
89	EMEA-000337-PIP01-08	Aqueous extract of DG, FP, HL, LP, PP and POP	SL

AE, Allergen extract; *AHADGP*, aluminum hydroxide adsorbed, depgimented glutaraldehyde polymerized; *BA*, betula alba; *BV*, betula verrucosa; *APP*, way of application; *CP*, cutaneous patch; *DG*, dactylis glomerata; *DP*, dermatophagoides; *FE*, festuca elatior; *FP*, festuca pratensis; *HDM*, house dust mites; *HL*, holcus lanatus; *ID*, intradermal; *LP*, lolium perenne; *OS*, oral solution; *POP*, poa pratensis; *PP*, phleum pratense; *SC*, subcutaneous; *SL*, sublingual.

of methods for their quantification) was supported with generous funding from the EU [23].

Since 1985, every few years regulators from the FDA, European countries, academic researchers on ASIT, and representatives of allergen producing manufacturers meet at an international Paul-Ehrlich Seminar (IPES). The last such event took place in 2017 in Bonn, Germany, the next one is planned for 2020, again in Bonn, Germany [67–70].

These were and are not meetings on eye level. Everybody participating in such a meeting is aware of its fundamental rules. In controversial questions, the regulatory authorities decide. Regulatory authorities act within the legal and political framework set by their respective national or regional government. Within this framework, they have some autonomy of decision. Specifically for the representatives of the manufacturers, these meetings are a tightrope walk. Regarding the "pediatric" studies demanded by the EMA, most scientists working in companies that manufacture ASIT products are aware that there is no medical sense in them—they get negative feedback from discussions with countless clinicians. They also know that the EMA is adamant and that its representatives *speak* of "close collaboration between academia, industry and drug regulators." But they *mean* that they expect obedience [63]. Double-blind placebo-controlled ASIT studies in young patients have already been characterized as clinically and ethically questionable [64], without changing the EMA position. Thus, the controversial positions will be presented in 2020 in a "Pro-Con-Session," in a friendly, academic atmosphere [69], with no substantial movements or results to be expected.

Pediatric ASIT studies in www.clinicaltrials.gov

As of April 2020, the search terms "allergic rhinoconjunctivitis," "child," and "industry-funded" resulted in 31 studies listed in www.clinicaltrials.gov. The search terms "sublingual," "child," "industry-funded" and "allergic rhinoconjunctivitis" resulted in 8 studies in www.clinicaltrials.gov, and the search terms "allergic rhinitis," "child," and "industry-funded" resulted in 273 studies. Of these 273 studies, the vast majority investigated antihistamines, corticosteroids, montelukast and several other drugs and biologics in various formulations (nasal sprach, inhalation, tablets, drops, sirup, and more). Those studies that investigat(ed) ASIT products are listed in Table 4.6.2 and Table 4.6.3.

Apart from some small ASIT studies [83], "pediatric" studies were performed almost only with SLIT, see Table 4.6.2. One house dust mites study in 5–17 year old patients was terminated following a drug safety monitoring board decision (study 7, Table 4.6.2). One SCIT study in children aged 3–11 years (study 4, Table 4.6.2) and one SLIT study in children aged 5–11 years are recruiting, furthermore one SLIT study in "children" aged 5–17 years is recruiting (study 9, Table 4.6.2). A relevant part of the patients in study 9 are physiologically no longer children.

Table 4.6.3 lists the ASIT studies that include minors that are listed in www.clinicaltrials.gov. We observe the tendency to include adults and minor patients into pivotal studies, away from recruiting exclusively "children," administratively defined by the age limit of <18 years.

TABLE 4.6.2 "Pediatric" ASIT studies in patiens < 17y including minors in ARC, AR, and asthma.

	NCT #	Study	# of ctrs/pts	Age	Status
1	NCT00841256	DB R PC grass pollen SLIT	1/ 207	4-11y	Completed [71]
2	NCT00409409	R DB PC S + E study of SLIT in GP ARC	1/ 278	5–17y	Completed [72]
3	NCT02478398	R PC RAGWITEK SLIT E + S in RI ARC	?/ 1025	4–17y	Completed
4	NCT03963947	S + E of Beltavac HDM SCIT	1/ 97	3–11y	Recruiting
5	NCT04145219	DB PC E + S study of SLIT in HDMI AR	4/ 1370	5–11y	Recruiting
6	NCT01921257	S of Cat-PAD SCIT in cat-allergic pts	3/17	5–11y	Completed [73]
7	NCT01199133	SLIT in house dust mite allergy	471	5–17y	Terminated
8	NCT01919554	SLIT in house dust mit allergy	37	12–17y	Completed
9	NCT03654976	R DB PC E study of HDM SLIT	600	5–17y	Recruiting
10	NCT04004351	SLIT in HDMI AR and/or Asthma	1'531	5–17y	Completed
11	NCT02295969	SLIT in GPI AR	307	5–9y	Completed
12	NCT00408616	DB PC Grazax SLIT in GPI ARC	253	5–16y	Completed [74]
13	NCT00550550	DB PC study of grass SLIT in ARC	345	5–17	Completed [75]

(Continued)

TABLE 4.6.2 (Continued)

	NCT #	Study	# of ctrs/pts	Age	Status
14	NCT01678807	DB PC S study of HDM SLIT tablets	195	12–17	Completed [76]
15	NCT01061203	Asthma prevention by grazax SLIT	812	5–12	Completed [77]

AC, Active controlled; *AIT*, allergen-specific immunotherapy; *AnR*, active not recruiting; *ARC*, allergic rhinoconjunctivitis; *cSMS*, combined Symptom Medication Score; *DB*, double blind; *Depiquick Birch*, Depigmented Glutaraldehyde Polymerized Birch Pollen Allergenic Extract; *E*, efficacy; *ES*, extension study; *GP*, grass pollen; *GPI*, grass pollen induced; *HDM*, house dust mites; *HDMI*, house dust mites induced; *LT*, long term; *NS*, nasal spray; *OL*, open label; *R*, randomized; *RI*, ragweed-induced; *S*, safety; *SAR*, seasonal allergic rhinitis; *SCIT*, subcutaneous immunotherapy; *SIT*, specific immunotherapy; *T*, tolerability; *TM*, treatment modalities.

TABLE 4.6.3 ASIT studies including minors in ARC, AR, and asthma.

	NCT #	Study	# of ctrs/pts	Age	Status
1	NCT02844842	T + S of SCIT Allergovac Poliplus	15/152	5–60y	Completed
2	NCT01902992	DB R PC E + S Depiquick Birch SCIT study	36/202	12–70y	Completed
3	NCT01918956	OL R Birch SCIT study	8/120	> 12y	Completed
4	NCT03850626	Validation of cSMS in Depigoid AIT	1/200	> 12y	Recruiting
5	NCT00501527	DB PC E study of DEPI grass allergen SLIT	1/80	12–50y	Completed
6	NCT00803244	R DB PC S + E study of SLIT in GP ARC	6/381	12–65y	Completed
7	NCT01694836	MC PC LT study of DPI Birch SCIT	2/634	12–70y	Completed*
8	NCT03821077	E + S of "Allergovac Poliplus" SCIT in ARC	10/150	5–60y	Recruiting

(*Continued*)

TABLE 4.6.3 (Continued)

	NCT #	Study	# of ctrs/pts	Age	Status
9	NCT01700192	PC R SLIT study in HDMI ARC	1482	>12y	Completed [78–80]
10	NCT01353755	DB PC E + T study of SCIT in GPI ARC	195	12–65y	Completed
11	NCT04207697	S + E of Beltavac Cat Dander SCIT	4/50	12–65y	Recruiting
12	NCT03604718	S + E of Beltavac Alternaria alternata SCIT	11/100	>5y	Recruiting
13	NCT01620762	DB R PC MC E + S study of Cat-PAD SCIT in ARC	118/1408	12–65	Completed
14	NCT01385371	DB PC PG E + S of grass SLIT in ARC	?/1501	5–65y	Completed [76,81,82]
15	NCT01603056	PC E study of HDM SLIT tablets	617	5–55	Completed
16	NCT04125888	Retrospective study of AIT in AR + asthma	100,000	All ages	AnR
17	NCT02443805	PC S + E of STG320 SLIT in HDM allergy	1607	12–65y	Completed
18	NCT00422149	DB PC E SUBLIVAC grass SLIT drops in AR	60/350	>12y	Completed

AC, Active controlled; *AIT*, allergen-specific immunotherapy; *AnR*, active not recruiting; *ARC*, allergic rhinoconjunctivitis; *cSMS*, combined Symptom Medication Score; *DB*, double blind; *Depiquick Birch*, Depigmented Glutaraldehyde Polymerized Birch Pollen Allergenic Extract; *E*, efficacy; *ES*, extension study; *GP*, grass pollen; *GPI*, grass pollen induced; *HDM*, house dust mites; *HDMI*, house dust mites induced; *LT*, long term; *NS*, nasal spray; *OL*, open label; *R*, randomized; *RI*, ragweed-induced; *S*, safety; *SAR*, seasonal allergic rhinitis; *SCIT*, subcutaneous immunotherapy; *SIT*, specific immunotherapy; *T*, tolerability; *TM*, treatment modalities.
**Total study duration per patient 5 years: 3 years of perennial treatment (application of study medication at intervals of 4-6 weeks) followed by a treatment-free observational phase of 2 years (seasons).*

In 2018, the PEI announced under the headline "Therapy Allergen Regulation bearing fruit," that the first therapy allergens assessed in accordance with the Therapy Allergen Regulation received a marketing authorization in Germany [84]. This announcement is misleading. Table 4.6.4 lists the number of ASIT products PEI-approved until April 2020. Since 2008,

TABLE 4.6.4 PEI-approved ASIT products in April 2020.

Description	#	Approval date	Approved in/after 2008
Tree pollen SCIT	42	1989–1997	
Grass pollen SCIT	53	1976–2005	
House dust mites SCIT	25	1990–2004	
Insects venom SCIT	18	1980–1997	
Tree pollen SLIT	7	2004–2019	3
Grass pollen SLIT	32	2006–2019	32
House dust mites SLIT	4	2015–2019	4

i.e. the enactment of the German TAO, not one SCIT product was approved in Germany. But there are now 32 SLIT allergen products approved in Germany, see Table 4.6.4. The claim that the TAO is bearing fruit is ridiculous. There are no fruits.

Table 4.6.5 lists the 7 companies that sell "marketable" ASIT SCIT and SLIT products, and the 17 companies that sell approved SLIT products in Germany.

"Marketable" means that the companies have submitted their PIPs and are allowed to continue selling their products. However, PEI and EMA still expect them to perform the 58 demanded "pediatric" studies in tens of thousands of young patients [63,65]. Among the 17 companies that sell approved ASIT products, there are just two who also sell "marketable" products, and 15 that sell Grazax and/or Oralair SLIT products. As can be seen from the product names, these products are identical to the original products of the companies ALK-Abelló and Stallergenes. The 15 companies in the left column of Table 4.6.5 buy the products in EU countries where the drug prices are lower, and reimport them into Germany ("parallel import"). This is a legal procedure and a peculiarity of the complex EU legal system that here we will not discuss further. The point here is that of the seven manufacturers that submitted PIPs in 2010, only two sell SLIT products that are approved in Germany. The clinical studies that resulted in FDA approval of these SLIT products were primarily not driven by the EU regulatory framework, but were the result of companies' expectation that the investments for FDA approval would justify the costs for clinical ASIT studies. Of course, additional sales in any market are welcome.

TABLE 4.6.5 Manufacturers of "marketable" versus manufacturers of approved ASIT products in Germany [13,85].

Manufacturers of "marketable" ASIT products	Manufacturers of approved ASIT products
• ALK-Abelló Arzneimittel GmbH • Allergopharma GmbH & Co. KG • ATL (UK) / BENCARD Allergie GmbH • HAL Allergie GmbH • LETI Pharma GmbH • Lofarma SpA • ROXALL Medizin GmbH	• ALK-Abelló Arzneimittel GmbH (Grazax, RAGWIZAX, ACARIZAX, AITARO, AMITEND) • Stallergenes GmbH (Grazax, Oralair) • HAL Allergie GmbH (Grazax) • EMRAmed Arzneimittel GmbH (Grazax, Oralair) • CC-Pharma GmbH (Grazax, Oralair) • PB Pharma GmbH (Grazax) • Orifarm GmbH (Grazax, Oralair) • Abacus Medicine A/S (Grazax, Oralair) • kohlpharma GmbH (Grazax, Oralair) • A.C.A Müller ADAG Pharma AG (Grazax, Oralair) • Haemato Pharm GmbH (Grazax, Oralair) • AxiCorp Pharma GmbH (Grazax, Oralair) • Medicopharm AG (Grazax, Oralair) • Pharma Gerke GmbH (Grazax) • European Pharma B.V., Niederlande (Oralair) • EurimPharm Arzneimittel GmbH (Oralair)

Academic helplessness

In 2018, the European Academy of Allergy and Clinical Immunology (EAACI) and its Future of the Allergists and Specific Immunotherapy (FASIT) working group criticized the EMA demands for five-year double-blind placebo-controlled allergen immunotherapy efficacy trials in children. In the placebo group, these studies prevent effective treatment and increase the risk of asthma [64]. The authors, however, also describe the EU pediatric regulation as "enshrining the right for children to receive evidence-based medicine." The EAACI correctly criticizes the use of placebo-controlled clinical studies in young patients in a clinical area where effective treatment is already well established. However, the EAACI has so far not addressed the blur of using the different meanings of the term "child."

Discussion

Although the intellectual fundaments of separate drug approval in adults and children evolved in a collaboration between the AAP and the DA, the FDA has in ASIT not developed any "pediatric" activism comparable to EMA and PEI. Where manufacturers performed clinical studies in young and older patients, the

FDA approved the respective products down to young ages: grasstek from >5 years of age on, oral air from >10 years of age on [31–33].

The combined EMA and PEI demand for separate "pediatric" ASIT SCIT studies did not emerge from a clinical crisis in treating and preventing allergic diseases in young patients. This is a parallel to all other analyzed clinical areas in this book. But the special case of ASIT is that the "pediatric" challenge was imported into the therapeutic arena of ASIT that for decades had enjoyed a special niche situation aside from mainstream drug development and control by regulatory authorities. On a technical and scientific level, today a worldwide standardization of allergen products would be technically possible. Obviously, the public pressure on the regulatory authorities, academic researchers, manufacturers, and other involved institutions including learned societies and the WHO are not sufficient. However, the challenge of "pediatric" studies in ASIT goes even farther than in other clinical areas.

There is a strong mismatch between the regulatory demands for separate "pediatric" studies in ASIT and the number of SCIT studies that have been completed or are recruiting (Table 4.6.2). There is just one study currently recruiting patients into a "pediatric" SCIT study (Table 4.6.1, study 4), and one study is completed. SCIT ASIT products are in Germany only approved in adults, with a long, long list of products that are in the limbo of being "marketable," but without approval [85]. The 116 PIPs issued in 2010 have so far not led to a single "pediatric" registration [63,65]. There are several reasons for this mismatch. In many other clinical areas, the PIPs were demanded for products that provided enough financial benefit for the companies that had developed them, so they could afford to invest the € or $ US millions to finance such medical senseless or even harmful studies. But the majority of ASIT allergen manufacturers are of a completely different dimension than the large pharmaceutical companies. The PEI lists for the marketable allergen products that have no registration, seven producers: ALK-Abelló, Allergopharma, ATL (UK)/Bencard; HAL Allergie; Leti Pharma, Lofarma, and Roxall (see Table 4.6.5). Compared to "big pharma," these seven companies belong to another class. They are simply much smaller. They could not afford the costs of roughly €20 million for each PIP, the costs that the EU Commission estimates as the costs of each fulfilled PIP [86]. Another reason for this mismatch is probably that clinicians will have deeper hesitations to tell parents and patients that these demanded studies would make any medical sense.

Clinical reviews recommend for ASIT a relative lower age limit of five years, but more based on pragmatic considerations, and as an absolute counterindication the age limit of two years [87]. Clinical reviews also reveal the trouble of many authors to maneuver between the official regulatory situation and medical common sense [64,88]. Others try to focus on technical and clinical questions only [1,89,90]. Young children still have no teeth, need predominantly fluid food, and cannot swallow tablets. The typical neonatal toxicities are, however, no longer threatening young children. Any drug is dangerous if it is administered in wrong doses.

In the medical literature, a first critical discussion of stimulating pediatric studies dates back to 2007, showing that US-rewarded pediatric studies predominantly examined the use of drugs for adult diseases in young patients, i.e. they did not meet medical needs in children [91]. The obsession of clinicians with clinical studies as opposed to common sense was ridiculed in a paper that apparently seriously criticized the efficacy of parachutes because they had not been proven to be efficacious in double-blind randomized placebo-controlled trials [92]. The unease expressed in this paper was partially due to regulatory clinical studies that are formally well organized, can advance academic careers, but lack medical sense. Nevertheless, the authors did not go beyond expressing unease and mocking clinicians' obsession. The first papers on the EMA's unrealistic assumptions of the number of "pediatric" patients with metastatic melanoma were published in 2014 [93,94]. The first academic criticism of PIP-demanded ASIT studies dates from 2015 [65]. In the meantime, several systematic analyses of the fundamental flaws of the PIP system have been published [53–55,95–101].

The lack of medical sense of all the EMA-demanded clinical studies in young allergic patients in almost astronomical numbers is obvious, as five years of placebo treatment deny effective treatment and allow the progression to asthma and other allergic diseases.

Also the careful coding in official regulatory documents and in the literature needs to be addressed. The authorities claim that off-label use of drugs in children is dangerous, and that their crusade for pediatric labels advances child healthcare. The regulatory authorities' statements must not be taken at face value. Also the conflicts of interest within academic allergy need to be addressed. "Pediatric" studies should not be performed without explicitly mentioning that these studies are based on PIP demands. Most ASIT studies that are not triggered by PIPs recruit both adults and children, see Table 4.6.4. Obviously, the sponsoring companies, respectively, have decided that the financial investment to perform the ongoing studies is worthwhile. Participation in these studies is a temptation for clinicians as the results are published in high-ranking journals, study participation means participation at international investigator meetings and funding.

There are two reasons that so many pediatric oncology regulatory studies were and are performed, and relatively few ASIT studies. Firstly, young patients with cancer are in immediate danger of death and often no safe effective treatment exists yet. Secondly, companies forced by the EMA to perform "pediatric" oncology studies have no choice but to finance these studies, even if they are fully aware that they are senseless. For each company, this is a business decision. Everybody appears to profit: researchers, authorities, companies. But the real price is paid by abused young patients and their families.

In 2011, the European Academy of Allergy and Clinical Immunology (EAACI) tried to find a common position with the EMA [102]. However, the EAACI failed to address the key question regarding how to define children physiologically. The EMA/EAACI meeting was followed by a publication with a diplomatic, but in reality cynical title that shows that for the authors, both EMA employees, "close collaboration" is simply obedience [63]. Two leading EU regulatory employees seriously criticized pediatric oncology, because, although it admittedly saved lives, it did not result in pediatric labels [103]. An EMA position paper claims that off-label use in children is always dangerous [104], without addressing the life-saving achievements of pediatric oncology, neonatology and further pediatric sub-disciplines.

The report of the FASIT workshop in 2017 shows the helplessness of academic allergy clinicians. It describes the current PIP situation as unsatisfactory, with a number of questions that need resolution. But it also uncritically repeats flawed EMA key statements. Unfortunately, the conclusion that stakeholders should further discuss is not correct. Such discussions would not put an end to these wasteful and potentially harmful studies. As long as EMA statements are taken at face value and as long as conflicts of interest of FDA, AAP, EMA, PEI, and parts of pediatric academia, including allergy, are not addressed, conferences will carry on without results.

Most companies that develop new, innovative ASIT therapies such as SLIT tablets simply include adults and younger patients into the same studies, see the FDA-approved SLIT products [30–35], and see the completed and the currently recruiting studies listed in Table 4.6.3.

Meta-analyzes of "pediatric" ASIT studies have the common weakness and flaw that they accept blindly the administrative inclusion criteria by age [105,106]. As physicians treat patients, not their legal or administrative status, the conclusions from such meta-analyses are worthless for an assessment of the scientific foundations for ASIT in young patients.

The placebo-controlled "pediatric" asthma study NCT03654976 is now recruiting. Its brief summary: "The trial aims to demonstrate efficacy of the House Dust Mite SLIT-tablet versus placebo as add-on treatment in children and adolescents (5–17 years) with House Dust Mite allergic asthma based on clinically relevant asthma worsening." [107] This and other "pediatric" studies deny young patients effective treatment.

Conclusions

Statements that there is limited data on "pediatric" rhinoconjunctivitis are of limited relevance once we agree that physicians treat physical patients, and not patients' legal status [88]. The term "pediatric" rhinoconjunctivitis blurs different meanings of the term "child." Medical treatment should always consider that the patient's mind plays a major role. Treatment is (hopefully) never limited to physical treatment. However, the legal status of the patient should not influence therapeutic decisions, irrespectively if the respective patient is treated on a pediatric or an adult ward, by an adult or a "pediatric" allergist, or is in the respective country legally still a child or already an adult.

The combined effects of the EU pediatric regulation and the German TAO have resulted in a bizarre situation that the central European Medicines Agency EMA demands clinical studies literally in tens of thousands of patients that would, if initiated, be without exception medically senseless, questionable, and harmful for the patients [63,65]. Few, if any of these studies will ever be initiated. They even fall short of the EMA's coding that lists drugs as having become "available" for "children" as a result of the EMA's "pediatric" activism, a claim made for drugs in rheumatology, cardiovascular diseases, infectious diseases, and pediatric oncology [108]. Not one SCIT product has become "available" for young patients as a result of the ASIT PIP orgy of 2010, which so far has produced nothing but administrative costs to manufacturers, to the regulatory authorities, and a number of academic papers.

The PEI claims that now the TAO is bearing fruit [84]. This is ridiculous. It reminds of official statements of the Soviet Union during the cold war about "successes" or "achievements" of the centrally planned economy.

We can discuss to what degree these studies are a larger abuse of patients than the many questionable studies unveiled in 1966 by Beecher that had been performed by US clinical academic research and that led to the creation of the Belmont declaration, the office of patient protection, and the establishment of Institutional Review Boards (IRBs)/ ethics committees (ECs) [40,41].

Even more bizarre is that neither do enough patients for all EMA/PIP-demanded allegedly "pediatric" studies exist, nor would parents allow to let their children participate, nor have the allergen manufacturers the necessary funds to sponsor even only a fraction of these EMA/PIP-demanded studies. And even more bizarre is that academic researchers are unhappy with this situation, have relatively openly criticized it, but have until now not dared to do the only thing that has a chance to change the situation: openly challenge the ethics of the EMA-demanded "pediatric" studies in general and specifically in ASIT [52,63,65,93–102].

References

[1] Ring J. History of allergy in antiquity. In: Bergmann KC, Ring J, editors. History of Allergy. Basel, Switzerland: Karger; 2014. p. 2–14.

[2] Bergmann KC. Milestones in the 20th century. In: Bergmann KC, Ring J, editors. History of Allergy. Switzerland: Karger, Basel; 2014. p. 29–45.

[3] Jackson M. Allergy. The history of a modern malady. London, UK: Reaktion Books; 2006.

[4] Noon L. Prophylactic inoculation against hay fever. Lancet 1911;i:1572–3.

[5] Alam R. A brief review of the immune system. Prim Care 1998;25(4):727–38.

[6] Pradeu T, Du, Pasquier L. Immunological memory: what's in a name? Immunol Rev 2018;283(1):7–20.

[7] Chaplin DD. Overview of the immune response. J Allergy Clin Immunol 2010;125:S3−23 (2 Suppl 2) <https://www.ncbi.nlm.nih.gov/pmc/articles/PMC2923430/pdf/nihms225107.pdf>.

[8] Okada H, Kuhn C, Feillet H, et al. The 'hygiene hypothesis' for autoimmune and allergic diseases:an update. Clin Exp Immunol 2010;160(1):1−9. <https://www.ncbi.nlm.nih.gov/pmc/articles/PMC2841828/pdf/cei0160-0001.pdf>.

[9] Hill DA, Spergel JM. The atopic march: critical evidence and clinical relevance. Ann Allergy Asthma Immunol 2018;120(2):131−7. <https://www.ncbi.nlm.nih.gov/pmc/articles/PMC5806141/pdf/nihms919894.pdf>.

[10] Paller AS, Spergel JM, Mina-Osorio P. The atopic march and atopic multimorbidity: many trajectories, many pathways. J Allergy Clin Immunol 2019;143(1):46−55.

[11] What is the atopic march? <https://atopicdermatitis.net/clinical/what-is-the-atopic-march/>.

[12] FDA 2020. Allergenics. <https://www.fda.gov/vaccines-blood-biologics/allergenics>.

[13] PEI 2020. Allergens. <https://www.pei.de/EN/medicinal-products/allergens/allergens-node.html>.

[14] Ring J, Gutermuth J. 100 years of hyposensitization: history of allergen-specific immunotherapy (ASIT). Allergy 2011;66(6):713−24 <https://onlinelibrary.wiley.com/doi/pdf/10.1111/j.1398-9995.2010.02541.x>.

[15] Cox LS, Larenas Linnemann D, Nolte H, et al. Sublingual immunotherapy: a comprehensive review. J Allergy Clin Immunol 2006;117(5):1021−35. <https://www.jacionline.org/article/S0091-6749(06)00518-5/pdf>.

[16] Cox LS. Sublingual immunotherapy: historical perspective and practical guidance. J Allergy Clin Immunol Pract 2017;5(1):63−5.

[17] Wilson DR, Torres Lima M, Durham SR. Sublingual immunotherapy for allergic rhinitis: systematic review and meta-analysis. Allergy 2005;60(1):4−12. <https://onlinelibrary.wiley.com/doi/epdf/10.1111/j.1398-9995.2005.00699.x>.

[18] Passalaqua G, Bagnasco D, Canonica GW. 30 years of sublingual immunotherapy. Allergy 2019;.

[19] Giannini EH, Cawkwell GD. Drug treatment in children with juvenile rheumatoid arthritis. Past, present, and future. Pediatr Clin North Am 1995;42(5):1099−125.

[20] Higgins GC. Complications of treatments for pediatric rheumatic diseases. Pediatr Clin North Am 2018;65(4):827−54.

[21] Skoner JD, Schaffner TJ, Schad CA, et al. Addressing steroid phobia: improving the risk-benefit ratio with new agents. Allergy Asthma Proc 2008;29(4):358−64.

[22] Li AW, Yin ES, Antaya RJ. Topical corticosteroid phobia in atopic dermatitis: a systematic review. JAMA Dermatol 2017;153(10):1036−42.

[23] Løwenstein H. Characterization and standardization of allergen extracts. In: Bergmann KC, Ring J, editors. History of Allergy. Switzerland: Karger, Basel; 2014. p. 323−32.

[24] Esch RE, White W. Standardization: dreams, myths and reality. In: Kurth R, Haustein D, Lin Y, editors. Regulatory control and standardization of allergenic extracts. Stuttgart: Gustav Fischer Publishers; 1997. p. 134−6.

[25] De Weck A. Allergen standardization at a crossroads? In: Kurth R, Haustein D, Lin Y, editors. Regulatory control and standardization of allergenic extracts. Stuttgart: Gustav Fischer Publishers; 1997. p. 183.

[26] Zimmer J, Vieths S, Kaul S. Standardization and regulation of allergen products in the European Union. Curr Allergy Asthma Rep 2016;16(3):21.

[27] Larsen JN, Dreborg S. Standardization of allergen extracts. Methods Mol Biol 2019;2020:63−76.

[28] Van Ree R, Chapman MD, Ferreira F, et al. The CREATE project: development of certified reference materials for allergenic products and validation of methods for their quantification. Allergy 2008;63(3):310−26.

[29] Nelson HS, Norman PS. Allergen-specific immunotherapy. In: Bergmann KC, Ring J, editors. History of allergy. Switzerland: Karger, Basel; 2014. p. 333–8.

[30] American Academy of Allergy, Asthma & Immunology (AAAAI) 2020. SLIT treatment (allergy tablets) for allergic rhinitis nothing to sneeze about. <https://www.aaaai.org/conditions-and-treatments/library/allergy-library/sublingual-immunotherapy-for-allergic-rhinitis>.

[31] Lee VS, Lin SY. Allergy and the pediatric otolaryngologist. Otolaryngol Clin North Am 2019;52(5):863–73.

[32] FDA 2014. Grasstec label. <https://www.fda.gov/media/88510/download>.

[33] FDA 2014. Oralair label. <https://www.fda.gov/media/87935/download>.

[34] FDA 2017. Odacra label. <https://www.fda.gov/media/103380/download>.

[35] FDA 2014. Ragwiteck label. <https://www.fda.gov/media/88712/download>.

[36] Rooke M. Regulations of allergen products in Europe: what now? Where next? In: Kurth R, Haustein D, Lin Y, editors. Regulatory control and standardization of allergenic extracts. Stuttgart, Germany: Gustav Fischer Publishers; 1997. p. 138–44.

[37] Janssen WM A historical perspective on off-label medicine: from regulation, promotion, and the first amendment to the next frontiers. Food and drug law institute, Levy, M.C. (Editor). First Washington, D.C., USA Off-Label Communications (2008).

[38] Rägo L, Santo B. Drug regulation: history, present and future. In: van Boxtel CJ, Santo B, Edwards IR, editors. Drug benefits and risks: international textbook of clinical pharmacology. revised 2nd edition Uppsala, Sweden: IOS Press & Uppsala Monitoring Centre; 2008. p. 65–77. Chapter 6.

[39] Yad Vashem 2020. The nuremberg trials. <https://www.yadvashem.org/holocaust/about/end-of-war-aftermath/nuremberg-trials.html>.

[40] Beecher HK. Ethics and clinical research. N Engl J Med 1966;274(24):1354–60 <https://www.observatoriobioetica.org/wp-content/uploads/2016/09/Beecher_Ethics_and_Clinical_Research_1966.pdf>.

[41] Adashi EY, Walters LB, Menikoff JA. The belmont report at 40: reckoning with time. Am J Public Health 2018;108(10):1345–8.

[42] Harriet A. Washington. Medical apartheid: the dark history of medical experimentation on Black Americans from colonial times to the present. New York, USA: Anchor Books; 2008.

[43] Rose K. Ethical, regulatory and scientific challenges in paediatric drug development. Pharm Med 2008;22(4):221–34.

[44] International Council for Harmonisation of Technical Requirements for Pharmaceuticals for Human Use (ICH). <https://en.wikipedia.org/wiki/International_Council_for_Harmonisation_of_Technical_Requirements_for_Pharmaceuticals_for_Human_Use>.

[45] International Council For Harmonisation Of Technical Requirements For Pharmaceuticals For Human Use (ICH) 2016. ICH harmonised guideline integrated addendum to ICH E6 (R1): guideline for good clinical practice E6(R2). <https://database.ich.org/sites/default/files/E6_R2_Addendum.pdf>.

[46] The Council of the European Communities. Council Directive 89/342/EEC of 3 May 1989 extending the scope of Directives 65/65/EEC and 75/319/EEC and laying down additional provisions for immunological medicinal products consisting of vaccines, toxins or serums and allergens. 1989: official journal of the European Communities. <https://eur-lex.europa.eu/legal-content/EN/TXT/PDF/?uri = CELEX:31989L0342&from = GA>.

[47] Lorenz AR, Lüttkopf D, Seitz R, Vieths S. The regulatory system in Europe with special emphasis on allergen products. Int Arch Allergy Immunol 2008;147:263–75.

[48] Regulation (EC) No 1901/2006 of the European Parliament and of the council of 12 December 2006 on medicinal products for paediatric use. <https://ec.europa.eu/health//sites/health/files/files/eudralex/vol-1/reg_2006_1901/reg_2006_1901_en.pdf>.

[49] Simon AK, Hollander GA, McMichael A. Evolution of the immune system in humans from infancy to old age. Proc Biol Sci 2015;282(1821):20143085 <https://royalsociety-publishing.org/doi/pdf/10.1098/rspb.2014.3085>.

[50] Holt PG, Jones CA. The development of the immune system during pregnancy and early life. Allergy. 2000;55(8):688–97.

[51] Lai L, Casale TB, Stokes J. Pediatric allergic rhinitis: treatment. Immunol Allergy Clin North Am 2005;25(2):283–99 vi.

[52] AAP. Guidelines for the ethical conduct of studies to evaluate drugs in pediatric populations, committee on drugs. Am Acad Pediatrics, Pediatrics 1995;95 (2):286–94 1995.

[53] Rose K, Neubauer D, Grant-Kels JM. Rational use of medicine in children—the conflict of interests story. A Rev Rambam Maimonides Med J 2019;10(3):e0018. Available from: https://doi.org/10.5041/RMMJ.10371 Review <https://www.rmmj.org.il/userimages/928/2/PublishFiles/953Article.pdf>.

[54] Rose K. The challenges of pediatric drug development. Curr Ther Res Clin Exp 2019;. Available from: https://doi.org/10.1016/j.curtheres.2019.01.007.

[55] Rose K, Grant-Kels JM. The meanings of "pediatric drug development." A review. Ther Innov Regul Sci 2019;53(6):767–74.

[56] British National Formulary (BNF) for children. Royal pharmaceutical society, London, UK, 2009.

[57] Blaiss MS. Pediatric allergic rhinitis: physical and mental complications. Allergy Asthma Proc 2008;29(1):1–6.

[58] Lack G. Pediatric allergic rhinitis and comorbid disorders. J Allergy Clin Immunol 2001;108(1 Suppl):S9–15 <https://www.jacionline.org/action/showPdf?pii = S0091-6749%2801%2946616-4>.

[59] Tharpe CA, Kemp SF. Pediatric allergic rhinitis. Immunol Allergy Clin North Am 2015;35(1):185–98.

[60] Verordnung über die Ausdehnung der Vorschriften über die Zulassung der Arzneimittel auf Therapieallergene, die für einzelne Personen auf Grund einer Rezeptur hergestellt werden, sowie über Verfahrensregelungen der staatlichen Chargenprüfung (Therapieallergene-Verordnung). Vom 7. November 2008. <https://www.bgbl.de/xaver/bgbl/text.xav?SID = &tf = xaver.component.Text_0&tocf = &qmf = &hlf = xaver.component.Hitlist_0&bk = bgbl&start = %2F%2F*%5B%40node_id%3D%27362565%27%5D&skin = pdf&tlevel = -2&nohist = 1>.

[61] Englert L., May S., Kaul S., Vieths S. Die Therapieallergene-Verordnung. Hintergrund und Auswirkungen. Bundesgesundheitsbl 2012 55:351–357.

[62] Döring C. Regulatory burden, adequate to allergen specific immunotherapy? Wissenschaftliche Prüfungsarbeit zur Erlangung des Titels "Master of Drug Regulatory Affairs" an der Mathematisch-Naturwissenschaftlichen Fakultät der Rheinischen Friedrich-Wilhelms-Universität Bonn, 2014 <https://dgra.de/media/pdf/studium/masterthesis/master_doering_c.pdf>.

[63] Eichler I, Soriano ES. Close collaboration between academia, industry and drug regulators is required in the development of allergen products for specific immunotherapy in children. Allergy. 2011;66(8):999–1004.

[64] Pfaar O, Bonini S, Cardona V, et al. Perspectives in allergen immunotherapy: 2017 and beyond. Allergy 2018;73(Suppl 104):5–23.

[65] Rose K, Kopp MV. Pediatric investigation plans for specific immunotherapy: questionable contributions to childhood health. Pediatr Allergy Immunol 2015;26(8):695–701.

[66] Swissmedic 2014. AW-Verwaltungsverordnung—HD-Wegleitung Zulassung von Allergenpräparaten. <https://www.swissmedic.ch/ZL000_00_009d_WL>.

[67] PEI 2017. 15th International Paul-Ehrlich-Seminar 2017. IPES 2017: 15. Internationales Paul-Ehrlich-Seminar zu Diagnostik und Therapie von Allergien. <https://www.pei.de/DE/newsroom/pm/jahr/2017/11-ipes-2017-15-internationales-paul-ehrlich-seminar-diagnostik-therapie-allergien.html> (in German only).

[68] PEI 2021. 16th International Paul-Ehrlich-Seminar 2021. Draft Programme. <https://www.pei.de/SharedDocs/Downloads/EN/newsroom-en/events/ipes-2021-draft-programme.pdf?__blob = publicationFile&v = 6>.

[69] PEI 2021. 16th International Paul-Ehrlich-Seminar 2021. <www.pei.de/ipes2021> and <https://www.pei.de/EN/newsroom/events/ipes-2021/ipes-2021-node.html>.

[70] PEI Biannual Report 2017/18. <https://www.pei.de/SharedDocs/Downloads/EN/newsroom-en/biennialreports/biennial-report-2017-2018.pdf?__blob = publicationFile&v = 4>.

[71] Wahn U, Klimek L, Ploszczuk A, et al. High-dose sublingual immunotherapy with single-dose aqueous grass pollen extract in children is effective and safe: a double-blind, placebo-controlled study. J Allergy Clin Immunol 2012;130(4):886–93 e5.

[72] Wahn U, Tabar A, Kuna P, et al. Efficacy and safety of 5-grass-pollen sublingual immunotherapy tablets in pediatric allergic rhinoconjunctivitis. J Allergy Clin Immunol 2009;123(1):160–6 e3.

[73] Pawsey S, Hafner RP, Casale TB, et al. Safety, Tolerability and Efficacy of Cat-PeptideAntigen Desensitisation (Cat-PAD) in cat-allergicchildren—findings from a pilot study. J Allergy Clin Immunol 2017; <https://www.jacionline.org/article/S0091-6749(16)32341-7/pdf>.

[74] Bufe A, Eberle P, Franke-Beckmann E, Funck J, Kimmig M, Klimek L, et al. Safety and efficacy in children of an SQ-standardized grass allergen tablet for sublingual immunotherapy. J Allergy Clin Immunol 2009;123(1):167–73 e7.

[75] Blaiss M, Maloney J, Nolte H, Gawchik S, Yao R, Skoner DP. Efficacy and safety of timothy grass allergy immunotherapy tablets in North American children and adolescents. J Allergy Clin Immunol 2011;127(1):64–71 71.e1-4.

[76] Maloney J, Bernstein DI, Nelson H, Creticos P, Hébert J, Noonan M, et al. Efficacy and safety of grass sublingual immunotherapy tablet, MK-7243: a large randomized controlled trial. Ann Allergy Asthma Immunol 2014;112(2):146–53 e2.

[77] Valovirta E, Petersen TH, Piotrowska T, et al. Results from the 5-year SQ grass sublingual immunotherapy tablet asthma prevention (GAP) trial in children with grass pollen allergy. J Allergy Clin Immunol 2017.

[78] Nolte H, Bernstein DI, Nelson HS, et al. Efficacy of house dust mite sublingual immunotherapy tablet in North American adolescents and adults in a randomized, placebo-controlled trial. J Allergy Clin Immunol 2016;138(6):1631–8.

[79] Bernstein DI, Kleine-Tebbe J, Nelson HS, et al. SQ house dust mite sublingual immunotherapy tablet subgroup efficacy and local application site reaction duration. Ann Allergy Asthma Immunol 2018;121(1):105–10.

[80] Nolte H, Bernstein DI, Sussman GL, et al. Impact of adverse event solicitation on the safety profile of SQ house dust mite sublingual immunotherapy tablet. J Allergy Clin Immunol Pract 2018;6(6):2081–6 e1.

[81] Nolte M, Barber D, Maloney J, et al. Timothy specific IgE levels are associated with efficacy and safety of timothy grass sublingual immunotherapy tablet. Ann Allergy Asthma Immunol

2015;115(6):509–515.e2. Available from: https://doi.org/10.1016/j.anai.2015.09.018 Epub 2015 Oct 21.

[82] Hébert J, Blaiss M, Waserman S, et al. The efficacy and safety of the Timothy grass allergy sublingual immunotherapy tablet in Canadian adults and children. Allergy Asthma Clin Immunol 2014;10(1):53.

[83] Valovirta E. Effect of AIT in children including potential to prevent the development of asthma. Allergy 2011;66(Suppl 95):53–4.

[84] PEI 2018—Therapy Allergen Regulation bearing fruit. <https://www.pei.de/EN/newsroom/press-releases/year/2018/13-therapy-allergen-regulation-bearing-fruit.html>.

[85] PEI 2020. Marketable therapeutic allergens with active marketing authorization application under the development program of the therapy allergens ordinance. <https://www.pei.de/SharedDocs/Downloads/DE/arzneimittel/liste-therapie-allergen-nach-tav-de-en.pdf?__blob = publicationFile&v = 5> (Products of 7 companies).

[86] Commission Report On The Paediatric Regulation (Article 50(3) Of Regulation (EC) No 1901/2006). Consultation document. <https://ec.europa.eu/health/sites/health/files/files/paediatrics/2016_pc_report_2017/paediatric_consultation_document.pdf>.

[87] Pitsios C, Demoly P, Bilò MB, Gerth van Wijk R, Pfaar O, Sturm GJ, et al. Clinical contraindications to allergen immunotherapy: an EAACI position paper. Allergy 2015;70 (8):897–909.

[88] Szépfalusi Z, Horak F, Eiwegger T, et al. Allergenspezifische Immuntherapie bei IgEvermittelten Erkrankungen im Kindes- und Jugendalter. Übersicht über in Österreich zugelassene Allergenpräparate—Update 2017. Monatsschr Kinderheilkd 2018.

[89] Rice JL, Diette GB, Suarez-Cuervo C, Brigham EP, Lin SY, Ramanathan M, et al. Allergen-specific immunotherapy in the treatment of pediatric asthma: a systematic review. Pediatrics 2018;141(5) pii: e20173833.

[90] Pleskovic N, Bartholow A, Skoner DP. Sublingual immunotherapy in children: the recent experiences. Curr Opin Allergy Clin Immunol 2014;14(6):582–90.

[91] Boots I, Sukhai RN, Klein RH, et al. Stimulation programs for pediatric drug research—do children really benefit? Eur J Pediatr 2007;166(8):849–55.

[92] Smith GC, Pell JP. Parachute use to prevent death and major trauma related to gravitational challenge: systematic review of randomized controlled trials. BMJ 2003;237 (7427):1459–61.

[93] Rose K. European Union pediatric legislation jeopardizes worldwide, timely future advances in the care of children with cancer. Clin Therapeutics 2014;36(2):163–77.

[94] Rose K, Senn S. Drug development: EU paediatric legislation, the European medicines agency and its paediatric committee—adolescents' melanoma as a paradigm. Pharm Stat 2014;13(4):211–13.

[95] Rose K, Walson PD. Do Pediatric Investigation Plans (PIPs) advance pediatric healthcare? Pediatr Drugs 2017;19(6):515–22.

[96] Rose K, Grant-Kels JM. Questionable international pediatric studies in the United States and Russia triggered by regulatory authorities. Asian J Res Med Pharm Sci 2018;3(3) <http://www.journalrepository.org/media/journals/AJRIMPS_63/2018/Apr/Rose332018AJRIMPS40776.pdf>.

[97] Rose K, Grant-Kels JM. Questionable industry-sponsored pediatric studies in China triggered by United States of America (US) and European Union (EU) regulatory authorities. SF Pharma J 2018;1:1 <https://www.scifedpublishers.com/open-access/questionable-industry-sponsored-pediatric-studies-in-china-triggeredby-united-states-of-america-us-and-european-union-eu-regulatoryauthorities.pdf>.

[98] Rose K, Grant-Kels JM. Pediatric melanoma—the whole (conflicts of interest) story. Int J Womens Dermatol 2018;5(2):110–15. Available from: https://doi.org/10.1016/j.ijwd.2018.10.020 <https://www.ncbi.nlm.nih.gov/pmc/articles/PMC6451736/pdf/main.pdf>.

[99] Rose K, Neubauer D, Fumi L, Grant-Kels JM. Comment on: Mumme M et al. Tissue engineering for paediatric patients. Swiss Med Wkly 2020; (in press).

[100] Rose K, Neubauer D, Grant-Kels JM. Ethical issues in pediatric regulatory studies involving placebo treatment. J Pediatr Epilepsy 2020; (in press).

[101] Rose K, Neubauer D, Grant-Kels JM. Too many avoidable suicides occur worldwide in young patients. A review. Rambam Maimonides Med J 2019; <https://www.rmmj.org.il/userimages/965/1/PublishFiles/977OnlineFirst.pdf>.

[102] Calderon MA, Gerth van Wijk R, Eichler I, et al. Perspectives on allergen-specific immunotherapy in childhood: an EAACI position statement. Pediatr Allergy Immunol 2012;23:300–6.

[103] Saint-Raymond A, Brasseur D. Development of medicines for children in Europe: ethical implications. Paediatr Respir Rev 2005;6(1):45–51.

[104] EMA 2004: Evidence of harm from off-label or unlicensed medicines in children. <http://www.ema.europa.eu/docs/en_GB/document_library/Other/2009/10/WC500004021.pdf>.

[105] Olaguíbel JM, Alvarez Puebla MJ. Efficacy of sublingual allergen vaccination for respiratory allergy in children. Conclusions from one meta-analysis. J Investig Allergol Clin Immunol 2005;15(1):9–16.

[106] Penagos M, Compalati E, Tarantini F, et al. Efficacy of sublingual immunotherapy in the treatment of allergic rhinitis in pediatric patients 3 to 18 years of age: a meta-analysis of randomized, placebo-controlled, double-blind trials. Ann Allergy Asthma Immunol 2006;97(2):141–8.

[107] Mite Asthma Pediatric Immunotherapy Trial (MAPIT). <https://clinicaltrials.gov/ct2/show/NCT03654976>.

[108] EMA 2016: 10-year Report to the European Commission. <https://ec.europa.eu/health/sites/health/files/files/paediatrics/2016_pc_report_2017/ema_10_year_report_for_consultation.pdf>.

Subchapter 4.7

Epilepsy

Introduction

Epilepsy is characterized by transient epileptic seizures that are caused by abnormal excessive or synchronous neuronal activity in the brain [1]. It can be caused by many different underlying diseases, syndromes and other factors, including stroke, traumatic brain injury, infectious diseases, autoimmune diseases, genetic mutations, stress, and more. Epilepsy is characterized by epileptic seizures and associated cognitive, psychological and social consequences [2].

Thanks to modern antiepileptic drugs (AEDs), epilepsy is no longer the "falling sickness," an event that in the past occurred relatively frequently in the public, mostly by epileptic seizures that were unprovoked by external circumstances and could not be explained rationally. This gave epilepsy a prominent position compared to most other diseases. Today, AEDs prevent many, but not all epileptic attacks. Despite the availability of many new effective AEDs with diverse mechanisms of action, many challenges remain, including drug resistance and side effects [3,4]. Although epilepsy is more treatable and preventable than ever, it has to this day also maintained a degree of eeriness, despite the Enlightenment and partially even because of the Enlightenment. Without the enlightment, modern effective drugs would not exist.

Ambulance services receive many calls for epileptic seizures, often by concerned citizens who want to help but are unaware of the basics of epilepsy. Ambulances often transport patients to accident and emergency (A&E) centers not because of solid medical reasons, but because of public expectations, fear of litigation, and limited on-scene access to relevant patient information [5,6]. Most epileptic seizures resolve on their own, while status epilepticus is an emergency that requires fast and decisive treatment. More knowledge in the public about the basics of epilepsy would be desirable. In this regard, epilepsy is both a medical and a social and societal challenge.

Epilepsy occurs both in old and young humans (and animals). Partial-onset seizures (POS) are the most frequent form. Other seizure types and syndromes occur in childhood only. Two key characteristics distinguish today's drugs from the few effective medications that existed since classical times. Drug approval is today based on regulatory clinical studies. The United States (US) introduced this principle in 1962 in the wake of the thalidomide disaster with thousands of malformed babies born worldwide because the mothers had taken an apparently harmless sleeping pill during pregnancy; [7] today it is in effect worldwide [8]. To work, this principle requires a functional public administration, social trust, and a societal balance of influence of the classical healthcare professions, drug manufacturers, regulatory authorities, the public opinion, patients, and, for underage patients, parents. The regulatory authorities approve drugs today separately in children, including AEDs. This did not emerge specifically with AEDs in the framework of a historical crisis in the treatment of children with epilepsy, but within the general concept of "pediatric drug development" that has emerged as part of overcoming the thalidomide disaster, and the concept of children as "therapeutic orphans" [9]. On a general level, this concept has until today remained largely unquestioned, comparable to the firm belief that existed several decades earlier that spinach contains high amounts of iron and makes people strong, exemplified by the sailor Popeye [10,11].

The International League Against Epilepsy (ILAE) has addressed since 1973 the testing of AEDs in children. Its early publications reflected hands-on clinical common sense [12,13]. In 1994, the US National Institute of Health (NIH) organized a conference on pharmaceutical treatment of children with epilepsy, as part of the emerging movement of "pediatric drug development." The conference departed from noting that most new AEDs were not approved in "children," had no "pediatric" PK or safety data, and were nevertheless used in "children," as this occurred also with the drugs in other clinical areas [14]. The conference was not triggered by specific clinical challenges in young patients with epilepsy, but as part of a general *regulatory* challenge which in the regulators' view had a high clinical relevance. The report outlines that new AEDs were given to "children" once approved in adults; that dosing recommendations based upon safety and PK data in "children" would be desirable; and that dosing recommendations for "children" should not be given without controlled trials. Several times the report reiterates that clinicians use AEDs in "children" with or without separate approval, while a regulatory perspective prefers proof that partial seizures are the same in adults and "children," and that drugs that are effective in adults are also effective in "children." Specific challenges in infants and very young children were addressed. At the end of the meeting, the nongovernment participants opined, among other issues, that effectiveness of drugs for partial seizures in adults justifies their approval for this type of seizures in young patients as well, provided safety and PK are ensured [14]. The word "children" is put in parentheses because the study report uses the term "children" unquestioningly.

Since 2019 the FDA accepts extrapolation of efficacy for POS-type epilepsy in young patients down to the age of two years [15], after it had in

2015 already accepted extrapolation of efficacy down to the age of four years [16]. The FDA justifies its shifts of opinion "by the advance in understanding disease pathophysiology and progression" in epilepsy research [16]. The background for this change of opinion was that the EMA had asked clinicians for guidance in the approval process of brivaracetam. When these clinicians investigated all clinical studies that had been performed from 1970 to 2010 on adjunctive therapy in POS in adults and children aged two to 18 years, they concluded that AEDs are effective for POS in children as well, once efficacy is shown in adults [17–19]. In children under 2 years old, the number of patients and trials was not sufficient for an analysis. In the following, the FDA decided to accept this conclusion and shifted its position in two steps, first down to four, then to two years.

The clinicians at the NIH-hosted conference in 1994 had then claimed what was finally accepted by the FDA more than two decades later [14,17–20]. Another clinical paper openly asks the heretic question if pediatric patients are just small adults, and answers this positively for AEDs: the underlying pathophysiological process is the same for patients ≥ 2 years. Young patients will respond similarly to AEDs, provided an equivalent serum concentration–time profile by adequate dosing [21].

With these clinical positions published in recognized international peer-reviewed journals, epileptology was and is one of the first clinical disciplines to openly challenge the concept of children as "therapeutic orphans" that since 1968 is the backbone of first US and then EU pediatric legislation [9,22]. Another such discipline is rheumatology, where it has been stated that separate "pediatric" and adult rheumatoid arthritis do not exist; [23] the disease types summarized under the umbrella term "juvenile idiopathic arthritis" (JIA) are in reality several types of rheumatoid disorders that start early in life, but persist into adulthood [23–26]. A patient with systemic juvenile idiopathic arthritis (sJIA, one of the currently seven subtypes of JIA) as an adolescent does not switch into adult rheumatoid arthritis at the 17th, 18th, or 21st birthday. His *legal* and *administrative* status changes, but the disease remains the same. Hopefully, he will find a rheumatologist who will not re-classify him and change the medication, as this occurs frequently [23], and will continue to occur as long as mainstream medicine uses chronological age ranges for inappropriate purposes. Also in oncology times are changing. Conventional malignant melanoma in an adolescent is the same disease as in much older patients [27–30], and needs the same type of treatment.

In the US, each member state decides about the age of majority. In 1979, the FDA defined administratively on a federal level "children" as <17-years-old [31]. The EU pediatric law, in force since 2007, even defines "children" as <18-years-old [32]. When we talk about children, we associate with this word young, vulnerable babies or infants, and not a 15-years-old mammoth athlete or a young mother. "Pediatric drug development" (PDD) blurs the difference between legal and administrative meanings of "child" versus its physiological and bodily [33,34].

To address this blur it is necessary to put AED treatment in young patients on a scientific basis. The use of the term "extrapolation" of efficacy of AEDs from adults to "children" is inadequate and misleading [15,19,20,35,36]. "Extrapolation" implies a fundamental difference between adults and "children." There is indeed a fundamental difference between infants and adults, but children grow. They do not remain newborn and vulnerable until they reach the official age limit of maturity, which furthermore is different in each US member state and in states outside of the US. *Legally* and *administratively*, humans remain children until they officially come of age. Bodily, they become mature earlier. Furthermore, the process of physiological maturation has become considerably faster during the last century [37,38]. A clinical study in 12–17-year-old patients is scientifically and medically not a "pediatric" study. It is a "pediatric" study by today's flawed regulatory terms.

There is today scientific agreement that adjunctive AED therapy in POS does not need separate proof of efficacy in young patients. From there the next logical step is to review and to re-examine the "pediatric" studies performed during the last decades and analyzed in critical publications [17–19]. The FDA's claim that the shifts of position regarding age ranges first down to four and then to two years occurred "by the advance in understanding disease pathophysiology and progression" in epilepsy research is not sincere. After more than two decades, the FDA has finally reached the position expressed by the clinicians in 1994 at the NIH-hosted conference [14]. The Declaration of Helsinki (DoH) limits clinical studies in humans to improve understanding, diagnosis and therapy of diseases. It does not make exceptions for the senseless repetition of clinical studies in young patients for regulatory purposes and for "pediatric" labels [39]. Such studies produce again knowledge that exists already before the respective study starts. All these studies were unnecessary and therefore unethical and in breach of the DoH. Already today, parents have become rather reluctant to allow participation of their loved ones into "pediatric" epilepsy studies [40]. Their gut feeling has protected many young patients from senseless studies. Now the time has come to progress to a fundamental analysis of PDD, ask even more heretic questions, and develop tentative recommendations how to proceed in epilepsy research in the future.

When Shirkey characterized children as "therapeutic orphans," he claimed that this was due to an "odd and unfortunate twist of fate" [9]. But the pediatric warnings in the new drug labels followed the Drug Efficacy Amendment of 1962 to the US Federal Food, Drug, and Cosmetic Act [8,41]. The pediatric warnings had less a *medical* or *scientific* and more a *legal* rationale. The US legal system is rather litigious, specifically so in medical malpractice. This is well known and therefore feared by pharmaceutical manufacturers [42–46]. The pediatric warnings' primary aim was *legal* protection [20,33,34]. This did not occur by an "odd and unfortunate twist of fate," but resulted from the beginning of modern drug development and the emergence of a new profitable branch of industry, and the US legal system in which modern drug development took place. Furthermore, new branches of science were emerging, including neonatology, pediatric pharmacology, pediatric clinical pharmacology, and many more. All these new branches needed research projects and funds. They welcomed the children-are-therapeutic-orphans and the children-are-not-small-adults concepts, now twisted into the demand for and justification of "pediatric" studies far beyond what was reasonable. Toxicities in preterm newborns and newborns had occurred [47,48]. There was no major pediatric disaster after the thalidomide catastrophe. But the thalidomide disaster helped to paint the devil on the wall and to justify the call for more research for "children." It was also facilitated by public discussions during the cold war that strived to find minimal common grounds in the United Nations, leading e.g. to a pathetic declaration of the rights of the child in 1959 [49], also supported by the Soviet Union that continued its Gulag system during the cold war [50]. There was no mercy for the children of parents who were sent to the Gulag concentration camps [51]. The wish to do something good for "children" hit the nerve of the time. In hindsight, we can criticize that the pediatric warnings, inserted by drug manufacturers into the new labels since 1962, had used the term "children" in an undifferentiated way. But it was Shirkey who extrapolated the observed toxicities into an alleged danger of modern drugs for all "children." His new concept was adopted by the American Academy of Pediatrics (AAP), where Shirkey had a prominent position, then by the FDA, and finally by the US law makers. In the ensuing discussion all contemporary main players in healthcare, i.e. researchers, FDA and pharmaceutical industry agreed that "children" needed separate studies. This movement reached also the drug treatment of epilepsy.

When in 1997 the first US pediatric law was enacted, diseases in the newly labeled "pediatric population" were now regarded as being of a fundamentally different nature, although most diseases' names in adults and "children" remained the same. The bizarre consequence was that many drugs were approved in adults, but not in "children" one day before their 18th birthday, although a study by FDA employees showed that in adolescents the recommend drug doses were with few exceptions identical to the adult doses [52]. Separate "pediatric" studies were justified by referring to children's different absorption, distribution, metabolism and excretion (ADME), which is correct for preterm newborns and newborns, but not for all "children." Separate PDD, irrespective of the degree of maturation of the respective patient's body, continues to be justified on a regular base [53–56]. The justifications for these "pediatric" studies are convincing as long as the blur between the different meanings of the term "child" is not noted. But there is no scientific or clinical sense in these studies. Drugs, including AEDs, treat the body, not the legal or the administrative status of the respective patient.

The EU pediatric regulation, in force since 2007, was inspired by the US precedence, but is more ambitious. The FDA cannot mandate "pediatric" studies in rare diseases, vaccines and biologics. The EU law has no such restrictions. For all new drugs with the exception of those that target a disease that officially is classified not exist in "children," the EU demands a "pediatric investigation plan" (PIP) in which companies have to commit to juvenile animal studies, pediatric formulations, and studies in "children," defined as anybody below 18 years. Essentially, the EU PIPs demand in addition to the adult pivotal studies once more an entire clinical development program in "children."

The FDA has issued "written requests" (WRs) for carbamazepine, eslicarbazepine, oxcarbazepine, valproate, gabapentin and other AEDs. The internet shows for which drugs WRs were issued [57,58], but the WRs for AEDs are not on the internet. Many AEDs were already in 1997 out of patent and thus the FDA could not reward or order separate "pediatric" studies. But for those drugs where the FDA had a mandate, it requested/demanded that efficacy of AEDs be shown again in "children." From 2015 on, the FDA accepted "extrapolation" of efficacy from adults to "children" aged 4–17 years, since 2019 down to two years. An example is the FDA clinical review of an extended-release version of oxcarbazepine in 2011 [59]. Study 804P107 investigated 18 "children" aged 4–17 years with epilepsy, of which a 12 years old weighed 70.4 kg and a 16 years old 69 kg. Bodily, these young patients were no longer "children," but regulatorily they were. The FDA review of eslicarbazepine in 2017 shows how "extrapolation" of efficacy was now accepted down to 4 years [60].

Table 4.7.1 lists completed placebo-controlled studies in young patients with various forms of epilepsy. Those that started before 2007 were most probably triggered by FDA requests or demands. Those in patients >2 y old were by today's standards senseless. They showed again efficacy in patients. But medically, this was not necessary. They exposed patients useless studies, and to placebo treatment, i.e. no treatment.

The EMA has issued PIPs for most modern AEDs, see Table 4.7.2. The demanded studies show as a pattern study demands in "children" aged up to 17 years, see Table 4.7.2.

Scientifically and medically, those for POS never made sense. For almost two decades, also pediatric epilepsy accepted the "children-are-not-small-adults" mantra, although from the very beginning clinicians were at least skeptical toward the regulatory expectations [14].

The EMA demands a complete separate development program in the population labeled "pediatric" for each single AED. One consequence is that the EMA-demanded clinical studies demand more "pediatric" patients than exist on this planet [20,33,34].

TABLE 4.7.1 Completed placebo-controlled clinicaltrials.gov-listed studies in young patients.

NCT#	Study description	Age	When	#Patiens/#centers	Publications
NCT01921205	E Lacosamide + 1-2 other AEDs in UPOS	≥4–<17 y	2013–2017	404/118	
NCT00175890	S + E of adjunctive levetiracetam in POS	1mo–<4 y	2004–2007	116/88	[40,41]
NCT00437281	ED MD E, S, T, PK of pregabalin in POS	1mo–16y	2007–2012	65/18	
NCT01527513	Add-on eslicarbazepine in POS: DB R PG MC	6–16 y	2010–2013	123/36	
NCT00566254	Zonisamide S&E study	6–17 y	2008–2011	207/43	
NCT00105040	Add-on Levetiracetam in refractory POS	4–16 y	2004–2007	87/45	[42,43]
NCT02091206	DR PK + S of Cannabidiol in Dravet syndrome	4–10 y	2014–2015	34/11	[44]
NCT00113815	Topiramate in refractory POS	1–24mo	2005–2007	118/94	[45–47]
NCT01161524	Perampanel in POS	12–18 y	2010–2014	133/38	[48,49]
NCT02224703	Cannabidiol in Dravet syndrome	2–18 y	2015–2018	199/38	
NCT02091375	Cannabidiol in Dravet syndrome	2–18 y	2015–2015	120/22	[50]
NCT02926898	Add-on fenfluramine in Dravet syndrome	2–18 y	2016–2019	105/32	[51]
NCT01146951	DB Add-on pregabalin in POS	4–30 y	2010–2011	66/23	
NCT02072824	Add-on pregabalin in POS: S E T	1mo–3y	2014–2018	175/72	

AEDs, Antiepileptic drugs; *DB*, double blind; *DR*, dose ranging; *E*, efficacy; *ED*, escalating dose; *MC*, multicenter; *MD*, multiple dose; *mo*, month; *PG*, parallel group; *PK*, pharmacokinetics; *POS*, partial onset seizures; *R*, randomized; *S*, safety; *T*, tolerability; *UPOS*, uncontrolled partial onset seizures; *y*, year.

TABLE 4.7.2 EMA epilepsy PIPs.

Drug	PIP#	Indication	Clinical studies	TBFU
Brivaracetame	EMEA-000332-PIP01-08-M14	Neonatal seizures	1. In silico study to predict disposition in children 2. M&S of i.v. PK in children to evaluate dose adaptation rules 3. OL S, PK,A study in neonates with repeated EEG seizures assessed by video-EEG 4. OL SA LT FU study in children with epilepsy	2022
		POS	1. OL SA MC PK,S,E study of AT in 1mo-15y with RPES or epilepsy 2. OL SA LT FU study in children with epilepsy 3. OL S, PK,A study in neonates with repeated EEG seizures assessed by video-EEG 1. Systematic literature review on the possibility to extrapolate E from adults to children with POS	
Brivaracetame	EMEA-000332-PIP02-17	RPESs	1. In silico study to predict disposition in children 2. OL SA MC PK,S,E study of AT in 1mo-15y with RPES or epilepsy 3. R DB PC PG MC E,S,T study as AT in 1mo-15y with a PES based results of study 1 5. OL SA LT FU study in children with epilepsy	2019
Carisbamate	EMEA-000360-PIP01-08	POS	2. OL i.v. S&RD PK,S,T study in HAS 3. OL S&MD study on PK S T as AT in 4-16 y, followed by a 15mo OL ES 4. OL S&MD study on PK S T as AT on PK S T in 1mo-4y, followed by a 15mo OL ES 5. OL MD i.v. study on PK S T in 1mo-17y + a 15mo OL ES 6. R DB PC PG MC study on E,S,T (OS + tablets) as AT in 4-15 y, followed by a 15mo OL ES 7. R DB PC PG MC study on E S T of OS as AT in 1mo-3y, followed by a 15mo OL ES	2017
		Neonatal seizures	1. OL MD PK,S,T study as AT in neonates <28days + a 15mo OL ES 2. OL MD i.v. PK,S,T study as AT in neonates <28days, with a 15mo OL ES	
		ISs (WS), LGS + OPES such as DS, MAS, EWCSWIS, IPE, AE	1. Observational OL (arm 1) PC COD (arm 2 and 3) study on E,S,T as AT in 1mo-18y with ISs (arm 1), LGS (arm 2) and OPES such as DS, MAS, EWCSWIS, IPE, AE (arm 3) followed by a 15mo OL ES 2. R DB PC PG MC study on E,S,T (OS + T) as AT in 1mo-18y with a PES based on the results of the observational study with 15mo OL ES	

Eslicarba-mazepine	EMEA-000696-PIP02-10-M06	POS	1. OL MD PK,S,T study in 2-17 y 2. DB PG R PC MC two part E&S + EOCF study in 6-15 y, as AT with an OL ES (48 weeks) 3. DB R PC PG MC E + S study as AT for refractory POS in 2-17 y with a 1 y OL ES 4. OL 2-dose-level PK,S,T study as AT in infants with RPOS 1mo-2y 5. DB R PC PG MC E&S study as AT for RPOS in 7mo—2 y with a 1 y OL ES 6. DB R PC PG MC S + T study as AT for RPOS in 1-6mo with a 1 y OL ES 7. DB R PG MC E&S study as monotherapy in 4-17 y with newly diagnosed POS 8. OL MC T&S study as monotherapy in 1mo-4y with newly diagnosed POS 9. DB study in 5-7 y to compare oral suspension formulation with alternative flavors	2020
Ethosuximide	EMEA-001617-PIP01-14	Childhood absence epilepsy	1. R 3-way CO PB study in HS on PK, PD, P,S,T of a NOF versus placebo and the marketed sirup 2. R 3-period SD CO OL study in health subjects on PK,S,T of a NOF versus Sirup + versus capsules. 3. Ph2b R OL 2-way CO MC study on P, A, PK, PD, S, T + compliance of MD MT or in CT 4. Pop PK study	2017
Fenfluramine	EMEA-001990-PIP01-16	Dravet Syndrome	1. MC R DB PC PG study of two fixed doses as AT in 2-17 y 2. MC R DB PC PG study of two fixed doses as AT in 2-17 y 3. OL LTS ES on LTS 4. TCS on PK + S of a SD when added to SOC + a R DB PC PG E,S,T study as AT to stiripentol in 2-17 y 5. M&S study in 1-17 y with DS	2021
Lacosamide	EMEA-000402-PIP03-17-M03	Epilepsy and epileptic syndromes	1. OL MC PK study (tablet or oral solution) in 1mo—17 y 2. Exploratory OL S,T, preliminary E AT in epilepsy syndromes with generalized seizures, excluding PGTCSWIE, TA Type IIA1 or AA Type IIA2 seizures 3. OL MC PG non-inferiority E,S,T study of AT of NS in term neonates 4. OL LTS, T, PK study in 1mo-17y 5. DB R PC PG MC E&S AT study for UPGTCS in 4-17 y with IGE 6. OL MC AT ES in IGE with UPGTCS in 4-17 y with IGE 7. PBPK prediction of oral PK and dose adaptations from birth to 17 y 8. POP PK in POS in 1mo—17 y 9. PBPK predicion of i.v. PK + dose adaptations in neonates (birth to 28 days) 10. Predictive pop PK of i.v. treatment from birth to 17 y	2024

(Continued)

TABLE 4.7.2 (Continued)

Drug	PIP#	Indication	Clinical studies	TBFU
			11. Final retrospective POP PK model birth to 17 y combining all available data	
Perampanel	EMEA-000467-PIP01-08-M11	RPOS + other epilepsies	1. Pooled subgroup analyses of E, PK, S in adolescents included in 3 DB PC studies in RPOS 2. OL ES to DB PC DE PG studies on E, PK, S as AT in A&As with RPOS 3. R DB PC PG with OL ES on cognition, S, T, PK as AT in 12-17 y with ICPOS 4. R OL COS on comparing bioavailability of 4 mg OR with 4 mg tablet in HAS 5. OL pilot PK + preliminary S,T,E study of oral suspension as AT in AT in 2-11 y + ES 6. Exploratory OL PK + preliminary S,T,E study as AT in 1mo-18y with epilepsy + ES 7. OL MC single-arm S, T, PK, PK/PD study in AT + ES in 4-11 y with ICPOS or PGTCS 8. OL MD S, T, PK study as AT in neonates with seizures birth to 27days + OL ES up to 1 y 9. OL pilot PK + preliminary S,T,E study of OS as AT in 1-24mo + ES 10. Pop PK and PK/PD analyses for study 7, patients 4-12 years) 11. Pop PK analysis (regarding study 9); patients 1-24 month 12. Extrapolation study in 4–11 y with PGTCS 13. Literature meta-analysis on extrapolating E from adults to children with PGCTS	2022
Rufinamide	EMEA-000709-PIP01-09-M05	LGS	1. MC R OL study on cognitive development, S, PK as AT in 1-3 y inadequately controlled LGS	2017
Vigabatrin	EMEA-000717-PIP02-13-M02	IS, RPOS	1. OL acceptability study on A/P,S,T of a new soluble tablet in 1mo—7 y with seizures (infantile spasms, RPOS) + FU of 4 weeks	2016

Retigabine	EMEA-000116-PIP01-07-M08	POS	1. OL MD PK S T study as AT in 12-17 y with POS or LGS 2. OL MD PK S T study as AT in 2-12 y with POS or LGS 3. OL MD PK S T study as AT in 1-23mo with mixed or POS 4. OL MD PK S T study as AT from birth to <1mo with MST 5. OL uncontrolled ES on LTS + E in 12-17 y olds who participated in retigabine pediatric studies. 6. R DB PC MC E + S study as AT in 12-17 y with POS 7. R DB PC MC E + S study as AT in 1-23mo with POS 8. R DB PC MC E + S study as AT from birth to <1mo with MST 9. R DB PC MC E + S study as AT in 2-11 y with POS 10. OL LT S + T study in POS (<12 y) or LGS (2-29 y) 11. OL uncontrolled ES on LTS + E as AT in POS (12-17 y) or LGS (12-29 y) who participated in retigabine pediatric studies.	2035
		LGS	1. OL MD PK S T study as AT in 12-17 y with POS or LGS 2. OL MD PK S T study as AT in 2-12 y with POS or LGS 3. OL MD PK S T study as AT in 1-23mo with mixed or POS 4. OL MD PK S T study as AT from birth to <1mo with MST 5. OL uncontrolled ES on LTS + E in 12-17 y olds who participated in retigabine pediatric studies. 6. R DB PC MC E + S study as AT in 12-17 y with POS 7. R DB PC MC E + S study as AT in 1-23mo with POS 8. R DB PC MC PG E + S study as AT for LGS patients 12-29 y 9. R DB PC MC PG E + S study as AT for LGS patients 2-11 y	

AA, Atypical absence; *A/P*, acceptability/ palatability; *AE*, absence epilepsy; *AT*, adjunctive therapy; *CO*, cross-over; *COD*, cross-over design; *CT*, combination treatment; *DB*, double blind; *DS*, dravet syndrome; *EOCF*, effect on cognitive function; *ES*, extension study; *EWCSWIS*, epilepsy with continuous sharp-waves in sleep; *FU*, follow-up; *HAS*, healthy adult subjects; *HS*, healthy subjects; *ICPOS*, inadequately controlled POS; *IGE*, idiopathic generalized epilepsy; *IPE*, idiopathic partial epilepsy; *IS*, infantile spasms; *i.v.*, intravenous; *LGS*, Lennox-Gastaut Syndrome; *LT*, long term; *LTS*, long-term safety; *MAS*, myoclonic astatic syndrome; *mo*, month; *NOF*, new oral formulation; *P*, palatability; *MC*, multicenter; *M&S*, modeling & simulation; *MST*, multiple seizure types; *MT*, monotherapy; *NS*, neonatal seizures; *OL*, open label; *OPES*, other pediatric epilepsy syndromes; *OS*, oral suspension; *PATMS*, placebo and the marketed sirup; *PBPK*, physiologically based pharmacokinetic modeling; *PC*, placebo-controlled; *PD*, pharmacodynamics; *PES*, pediatric epileptic syndrome; *PG*, parallel group; *PGTCSWIGE*, primary generalized tonic-clonic seizures with Idiopathic Generalized Epilepsy; *PK*, pharmacokinetics; *POP PK*, population pharmacokinetics; *R*, randomized; *RPES*, refractory pediatric epilepsy syndromes; *SA*, single-arm; *SD*, single dose; *S&MD*, single- and multiple-dose; *S&RD*, single & repeat dose; *SOC*, standard-of-care; *TA*, typical absence; *TBFU*, to be finalized until; *TCS*, two-cohort-study; *UPGTCS*, uncontrolled primary generalized tonicclonic seizures; *WS*, West syndrome; *y*, year.

Another aspect is the PIP timelines. The most extreme case was retigabine, where the PIP until its 8th modification demanded 20 (in words: twenty) clinical studies in "children" of all ages to be concluded until 2035, i.e. an overall duration of more than 20 years [61].

With the 9th modification, the EMA issued a complete waiver that released the company of all "pediatric" studies [62]. The twenty demanded retigabine "pediatric" studies would never have been completed. "Pediatric" studies that would take decades to be completed occur also in other therapeutic areas, see PIPs demanding "pediatric" allergen studies to be completed until 2031 [63]. At the end of the PIP number, an "M" with a number indicates in which modification the PIP is currently. PIP negotiations take routinely roughly one year. If the company cannot recruit the demanded patients, it must request a modification, which is than negotiated in a procedure of half a year. Retigabine was relieved of "pediatric" demands, but brivaracetame, now in its 14th modification, was not, as shown in Table 4.7.2.

The EMA is well aware of the lack of feasibility of the studies it demands [64]. So far, this had not resulted in conclusions to fundamentally change the PIP system.

Most studies for epileptic syndromes beyond POS lack medical sense as well. Lacosamide studies are asked for patients between 1 month and 17 years, as shown in Table 4.7.2. But 17-year-old young people are physiologically no longer children.

Ongoing pediatric epilepsy studies

Table 4.7.3 lists exemplarily ongoing "pediatric" studies. Most lack medical sense. The inclusion criteria by age limits are based on regulatory thinking, not on therapeutic intentions.

The concept of "pediatric drug development" (PDD) first emerged in the US [53]. It was initially supported by all parties in pediatric research and healthcare. It was amplified by the EU EMA into an orgy of allegedly "pediatric" clinical studies, justified by alleged clinical needs of the "pediatric" population. Once the semantic blur of different meanings of the term "child" is noted, it does not take an Einstein genius to see the systematic deceit that is currently guiding "PDD" [65]. In epilepsy, the FDA has given in to clinical criticism. Also in pediatric cancer now the FDA recommends the inclusion of adolescents into adult pivotal cancer studies [30,66]. Another area where the FDA has relented is birth control [16]. But for the efficacy of contraceptives in young women extrapolation of efficacy is an inappropriate description. Contraceptives simply work in women before as well as after the 17th birthday.

The EMA claims "off-label" use in "children" to be always harmful [67]. Scientifically, medically and historically, this is untrue. Pediatric oncology did not advance through new drugs approved in "children," but by chemotherapy

TABLE 4.7.3 Ongoing industry-sponsored epilepsy studies in "children" in www.clinicaltrials.gov (including studies not yet recruiting).

#	NCT#	Drug	Design/status	Age	# Patients/ctrs
1	NCT01964560	Adj lacosamide	LT S + T, 1-3 other AEDs/EbI	1mo–17 y	500/129
2	NCT03222349	Diazepam	PK + S of buccal soluble film/r	2–17 y	18/10
3	NCT02914314	Adj Perampanel	PK/r	1–24mo	16/24
4	NCT03405714	Brivaracetam	PK, S, T in epilepsy/r	1mo–16y	50/39
5	NCT02201251	Topiramate	R vs levetiracetam (monother)/AnR	2–15 y	63/42
6	NCT03865732	Adj ganoxolone	PC in PCDH19-rE/r	♀1–17 y	70/15
7	NCT01364597	Adj brivaracetam	OL LT/EbI	< 17 y	600/71
8	NCT00938912	Adj lacosamide	OL S, T, E in epilepsy/AnR	1mo–17 y	366/7
9	NCT03650452	Adj TAK-935	R DB PC on S,E,T in dev a/o ep Encep/r	2–17 y	126/44
10	NCT02477839	Adj lacosamide	PC E + S/r	1–47mo	179/244
11	NCT02758626	Ataluren	NM in CDKL5 + Dravet Syn; R, PC,c-o/AnR	2–12 y	16/1
12	NCT02358538	Adj ganoxolone	♀ PCDH19-rE + other RET/AnR	2–18 y	30/10
13	NCT03355300	Cannabidiol	LT S + T in TRCAS/r	3–17 y	30/8
14	NCT03336242	Cannabidiol	E in TRCAS/r	3–17 y	30/12
15	NCT04320940	Phenobarbital	E&S of i.v. phenobarbital in neonatal seizures	36– < 43 wGA	490/?
16	NCT02983695	Adj CBD	OL S + DFS in SDRE due to DS	1–18 y	20/1
17	NCT03059381	Fycompa	S + E/AnR	12–17 y	519/?

(Continued)

TABLE 4.7.3 (Continued)

#	NCT#	Drug	Design/status	Age	# Patients/ctrs
18	NCT02655198	Adj fenfluramine	Lennox-Gastaut	3–18 y	13/1
19	NCT04015141	Adj perampanel	E + S in PES (Cohort 1) + POS (Cohort 2)/r	1mo–18y	100/48
20	NCT03340064	Levetiracetam	Partial seizures	1mo–3y	48 /22
21	NCT02682927	Adj fenfluramine	MC PC DB PG study in Dravet Sy/AnR	2–18 y	130/21
22	NCT02826863	Adj fenfluramine	MC PC DB PG study in Dravet Sy/r	2–18 y	130/34
23	NCT02823145	Adj fenfluraime	OL extension/Ebl	2–35 y	340/64
24	NCT03467113	Adj fenfluramine	DS or LGS who are receiving CBD	2–18 y	25/2
25	NCT02849626	Adj perampanel	FOS or PGTCS	4–12 y	208/92
26	NCT04133480	CBD	Cognitive outcomes under CBD	3–10 y	116/16
27	NCT03572933	Adj ganoxolone	PC study in CDKL5 gene mutation/r	2–21 y	100/38
28	NCT03976076	JBPOS0101	Refractory infantile spasms	6–24mo	35/1
29	NCT03421496	CBD + vigabatrin	Infantile spasms/AnR	1–24mo	190/5
30	NCT02954887	CBD	R DB PC in Infantile spasms—OLE/AnR	1–24mo	202/6
31	NCT02953548	CBD	Infantile spasms/AnR	1–24mo	10/6
32[a]	NCT03325439	Brivaracetam	PK, E, S in newborns with RES	<28days	42/15

♀, Female; *a/o*, and/or; *AnR*, active, not recruiting; *Adj*, adjunctive; *CBD*, cannabidiol; *CDKL5*, cyclin-dependent kinase-like 5 deficiency; *c-o*, cross-over; *DBSF*, Diazepam Buccal Soluble Film; *DS*, Dravet syndrome; *EbI*, enrolling by invitation; *dev*, developmental; *Encep*, encephalopathies; *ep*, epileptic; *IGEWAS*, Idiopathic Generalized Epilepsy With Absence Seizures; *NM*, nonsense mutation; *LGS*, Lennox-Gastaut Syndrome; *mo*, month; *OLE*, open label extension; *PCDH19-r*, Protocadherin 19 related; *PC*, placebo-controlled; *PES*, pediatric epileptic syndrome; *PGCTS*, Primary Generalized Tonic Clonic Seizures; *POS*, partial onset seizures; *R*, randomized; *r*, recruiting; *RES*, repeated electroencephalographic seizures; *RET*, rare epilepsy types; *S*, safety; *SDRE*, severe drug resistant epilepsy; *Sy*, Syndrome; *T*, tolerability; *TRCAS*, Treatment-Resistant Childhood Absence Seizures; *wGA*, weeks gestational age; *y*, year.

[a]*Recruitment temporarily halted as a precautionary measure due to the COVID-19 pandemic.*

drugs, already approved for adult cancers, that were administered to young patients [30,68]. Neonatology always used whatever was available [69]. The EMA claims to have made drugs "available" for "children." Some of these drugs were "available" and used already decades ago, e.g. asparaginase against acute lymphoblastic leukemia (ALL) [70]. Why should a new recombinant asparaginase not work in patients younger than 18 years?

The justification of a general fundamental difference of adults and "children," irrespective of their physiological maturity, has created massive conflicts of interest [20,33,34]. "PDD" has channeled billions of $ US and € into clinical research programs for clinicians and into financial rewards by patent extensions into pharmaceutical companies. A coalition of industry, academia and regulatory authorities emerged, building an academy-based "industry" where numerous "pediatric" careers are based on continuing questionable "pediatric" studies [65].

Should parents allow their 3-4y-old child to participate in a placebo-controlled study? The EMA still demands these studies. Not out of concern for the young patients, but because as a large and powerful administration it has committed to a concept where it cannot retreat without losing face. The EMA is more insulated from the mainstream of public and scientific thinking than the FDA. The EMA puts dogma first and disregards patients' rights, breaching daily the Declaration of Helsinki with hypocrisy. We urgently need to establish from which age on AEDs can be considered to be effective in young patients. Even the lower age limit of 2 years should not be regarded as cast in stone.

In epilepsy, an increasing number of new innovative drugs is licensed in adults and are increasingly also used in children. Daily new complex syndromes are identified. Is it in young patients' interest that drug developers must apply for an approved indication in every single rare indication? Clinicians should challenge the regulatory authorities, but so far they are hesitant.

New AEDs have improved treatment of old and young patients. Conflicts of interest are part of modern society. The ICMJE accepts in its recommendations non-financial conflicts of interest, but nothing is outlined for alleged "PDD." This needs to be urgently addressed, in epileptology, in other areas of neurology, including multiple sclerosis where the pediatric specialists strongly criticize placebo-controlled studies in young patients [71,72], and in rheumatology [24]. But to change the course of science, we have to crack the myth of allegedly needed "PDD." This affects every single clinical area, at the interface of law and medicine. It will require a discussion beyond clinicians only. Pharmaceutical companies are as greedy as all other businesses, or they would not survive. They have become a convenient scapegoat [73–75]. Those with a beam in their own eye point comfortably to the speck in the eye of the scapegoat [76].

Twenty years ago, the clinical world expected that a growing number of AEDs also approved in children would fundamentally improve treatment of childhood epilepsy. The current focus of "pediatric" research in epilepsy is too much on large international regulatory studies in young patients. These studies require very complex and expensive logistics, see the number of patients and clinical centers listed in the tables. These studies do not contribute to better treatment of young people with epilepsy.

The ILAE recommendations fall short of identifying the underlying errors of separate approval of AEDs in "children" [40]. In the balance of influence between regulatory authorities, pharmaceutical industry and clinicians, the clinical world has for too long accepted regulatory positions.

Today, there is already reluctance to allow participation in young patients' epilepsy studies [39]. This reluctance will continue and increase until the underlying questions are addressed in a transparent and candid way. It was patients protests during the initial phase of the HIV epidemy who caused the establishment of the first clinical studies database www.clinicaltrials.org. Every clinician and every single patient with internet access can check PIP decisions and clinical studies.

Probably one major element will be research how to better integrate parents into prospective care of children that are at risk for epileptic seizures or had already first seizures [77]. It would be desirable to see more funds invested into such projects, instead of throwing time and money out of the window for medically questionable and even harmful clinical studies that, however, also help to solidify the positions of those academic clinicians that have established a comfortable position in the current "PDD" clinical studies machinery.

In 1994, when the NIH-hosted conference took place, reimbursement of drugs not approved for "pediatric" use was not a problem [14]. This has partially changed. Today, administrative aspects have acquired a much higher role in medical care. But the lack of "pediatric" approval of a new AED is no valid medical reason to perform separate "pediatric" efficacy studies.

References

[1] Fisher RS, Acevedo C, Arzimanoglou A, et al. ILAE official report: a practical clinical definition of epilepsy. Epilepsia 2014;55(4):475–82. Apr <https://onlinelibrary.wiley.com/doi/epdf/10.1111/epi.12550>.

[2] Devinski O, Vezzani A, O'Brien TJ, et al. Epilepsy. Nat Rev Dis Prim 2018;4:18024 May 3.

[3] Wang Y, Chen Z. An update for epilepsy research and antiepileptic drug development: toward precise circuit therapy. Pharmacol Ther 2019;201:77–93 Sep.

[4] Chen Z, Brodie MJ, Kwan P. What has been the impact of new drug treatments on epilepsy? Curr Opin Neurol 2020;11 Feb.

[5] Burrell L, Noble A, Ridsdale L. Decision-making by ambulance clinicians in London when managing patients with epilepsy: a qualitative study. Emerg Med J 2013;30(3):236–40 Mar <https://www.ncbi.nlm.nih.gov/pubmed/22433590>.

[6] Berry M., Sander L. Not always A&E. <https://www.epilepsysociety.org.uk/sites/default/files/Ambulance%20service%20ER%20Issue%2010%20Summer%202014%20spreads-3_0.pdf>.

[7] Vargesson N. Thalidomide-induced teratogenesis: history and mechanisms. Birth Defects Res C Embryo Today 2015;105(2):140–56 Jun.

[8] Rägo L, Santo B. Drug regulation: history, present and future. In: 2nd edition van Boxtel CJ, Santo B, Edwards IR, editors. Drug benefits andrisks: international textbook of clinical pharmacology, revised, 6. Uppsala, Sweden: IOS Press & Uppsala Monitoring Centre; 2008. p. 65–77. chapter.

[9] Shirkey H. Therapeutic orphans. J Pediatr 1968;72(1):119–20 Jan <https://pdfs.semanticscholar.org/f1cb/acdbac19fa56236b919fb7799eaacaa10c77.pdf>.

[10] Lovett L. The Popeye principle: selling child health in the first nutrition crisis. J Health Polit Policy Law 2005;30(5):803–38. Available from: https://doi.org/10.1215/03616878-30-5-803.

[11] Griffiths S. Sorry Popeye, spinach DOESN'T make your muscles big: expert reveals sailor's love of the food was due to a misplaced decimal point. UK Dly Mail 2013; <https://www.dailymail.co.uk/sciencetech/article-2354580/Popeyes-legendary-love-spinach-actually-misplaced-decimal-point.html>.

[12] Penry JK. International league against epilepsy, first commission on antiepileptic drugs. Princ Clin Test antiepileptic drugs, Epilepsia 1973;14:451–8.

[13] Commission on antiepileptic drugs of the international league against epilepsy, workshop on antiepileptic drug trials in children, Epilepsia, 32 (1991) 284-285.

[14] Sheridan PH, Jacobs MP The development of antiepileptic drugs for children. Report from the NIH workshop, Bethesda, Maryland, February 17–18, 1994. Epilepsy Res. 1996 Feb;23(1):87–92.

[15] FDA 2019. Drugs for treatment of partial onset seizures: full extrapolation of efficacy from adults to pediatric patients 2 years of age and olderguidance for industry. <https://www.fda.gov/media/130449/download>.

[16] Sun H, Temeck JW, Chambers W, Perkins G, Bonnel R, Murphy D. Extrapolation of efficacy in pediatric drug development and evidence-based medicine: progress and lessons learned. Ther Innov Regul Sci 2017;2017:1–7 <https://www.ncbi.nlm.nih.gov/pmc/articles/PMC5587157/pdf/nihms901908.pdf>.

[17] Pellock JM, Carman WJ, Thyagarajan V, Daniels T, Morris DL, D'Cruz O. Efficacy of antiepileptic drugs in adults predicts efficacy in children: a systematic review. Neurology. 2012;79(14):1482–9 Oct 2 <https://www.ncbi.nlm.nih.gov/pmc/articles/PMC4098824/pdf/znl1482.pdf>.

[18] Pellock JM, Arzimanoglu A, D'Cruz O, et al. Extrapolating evidence of antiepileptic drug efficacy in adults to children ≥2 years of age with focal seizures: the case for disease similarity. Epilepsia. 2017;58(10):1686–96 Oct <https://onlinelibrary.wiley.com/doi/epdf/10.1111/epi.13859>.

[19] Arzimanoglou A, D'Cruz O, Nordli D, et al. A review of the new antiepileptic drugs for focal-onset seizures in pediatrics: role of extrapolation. Paediatr Drugs 2018;20(3):249–64. Available from: https://doi.org/10.1007/s40272-018-0286-0 Jun.

[20] Rose K, Neubauer D, Grant-Kels JM. Ethical issues in pediatric regulatory studies involving placebo treatment. J Pediatr Epilepsy 2020; (in press).

[21] Wadsworth I, Jaki T, Sills GJ, et al. Clinical drug development in epilepsy revisited: a proposal for a new paradigm streamlined using extrapolation. CNS Drugs 2016;30(11):1011–17 Nov <https://www.ncbi.nlm.nih.gov/pmc/articles/PMC5078157/pdf/40263_2016_Article_383.pdf>.

[22] Hirschfeld S, Saint-Raymond A. Pediatric regulatory initiatives. Handb Exp Pharmacol 2011;205:245–68.

[23] Nigrovic PA, Raychaudhuri S, Thompson SD. Review: genetics and the classification of arthritis in adults and children. Arthritis Rheumatol 2018;70(1):7–17 Jan <https://onlinelibrary.wiley.com/doi/epdf/10.1002/art.40350>.

[24] Feger DM, Longson N, Dodanwala H, et al. Comparison of adults with polyarticular juvenile idiopathic arthritis to adults with rheumatoid arthritis: a cross-sectional analysis of clinical features and medication use. J Clin Rheumatol 2019;25(4):163–70 Jun <https://www.ncbi.nlm.nih.gov/pmc/articles/PMC6240403/pdf/rhu-25-163.pdf>.

[25] Oliveira-Ramos F, Eusébio M, Martins FM, et al. Juvenile idiopathic arthritis in adulthood: fulfilment of classification criteria for adult rheumatic diseases, long-term outcomes and predictors of inactive disease, functional status and damage. RMD Open 2016;2(2): e000304 Sep 22 <https://rmdopen.bmj.com/content/2/2/e000304>.

[26] Packham JC, Hall MA. Long-term follow-up of 246 adults with juvenile idiopathic arthritis: functional outcome. Rheumatol (Oxf) 2002;41(12):1428–35 Dec.

[27] Pappo AS. Pediatric melanoma: the whole (genome) story. Am Soc Clin Oncolology Educ Book 2014;e432–5.

[28] Rose K, Walson PD. Are regulatory age limits in pediatric melanoma justified? Curr Ther Res Clin Exp 2019; <https://www.ncbi.nlm.nih.gov/pmc/articles/PMC6677782/pdf/main.pdf>.

[29] Rose K, Walson PD. Do the European Medicines Agency (EMA) decisions hurt pediatric melanoma patients? Clin Therapeutics 2017;39(2):253–65 <https://www.clinicaltherapeutics.com/article/S0149-2918(17)30047-4/pdf>.

[30] Rose K, Grant-Kels JM. Pediatric melanoma—the whole (conflicts of interest) story. Int J Womens Dermatol 2018;5(2):110–15 <https://doi.org/10.1016/j.ijwd.2018.10.020>Nov 19 <https://www.ncbi.nlm.nih.gov/pmc/articles/PMC6451736/pdf/main.pdf>.

[31] Hirschfeld S. History pediatric labeling 2012; <https://www.slideserve.com/marlin/history-of-pediatric-labeling>.

[32] Regulation (EC) No 1901/2006 of the European Parliament and of the Council of 12 December 2006 on Medicinal Products for Paediatric Use and Amending Regulation (EEC) No 1768/92, Directive 2001/20/EC, Directive 2001/83/EC and Regulation (EC) No 726/2004. <http://ec.europa.eu/health/files/eudralex/vol-1/reg_2006_1901/reg_2006_1901_en.pdf>.

[33] Rose K, Grant-Kels JM. The meanings of "pediatric drug development." A review. Ther Innov Regul Sci 2019;53(6):767–74 Nov.

[34] Rose K. The challenges of pediatric drug development. Curr Ther Res Clin Exp 2019;. Available from: https://doi.org/10.1016/j.curtheres.2019.01.007.

[35] EMA 2018. Guideline on clinical investigation of medicinal products in the treatment of epileptic disorders. <https://www.ema.europa.eu/en/documents/scientific-guideline/draft-guideline-clinical-investigation-medicinal-products-treatment-epileptic-disorders-revision-3_en.pdf>

[36] Dunne J, Rodriguez WJ, Murphy MD, et al. Extrapolation of adult data and other data in pediatric drug-development programs. Pediatrics. 2011;128:e1242–9.

[37] Cone Jr. TE. Secular acceleration of height and biologic maturation in children during the past century. J Pediatr 1961;59:736–40 Nov.

[38] Komlos J, Lauderdale BE. The mysterious trend in American heights in the 20th century. Ann Hum Biol 2007;34(2):206–15 Mar-Apr.

[39] World Medical Association (WMA) Declaration of Helsinki—Ethical Principles for Medical Research Involving Human Subjects. Adopted by the 18th WMA General Assembly, Helsinki, Finland, June 1964, and amended by the 64th WMA General Assembly, Fortaleza,

Brazil, October 2013. <https://www.wma.net/policies-post/wma-declaration-of-helsinki-ethical-principles-for-medical-research-involving-human-subjects/>.

[40] Auvin S, French J, Dlugos D, et al. Novel study design to assess the efficacy and tolerability of antiseizure medications for focal-onset seizures in infants and young children: A consensus document from the regulatory task force and the pediatric commission of the International League against Epilepsy (ILAE), in collaboration with the Pediatric Epilepsy Research Consortium (PERC). Epilepsia Open 2019;4(4):537–43. Available from: https://doi.org/10.1002/epi4.12356 eCollection 2019 Dec.

[41] Janssen WM. A historical perspective on off-label medicine: from regulation, promotion, and the first amendment to the next frontiers. In: Levy MC, editor. Food and Drug Law Institute. First Washington, D.C.: USA Off-Label Communications; 2008.

[42] Kritzer HM. Propensity to Sue in England and the United States of America: blaming and claiming in tort cases. J. Law Soc. 1991;18(4):400–27.

[43] Lochlann Jain SS. Injury: the politics of product design and safety law in the United States. Princeton, NJ, USA: Princeton University Press; 2006.

[44] McGovern F. Punitive damages and class actions. Lousiana Law Rev 2010;70:435–62 <https://scholarship.law.duke.edu/cgi/viewcontent.cgi?article = 2762&context = faculty_scholarship>.

[45] Bal BS. An introduction to medical malpractice in the United States. Clin Orthop Relat Res 2009;467(2):339–47 Feb <https://www.ncbi.nlm.nih.gov/pmc/articles/PMC2628513/>.

[46] Kass JS, Rose RV. Medical malpractice reform: historical approaches, alternative models, and communication and resolution programs. AMA J Ethics 2016;18(3):299–310 <https://journalofethics.ama-assn.org/sites/journalofethics.ama-assn.org/files/2019-12/pfor6-1603.pdf>.

[47] AAP. Guidelines for the ethical conduct of studies to evaluate drugs in pediatric populations, committee on drugs. Am Acad Pediatrics, Pediatrics 1995;95(2):286–94 1995 Feb.

[48] Shaddy RE, Denne SC. Committee on drugs and committee on pediatric research. Clinical report—guidelines for the ethical conduct of studies to evaluate drugs in pediatric populations. Pediatrics 2010;125(4):850–60 Apr <https://pediatrics.aappublications.org/content/pediatrics/125/4/850.full.pdf>.

[49] UN declaration of the rights of the child 1959 <https://www.humanium.org/en/declaration-rights-child-2/>.

[50] Gulag <https://www.history.com/topics/russia/gulag>.

[51] Frierson CA, Vilensky SS. Children of the Gulag. New Haven, CT, USA: Yale University Press; 2010.

[52] Momper JD, Mulugeta Y, Green DJ, et al. Adolescent dosing and labeling since the Food and Drug Administration Amendments Act of 2007. JAMA Pediatr 2013;167(10):926–32 Oct.

[53] Ward RM, Benjamin Jr DK, Davis JM, Gorman RL, Kauffman R, Kearns GL, et al. The need for pediatric drug development. J Pediatr 2018;192:13–21 Jan.

[54] Tsang VWL, West L, Woods C, et al. Role of patients and parents in pediatric drug development. Ther Innov Regul Sci 2019;53(5):601–8 Sep.

[55] McCune S, Portman R. Innovation and opportunities in pediatric therapeutic development. Ther Innov Regul Sci 2019;53(5):564–6 Sep.

[56] McCune S. 2019. FDA overview of the pediatric legislation. <https://www.fda.gov/media/132890/download>.

[57] FDA Written requests issued. <https://www.fda.gov/Drugs/DevelopmentApprovalProcess/DevelopmentResources/ucm050002.htm>

[58] FDA. The pediatric exclusivity provision. January 2001. Status Rep Congr 2001; <https://www.fda.gov/downloads/Drugs/DevelopmentApprovalProcess/DevelopmentResources/UCM049915.pdf>.

[59] <https://www.fda.gov/media/84835/download>

[60] <https://www.fda.gov/media/109082/download>.

[61] Retigabine PIP EMEA-000116-PIP01-07-M08 <https://www.ema.europa.eu/en/documents/pip-decision/p/0009/2016-ema-decision-29-january-2016-acceptance-modification-agreed-paediatric-investigation-plan_en.pdf>.

[62] Retigabine PIP EMEA-000116-PIP01-07-M09 <https://www.ema.europa.eu/en/medicines/human/paediatric-investigation-plans/emea-000116-pip01-07-m09>.

[63] EMA 2010. Allergen extract of Secale cereale pollen PIP. EMEA-000910-PIP01-10. <https://www.ema.europa.eu/en/documents/pip-decision/p/282/2010-ema-decision-3-december-2010-agreement-paediatric-investigation-plan-granting-deferral-granting_en.pdf>.

[64] Hwang TJ, Tomasi PA, Bourgeois FT. Delays in completion and results reporting of clinical trials under the Paediatric Regulation in the European Union: a cohort study. PLoS Med 2018;15(3):e1002520 Mar 1 <https://www.ncbi.nlm.nih.gov/pmc/articles/PMC5832187/pdf/pmed.1002520.pdf>.

[65] Molloy EJ, Modi N, Greenough A, et al. The future of pediatric research: European perspective. Pediatr Res 2017;81(1-2):138–9 Jan <https://www.nature.com/articles/pr2016225.pdf>.

[66] FDA 2019. Considerations for the inclusion of adolescent patients in adult oncology clinical trials. Guidance for industry. <https://www.fda.gov/media/113499/download>.

[67] EMA 2004 Evidence of harm from off-label or unlicensed medicines in children EMEA. <https://www.ema.europa.eu/en/documents/other/evidence-harm-label-unlicensed-medicines-children_en.pdf>.

[68] Adamson PC. Improving the outcome for children with cancer: development of targeted new agents. CA Cancer J Cli 2015;65(3):212–20 May-Jun.

[69] Philip AG. The evolution of neonatology. Pediatr Res 2005;58(4):799–815 Oct.

[70] EMA 2016: 10-year Report to the European Commission. <https://ec.europa.eu/health/sites/health/files/files/paediatrics/2016_pc_report_2017/ema_10_year_report_for_consultation.pdf>.

[71] Waubant E, Banwell B, Wassmer E, Sormani MP, Amato MP, Hintzen R, et al. Clinical trials of disease-modifying agents in pediatric MS: opportunities, challenges, and recommendations from the IPMSSG. Neurology 2019; May 1.

[72] Krysko KM, Graves JS, Rensel M, et al. Real-world effectiveness of initial disease-modifying therapies in pediatric MS. Ann Neurol 2020; Apr 8.

[73] Goldacre B. Bad pharma: how drug companies mislead doctors and harm patients. London, UK: HarperCollinsPublishers; 2012.

[74] Angell M. The truth about the drug companies: how they deceive us and what to do about it. New York, USA: Random House Publishers; 2004.

[75] Gøtzsche P. Deadly medicines and organised crime: how big pharma has corrupted healthcare. London, UK: Routledge; 2013.

[76] Bible, Matthew 7:5.

[77] Berg AT, Baca CB, Loddenkemper T, et al. Priorities in pediatric epilepsy research: improving children's futures today. Neurology. 2013;81(13):1166–75 Sep 24 <https://www.ncbi.nlm.nih.gov/pmc/articles/PMC3795602/pdf/WNL205431.pdf>.

Subchapter 4.8

Multiple sclerosis

Introduction

Multiple sclerosis (MS) is a chronic autoimmune, inflammatory neurodegenerative disease. It damages and destroys to various degrees the insulating covers (myelin) of the nerve cells' axons and the axons themselves in the brain and in the spinal cord. MS thereby disrupts the ability of parts of the nervous system to transmit signals, which can result in a multitude of very different signs and symptoms, including double vision, blindness in one eye, muscle weakness, problems with sensation and coordination, and many more. The course of MS is highly varied. In most patients, it begins with episodes of reversible neurological deficits, often followed by progressive neurological deterioration over time. In the most common form, relapsing-remitting MS, symptoms flare up and are followed by periods of remission, during which the symptoms improve or disappear. In other forms it is progressive, i.e., symptoms build up over time. At present, MS definitions place artificial distinctions between patients with progressive and those with relapsing disease. Instead, these subtypes should be seen as points on a continuum of disease, which might be expanded to include presymptomatic disease before clinical symptoms develop, but have already organ damage documented radiologically or by magnetic resonance imaging (MRI) [1–3].

MS is mainly found in individuals of European descent, is more frequent in women, and is less frequent in black persons, persons of Asian origin, or native Americans. Migrants from low risk countries, such as the West Indies to Europe, are at low risk of developing MS; however, children born to migrants in Europe are at high risk [2]. The prevalence of MS has increased since the 1950s. This might be a true increase in disease frequency, or might reflect easier access to medical facilities, combined with improvements in diagnostic procedures [1–3].

MS is a complex, multifactorial disease with genetic, epigenetic, environmental, nutritional, behavioral, and more contributing factors, including low serum levels of vitamin D, exposure to ultraviolet B (UVB) light, Epstein–Barr virus (EBV), obesity, smoking, and more [2,4]. The interplay between genetic and environmental factors leads to chronic inflammation of the central nervous system and immune dysregulation, and ultimately manifests as demyelinating lesions and progressive neurologic dysfunction [5].

A recent concept is "no evidence of disease activity" (NEDA), developed from the understanding that clinical relapses are only the tip of the iceberg of MS disease activity. Ongoing inflammatory activity occurs in excess of clinical relapses; brain damage can progress in the absence of overt inflammatory disease activity [2].

Age of onset of MS and the meanings of the term "child"

MS affects predominantly young adults. However, it is estimated that up to ten percent of adults with MS have their first clinical event before the age of 18 years [5–7]. The youngest reported age of MS onset is two years, but the majority of MS diagnosed in young persons occurs in childhood and early adolescence [5]. The term "pediatric multiple sclerosis" is frequently used as a review headline [5–14], but this term is misleading. It also reflects that child neurologists see young patients, and adult neurologists adult patients. But this division is administrative. The treating physician has to consider the patient's body and mind, not his legal or administrative status. A better term is "pediatric-onset multiple sclerosis" (POMS) [4,10]. In 2012, the International Pediatric MS Study Group (IPMSSG) established diagnostic criteria for POMS [4].

We have here the same challenge as in all diseases that occur both in young and in adult patients. It is misleading to describe MS in a young person as a "pediatric" disease. Firstly, careful examination of the disease history in patients that are adult when they consult a first time a neurologist shows that often there were first flares in the respective patient's past when he was younger. These flares went away and were not further investigated. But this does not mean that the respective person should now be diagnosed in hindsight with "pediatric" MS. Secondly, better access to modern diagnostics allows today in general an earlier diagnosis. Thirdly, MS is an inflammatory disease that begins before the first clinical attack; most patients presenting with a clinically isolated syndrome have older, inactive lesions on their MRI. Radiologically isolated syndrome or asymptomatic MS is often detected on MRIs when such examinations are performed for unrelated reasons, such as headache, head injury, or screening in the airline industry. But even in these earliest stages there is evidence of end-organ damage [2].

There is a fundamental blur in today's medicine when we discuss "children." Of course, pediatric neurologists see almost only young patients, and adult neurologists mostly adult patients. But that does not make every single disease seen by pediatric neurologists a "pediatric" disease. Furthermore, the spectrum of patients seen by pediatric neurologists is administratively defined. Like other pediatric disciplines, child neurology evolved into a distinct clinical and scientific specialty early in the 20th century [15,16]. But that a patient is seen by a pediatrician or a pediatric neurologist does not make him *physiologically* a child. The age limit of 18 years used for POMS or "pediatric" multiple sclerosis is administrative in nature.

All reviews of "pediatric" MS emphasize correctly that MS in young patients differs in many aspects clinically from MS in older patients. In young patients, MS is more active, often shows a more inflammatory disease course within the first several years of diagnosis, is associated with greater frequency of clinical relapses, a high risk of developing early physical disabilities, and early cognitive impairment [4,7]. Young patients have a predilection toward a polyfocal onset of symptoms [17]. Also the question if both children and adolescents should be included in the same "pediatric" category has been discussed in the literature. That most societies have for "social, judicial, ethical and educational purposes" defined "pediatric" MS for those under the age of 16 to 18 years reflects current agreement among researchers and clinicians [17], but falls short of addressing the blur between different meanings of the term "child." There are not two different diseases, a "pediatric" MS, and an "adult" MS, divided by an administrative age limit, for which at present the 18th birthday is used both by the FDA and the EMA. MS is a chronic inflammation of the central nervous system, based on immune dysregulation [5], that today is regarded to begin in young age in roughly ten percent of the patients [5,6]. Further improvements in access to modern diagnostics and consideration of a "presymptomatic MS" might in the near future result in therapeutic consequences [2]. This would certainly further increase the percentage of patients diagnosed with MS before the 18th birthday.

The core of the challenge is that the physiological maturation of young persons progresses during the period of *legal* and *administrative* childhood [18–24]. When puberty is over, the body is mature, although the respective person is not yet legally or administratively of age. Furthermore, the process of bodily and mental maturation has accelerated in developed countries during the last hundred years [19,25,26].

A key question will be if we are ready for presymptomatic diagnosis and treatment of MS, other neurodegenerative diseases, and other diseases that can today be diagnosed at birth or even before birth, such as cystic fibrosis [27,28]. In the past, the mainstream thinking was that treatment should only begin when clinical symptoms develop and organ damage is visible. Today, there is more discussion that treatment should begin as early as possible in diseases such as MS where organ damage can occur before showing external clinical symptoms. Evidence of organ damage before clinical symptoms occur would of course result in many patients previously diagnosed with clinically isolated syndrome only now to meet the diagnostic criteria for MS. This would result in changes in clinical practice, changes of treatment guidelines, and reclassification of eligibility criteria for treatment if MS [2].

Treatment of MS

As MS represents a serious socioeconomic challenge, scientific research and pharmaceutical industry have invested considerable efforts in developing effective treatments. New and more effective treatments become increasingly available. Although there is no cure, treatment can improve bodily functions and quality of life after attacks, can to some degree prevent new attacks, and can thus at least slow down the progression of the disease.

The treatment of MS can be divided into disease-modifying therapies (DMTs) that tend to be MS-specific and symptomatic therapies that are often used in different disease areas to treat symptoms resulting from neurological dysfunction [2].

It is common practice to treat acute relapses of MS with a short course (typically three to five days) of a corticosteroid that has a rapid onset of action and that produces few adverse drug effects [1]. This is a symptomatic therapy also used in many other inflammatory diseases.

There are now several types of DMTs available. Beta-interferons are naturally occurring cytokines secreted by immune cells. Several beta-interferons are FDA-approved in MS. Although their mechanisms of action is not precisely known, these cytokines perform regulatory functions in the immune system. Their antiinflammatory properties are beneficial in MS, and they improve quality of life and cognitive function. Side effects of beta-interferons include flu-like symptoms and developing neutralizing antibodies. Glatiramer acetate, a synthesized copolymer polypeptide mixture, reduces the rate of attacks in patients with relapsing-remitting MS. Mitoxantrone is a cytotoxic agent that is broadly used in cancer treatment. It is effective in progressive forms of MS. As a cytotoxic agent, careful monitoring and awareness of a lifetime maximum cumulative dose are important. Natalizumab is a recombinant humanized immunoglobulin monoclonal antibody (MAB). Like the beta-interferons and glatiramer acetate, its precise mechanism of action in patients with MS has not been fully defined. Natalizumab reduces the attack rate in patients with MS and significantly improves all measures of severity. Fingolimod is the first orally administered, disease-modifying FDA-approved drug to reduce relapses and to delay the progression of disability in patients with relapsing forms of MS. Fingolimod blocks the migration of lymphocytes from lymph nodes, reducing the number of lymphocytes in peripheral blood [1].

In adult MS patients, today, the "treat-to-target" or "tiered-escalation" approach begins with less toxic, but often also less effective medications. Treatment is then escalated to more effective but potentially more harmful therapies if the disease activity continues. In contrast, a "maximal efficacy" or "early intensive" approach uses the most effective treatments early in the hope to better control relapsing activity and therefore to prevent tissue injury in patients that experience breakthrough disease activity despite treatment with less effective drugs [3,29].

Injectable disease-modifying treatments, such as beta-interferons or glatiramer acetate, have been the main first-line treatment option for two decades, also because they cost much less than newer drugs. But their clinical efficacy is only moderate, and they can product injection-related adverse effects, such as flu-like symptoms with beta-interferons and injection site inflammation. A new treatment strategy, "induction therapy," uses more effective drugs earlier to prevent the accumulation of irreversible CNS damage and clinical disability. Induction therapy starts soon after a confirmed diagnosis [3].

Monoclonal antibodies (MABs) have become important in MS treatment. MABs bind to characteristic surface areas of larger proteins, which allows them to act on very specific pathways. In MS, MABs are able to specifically neutralize structures and cells that are involved in the attack of the immune system against nerve cells in the central nervous system. Because of their specificity, they also tend to have less side effects and less drug–drug interactions than classical drugs. First MABs were developed from other species like mice. To reduce their potential immunogenicity, i.e., attacks of the immune system, modern MABs use the technique of chimerization. Some or even all regions of the respective MAB are replaced by human regions that are produced by transgenic animal cells. These partly or completely "humanized" modern antibodies are less susceptible to be attacked as bodies of foreign origin. MABs against MS have a much more targeted antiinflammatory effect than corticosteroids. Natalizumab was FDA-approved for MS in 2004, followed by alemtuzumab and ocrelizumab. Rituximab and ofatumumab have been used off label in the treatment of MS; further MABs are in late clinical development against MS [29,30].

Another modern approach are sphingosine-1-phosphate receptor (S1PR) modulators. A subtype of S1PR is expressed on the surface of lymphocytes and is involved in regulating the exit of lymphocytes from lymph nodes. S1PR modulators antagonize the S1PR function and thus help to keep lymphocytes more in the lymph nodes. S1PR modulators have in comparison to MABs the advantage that they can be taken orally. Fingolimod, the first S1PR modulator, was FDA-approved in 2010 [31], ponesimod in 2019 [32], ozanimod in 2020 [33]. Further S1PR modulators are in various stages of clinical development [34,35].

Separate drug approval in adults and "children"

Both FDA and EMA demand for drug approval for the treatment of MS in "children" separate "pediatric" regulatory studies. In 1979, the FDA defined "children" as persons younger than 17 years, in 2006 the EU as persons younger than 18 years. In MS, both regulatory authorities use the age limit of the 18th birthday to define "children." However, physicians treat the patient's body, and hopefully also his mind, but not his legal or administrative status. Separate "pediatric" drug approval is discussed in other chapters and in the literature [21–24]. The separation of the population into an adult and a "pediatric" population is not based on physiology. Patients become bodily mature long before they become legally and administratively of age. "Children-are-therapeutic-orphans" and "children-are-not-small-adults" are two mantras that originated on the basis of toxicities in preterm and term newborns in the 1950s. But young persons do not remain as vulnerable and immature as newborns until they come of age [21–24].

There is no solid scientific rationale of approving drugs against MS in a first round only in adults. All FDA/EMA-demanded "pediatric" studies in MS demand patients 10 to 17 years of age, which are artificial inclusion criteria and do medically not make any sense. Neither the body's cells, nor the involved receptors change their weight, size or any other characteristic in the night of the 18th birthday. That many drugs are not approved in patients until the 18th birthday, but are approved one night after the 18th birthday is ridiculous.

FDA-demanded "pediatric" MS studies

Table 4.8.1 lists the FDA-demanded "pediatric" studies in MS.

TABLE 4.8.1 **FDA-demanded "pediatric" multiple sclerosis studies. All studies in patients 10 to 17 years of age.**

Compound	Abbreviated study title	FSR
Glatiramer acetate (copaxone) [36]	R PG superiority S&E study compared to an appropriate control	2021
Teriflunomide (Aubagio) [37]	R PG superiority trial on single + MD PK, S&E compared to appropriate control	2017
Fingolimod (Gilenya) [38]	24-month, R AC PG study on single + MD PK, + S&E of MDs compared to IFβ 1-a-IM (Avonex). Efficacy portion of study to be designed to show superiority over AC	2016
Dimethyl fumarate (Tecfidera) [39]	R C PG superiority PK, S&E study compared to an appropriate control	2020
Ozanimod (Zeposia) [40]	1. OL S T PK PD study 2. R DB PG E& S study compared to an appropriate comparator	2034
Siponimod (Mayzent) [41]	1. OL S T PK PD study 2. R DB PG E&S study compared to an appropriate control	2026

AC, Active control(led); *DB*, double-blind; *E*, efficacy; *E&S*, efficacy and safety; *FSR*, Final Study Report; *Ifβ*, interferon beta; *IM*, intramuscular; *MD*, multiple dose(s); *OL*, open label; *PD*, pharmacodynamic(s); *PG*, parallel group; *PK*, pharmacokinetic(s); *R*, randomized; *R/R*, relapsing-remitting; *S*, safety; *T*, tolerability.

From Table 4.8.1 we can see that the FDA demands "pediatric" studies that compare new, highly effective MABs against older, less effective treatments. The "pediatric" studies for siponimod are supposed to be reported until 2026, the ones for ozanimod until 2034 (2026 and 2034 are the dates of the final study report; the studies must be finalized a year earlier). Hopefully, there will be much advanced therapeutic options for young patients with MS until 2026 and 2034. Hopefully, parents will refuse to let their children participate in any of these studies.

In 2018, the FDA-approved fingolimod for relapsing MS in patients aged 10 years and older [42].

EU PIPs

Table two lists the pediatric investigation plans (PIPs) that so far have been issued by the EMA (Table 4.8.2).

Table 4.8.3 lists the clinical studies demanded for "pediatric" patients with MS. These studies demand recruitment of patients until 2024.

TABLE 4.8.2 MS PIPs, number of demanded clinical studies, and their time horizon[a].

#	PIP #	Compound	Studies	Until
1	EMEA-000087-PIP01-07-M05	Fingolimod	1	2018
2	EMEA-000802-PIP01-09	Tabalumab	1	2023
3	EMEA-000798-PIP01-09	Ponesimod	1	2022
4	EMEA-000716-PIP01-09-M01	Siponimod	1	2024
5	EMEA-001072-PIP01-10-M02	Alemtuzumab	1	2024
6	EMEA-000832-PIP01-10-M04	Dimethyl fumarate	1	2020
7	EMEA-000972-PIP01-10-M04	Laquinimod	2	2018
8	EMEA-000310-PIP03-10-M03	Ocrelizumab	2	2025
9	EMEA-001094-PIP01-10-M04	Teriflunomide	1	2021
10	EMEA-001129-PIP01-11-M04	Pegylated interferon β	1	2023
11	EMEA-001349-PIP01-12-M01	Daclizumab	1	2019
12	EMEA-001095-PIP02-12	Natalizumab	2	2015
13	EMEA-001710-PIP02-14-M02	Ozanimod	2	2022

Explanation: Six PIPs came up at the EMA website when the PIPs were searched for "treatment of multiple sclerosis". The other PIPs were listed in Rose & Müller; [43] some have undergone further modifications since 2016.
[a]***Order of listing:*** *by date of PIP submission, visible as the two numbers at the end of the original PIP. "07" stands for 2007, "18" for 2018.*

TABLE 4.8.3 Multiple sclerosis PIP-demanded studies. All studies demand patients aged 10–17 years.

#	Compound & PIP#	Abbreviated study description	Until
1	Alemtuzumab	1. R PG E S T study compared to an ApprCom in R/R MS w/prior DMT	2018
2	Tabalumab	1. MC OL R AC (IFβ-1a) study on S, T, PK & E in R/R MS	2023
3	Daclizumab	1. OL R AC E; S & T study w/R/R MS followed by a 24 months ES	2019
4	Dimethyl fumarate	1. OL R MC MD AC PG E&S study in w/R/R MS	2016
5	Fingolimod	1. DB R MC MD AC (IFβ-1) PG PK, S & E trial followed by a LTE	2019
6	Laquinimod	1. OL SA PK S&T single oral dose study in 10 to < 18 y w/R/R MS 2. R MC PG AC S,T&E AC trial in R/R MS; blinded MRI assessment	2018
7	Natalizumab	1. OL RD PK & S study in 10 to <18 y w/R/R MS 2. Meta-analysis of natalizumab S&E in ped MS patients	2015
8	Ocrelizumab	1. OL PG SD S,T, PK&E of 3 ascending doses in 10– < 18 y w/R/R MS 2. R OL AC (IFβ-1a) PG S&E study in children 10– < 18 y w/R/R MS	2023
9	Ozanimod	1. DB DD R AC S&E trial compared to IFβ-1a in 10– < 18 y w/R/R MS 2. Develop a pop PK/PD model to support dosing in the S&E study R/R MS	2022
10	Pegylated interferon β	1. OL R AC S&E trial in R/R MS	2021
11	Ponesimod	1. MC R OL AC (interferon β-1a) PG PK, PD, E,S&T study in R/R MS	2022
12	Siponimod	1. OL R MC MD AC PG E&S study in 10– < 18 y w/R/R MS	2024
13	Teriflunomide	1. DB R MC PC PG E, PK, S&T trial in 10– < 18 y w/R/R MS, followed by LTE	2020

AC, Active controlled; *ApprCom*, appropriate comparator; *DD*, double dummy; *E*, efficacy; *ES*, extension study; *Ifβ*, Interferon beta; *DMT*, disease-modifying treatment; *LTE*, long-term extension; *MC*, multicenter; *OL*, open label; *PD*, pharmacodynamic(s); *PG*, parallel group; *PK*, pharmacokinetic(s); *PK/PD*, pharmacokinetics/pharmacodynamics; *R*, randomized; *R/R*, relapsing/remitting; *S*, safety; *S&E*, safety and efficacy; *T*, tolerability; *w*, with.

All MS PIPs demand patients aged ten to 17 years old. All PIP studies demand comparison of advanced modern therapies against outdated older treatments. Study 13, Table 4.8.3, even demands a placebo-controlled trial. All these studies deny young patients the treatment with advanced modern drugs. The Declaration of Helsinki, which should bind physicians in all countries, does not allow clinical studies that withhold effective treatment based on regulatory grounds [44].

Ongoing "pediatric" MS studies worldwide

Table 4.8.4 lists currently ongoing "pediatric" MS studies listed in www.clinicaltrials.gov that investigate drugs. Most recruit patients aged 10 to 17 years, study 1 patients aged 5 to 17 years, the last 3 studies patients 10 to 18 years of age.

Discussion

Both FDA and EMA demanded and continue to demand "pediatric" MS studies in patients who to a relevant part are already physiologically mature. MS in adults is a relatively frequent disease, but is detected much less in young patients. The "pediatric" studies requested and/or demanded by the FDA and the EMA will not improve the treatment of young patients with MS. Those patients that are bodily already mature need adult doses. For those that are younger and weigh less, appropriate dosing could and should be determined by small "opportunistic" studies, accompanied by PD/PD analysis by additional blood samples [44,45].

To demand a placebo-controlled study for teriflunamide means to expose the patients in the placebo group to no treatment at all (Table 4.8.3, study 13, Table 4.8.4, study 7). This is unethical.

Probably, worldwide not enough young patients exist for all the FDA/EMA-demanded "pediatric" MS studies. Companies and clinical research organization compete worldwide for these rare patients. These studies promote "pediatric" careers in academia, in regulatory authorities, in commercial clinical research, and in pharmaceutical industry. But they withhold effective treatment to young patients with MS. Although the clinical features of MS in young and older patients are not identical, they are no two different diseases, one that would be "pediatric" and the other one that would be "adult." MS is simply a disease in humans.

There are indeed diseases that are different in nature if they are detected in young patients. The umbrella term of "juvenile idiopathic arthritis" comprises seven different diseases. When somebody at young age contracts one of them, after the 18th birthday his disease does not become adult rheumatoid arthritis. Instead, it continues as a distinct disease that is frequently misdiagnosed by adult rheumatologists [46–51]. The term "juvenile idiopathic

TABLE 4.8.4 "Pediatric" MS studies in www.clinicaltrials.gov.

#	NCT#	Compound	Abbreviated study description	Age	centers/ pts	Status
1	NCT02200718	NeuroVax™	R DB Ph1 S&E study vs. IFA Incomplete Freund's Adjuvant	5–17 y	1/12	nyr
2	NCT01892722	Fingolimod	R DB PC AC study vs. weekly Ifβ-1a + 5 y EP	10–17	86/217	anr
3	NCT03870763	Tecfidera[a]/ Plegridy[b]	R DB PC DD 3-arm PG to compare S&E Tecfidera, plegridy, and placebo	10–17	13/260	recr
4	NCT02283853	Tecfidera[a]	OL R MC MD AC PG E&S study vs. Ifβ-1a; OL EP	10–17	62/142	anr
5	NCT03368664	Alemtuzumab	MC OL SA study in pts on prior DMT, comparing before + after switch	10–17	34/50	recr
6	NCT04075266	Ocrelizumab	OL PG S T PK + PD study	10–18	22/12	recr
7	NCT02201108	Teriflunomide	DB PC R	10–18	59/165	anr
8	NCT03958877	Peginterferon Beta-1a	OL MC AC PG BIIB017[c] vs. Avonex[d]	10–18	59/142	recr

AC, Active controlled; *DD*, double dummy; *DMT*, disease-modifying treatment; *E*, efficacy; *Ifβ*, interferon beta; *MAB*, monoclonal antibody; *MC*, multicenter; *OL*, open label; *PG*, parallel group; *PK/PD*, pharmacokinetics/pharmacodynamics; *pts*, patients; *R*, randomized; *S*, safety; *SA*, single arm; *T*, tolerability.
MS, than advanced research, and ☑ child (birth-17) ☑ Funder type: industry, and ☑ recruiting ☑ not yet recruiting ☑ Enrolling by invitation ☑ Active, not recruiting → 61 studies. Only the first 11 studies are "pediatric" studies, and of these nine are drug studies.
[a]*Tecfidera: dimethyl fumarate.*
[b]*Plegridy: Peginterferon Beta-1a.*
[c]*BIIB017: peginterferon beta-1a.*
[d]*Avonex: Interferon beta type 1a.*

arthritis" itself is flawed [49]. It conveys the impression of a disease that exists in juvenile patients only, which is simply wrong.

Many academic publications advocate for more double-blind randomized clinical trials in "children" with MS [4,5,9–12]. This is not the appropriate way forward. Instead, clinicians should return to the roots of the medical profession: help with all means that are available. Modern disease-modifying drugs are increasingly prescribed by clinicians [9], but this off-label prescribing is still mostly described as if it were a barely accepted break of rules. Regulatory studies prove that drugs work better than placebo or better than another drug. But they document patient treatment over a limited period of time. They do not mirror patients' fight with a disease over decades. Today, we have already several rather effective treatments for MS. Instead of using them and investigate how they can be used today as early as possible, and how treatment can and should continuously be improved over the decades of life that young patients still have ahead of them, resources are wasted for questionable and even harmful "pediatric" regulatory MS studies.

The IPMSSG reports that convincing evidence has emerged that the biological processes involved in MS are largely the same in all MS patients. Treatments that have proven efficacious for the care of adults with MS have a biological rationale for use in "pediatric" MS as well. Furthermore, the IPMSSG is highly critical of placebo-controlled studies in young patients that withhold active treatment. It explicitly states that phase 3 trials for every newly approved drug in adult MS in the pediatric MS population are simply not feasible. The IPMSSG also reports an increasing resistance of parents against letting their children participate in such studies [52].

Conclusions

The core of the challenge of separate "pediatric" drug approval and separate "pediatric" regulatory studies is *semantically* a blur between the different meanings of the term "child." We associate with children more young, vulnerable babies and infants, and less adolescent athletes that can already be stronger and taller than one or both parents. This challenge affects the entire medical care in our modern world. Behind the semantic blur hide strong conflicts of interest. The crusade for separate "pediatric" studies has advanced "pediatric" careers in academia, regulatory authorities, industry and commercial clinical research operations for more than two decades. Every single clinical sub-discipline faces this challenge. In epilepsy, the critical feedback of clinicians had positive results [53–56]. The FDA has lowered the age limit for accepting "extrapolation" of efficacy in partial-onset seizures (POS) of antiepileptic drugs down to the age of two years, the EMA has for now lowered the age limit to four years. With the usual delay of a few years the EMA will probably follow the FDA also in this regard.

It is good that finally the IPMSSG recommends the use of effective modern drugs also in patients before the 18th birthday [52]. The IPMSSG still argues from the point of view of specialized academic researchers, reflecting the compartmentalization of today's medical system. But the semantic blur between the administrative and the physiological meanings of the terms "child" and "pediatric," and the deep conflicts of interest behind this blur keep it alive since decades beyond one or a few clinical subspecialties.

The FDA might in the next years allow "extrapolation" of efficacy to adolescents with MS. Hopefully, parents will decline even more than now to let their children participate in "pediatric" MS studies that lack medical and scientific sense. Maybe, first lawyers will sue pharmaceutical companies, commercial clinical research organizations, or academic clinical research centers for damage done to young patients that were treated with suboptimal therapies during one of the "pediatric" studies. It would be desirable if the IPMSSG would become even more explicit in its resistance against separate regulatory "pediatric" studies.

Academic researchers should cease to compete for participation in questionable and even harmful "pediatric" regulatory studies in young patients with MS. Instead, they should advocate for reasonable studies that would accompany early start of treatment and continuous improvement of treatment over more than the short period of time required for regulatory studies.

Institution Review Boards (IRBs)/ethics committees (ECs) should reanalyze all ongoing "pediatric" studies in MS. Those found to be questionable or even harming young patients should be suspended. Further "pediatric" MS studies newly submitted for IRB/EC approval should be rejected.

Eventually, pediatric laws both in the US and the EU need revision.

References

[1] Goldenberg MM. Multiple sclerosis review. P&T 2012;37(3):175–84 Mar <https://www.ncbi.nlm.nih.gov/pmc/articles/PMC3351877/pdf/ptj3703175.pdf>.

[2] Dobson R, Giovannoni G. Multiple sclerosis—a review. Eur J Neurol 2019;26(1):27–40.

[3] Filippi M, Bar-Or A, Piehl F, et al. Multiple sclerosis. Nat Rev Dis Prim 2018;.

[4] Deiva K. Pediatric onset multiple sclerosis. Rev Neurol (Paris) 2020;176(1-2):30–6 Jan-Feb.

[5] Lee JY, Chitnis T. Pediatric multiple sclerosis. Semin Neurol 2016;36(2):148–53 Apr.

[6] Yeshokumar AK, Narula S, Banwell B. Pediatric multiple sclerosis. Curr Opin Neurol 2017;30(3):216–21 Jun.

[7] Cappa R, Theroux L, Brenton JN. Pediatric multiple sclerosis: genes, environment, and a comprehensive therapeutic approach. Pediatr Neurol 2017;75:17–28 Oct.

[8] Galardi MM, Gaudioso C, Ahmadi S, et al. Differential diagnosis of pediatric multiple sclerosis. Children (Basel) 2019;6(6):75 Jun 3 <https://www.ncbi.nlm.nih.gov/pmc/articles/PMC6617098/pdf/children-06-00075.pdf>.

[9] Macaron G, Feng J, Moodley M, et al. Newer treatment approaches in pediatric-onset multiple sclerosis. Curr Treat Options Neurol 2019;.

[10] Ruet A. Update on pediatric-onset multiple sclerosis. Rev Neurol (Paris) 2018;174 (6):398–407 Jun.

[11] Otallah S, Banwell B. Pediatric multiple sclerosis: an update. Curr Neurol Neurosci Rep 2018;18(11):76 Sep 18.

[12] Langille MM, Rutatangwa A, Francisco C. Pediatric multiple sclerosis: a review. Adv Pediatr 2019;66:209–29 Aug.

[13] Waldman A, Ness J, Pohl D, et al. Pediatric multiple sclerosis: clinical features and outcome. Neurology. 2016;87(9 Suppl 2):S74–81 Aug 30.

[14] Alroughani R, Boyko A. Pediatric multiple sclerosis: a review. BMC Neurol 2018;18 (1):27 Mar 9 <https://www.ncbi.nlm.nih.gov/pmc/articles/PMC5845207/pdf/12883_2018_Article_1026.pdf>.

[15] Ashwal S, Rust R. Child neurology in the 20th century. Pediatr Res 2003;53 (2):345–61 Feb <https://www.nature.com/articles/pr2003231.pdf?origin = ppub>.

[16] Millichap JJ, Millichap JG. Child neurology: past, present, and future. Part 1: history. Neurology 2009;73(7):e31–3 Aug 18.

[17] Chitnis T. Paediatric MS is the same disease as adult MS: no. Mult Scler 2013;19 (10):1255–6 Sep.

[18] Coleman L, Coleman J. The measurement of puberty: a review. J Adolesc 2002;25 (5):535–50 Oct.

[19] Cheng HL, Harris SR, Sritharan M, et al. The tempo of puberty and its relationship to adolescent health and wellbeing: a systematic review. Acta Paediatr 2020;109(5):900–13 May.

[20] Kearns GL, Abdel-Rahman SM, Alander SW, Blowey DL, Leeder JS, Kauffman RE. Developmental pharmacology—drug disposition, action, and therapy in infants and children. N Engl J Med 2003;349(12):1157–67 Sep 18.

[21] Rose K. The challenges of pediatric drug development. Curr Ther Res Clin Exp 2019;. Available from: https://doi.org/10.1016/j.curtheres.2019.01.007.

[22] Rose K, Grant-Kels JM. The meanings of "pediatric drug development". A Rev Ther Innov Regul Sci 2019;53(6):767–74 Nov.

[23] Rose K, Neubauer D, Grant-Kels JM. Rational use of medicine in children—the conflict of interests story. A review. R Med J 2019;10(3):e0018 Review. <10.5041/RMMJ.10371> <https://www.rmmj.org.il/userimages/928/2/PublishFiles/953Article.pdf>.

[24] Rose K, Neubauer D, Grant-Kels JM. Too many avoidable suicides occur worldwide in young patients. A review. Rambam Maimonides Med J 2019; Sep 18 <https://www.rmmj.org.il/userimages/965/1/PublishFiles/977OnlineFirst.pdf>.

[25] Cone Jr. TE. Secular acceleration of height and biologic maturation in children during the past century. J Pediatr 1961;59:736–40 Nov.

[26] Komlos J, Lauderdale BE. The mysterious trend in American heights in the 20th century. Ann Hum Biol 2007;34(2):206–15 Mar-Apr.

[27] Fedick AM, Zhang J, Edelmann L, et al. Prenatal diagnosis of cystic fibrosis. Methods Mol Biol 2019;1885:221–31.

[28] Course CW, Hanks R. Newborn screening for cystic fibrosis: is there benefit for everyone? Paediatr Respir Rev 2019;31:3–5 Aug.

[29] Cree BAC, Mares J, Hartung HP. Current therapeutic landscape in multiple sclerosis: an evolving treatment paradigm. Curr Opin Neurol 2019;32(3):365–77 Jun.

[30] Voge NV, Alvarez E. Monoclonal antibodies in multiple sclerosis: present and future. Biomedicines 2019;7(1):20 Mar 14 <https://www.ncbi.nlm.nih.gov/pmc/articles/PMC6466331/pdf/biomedicines-07-00020.pdf>.

[31] FDA 2019. Fingolimod (gilenya) label. <https://www.accessdata.fda.gov/drugsatfda_docs/label/2019/022527s26lbl.pdf>.

[32] FDA 2019. Ponesimod label. <https://www.accessdata.fda.gov/drugsatfda_docs/label/2019/209884s000lbl.pdf>.

[33] FDA 2020. Ozanimod label. <https://www.accessdata.fda.gov/drugsatfda_docs/label/2020/209899s000lbl.pdf>.

[34] Vermersch P. Sphingosine-1-phosphate receptor modulators in multiple sclerosis. Eur Neurol Rev 2018;13(1):25−30 <https://www.touchneurology.com/wp-content/uploads/sites/3/2018/06/private_articles_12344_pdf_EU-NEURO-13_1_p25-30.pdf>.

[35] Chaudhry BZ, Cohen JA, Conway DS. Sphingosine 1-phosphate receptor modulators for the treatment of multiple sclerosis. Neurotherapeutics. 2017;14(4):859−73. Oct <https://www.ncbi.nlm.nih.gov/pmc/articles/PMC5722770/pdf/13311_2017_Article_565.pdf>.

[36] FDA 2014. Copaxone approval letter. <https://www.accessdata.fda.gov/drugsatfda_docs/appletter/2014/020622Orig1s089ltr.pdf>.

[37] FDA 2012. Teriflunamide approval letter. <https://www.accessdata.fda.gov/drugsatfda_-docs/appletter/2012/202992Orig1s000ltr.pdf>

[38] FDA 2010. Fingolimod approval letter. <https://www.accessdata.fda.gov/drugsatfda_docs/nda/2010/022527Orig1s000ltr.pdf>.

[39] FDA 2013. Tecfidera approval letter. <https://www.accessdata.fda.gov/drugsatfda_docs/nda/2013/204063Orig1s000Approv.pdf.>

[40] FDA 2020. Ozanimod (zeposia) approval package including approval letter. <https://www.accessdata.fda.gov/drugsatfda_docs/nda/2020/209899Orig1s000Approv.pdf>.

[41] FDA 2019. Siponimod (mayzent) approval package, including the approval letter. <https://www.accessdata.fda.gov/drugsatfda_docs/nda/2019/209884Orig1s000Approv.pdf.>

[42] FDA 2018. FDA expands approval of Gilenya to treat multiple sclerosis in pediatric patients. <https://www.fda.gov/news-events/press-announcements/fda-expands-approval-gilenya-treat-multiple-sclerosis-pediatric-patients>.

[43] Rose K, Mueller T. Children with multiple sclerosis should not become therapeutic hostages. Ther Adv Neurol Disord 2016;9(5):389−95. <https://www.ncbi.nlm.nih.gov/pmc/articles/PMC4994785/pdf/10.1177_1756285616656592.pdf>.

[44] World Medical Association (WMA) Declaration of Helsinki—Ethical Principles for Medical Research Involving Human Subjects. Adopted by the 18th WMA General Assembly, Helsinki, Finland, June 1964, and amended by the 64th WMA General Assembly, Fortaleza, Brazil, October 2013. <https://www.wma.net/policies-post/wma-declaration-of-helsinki-ethical-principles-for-medical-research-involving-human-subjects/>.

[45] Laughon MM, Benjamin DK. Mechanisms to provide safe and effective drugs for children. Pediatrics. 2014;134(2):e562−3 Aug.

[46] Feger DM, Longson N, Dodanwala H, et al. Comparison of adults with polyarticular juvenile idiopathic arthritis to adults with rheumatoid arthritis: a cross-sectional analysis of clinical features and medication use. J Clin Rheumatol 2019;25(4):163−70 Jun <https://www.ncbi.nlm.nih.gov/pmc/articles/PMC6240403/pdf/rhu-25-163.pdf>.

[47] Nigrovic PA 2013 What adult rheumatologists need to know about juvenile arthritis. <https://www.the-rheumatologist.org/article/what-adult-rheumatologists-need-to-know-about-juvenile-arthritis/?singlepage = 1&theme = print-friendly>.

[48] Nigrovic PA, White PH. Care of the adult with juvenile rheumatoid arthritis. Arthritis Rheum 2006;55(2):208−16 Apr 15 <https://onlinelibrary.wiley.com/doi/pdf/10.1002/art.21857>.

[49] Nigrovic PA, Raychaudhuri S, Thompson SD. Review: genetics and the classification of arthritis in adults and children. Arthritis Rheumatol 2018;70(1):7–17. Jan <https://onlinelibrary.wiley.com/doi/epdf/10.1002/art.40350>.

[50] Oliveira-Ramos F, Eusébio M, Martins FM, et al. Juvenile idiopathic arthritis in adulthood: fulfilment of classification criteria for adult rheumatic diseases, long-term outcomes and predictors of inactive disease, functional status and damage. RMD Open 2016;2(2):e000304 Sep 22 <https://rmdopen.bmj.com/content/2/2/e000304>.

[51] Packham JC, Hall MA. Long-term follow-up of 246 adults with juvenile idiopathic arthritis: functional outcome. Rheumatol (Oxf) 2002;41(12):1428–35 Dec.

[52] Waubant E, Banwell B, Wassmer E, et al. Clinical trials of disease-modifying agents in pediatric MS. Neurology 2019;92(22):e2538–49 May 28.

[53] Wadsworth I, Jaki T, Sills GJ, et al. Clinical drug development in epilepsy revisited: a proposal for a new paradigm streamlined using extrapolation. CNS Drugs 2016;30 (11):1011–1017. Nov <https://www.ncbi.nlm.nih.gov/pmc/articles/PMC5078157/pdf/40263_2016_Article_383.pdf>.

[54] Pellock JM, Arzimanoglu A, D'Cruz O, et al. Extrapolating evidence of antiepileptic drug efficacy in adults to children ≥2 years of age with focal seizures: the case for disease similarity. Epilepsia 2017;58(10):1686–96. Oct <https://onlinelibrary.wiley.com/doi/epdf/10.1111/epi.13859>.

[55] Arzimanoglou A, D'Cruz O, Nordli D, et al. A review of the new antiepileptic drugs for focal-onset seizures in pediatrics: role of extrapolation Paediatr Drugs 2018;20 (3):249–64Jun. Available from: https://doi.org/10.1007/s40272-018-0286-0.

[56] Rose K, Neubauer D, Grant-Kels JM. Ethical issues in pediatric regulatory studies involving placebo treatment. J Pediatr Epilepsy 2020; in press.

Subchapter 4.9

Atopic dermatitis and psoriasis

Introduction

Atopic dermatitis (AD) and psoriasis are the two most common skin conditions seen both by primary care physicians and dermatologists [1].

AD is an inflammatory skin disease that affects 3%–10% of adults and 20%–30% of young persons [2]. AD is characterized by dry skin and severe pruritus. The clinical signs can vary considerably. AD typically begins in early childhood, but a large percentage of cases goes into remission eventually [3]. AD has long been associated with other diseases that have autoimmune and allergic causes, including food allergies, asthma, and allergic rhinitis [4]. Although its exact causes are not completely understood, it is thought to result from a complex interaction of genetic and environmental factors that ultimately lead to impaired epidermal barrier function and immune dysregulation. As sensitization to external substances often is the result of a more porous skin barrier, it was a common misconception that allergy is at the root of AD. AD tends indeed to be the first manifestation of the atopic march [5]. Sensitization through the skin is probably an important initial step in the development of further allergic diseases. Impairment of the outermost layer of the skin (the stratum corneum) results in an increase in transepidermal water loss or a decrease in the skin's ability to hold water. This disruption of the skin barrier is associated with the release of proinflammatory cytokines that promote chemoattractants and adhesional molecules to recruit T-cells to cutaneous sites [3].

Psoriasis is a chronic, systemic, immune-mediated disease characterized by red, indurated, scaly, pruritic, and often painful skin plaques. It affects up to 2%–5% of the general population; in up to one-third of cases, psoriasis begins already in childhood. Psoriasis can range from small, localized patches up to affecting the entire body. There are several sub-types. The most frequent form is plaque psoriasis, also known as psoriasis vulgaris. Psoriasis is driven by proinflammatory cytokines. Also psoriasis is associated with other diseases, including psoriatic arthritis, cardiovascular disease, diabetes mellitus, obesity, inflammatory bowel disease and nonalcoholic fatty liver disease [6,7]. Twenty to thirty percent of psoriasis patients will also develop psoriatic arthritis.

Both AD and psoriasis significantly affect patients' quality of life. The majority of patients with each condition is still treated with topical therapies, with varying degrees of efficacy and patient satisfaction. However, severe cases can present therapeutic challenges, with patients failing multiple lines of treatment [1].

Historically, both AD and psoriasis were considered predominantly as skin diseases. Today, we recognize in both diseases systemic autoinflammatory roots based on a dysregulated immune system. In moderate-to-severe psoriasis, elevated levels of multiple proinflammatory cytokines are found not only in skin lesions, but also in the blood. Today, in treating psoriasis we focus beyond controlling the visible skin inflammation also on the systemic inflammation with two goals: prevent damage associated with systemic inflammation and the progression of psoriasis and its comorbidities; and potentially reverse existing inflammatory damage and signs and symptoms of comorbidities [6]. Biologics have dramatically changed treatment due to their high efficacy and tolerable safety. In addition, their efficacy is also helping us to better understand the underlying causes of psoriasis [8].

Both diseases have different mechanisms of disease. But as in both diseases we consider increasingly the systemic inflammation and the dysregulation of the immune system as a key element, this is not only changing our understanding of AD and psoriasis, but also makes the artificial differentiation of a separate, administratively defined "pediatric" population for treatment and regulatory approval increasingly questionable.

Treatment of AD and psoriasis

Cleansing and moisturization are still the mainstay of treatment in AD. Current guidelines often recommend a short bath or shower followed immediately by the application of emollient moisturizer when the skin is still slightly wet. Avoiding exposure to allergens does not result in a significant reduction of AD severity [3]. Historically, treatment of AD has evolved from topical emollients in the early 1930s to topical steroids in the 1960s, to calcineurin inhibitors in the 2000s, and now increasingly new biologic agents including monoclonal antibodies (MABs) against various interleukins (ILs), specifically IL-4 and IL-13 [1,9].

Crisaborole is a topical low-molecular-weight phosphodiesterase 4 (PDE4) inhibitor that effectively penetrates into the human skin and results in good local antiinflammatory efficacy in AD. PDE4 activity is increased in AD skin, which results in increased production of proinflammatory cytokines [9].

Dupilumab is the only biologic agent currently approved by the FDA for systemic treatment of AD. Dupilumab received FDA approval in March 2017 for adult patients ($>$ 18 years old) with moderate-to-severe AD whose disease is not adequately controlled with topical prescription therapies or when those therapies are not advisable. It can be used with or without topical corticosteroids [9,10].

Also psoriasis is often successfully managed by medications that have been on the market for decades. While topical therapy alone may be sufficient in many patients, others do not achieve treatment success with topicals alone and are therefore candidates for systemic therapy [1].

Biologic agents commonly used for the treatment of psoriasis are categorized into tumor necrosis factor (TNF)-alpha inhibitors and interleukin inhibitors. Infliximab, adalimumab, etanercept, certolizumab-pegol, and golimumab are TNF-alpha inhibitors. Golimumab is used only for psoriatic arthritis. Ustekinumab is an anti-IL-12/ IL-23 monoclonal antibody. Guselkumab, Risankizumab, and tildrakizumab are antibodies against IL-23. Secukinumab, mirikizumab, ixekizumab, and brodalumab are antibodies against IL-17A [8].

Several biological agents that today are FDA-approved for the treatment of moderate-to-severe psoriasis are also approved for the treatment of rheumatoid arthritis, including etanercept, adalimumab, certolizumab and infliximab, and/or for the treatment of Crohn's disease, including adalimumab, infliximab, certolizumab and ustekinumab, as they moderate key elements of the immune cascade [6].

Treatment of AD and psoriasis in young patients

While the number of biologic agents to treat dermatologic conditions in adult patients has expanded in the past decade, biologic options available for "pediatric" AD and psoriasis remain limited. Physicians may consider prescribing these biologics off-label. There is no physiological change in the body in the night of the 18th birthday. There is no scientific basis to argue against off-label prescription, and it is physicians' right and duty to prescribe off-label. Today's system of modern medicine would not work without off-label prescribing. The on-label/off-label framework is complex, and there are good arguments for and against it [11,12], which will not be discussed here more in depth. Here, we discuss the consequences of imposing the on-label/off-label framework to the administratively defined "pediatric" population. Although off-label prescribing is legitimate, it can result in issues with insurance coverage [13]. Furthermore, physicians also fear lawsuits for damage and/or medical malpractice [14–18]. At present, only etanarcept, ustekinumab and adalimumab are EMA-approved for psoriasis in "children." Dupilumab is FDA- and EMA-approved for adult AD, but not yet in "children" [13].

The concept of "pediatric drug development" and separate "pediatric" studies

Separate approval of drugs in "children" defined by an administrative age limit of under 17/18 years of age goes back to the children-are-therapeutic-orphans concept expressed a first time by Shirkey in 1968 [19]. This concept is flawed, as it blurs different meanings of the term "child." Persons that are administratively and legally still children usually become bodily mature long before the 18th birthday [20]. Furthermore, the bodily maturation of young persons in the western world has accelerated considerably over the last hundred years [21,22]. The use of the on-label/off-label framework on the administratively defined "pediatric" population appeals to protective feelings we have when we discuss "children." However, only newborns and young infants are so vulnerable and immature that typical neonate toxicities occur. Young persons do not remain as immature and vulnerable as preterm newborns and newborns until they become legally and administratively of age [23–27].

The US system has two pediatric laws and legal pathways to promote "pediatric" studies. The voluntary pathway goes back to the FDA Modernization Act (FDAMA) in 1997; in 2002, this approach became the "Best Pharmaceuticals For Children Act" (BPCA). The mandatory pathway "Pediatric Research Equity Act" (PREA) goes back to 2003. Both had for a while to be re-authorized every five years, but became permanent in 2012 as the "Food and Drug Administration Safety and Innovation Act" (FDASIA). The FDA has no authority to demand "pediatric" studies for rare and orphan diseases, but it can offer a voluntary reward of six months patent extension for "pediatric" studies. For diseases that occur commonly in both adults and "children," the FDA can demand "pediatric" studies based on PREA. This is the case for AD, psoriasis, and juvenile idiopathic arthritis [23–28].

The EU has taken up the US model and has introduced one single "pediatric" law which came into force in 2007. For new drugs, companies must submit a "pediatric investigation plan" (PIP) at the end of phase 1 studies. This submitted draft PIP is negotiated with the EMA of a standard procedure of one year. In this PIP the company must commit to juvenile animal studies, pediatric formulations (e.g. liquids versus tablets), and "pediatric" clinical studies. "Children" are EU-defined as anybody younger than 18 years [23–28].

In AD and psoriasis, both the FDA and the EMA use the age limit of the 18th birthday in their demands for clinical studies, see the following tables.

FDA-demanded "pediatric" studies for modern drugs used in psoriasis and AD

Table 4.9.1 lists exemplarily "pediatric" studies demanded by the FDA for dupilumab [29], brodalumab [30], and tofacitinib [31]. For all three compounds, the FDA has the authority to demand "pediatric" studies based on the mandatory law PREA. The list of demanded "pediatric" studies is given in the approval letter of the respective compound [29–31].

TABLE 4.9.1 FDA-demanded "pediatric" studies.

Compound	Disease		FSRS
Dupilumab [29]	Atopic dermatitis	1. R DB PC E&S study w/ topical therapy in 6–11 y w/ SAD 2. R DB PC E&S study in 12–17 y w/ MTSAD 3. OL LT safety study in 6 mo–17 y w/ MAOSAD 4. S, PK, E study in 6mo–5 y w/ SAD	09/2019 05/2019 03/2023 11/2021
Brodalumab: [30]	Severe plaque psoriasis	1. OL PK study 6–17 y patients with SPP 2. DB AC MC S&E study in pts 12–17 y with SPP 3. OL SA S&E study in pts 6–11 y with SPP	06/2019 06/2024 06/2029
Tofacitinib [31]	JIA	1. PK study in pts 2–17 y with (JIA) 2. R DB PC E&S study in pts 2–17 y	09/2014 09/2017

AD, Atopic dermatitis; *DB*, double-blind; *DS*, dietary supplement; *ES*, extension study; *E&S*, efficacy and safety; *FSRS*, final study report submission; *JIA*, juvenile idiopathic arthritis; *LT*, long term; *MAOAD*, moderate and/or severe atopic dermatitis; *MTSAD*, moderate-to-severe atopic dermatitis; *OL*, open label; *PC*, placebo-controlled; *R*, randomized; *SAD*, severe atopic dermatitis; *SPP*, severe plaque psoriasis; *y*, year.

Dupilumab is a fully human monoclonal antibody targeting the alpha subunit shared by IL-4 and IL-13 receptors, thereby inhibiting their downstream signaling [10,13]. There is no change of the body in the night of the 18th birthday that would influence the action of dupilumab on the alpha subunit of the IL-4/IL-13 receptors. The antiinflammatory characteristics of dupilumab are identical before and after the 18th birthday. The randomized, placebo-controlled studies no. 1 and 2 in the FDA approval letter expose young patients with severe (study 1) and moderate-to-severe (study 2) patients to placebo, i.e. they deny these patients effective treatment. The last final study report of the four dupilimab "pediatric" studies is expected until 2023 (study # 3).

The brodalumab studies demand "pediatric" patients with severe plaque psoriasis. Study # 2 is asking for patients aged 12–17 years. At this age, the body can already be considered mature, and adult doses for treatment of any disease is adequate [20,23–26]. The last final study report for the FDA-demanded "pediatric" studies in severe plaque psoriasis is expected to be submitted until 2029.

The tofacitinib "pediatric" studies are demanded for juvenile idiopathic arthritis (JIA). JIA is an umbrella term for different types of arthritis that begin before the 16th birthday. For more details on JIA, see the separate chapter in this book.

EMA PIPs in psoriasis and AD

While the FDA asks for "pediatric" studies relatively late in the process of drug development, the EU and its EMA demand a submission of a "pediatric investigation plan" (PIP) at the end of phase 1 studies. The submitted draft PIP is then negotiated with the EMA over a standard period of one year. As the PIPs are demanded so early in the drug development process, many PIPs have been issued for psoriasis and AD.

Table 4.9.2 lists the EMA-issued PIPs for psoriasis.

Table 4.9.3 lists the EMA-issued PIPs for AD.

Table 4.9.4 lists exemplary PIP-demanded "pediatric" studies for psoriasis

Table 4.9.5 lists exemplary PIP-demanded "pediatric" studies for AD

Table 4.9.6 lists ongoing industry-sponsored "pediatric" studies for psoriasis

Table 4.9.7 lists ongoing industry-sponsored "pediatric" studies for AD.

Discussion

Modern antiinflammatory compounds are efficacious also in young persons. The children-are-therapeutic-orphans mantra developed following pediatric

TABLE 4.9.2 Psoriasis pediatric investigation plans (PIPs).

PIP#	Compound	Studies	Age	Until
EMEA-000366-PIP01-08-M06	Adalimumab	1	4–17 y	2014
EMEA-001451-PIP01-13	Tildrakizumab	1	6–17 y	2024
EMEA-000715-PIP03-11-M05	Apremilast	2	6–17 y	2021
EMEA-00552-PIP01-09-M01	Briakinumab	2	4–17 y	2019
EMEA-001089-PIP02-13-M01	Brodalumab	3	6–17 y	2027
EMEA-00299-PIP01-08-M03	Etanercept	3	1–17 y	2011
EMEA-000380-PIP01-08-M04	Secukinumab	3	6–17 y	2023
EMEA-000576-PIP02-11-M04	Tofacitinib	4	6–17 y	2025
EMEA-000311-PIP01-08-M04	Ustekinumab	3	6–17 y	2020
EMEA-002819-PIP01-17-M01	Bimekizumab	3	6–17 y	2030
EMEA-001050-PIP01-10-M04	Ixekizumab	1	6–17 y	2023
EMEA-001523-PIP02-14-M02	Guselkumab	3	6–17 y	2023
EMEA-001776-PIP01-15	Risankizumab	1	6–17 y	2026
EMEA-002350-PIP01-18	BMS-986165	3	6–17 y	2028
EMEA-002208-PIP01-17	Mirikizumab	1	6–17 y	2027

TABLE 4.9.3 AD PIPs.

PIP#	Compound	Studies	Age	Until
EMEA-001501-PIP01-13-M06	Dupilumab	5	6mo–17y	2022
EMEA-001220-PIP03-16-M01	Baricitinib	1	2–17 y	2021
EMEA-001900-PIP02-17-M02	Tralokinumab	5	2–17 y	2025
EMEA-002065-PIP01-16-M01	Crisaborole	5	1mo–17y	2021
EMEA-001624-PIP01-14	Nemolizumab	8	2–17 y	2022
EMEA-000993-PIP01-10	Prednicarbate/ octenidine	2	1mo–17y	2014
EMEA-002464-PIP01-18	LY337588	2	6mo–17y	2027
EMEA-002364-PIP02-18	Diroleuton	3	1mo–17y	2024
EMEA-001741-PIP04-17	Upadacitinib	8	2–17 y	2023
EMEA-002312-PIP01-17	Abrocitinib	8	2–17 y	2029

mo, Month; *y*, year.

TABLE 4.9.4 Exemplary "pediatric" psoriasis studies demanded in EMA PIPs.

Adalimumab	1. MC R DD DB study 2 doses adalimumab versus MTX in pediatric patients with CPP
Brodalumab	1. OL PK, S & T brodalumab study in 4–17 y old patients with SPP 2. R DB AC E&S study in adolescents 12–17 y with SPP 3. SA OL E&S study in children 4–11 y with SPP
Tofacitinib	1. R DB PC E&S study in 6–17 y old patients w/ psoriasis 2. Population PK and exposure-response model in adult psoriasis patients 3. Population PK model in pediatric psoriasis patients 4. Extrapolation of PK characteristics for determining starting dose in pts 12–16 y and 6–11 y

AC, active controlled; *CPP*, chronic plaque psoriasis; *DB*, double-blind; *DD*, double dummy; *E*, efficacy; *E&S*, efficacy and safety; *MC*, multicenter; *MTX*, methotrexate; *mo*, month; *OL*, open label; *PC*, placebo-controlled; *PIP*, pediatric investigation plan; *PK*, pharmacokinetic(s); *R*, randomized; *S*, safety; *SA*, single arm; *SPP*, severe plaque psoriasis; *T*, tolerability; *y*, year.

warnings in new drug labels from 1962 on after the introduction of the Drug Efficacy Amendment (Kefauver-Harris Amendment) to the Federal Food, Drug, and Cosmetics Act in 1962 [11]. The pediatric warnings were triggered by toxicities of antibiotics in newborns observed earlier, in the 1950s [23–27,32]. These pediatric warnings had predominantly the legal purpose to protect manufacturers against damage lawsuits in the litigious US

TABLE 4.9.5 Exemplary "pediatric" studies in AD demanded in EMA PIPs.

Dupilumab	1. OL S & PK study in pts 6–17 y 2. R DB PC E & LT S in pts 12–17 y with MTSAD 3. S, PK & E study in pts 6 mo–5 y with SAD 4. R DB PC E & LT S study in pts 6–11 y with SAD 5. R DB PC E study in pts 6 mo–5 y with SAD
Nemolizumab	1. R PC MC E&S study 2. R PC MC E&S study 3. SA OL LT E&S study 4. SA OL LT E&S study 5. R DB PC MC SD study on systemic exposure and T profile 6. SA OL RD extension study 7. SA OL LT study 8. One-compartment model with first-order absorption (PK)
Abrocitinib	1. DB R PC PG E&S study in adolescents (and adults) with MTSAD 2. DB R PC PG E&S study in adolescents (and adults) with MTSAD 3. DB R PC E&S study as add-on to topical treatment in pts 6–11 y with MTSAD 4. DB R PC PG E&S study as add-on to topical treatment in pts 2–5 y with MTSAD 5. OL uncontrolled LT S study in pts 2–11 y who participated in studies 3 and 4 6. Pop PK analysis and exposure-response modeling of E measures in As & As with MTSAD 7. Pop PK in pediatric patients with MTSAD 8. Extrapolation of PK for determining starting dose in pts 2–11 y

AC, Active controlled; *As & As*, adolescents and adults; *CPP*, chronic plaque psoriasis; *DB*, double-blind; *DD*, double dummy; *E*, efficacy; *E&S*, efficacy and safety; *LT*, long term; *MC*, multicenter; *MTSAD*, moderate-to-severe atopic dermatitis; *OL*, open label; *PC*, placebo-controlled; *PIP*, pediatric investigation plan; *PK*, pharmacokinetic(s); *Pop PK*, population pharmacokinetic(s); *pts*, patients; *R*, randomized; *RD*, repeat dose; *S*, safety; *SA*, single arm; *SAD*, severe atopic dermatitis; *T*, tolerability; *y*, year.

[14–18,23–26]. The FDA/EMA-demanded "pediatric" studies do not aim at improving healthcare of young patients. The only area with justified additional safety concerns in children are newborns and young infants. The PIP-demanded "pediatric" studies in psoriasis (Table 4.9.4) and AD (Table 4.9.5) demand studies in young persons aged over 4 and 6 years (Table 4.9.4) and 6 months and older (Table 4.9.5). Of course, treating inflammatory disease at very young age requires caution. General practitioners will hopefully refuse to treat babies a few months of age with modern drugs that have only recently been approved in adults. But there is no reason to believe that monoclonal antibodies and other modern compounds should not work at all in younger patients and therefore need randomized, double-blind, placebo-controlled studies. There are no "pediatric" interleukins and no "pediatric" IL receptor antagonists. Proteins, blood cells, interleukins, interleukin

TABLE 4.9.6 **Ongoing "pediatric" industry-sponsored clinical trials in psoriasis at clinicaltrials.gov. Terms "psoriasis," "child," industry-sponsored. 39 Hits.**

	NCT#	Compound	Study description	Age (y)	Centers/pts	Status
1	NCT03988439	IDP-118 Lotion	Ph4 OL MC PK + S study in MTSPP	4–17	8/45	recr
2	NCT03987763	IDP-122 Lotion	Ph4 OL MC PK + S study in MTSPP	6–17	4/45	recr
3	NCT04175613	Apremilast	MC OL LT ES in MTSPP	6–17	?/140	recr
4	NCT02698475	Ustekinumab	OL E S PK study in MTSCPP	6–11	31/44	anr
5	NCT03701763	Apremilast	E&S study in MTSPP	6–17	109/230	recr
6	NCT03073200	Ixekizumab	MC DB PC S,T,E study in MTSPP	6–17	69/201	anr
7	NCT04305327	Brodalumab	R DB MC study vs placebo vs. ustekinumab in MTSPP	12–17	?/120	nyr
8	NCT03218488	Ustekinumab	Observational study in MTSPP	12–17	32/75	recr
9	NCT02471144	Secukiumab	R DB MC PC + AC (placebo, etanercept) in SPP	6–17	58/162	anr
10	NCT02970331	Pefcalcitol Ointment	S T PK/PD study in PP	12–16	?/50	nyr
11	NCT03668613	Secukiumab	OL LT S T E in MTSPP	6–17	26/84	anr
12	NCT03997786	Tildrakizumab	MC R E,S, PK, PC + AC (etanercept) study in MTSPP	6–17	9/120	recr
13	NCT03179605	Clobetasol propionate	OL MC study in MTSPP on HPAAS	6–17	9/50	recr
14	NCT03819218	MC2-01 cream	OL S + PK study in EPV	12–16	2/30	recr
15	NCT03240809	Brodalumab	OL S,T, PK study in SPP	6–18	5/16	recr

anr, active, not recruiting; *CPP*, Chronic plaque psoriasis; *DB*, double-blind; *E*, efficacy; *EPV*, extensive psoriasis vulgaris; *E&S*, efficacy & safety; *HPAAS*, hypothalamic-pituitary-adrenal axis suppression; *MC*, multicenter; *MTSP*, moderate-to-severe psoriasis; *MTSCPP*, moderate-to-severe chronic plaque psoriasis; *MTSPP*, moderate-to-severe plaque psoriasis; *nyr*, not yet recruiting; *OL*, open label; *PC*, placebo-controlled; *PD*, pharmacokinetic(s); *PK*, pharmacokinetic(s); *R*, randomized; *recr*, recruiting; *S*, safety; *SCPP*, severe chronic plaque psoriasis; *SPP*, severe plaque psoriasis; *T*, tolerability.

TABLE 4.9.7 Industry-sponsored "pediatric" AD studies listed in www.clinicaltrials.gov.

	NCT#	Compound	Study description	Age	Ctrs/pts	Status
1	NCT03952559	Baricitinib	DB R PC PK E&S study in MTSAD	2–17 y	91/465	recr
2	NCT02612454	Dupilumab	OL ES on LT E&S in AD	6mo–17y	102/800	ebi
3	NCT03822624	Probiotic DS	R DB PC E&S study in AD	4–17 y	3/70	recr
4	NCT04398758	SanaCutan Cream	OL E study cream vs. no cream in preventing AD in high risk pts	< 21days	5/360	recr
5	NCT03257644	Ruxolitinib Cream	OL PK study in AD	2–17 y	13/60	recr
6	NCT03646604	Upadacitinib	S PK T study in severe AD	6mo–12y	15/40	recr
7	NCT03921411	Nemolizumab	PK S study in MTSAD	12–17 y	10/20	anr
8	NCT03526861	Tralokinumab	MC R DB PC E S T study in MTSAD	12–17 y	87/294	anr
9	NCT00568997	Pimecrolimus	OR in AD pts treated w/pimecrolimus	2–17 y	?/8000	recr
10	NCT04156191	ARQ-151 cream	OL PK S E study in MTSAD	2–17 y	5/22	recr
11	NCT03847389	Clobetasol oil	OL PK S study in MTSAD	2–18 y	7/72	recr
12	NCT04265716	Topical LR	R DB PC in MMAD	1–8 y	1/102	recr
13	NCT03346434	Dupilumab	OL PK,S,E study in MTSAD	6 mo–5 y	28/200	recr
14	NCT04023084	Eucrisa	OL BS study response to Eucrisa	5–17 y	1/30	nyr
15	NCT02906475	Emollient	R CO study	< 14days	1/160	anr
16	NCT03808532	Cura + MoisC	R OL study MoisC vs. no MoisC to prevent AD	< 5days	?/290	recr
17	NCT03687359	SP	Observational 5 y study in MTSAD	< 11 y	17/1300	recr
18	NCT03907228	RHT-3201 Probiotic	DB PC E&S in AD	1–12 y	1/102	recr

AD, Atopic dermatitis; *anr*, active not recruiting; *BS*, biomarker searching; *CO*, crossover; *Ctrs*, centers; *DB*, double-blind; *DS*, dietary supplement; *ebi*, enrollment by invitation; *ES*, extension study; *E&S*, efficacy and safety; *LR*, lactobacillus reuteri; *LT*, long term; *MC*, multicenter; *MoisC*, moisturizing cream; *MMAD*, mild or moderate atopic dermatitis; *MTSAD*, moderate-to-severe atopic dermatitis; *nyr*, not yet recruiting; *OL*, open label; *PC*, placebo-controlled; *PK*, pharmacokinetic(s); *pts*, patients; *R*, randomized; *recr*, recruiting; *SP*, standard practice; *T*, tolerability; *w*, with; *y*, year.

receptors and interleukin receptor antagonists have the same size in babies, infants, children and adults.

The EU-demanded early PIP submissions force companies to commit to "pediatric" studies many years before the respective new compound has proven efficacy and reaches the market, if it reaches the market at all. Table 4.9.2 shows that companies have to commit to perform "pediatric" studies in psoriasis until 2030, Table 4.9.3 that companies have to commit to "pediatric" studies in AD until 2029. As the EMA is asking for commitment to "pediatric" studies years before the pivotal studies have even started, the number of EMA-demanded "pediatric" studies is already high today. And many more effective drugs are in development. In the framework of modern drug development, within ten years pharmaceutical treatment of most diseases undergoes profound changes. To demand commitments for clinical studies in young patients over a span of ten years shows that the primary focus of the "pediatric" demands is not the wellbeing of young patients.

To discuss all EMA-demanded "pediatric" studies in psoriasis and AD would require an entire book, which might be written at a later date by academic researchers. Here we have chosen just a few examples.

The PIP-demanded "pediatric" study for adalimumab demanded a study of adalimumab vs. methotrexate. Methotrexate was originally developed in cancer treatment as it inhibits proliferation and turnover of malignant cells. Since then, it has been broadly used also in many inflammatory diseases with a high turnover of inflammatory cells, such as T lymphocytes. The antiproliferative effects of MTX also explain many of its side effects, including bone marrow suppression, alopecia, inflammation of the stomach, liver fibrosis, or liver cirrhosis [33,34]. The PIP-demanded adalimumab "pediatric" study was performed in 38 centers in 13 countries, and has been published [35]. It was followed by a publication on an extension study [36]. In the first publication, comparison of adalimumab vs. methotrexate, the authors proudly report that although methotrexate is commonly used in daily practice for young patients with plaque psoriasis showing inadequate response to other treatments, there had been no previous randomized controlled trials. The study result was that adalimumab provides greater efficacy than methotrexate [35]. The one key question not discussed in this paper is if this study made scientific and medical sense. It discusses the treatment of "children" without reflecting that the administrative meaning of the term "children" means that many of the study participants were bodily no longer children. Bodily, many were already mature. Roughly half of the participants were adolescents between 12 and 17 years of age [35]. That adalimumab was effective was no surprise. This study is a good example for the myriad of "pediatric" clinical studies that are declared to be "pediatric" studies, although many of the recruited patients were physiologically no longer children. This study was published in 2017 in the Lancet, a journal of highest reputation, showing that the concept of "pediatric drug development" has to this day remained largely unchallenged.

The brodalumab "pediatric" psoriasis studies in Table 4.9.4 demand comparison of brodalumab against an active control (Table 4.9.4, study 2). Brodalumab is FDA-approved in adult patients with moderate-to-severe plaque psoriasis who are candidates for systemic therapy or phototherapy and have failed to respond or have lost response to other systemic therapies [37]. Both the FDA and the EMA demand separate "pediatric" studies, as if patients younger than 18 years were another species.

For tofacitinib, the PIP demands a "pediatric" placebo-controlled study in psoriasis (Table 4.9.4, study 3). Tofacitinib is FDA-approved in adults with rheumatic arthritis, psoriatic arthritis, and ulcerative colitis [38]. In 2012, the FDA-demanded "pediatric" studies in patients 2 to 17 years old with juvenile idiopathic arthritis. The EMA PIP-demanded studies include a double-blind placebo-controlled study in patients 6 to 17 years old with psoriasis. There is no pharmacological reason to assume that tofacitinib should only work in patients after the 18th birthday. The antiinflammatory characteristics of tofacitinib are well known. To demand a placebo-controlled study with this medication denies young patient effective treatment.

PIPs demand separate placebo-controlled "pediatric" studies for dupilumab (Table 4.9.5, dupilumab studies 2, 4, 5) and abrocitinib (Table 4.9.5, abrocitinib studies 3 and 4). For abrocitinib, the PIP accepts the inclusion of adolescents into the pivotal studies (Table 4.9.5, studies 1 and 2). For nemolizumab, the PIP does not give the patients' age of the demanded studies in the list of studies, but lists the age of concerned patients as from 2 to 17 years.

Table 4.9.6 and 4.9.7 list all industry-sponsored studies that currently recruit patients up to 18 years worldwide, are still in preparation, are still active but do no longer recruit, or enroll by invitation. Drug development is commercial. Studies 4, 15, and 16 in Table 4.9.7 examine if AD in newborns can be prevented, which is a legitimate question. It is good that pharmaceutical companies try to find new ways to prevent AD. Other studies are open label safety studies, or they examine probiotic dietary supplement against placebo. Probiotics are not approved as drugs. That companies give them a try in preventing AD is acceptable. But the questionable studies in Table 4.9.6 and 4.9.7 are those that compare compounds with already well-established efficacy in humans against placebo. Once pivotal studies in humans have shown efficacy of a new compound, usually in two separate studies, the compound's efficacy can be regarded as proven. To demand additional placebo-controlled studies in young patients is abuse of the patients and of the trust their parents still put into the medical system.

Table 4.9.6 lists the currently ongoing "pediatric" studies in AD listed in www.clinicaltrials.gov. The studies # 2 (baricitinib) and # 8 (tralokinumab) compare compounds with well-known antiinflammatory characteristics against placebo, which means that they deny young patients treatment known already to be effective.

Table 4.9.7 lists the currently ongoing "pediatric" studies in psoriasis listed in www.clinicaltrials.gov. Studies # 6 (ixekizumab), # 7 (brodalumab), # 9 (secukinimab) and # 12 (tildrakizumab) compare compounds with well-known antiinflammatory characteristics against placebo. These studies deny young patients treatment known already to be effective in human beings.

To perform randomized controlled clinical trials against placebo or against another active compound should not be a self-purpose. These trials were introduced into the medical system to prevent quack or dangerous compounds to be sold as medicines. Unfortunately, today's medical system has made the performance of clinical studies almost a self-purpose. The authors of the adalimumab vs. methotrexate study report proudly that this was the first randomized controlled study of either adalimumab or methotrexate in children and adolescents with psoriasis [35]. This study did not make medical or scientific sense. The study report is still accepting the administrative use of the term "children" without reflecting that bodily many patients were no longer children.

A recent academic paper discusses developing drugs for treatment of AD in "children," defining "children" three months of age or older up to 17 years old in the paper's headline [39]. This is an administrative, not a physiological definition. Many of the authors are dermatologists with a high reputation in the scientific world. By accepting and using this administrative definition of "children," they take for granted that these separate studies are a given. This helps to justify questionable studies demanded by the FDA and the EMA, but does not advance child healthcare. Furthermore, there is a massive conflict of interest. Publications of papers in high ranking medical journals have a strong impact on academic careers.

Conclusion

While for adults and children continuously better drugs are developed, the regulatory authorities have adopted the concept of separate "pediatric drug development," which is not justified on clinical grounds, and withholds modern efficacious drugs against AD and psoriasis from young patients. Resulting "pediatric" studies are at best medically and scientifically senseless, which is already bad enough. Many even harm young patients by exposing them to placebo or to sub-optimal standard-of-care treatment.

This alone is bad enough. However, the true tragedy here is that in the name of child healthcare time and resources are wasted. There was a time that there were no or almost no effective drugs against AD and psoriasis. Today, we have plenty of them, and companies are developing more. The aim of true pediatric research should not be to achieve separate "pediatric" drug labels based on the flawed concepts of children-are-therapeutic-orphans or children-are-not-small-adults, but to improve the ways how young persons get access to advanced treatment, and how to continue optimal treatment for decades.

Young physicians and other healthcare professionals are full of energy and full of good intentions. At present, much of this energy is wasted for medically and scientifically useless studies, of which many even harm young patients. We can discuss what is worse: the abuse of young patients in questionable and harmful clinical studies, or that the energy, funds and time invested into these studies deter from research that would have the potential to really improve healthcare in young patients. Such improvements are today technically possible, but are hindered by the regulatory authorities, pediatric researchers, healthcare professionals in clinical research organizations and employees of pharmaceutical companies that have found a niche within which they defend and justify senseless allegedly "pediatric" studies.

References

[1] Psomadakis CE, Han G. New and emerging topical therapies for psoriasis and atopic dermatitis. J Clin Aesthet Dermatol 2019;12(12):28–34 Dec <https://www.ncbi.nlm.nih.gov/pmc/articles/PMC7002051/pdf/jcad_12_12_28.pdf>.

[2] Oliveira C, Torres T. More than skin deep: the systemic nature of atopic dermatitis. Eur J Dermatol 2019;29(3):250–8 Jun 1.

[3] Kraft MT, Prince BT. Atopic dermatitis is a barrier issue, not an allergy issue. Immunol Allergy Clin North Am 2019;39(4):507–19 Nov.

[4] de la O-Escamilla NO, Sidbury R. Atopic dermatitis: update on pathogenesis and therapy. Pediatr Ann 2020;49(3):e140–6 Mar 1.

[5] Schneider L, Hanifin J, Boguniewicz M, et al. Study of the atopic march: development of atopic comorbidities. Pediatr Dermatol 2016;33:388–98 <https://www.ncbi.nlm.nih.gov/pmc/articles/PMC5649252/pdf/nihms912001.pdf>.

[6] Korman NJ. Management of psoriasis as a systemic disease: what is the evidence? Br J Dermatol 2020;182(4):840–8. Apr <https://www.ncbi.nlm.nih.gov/pmc/articles/PMC7187293/pdf/BJD-182-840.pdf>.

[7] Lansang P, Bergman JN, Fiorillo L, et al. Management of pediatric plaque psoriasis using biologics. J Am Acad Dermatol 2020;82(1):213–21 Jan.

[8] Kamata M, Tada Y. Efficacy and safety of biologics for psoriasis and psoriatic arthritis and their impact on comorbidities: a literature review. Int J Mol Sci 2020;21(5):1690 Mar 1 <https://www.ncbi.nlm.nih.gov/pmc/articles/PMC7084606/pdf/ijms-21-01690.pdf>.

[9] Saini S, Pansare M. New insights and treatments in atopic dermatitis. Pediatr Clin North Am 2019;66(5):1021–33 Oct.

[10] FDA 2018. Dupilumab (Dupixent®) label. <https://www.accessdata.fda.gov/drugsatfda_docs/label/2018/761055s007lbl.pdf>.

[11] Janssen WM. A historical perspective on off-label medicine: from regulation, promotion, and the first amendment to the next frontiers. In: Levy MC, editor. Food and Drug Law Institute. First Washington, D.C.: USA Off-Label Communications; 2008.

[12] Mazina N Recent developments in off-label use and legal implications to physicians. American Bar Association, Health Law Section, No. 14 Vol. 3, Available at: <https://www.americanbar.org/groups/health_law/publications/aba_health_esource/2016-2017/november2017/offlabeluse.html>.

[13] Cline A, Bartos GJ, Strowd LC, et al. Biologic treatment options for pediatric psoriasis and atopic dermatitis. Child (Basel) 2019;6(9):103 Sep 11 <https://www.ncbi.nlm.nih.gov/pmc/articles/PMC6769539/pdf/children-06-00103.pdf>.

[14] Kritzer HM. Propensity to Sue in England and the United States of America: blaming and claiming in tort cases. J Law Soc 1991;18(4):400–27.

[15] Lochlann Jain SS. Injury: the politics of product design and safety law in the United States. Princeton, NJ, USA: Princeton University Press; 2006.

[16] McGovern F. Punitive damages and class actions. Lousiana Law Rev 2010;70:435–62 <https://scholarship.law.duke.edu/cgi/viewcontent.cgi?article = 2762&context = faculty_scholarship>.

[17] Bal BS. An introduction to medical malpractice in the United States. Clin Orthop Relat Res 2009;467(2):339–47 Feb <https://www.ncbi.nlm.nih.gov/pmc/articles/PMC2628513/>.

[18] Kass JS, Rose RV. Medical malpractice reform: historical approaches, alternative models, and communication and resolution programs. AMA J Ethics 2016;18(3):299–310 <https://journalofethics.ama-assn.org/sites/journalofethics.ama-assn.org/files/2019-12/pfor6-1603.pdf>.

[19] Shirkey H. Therapeutic orphans. J Pediatr 1968;72(1):119–20 Jan <https://pdfs.semanticscholar.org/f1cb/acdbac19fa56236b919fb7799eaacaa10c77.pdf>.

[20] Kearns GL, Abdel-Rahman SM, Alander SW, Blowey DL, Leeder JS, Kauffman RE. Developmental pharmacology—drug disposition, action, and therapy in infants and children. N Engl J Med 2003;349(12):1157–67 Sep 18.

[21] Cone Jr. TE. Secular acceleration of height and biologic maturation in children during the past century. J Pediatr 1961;59:736–40 Nov.

[22] Komlos J, Lauderdale BE. The mysterious trend in American heights in the 20th century. Ann Hum Biol 2007;34(2):206–15 Mar-Apr.

[23] Rose K. The challenges of pediatric drug development. Curr Ther Res Clin Exp 2019;. Available from: https://doi.org/10.1016/j.curtheres.2019.01.007.

[24] Rose K, Grant-Kels JM. The meanings of "pediatric drug development." A review. Ther Innov Regul Sci 2019;53(6):767–74 Nov.

[25] Rose K, Neubauer D, Grant-Kels JM. Rational use of medicine in children—the conflict of interests story. A review. Rambam Maimonides Med J 2019;10(3):e0018. Available from: https://doi.org/10.5041/RMMJ.10371 Review <https://www.rmmj.org.il/userimages/928/2/PublishFiles/953Article.pdf>.

[26] Rose K, Neubauer D, Grant-Kels JM. Too many avoidable suicides occur worldwide in young patients. A review. Rambam Maimonides Med J 2019; Sep 18 <https://www.rmmj.org.il/userimages/965/1/PublishFiles/977OnlineFirst.pdf>.

[27] Rose K, Happle R. The impact of regulation on pediatric psoriasis drug approvals: the challenge of the European Union (EU) pediatric investigation plans. Pediatr Dermatol 2017;34(3):e154–9 May.

[28] Hirschfeld S, Saint-Raymond A. Pediatric regulatory initiatives. Handb Exp Pharmacol 2011;205:245–68.

[29] FDA 2017. Dupilumab approval letter atopic dermatitis <https://www.accessdata.fda.gov/drugsatfda_docs/appletter/2017/761055Orig1s000ltr.pdf>.

[30] FDA 2017. Brodalumab approval letter. <https://www.accessdata.fda.gov/drugsatfda_-docs/nda/2017/761032Orig1s000Approv.pdf>

[31] FDA 2012. Tofacitinib approval letter. <https://www.accessdata.fda.gov/drugsatfda_docs/nda/2012/203214Orig1s000Approv.pdf>

[32] AAP. Guidelines for the ethical conduct of studies to evaluate drugs in pediatric populations, committee on drugs. Am Acad Pediatrics, Pediatrics 1995;95(2):286–94 1995 Feb.

[33] Cronstein BN, Aune TM. Methotrexate and its mechanisms of action in inflammatory arthritis. Nat Rev Rheumatol 2020;16(3):145–54 Mar.

[34] Chan ESL, Cronstein BN. Molecular action of methotrexate in inflammatory diseases. Bull Hosp Jt Dis 2013;71(Suppl 1):S5–8. <http://presentationgrafix.com/_dev/cake/files/archive/pdfs/52.pdf>.

[35] Papp K, Thaçi D, Marcoux D, et al. Efficacy and safety of adalimumab every other week versus methotrexate once weekly in children and adolescents with severe chronic plaque psoriasis: a randomised, double-blind, phase 3 trial. Lancet. 2017;390(10089):40–9 Jul 1.

[36] Thaçi D, Papp K, Marcoux D, et al. Sustained long-term efficacy and safety of adalimumab in paediatric patients with severe chronic plaque psoriasis from a randomized, double-blind, phase III study. Br J Dermatol 2019;181(6):1177–89. Dec <https://www.ncbi.nlm.nih.gov/pmc/articles/PMC6916374/pdf/BJD-181-1177.pdf>.

[37] FDA 2017. Brodalumab label. <https://www.accessdata.fda.gov/drugsatfda_docs/label/2017/761032lbl.pdf>.

[38] FDA 2012. Tofacitinib label. <https://www.accessdata.fda.gov/drugsatfda_docs/label/2018/203214s018lbl.pdf>.

[39] Siegfried EC, Jaworski JC, Eichenfield LF, Paller A, Hebert AA, Simpson EL, et al. Developing drugs for treatment of atopic dermatitis in children (≥3 months to < 18 years of age): Draft guidance for industry. Pediatr Dermatol 2018;35(3):303–22 May.

Subchapter 4.10

Cystic fibrosis

Introduction

Persons with cystic fibrosis (CF) cannot produce normal sweat, digestive fluids, mucus, or other fluids needed for all the bodily processes that work smoothly in healthy persons without anybody paying much attention. CF affects the lungs, the pancreas, the liver, the kidneys, the intestines, and other parts of the body. Before modern treatments emerged, it was a lethal disease early in childhood. In the centuries before the Enlightenment, midwives knew that babies who tasted salty from kissing or licking the brow often had to die soon; in these days, the common belief was that they were cursed [1]. CF was first described scientifically in 1938, based on observations of infants and children on whom postmortem examination had been done. Such childrens' medical history was described as been born looking well with proper weight, fed with care but did not gain weight; pulmonary infection supervened; there was no vomiting, but the infants simply refused to survive. Dr. Anderson found comparable scars and tissue damages in the lungs and in the pancreas and concluded that these damages came from the same disease which she called "cystic fibrosis of the pancreas" [2].

Babies with CF died usually before their first birthday from malnutrition due to pancreatic insufficiency. Pancreatic enzyme supplementation to improve digestion was the first major therapeutic step forward, but children still died early from chronic bacterial respiratory infections, predominantly staphylococcus aureus and pseudomonas aeruginosa. Over the following decades, treatment of the airways was added to the armamentarium, including systemic and inhaled antibiotics, drugs able to ease the high viscosity of the lung secretions such as recombinant deoxyribonuclease which breaks down deoxyribonucleic acid (DNA) in the sputum and in the lung mucosa and thus decreases its viscosity, and hypertonic saline. Increasingly, treatment intensity and standardized patient follow-up improved outcomes further. CF is the most common lethal genetic autosomal recessive disease in the Caucasian ("white") population, but affects persons of any racial background, although with a lower frequency [3,4].

The cause of CF

CF is caused by a defective transport protein, the CF Transmembrane Conductance Regulator (CFTR). The gene for the CFTR was identified in

1989 [5]. CFTR works as an ion transport channel on the outside surface of specialized epithelial cells, including sweat glands, the internal surface of the pancreas, the gastrointestinal and reproductive tracts, airway epithelia, submucosal glands, and other organs. Apart from working as a transport channel, the CFTR has several other regulatory roles within cells and between cells and organs. When the CFTR does not work properly, secretions, which in healthy persons are relatively thin, are instead thick and of high viscosity. Not all persons with defective CFTR genes have full CF. Some persons develop CF symptoms late or only have lung trouble, liver disease, or are infertile. In these persons, diagnosis of CF used to be made in adulthood. Nevertheless, they also can get respiratory problems, and symptomatic CF treatment helps. If CF goes undiagnosed and untreated in early life, severe lung problems can already be present at diagnosis. Prevention of progression of lung disease and its complications is highly important. Today we know CF newborn screening is overall beneficial [4,6–8]. Newborn screening programs, including screening for CF, have been introduced in the developed world, including most European countries and the US, although screening protocols still vary substantially, and there is little consensus about the optimal screening pathway [9,10]. Testing for CF is recommended for parents with a known higher risk to get a child with CF [5].

We receive our genes from both mother and father. Persons in which only one gene ("allele") that encodes for the CFTR is defective are clinically healthy. One gene is enough to have sufficient CFTR. Such a person is "only" a "carrier." However, if both parents have defective genes, i.e., are "carriers," their child may not have enough working CFTR, resulting in CF. CF is an "autosomal recessive" disease. Parents with a child that has CF can also get healthy children, but the chance for another child with CF depends of the parents' genes and a number of further factors. Genetic counseling is recommended. Genetic counselors translate the results of genetic testing to people with CF, their parents, their family, and the involved care teams. This expertise is today becoming more important as the lifespan of persons with CF is currently massively increasing. With their dual psychosocial and medical roles, genetic counselors can provide an important bridge between scientific advancement and real-world application for a life with CF [11]. Also prenatal diagnosis of CF is increasingly offered and practiced today [5].

The cystic fibrosis foundation

Faced with insurmountable odds, but determined to fight for the lives of their children, a group of US parents of CF children established the Cystic Fibrosis Foundation (CFF) in 1955 [12,13]. In 1961, the CFF created two centers devoted to treating CF and thus established a care center network. In 1962, the predicted age survival of children with CF was ten years, in 1970 sixteen years, in 1980 eighteen years. In 1978, the number of CFF-accredited care centers was already more than one hundred. The team of scientists that detected the CFTR gene had been supported by the CFF [13].

The CF Foundation developed the concept of "venture philanthropy": funding drug development in for-profit companies. Until then, most disease nonprofit organization had focused their fundraising on academic and medical research. In 2000, the CFF invested $ US 40 million into Aurora Biosciences (now Vertex) to discover and develop compounds that might correct CFTR mutations. In these days, such compounds did not exist. Thus, this investment was a gamble. After ivacaftor had been FDA-approved, the CFF sold in 2014 royalty rights for CF treatments developed by Vertex for $US 3.3 billion. In the future, the CFF might receive additional payments. Today the CFF is funding research programs with several more leading biopharmaceutical companies worldwide. So far, it has invested $ US 425 million as part of its venture philanthropy model to accelerate drug development for CF. The CFF approach has also been emulated by other rare disease nonprofit organizations. A US National Institutes of Health (NIH) initiative has adopted CFF strategies to advance drug development for rare and neglected diseases [14–16].

Modern CF treatment

Before the CFTR was identified, treatment could only be symptomatic. Treatment was from the beginning multidisciplinary, including nutritional support, drug therapy, ergotherapy, psychological support of patients and parents, and more. The four key components were (1) nutritional repletion, (2) relief of airway obstruction, (3) treatment of airway infections, and (4) suppression of inflammation. Originally, the intense inflammation in the CF lung had been considered the body's reasonable response to infection. Eventually, inflammation began to be considered as an independent challenge that needed pharmacological treatment. Suppression of inflammation was for a while done by alternate-day steroids or by high-dose ibuprofen, which reduced the rate of decline of pulmonary function in young, otherwise still healthy CF patients. But alternate-day steroids were associated with unacceptable rates of growth failure, cataracts, and diabetes. Ibuprofen showed greater improvement in rate of decline of pulmonary function and had fewer adverse effects, but is associated with increased incidence of gastrointestinal bleeding [17,18]. Pharmacological interventions require a good awareness of both the therapeutic potential of the respective drugs, a careful balance against well-known potential side effects, and a continuous alertness toward unexpected side effects.

When the CFTR gene was identified in 1989 [5,19], the idea emerged to help the defective CFTR protein to work properly. CFTR deficiencies range from complete absence of CFTR from the cell surface to defective or reduced channel activity.

There are today more than 2,000 different types of mutations known that lead to a defective CFTR and hence to CF. A missing phenylalanine molecule at position 508 (F508del) is the most common gene mutation. Many further mutations cause CF. Most are rare, and only roughly 20 mutations reach a frequency of 0.1%. Furthermore, the severity of CF is influenced by many factors beyond CFTR mutation such as modifier genes, environment, and lifestyle. To make things even more complicated, different CFTR mutations may be found on the two alleles of a CF patient with CF [18,19].

Understanding the CFTR structure and function helped in the development of small-molecule compounds to improve or restore the activity of mutant CFTR. Such compounds are termed CFTR modulators, CFTR potentiators, and/or CFTR correctors. Several further CFTR modulators/potentiators/correctors beyond ivacaftor, tezakaftor, lumacaftor and elexacaftor are currently in development in several stages [19].

The first CFTR modulator was ivacaftor, able to improve the CFTR activity in patients with the G551D mutation, who account for 4%–5% of patients with CF. It was developed in collaboration with the CFF. Ivacaftor was approved by the FDA and the EMA in 2012 in CF patients 6 years and older. Ivacaftor was the first drug to treat the underlying cause rather than the symptoms of the disease. Later on, ivacaftor was approved for several more mutations responsible for CF [19].

Table 4.10.1 gives an overview over the history of the CFTR potentiator ivacaftor and its follow-up substances lumacaftor, tezakaftor, and elexacaftor.

Today, three oral drugs are FDA-approved to treat the underlying defect in CF: ivacaftor (kalydeco), lumacaftor + ivacaftor (orkambi) and tezacaftor + ivacaftor (symdeco), for details see Table 4.10.1. In October 2019, the elexacaftor, ivacaftor, tezacaftor (Trikafta) triple combination was approved by the FDA [20,21]. Essentially, the EMA followed the FDA in approving ivacaftor and its follow-up substances. The triple combination of elexaftor + tezacaftor + ivacaftor (Trikafta) was not EMA-approved in May 2020.

US and EU pediatric legislation and its contribution to treating CF

The FDA offered a pediatric written request for ivacaftor, i.e. six months patent extension for sponsoring/performing "pediatric" studies in patients <17 years of age [23]. Ivacaftor was from the very beginning approved for patients six years or older [24].

Table 4.10.2 lists the pediatric investigation plans (PIPs) that the EMA has issued for compounds intended to help in CF.

TABLE 4.10.1 Approval history of CF correctors in the US [13].

2012	The FDA approves ivacaftor for CF patients >6 years with the G551D mutation.
2014	The FDA approves ivacaftor for CF patients aged >6 years with one of eight further CF mutations *(G1244E, G1349D, G178R, G551S, S1251N, S1255P, S549N, S549R).*
2015	The FDA approves lumacaftor + ivacaftor (Orkambi) for CF patients >12 years with two copies of F508del, the most common CF mutation, representing about a third of CF patients in the US.
2016	The FDA approves the lumacaftor + ivacaftor in CF patients 6–11 years with two copies of the F508del mutation.
2017	The FDA approves ivacaftor in CF patients >2 years with at least one of 23 residual function mutations in the CFTR gene.
2018	The FDA approves tezacaftor + ivacaftor (Symdeko) in CF patients >12 years with two copies of the F508del mutation.
2018	Tezacaftor + ivacaftor (Symdeko) is approved for CF patients with a single copy of one of 26 specified mutations, regardless of their other mutation.
2019	The FDA approves ivacaftor in CF patients >6 months with certain mutations. Study data indicate that starting modulators at a young age has the potential to slow or even prevent disease progression.
2019	The FDA approves tezacaftor + ivacaftor (Symdeko) in CF patients 6 to 11 years with two copies of the F508del mutation or a single copy of one of 26 specified mutations.
2019	The FDA approves the triple combination elexacaftor + tezacaftor + ivacaftor (Trikafta) for CF patients > 12 years with at least one copy of the F508del mutation, regardless of their other mutation. For the first time the majority of CF patients can potentially have a highly effective therapy.

Table 4.10.3 lists exemplarily "pediatric" clinical studies demanded in EU PIPs.

CF used to be a predominantly pediatric disease

When CF was described a first time in 1938, babies and infants with CF died early. After initial advances in treatment, followed by the breakthrough in CFTR modulation, CF has started to turn from a lethal disease toward a chronic condition that increasingly allows a normal life, which constitutes a veritable medical revolution comparable to the early breakthroughs in pediatric oncology emerging from the 1960s on [25], the development of effective antidepressants [26], or the successful introduction of CAR-T cell therapy in treating relapsed or refractory acute lymphoblastic leukemia [27,28].

TABLE 4.10.2 CF PIPs, number of demanded clinical studies, and their time horizon[a].

#	PIP #	Product	Studies	Until
1	EMEA-000035-PIP01-07-M05	Tiotropium bromide	4	2012
2	EMEA-000176-PIP01-07-M04	Colistimethate sodium	6	2018
3	EMEA-000335-PIP01-08-M13	Ivacaftor	9	2020
4	EMEA-000436-PIP01-08	Mannitol	4	2011
5	EMEA-000184-PIP01-08-M01	Tobramycin	2	2015
6	EMEA-000525-PIP01-08-M06	Amikacin sulfate	7	2023
7	EMEA-000115-PIP02-09-M03	Ataluren	5	2019
8	EMEA-000827-PIP01-09-M04	Aztreonam	4	2021
9	EMEA-001211-PIP01-11-M01	Levofloxacin	6	2019
10	EMEA-001173-PIP01-11-M01	Lumacaftor	8	2017
11	EMEA-001582-PIP01-13-M09	Lumacaftor + ivacaftor	10	2024
12	EMEA-001640-PIP01-14-M05	Tezakaftor + ivacaftor	11	2024
13	EMEA-001965-PIP01-16	Olodaterol	4	2021
14	EMEA-002082-PIP01-16	BI 443651	8	2025
15	EMEA-002191-PIP02-17	Ivacaftor + tezacaftor + VX-659	11	2029
16	EMEA-002324-PIP01-17	Elexacaftor + tezacaftor + ivacaftor	11	2029
17	EMEA-002398-PIP01-18	PTI-428	8	2027

Explanation: Twelve PIPs came up at the EMA website when the PIPs were searched for "treatment of cystic fibrosis." The other PIPs were listed in Rose & Spigarelli [22] some have undergone further modifications since 2015.
[a]***Order of listing:*** *by date of PIP submission, visible as the two numbers at the end of the original PIP. "07" stands for 2007, "18" for 2018.*

The justification for US and EU pediatric legislation is that drugs are developed and clinical tested in adults and not in "children" [29–34]. But CF is a disease that used to be predominantly pediatric. Aurora Biosciences/ Vertex investigated from the very beginning a disease for which pediatric expertise was a key component.

CF treatment has undergone a veritable revolution over the last years. This leads us to the following critical questions:

- What were the results of the EMA PIP activities for compounds intended to treat CF?

TABLE 4.10.3 Exemplary PIP-demanded clinical studies in cystic fibrosis.

Ivacaftor	1. R DB PC PG S&E study in pts 12–17 y (and adults) with G551D Mutation 2. R DB PC PG E&S study in pts 6–11 y with G551D mutation 3. randomized, double-blind, placebo-controlled, multicenter study in patients with CF with at least 1 Allele of a R117H-CFTR mutation, age 6 years and older 4. R double-blind, placebo-controlled, multicenter study in pts 12–17 y (and adults) with CF with the ΔF508/ΔF508-CFTR mutation 5. Rollover long-term safety and efficacy study in (adults) and children with CF age 6 years and older with at least one allele of G551D-CFTR mutation 6. R double-blind, placebo-controlled, crossover study to evaluate the effect of ivacaftor (VX-770) on lung clearance index in subjects with cystic fibrosis with the G551D mutation and a FEV1 above 90% predicted, 6 years and older 7. A 2-part open-label study to evaluate the safety, PK, and PD of ivacaftor (VX-770) in subjects with cystic fibrosis and a CFTR gating mutation, aged 2 to less than 6 years 8. A 2-part open-label study to evaluate the safety, PK, and PD of ivacaftor in subjects with cystic fibrosis who are less than 24 months of age and have a CFTR gating mutation 9. Two-part, randomized, double-blind, placebo-controlled, crossover study with an open-label period to evaluate the efficacy and safety of ivacaftor in patients with Cystic Fibrosis aged 6 years or older, who have a non-G551D CFTR gating mutation
Lumacaftor	1. OL MC PK + S study in combination with ivacaftor and their respective major circulating metabolites in pts 6–11 y homozygous for the F508del-CFTR mutation 2. R DB PC E,S, PK study in pts 6–11 y homozygous for the F508del-CFTR mutation 3. R DB PC E&S study in pts 11-17 y (+ adults) homozygous for the F508del-CFTR mutation 4. R DB PC E&S study in pts 12–17 y (and adults homozygous for the F508del-CFTR mutation) 5. Rollover OL LT E&S study in pts 6-17 y (and adults) homozygous for the F508del-CFTR mutation 6. Pharmacokinetic and safety study in subjects with CF who are homozygous for the F508del-CFTR mutation aged 2 to less than 6 years (Study 15). 7. Pharmacokinetic and safety study in subjects with CF who are homozygous for the F508del-CFTR mutation from birth to less than 2 years of age (Study 16). 8. Relative bioavailability study to characterize the PK of the pediatric age appropriate formulation relative to the tablet formulation in healthy adults.

(*Continued*)

TABLE 4.10.3 (Continued)

L + I	1. Open-label, multidose study to evaluate the pharmacokinetics (PK) and safety of lumacaftor in combination with ivacaftor and their respective major circulating metabolites in subjects with Cystic Fibrosis (CF) who are homozygous for the F508del-CFTR mutation aged 6 to less than 12 years 2. Randomized, double-blind, placebo-controlled study to evaluate efficacy and safety and PK in subjects with CF homozygous for the F508del-CFTR mutation aged 6 to less than 12 years 3. Randomized, double-blind, placebo-controlled study to evaluate efficacy and safety in subjects with CF who are homozygous for the F508del-CFTR mutation aged 12 to less than 18 years (and adults) 4. Randomized, double-blind, placebo-controlled study to evaluate efficacy and safety in subjects with CF who are homozygous for the F508del-CFTR mutation aged 12 to less than 18 years (and adults) 5. RO LT S&E study in pts 12–17 y (and adults) homozygous for the F508del-CFTR mutation 6. PK + S study in pts 2-5 y homozygous for the F508del-CFTR mutation 7. PK + S study in pts 1 y old homozygous for the F508del-CFTR mutation
T + I	1. DB PC PG MC E and LT S study in pts 12–17 y (and adults) homozygous for the F508del-CFTR mutation 2. DB PC MC E&S in F508del-CFTR heterozygous pts 12–17 y (and adults) with a T + I nonresponsive mutation on the second allele 3. DB P + AC 6-sequence, 8 week CO S&E study in F508del-CFTR heterozygous subjects with a residual function mutation that is potentially ivacaftor-responsive on the second allele, in pts 12–17 y (and adults). 4. DB AC MC PA E&S study in F508del-CFTR heterozygous pts 12–17 y (and adults) with a clinically proven ivacaftor-responsive mutation with a gating defect on the second allele 5. OL MC S + PK study of two weeks treatment with single oral doses in pts 6–11 y homozygous or heterozygous for the F508del-CFTR mutation 6. R DB P + AC parallel MC E,S, PK study of 8 in pts 6–11 y homozygous or heterozygous for the F508-del-CFTR mutation 7. RO OL LT S&E study in pts 12–17 y (and adults) 8. Two-part UC MC S, PK, PD, E study in pts 2-5 y HOH for the F508del-CFTR mutation 9. Two-part, UC, MC study on LT S + PK in pts from birth to <2 y homozygous or heterozygous for the F508del CFTR mutation. 10. R SD crossover, relative bioavailability study in healthy adults to characterize PK of age appropriate pediatric formulation relative to the adult formulation. 11. OL RO S&E study of LT treatment in pts 6–11 y at the beginning of this study homozygous or heterozygous for the F508del mutation 12. M&S study for dose selection in pts from birth to 11 y

(Continued)

TABLE 4.10.3 (Continued)

E + T + I	1. R DB PC PG MC E&S study in pts 12–17 y heterozygous for F508del and minimal CFTR function mutation (F/MF genotypes). 2. R DB AC PG MC E&S study in pts homozygous for F508del mutation (F/F genotype). 3. RO OL 96-week LT S&E study inputs 12–17 y (and adults) who have completed studies 1 or 2 4. Two-part SA MC S, PK, PD + E study in pts 6–11 y who have F/MF or F/F genotypes. 5. RO OL 96-week LT S&E study in pts 6–11 y who have completed part B of study 4. 6. Two-part SA MC S, PK, PD + E study in pts 2-5 y with F/MF or F/F genotypes. 7. Two-part SA MC S, PK, PD + E study in pts from birth to <2 y with F/MF or F/F genotypes. 8. M&S study for dose selection in children from birth to 11 y 9. ES by M&S of E + PD endpoints using data obtained in A + A to support extrapolation of E to pts <12 y 10. Meta-analysis of E + T + I and T + I study data to provide comparative 24-week E data in pts with the F/F genotype. 11. Descriptive comparison of E&S outputs for 2 studies evaluating the respective TCR in pts with an F/MF genotype

A + A, Adolescents and adults; *CO*, cross-over, *DB*, double bline; *E*, efficacy; *ES*, extrapolation study; *E + T + I*, elexacaftor + tezacaftor + ivacaftor; *HOH*, homozygous or heterozygous; *L + I*, Lumacaftor + ivacaftor; *LT*, long-term; *MC*, multicenter; *M&S*, modeling & simulation; *OL*, open-label; *P + AC*, placebo and active control; *PA*, parallel arm; *PC*, placebo-controlled; *PD*, pharmacodynamic(s); *PG*, parallel group; *PK*, pharmacokinetic(s); *pts*, patients; *R*, randomized; *RO*, rollover; *S*, safety; *S&E*, safety & efficacy; *SA*, single arm; *SD*, single dose; *TCR*, triple combination regimen; *T + I*, tezakaftor + ivacaftor; *UC*, uncontrolled; *y*, year.

- Was there any benefit for CF patients?
- Did the immense additional workload for submitting and negotiating at least 17 PIPs with altogether 52 PIP modifications, leading to altogether 110 demanded "pediatric" clinical studies (Table 4.10.2), result in any tangible advance of CF treatment in young patients in the EU as compared to the US? This was additional workload for pharmaceutical companies developing CF treatments, regulatory authorities, clinical scientists that were asked for advice, and more.
- Does it make sense that the EMA is demanding studies in young CF patients for PIP "pediatric" studies until 2029? See Table 4.10.2. These studies compete and will further compete with studies for next generation CF treatments that will certainly emerge over the next years.
- Does it make sense to demand a binding commitment to compounds at an early time point of development when it is still unknown if the compound will ever pass successfully phase 3 pivotal studies and will eventually become an approved drug? One PIP demands "pediatric" studies for

combinations that include VX-659. But this compound has been abandoned by the developing company Vertex.

In 2015, a paper analyzed the EMA's ivacaftor PIP and compared it to the clinical studies the FDA had used for their approval of CFTR modulators and potentiators, documented in FDA ivacaftor medical review [35]. Beyond the studies Vertex had used to support the US registration, there was no relevant additional input from the EMA [22]. The many clinical studies demanded in young patients are for a disease that historically used to be a pediatric disease only. This is a disease where today we know that early treatment has the potential to prevent disease progression from the very moment of diagnosis.

Discussion

There are several challenges in the regulatory handling of CTFR modulators. Firstly, the term "children," defined as <17 years of age (FDA) and <18 years of age (EU/EMA) does not correspond to a physiological age barrier [36–40]. The pivotal study of tezacaftor + ivacaftor (US: symdeco; EU: symkevi) was performed in patients > 12 years, which was reasonable approach, as the body of patients 12 years old are mature enough to be treated with adult doses. A review of 92 drugs FDA-approved in adults and adolescents found that 87 (94.5%) had identical adolescent and adult dosing [41]. There is no scientifically defendable justification for separate "pediatric" studies in adolescents.

Regulatory authorities must task to prevent worthless or even dangerous compounds to be sold as medicines. Thus, the benefit of new drugs and treatments needs to be proven in a reproducible way. The traditional approach to measure the amount of air that a person can force out of their lungs in one second (forced expiratory volume [FEV1]). This works in adults, adolescents, and children of school age, but not in younger children, infants and babies, where new methods to measure efficacy are needed [42,43].

Current CF therapies aim at treating existing disease and at slowing disease progression. However, CF provides a striking opportunity for prevention and initiation of therapies in CF patients before the disease has produced damage [44]. Implementation of prenatal and neonatal screening can ensure that babies and infants are diagnosed very early. The emerging novel therapies that target CF basic defects allows the hope that progression of CF can be prevented before respiratory symptoms [18], and of course all other symptoms. Today, there is broad agreement that the benefits of CF newborn screening outweigh the harm and that CF newborn screening leads to better survival [4].

The FDA has licensed symkevi for now only in patients > 12 years and will expect for registration in younger patients double-blind placebo-controlled proof of efficacy studies, which makes medically no sense. There are enough CF patients younger than 12 years of age. Today, the correct dose can be calculated by physiology-based modeling and simulation. Confirmation of the calculated dose in younger patients can and should be done in an opportunistic setting [45,46], i.e., treat young patients, ask for permission for additional blood samples for PK/PD assessment, and confirm/adjust the calculated dose.

If we look at the PIP-demanded "pediatric" studies in CF, we see that for ivacaftor, lumacaftor, lumacaftor + ivacaftor, tezakaftor + ivacaftor, and elexacaftor + tezacaftor + ivacaftor "pediatric" studies in adolescents (and adults) are demanded, see Table 4.10.3. Studies in patients 12−17 years old are physiologically not pediatric studies. The term "pediatric" refers in this context to the legal status of the patients. But drugs treat the physical patient, not the legal status.

There was no additional input by the EMA and its "pediatric committee" (PDCO) that would have helped Vertex to investigate its compounds in young patients. The company had sufficient expertise to address this challenge also without the EMA. The EMA demanded and still additional "pediatric" studies in compounds that are already licensed in the treatment of CF.

Ivacaftor was approved by FDA and EMA in 2012 for CF patients with G551D mutation, who account for 4%−5% of patients with CF, i.e., only a tiny fraction of all CF patients. The combination of lumacaftor + ivacaftor (orkambi), FDA-approved in 2015, works in CF patients with two copies of the F508del mutation, which is already roughly a third of all CF patients. The triple combination of elexacaftor + tezacaftor + ivacaftor (Trikafta), FDA-approved in 2019, works in CF patients with at least one copy of the F508del mutation, regardless of their other mutation. This is already the vast majority of all CF patients. For the approval of the triple combination Trikafta, the EMA will probably take roughly a year longer.

There is no medical sense in demanding "pediatric" Trikafta studies to be performed until 2029, see Table 4.10.2. Considering the years since the FDA approval of the first CTFR modulator, we can expect more breakthrough innovations that will make EU PIP-demanded studies even more obsolete and superfluous than they are already today.

PIP no. 16, Table 4.10.2, demands "pediatric" studies for the triple combination Ivacaftor + tezacaftor + VX-659, to be completed until 2029. Vertex has abandoned the development of VX-659 and will also not license it out [47]. To demand "pediatric" clinical studies for the coming ten years for breakthrough medications is irrational. Drug development for CF and any other serious disease needs speed and flexibility, and not "pediatric" ten-year-development-plans.

The EU concept for "pediatric drug development" demands for the vast majority of new drugs additional "pediatric" studies that at best are useless in adolescents, as these have already a mature body that needs the same doses as adults [36–40]. Where they demand placebo-controlled studies, they deny effective treatment. For younger patients, the PIP-demanded studies are massively exaggerated, as the same information could be obtained by "opportunistic" studies in a fraction of the needed patients [45,46]. Also the costs for these would be only a fraction of the costs for PIP-demanded additional regulatory studies. In case of safety concerns, drug registries are the appropriate approach. Drug registries are able to catch real-life challenges, in contrast to regulatory studies.

The PIPs for drugs that treat CF reflect the same automatism that is used for all drugs in general. While the FDA is at present at the forefront to support drug development for young patients, the FDA is still caught in the concept that "children" are "therapeutic orphans," resulting in the flawed concept of "pediatric drug development." Adopted and amplified by the EMA, the CF PIPs follow the same logic that is used for all drugs. They demand "pediatric" studies in patients that are physiologically already mature. They do not translate the learnings from developmental clinical pharmacology. Instead, they demand a multitude of "pediatric" clinical studies that are superfluous in adolescents and exaggerated in most young patients. Where they demand comparison against placebo or outdated standard-of-care, they harm young patients by omission, as they deny existing, available effective treatment. The PIP approach is without therapeutic intentions. It is drug-centered and reflects a regulatory dogmatism that needs to be overcome.

Conclusions

The CFF has established the new concept of venture philanthropy [13–16]. With this concept, it has replaced the "moral imperative" proclaimed by the AAP [48,49] and translated into the "pediatric imperative" proclaimed by the European Society of Developmental Perinatal and Pediatric Pharmacology (ESDPPP) at its biannual conference in 2019 [50,51]. In contrast to the "pediatric drug development" concept, which is full of conflicts of interest and advances "pediatric" careers in academia, pharmaceutical industry and regulatory authorities [37–40], but does not advance healthcare for young patients, the CFF has already changed the fate of a formerly lethal disease and continues to go ahead on this path [12,13].

For a first time, a causal treatment of CF is possible. Treatment will for the next years continue to focus on preventing organ damage by supporting the defective CFTR. This is already possible for roughly 90% of patients, and research will hopefully soon find ways to help also the remaining ten percent of patients. Furthermore, earlier or later, CF gene therapy will be possible [52].

Truly new challenges like the treatment of CF and the prevention of organ damage from birth on or even already before birth [53] cannot be advanced by stone age methodology. Both the FDA and the EU concept of children as "therapeutic orphans" is flawed. Specifically the EU PIP approach is drug-centered and reflects regulatory dogmatism that needs to be overcome.

References

[1] Busch R. On the history of cystic fibrosis. Acta Univ Carol Med 1990;36(1-4):13–15 Jan 1.

[2] Andersen DH. Cystic fibrosis of the pancreas and its relation to celiac disease. A clinical and pathological study. Am J Dis Child 1938;56(2):344–99.

[3] O'Sullivan BP, Freedman SD. Cystic fibrosis. Lancet. 2009;373(9678):1891–904 May 30.

[4] De Boeck K. Cystic fibrosis in the year 2020: a disease with a new face. Acta Paediatr 2020;109(5):893–9 May.

[5] Fedick AM, Zhang J, Edelmann L, et al. Prenatal diagnosis of cystic fibrosis. Methods Mol Biol 2019;1885:221–31.

[6] Doull I. Cystic fibrosis 2019: year in review. Paediatr Respir Rev 2020; Apr 9. pii: S1526-0542(20)30031-2.

[7] Flume PA, Van Devanter DR. State of progress in treating cystic fibrosis respiratory disease. BMC Med 2012;10:88. Available at: <http://www.ncbi.nlm.nih.gov/pmc/articles/PMC3425089/>.

[8] Rowe SM, Borowitz DS, Burns JL, et al. Progress in cystic fibrosis and the CF therapeutics development network. Thorax 2012;67:882–90.

[9] Course CW, Hanks R. Newborn screening for cystic fibrosis: is there benefit for everyone? Paediatr Respir Rev 2019;31:3–5 Aug.

[10] Newborn screening for CF. <https://www.cff.org/What-is-CF/Testing/Newborn-Screening-for-CF/>.

[11] Foil KE, Powers A, Raraigh KS, et al. The increasing challenge of genetic counseling for cystic fibrosis. J Cyst Fibros 2019;18(2):167–74 Mar.

[12] Cystic fibrosis foundation. <https://www.cff.org/>.

[13] Cystic fibrosis foundation. Our history. <https://www.cff.org/About-Us/About-the-Cystic-Fibrosis-Foundation/Our-History/>.

[14] CF Foundation Venture Philanthropy Model. <https://www.cff.org/About-Us/About-the-Cystic-Fibrosis-Foundation/CF-Foundation-Venture-Philanthropy-Model/>.

[15] Feuerstein A, Herper M. 'A game-changer': how vertex delivered on cystic fibrosis. Statnews 2019; <https://www.statnews.com/2019/10/23/we-conquered-a-disease-how-vertex-delivered-a-transformative-medicine-for-cystic-fibrosis/>.

[16] Cystic Fibrosis Foundation Receives $3.3 Billion Royalty Pay Out. Philanthropynewdigest 2014. <https://philanthropynewsdigest.org/news/cystic-fibrosis-foundation-receives-3.3-billion-royalty-pay-out>.

[17] Davis PB. Cystic fibrosis since 1938. Am J Respir Crit Care Med 2006;173(5):475–82 Mar 1 <https://www.ecfs.eu/society-details/about>.

[18] Pittman JE, Ferkol TW. The evolution of cystic fibrosis care. Chest 2015; 148(2):533–42 Aug <https://www.ncbi.nlm.nih.gov/pmc/articles/PMC4524331/pdf/chest_148_2_533.pdf>.

[19] Gentzsch M, Mall MA. Ion channel modulators in cystic fibrosis. Chest. 2018;154(2):383–93 Aug <https://www.ncbi.nlm.nih.gov/pmc/articles/PMC6113631/pdf/main.pdf>.

[20] Joshi D, Ehrhardt A, Hong JS, Sorscher EJ. Cystic fibrosis precision therapeutics: emerging considerations. Pediatr Pulmonol 2019;54(Suppl 3):S13–17 Nov <https://onlinelibrary.wiley.com/doi/epdf/10.1002/ppul.24547>.

[21] FDA 2019. Trikafta label. <https://www.accessdata.fda.gov/drugsatfda_docs/label/2019/212273s000lbl.pdf>.

[22] Rose K, Spigarelli MG. Cystic fibrosis treatment: a paradigm for new pediatric medicines, globalization of drug development and the role of the european medicines agency. Children (Basel) 2015;2:108–30 <https://www.mdpi.com/2227-9067/2/1/108>.

[23] FDA written requests issued. <https://www.fda.gov/drugs/development-resources/written-requests-issued.>

[24] FDA 2017. Kalydeco® (ivacaftor) label. <https://www.accessdata.fda.gov/drugsatfda_-docs/label/2017/203188s019lbl.pdf>.

[25] Adamson PC. Improving the outcome for children with cancer: development of targeted new agents. CA Cancer J Cli 2015;65(3):212–20 May-Jun.

[26] López-Muñoz F, Alamo C. Monoaminergic neurotransmission: the history of the discovery of antidepressants from 1950s until today. Curr Pharm Des 2009; 15(14):1563–86.

[27] Maude SL, Laetsch TW, Buechner J, Rives S, Boyer M, Bittencourt H. Tisagenlecleucel in children and young adults with b-cell lymphoblastic leukemia. N Engl J Med 2018; 378(5):439–48 Feb 1.

[28] Emily Whitehead: A young girl beats cancer with immunotherapy. <https://www.cancer-research.org/immunotherapy/stories/patients/emily-whitehead>.

[29] Tomasi PA, Egger GF, Pallidis C, Saint-Raymond A. Enabling development of paediatric medicines in Europe: 10 years of the EU paediatric regulation. Pediatr Drugs 2017; 19(6):505–13 Dec.

[30] Mentzer D. Progress review of the European paediatric regulatory framework after six years of implementation. Int J Pharm 2014;469(2):240–3 Aug 5.

[31] Rocchi F, Tomasi P. The development of medicines for children. Pharmacol Res 2011;64:169–75.

[32] Ward RM, Benjamin Jr DK, Davis JM, Gorman RL, Kauffman R, Kearns GL, et al. The need for pediatric drug development. J Pediatr 2018;192:13–21 Jan.

[33] Hirschfeld S, Saint-Raymond A. Pediatric regulatory initiatives. Handb Exp Pharmacol 2011;205:245–68.

[34] EMA 2016: 10-year report to the European Commission. <https://ec.europa.eu/health/sites/health/files/files/paediatrics/2016_pc_report_2017/ema_10_year_report_for_consultation.pdf>.

[35] FDA 2011. Medical review ivacaftor. <http://www.accessdata.fda.gov/drugsatfda_docs/nda/2012/203188Orig1s000MedR.pdf>.

[36] Kearns GL, Abdel-Rahman SM, Alander SW, Blowey DL, Leeder JS, Kauffman RE. Developmental pharmacology—drug disposition, action, and therapy in infants and children. N Engl J Med 2003;349(12):1157–67 Sep 18.

[37] Rose K. The challenges of pediatric drug development. Curr Ther Res Clin Exp 2019;. Available from: https://doi.org/10.1016/j.curtheres.2019.01.007.

[38] Rose K, Grant-Kels JM. The meanings of "pediatric drug development." A review. Ther Innov Regul Sci 2019;53(6):767–74 Nov.

[39] Rose K, Neubauer D, Grant-Kels JM. Rational use of medicine in children—the conflict of interests story. A review. Rambam Maimonides Med J 2019;10(3):e0018. Available from: https://doi.org/10.5041/RMMJ.10371 Review <https://www.rmmj.org.il/userimages/928/2/PublishFiles/953Article.pdf>.

[40] Rose K, Neubauer D, Grant-Kels JM. Too many avoidable suicides occur worldwide in young patients. A review. Rambam Maimonides Med J 2019; Sep 18 <https://www.rmmj.org.il/userimages/965/1/PublishFiles/977OnlineFirst.pdf>.

[41] Momper JD, Mulugeta Y, Green DJ, et al. Adolescent dosing and labeling since the food and drug administration amendments act of 2007. JAMA Pediatr 2013;167(10):926–32 Oct.

[42] Eichler I. 2012. Difficulties encountered. Paediatric investigation plan. EMA workshop on endpoints for CF clinical trials 27 & 28 September 2012. <https://www.ema.europa.eu/

en/documents/presentation/presentation-difficulties-encountered-regulatory-perspective-paediatric-investigation-plans-irmgard_en.pdf>.

[43] EMA 2012. Report of the workshop on endpoints for cystic fibrosis clinical trials. <https://www.ema.europa.eu/en/documents/report/report-workshop-endpoints-cystic-fibrosis-clinical-trials_en.pdf>.

[44] Pittman JE, Cutting G, Davis SD, et al. Cystic fibrosis: NHLBI workshop on the primary prevention of chronic lung diseases. Ann Am Thorac Soc 2014;11(Suppl 3):S161–8 Apr <https://www.ncbi.nlm.nih.gov/pmc/articles/PMC5473656/pdf/AnnalsATS.201312-444LD.pdf>.

[45] Gonzalez D, Melloni C, Yogev R, et al. Use of opportunistic clinical data and a population pharmacokinetic model to support dosing of clindamycin for premature infants to adolescents. Clin Pharmacol Ther 2014;96(4):429–37 Oct.

[46] Laughon MM, Benjamin DK. Mechanisms to provide safe and effective drugs for children. Pediatrics. 2014;134(2):e562–3 Aug.

[47] Biopharmadive 2019. Vertex chooses its cystic fibrosis future. <https://www.biopharmadive.com/news/vertex-chooses-its-cystic-fibrosis-future/555851/>.

[48] AAP. Guidelines for the ethical conduct of studies to evaluate drugs in pediatric populations, committee on drugs. Am Acad Pediatrics, Pediatrics 1995;95(2):286–94 1995 Feb <https://pediatrics.aappublications.org/content/pediatrics/95/2/286.full.pdf>.

[49] Shaddy RE, Denne SC. Committee on drugs and committee on pediatric research. Clinical report—guidelines for the ethical conduct of studies to evaluate drugs in pediatric populations. Pediatrics. 2010;125(4):850–60 Apr.

[50] European society of development, perinatal and pediatric pharmacology. www.esdppp.org.

[51] ESDPPP conference 2019 website: removed from the internet. The search term "paediatric imperative" still results in a google hit (03APR2020) with its first words ("The Paediatric Imperative. No matter if a company has no specific portfolio interest in paediatric medicines new EMA and FDA regulatory requirements demand . . ."). Archived by Klaus Rose.

[52] Cooncy AL, McCray Jr PB, Sinn PL. Cystic fibrosis gene therapy: looking back, looking forward. Genes (Basel) 2018;9(11):538 Nov 7 <https://www.ncbi.nlm.nih.gov/pmc/articles/PMC6266271/pdf/genes-09-00538.pdf>.

[53] Clancy JP, Cotton CU, Donaldson SH, et al. CFTR modulator theratyping: current status, gaps and future directions. J Cyst Fibros 2019;18(1):22–34 Jan.

Subchapter 4.11

Vaccines and antiinfectives

Introduction

The introduction of vaccines and antiinfective drugs has revolutionized medical care of patients of all ages. Vaccines protect against viral infections. Antibiotics treat bacterial, antivirals viral, and antifungals fungal infections. For the approval of new antiinfectives in "children" defined by an administrative age limit the FDA and the EMA demand "pediatric" studies. The EMA demands the submission of a draft pediatric investigation plan (PIP) that must be negotiated with the EMA during a one year negotiation procedure for vaccines, antibiotic, antiviral, and antifungal drugs.

The pediatric warnings in US drug labels from 1962 on that followed the US processing of the thalidomide disaster by the "Drug Efficacy Amendment" of 1962 to the US Federal Food, Drug, and Cosmetic Act had their origin in toxicities that had been observed in the 1950s. These toxicities had occurred in preterm newborns treated with antibiotics [1–3]. Although these warnings had the preliminary legal purpose of preventing damage lawsuits in the litigious US legal environment [4–8], their medical interpretation led to the concept that children are therapeutic orphans [9]. There are specific toxicities in neonates and babies [10], but the extrapolation of these dangers into the entire "pediatric population" defined by the FDA as younger than 17 years and later by the EMA as younger than 18 years was a medically and scientifically unjustified exaggeration that has over the following decades resulted in an unprecedented number of "pediatric" studies that, however, mostly lack medical and scientific sense and often even harm young patients [11–14].

Antibiotics are the therapeutic agents most frequently used in young patients. Most antibiotic prescriptions aim at common pediatric infections such as otitis media, pharyngitis, pneumonia, and other respiratory infections that are diagnosed primarily in the ambulatory setting. Often antibiotics are inappropriately prescribed and antibiotic overuse is a persistent problem specifically in outpatient pediatric practices [15].

Pediatric legislation and antiinfectives

Both the FDA and the EMA approve antiinfectives routinely only in adults and demand separate "pediatric" studies in "children", without taking into account that many of the administratively defined "children" are already bodily mature [11–14].

EU pediatric investigation plans (PIPs) for vaccines

The introduction of the EU pediatric regulation was justified by the claim that drugs were usually developed in adults first and only later in children [16]. This statement is certainly wrong in vaccines that today are routinely given predominantly in young persons. Most vaccines are given before a person has contracted a disease. Vaccines help the immune system to prevent future infections. Most vaccines are given by injection, some are administered after the patient already has contracted a disease. While vaccination provides a lasting effect, the protection usually takes several weeks to develop.

Vaccination against smallpox was developed and made compulsory in the UK in the 19th century. Tetanus toxoid, diphtheria toxoid and a pertussis (whooping cough) vaccine (DPT) was developed in 1931 and has remained a key component of infant immunization across the planet. DPT is now used widely in combination with hepatitis B and Hemophilus influenzae type B vaccines, a combination widely known as pentavalent vaccine. Several further new vaccines were introduced into routine use in industrialized countries including vaccines against hepatitis B, Hemophilus influenzae serotype B, pneumococcal and meningococcal infections, rotavirus and human papilloma virus (HPV) [17].

Initially, vaccines were developed mostly against infectious diseases that were a major cause of mortality in children and infants. Thanks to their success, today people live longer and there are only a few major infectious agents still causing life-threatening diseases in infants living in developed countries [18,19]. Today, young children undergo in developed countries a routine program of vaccinations. In adolescents, a booster is needed to increase the protective levels of antibodies against pertussis, meningococcus, diphtheria, tetanus, and influenza. Furthermore, female adolescents are vaccinated to prevent infection with human papilloma virus, which can lead to cervical cancer later in life. For some diseases, also adults should repeat their booster injections on a regular base, including tetanus. Today, new and better vaccines are developed also for elderly persons whose aged immune system might need more potent vaccines [18].

Development of vaccines has worked well since the 20th century. The added obligation to submit a PIP for vaccines has added another bureaucratic layer to vaccine development. From 2007 to 2016, a total of 52 PIPs/ waivers on vaccines were issued by the EMA. Of these PIPs, 12 were completed, leading to the approval of 12 "pediatric" vaccine indications [20]. The EMA has also developed a document with expected key elements and requirements for a new diphtheria, tetanus, and acellular pertussis (DTaP) containing combination vaccine [21].

Table 4.11.1 lists the numbers for the 17 PIP for vaccines against the influenza virus. Influenza, mostly referred to as "flu," is a contagious viral infection caused mostly by the influenza virus A or B. It affects mainly the organs of the upper respiratory tract including nose, throat, bronchi, and lungs; other organs can also be involved. It causes worldwide considerable morbidity and mortality with pandemic, epidemic, or seasonal patterns. Annual vaccination against seasonal influenza is an important strategy to prevent influenza. The influenza virus is characterized for a high rate of mutation, beating the immune system's function against new variants. New vaccines are produced annually to match circulating viruses. The selection of influenza antigens for these vaccines is based upon the global surveillance of influenza viruses in circulation and the spread of new strains around the world [22]. The PIP documents can be retrieved from the internet by entering the PIP number into any search engine.

Table 4.11.2 lists exemplarily the "pediatric" studies demanded in PIP EMEA.000160-PIP01-07-M05 for a vaccine against an influenza virus. Influenza affects persons of all ages. The 18th birthday is not, as study 2 in Table 4.11.2 appears to suggest, a physiological age limit where the body undergoes a profound transformation. Instead, the 18th birthday is an administrative and legal age limit. Medicines and vaccines treat the body, and not the legal status of a patient.

PIPs for antibiotics

Several papers discuss the approval situation of antibiotics in the "pediatric population," complain about a lower number of clinical studies in "children" and praise the US and the EU pediatric legislation for enforcing more "pediatric" studies [23,24]. As in all other clinical areas, this sounds appealing as long as we do not ask what the authors mean with "children."

Table 4.11.3 lists a "pediatric" study demanded by the moxifloxacin PIP EMEA-000492-PIP01-08-M01 for the indication of pelvic inflammatory disease. But an extrapolation study on existing adult and pediatric data in female adolescents aged 12–17 years does not make sense. The cover picture of this book shows a young woman. In the days of Rumpelstiltskin young women were often married at a young age. If under 18 years old, she would for the EMA still be a "child." But bodily, a young woman of 15, 16, or 17 years is no longer a child. There is no difference in pelvic inflammatory disease of an 18 years old woman as compared to a 17 years old woman. This study lacks medical sense.

The moxifloxacin PIP further demands four "pediatric" clinical studies for complicated intra-abdominal infection in persons aged from 3 months to 17 years, see Table 4.11.4.

Bodily, a relevant part of the patients demanded in the studies listed in Table 4.11.4 are no longer children. Physiologically, there is no difference between a patients one day before and one day after his 18th birthday. Study 1, Table 4.11.4 is a comparison of the bioavailability of the oral tablet and

TABLE 4.11.1 PIPs for influenza virus vaccines (June 2020).

1. EMEA-001715-PIP01-14-M03
2. EMEA-002359-PIP01-19-M01
3. EMEA-001894-PIP01-15-M01
4. EMEA-002027-PIP02-17-M01
5. EMEA-000160-PIP01-07-M05
6. EMEA-002418-PIP01-18-M01
7. EMEA-001830-PIP01-15-M01
8. EMEA-001782-PIP01-15-M03
9. EMEA-001133-PIP01-11
10. EMEA-001254-PIP01-11-M02
11. EMEA-000178-PIP01-07-M04
12. EMEA-001559-PIP01-13
13. EMEA-001051-PIP01-10-M03
14. EMEA-000817-PIP02-11-M01
15. EMEA-00249-PIP01-10
16. EMEA-002353-PIP01-18
17. EMEA-002440-PIP01-18

the pediatric formulation, which makes sense. However, studies 2, 3, and 4 in Table 4.11.4 demand "pediatric" patients aged 3 months to 17 years. Medically, clinically and scientifically, these studies lack sense.

Study no. 4, Table 4.11.4 has been performed and published. In this multicenter, randomized, double-blind, controlled study, 451 "pediatric" patients aged 3 months to 17 years with complicated intra-abdominal infection were treated either with intravenous/oral moxifloxacin (N = 301) or with intravenous ertapenem followed by oral amoxicillin/clavulanate (N = 150) for 5 to 14 days. Both treatments worked, but a lower clinical cure rate was observed with moxifloxacin treatment. The authors recommend for "children" with complicated intraabdominal infection not to use moxifloxacin when alternative more efficacious antibiotics with better safety profile are available [25]. This study was not a study in "children." Its inclusion criteria were not based on science, but on regulatory demands within the framework of pediatric legislation. Other authors went another way. Moxifloxacin is FDA-approved in adults of 18 years and older, but not in "children" [26]. However, its high oral bioavailability, broad-spectrum coverage, and penetration of the central nervous system give it a unique niche. Uses of moxifloxacin in young patients include treatment and prophylaxis of multidrug-resistant tuberculosis, treatment of other mycobacterial infections, atypical pneumonia, and neonatal mycoplasma hominis meningitis. In this study, the use of moxifloxacin was investigated retrospectively in young patients younger than 18 years. The authors conclude that moxifloxacin is generally well tolerated in young patients and that related adverse event rarely lead to the

TABLE 4.11.2 PIP-demanded studies in EMEA-000160-PIP01-07-M05.

1. OL S and IG study of the pediatric formulation of the (pre)pandemic H5N1 influenza candidate vaccine following a heterologous prime-boost schedule (six months apart) in children 6mo to <36 mo (H5N1-013)
2. R OL S and IG study of a prime-boost schedule of the pediatric formulation of H5N1 candidate vaccine administered to subjects 3 y to <18 y (H5N1-032).
3. R, observer-blind, DR IG and S study of varying quantities of the Quebec manufactured H5N1 HA antigen (Q-Pan) adjuvanted with varying quantities of AS03 versus the reference vaccine dose of 1.9 μg HA with AS03B (Q-Pan-H5N1-023).

DR, Dose range; *IG*, immunogenicity; *OL*, open label; *PK*, pharmacokinetics; *R*, randomized; *S*, safety; *T*, tolerability.

TABLE 4.11.3 PIP-demanded "pediatric" moxifloxacin study in pelvic inflammatory disease (EMEA-000492-PIP01-08-M01).

- Indication: pelvic inflammatory disease
- Concerned patients: Female adolescents from 12 to <18 y
- Study: Extrapolation of existing adult and pediatric data

DR, Dose range; *IG*, immunogenicity; *OL*, open label; *PK*, pharmacokinetics; *R*, randomized; *S*, safety; *T*, tolerability; *y*, year.

discontinuation of treatment [27]. These authors do not address the blur of different meanings of the terms "child" and "pediatric." But they investigated the use of this drug in a therapeutic framework where responsible physicians had decided to use it in young patients despite "pediatric" nonapproved.

Table 4.11.5 lists the "pediatric" studies demanded for the antibiotic doripenem in PIP EMEA-000015-PIP01-07-M04. Doripenem is FDA-approved in adults > 18 years old, but not in "children" [28].

A relevant part of the patients demanded in this PIP are bodily no longer "children." There is no medical reason to assume that doripenem should work from the 18th birthday on, but not in persons one day younger. The "pediatric" studies in the doripenem PIP are partially open label, partially double-blind, placebo-controlled studies. These separate "pediatric" studies do not make medical sense. A report about three doripenem "pediatric" studies reports that these studies had to be terminated prematurely for "nonsafety reasons": "Low enrollment limited ability to assess benefits and risks of doripenem in children" [29].

An EMA document from 2018 outlines the general requirements for PIPs in antibiotics. In general, it accepts extrapolation of the efficacy of an antibacterial agent across age ranges, but also lists some exceptions [30,31]. However, the term "extrapolation" is misleading. Young patients are not another species. When the body has passed the slow process of puberty

TABLE 4.11.4 PIP-demanded moxifloxacin "pediatric" studies in complicated intra-abdominal infection.

1. Comparative BA study in healthy adult volunteers following non-blinded, R, single dose, cross over oral administration of the approved 400 mg tablet and the pediatric oral formulations.
2. Subprotocol for characterization of oral PK and absolute BA in pediatric patients with cIAI
3. Single dose S, T, PK in pediatric patients
4. Prospective, R, active-controlled, multinational, multicenter study in pediatric patients with cIAI.

BA, Bioavailability; *cIAI*, complicated intra-abdominal infection; *PK*, pharmacokinetics; *R*, randomized; *S*, safety; *T*, tolerability.

[32–36], it becomes mature, and there is no reason why an antibiotic should work differently before and after the 18th birthday.

PIPs for antifungals

Table 4.11.6 lists the "pediatric" voriconazole studies demanded by PIP EMEA-000191-PIP01-08-M05. Voriconazole is an drug effective against a multitude of fungal infections. It can be administered orally or intravenously.

Again, one study demands patients aged 12 to 17 years (Table 4.11.6, study 3), as if the 18th birthday would transform minors into members of another species.

PIPs for antiviral compounds

Altogether, the EMA website listed in June 2020 38 PIPs for the treatment of human immunodeficiency virus (HIV).

Table 4.11.7 lists the PIP-demanded studies for baloxavir marboxil.

The first four studies are clinical studies, studies 5 to 12 demand modeling & simulation. Study no. 13 is a randomized, double-blind placebo-controlled study. Baloxavir marboxil is an antiviral medication for treatment of influenza A and influenza B flu. It was FDA-approved in 2018 in patients down to the age of 12 years [37]. To ask for a placebo-controlled study for drug whose efficacy has already been shown in humans is unethical and in breach of the declaration of Helsinki [38]. The PIP also documents that these studies should be concluded until 2029.

Table 4.11.8 lists the "pediatric" studies EMA-demanded for raltegravir. Raltegravir is an anti-HIV compound FDA-approved for the treatment of HIV in adults [39].

Table 4.11.9 lists the "pediatric" studies for ibalizumab, a non-immunosuppressive humanized monoclonal antibody that binds CD4, the primary

TABLE 4.11.5 PIP-demanded doripenem "pediatric" studies.

1.	MC OL PK, S T and to identify the appropriate dose for children from 3 months to <18 y
2.	R DB MC comparative study in hospitalized children 3 months to <18 y with cIAI requiring i.v. AT
3.	R DB MC comparative study in hospitalized children 3 mo to <18 y with cUTI requiring i.v. AT
4.	R DB MC comparative study in hospitalized children 3 mo to <18 y with pneumonia requiring i.v. AT
5.	MC OL PK, S, T study in neonates, preterm infants with GA <28 weeks and in infants <3mo
6.	MC OL descriptive S, T, E study in neonates, preterm infants with GA <28 weeks, and infants <3mo

AT, Antibiotic therapy; *BA*, bioavailability; cIAI complicated intra-abdominal infection; cUTI complicated urinary tract infections; GA gestational age; i.v. intravenous; *mo*, month; *OL*, open label; PK pharmacokinetics; R randomized; S safety; T tolerability; *y*, year.

receptor for HIV, and prevents the HIV virus from entering cells. Ibalizumab is FDA-approved for multidrug-resistant HIV-1 in adults [40].

Why should the 18th birthday change the mode of action of the monoclonal antibody? Not all patients aged 6 to 17 years are "children".

Even for potential treatments and vaccines against COVID-19 the EMA demands a PIP

For the COVID-19 pandemic, the EMA has released a document for acceleration of development support and evaluation procedures for COVID-19 treatments and vaccines. The document addresses (1) rapid scientific advice, (2) rapid agreement of a pediatric investigation plan and rapid compliance check, (3) rolling review, (4) marketing authorization (5) extension of indication and extension of marketing authorization, (6) compassionate use, and (7) other considerations [41]. Specifically for PIPs, the EMA offers: no prespecified submission deadlines; PIP review reduced to a minimum of 20 days (from 120 days). Exact timeline depends on complexity of PIP and the preparedness by the sponsor to respond to questions; EMA decision following a review is reduced to 2 days (from 10 days); the possibility for developers to provide a focused scientific documentation, agreed on a case-by-case basis; the compliance check can be reduced to 4 days if necessary [42].

Discussion

Separate "pediatric" studies resulted in roughly 95% of drugs in the same recommended doses for adolescents as compared to adults [43]. Bodily, adolescents are already mature, but not yet administratively and legally. Study 3

TABLE 4.11.6 PIP EMEA-000191-PIP01-08-M05 Voriconazole.

1. OL multiple i.v. dose, MC PK, S, T study in children 2 to 11 y who need treatment for the prevention of SFI
2. OL MC PK, S, T study of increasing i.v. doses and following a switch to oral voriconazole in immunocompromised subjects 2- 11 y who need treatment for the prevention of SFI
3. OL i.v. to oral switch, MD PK, S, T study in immunocompromised adolescents 12 to <17 y at high risk for SFI
4. OL i.v. to oral switch, MD PK, S, T study in immunocompromised children aged 2 to 11 y at high risk for SFI
5. Pop PK in children, adolescents and adults based on the results of the 4 studies listed above
6. Extrapolation of E & S data from two adults studies to the subset of patients 2-17 y

E, Efficacy; *i.v.*, intravenous; *MC*, multicenter; *MD*, multiple dose; *OL*, open label; *Pop PK*, population pharmacokinetics; *PK*, pharmacokinetics; *R*, randomized; *S*, safety; *SFI*, systemic fungal infection; *T*, tolerability; *y*, year.

in Table 4.11.3 lacks medical and scientific sense because the demanded adolescent patients are already bodily mature. Studies 1, 2, and 4 are massively exaggerated. These data could be generated in an opportunistic framework where voriconazole is administered for therapeutic reasons anyway [44,45].

When authors complain about unlicensed and off-label prescribing in pediatric patients, this sounds at first horrifying [24]. But is this really a *clinical* challenge? The entire discipline of pediatric medicine developed off-label with the emergence of effective antiintective drugs decades before the term “off-label” was used a first time in 1988 [46,47]. When authors make compelling and inflammatory appeals to approach this situation, they mention that is unclear whether the current neonatal and pediatric antibiotic research pipeline is adequate to inform optimal drug dosing in neonatal and pediatric patients [24]. But at present, in this framework the use of the term “pediatric” is blurred. The entire pediatric discipline has emerged successfully since the American Academy of Pediatrics (AAP) was established [47]. Pediatric healthcare has continuously improved with the availability of modern antiinfective drugs. The call for more “pediatric” research does not aim at improving pediatric bedside healthcare, but to trigger even more “pediatric” studies that are based on an semantic blur, and to translate these studies into “pediatric” labels. This semantic blur has produced massive conflicts of interest. The true challenge is not that we do not know the right doses to treat young patients, but that the regulatory authorities, powerful institutions representing pediatric research, and large parts of the academic clinical community have established a coalition that continuously asks for more “pediatric” studies [11–14].

TABLE 4.11.7 "Pediatric" studies demanded PIP EMEA-002440-PIP01-18 (baloxavir marboxil).

1. MC SA OL S, PK, E study in infants from birth to <1 y with influenza-like symptoms.
2. MC R DB AC S, PK, E study compared to oseltamivir in children 1 to 11 y with influenza-like symptoms
3. R DB PC MC E, S, PK study combined with a SOCNAI vs. placebo combined with a SOCNAI in adolescents who need hospitalization for SI or who contract severe influenza during hospitalization (and adults).
4. MC SA OL single and MD PK & S study in combination with a SOCNAI in pediatric patients from birth to <18 y hospitalized for SI and present within 96 hours of symptom onset.
5. Pop PK model in otherwise healthy and high risk adult and pediatric subjects, evaluating relevant demographic covariates that may influence systemic drug exposure.
6. Pop PK model in adult, adolescent and pediatric hospitalized population. Linear pop PK model accounting for relevant demographic covariates that may influence systemic drug exposure.
7. M&S study in otherwise healthy and high risk patients evaluating exposure-response using viral kinetic modeling and primary efficacy endpoints.
8. M&S study in hospitalized adult and adolescent patients evaluating exposure-response using viral kinetic modeling and primary efficacy endpoints PK-Viral kinetic modeling.
9. PBPK model for baloxavir
10. Partial extrapolation of PK, PD (virology, virus titers) and efficacy (primary endpoint, time to symptom alleviation) in otherwise healthy pediatric patients from birth to <12 y
11. Complete extrapolation of PD and efficacy (primary endpoint, time to symptom alleviation) in High Risk pediatric patients from birth to <12 y
12. Extrapolation of PK, PD (virology, virus titers) and efficacy (primary endpoint, time to symptom alleviation) in hospitalized pediatric patients from birth to <12 y
13. R DB MC PG PC E & S of a single oral dose in the prevention of IVI in children from birth to <18 y who are household members of influenza-infected index patients.

AT, Antibiotic therapy; *BA*, bioavailability; *E*, efficacy; *GA*, gestational age; *i.v.*, intravenous; *IVI*, influenza virus infections; *MC*, multicenter; *MD*, multiple dose; *M&S*, modeling & simulation; *OL*, open label; *PD*, pharmacodynamic(s); *PBPK*, Physiologically based pharmacokinetic(s); *PK*, pharmacokinetic(s); *pop PK*, population pharmacokinetic(s); *R*, randomized; *S*, safety; *SA*, single arm; *SI*, severe influenza; *SOCNAI*, standard of care neuraminidase inhibitor; *T*, tolerability; *y*, year.

In the tables of this chapter, we see that the EMA's general approach to PIP-demanded "pediatric" studies is the same for antiinfective compounds and for vaccines as for all other clinical areas discussed in this book. The terms "children" and "pediatric" are used to trigger concerns for the wellbeing of young patients. But a close look shows that these demands reflect regulatory dogmatism. Based on the children-are-not-small-adults and children-are-therapeutic-orphans mantras that originated in the US but were taken up and extended by the EU and its EMA, they demand a repetition of proof-of-efficacy in young patients

TABLE 4.11.8 "Pediatric" studies demanded for raltegravir (EMEA-000279-PIP01-08-M05).

1. OL noncomparative trial on PK, S, T and anti-retroviral activity of raltegravir in HIV-1 infected, treatment experienced patients 6mo to 17 y
2. OL, noncomparative trial on PK, S, T of raltegravir granules for oral suspension in neonates and infants less than 6 weeks of age (enrolled within 48 hours of birth) born to HIV infected mothers.
3. OL, noncomparative trial on PK, S, T, and antiretroviral activity of raltegravir with optimized background therapy (OBT) in HIV-1 infected treatment-naive children from 4 weeks to <6 months of age.

mo, Month; *OL*, open label; *PD*, pharmacodynamic(s); *PK*, pharmacokinetic(s); *S*, safety; *T*, tolerability; *y*, year.

TABLE 4.11.9 "Pediatric" studies demanded for ibalizumab (EMEA-002311-PIP01-17).

1. OL MD uncontrolled PK, PD, S and T study in children from 6 to 17 y with HIV-1 infection to provide PK/PD data to support the extrapolation of efficacy from adults.
2. M&S study to evaluate the use of ibalizumab in the treatment HIV-1 infection resistant to at least one agent in three different classes in children from 6 to 17 y

HIV, human immunodeficiency virus; *MD*, multiple dose; *M&S*, modeling & simulation; *OL*, open label; *PD*, pharmacodynamic(s); *PK*, pharmacokinetic(s); *S*, safety; *T*, tolerability.

as if these were another species [11–14]. As long as the blur of the different meanings of the terms "child" and "pediatric" is not challenged, the justification for these studies appear to be based on legitimate concern for childrens' health. However, these justifications collapse like a house of cards once the key question is asked: what do they mean with "children"? The pseudoscientific justification for "pediatric" studies in young persons beyond the period of time when they are still small babies is scientifically not solid. This is the parallel to the Rumpelstiltskin fairy tale. Rumpelstiltskin maintains his power as long as the miller's daughter does not know his name. The moment she speaks his name, the spell is broken, and his power is gone. In the fairy tale, Rumpelstiltskin is so angry about his loss of power that he rips himself up and disappears.

This is not a challenge of the FDA and the EMA alone. A flawed concept has invaded those structures and institutions that should protect patients. The pediatric laws have created massive conflicts of interest. The questionable "pediatric" studies can also continue because the clinical academic world support a flawed concept. Editors-in-chief accept reports about separate "pediatric" studies, see the publications of the moxifloxacin and the doripenem studies [25,29]. Research institutions get funds from industry for these "pediatric" studies. Institutional Review Boards (IRBs)/ethics committees (ECs) should not approve such allegedly "pediatric" studies. Editors-in-chief should refuse to publish such studies.

Many parents have already become skeptical toward "pediatric" studies. Hopefully, this book will contribute to more parents refusing participation of the loved ones in questionable "pediatric" studies.

Furthermore, also in the studies demanded for antiinfectives, "pediatric" patients are blocked by regulatory authorities' demand for the coming ten years, see the PIP for baloxavir marboxil (Table 4.11.7). Within the next ten years, hopefully the treatment of HIV will have progressed massively. Parents would be ill advised to allow participation of their loved ones in studies that are planned for an entire decade.

Conclusions

Science, research, and pharmaceutical companies have revolutionized and advanced drug development. Already today, a huge array of effective antiinfective medicines is available. It was a fundamental historical mistake to separate the human population into two groups, and adults vs. a "pediatric" population defined by an administrative age limit. This age limit is based on administrative and legal grounds, but it does not have a physiological basis. This chapter shows that the regulatory logic to demand separate "pediatric" studies for vaccines and antiinfectives is flawed.

Here the parallel to the Rumpelstiltskin fairy tale ends. This real world challenge will not disappear overnight like Rumpelstiltskin did when the miller's daughter spoke his name. The FDA and the EMA have already started to gradually and slowly step back from the children-are-not-small-adults and children-are-therapeutic-orphans mantras in several clinical areas, allowing to some degree "extrapolation" of efficacy. But also this term is misleading. We need a clear rejection of the two flawed mantras, and a revision of the "pediatric" laws both in the US and in the EU, for vaccines, antiinfectives, and all other drugs.

References

[1] Silverman WA, Andersen DH, Blanc WA, Crozier DN. A difference in mortality rate and incidence of kernicterus among premature infants allotted to two prophylactic antibacterial regimens. Pediatrics. 1956;18:614.

[2] Burns LE, Hodgman JE, Cass AB. Fatal circulatory collapse in premature infants receiving chloramphenicol. N Engl 1 Med 1959;261:1318–21.

[3] AAP. Guidelines for the ethical conduct of studies to evaluate drugs in pediatric populations, committee on drugs. Am Acad Pediatrics, Pediatrics 1995;95(2):286–94 1995 Feb.

[4] Kritzer HM. Propensity to Sue in England and the United States of America: blaming and claiming in tort cases. J Law Soc 1991;18(4):400–27.

[5] Lochlann Jain SS. Injury: the politics of product design and safety law in the United States. Princeton, NJ, USA: Princeton University Press; 2006.

[6] McGovern F. Punitive damages and class actions. Lousiana Law Rev 2010;70:435–62 <https://scholarship.law.duke.edu/cgi/viewcontent.cgi?article = 2762&context = faculty_scholarship>.

[7] Bal BS. An introduction to medical malpractice in the United States. Clin Orthop Relat Res 2009;467(2):339–47 Feb <https://www.ncbi.nlm.nih.gov/pmc/articles/PMC2628513/>.

[8] Kass JS, Rose RV. Medical malpractice reform: historical approaches, alternative models, and communication and resolution programs. AMA J Ethics 2016;18(3):299–310 <https://journalofethics.ama-assn.org/sites/journalofethics.ama-assn.org/files/2019-12/pfor6-1603.pdf>.

[9] Shirkey H. Therapeutic orphans. J Pediatrics 1968;72(1):119–20 Reprinted in Pediatrics 1999;104(3) (Suppl), 583-584.

[10] Christensen ML, Helms RA, Chesney RW. Is pediatric labelling really necessary? Pediatrics 1999;104(3 Pt 2):593–7 Sep <https://pediatrics.aappublications.org/content/pediatrics/104/Supplement_3/598.full.pdf>.

[11] Rose K, Grant-Kels JM. The meanings of "pediatric drug development". A review. Ther Innov Regul Sci 2019;53(6):767–74 Nov.

[12] Rose K. The challenges of pediatric drug development. Curr Ther Res Clin Exp 2019;. Available from: https://doi.org/10.1016/j.curtheres.2019.01.007.

[13] Rose K, Neubauer D, Grant-Kels JM. Rational use of medicine in children—the conflict of interests story. A Rev Rambam Maimonides Med J 2019;10(3):e0018. Available from: https://doi.org/10.5041/RMMJ.10371 Review <https://www.rmmj.org.il/userimages/928/2/PublishFiles/953Article.pdf>.

[14] Rose K, Grant-Kels JM. Pediatric Melanoma—the whole (conflicts of interest) story. Int J Womens Dermatol 2018;5(2):110–15. Available from: https://doi.org/10.1016/j.ijwd.2018.10.020 Nov 19 <https://www.ncbi.nlm.nih.gov/pmc/articles/PMC6451736/pdf/main.pdf>.

[15] Chavez-Bueno S, Stull TL. Antibacterial agents in pediatrics. Infect Dis Clin North Am 2009;23(4):865–80 Dec.

[16] Regulation (EC) No 1901/2006 of the European Parliament and of the Council of 12 December 2006 on Medicinal Products for Paediatric Use and Amending Regulation (EEC) No 1768/92, Directive 2001/20/EC, Directive 2001/83/EC and Regulation (EC) No 726/2004. <http://ec.europa.eu/health/files/eudralex/vol-1/reg_2006_1901/reg_2006_1901_en.pdf>.

[17] Greenwood B. The contribution of vaccination to global health: past, present and future. Philos Trans R Soc Lond B Biol Sci 2014;369(1645):20130433 May 12 <https://www.ncbi.nlm.nih.gov/pmc/articles/PMC4024226/pdf/rstb20130433.pdf>.

[18] Rappuoli R, Pizza M, Del Giudice G, et al. Vaccines, new opportunities for a new society. Proc Natl Acad Sci USA 2014;111(34):12288–93 Aug 26.

[19] Piot P, Larson HJ, O'Brien KL, et al. Immunization: vital progress, unfinished agenda. Nature. 2019;575(7781):119–29 Nov.

[20] Giaquinto G, Rocchi F. Registration of vaccines, safety follow-up, and pediatric investigation plan. In: Vesikari T, Van Damme P, editors. Pediatric Vaccines and Vaccinations: A European Textbook. NY, USA: Springer Publishers; 2017. p. 254–7.

[21] EMA 2015. Final paediatric investigation plan: expected key elements and requirements for a new DTaP-containing combination vaccine for primary and booster vaccination in infants and toddlers. <https://www.ema.europa.eu/en/documents/regulatory-procedural-guideline/final-paediatric-investigation-plan-expected-key-elements-requirements-new-dtap-containing_en.pdf>.

[22] Moghadami M. Narrative review of influenza: a seasonal and pandemic disease. Iran J Med Sci 2017;42(1):2–13 Jan <https://www.ncbi.nlm.nih.gov/pmc/articles/PMC5337761/pdf/IJMS-42-2.pdf>.

[23] Garazzino S, Lutsar I, Bertaina C, et al. New antibiotics for paediatric use: a review of a decade of regulatory trials submitted to the European medicines agency from 2000—why aren't we doing better? Int J Antimicrob Agents 2013;42(2):99–118 Aug.

[24] Thompson G, Barker C, Folgori L, et al. Global shortage of neonatal and paediatric antibiotic trials: rapid review. BMJ Open 2017;7(10):e016293 Oct 13 <https://www.ncbi.nlm.nih.gov/pmc/articles/PMC5652566/pdf/bmjopen-2017-016293.pdf>.

[25] Wirth S, Emil SGS, Engelis A, et al. Moxifloxacin in pediatric patients with complicated intra-abdominal infections: results of the MOXIPEDIA randomized controlled study. Pediatr Infect Dis 2018;37(8):e207–13 Aug.

[26] FDA 2016. Moxifloxacin label. <https://www.accessdata.fda.gov/drugsatfda_docs/label/2016/021085s063lbl.pdf>.

[27] Dixit A, Karandikar MV, Jones S, et al. Safety and tolerability of moxifloxacin in children. J Pediatric Infect Dis Soc 2018;7(3):e92–e101 Aug 17.

[28] FDA 2008. Doripenem Label. <https://www.accessdata.fda.gov/drugsatfda_docs/label/2009/022106s002s005lbl.pdf>

[29] Cannavino CR, Castaneda-Ruiz B, Redman R, et al. Safety and tolerability of doripenem in hospitalized children with complicated intra-abdominal infection, complicated urinary tract infections and pneumonia. Pediatr Infect Dis J 2015;34(11):1264–7 Nov.

[30] EMA 2019 Guideline on the evaluation of medicinal products indicated for treatment of bacterial infections, Rev. 3. <https://www.ema.europa.eu/en/documents/scientific-guideline/draft-guideline-evaluation-medicinal-products-indicated-treatment-bacterial-infections-revision-3_en.pdf>.

[31] EMA 2018. Addendum to the guideline on the evaluation of medicinal products indicated for treatment of bacterial infections to address paediatric-specific clinical data requirements. <https://www.ema.europa.eu/en/documents/scientific-guideline/draft-addendum-guideline-evaluation-medicinal-products-indicated-treatment-bacterial-infections_en.pdf>.

[32] Cheng HL, Harris SR, Sritharan M, et al. The tempo of puberty and its relationship to adolescent health and wellbeing: a systematic review. Acta Paediatr 2019; Nov 15.

[33] Khan L. Puberty: onset and progression. Pediatr Ann 2019;48(4):e141–5 Apr 1.

[34] Abreu AP, Kaiser UB. Pubertal development and regulation. Lancet Diabetes Endocrinol 2016;4(3):254–64 Mar.

[35] Snyder CK. Puberty: an overview for pediatric nurses. J Pediatr Nurs 2016;31(6):757–9 Nov-Dec.

[36] Wood CL, Lane LC, Cheetham T. Puberty: normal physiology (brief overview). Best Pract Res Clin Endocrinol Metab 2019;33(3):101265 Jun.

[37] FDA 2018. Baloxavir marboxil label. <https://www.accessdata.fda.gov/drugsatfda_docs/label/2018/210854s000lbl.pdf>.

[38] World Medical Association (WMA) Declaration of Helsinki—ethical principles for medical research involving human subjects. Adopted by the 18th WMA general assembly, Helsinki, Finland, June 1964, and amended by the 64th WMA General Assembly, Fortaleza, Brazil, October 2013. <https://www.wma.net/policies-post/wma-declaration-of-helsinki-ethical-principles-for-medical-research-involving-human-subjects/>.

[39] FDA 2011. Raltegravir label. <https://www.accessdata.fda.gov/drugsatfda_docs/label/2011/022145s018lbl.pdf>.

[40] FDA 2018. Ibalizumab label. <https://www.accessdata.fda.gov/drugsatfda_docs/label/2018/761065lbl.pdf>.

[41] EMA 2020. EMA initiatives for acceleration of development support and evaluation procedures for COVID-19 treatments and vaccines. <https://www.ema.europa.eu/en/

documents/other/ema-initiatives-acceleration-development-support-evaluation-procedures-covid-19-treatments-vaccines_en.pdf>.

[42] EMA 2020. Guidance for medicine developers and companies on COVID-19. Includes rules rapid Agreem PIPs. <https://www.ema.europa.eu/en/human-regulatory/overview/public-health-threats/coronavirus-disease-covid-19/guidance-medicine-developers-companies-covid-19#accelerated-procedures-for-covid-19-treatments-and-vaccines-section>.

[43] Momper JD, Mulugeta Y, Green DJ, et al. Adolescent dosing and labeling since the food and drug administration amendments act of 2007. JAMA Pediatr 2013;167(10):926–32 Oct.

[44] Gonzalez D, Melloni C, Yogev R, et al. Use of opportunistic clinical data and a population pharmacokinetic model to support dosing of clindamycin for premature infants to adolescents. Clin Pharmacol Ther 2014;96(4):429–37 Oct.

[45] Laughon MM, Benjamin DK. Mechanisms to provide safe and effective drugs for children. Pediatrics. 2014;134(2):e562–3 Aug.

[46] Plate V. The impact of off-label, compassionate and unlicensed use on health care laws in preselected countries. <http://hss.ulb.uni-bonn.de/2009/1936/1936.pdf>.

[47] Colón AR. Nurturing childen. A history of pediatrics. Westport, CT: Greenwood Press; 1999.

Chapter 5

Neonatology

Introduction

Neonatology is the hospital-based subspecialty of pediatric medicine that cares for newborns that are ill or born prematurely with low birth weight, intrauterine growth restriction, birth defects, sepsis, pulmonary hypoplasia, birth asphyxia, and more [1]. Among all pediatric sub-specialties, neonatology might be the youngest one. Its challenges reach across all medical areas that in older patients are differentiated into a multitude of different subspecialties. Neonates are very small, very immature, and very vulnerable patients. One of the key elements that eventually led to the characterization of all children as "therapeutic orphans" were the toxicities observed in preterm newborns in the 1950s [2–4]. Additional elements were the thalidomide catastrophe [5–7], which triggered the efficacy amendment of 1962 to the Federal Food, Drug, and Cosmetic Act [8]; the medical warnings inserted into drug labels by pharmaceutical manufacturers to prevent damage lawsuits in the litigious US legal culture [9–13]; the *medical* interpretation of these predominantly *legal* warnings and the creation of the concept that all children are "therapeutic orphans" [14]; the adoption of this concept by the committee on drugs of the American Academy of Pediatrics (AAP) [4,15–18]; and eventually the translation of this concept into law first by the US and eventually by the EU [19–22]. Neonatology was at its very beginnings when the children-are-therapeutic-orphans concept emerged.

Neonatology began as a pioneer discipline

Key steps in improving the care of newborns included the introduction of thermoregulation by incubators, parenteral nutrition, steroid injections for pregnant women to encourage the fetus at risk for premature birth to speed up the production of natural surfactant, development of external surfactant that could be instilled into the lungs of babies born before they were able to produce this surfactant on their own, respiratory support, cardiopulmonary support, and effective pharmaceutical treatment of bacterial, viral, and fungal neonatal infections. Furthermore, a fundamental change in the attitudes of physicians and nurses toward parents occurred. Parents were initially allowed to view their infants only through a glass partition due to fear of infections.

Considering the Patient in Pediatric Drug Development. DOI: https://doi.org/10.1016/B978-0-12-823888-2.00020-X

Eventually, the key role of emotional bonding between the tiny patients and the parents became accepted, and the attitude of physicians and other healthcare professionals toward the parents softened [23,24]. The term "neonatology" was coined in 1961 [25]. In 1975, the first examination of the subboard of neonatal-perinatal medicine of the American Board of Pediatrics and the first meeting of the perinatal section of the AAP took place [24]. The first neonatal intensive care unit (NICU) was established in the US in 1965 [23]. Today, neonatology is usually performed in NICUs.

Neonatology is a successful clinical subspecialty

Many publications complain about a lack of "pediatric" studies in general, and even more so in the neonatal population [26–38]. But there is a logical break in the continuously repeated lament of the protagonists of "pediatric drug development" [39]. Over the past century, the outlook for infants with birth weights of 1 kg has changed from 95% mortality to 95% survival [23,24]. Many of the major advances in care that have transformed outcomes for preterm and sick newborns were achieved by empirical and applied health research [40]. Errors occurred, such a exposing the neonates to too much oxygen resulting in eye damage [41,42], or the mentioned toxicities in preterm newborns [2–4]. Such errors were eventually corrected. There is no pioneer medicine without mistakes. Altogether, the work of neonatology and the NICUs was and is highly successful. More neonates than ever survive.

Neonatology and drug approval

The emotional power of small and vulnerable tiny children has played a major role in the justification and the development of "pediatric drug development." However, drug approval for neonates has not played a major role in preparing and discussing US and EU pediatric legislation. Historical overviews over the development of neonatology do not even mention the role of the regulatory authorities [23–25]. The vast majority of "pediatric" clinical studies are requested/demanded by the FDA and the EMA in minors from 1 to 17 years of age, not in neonates. When lung surfactants, intravenous nutrition, antibiotics, and other life-saving measures were first used in neonatology, they were used to help the little patients. Over time, such measures proved to be successful. Errors occurred but were eventually corrected [2–4,41,42]. When the first incubators were introduced, nobody gave much thought about an approval as medical devices. Such an attitude is usual in pioneering disciplines. When the first iron lungs were constructed to save children with polio, the treating physicians' last concern was if the iron lung would ever be certified [43]. Comparably to the attempts of, first, the FDA, and then the EMA to also play a major role in pediatric oncology, there are many publications that argue for more regulatory studies in neonatology [26–38]. "The magnitude of the problem is demonstrated by the fact that today over 90% of neonatal intensive care unit (NICU) prescribing remains off-label. Importantly, this means that prescribing of drugs in the NICU is routinely occurring without an adequate evidence base for their use in this neonatal population" [44]. If we would have enormous death rates in the NICUs, we might consider that there might be a truly clinical problem. But neonatology has become a successful pediatric subdiscipline. The first textbook of neonatology was published in 1922 [23]. Today's textbooks on neonatology are as thick and impressive as the textbooks in all other medical and pediatric subdisciplines. The demand for more labels also in neonatology is a *regulatory* demand supported by clinicians and others who plead for more "pediatric" studies without mentioning that most lack medical sense or are massively exaggerated. Neonatology emerged like many other pediatric subspecialties entirely "off-label," decades before the term off-label emerged a first time in 1988 [45].

The key issue is the same as discussed for other pediatric subspecialties. The treatment of very young patients has continuously improved during the 20th century. Despite fierce resistance both from pharmaceutical manufacturers and the medical profession [46], the intellectual and administrative processing of the thalidomide catastrophe by the drug efficacy amendment of 1962 to the Federal Food, Drug, and Cosmetic Act [8] was decisive in advancing modern drug development. All pediatric subspecialties used whatever was available to improve hands-on bedside treatment. Of course, they all used modern drugs. There was no specific role of the FDA in the early years of neonatology. Relatively few drugs used in the NICUs are FDA approved. A paper from 2014 reports that 13 drugs studied in neonates were not used at all among over 400,000 hospitalized neonates. It concludes that study designs and procedures that are appropriate in adults and older children may not be appropriate in neonates [47]. This is a correct conclusion for neonatology, but short-sighted regarding all regulatorily demanded "pediatric" studies. Most studies performed in the "pediatric population" lack medical sense. They would lack even more sense in neonatology where the appropriate dose of a given drug may have to be corrected a few hours after its first use during the same day, due to the rapidly developing body of the neonate.

Neonatology uses all drugs that are available. But neonatology is also part of our real world. Some developmental pharmacologists and neonatologists have realized that the call for "more" pediatric studies also in neonatology is a relatively easy strategy to ask for research funds. The demand for more pediatric labels and more regulatory studies in neonatology is based on the assumption that the separate regulatory clinical studies in the "pediatric population" were and are a huge success story. This assumption is wrong. Clinical healthcare of young patients has not improved through better labels, but through better medicines, through the medical profession's learning how to use them, better guidelines and dosing recommendations, and better available formulations. Such learning has often taken many years, as we see in the survival rates of children with cancer that improved by ten percent per decade during the last decades of the 20th century until they reached a plateau [48,49].

Regulatory studies prove that a new drug works better than placebo or comparison treatment *in humans*. Unless they are toxic, antibiotics, antifungals and antivirals work also in premature newborns. Their administration must be handled with extreme care. Neonatology has learned this stepwise through the last half century. The call for the expansion of separate proof-of-efficacy studies from the general "pediatric population" into the field of neonatology has the same material conflict of interest that forms the basis of the entire "pediatric drug development" [39]. These "pediatric" studies have created an entire industry of "pediatric" studies that have advanced careers in regulatory authorities, clinical academia, pharmaceutical industry, and commercial clinical research organizations [20–22,50]. But they have not advanced pediatric healthcare.

Conclusion

As in all other medical subspecialties, researchers need funds. There is nothing bad about this, but justification for pediatric research, including in neonatology should differentiate between reasonable research aimed at improving healthcare, and research projects that aim at pediatric labels only and are medically questionable or even harm patients. No physician should prescribe medicines to young patients without pediatric expertise. Regulatory clinical studies have protected mankind from further disasters like the thalidomide one [5–7]. But the desire to protect young patients by specific "pediatric" drug approval is a dead end. The degree to which drug developers should producc dosing rccommendations for young and very young patients needs to be balanced against understandable, but exaggerated desires for funding of pediatric and neonatal research.

That neonatologists use available modern and effective drugs in daily practice is good. It contradicts current regulatory logic. There are two logics, a clinical one, and a regulatory one. Exaggerated and blind regulatory logic has invaded relevant parts of medical thinking. It is time to reverse this. Regulatory logic should help and support hands-on bedside clinical care. The committed errors were not done by individuals with bad intentions. Nevertheless, in the process of correcting these errors, issues must be addressed candidly.

References

[1] Wikipedia. Neonatology. <https://en.wikipedia.org/wiki/Neonatology>

[2] Silverman WA, Andersen DH, Blanc WA, Crozier DN. A difference in mortality rate and incidence of kernicterus among premature infants allotted to two prophylactic antibacterial regimens. Pediatrics. 1956;18:614.

[3] Burns LE, Hodgman JE, Cass AB. Fatal circulatory collapse in premature infants receiving chloramphenicol. N Engl J Med 1959;261:1318–21.

[4] AAP. Guidelines for the ethical conduct of studies to evaluate drugs in pediatric populations, committee on drugs 1995 Am Acad Pediatrics, Pediatrics 1995;95(2):286–94 <https://pediatrics.aappublications.org/content/pediatrics/95/2/286.full.pdf>.

[5] Vargesson N. Thalidomide-induced teratogenesis: History and mechanisms. Birth Defects Res C Embryo Today 2015;105(2):140–56 <https://www.ncbi.nlm.nih.gov/pmc/articles/PMC4737249/>.

[6] Ridings JE. The thalidomide disaster, lessons from the past. Methods Mol Biol 2013; 947:575–86.

[7] Thomann KD. Die Contergan-Katastrophe. DÄ 2007;104(41):A2778–82 <https://www.aerzteblatt.de/pdf.asp?id = 57224>.

[8] Janssen WM. A historical perspective on off-label medicine: from regulation, promotion, and the first amendment to the next frontiers. Food and Drug Law Institute, Levy M.C. (Editor). First Washington, D.C., USA *Off-Label Communications* (2008)

[9] Kritzer HM. Propensity to Sue in England and the United States of America: blaming and claiming in tort cases. J Law Soc 1991;18(4):400–27.

[10] Lochlann Jain SS. Injury: the politics of product design and safety law in the United States. Princeton, NJ, USA: Princeton University Press; 2006.

[11] McGovern F. Punitive damages and class actions. Lousiana Law Rev 2010;70:435–62 <https://scholarship.law.duke.edu/cgi/viewcontent.cgi?article = 2762&context = faculty_scholarship>.

[12] Bal BS. An introduction to medical malpractice in the United States. Clin Orthop Relat Res 2009;467(2):339–47 <https://www.ncbi.nlm.nih.gov/pmc/articles/PMC2628513/>.

[13] Kass JS, Rose RV. Medical malpractice reform: historical approaches, alternative models, and communication and resolution programs. AMA J Ethics 2016;18(3):299–310 <https://journalofethics.ama-assn.org/sites/journalofethics.ama-assn.org/files/2019-12/pfor6-1603.pdf>.

[14] Shirkey H. Therapeutic orphans. J Pediatr 1968;72(1):119–20 <https://pdfs.semanticscholar.org/f1cb/acdbac19fa56236b919fb7799eaacaa10c77.pdf>.

[15] Yaffe SJ, Avery ME, Gold AP, et al. American academy of pediatrics. Committee on drugs. Drug testing in children: FDA regulations. Pediatrics 1969;43(3):463–5 <https://pediatrics.aappublications.org/content/pediatrics/43/3/463.full.pdf>.

[16] AAP. Committee on drugs. Guidelines for the ethical conduct of studies to evaluate drugs in pediatric populations 1977 Pediatrics 1977;60(1):91–101 <https://pediatrics.aappublications.org/content/pediatrics/60/1/91.full.pdf>.

[17] Shaddy RE, Denne SC. Committee on drugs and committee on pediatric research. Clinical report--guidelines for the ethical conduct of studies to evaluate drugs in pediatric populations. Pediatrics 2010;125(4):850–60 <https://pediatrics.aappublications.org/content/pediatrics/125/4/850.full.pdf>.

[18] Christensen ML, Helms RA, Chesney RW. Is pediatric labelling really necessary? Pediatrics 1999;104(3 Pt 2):593–7 <https://pediatrics.aappublications.org/content/pediatrics/104/Supplement_3/598.full.pdf>.

[19] Hirschfeld S, Saint-Raymond A. Pediatric regulatory initiatives. Handb Exp Pharmacol 2011;205:245–68.

[20] Rose K, Neubauer D, Grant-Kels JM. Rational use of medicine in children – The conflict of interests story. A review. Rambam Maimonides Med J 2019;10(3):e0018. Available from: https://doi.org/10.5041/RMMJ.10371 Review <https://www.rmmj.org.il/userimages/928/2/PublishFiles/953Article.pdf>.

[21] Rose K, Grant-Kels JM. The meanings of "pediatric drug development". A review. Ther Innov Regul Sci 2019;53(6):767–74.

[22] Rose K. The challenges of pediatric drug development. Curr Ther Res Clin Exp 2019;. Available from: https://doi.org/10.1016/j.curtheres.2019.01.007.

[23] Jorgensen AM. Born in the USA – The history of neonatology in the United States: A century of caring. <http://images.abbottnutrition.com/ANHI/MEDIA/Nurse%20Currents%20NICU%20History%20June%202010.pdf>.

[24] Philip AG. The evolution of neonatology. Pediatr Res 2005;58(4):799–815 <https://www.nature.com/articles/pr2005743.pdf?origin = ppub>.

[25] Vidyasagar D. Half a century of evolution of neonatology: A witness's story" Dr. K. C. Chaudhuri Lifetime Achievement Award Oration Delivered at AIIMS, New Delhi on 7th September 2014Indian J Pediatr 2015;82(12):1117–25. Available from: https://doi.org/10.1007/s12098-015-1838-8.

[26] Stiers J, Ward RM. Newborns, one of the last therapeutic orphans to be adopted. JAMA Pediatr 2014;168(2):106–8.

[27] Barrett JS, Bishai R, Bucci-Rechtweg C, et al. Challenges and opportunities in the development of medical therapies for pediatric populations and the role of extrapolation. Clin Pharmacol Ther 2018;103(3):419–33. Available from: https://doi.org/10.1002/cpt.1000 Epub 2018.

[28] Ward RM, Benjamin D, Barrett JS, et al. Safety, dosing, and pharmaceutical quality for studies that evaluate medicinal products (including biological products) in neonates. 2016

[29] Ward RM, Benjamin D, Barrett JS, et al. Safety, dosing, and pharmaceutical quality for studies that evaluate medicinal products (including biological products) in neonates. Pediatr Res 2017;81(5):692–711.

[30] Dotta A, Braguglia A, Salvatori G. Pharmacological research in neonatology. J Matern Fetal Neonatal Med 2011;24(Suppl 1):44–6.

[31] Sivanandan S, Jain K, Plakkal N, et al. Issues, challenges, and the way forward in conducting clinical trials among neonates: investigators' perspective. J Perinatol 2019;39 (Suppl 1):20–30. Available from: https://doi.org/10.1038/s41372-019-0469-8.

[32] Wang J, Avant D, Green D, et al. A survey of neonatal pharmacokinetic and pharmacodynamic studies in pediatric drug development. Clin Pharmacol Ther 2015;98(3):328–35.

[33] Smith AM, Davis JM. Challenges and opportunities to enhance global drug development in neonates. Curr Opin Pediatr 2017;29(2):149–52.

[34] Giacoia GP, Taylor-Zapata P, Zajicek A. Drug Studies in Newborns: A Therapeutic Imperative. Clin Perinatol 2012;39(1):11–23.

[35] O'Hara K, Martin JH, Schneider JJ. Barriers and challenges in performing pharmacokinetic studies to inform dosing in the neonatal population. Pharm (Basel) 2020;8(1):16 <https://www.ncbi.nlm.nih.gov/pmc/articles/PMC7151681/pdf/pharmacy-08-00016.pdf>.

[36] Allegaert K, van den Anker JN. Perinatal clinical pharmacology: optimizing pharmacotherapy for pregnant women, their fetuses and infants. Curr Pharm Des 2019;25 (5):467–8. Available from: https://doi.org/10.2174/138161282504190516090723.

[37] van den Anker JN, Coppes MJ, Koren G. Neonatal and pediatric clinical pharmacology. Pediatr Clin North Am 2012;59(5):xv–xviii. Available from: https://doi.org/10.1016/j.pcl.2012.07.014 Epub 2012.

[38] Allegaert K. Rational use of medicines in neonates: current observations, areas for research and perspectives. Healthc (Basel) 2018;6(3):115 <https://www.ncbi.nlm.nih.gov/pmc/articles/PMC6165407/pdf/healthcare-06-00115.pdf>.

[39] Ward RM, Benjamin Jr DK, Davis JM, Gorman RL, Kauffman R, Kearns GL, et al. The need for pediatric drug development. J Pediatr 2018;192:13–21.

[40] McGuire W, Halliday HL. The research cycle: improving care and outcomes for newborn infants. Neonatology 2018;114(1):2–6.

[41] Patz A. The role of oxygen in retrolental fibroplasia. Trans Am Ophthalmol Soc 1968; 66:940–85 <https://www.ncbi.nlm.nih.gov/pmc/articles/PMC1310320/pdf/taos00033-0953.pdf>.

[42] Tasman W, Patz A, McNamara JA, et al. Retinopathy of prematurity: the life of a lifetime disease. Am J Ophthalmol 2006;141(1):167–74.

[43] Odessa R. Breath is life: the fascinating history of the iron lung. The Wisdom Daily, 13th July 2017. <http://thewisdomdaily.com/breath-is-life-the-fascinating-history-of-the-iron-lung/>.

[44] Bucci-Rechtweg CM, Ward RM. Tiny and forgotten: a call for focused neonatal policy reform. Ther Innov Regul Sci 2019;53(5):615–17.

[45] Plate V. The impact of off-label, compassionate and unlicensed use on health care laws in preselected countries. <http://hss.ulb.uni-bonn.de/2009/1936/1936.pdf>.

[46] Hilts PJ. Protecting America's health: the FDA, business, and one hundred years of regulation. New York: Alfred A Knopf Publishers; 2003.

[47] Laughon MW, Avant D, Tripathi N, et al. Drug labeling and exposure in neonates. JAMA Pediatr 2014;168(2):130–6 <https://www.ncbi.nlm.nih.gov/pmc/articles/PMC3927948/pdf/nihms551236.pdf>.

[48] Norris RE, Adamson PC. Challenges and opportunities in childhood cancer drug development. Nat Rev Cancer 2012;12(11):776–82.

[49] Adamson PC. Improving the outcome for children with cancer: development of targeted new agents. CA Cancer J Clin 2015;65(3):212–20.

[50] Severin T, Corriol-Rohou S, Bucci-Rechtweg C, et al. How is the pharmaceutical industry structured to optimize pediatric drug development? Existing pediatric structure models and proposed recommendations for structural enhancement. Ther Innov Regul Sci 2020.

Chapter 6

Challenges at the interface of science, drug development, and drug approval beyond specific disease areas

In contrast to the clinical areas discussed in Chapter 4, the subchapters in this chapter address "pediatric drug development" from very different points of view. "PDD" has now already a history of half a century, and thus has invaded many areas of medicine and science. Uncountable numbers of papers, and many books have been published that repeat and try to solidify wrong statements. "Pediatric drug development" is not only discussed in scientific and pseudoscientific publications, but lures people of good will with appeals that are more emotional than scientific in nature. Otherwise, lawmakers on both sides of the Atlantic would not have enacted pediatric laws. This chapter addresses several manyfold blurs used to justify and defend "pediatric drug development."

One of the most frequently used arguments for "pediatric drug development" is that many drugs in young patients are used "off-label." But the entire discipline of pediatrics and many of its subdisciplines emerged and developed "off-label" even before this term was used for the first time in 1988.

Developmental pharmacology/pediatric clinical pharmacology is a science that goes across specific disease areas and investigates how body and drugs interact. Representatives of developmental pharmacology have played a major role in advancing "pediatric drug development" and to transform it into a worldwide movement with numerous international institutions, initiatives, and structures.

Extrapolation and similar methods are useful techniques of developmental pharmacology. Where the FDA and the EMA accept that separate proof of efficacy is not necessary, they nevertheless demand "extrapolation," for example, from adults into adolescents, as if these two were different species. But they are not. Adolescents are already bodily mature and do not need different dose recommendations. The FDA has found this out on its own when it compared dosing recommendations for adults and adolescents. But it has not drawn the necessary conclusions and continues to use the term "extrapolation," as does the EMA.

Considering the Patient in Pediatric Drug Development. DOI: https://doi.org/10.1016/B978-0-12-823888-2.00032-6

Fraud in research is, in general, perceived as deception by individuals who know what they are doing and hope they will never get caught. Here we introduce a new type of deceit in the 21st century where the regulatory authorities, leading academic clinicians, and representatives from large research-based pharmaceutical companies and from commercial clinical trial organizations tell the same story to justify "pediatric drug development." This new type of deceit would be impossible without the scientific, academic, and governmental structures and institutions that have developed during the last half century and have developed partially a life and interests of their own.

In the fairy tale, the speaking out of Rumpelstiltskin's name is a total and final game changer. One of the two reasons for choosing the picture of the miller's daughter on the book cover is that a similar effect is expected by addressing what the term "child" means, and how its different meanings are carefully used to blur and to produce wrong impressions.

Last but not least, myths and misunderstandings in today's medical world are discussed. Such myths include the claim that "off-label" use of drugs in "children" is always dangerous, that the market of the "pediatric population" is too small for commercial drug development, that only state-mandated "pediatric" clinical studies are able to fulfill the needs of young patients, that all "pediatric" studies are evidenced-based and scientifically sound, and that the hesitance of reimbursement institutions to pay for off-label treatment in "children" is a medically and scientifically sound and acceptable justification for separate regulatory "pediatric" studies.

Enjoy reading!

Subchapter 6.1

The on-label/off-label framework in adults and young patients

On-label and off-label in adults and "children"

One of the most common arguments for separate "pediatric" studies is that the respective drug is not approved in "children." The FDA defines "children" as persons younger than 17 [1], the EU as younger than 18 years [2,3]. At first glance this argument may sound quite plausible, but it does not stand up to critical analysis.

A label is in everyday life the product description on a package. In medicine, this term has become a synonym for the information that describes for the respective drug the diseases it is approved to treat; its effects and side effects; the clinical studies that have been carried out, and more. Although patients may obtain useful information from prescription drug labeling, its primary purpose is to give healthcare professionals the information they need to prescribe the drug appropriately [4]. Today's labels must describe correctly the content of the respective drug and must not be misleading. It took decades until this level of honesty was reached. In the first decades of the 20th century the courts allowed misleading information given in the labels [5].

Today's US label system began in 1906 when the US Congress enacted the federal Pure Food and Drugs Act [6]. It gave the predecessor of today's FDA, the Bureau of Chemistry the power to seize "adulterated" and "misbranded" food and drugs. To understand the situation in 1906, in which the US could be described as "the world's dumping ground for counterfeit, contaminated, diluted, and decomposed drug materials" [7]. US drug legislation regulated from its beginning the *trading* of drugs, not their prescription. The Bureau of Chemistry was reorganized in 1927 and named the "Food, Drug, and Insecticide Administration." Finally it was renamed in 1931 as the Food and Drug Administration (FDA) [7].

We can differentiate three different subterms: off-label use, off-label prescription, and off-label promotion. Off-label use is if a patients gets a prescription for a specific health problem, but uses it for a different challenge. Off-label use is not regulated by the FDA. Off-label prescription is if a physician prescribes a drug for a different purpose. Off-label prescription is not regulated by the FDA. Off-label promotion is when a company promotes the use of a given drug for another purpose than officially approved by the FDA. Off-label promotion is heavily sanctioned by the FDA and has resulted in fines of $US billions for pharmaceutical companies [6].

The focus of the US federal regulatory scheme was from the beginning conceived to be on the *supply* of medical products. This essential feature remains until today. The US federal laws ensure that pharmaceuticals and medical devices are not made available to the market unless they have been examined and approved by the FDA. The US federal laws are decidedly not intended to reach further into the realm of physicians' professional decisions to prescribe drugs [6].

Off-label prescription is well documented in the medical and legal literature and has become part of today's complex medical system. The US supreme court has declared off-label prescribing to be "an accepted and necessary corollary of FDA's mission to regulate in this area without directly interfering with the practice of medicine." Off-label prescribing is described as "quite common," "generally accepted," and "an established aspect" of the practice of medicine. Not only is it commonplace. Off-label treatment may not only be merely acceptable, but may even represent the current therapeutic standard-of-care. In such cases, a physician's failure to make an appropriate off-label prescription may be regarded as medical malpractice [6].

There are good arguments for the FDA's strict controls of off-label promotion, and good arguments against them. For a while, it was forbidden for pharmaceutical companies to hand out peer-reviewed scientific publications on off-label use of drugs. This restricted the freedom of speech, and is since decades heavily fought over in the US courts [6,8]. This is a debate on which here we will not focus further.

Much of today's drug approval goes back to industrial societies' coping with the 1962 thalidomide disaster. Thalidomide, a supposedly harmless sedative, had caused massive malformations of the children in the womb in pregnant women. In Germany, thalidomide could be bought over the counter (OTC) in the pharmacy from the start, so the number of affected children was very high, but this catastrophe occurred worldwide wherever thalidomide was sold or made otherwise available to patients [9–11]. It was not approved in the US in the 1960s, but a few babies with malformed limbs were also born in the US, since thalidomide had been distributed in so-called "clinical studies" that amounted to medical doctors dispensing the tablets to patients as sleeping pills or tranquilizers without any control and documentation [5]. The US was the country that took the most resolute action compared to other countries' hesitant response. The US gave the FDA the authority to approve drugs from now on only based on clinical trials that demonstrated efficacy and safety. These studies had to be completed before submitting a marketing authorization application admission. This principle of proving efficacy and safety through completed clinical studies has meanwhile become established worldwide [12]. It has fundamentally changed drug development, medicine and the health system. The effort to put medical action on a scientific basis has found its way into all medical disciplines. That was not always a matter of course, especially in areas where ideology, religion, belief and traditions play(ed) a major role. Homosexuality was in the middle ages considered a sin, and in modern times a disease. The diagnosis of homosexuality was removed from the Diagnostic and Statistical Manual of Mental Disorders (DSM) in 1973 and from the International Classification of Diseases (ICD) in 1991 [13,14]. The first birth control pill in Germany was initially approved for menstrual cramps; for contraception only for married women [15]. Being married is not a physical condition, but a legal position. The restriction of approval for contraception to married women only was a concession by the regulatory authorities to a social code that threatened parents with criminal proceedings for procuration if they allowed the son to keep his girlfriend or the daughter to keep her boyfriend at home for the night. It was not long ago that women in general, men and women of black skin, or persons of Jewish religion could not do military service or study medicine.

The term "off-label" for the use of a drug outside of the officially approved indication appeared a first time in 1988 [15]. Off-label use of medication does not mean that this use is medically wrong. An Israeli doctor who still had thalidomide packs in his office gave it to patients with leprosy who could not sleep. To his surprise, leprosy lesions disappeared almost overnight in these patients. This observation triggered a compassionate use program at the FDA that allowed thalidomide to be delivered to patients who had skin problems caused by leprosy. Today, thalidomide is approved by the FDA for the treatment of multiple myeloma (a cancer) and skin problems in leprosy [9–11,16,17]. The use and prescription of medication for a problem or illness other than the one originally intended and also approved is an elementary part of medical practice. The Israeli doctor who gave thalidomide to his first leprosy patients acted responsibly. He knew very well that these patients were not planning to get pregnant. This delivery of thalidomide happened "off-label" at a time when this expression did not yet exist. Pediatric oncology, the successful treatment of young patients with cancer, developed entirely "off-label," decades before the term "off-label" first appeared [15,18,19].

The separate approval of medicines for adults and minors, which the authorities classify as "children," even if they are no longer physically children, developed after the thalidomide disaster, triggered by toxicities in newborns in the 1950s that had been treated with antibiotics [20,21]. Pediatric warnings in drug labels since 1962 served predominantly as a legal protection against damage lawsuits in the litigious US legal environment [22–26]. But these pediatric warnings led to the new concept of children as "therapeutic orphans" [27]. Before that, children and adults had been correctly perceived as human beings. The children-are-therapeutic-orphans and children-are-not-small-adults mantras emerged with the growing awareness that in very small children the dosage of medication cannot simply be adapted to the lower body weight, but that additional measurements are necessary [28,29]. The American Academy of Pediatrics (AAP) began to demand "pediatric" studies [30–33]. In these AAP demands the difference between the legal and the physiological meaning of the term "child" became blurred [34–36]. On one side the AAP emphasized that off-label use of drugs in "children" is legitimate [37,38], but nevertheless it emphasized the need for "pediatric" studies and the "moral imperative" that demanded such studies [30,31]. The FDA began to demand clinical data in "children" and eventually began to approve drugs separately in "children" [1,2], followed by the EU [2,3], and other regulatory agencies worldwide. But the definition of "children" was administrative. It extrapolated the toxicities observed in neonates into all administratively defined "children," as if "children" remain as vulnerable and immature as preterm newborns until they come of age.

Today, the medical system is already responsible for a relevant part of economic output, and the trend is rising. And people are getting older because more and more things that used to lead to death with high certainty can now be treated routinely.

In the past, a doctor's decision to prescribe a medication for another purpose other than the one for which it was approved was sufficient, but the focus has shifted in recent decades. A physician can get into trouble with the institutions responsible for reimbursement. This trouble can occur directly, if he is independent; indirectly, if he works in a hospital, and the hospital administration is concerned regarding reimbursement. Today's modern effective drugs can be very expensive. The emergence of the "off-label" term in 1988 also stands for the increase in power of the medical system's administration and for the need to carefully control the resources invested into the healthcare system.

Imposing the on-label/ off-label framework on the administratively defined "children" is a completely different issue than the question if a given drug should be approved or not. This question is answered by the pivotal regulatory studies organized for drug approval. There are two potential scenarios for the fact that medication is initially only approved for adults, i.e., over 18 years of age, and not for "children": either the lack of regulatory approval for "children" is based on science, or this is not the case. If this is not the case, there must be reasons why this practice has been unquestioned for many years.

Authorities, researching pediatricians, developmental pharmacologists, and representatives of "pediatric" research in industry and contract research organizations claim that there are no data for the respective medication in "children," and therefore require repetition of proof-of-effectiveness and safety studies in the "pediatric population." But there is a twist in this demand. We do not require that red-haired people are only treated with drugs for which studies have been performed only in red-haired people. Or that people whose first or last name begin with the letter "R" or "K" are only treated with drugs that have been tested in persons with the same initials. Or that 23-year-olds are only treated with drugs that have been tested in 23-year-old patients. Instead, the limitations of approval of drugs in specific sub-groups of patients need to be based on rational grounds and lead to reproducible data, provided these grounds are reasonable.

Is there a fundamental bodily difference between "children" and adults? There is a fundamental difference between babies and adults; an even bigger difference between premature babies and adults; and an even bigger difference between extremely immature premature babies and adults [28]. But not between young people whose bodies are already mature when they have passed puberty [39–42]. After puberty, young persons are *legally* still minors. They are *administratively* young adults one hour, one day, one week, one month, or one year after the 17th/18th birthday. A birthday can change the *legal* and *administrative* status of a person, but the body does not change overnight. The demand for separate studies and for separate "data" appears to be plausible as long as we do not look closely what the term "child" means. It has different meanings that should not be blurred. Young persons are not another species in which the efficacy of antidepressants, antibiotics, antiepileptics and many more drugs has to be proven again. Drugs work the same before and after the 17th/18th birthday.

There are a several more questions: dosage, safety, newborns, and premature newborns. Many premature newborns that survive today did not survive in the 1960s. Neonatology has become a successful and respected discipline [43]. When it comes to dosing, separate "pediatric" studies are superfluous as soon as the body has grown up, regardless of the legal status of the individual. A comparison of adult and adolescent doses showed that in roughly 95% of drugs the FDA-recommended doses are identical [44]. Dosing in younger children does not require extensive, international, randomized, and complicated studies. Additional blood sampling is sufficient for some patients for whom there are compelling medical reasons for the administration of the respective medication. Such studies are called "opportunistic" studies [45,46]. Today, the necessary dosages in young people can be calculated very precisely in computer models; there are numerous companies that offer such a service if the respective company does not have these skills in-house.

The vast majority of "pediatric" studies requested/ demanded by the FDA and EMA are not in newborns, but are in "children" from birth to 17 years. As far as medication will play a role in the treatment of newborns and premature babies, separate studies make sense. But not if the result is clear from the start. Pain killers, opiates, and antibiotics also work in newborns. We need to be alert on toxicities, and the doses must be correct. But this is precisely the reason what newborns and preterm newborns are treated in specialized neonate wards.

Lack of approval of drugs in "children" and demands for separate additional "pediatric" studies can either mean that necessary studies are indeed missing, or that the demand for additional "pediatric" studies is flawed. Regulatory authorities, researchers, academics, and other institutions that support the demand for additional "pediatric" studies have developed strong, material, hidden interests. The concept of "pediatric drug development" has gradually became a social reality. The EU followed the US precedence, even wanted to outperform the United States, and extended the call for "pediatric" studies to everyone under the age of 18. The EMA also extended the call for "pediatric" studies to numerous disease areas where the FDA could not mandate "pediatric" studies, including drugs for rare diseases, vaccines, biologicals, therapeutic allergens, and tissue-engineered products to support surgical treatment of joint injuries and other tissue challenges [47,48].

This concept is enforced by the regulatory authorities. But without the support of academic research medicine, FDA and EMA could not continue. The thousands of Institutional Review Boards (IRBs)/ethics committees (ECs) that review every single clinical study worldwide have overlooked this challenge. How is that possible?

Trust in official and state institutions is strong worldwide. That authority-demanded studies lack medical sense and even harm patients may appear to most persons as conceivable in theory, but not in something as elementary as children's health. Lack of medical sense in most government-demanded "pediatric" studies has a dimension that is almost unimaginable. But what is new here? During the first years of the thalidomide disaster the entire professional world in Germany repeatedly assured the public that there was no increase in malformations. And if really something should be wrong, it was probably caused by the US nuclear bombs detonated over Japan [9]. At the end, it took one pediatrician in one city who questioned a number of mothers, inspected their homes and the drugs these mothers had used, until the penny dropped. When he presented his findings at a medical conference and a major newspaper printed the suspicion, the next Monday thalidomide had disappeared from pharmacies [9–11]. Another factor is that supporters of the concept of "pediatric drug development" are members of the editorial boards of many scientific journals and of the governing body of many scientific conferences. Critical manuscripts and abstracts that address elementary questions are simply rejected.

What originally probably emerged out of genuine concern for young patients has evolved into a worldwide orgy of senseless "pediatric" studies. The EU has augmented and expanded the flaws that existed already in the US pediatric laws to such an extent that we are now finally able to see the dimension and the downside of this "pediatric" activism [34–36].

The "off-label" classification of effective drugs in officially defined "children" means that for serious and life-threatening diseases effective treatment is withheld from young patients. The "pediatric" studies requested/demanded by the FDA and even more so by the EU are together probably the largest and most extensive systematic abuse of patients in medical research in human history.

The banality of evil is often breathtaking. When black, illiterate men with syphilis in the United States fell into the hands of the National Health Service (NHS), which monitored these men for a total of forty years, they were told they had "bad blood". Antibiotics help against syphilis. But when antibiotics became available, these men were not treated. This study (now notoriously known as the Tuskegee Study) was reported on at conferences of the American Medical Association (AMA) long before it was finally exposed in 1972. But at that time, black physicians had no access to these conferences [49]. No one protested. The NHS employees were allowed to observe the autopsies of the men who died from syphilis and published about them in medical journals. Of course, the scientific level of these publications was mediocre. But the employees achieved their annual goals, received their year-end bonus, and received their annual pay rise. For such banal reasons, effective treatment can be withheld from people with fatal diseases [50].

The employees that coordinate the demand for "pediatric" studies in the EMA and coordinate with the EU national regulatory authorities are well paid. Questionable, but apparently scientific publications appear regularly, justifying the need for separate "pediatric" studies [29−33,51−56]. Authors assure that they have no conflicts of interest [52,56]. Peter Buxtun, a US Public Health Service (PHS) employee, tried to convince the PHS management to terminate the study. After having been stonewalled for seven years, he finally understood that he could continue internally for another hundred years without success. Finally he turned to the press. The spook was over in weeks. Then it took another decades for a US president to apologize to the last survivors of the Tuskegee trial [57,58].

The results of "pediatric" studies are published in medical journals of highest medical reputation [59,60]. In joined publications with representatives of the EU regulatory authorities, "pediatric" researchers praise the fight against "off-label" use of medicines in "children" and claim that this constantly improves child healthcare [54,61].

The terminated and ongoing "pediatric" studies are already bad enough. But their two worst consequence are firstly that they block reasonable research in young patients. Modern drugs work in young patients, but parents with children with a chronic disease do not get the support they could get. Resources are wasted for clinical studies aiming at "pediatric" drug approval. Children with complex chronic diseases need support over decades. At present, the parents are largely left alone.

The second consequence is that the EU enforcement of "pediatric" studies is damaging and even destroying entire branches of industry in Europe, specifically fledgling companies dedicated to providing allergen products for ASIT and tissue-engineered products for joint repair and many other tissue challenges in adults and children [47,48]. Europe has *technically* and *scientifically* the potential to be a world leader in tissue-engineered modern medical products, allergen products for allergen-specific autoimmune treatment, and many other clinical areas and medical challenges. But not as long as the European Medicines Agency continues to block development.

References

[1] Hirschfeld S. History of pediatric labeling. Available from: https://slideplayer.com/slide/8600310/.

[2] Hirschfeld S, Saint-Raymond A. Pediatric regulatory initiatives. Handb Exp Pharmacol 2011;205:245–68.

[3] Regulation (EC) No 1901/2006 of the European Parliament and of the Council of 12 December 2006 on medicinal products for paediatric use and amending regulation (EEC) No 1768/92, Directive 2001/20/EC, Directive 2001/83/EC and Regulation (EC) No 726/2004. Available from:http://ec.europa.eu/health/files/eudralex/vol-1/reg_2006_1901/reg_2006_1901_en.pdf.

[4] Kremzner ME, Osborne SF. 2006. An introduction to the improved fda prescription drug labeling. Available from: https://www.fda.gov/media/72979/download.

[5] Hilts PJ. Protecting America's health: the FDA, business, and one hundred years of regulation. New York: Alfred A Knopf Publishers; 2003.

[6] Janssen WM. A historical perspective on off-label medicine: from regulation, promotion, and the first amendment to the next frontiers First In: Levy MC, editor. Off-Label Communications. Washington, D.C., USA: Food and Drug Law Institute; 2008.

[7] Janssen WF. The story of the laws behind the labels. FDA consumer magazine (June 1981). Available from: https://www.fda.gov/media/116890/download.

[8] Mazina N. Recent developments in off-label use and legal implications to physicians. American bar association, health law section, No. 14 Vol. 3, Available from: https://www.americanbar.org/groups/health_law/publications/aba_health_esource/2016-2017/november2017/offlabeluse.html.

[9] Thomann KD. Die contergan-katastrophe. DÄ 2007;104(41):A2778–82. Available from: https://www.aerzteblatt.de/pdf.asp?id=57224.

[10] Vargesson N. Thalidomide-induced teratogenesis: history and mechanisms. Birth Defects Res C Embryo Today 2015;105(2):140–56. Available from: https://www.ncbi.nlm.nih.gov/pmc/articles/PMC4737249/.

[11] Ridings JE. The thalidomide disaster, lessons from the past. Methods Mol Biol 2013;947:575–86.

[12] Rägo L, Santo B. Drug regulation: history, present and future. Available from: https://www.who.int/medicines/technical_briefing/tbs/Drug_Regulation_History_Present_Future.pdf.

[13] van de Water T, Suliman S, Seedat S. Gender and cultural issues in psychiatric nosological classification systems. CNS Spectr 2016;21(4):334–40.

[14] Mahler L, Mundle G, Plöderl M. Wirkungen und Nebenwirkungen des Krankheitskonzepts "Homosexualität" (Effects and side effects of the disease concept "Homosexuality"). Fortschr Neurol Psychiatr 2018;86(8):469–76.

[15] Plate V. 2009. The impact of off-label, compassionate and unlicensed use on health care laws in preselected countries. Dissertation to obtain a doctoral degree (Dr. rer. Nat.) From the faculty of mathematics and natural sciences at the rheinische friedrich-wilhelms-universität bonn. Available from: https://hss.ulb.uni-bonn.de/2009/1936/1936.pdf.

[16] FDA 1998 Thalidomide label. Available from: https://www.accessdata.fda.gov/drugsatfda_docs/label/2014/020785s055lbl.pdf.

[17] Pushpakom S, Iorio F, Eyers PA, et al. Drug repurposing: progress, challenges and recommendations. Nat Rev Drug Discov 2019;18(1):41–58.

[18] Adamson PC. Improving the outcome for children with cancer: development of targeted new agents. CA Cancer J Cli 2015;65(3):212–20.

[19] Rose K, Grant-Kels JM. Pediatric melanoma – the whole (conflicts of interest) story. Int J Womens Dermatol 2018;5(2):110–15. Available from: https://doi.org/10.1016/j.ijwd.2018.10.020. Available from: https://www.ncbi.nlm.nih.gov/pmc/articles/PMC6451736/pdf/main.pdf.

[20] Silverman WA, Andersen DH, Blanc WA, Crozier DN. A difference in mortality rate and incidence of kernicterus among premature infants allotted to two prophylactic antibacterial regimens. Pediatrics 1956;18:614.

[21] Burns LE, Hodgman JE, Cass AB. Fatal circulatory collapse in premature infants receiving chloramphenicol. N Engl 1 Med 1959;261:1318–21.

[22] Kritzer HM. Propensity to sue in England and the United States of America: blaming and claiming in tort cases. J Law Soc 1991;18(4):400–27.

[23] Lochlann Jain SS. Injury: the politics of product design and safety law in the United States. Princeton, NJ, USA: Princeton University Press; 2006.

[24] McGovern F. Punitive damages and class actions. Lousiana Law Rev 2010;70:435–62. Available from: https://scholarship.law.duke.edu/cgi/viewcontent.cgi?article=2762&context=faculty_scholarship.

[25] Bal BS. An introduction to medical malpractice in the United States. Clin Orthop Relat Res 2009;467(2):339–47. Available from: https://www.ncbi.nlm.nih.gov/pmc/articles/PMC2628513/.

[26] Kass JS, Rose RV. Medical malpractice reform: historical approaches, alternative models, and communication and resolution programs. AMA J Ethics 2016;18(3):299–310. Available from: https://journalofethics.ama-assn.org/sites/journalofethics.ama-assn.org/files/2019-12/pfor6-1603.pdf.

[27] Shirkey H. Therapeutic orphans. J Pediatr 1968;72(1):119–20. Available from: https://pdfs.semanticscholar.org/f1cb/acdbac19fa56236b919fb7799eaacaa10c77.pdf.

[28] Kearns GL, Abdel-Rahman SM, Alander SW, Blowey DL, Leeder JS, Kauffman RE. Developmental pharmacology - drug disposition, action, and therapy in infants and children. N Engl J Med 2003;349(12):1157–67.

[29] Ward RM, Benjamin Jr DK, Davis JM, Gorman RL, Kauffman R, Kearns GL, et al. The need for pediatric drug development. J Pediatr 2018;192:13–21.

[30] AAP 1995. Guidelines for the ethical conduct of studies to evaluate drugs in pediatric populations, committee on drugs. Am Acad Pediatrics, Pediatrics 1995;95(2):286–94.

[31] Shaddy RE, Denne SC, Committee on Drugs and Committee on Pediatric Research. Clinical report--guidelines for the ethical conduct of studies to evaluate drugs in pediatric populations. Pediatrics 2010;125(4):850–60. Available from: https://pediatrics.aappublications.org/content/pediatrics/125/4/850.full.pdf.

[32] Yaffe SJ, Avery ME, Gold AP, et al. American academy of pediatrics. Committee on drugs. Drug testing in children: FDA regulations. Pediatrics 1969;43(3):463–5. Available from: https://pediatrics.aappublications.org/content/pediatrics/43/3/463.full.pdf.

[33] AAP 1977. Committee on drugs. Guidelines for the ethical conduct of studies to evaluate drugs in pediatric populations. Pediatrics 1977;60(1):91–101. Available from: https://pediatrics.aappublications.org/content/pediatrics/60/1/91.full.pdf.

[34] Rose K, Neubauer D, Grant-Kels JM. Rational use of medicine in children – the conflict of interests story. A review Rambam Maimonides Med J 2019;10(3):e0018. Available

from: https://doi.org/10.5041/RMMJ.10371Review. Available from: https://www.rmmj.org.il/userimages/928/2/PublishFiles/953Article.pdf.

[35] Rose K, Grant-Kels JM. The meanings of "pediatric drug development". A review. Ther Innov Regul Sci 2019;53(6):767–74.

[36] Rose K. The challenges of pediatric drug development. Curr Ther Res Clin Exp 2019. Available from: https://doi.org/10.1016/j.curtheres.2019.01.007.

[37] AAP 1996. Unapproved use of approved drugs: the physician, the package insert, and the food and drug administration: subject review. Pediatrics 1996;98(1):143–5. Available from: https://pediatrics.aappublications.org/content/pediatrics/98/1/143.full.pdf.

[38] Frattarelli DA, Galinkin JL, Green TP, et al. Off-label use of drugs in children. Pediatrics 2014;133(3):563–7. Available from: https://pediatrics.aappublications.org/content/pediatrics/133/3/563.full.pdf.

[39] Khan L. Puberty: onset and progression. Pediatr Ann 2019;48(4):e141–5.

[40] Abreu AP, Kaiser UB. Pubertal development and regulation. Lancet Diabetes Endocrinol 2016;4(3):254–64.

[41] Snyder CK. Puberty: an overview for pediatric nurses. J Pediatr Nurs 2016;31(6):757–9.

[42] Wood CL, Lane LC, Cheetham T. Puberty: normal physiology (brief overview). Best Pract Res Clin Endocrinol Metab 2019;33(3):101265.

[43] Philip AG. The evolution of neonatology. Pediatr Res 2005;58(4):799–815.

[44] Momper JD, Mulugeta Y, Green DJ, et al. Adolescent dosing and labeling since the food and drug administration amendments Act of 2007. JAMA Pediatr 2013;167(10) 926–32.

[45] Gonzalez D, Melloni C, Yogev R, et al. Use of opportunistic clinical data and a population pharmacokinetic model to support dosing of clindamycin for premature infants to adolescents. Clin Pharmacol Ther 2014;96(4):429–37.

[46] Laughon MM, Benjamin DK. Mechanisms to provide safe and effective drugs for children. Pediatrics 2014;134(2):e562–3.

[47] Mumme M, Wixmerten A, Miot S, Barbero A, Kaempfen A, Saxer F, et al. Tissue engineering for paediatric patients. Swiss Med Wkly 2019;149:w20032. Available from: https://smw.ch/article/doi/smw.2019.20032.

[48] Rose K, Neubauer D, Fumi L, Grant-Kels JM. Tissue engineering for paediatric patients Comment on: Mumme M et al Swiss Med Wkly 2020. Available from: https://smw.ch/article/doi/smw.2020.20239.

[49] Harriet A. Washington. Medical Apartheid: the dark history of medical experimentation on Black Americans from colonial times to the present. New York, USA: Anchor Books; 2008.

[50] Adashi EY, Walters LB, Menikoff JA. The belmont report at 40: reckoning with time. Am J Public Health 2018;108(10):1345–8.

[51] van Riet-Nales DA, Römkens EG, Saint-Raymond A, Kozarewicz P, Schobben AF, Egberts TC, et al. Oral medicines for children in the European paediatric investigation plans. PLoS One 2014;9(6):e98348.

[52] Rocchi F, Paolucci P, Ceci A, Rossi P. The european paediatric legislation: benefits and perspectives Italian J Pediatrics 2010;36:56 Link. Available from: http://www.ncbi.nlm.nih.gov/pmc/articles/PMC2933611/pdf/1824-7288-36-56.pdf.

[53] Rocchi F, Tomasi P. The development of medicines for children. Pharmacol Res 2011;64:169–75.

[54] Mentzer D. Progress review of the European paediatric regulatory framework after six years of implementation. Int J Pharm 2014;469(2):240–3.

[55] Vesely R. PReS13-SPK-1182: six years of eu paediatric regulation - what was achieved for paediatric rheumatology. Vesely Pediatric Rheumatol 2013;11(Suppl 2):I15. Available from: https://ped-rheum.biomedcentral.com/track/pdf/10.1186/1546-0096-11-S2-I15.
[56] Tomasi PA, Egger GF, Pallidis C, Saint-Raymond A. Enabling development of paediatric medicines in Europe: 10 years of the EU paediatric regulation. Pediatr Drugs 2017;19(6) 505–13.
[57] Rose K. Ethical, regulatory and scientific challenges in paediatric drug development. Pharm Med 2008;22(4):221–34.
[58] Wikipedia Peter Buxtun. Available from: https://en.wikipedia.org/wiki/Peter_Buxtun.
[59] Casanova M, Enis Özyar E, Patte C, Orbach D, Ferrari A, Veyrat-Follet C, et al. International randomized phase 2 study on the addition of docetaxel to the combination of cisplatin and 5-fluorouracil in the induction treatment for nasopharyngeal carcinoma in children and adolescents. Cancer Chemother Pharmacol 2016;77(2):289–98.
[60] Geoerger B, Bergeron C, Gore L, et al. Phase II study of ipilimumab in adolescents with unresectable stage III or IV malignant melanoma. Eur J Cancer 2017;86:358–63.
[61] Ruperto N, Eichler I, Herold R, et al. European network of paediatric research at the European Medicines Agency (Enpr-EMA). Arch Dis Child 2012;97(3):185–8.

Subchapter 6.2

Developmental pharmacology and the globalization of the children-are-therapeutic-orphans mantra

Introduction

The concept of children as "therapeutic orphans" was first published in 1968 [1]. It was adopted by the American Academy of Pediatrics (AAP) which soon supported the demand to prove efficacy of drugs in "children" by adequate clinical studies [2]. The demand for separate "pediatric" studies continued in the years to follow [3–5]. For hands-on clinical care, the AAP defined the pediatric population as up to 21 years of age [6], later also as older patients with special needs [7]. These classifications are reasonable for administrative purposes, but are inappropriate as decision criteria for pharmaceutical treatment and/or as inclusion criteria for "pediatric" clinical studies. To this day, the AAP does not differentiate between the administrative classification of young persons and the use of chronological age limits to define "children" for regulatory purposes, in contradiction to the meanwhile well-known physiological development of the human body [8]. Probably the most convincing element of the AAP's justification for separate studies in "children" was and is "*There is a moral imperative to formally study drugs in children so that they can enjoy equal access to existing as well as new therapeutic agents.*" (sic!) [4] This justification is not scientific, but applies to our feelings for children and their right to be treated with the same degree of goodwill as any human being. This argument has worked as a blind sport of western society for more than half a century. Unfortunately, is it not only cynical and hypocritical, but also factually wrong on at least two levels. Firstly, it disregards that young persons do not remain bodily as immature and vulnerable as preterm newborns and term newborns until they reach an administrative age limit that classifies them as adults. Secondly, it also disregards the acceleration of the growth and the maturation of the human body in the western world [9–11]. The AAP position statements of 1969, 1988, 1995, and 2010 helped to establish and solidify the blur between administrative classification of "children" and the use of this classification as inclusion criterion for clinical studies [2–5]. Probably, most AAP members, who are hard-working pediatricians, were never aware of this blur and still are not.

It was the AAP committee on drugs that was responsible for these policy statements. The AAP committee on drugs also provided guidance for physicians that prescribed medication off-label for young patients: Lack of approval for a specific use should not prevent physicians from prescribing an available drug in the best interests of their patients. The decision to prescribe a drug rests with the physician; he or she must weigh the risks and benefits of the drug in question whether or not it has full approval [12,13].

There are two theoretical possibilities for the demand for separate clinical studies and separate labels in children: either this demand is correct and justified, or it is mostly wrong and exaggerated. This book argues for the second option and claims that the demand for separate labels, based on separate studies, is flawed. It furthermore claims that the demand for separate "pediatric" studies is not based on a scientific assessment of the growing body, but that it extrapolates existing vulnerabilities in preterm newborns, term newborns and young infants into all "children", defined by an administratively age limit. But drugs treat the body, not the legal or administrative status of a patient.

This position makes most "pediatric" studies based on the blur between regulatory formalism and alleged clinical concerns questionable and unnecessary, or at least exaggerated. To substantiate this serious criticism further, in the following the development of the concept of children as "therapeutic orphans" and its adoption by the international key players is retraced in key documents of the AAP, of societies and research networks dedicated to pediatric clinical pharmacology, of the FDA, the EMA, and the "International Council for Harmonisation" of Technical Requirements for Pharmaceuticals for Human Use (ICH) [14], which coordinates worldwide regulatory authorities and pharmaceutical industry [15]. Furthermore, key textbooks on pediatric drug development, pediatric clinical research, and pediatric clinical pharmacology are presented and discussed. In addition, key elements of the "European Network of Paediatric Research at the European Medicines Agency" (Enpr-EMA) [16–21], of the "Taskforce in Europe for Drug Development of the Young" (TEDDY) [22–24], of the "European Paediatric Translational Research Infrastructure" (EPTRI) [25,26], the "Global Research in Paeditrics" (GRiP) [27–29], and a few more international "pediatric" networks and initiatives are addressed and discussed. This analysis covers roughly half a century. Many statements that justify the children-are-therapeutic-orphans and the children-are-not-small-adults mantra, respectively, have been repeated innumerable times. This analysis is focused on key documents, with the intention to makes it easier to keep an overview.

The early days of pediatric medicine

The body of newborns is different from adults. The most important changes in the organs responsible for absorption, distribution, metabolism, and excretion (ADME) occur during the first weeks and months of life [8]. To know this is not sufficient to understand the reasons that led to the children-are-therapeutic-orphans and the children-are-not-small-adults mantras.

Many key documents are available open source on the internet. Many key textbooks offer at least the table of contents, the introduction, and some more chapters open source on the internet as well, which makes it easier for readers and future researchers to confirm on their own the conclusions made here.

Initially, the blur between administrative classification of children and the degree of their bodily maturity was simply of semantic nature. Compared to general medicine, pediatrics was and is a young discipline. The first pediatric hospital in England, The Hospital for Sick Children in Great Ormond Street, London, was established in 1852, the first pediatric hospital in the US in 1855 in Philadelphia [30]. Until the first decades of the 20th century, maternal and infant mortality rates were extremely high compared with today [31]. The American Pediatric Society (APS) had been founded in 1888, but it remained a small club that confined its membership to 110 [32]. The AAP was established in 1930 [31,32]. Improved housing, nutrition, hygiene and vaccinations helped to prevent infectious diseases, who could from the end of world war II on also be treated [33]. Today's Pediatric Pharmacy Advocacy Group (PPAG) was established in 1985 as the Pharmacy Directors of Pediatric Hospitals (PDPH), re-named in 1987 as the PPAG, and got its current name in 1992 [34]. For the directors of the pharmacies of the pediatric hospitals, patients were of course defined administratively. Adulthood is *administratively* defined for different purposes at different age limits, including alcohol consumption, driving license, the right to vote and the right to get elected. Adulthood also has a multitude of further social, sociological, psychological and more aspects [35–37]. Physiologically and medically, adulthood cannot be defined by a chronological age limit. Instead, becoming adult physiologically and bodily is the well-known slow process of puberty [11,38–41].

A new concept at the interface of medicine and drug approval

The concept of children as "therapeutic orphans" emerged when the US had successfully established a new framework for new drugs to be approved by the FDA, based on the principle of clinical studies that proved efficacy and safety [42]. This was triggered by the first and until today deepest crisis of modern drug development, the thalidomide disaster [43–48]. It is today superfluous to speculate if and to what degree the founding fathers of pediatrics and pediatric clinical pharmacology were aware of future "side effects" of establishing a framework that would result in a myriad of "pediatric" studies and would advance careers in pediatric research, in regulatory authorities, in operational pediatric clinical research, and finally also in pharmaceutical industry.

As a discipline that covers all clinical areas, pediatric clinical pharmacology played a key role in establishing a broadly accepted scientific consensus of "pediatric drug development".

Clinical pharmacology addresses all aspects of the relationship between medicines and humans [49]. The International Union of Basic and Clinical Pharmacology (IUPHAR) has a section of pediatric clinical pharmacology [50]. Clinical pharmacology emerged in the mid-20th century [49]. Pediatric clinical pharmacology might in the first instance simply be understood as clinical pharmacology in children, but how does it define "children"? Pediatric clinical pharmacology has always accepted the administrative definition of "children" and the regulatory imposition of the on-label/off-label framework on the thus created "pediatric population," although pediatric pharmacologists are those that know best the processes of the maturation of the human body in terms of ADME.

The US Pediatric Pharmacology Research Units (PPRU) Network was established by the US National Institute of Health (NIH) in 1994. Until 2008, it grew from 7 to 13 sites at universities and children's hospitals. Its initial priority was "to conduct clinical trials that would lead to pediatric labeling of pharmaceuticals that were commonly used off-label to treat children." It also contributed to other areas of pediatric research. In 2010, the PPRU Network was discontinued [51]. The essential information here is that the PPRU Network's focus was pediatric labeling.

A key conference

In 1997, members of the US PPRU Network [51] met in Washington DC with representatives of the European Society for Developmental Pharmacology (today the European Society of Developmental, Perinatal, and Pediatric Pharmacology [ESDPPP]) [52], "to discuss the solution to the therapeutic orphan problem" [53]. The flawed children-are-therapeutic-orphans concept, supported by all speakers, was characterized as a *clinical* challenge, and all speakers emphasized that they wanted to improve pediatric healthcare [53–70]. The US pediatric legislation had just come into force. The participants perceived themselves as "a small group of dedicated and highly motivated pediatricians and pediatric clinical pharmacologists" that had worked tirelessly to ensure that sick and injured children were able to benefit from the remarkable advances in drug development [54]. All speakers proudly agreed that with the US legislation the foundations were established to perform all those clinical studies needed to improve child healthcare [53–70].

Beyond clinical challenges, speakers also discussed that "pediatric" labels would prevent denial of third-party reimbursement because of lack of labeling, would eliminate economic barrier to pediatric drug availability, and that malpractice insurance coverage would not be limited by off-label use [56]. Avoiding damage lawsuits had been the main purpose of the "pediatric warnings" [1,55]. But avoiding malpractice lawsuits and eliminating economic barriers to drug availability are not ethically acceptable justifications for separate pediatric studies in young persons. Other speakers openly addressed that now the pharmaceutical industry would fund "pediatric" studies [56], and European speakers expressed hope that somehow a "solution" similar to the US one should be found [57,61]. One speaker spoke about "CONTINUED PEDIATRIC THERAPEUTIC DISASTERS" [sic!], listing chloramphenicol toxicities in neonates, kernicterus in premature neonates by sulfonamide, a complex clinical syndrome including death in low birth weight infants exposed to E-Ferol, toxicity of propylene glycol in premature infants, and toxicity of benzyl alcohol in neonates [58]. He also mentioned the toxicity of oral propylene glycol in general, without elaborating that the well-known disaster of Elixir Sulphanimade had *not* been a specifically pediatric disaster; of the 105 deaths, 71 were adults, and 37 were children [71]. Nobody addressed the fact that the human body does not become mature overnight [53–70]. Birthdays change the *legal* and *administrative* status of persons, not their body.

The speakers addressed many real clinical challenges, including the lack of reliable dosing information for younger patients, the lack of liquid formulations for younger patients, and many more. But they all agreed that the way to resolve these challenges was to conduct separate "pediatric" studies in all "pediatric" age groups, including those "children" who had already a mature body, and those young patients who indeed needed smaller doses, but whose body was no longer as young, immature and vulnerable as a newborn. Already before this conference in 1997, a consensus existed that *clinical* concerns and challenges in drug treatment of young persons were translated into *regulatory* challenges and needed to be resolved by separate "pediatric" studies that would result in "pediatric" labels. This conference established a global consensus between US and European pediatricians and pediatric clinical pharmacologists. It solidified a regulatory-driven framework for "pediatric" pharmaceutical research for the next decades where the difference between the legal and the physiological meanings of the word "child" was blurred from the very beginning.

Pediatric legislation

One key factor for the situation in which this conference took place had been that the first US pediatric law now authorized the FDA to reward "pediatric" studies by 6 months patent extension for patent-protected drugs [72]. The positive financial outcome of these rewards for pharmaceutical companies has been discussed in the literature [73–75]. However, so far it has been neglected that these innumerable "pediatric" studies funded and advanced "pediatric" careers in academia, regulatory authorities, clinical research organizations, and pharmaceutical industry. Publications that critically address the costs of studies triggered by regulatory demands nevertheless emphasize that all these studies were beneficial for "children" [73–75]. In its first status report to congress in 2001 the FDA mused that pediatric exclusivity "should lead to significant advances in pediatric medicine. Superior drug treatment information is expected to permit quicker recoveries from childhood illnesses, with fewer attendant hospital stays, physician visits and parental work days lost" [76]. These were clinical, reasonable and measurable endpoints. But no data to direct medical improvement of pediatric healthcare by changes of labeling have been published. In the next FDA report to congress in 2016, these proposed endpoints were no longer mentioned and replaced by regulatory endpoints such as number of performed "pediatric" studies, number of label changes etc. [77].

The paper "Developmental Pharmacology: Drug Disposition, Action, and Therapy in Infants and Children" has become a standard reference [8]. It presents the contemporary knowledge of ADME in the developing body. Its figure 1 has been presented on hundreds of conferences. It discusses from when on the developing body can be regarded as mature. It explains that current gaps in knowledge preclude the use of simple dosage formulas and allometric scaling. "Such approaches may have potential clinical utility in children older than eight years of age and in adolescents, whose organ function and body composition approximate that of young adults." It also outlines that these formulas have limited value in very young infants and children with strong age-related differences in drug disposition. Its figure 1 shows developmental changes in physiologic factors that influence drug disposition in infants, children, and adolescents. The graph on changes in metabolic capacity spans from birth to ten years; the graph on developmental changes in distribution sites from birth to forty years; the graph on changes in gastrointestinal function from birth to adults; the graph on acquisition of renal function from birth to twelve years, and the graph on "integumentary development" (skin composition) from preterm newborns to adults [8]. Essentially, this paper outlines that the truly challenging pediatric period is the relatively short period of the first months after birth, not the administratively defined years where minors are administratively still "children." However, this paper is mostly quoted to confirm the validity of pediatric legislation.

In 2004, the EMA published a paper that claimed that off-label use of drugs in children is harmful [78], ignoring that the entire discipline of pediatrics emerged during its first decades without major regulatory impact [32], specifically including disciplines such as pediatric oncology [79], and neonatology [80].

The first textbook on pediatric clinical research was published in 2007 [81,82], a second edition in 2010 [83,84]. A first US-based textbook on pediatric drug development was published in 2009 [85], a second edition in 2013 [86,87]. In the meantime the main editor had moved to the FDA, and all coeditors of the second edition were FDA employees [87]. Several further textbooks have been published [88–90]. All these books welcomed US and

EU pediatric legislation in the belief that clinical care of children would improve through pediatric labels and more pediatric studies.

The standard textbook of pediatric clinical pharmacology classifies "children" into "preterm newborn infants" (<36 weeks of gestation), "term newborn infants" (0–27 days), "infants and toddlers" (28 days to 23 months, "children" (2 to 11 years), and "adolescents" (12 to 16–18 years, depending on the region) [91–93], referring to the FDA guidance for industry "E 11 Clinical Investigation of Medicinal Products in the Pediatric Population" [94], adopted from the ICH [14]. The mentioned textbook correctly characterizes the ICH E 11 definition as "to some extent arbitrary" [91,93], but does not elaborate the arbitrariness further.

Until 2014, publications on "pediatric drug development" accepted that its main aim was improvement of clinical care for children, although a few publications had started to ask critical questions [79,95]. Also in a first textbook on pediatric formulations in the framework of drug development some critical questions were asked [96].

The EMA has published many reports on its "pediatric drug development." On its website, the EMA claims that the EU pediatric regulation is "designed to better protect the health of children in the EU" [97]. On this website, there is also the link to a video titled "How to boost development of medicines for children" [97]. In the summary of its ten-year report to the EU commission, the EMA claims to have achieved "more medicines for children" (page 4) [98]. In the following, careful reading shows that with "more medicines for children" the EMA means more medicines *with an EMA "pediatric" approval*. Figure 1 (page 5) is titled "Number of new paediatric products and indications" for 2004–2006 and 2012–2014. But the EMA does not mean new pediatric products, but drugs with a new "pediatric" label. Figure 2 (page 6) is titled "Percentage of paediatric trials (of all trials, by start of year)". Indeed, the number of "pediatric" trials has increased. As shown in this book, most of them are needless and already in breach of the declaration of Helsinki for this reason, but many even harm patients by comparison to placebo or standard-of-care that in the meantime is outdated and inferior to available treatment. Also the high number of issued PIPs is used as documentation of "More ethical and high quality paediatric research" (page 5). The conclusion (page 9) claims that "The Paediatric Regulation has had a very positive impact on paediatric drug development." Page 14 lists "Examples of achievements through the Paediatric Regulation" from the clinical areas rheumatology, cardiovascular diseases, infectious diseases, and pediatric oncology. But the listed "achievements" are not clinical achievements, but merely a documentation of regulatory activities: PIPs issued for new drugs that successfully treated juvenile idiopathic arthritis (JIA). JIA is an umbrella term for diseases that begin before the age of 16 years [99]. JIA is *not* a "pediatric" disease. It may be administratively classified as "JIA" if it starts one day before the 16th birthday. And what about a patient in whom the symptoms of JIA start one day after the 16th birthday, or where the symptoms started, in hindsight, earlier, but a medical appointment occurs after the 16th birthday? There is no clearer way to express the key message of a review analysis of the genetics and the classification of arthritis in adults and children: "There is no such thing as juvenile idiopathic arthritis" [100]. The subdiseases of the umbrella term "JIA" and its symptoms do not stop at the 16th birthday. Many patients continue to suffer from JIA when they become adult. The true success story was and is *not* the EMA's separate "pediatric" approval of the drugs canakinumab, abatacept, etanercept, and adalimumab [98], but that these drugs were successfully developed. For JIA and cardiovascular diseases the EMA describes its "achievements" as having authorized new drugs for the treatment of JIA and cardiovascular diseases. For infectious diseases, the report claims that drugs were made "available after PIP completion" [98]. And for pediatric oncology, as an example "a new asparaginase (the first recombinant asparaginase) has become available for the treatment of acute lymphoblastic leukemia, the most frequent cancer in children" [98].

Decoding misleading information

To understand the description of the EMA's alleged "achievements," decoding of the used terminology is required. "Available" does in EMA speak *not* mean that a drug has become available, but that it now has a separate "pediatric" label, i.e. that it is now officially approved in the "pediatric" population, defined by anybody <18 years of age. Asparaginase is used in the treatment of acute lymphoblastic leukemia since decades. Why should a new first recombinant asparaginase not work in patients before their 18th birthday? Even if there would be serious safety concerns in young patients, this would not justify the demand for separate regulatory studies. Observation in a clinical registry would be sufficient.

When the FDA offered measurable clinical endpoints for the future results of US pediatric legislation in 2001, this expressed the current contemporaneous belief and excitement in "pediatric drug development" [76]. These endpoints were silently dropped in the next FDA report of 2016 [77]. But at no point has the FDA developed an elaborated and systematic terminology to disguise regulatory activism as clinical advances. It is time to read the EMA reports with the instruments of decoding outlined here.

In 2017, the EU commission published its 10-year-report to the EU parliament and the EU council [101], an excellent teaching example about modern communication. Its design is not as pseudo-scientific as the EMA report [98]. Instead, it summarizes the theories and concepts that justify "pediatric drug development" in lay language. It is structured into (1) "Introduction," (2) a description of the EU pediatric regulation, (3) "More medicines for children," (4) "Better Medicines for Children," (5) "Advancing Pure Pediatric Developments,"

(6) "The Costs of Paediatric Medicines," (7) "Improved Implementation," (8) "More Clinical Trials With Children," (9) "Future Challenges," and (10) "Conclusions."

In the introduction, it alleges that before the EU pediatric regulation "products used in children were prescribed and administered based on physicians' own experience rather than on the results of clinical research." It adds real-world challenges like the need to crush tablets in the past, and repeats the EMA position that off-label use can be dangerous in "children". It claims that until the 1980s the thought prevailed that "children should be protected from clinical research for ethical reasons". It also mentions that it is based on the EMA report of 2016 [98]. In the following chapters, illustrated by nice photographs that make it look like a glossy brochure, the EMA claims are repeated that make the pediatric regulation a large success story, including the claim that now we have "more medicines for children". Chapter 5, "Advancing Pure Pediatric Developments," explains one obvious failure. The "Pediatric Use Marketing Authorisation" (PUMA) program resulted until 2017 in just three specific pediatric approvals. It concludes: "This shows that the commercial success of a PUMA is influenced by complex factors that can be hardly addressed at EU level. They concern downstream decision-making at national level, which is outside the scope of EU law. Legislative incentives cannot compensate for economic success" [101]. In other words: this world is too evil for the EU's good intentions. But we live in this world. Chapter 6, "The Costs of Paediatric Medicines" estimates the research and development costs per pediatric investigation plan (PIP) at €18.9 mio. In chapter 9, "Future Challenges," it admits that companies might decide to divest into clinical areas where definitely no pediatric clinical trials can be demanded. The conclusions in chapter 10 are overall positive.

Without appropriate guidance, this report might be convincing at first glance. Replenished by nice, politically correct pictures of happy children, of a young white female medical doctor holding a brown baby, of a young woman that receives an intravenous infusion, and more, it is as well elaborated as the annual report of any major commercial company that praises its success during the last year. A glossy brochure probably produced by a commercial communication company. To decipher this report, we have to recapitulate a few basic questions: Has there been a crisis in child treatment in the last decades? Did child mortality increase again? Do we every day see dead or sick children on the street because there is no good medication for them and because nobody cares? Do more children die of infectious diseases, cancer, or traffic accidents than half a century ago? The answer to all these questions is no. The report of the EU Commission contains nothing but the *n*th repetition of the children-are-therapeutic-orphans and children-are-not-small-adults mantra, mixed with several fairy tales, including that off-label use of drugs in "children" is always dangerous, irrespective of the degree of maturity of the respective young person's body [78]. But it also includes some useful information, including an estimation of the costs of EU-enforced PIP-demanded "pediatric" studies. The costs of the EU pediatric regulation for all companies together is estimated as €2.1 billion per year. The average R&D costs per PIP are estimated at €18.9 million per PIP, assuming an average of three clinical studies per PIP. On top of this, companies' overhead costs are estimated as €720,000 for filing the initial PIP submission and for the subsequent modifications [101].

The picture of the young female patient in this report is the same as in a 2018 editorial of the *Lancet Child and Adolescent Health*, which also claims that "adolescents are often treated using off-label drugs, licensed for adults only, without full dosing knowledge" [102]. The young woman in this picture is no longer a child. She has a mature body and deserves adult dosing and treatment, irrespectively if for administrative reasons she is treated in a pediatric or an adult ward or hospital. She does not need separate "pediatric" studies, as the FDA has finally accepted in 2019 [103].

There are many further EMA and EU documents, whose additional description and analysis would add little new information.

The representative bodies of research-based pharmaceutical industry

The Pharmaceutical Research and Manufacturers of America (*PhRMA*) is the US representative body of the research-based biopharmaceutical biotechnological companies [104]. On its website, it praises the US pediatric legislation and emphasizes the industry's contributions to pediatric health care [105,106]. Unfortunately, it does not challenge the administrative definition of "children" for therapeutic purposes, resulting in "pediatric" studies in patients that are often bodily already mature, nor does it challenge the need for separate "pediatric" labels, irrespectively if the young person is physiologically and bodily still a child or not. It proudly list in its pediatric fact sheet the number of pediatric labeling changes since 1998 (>750), the number of "pediatric" studies completed within the framework of the US pediatric legislation (>680), the number of drugs that have received pediatric exclusivity (>250), and the number of industry-sponsored "pediatric" clinical studies that are underway (>2,100 with >1.2 mio patients) [106]. For now, the PhRMA accepts unconditionally the regulatory framework.

The European Federation of Pharmaceutical Industries and Associations (EFPIA), the representative body of the research-based pharmaceutical companies in Europe [107], has a comparable position. On a pragmatic level, it complains the heavy administrative burden of the PIPs and expresses the wish to make the handling of the PIPs more flexible, but all in all it emphasizes its commitment to "pediatric drug development" without a critical view of the current framework. In the eyes of its representatives, the EU pediatric regulation was and is a full success. EFPIA also applauded the EMA's pediatric ten-year report [98,108–110].

From the "moral imperative" to the "pediatric imperative"

On the website of its 2019 conference, the ESDPPP [52], had a subwebsite with industry information, titled "The Paediatric Imperative." This conference subwebsite has in the meantime been removed from the internet, but the search term "paediatric imperative" still results in a google hit [111]. This sub-website started with explaining that no matter if a company has a specific portfolio interest in pediatric medicines, EMA and FDA requirements demand pediatric studies. It ended with announcing the ESDPPP congress in May 2019 in Basel, Switzerland, as the "ideal opportunity to meet with many of the world's leading Paediatric Pharmacologists," emphasizing that these represent expertise and are "arbiters and advisors to industry and regulators alike" [111]. At least in this document we do not need decoding to see the conflict of interest that has systematically invaded pediatric clinical pharmacology on a global level. For the discipline of pediatric clinical pharmacology as represented in this ESDPPP conference, the mere existence of the US and the EU pediatric legislation is a guarantee for funds. Either by requests for advising from pharmaceutical companies and later executing the FDA-rewarded and/or EMA-PIP-demanded "pediatric" clinical studies, or by advising the EMA on questions of "pediatric" regulatory requirements.

International and global activism

The EMA has established the "European Network of Paediatric Research at the European Medicines Agency" (Enpr-EMA) as "a network of research networks, investigators and centers with recognized expertise in performing clinical studies in children," as a platform for sharing good practices as well as a pan-European voice for promoting research into medicines for children [16]. It describes its main objective as to facilitate studies in order "to increase the availability of authorized medicines for children" [17]. Enpr-EMA itself does not perform studies or fund studies directly [16]. However, funds for clinical studies in "children" are provided by the PIP-mandated clinical studies that companies have to sponsor as a condition for the approval of new effective drugs in adults [46–48,112]. The official objectives of Enpr-EMA make it clear this is not true pediatric research, but research in "children" defined within the EMA regulatory framework. On the EMA website are the Enpr-EMA mission statement [18], an Enpr-EMA brochure [19], and a presentation with background information [20]. As long as the reader is not prepared to decode the information in these documents, they appear convincing. However, decoding them shows that this is not research aimed at improving child healthcare, but a platform and network to allow academic scientists to network with the aim to participate in the movement of "pediatric drug development," allowing to advance careers by "pediatric" studies that mostly lack sense, and often even harm young patients. A key publication gives more insights and is easy to decode with the information outlined in this chapter and in the other chapters of this book [21].

Many participants in the Enpr-EMA network will either be not be aware of its questionable aims and the conflicts of interest participation brings upon each single participant, or prefer not to realize them. The number of partners in the Enpr-EMA network is considerable, but interestingly, the Enpr-EMA network database does no longer reveal all network members, but invites to ask the EMA directly for more details [113].

One of Enpr-EMA's newer members is TEDDY, a "network of excellence" to "support and strengthen scientific and technological excellence in the paediatric sector in Europe" [22,114]. TEDDY was funded by the EU 6th framework program for research and technological development (FP6) with €4 mio from 2005 to 2010 [24]. TEDDY now describes itself as operating as an allegedly independent multidisciplinary, multinational network including 28 centers in 15 EU and non-EU countries "to encourage the integration of paediatric pharmacological research activities, the implementation of adequate health policies, and the promotion of social awareness on the importance of pediatric medicines across Europe." TEDDY claims that its partners include pediatric clinical research centers and professionals (methodologists, pharmacologists, ethicists, regulators). TEDDY "offers its experience in the planning and management of clinical trials in the paediatric field and operates as a support network for the recruitment of patients" [23].

A follow-up to TEDDY is EPTRI, coordinated by CVBF (Consorzio per Valutazioni Biologiche e Farmacologiche [consortium for biologic and pharmacologic evaluations]) [25,115]. EPTRI is EU funded with €3 mio for two years [25]. On its website, the CVBP claims to create the framework for a new research infrastructure to enhance technology-driven pediatric research in drug discovery and early development phases to be translated into clinical research and pediatric use of medicines. The CVBF website further explains that EPTRI "arises from the need to find answers to the serious lack of medicines for children in EU and worldwide and to propose development models for paediatric medicines that integrates technology-driven aspects with clinical trials" [25].

A third project is GRiP, EU funded from 2011 to 2017 with €10 mio [28,29]. The justification of this funding reads almost as all official EMA justifications for "pediatric drug development". It claims that pediatric drugs lack appropriate testing, that most drugs have inadequate information about dosing regimen, dose adjustment and how to administer them. These challenges are described as "longstanding problems that unquestionably require concerted efforts at the international level", referring to both the US and the EU pediatric legislation. GRiP claims to mobilize 21 institutions as partners and at least 16 more networks, representing hundreds of clinical sites and more than thousand researchers worldwide. It also announces to work closely with families "to provide children with safe and effective medicines" [29].

Further networking activities include the "pediatric cluster", a coordination between the EMA and the FDA (together with Health Canada, PMDA [Japan], and TGA [Australia]) [97,116], the "Paediatric medicines Regulators' Network" (PmRN) [97,117]; and the initiative of the World Health Organization (WHO) "Make Medicines Child Size" [97,118,119].

First readings of the announcements and statements of all these networks, initiatives and clusters, respectively, trigger an appealing positive impression, as long as the reader is not prepared to decode them. There is no lack of pediatric medicines in the sense that such medicines do not exist. They do exist, they are effective, but their therapeutic use in young patients is prevented by the flawed concept of "children" as "therapeutic orphans." This concept does not look at the young persons' bodies, but classifies anybody younger than 17 or 18 years as part of the "pediatric population" whose subjection to questionable and harmful clinical studies is justified by repeating the children-are-not-small-adults mantra. The dimension of this worldwide cynical theater is breathtaking.

In many countries many things do not work properly, including the economy and the supply of medicines for persons of any age. This is an existing serious challenge, but a different one. The initiative for "pediatric drug development" originated in the richest countries of this planet. In these countries, effective treatment is withheld from young patients by a flawed concept that has created strong conflicts of interest.

There are many unmet medical needs. We are just beginning to understand the genetics roots of diseases. The coming decades and centuries will hopefully allow to diagnose diseases such as cystic fibrosis or sickle cell disease even before birth and correct the genetic code early in life. But the "pediatric" activism of the FDA, the EMA, and the WHO does not advance research. To the contrary. This activism and the studies it demands represent the dream of mediocre academic researchers: central bodies that distribute money and force "big bad pharma" to sponsor research for the alleged good of mankind. But the FDA/EMA-rewarded/mandated "pediatric" studies are mostly medically senseless, and often even harm young patients.

Tragedies

There are several tragedies in this pediatric activism caused by the dominance of the children-are-therapeutic-orphans and children-are-not-small-adults mantras that for decades have been taught in the education and training of medical doctors, pharmacists, pharmacologists, nurses, and other healthcare professionals. The first tragedy is that the vast majority of all these "pediatric" studies lack medical sense and many even harm young patients. The second tragedy is that many participants are not aware of the flaws in these mantras. The vast majority of healthcare professionals taking care of children and young patients are hard-working individuals that try to help young patients. Many participate in regulatory pediatric studies because they want approval for all those medications that otherwise must be given off-label. The primary job of healthcare professionals is not a fundamental discussion about the medical sense of regulatory studies. Some or many may feel uneasy with some studies, but the funds offered by such studies also contribute to pay the salaries and the research infrastructure. The third and worst tragedy is that all these studies have become an obstacle against the development of new effective drugs for the multitude of diseases that used to be a death sentence decades ago. Cystic fibrosis (CF) is one area where parents undertook reasonable and decisive steps. Today, the diagnosis of CF is no longer a death sentence. CF is on the way to become a manageable chronic disease. We are not yet there, but we are getting closer.

We have many effective drugs, and we are developing more and more. But instead of investigating how we can support families with a child that requires complex treatment, resources and funds are wasted for studies that lack medical sense and even harm patients. But they also advance some careers.

Conclusion

The most profound challenge of "pediatric drug development" and its justification by developmental pharmacology, the regulatory authorities, and a myriad of researchers and others is that there are no easily identifiable culprits. The world is no longer as easy as it used to be in biblical times, when one of two goats was sacrificed; the other one was left alive and cast into the desert as a scapegoat, bearing away all transgressions and sins of the community [120]. Powerful institutions have committed to the flawed concept of regulatory-driven "pediatric drug development" that primarily aims at separate labels in the "pediatric" population. The FDA, the EMA, and the WHO could not continue in their "pediatric" crusade without the support of researchers and institutions, of the hundreds of centers that participate in questionable "pediatric" studies, the thousands of Institutional Review Boards (IRBs)/ethics committees (ECs) that until now have approved countless questionable "pediatric" studies, and the many editors-in-chief that accept publication of questionable "pediatric" studies in scientific journals. The history of mankind is full of flawed concepts. They cannot and will not be overcome overnight. The most difficult job was to identify the outlined flaws. Now the second phase of overcoming them is beginning.

References

[1] Shirkey H. Therapeutic orphans. J Pediatr 1968;72(1):119–20. Available from: https://pdfs.semanticscholar.org/f1cb/acdbac19fa56236b919fb7799eaacaa10c77.pdf.

[2] Yaffe SJ, Avery ME, Gold AP, et al. American academy of pediatrics. Committee on drugs. Drug testing in children: FDA regulations. Pediatrics 1969;43(3):463–5. Available from: https://pediatrics.aappublications.org/content/pediatrics/43/3/463.full.pdf.

[3] AAP 1977. Committee on drugs. Guidelines for the ethical conduct of studies to evaluate drugs in pediatric populations. Pediatrics 1977;60(1):91–101. Available from: https://pediatrics.aappublications.org/content/pediatrics/60/1/91.full.pdf.

[4] Guidelines for the ethical conduct of studies to evaluate drugs in pediatric populations, committee on drugs. American academy of pediatrics; 1995. Pediatrics; 95:286–294. Available from: https://pediatrics.aappublications.org/content/pediatrics/95/2/286.full.pdf.

[5] Shaddy RE, Denne SC, Committee on Drugs and Committee on Pediatric Research. Clinical report--guidelines for the ethical conduct of studies to evaluate drugs in pediatric populations. Pediatrics 2010;125(4):850–60. Available from: https://pediatrics.aappublications.org/content/pediatrics/125/4/850.full.pdf.

[6] Holroyd HJ, Cohen HJ, Dyment PG, et al. AAP council on child and adolescent health. Age limits of pediatrics. Pediatrics 1988;81(5):736. Available from: https://pediatrics.aappublications.org/content/pediatrics/81/5/736.full.pdf.

[7] Hardin AP, Hackell JM. Committee on practice and ambulatory medicine. Age limit of pediatrics. Pediatrics 2017;140(3):e20172151. Available from: https://pediatrics.aappublications.org/content/pediatrics/140/3/e20172151.full.pdf.

[8] Kearns GL, Abdel-Rahman SM, Alander SW, Blowey DL, Leeder JS, Kauffman RE. Developmental pharmacology - drug disposition, action, and therapy in infants and children. N Engl J Med 2003;349(12):1157–67. Available from: https://pdfs.semanticscholar.org/55f8/1745303e9aaec7f4cb85f0b5921eec14a9c0.pdf.

[9] Cone Jr. TE. Secular acceleration of height and biologic maturation in children during the past century. J Pediatr 1961;59:736–40.

[10] Komlos J, Lauderdale BE. The mysterious trend in American heights in the 20th century. Ann Hum Biol 2007;34(2):206–15.

[11] Khan L. Puberty: onset and progression. Pediatr Ann 2019;48(4):e141–5.

[12] AAP 1996. Unapproved use of approved drugs: the physician, the package insert, and the food and drug administration: subject review. Pediatrics 1996;98(1):143–5. Available from: https://pediatrics.aappublications.org/content/pediatrics/98/1/143.full.pdf.

[13] Frattarelli DA, Galinkin JL, Green TP, et al. Off-label use of drugs in children. Pediatrics 2014;133(3):563–7. Available from: https://pediatrics.aappublications.org/content/pediatrics/133/3/563.full.pdf.

[14] International Council for Harmonisation of Technical Requirements for Pharmaceuticals for Human Use (ICH). Available from: www.ich.org.

[15] ICH wikipedia. Available from: https://en.wikipedia.org/wiki/International_Council_for_Harmonisation_of_Technical_Requirements_for_Pharmaceuticals_for_Human_Use.

[16] EMA 2020 Enpr-EMA. Available from: https://www.ema.europa.eu/en/partners-networks/networks/european-network-paediatric-research-european-medicines-agency-enpr-ema#objectives-section.

[17] EMA 2020 enpr-EMA objectives. Available from: https://www.ema.europa.eu/en/partners-networks/networks/european-network-paediatric-research-european-medicines-agency-enpr-ema#enpr-ema-network-database-section.

[18] EMA 2012 enpr-EMA mission statement. Available from: https://www.ema.europa.eu/en/documents/other/mission-statement-european-network-paediatric-research-european-medicines-agency-enpr-ema_en.pdf.

[19] EMA 2015 enpr-EMA brochure. Available from: https://www.ema.europa.eu/en/documents/leaflet/european-network-paediatric-research-european-medicines-agency_en.pdf.

[20] Eichler I. and EMA, no date. Enpr-EMA Background information. Available from: https://www.ema.europa.eu/en/documents/presentation/european-network-paediatric-research-european-medicines-agency-background-information_en.pdf.

[21] Ruperto N, Eichler I, Herold R, et al. A European network of paediatric research at the European Medicines Agency (Enpr-EMA). Arch Dis Child 2012;97(3):185–8.
[22] Ceci A, Giaquinto C, Aboulker JP, et al. The task-force in Europe for drug development for the young (TEDDY) Network of excellence. Paediatr Drugs 2009; 11(1):18–21.
[23] Consorzio per Valutazioni Biologiche e Farmacologiche (CVBF) 2018. TEDDY – task-force in Europe for drug development for the young. Available from: https://www.cvbf.net/teddy-task-force-in-europe-for-drug-development-for-the-young-2/.
[24] Cordis 2013. Taskforce in Europe for drug development of the young. Contains a downloadable fact sheet. Available from: https://cordis.europa.eu/project/id/5216.
[25] EPTRI. Available from: https://www.cvbf.net/eptri/.
[26] EPTRI. Available from: www.eptri.eu.
[27] Global Research in Pediatrics. Available from: https://cordis.europa.eu/project/id/261060.
[28] GRiP CVBF. Available from: https://www.cvbf.net/grip-global-research-in-paediatrics-2/.
[29] Cordis GRiP. Available from: https://cordis.europa.eu/project/id/261060/de.
[30] Radbill SX. A history of children's hospitals. AMA Am J Dis Child 1955;90(4):411–16.
[31] Hughes JG. Conception and creation of the American Academy of Pediatrics. Pediatrics 1993;92(3):469–70.
[32] Colón AR. Nurturing childen. A history of pediatrics. Westport, CT: Greenwood Press; 1999.
[33] Hilts PJ. Protecting America's health: The FDA, business, and one hundred years of regulation. New York: Alfred A Knopf Publishers; 2003.
[34] History of the Pediatric Pharmacy Association. Available from: https://www.ppag.org/index.cfm?pg=History.
[35] Blatterer H. Contemporary adulthood. Reconceptualizing an uncontested category. Curr Sociol 2007;55(6):771–92.
[36] Arnett JJ. Emerging adulthood. A theory of development from the late teens through the twenties. Am Psychol 2000;55(5):469–80. Available from: https://jeffreyarnett.com/ARNETT_Emerging_Adulthood_theory.pdf.
[37] Tagliabue S, Crocetti E, Lanz M. Emerging adulthood features and criteria for adulthood: variable- and person-centered approaches. J Youth Stud 2016;19(3):374–88. Available from: https://doi.org/10.1080/13676261.2015.1074985.
[38] Cheng HL, Harris SR, Sritharan M, et al. The tempo of puberty and its relationship to adolescent health and wellbeing: a systematic review. Acta Paediatr 2019.
[39] Abreu AP, Kaiser UB. Pubertal development and regulation. Lancet Diabetes Endocrinol 2016;4(3):254–64.
[40] Snyder CK. Puberty: an overview for pediatric nurses. J Pediatr Nurs 2016;31(6):757–9.
[41] Wood CL, Lane LC, Cheetham T. Puberty: normal physiology (brief overview). Best Pract Res Clin Endocrinol Metab 2019;33(3):101265.
[42] Rägo L, Santo B. Drug regulation: history, present and future. Available from: https://www.who.int/medicines/technical_briefing/tbs/Drug_Regulation_History_Present_Future.pdf.
[43] Thomann KD. Die contergan-katastrophe. DÄ 2007;104(41):A2778–82. Available from: https://www.aerzteblatt.de/pdf.asp?id=57224.
[44] Vargesson N. Thalidomide-induced teratogenesis: history and mechanisms. Birth Defects Res C Embryo Today 2015;105(2):140–56. Available from: https://www.ncbi.nlm.nih.gov/pmc/articles/PMC4737249/.
[45] Ridings JE. The thalidomide disaster, lessons from the past. Methods Mol Biol 2013;947:575–86.
[46] Rose K, Neubauer D, Grant-Kels JM. Rational use of medicine in children – the conflict of interests story. A review Rambam Maimonides Med J 2019;10(3):e0018. Available

from: https://doi.org/10.5041/RMMJ.10371Review. Available from: https://www.rmmj.org.il/userimages/928/2/PublishFiles/953Article.pdf.

[47] Rose K, Grant-Kels JM. The meanings of "pediatric drug development". A review. Ther Innov Regul Sci 2019;53(6):767–74.

[48] Rose K. The challenges of pediatric drug development. Curr Ther Res Clin Exp 2019. Available from: https://doi.org/10.1016/j.curtheres.2019.01.007.

[49] Birkett D, Brøsen K, Cascorbi I, et al. Clinical pharmacology in research, teaching and health care: considerations by IUPHAR, the international union of basic and clinical pharmacology. Basic Clin Pharmacol Toxicol 2010;107(1):531–59. Available from: https://onlinelibrary.wiley.com/doi/pdf/10.1111/j.1742-7843.2010.00602.x.

[50] Pediatric Clinical Pharmacology Section of the International Union of Basic and Clinical Pharmacology (IUPHAR). Available from: https://iuphar.org/sections-subcoms/pediatric/.

[51] National Institute of Child Health and Human Development 2010. Pediatric pharmacology research units (PPRU) network (for historical purposes only). Available from: https://www.nichd.nih.gov/research/supported/ppru.

[52] European Society of Development, Perinatal and Pediatric Pharmacology. Available from: www.esdppp.org.

[53] Yaffe SJ. Foreword. Pediatrics 1999;104(3 Pt 2):581. Available from: https://pediatrics.aappublications.org/content/104/Supplement_3.

[54] Blumer JL. Introduction. Pediatrics 1999;104(3 Pt 2):582. Available from: https://pediatrics.aappublications.org/content/pediatrics/104/Supplement_3/582.full.pdf.

[55] Shirkey H. Editorial comment: therapeutic orphans. Pediatrics 1999;104(3 Pt 2):583–4. Available from: https://pediatrics.aappublications.org/content/pediatrics/104/Supplement_3/583.full.pdf.

[56] Wilson JT. An update on the therapeutic orphan. Pediatrics 1999;104(3 Pt 2):585–90. Available from: https://pediatrics.aappublications.org/content/pediatrics/104/Supplement_3/585.full.pdf.

[57] Assael BM. Therapeutic orphans: European perspective. Pediatrics 1999;104(3 Pt 2):591–2. Available from: https://pediatrics.aappublications.org/content/pediatrics/104/Supplement_3/591.full.pdf.

[58] Christensen ML, Helms RA, Chesney RW. Is pediatric labelling really necessary? Pediatrics 1999;104(3 Pt 2):593–7. Available from: https://pediatrics.aappublications.org/content/pediatrics/104/Supplement_3/598.full.pdf.

[59] Blumer. Off-label uses of drugs in children. Pediatrics 1999;104(3 Pt 2):598–602. Available from: https://pediatrics.aappublications.org/content/pediatrics/104/Supplement_3/598.full.pdf.

[60] Kauffmann. Essential drugs for infants and children: North American perspective. Pediatrics 1999;104(3 Pt 2):603–5. Available from: https://pediatrics.aappublications.org/content/pediatrics/104/Supplement_3/603.full.pdf.

[61] Choonara I. Essential drugs for infants and children: European perspective. Pediatrics 1999;104(3 Pt 2):606. Available from: https://pediatrics.aappublications.org/content/pediatrics/104/Supplement_3/606.full.pdf.

[62] Nahara MC. Lack of pediatric drug formulations. Pediatrics 1999;104(3 Pt 2):607–9. Available from: https://pediatrics.aappublications.org/content/pediatrics/104/Supplement_3/607.full.pdf.

[63] Connor JD. A look at the future of pediatric therapeutics: an investigator's perspective of the new pediatric rule. Pediatrics 1999;104(3 Pt 2):610–13. Available from: https://pediatrics.aappublications.org/content/pediatrics/104/Supplement_3/610.full.pdf.

[64] Autret E. European regulatory authorities and pediatric labeling. Pediatrics 1999;104(3 Pt 2):614–18. Available from: https://pediatrics.aappublications.org/content/pediatrics/104/Supplement_3/614.full.pdf.

[65] Walson P. Patient recruitment: US perspective. Pediatrics 1999;104(3 Pt 2):619–22. Available from: https://pediatrics.aappublications.org/content/pediatrics/104/Supplement_3/619.full.pdf.

[66] Hoppu K. Patient recruitment: European perspective. Pediatrics 1999;104(3 Pt 2):623–6. Available from: https://pediatrics.aappublications.org/content/pediatrics/104/Supplement_3/623.full.pdf.

[67] Reed M. Optimal sampling theory: an overview of its application to pharmacokinetic studies in infants and children. Pediatrics 1999;104(3 Pt 2):627–32. Available from: https://pediatrics.aappublications.org/content/104/Supplement_3/627.long.

[68] Pons G, Rey E. Stable isotopes labeling of drugs in pediatric clinical pharmacology. Pediatrics 1999;104(3 Pt 2):633–9. Available from: https://pediatrics.aappublications.org/content/pediatrics/104/Supplement_3/633.full.pdf.

[69] Rane A. Phenotyping of drug metabolism in infants and children: potentials and problems. Pediatrics 1999;104(3 Pt 2):640–3. Available from: https://pediatrics.aappublications.org/content/pediatrics/104/Supplement_3/640.full.pdf.

[70] Cohen SN. The pediatric pharmacology research unit (PPRU) network and its role in meeting pediatric labeling needs. Pediatrics 1999;104(3 Pt 2):644–5. Available from: https://pediatrics.aappublications.org/content/pediatrics/104/Supplement_3/644.full.pdf.

[71] Wax PM. Elixirs, diluents, and the passage of the 1938 federal food, drug and cosmetic act. Ann Intern Med 1995;122(6):456–61.

[72] Li JS, Eisenstein EL, Grabowski HG, et al. Economic return of clinical trials performed under the pediatric exclusivity program. JAMA 2007;297(5):480–8.

[73] Kim J, Ross JS, Kapczynski A. Pediatric exclusivity and regulatory authority: implications of amgen v HHS. JAMA 2018;319(1):21–2.

[74] Sinha MS, Najafzadeh M, Rajasingh EK, Love J, Kesselheim AS. Labeling changes and costs for clinical trials performed under the US food and drug administration pediatric exclusivity extension, 2007 to 2012. JAMA Intern Med 2018;178(11):1458–66. Available from: https://www.ncbi.nlm.nih.gov/pmc/articles/PMC6248195/.

[75] Gore R, Chugh PK, Tripathi CD, Lhamo Y, Gautam S. Pediatric off-label and unlicensed drug use and its implications. Curr Clin Pharmacol 2017;12(1):18–25.

[76] FDA 2001. The pediatric exclusivity provision. January 2001. Status report to congress. Available from: https://www.fda.gov/downloads/Drugs/DevelopmentApprovalProcess/DevelopmentResources/UCM049915.pdf.

[77] FDA 2016. Best pharmaceuticals for children act and pediatric research equity act. Status report to congress. Available from: www.fda.gov/downloads/ScienceResearch/SpecialTopics/PediatricTherapeuticsResearch/UCM509815.pdf.

[78] EMA 2004. Evidence of harm from off-label or unlicensed medicines in children. Available from: https://www.ema.europa.eu/en/documents/other/evidence-harm-label-unlicensed-medicines-children_en.pdf.

[79] Adamson PC. Improving the outcome for children with cancer: development of targeted new agents. CA Cancer J Clin 2015;65(3):212–20.

[80] Philip AG. The evolution of neonatology. Pediatr Res 2005;58(4):799–815. Available from: https://www.nature.com/articles/pr2005743.pdf?origin=ppub.

[81] Rose K, van den Anker JN, editors. Guide to paediatric clinical research. Basel, Switzerland: Karger; 2007.

[82] Rose K, van den Anker JN, (Editors). Guide to paediatric clinical research. Table of contents, contributors, and introduction. Available from: https://www.karger.com/Article/Pdf/97766.

[83] Rose K, van den Anker JN, editors. Guide to paediatric drug development and clinical research. Basel, Switzerland: Karger; 2010.

[84] Rose K, van den Anker JN, (Editors): Guide to paediatric drug development and clinical research: contents, contributors, and introduction. Available from: https://www.karger.com/Article/Pdf/315565.

[85] Mulberg AE, Silber SA, van den Anker JN, editors. Pediatric drug development – concepts and applications. Hoboken, NJ: Wiley-Blackwell; 2009.

[86] Mulberg AE, Murphy D, Dunne J, Mathis L, editors. Pediatric drug development. 2nd edition Hoboken NJ: Wiley-Blackwell; 2013.

[87] Mulberg AE, Murphy D, Dunne J, Mathis L (Editors) Pediatric drug development, 2nd edition. Contents, contributors and preface. Available from: https://onlinelibrary.wiley.com/doi/pdf/10.1002/9781118312087.fmatter.

[88] Addressing the barriers to pediatric drug development: workshop summary. National Academies Press, Washington DC, USA, 2008. Available from: https://www.ncbi.nlm.nih.gov/books/NBK3994/.

[89] Byrns CD. Safety efforts in pediatric drug development pharmacology - research, safety testing and regulation. New York: Nova Science Publishers; 2010.

[90] Johnson F. Drug development & rare pediatric diseases (pharmacology-research, safety testing and regulation). New York: Nova Science Editors; 2016.

[91] Seyberth HW, Rane A, Schwab M. Pediatric clinical pharmacology. Handbook of experimental pharmacology, 205. Berlin, Germany: Springer; 2011.

[92] Seyberth HW, Rane A, Schwab M. Historical development of pediatric pharmacology. Handb Exp Pharmacol 2011;205:v–vi (Preface to reference #3).

[93] Seyberth HW, Kauffman RE. Basics and dynamics of neonatal and pediatric pharmacology. Handb Exp Pharmacol 2011;205:3–49 (First chapter of reference #3).

[94] FDA 2000. Guidance for industry. E 11 Clinical investigation of medicinal products in the pediatric population. Available from: https://www.fda.gov/media/71355/download.

[95] Rose K. European Union pediatric legislation jeopardizes worldwide, timely future advances in the care of children with cancer. Clin Therapeutics 2014;36(2):163–77. Available from: http://www.clinicaltherapeutics.com/article/S0149-2918(14)00018-6/pdf.

[96] Bar-Shalom D, Rose K, editors. Pediatric formulations – a roadmap. New York: AAPS Press & Springer; 2014Free download of introduction, sample pages, and tables of contents. Available from: http://www.springer.com/us/book/9781489980106#reviews.

[97] EMA. Paediatric medicines: overview. Available from: https://www.ema.europa.eu/en/human-regulatory/overview/paediatric-medicines-overview.

[98] EMA 2016. 10-year report to the European commission. General report on the experience acquired as a result of the application of the paediatric regulation. Available from: https://ec.europa.eu/health/sites/health/files/files/paediatrics/2016_pc_report_2017/ema_10_year_report_for_consultation.pdf.

[99] Cimaz R, Marino A, Martini A. How I treat juvenile idiopathic arthritis: a state of the art review. Autoimmun Rev 2017;16(10):1008–15.

[100] Nigrovic PA, Raychaudhuri S, Thompson SD. Review: genetics and the classification of arthritis in adults and children. Arthritis Rheumatol 2018;70(1):7–17. Available from: https://onlinelibrary.wiley.com/doi/epdf/10.1002/art.40350.

[101] State of Paediatric Medicines in the EU. 10 years of the EU paediatric regulation. Report from the commission to the European parliament and the council. COM (2017) 626. Available from: https://ec.europa.eu/health/sites/health/files/files/paediatrics/docs/2017_childrensmedicines_report_en.pdf.

[102] Cancer in the young: progress and priorities. Lancet child & adolescent health 2018 Mar;2(3):157. Available from: https://www.thelancet.com/action/showPdf?pii=S2352-4642%2818%2930041-5.

[103] FDA 2019. Considerations for the inclusion of adolescent patients in adult oncology clinical trials. Guidance for industry. Available from: https://www.fda.gov/media/113499/download.

[104] The Pharmaceutical Research and Manufacturers of America (PhRMA). Available from: https://www.phrma.org/en/About.

[105] PhRMA Research & Development. Pediatrics. Available from: https://www.phrma.org/Pediatrics.

[106] PhRMA 2020. Fact sheet. BPCA & PREA: Spurring pediatric drug development. Available from: https://www.phrma.org/-/media/Project/PhRMA/PhRMA-Org/PhRMA-Org/PDF/P-R/PREA_BPCA_OnePager2020.pdf.

[107] European Federation of Pharmaceutical Industries and Associations (EFPIA). Available from: www.efpia.eu.

[108] EFPIA 2018. Learnings from the first 10 years the paediatric regulation- back to inform on the future? A summary from a DIA Europe session. Available from: https://www.efpia.eu/news-events/the-efpia-view/blog-articles/20042018-learnings-from-the-first-10-years-the-paediatric-regulation-back-to-inform-on-the-future/.

[109] EFPIA 2019. Stimulating the development of new medicines for children. Available from: https://www.efpia.eu/news-events/the-efpia-view/blog-articles/stimulating-the-development-of-new-medicines-for-children/.

[110] EFPIA 2017. EFPIA welcomes paediatric medicines regulation report and reiterates its commitment to progress in this area. Available from: https://www.efpia.eu/news-events/the-efpia-view/statements-press-releases/27102017-efpia-welcomes-paediatric-medicines-regulation-report-and-reiterates-its-commitment-to-progress-in-this-area/.

[111] ESDPPP conference 2019 Website: removed from the Internet. Original link: Available from: https://www.esdppp2019.org/esdppp2019/industry-information/the-paediatric-imperative.html The search term "paediatric imperative" still results in a google hit (03APR2020) with its first words ("The Paediatric Imperative. No matter if a company has no specific portfolio interest in paediatric medicines new EMA and FDA regulatory requirements demand . . ."). Archived by the author.

[112] Hirschfeld S, Saint-Raymond A. Pediatric regulatory initiatives. Handb Exp Pharmacol 2011;205:245–68.

[113] Enpr-EMA network database Available from: http://enprema.ema.europa.eu/enprema/index.php.

[114] TEDDY is a new member of (Enpr-EMA) coordinating group Available from: https://www.teddynetwork.net/2020/05/04/teddy-is-a-new-member-of-enpr-ema-coordinating-group/.

[115] Consorzio per Valutazioni Biologiche e Farmacologiche (CVBF). Available from: www.cvbf.net.

[116] EMA 2017. Global collaboration between regulatory agencies with paediatric research networks. Available from: https://www.ema.europa.eu/en/documents/presentation/presentation-session-42-global-collaboration-between-regulatory-agencies-paediatric-research_en.pdf.

[117] Paediatric medicines Regulators' Network (PmRN). Available from: http://www.who.int/childmedicines/paediatric_regulators/en/.

[118] Watts G. WHO launches campaign to make drugs safer for children. BMJ 2007;335 (7632):1227.

[119] Hoppu K, Anabwani G, Garcia-Bournissen F, et al. The status of paediatric medicines initiatives around the world--What has happened and what has not? Eur J Clin Pharmacol 2012;68(1):1–10.

[120] The Bible, *Leviticus 16:21-22*.

Subchapter 6.3

Extrapolation

Introduction

Early in its crusade for separate labels and separate studies in the "pediatric" population, the FDA introduced the concept of extrapolation in the context of "pediatric use" labeling requirements. It defined (again) the "pediatric population" as from birth to 16 (=younger than 17) years. It claimed that practitioners might be reluctant to prescribe drugs for "children", or might prescribe them inappropriately, such as dosing "arbitrarily" based on the child's age, body weight, or body surface without specific information as to whether this is appropriate [1]. General practitioners and pediatricians have done such prescribing since effective modern drugs exist [2]. This is adequate and *not* arbitrary at all in young persons [3,4]. However, a medical doctor would act arbitrarily if he would prescribe effective drugs in preterm newborns, newborns or young infants without any experience with the respective drug and/or with only limited experience in the treatment of very young babies and infants. Early toxicities in newborns had been reported in the 1950s to warn off other physicians not to repeat this mistake [5–7]. Considering the US legal malpractice system [8–12], a physician would have to be almost suicidal to administer for example the antibiotic chloramphenicol to a preterm newborn after warnings had been reported in the literature.

But the FDA also emphasized that separate studies were not always required. Studies in adults might be sufficient if the FDA "concludes that the course of the disease and the drug's effects are sufficiently similar in the pediatric and adult populations to permit extrapolation from the adult efficacy data to pediatric patients." It also demanded pharmacokinetic (PK) studies for pediatric dosing and pediatric safety. Companies had either to submit separate "pediatric" studies, ask the FDA to waive such studies, or explicitly state that "pediatric" data did not exist for specific age groups, or as a general statement: "Safety and effectiveness in pediatric patients have not been established" [1].

With this, the published toxicities in preterm newborns, newborns and infants [5–7,13], and the increasing understanding of maturation of the organs responsible for absorption, distribution, metabolism, and excretion

(ADME) [3] had been extrapolated into an alleged danger for all administratively defined "children" if treated with drugs without "pediatric" labeling.

That the FDA accepted now the possibility not to repeat the entire clinical drug development in all age groups of the "pediatric population" added an element of science and common sense without, however, jeopardizing the now evolving concept of "pediatric drug development" [14].

From now on, "pediatric drug development" and extrapolation were exposed to at least five different dimensions

1. Pediatric researchers' dreams [15].
2. The regulatory authorities' willingness to conclude that "the course of the disease and the drug's effects are sufficiently similar in the pediatric and adult populations to permit extrapolation from the adult efficacy data to pediatric patients" [1].
3. Parents' willingness to expose their child to regulatory "pediatric" clinical studies.
4. The preparedness of regulatory authorities to describe and justify requests or demands for "pediatric" studies in appearantly scientific terms that could deceive a medical audience and a lay audience.
5. The willingness of pediatric researchers to justify and continue justifying separate "pediatric" studies.

Each of these five dimensions has its own history, its own conflicts of interest, its own dynamics, and its interaction with the other dimensions. Going in a first round through each of them individually, and then discussing them in their complex interaction with each other will hopefully help to give an overall idea of the role, achievements, promises, and limitations of extrapolation within "pediatric drug development".

Pediatric researchers' dreams

"In an ideal world, efficacy of each new drug would be established in every age group and for a broad range of clinical circumstances." With this phrase begins a report written by thought leaders in pediatric pain about an FDA-sponsored workshop that addressed current challenges [15]. The workshop was convened because parents were more concerned for the well-being of their children than for an ideal world. Many parents refused to let their child participate in placebo-controlled pain studies which the FDA had demanded until 2010 to "scientifically" proof pharmacokinetics, efficacy and safety of all painkillers and analgesics in all age groups. By denying the inclusion of their child, parents shattered researchers' dreams and led to a broader application of extrapolation. Key terms that in this context were used in an FDA presentation were "parental reluctance"; "fear of harm to children, especially extensive blood sampling"; and "emotional impact on parents of sick newborns" [16].

FDA/EMA's willingness to allow extrapolation of efficacy from adults to "children"

Only since the 1980s is has been fully appreciated that young persons can and do suffer significantly from depressive disorders [16]. When the existence of depression in young persons was accepted in the scientific, clinical, and general world, and when first effective antidepressants had been developed, the FDA requested separate "pediatric" studies in young patients. When study sponsors reported that participants talked about suicidal thoughts, regulatory authorities claimed that antidepressants in young patients caused "suicidality", and the FDA introduced a specific warning for all antidepressants. Maybe suicidality decreased worldwide, but the number of completed suicides increased [17,18].

Depression in young patients is an extremely complex challenge. Depression can result in suicide [4]. In young persons suicide is the second highest cause of death after accidents, far more frequent than cancer [19]. But depression, suicide, and the discussion of both occur in today's societal shark pool. In the company that had developed the antidepressant paroxetine, a selective serotonin reuptake inhibitor (SSRI), there had been internal reluctance to admit in the public that in the "pediatric" depression studies efficacy against placebo had not been statistically significant. "Suspecting cover-up of data by one of the big bad pharmaceutical companies, researchers now suspected that the addition of unpublished data indicated that risks could outweigh benefits of these drugs (except fluoxetine) to treat depression in children and young people" [20]. These researchers did not question the definition of "children" as younger than 17 years of age. In reaction to this publication, the Attorney General of the State of New York sued the manufacturer of paroxetine for having concealed clinical trial data that showed that paroxetine was ineffective in "pediatric patients", and could possibly be linked to inducing suicidal behavior [21–23]. The company settled the case in 2004, agreeing to pay $ US 2.5 million [23,24]. Compared to other settlements pharmaceutical companies had to agree to, this was a relatively small sum. It indicates that the legal case of the New York Attorney General was weak. Essentially, the company had no choice than to settle in view of the emotional weight of the accusations [23]. The lawsuit, however, had an important side effect. The company committed to make its trial data about paroxetine and "children" available on its website, and to establish a clinical trial register that would host summaries of all company-sponsored trials going back to 2000. In the following, other pharmaceutical companies joined this movement. Today, it is much easier to search clinical studies sponsored by pharmaceutical companies [25,26].

There was no scientific basis of the FDA's fundamental conviction that depression in persons before their 17th birthday was totally different from depression in persons after their 17th birthday. This is an extreme example where extrapolation under the condition that the FDA agrees that "the course of the disease and the drug's effects are sufficiently similar in the pediatric and adult populations to permit extrapolation from the adult efficacy data to pediatric patients" [1] is hampered by a rigid dogma. Extrapolation in "pediatric drug development" is a technique based on science as long as the questions to be answered are scientifically defined, e.g. which dose of an antidepressant should be administered to an underweight 10-year-old child with depression, and which dose of an antidepressant to an overweight 10-year-old child. Extrapolation is no remedy against adventuresome regulatory theories about the nature of diseases.

In type 2 diabetes mellitus (T2DM) the FDA rewarded separate "pediatric" studies with metformin, glimepiride, rosiglitazone, and the combination of metformin + glyburide. and approved only metformin. But T2DM is rare in young patients. T2DM develops when the body becomes used to too many calories and too much sugar, and hence to too much insulin. In reaction, the pancreas produces and distributes insulin and continuously increases insulin production, but tends to become exhausted after a while. Although the production and blood level of insulin are higher than in healthy individuals, the body is not able to achieve a normal sugar level. T2DM develops in young patients predominantly if they eat too much and in consequence become very obese. In all the FDA-rewarded "pediatric" diabetes studies, the investigated "children" were massively overweight. All drugs reduced the sugar level, but only metformin with statistical significance [4,27]. These studies were scientifically worthless. The inclusion criteria were based on administrative age levels, not on science. The studies did not investigate T2DM in young persons, which is almost nonexistent in otherwise healthy young persons. Instead, these studies investigated T2DM in a very special sub-population. However, the conclusions were not drawn for overweight young persons, but for alleged "children." Extrapolation might help to calculate the dose for extremely overweight young patients, or patients of any age. But not to establish doses in the "pediatric" population without making clear upfront that the inclusion criteria of the studies narrow the investigated population to a very small sub-part of young persons.

T2DM and depression in young patients are two examples where the FDA refused to use common sense, was fixated on its concept of "pediatric" labels and in consequence got lost in alleged "pediatric" studies that were scientifically and clinically worthless. The FDA did not allow extrapolation of efficacy from adults to younger patients. Separate "pediatric" studies in depression and diabetes are further addressed, respectively, in separate chapters of this book.

Parents' willingness to expose their child to regulatory "pediatric" clinical studies

As discussed in the context of the pain studies, parents refused to consent to their children's participation in "pediatric" studies. Their gut feelings protected their loved ones against the pseudo-scientific justifications used by researchers and regulators to justify their studies [15,16]. In epilepsy, parents' willingness to let their child participate in regulatory studies has significantly decreased during the last years [28].

Disguising "pediatric" study requests or demands

In the early days of "pediatric drug development," the FDA issued pediatric written requests for several individual chemotherapeutic agents. One of these written requests was for pemetrexed [29]. The efficacy of chemotherapy agents was well known from adult oncology. Chemotherapeutic agents are toxic in patients of any age. That is why they are also called cytotoxins (literately translated: cell poisons). But they are given with a therapeutic intention, because avoiding these toxicities would result in patients' prolonged suffering and/or death. The efficacy of cytotoxic compounds used in adult oncology had also been successfully shown in pediatric oncology over decades of clinical studies [30], although these studies did not have a regulatory focus. Their intent, instead, was purely therapeutic [31,32]. Many FDA-requested "pediatric" oncology studies asked for patients up to 21 years [33]. Here we quote from the pemetrexed written request, which justified: "because the majority of pediatric patients receive their cancer therapy as participants in clinical research protocols, participation in Phase 3 oncology trials has become the standard of care in pediatric oncology" [29]. But the requested pemetrexed studies were studies with a single chemotherapy agent whose efficacy was already well known. These requested pemetrexed studies could only repeat what was already well known. The FDA justification for its pediatric oncology studies was invalid.

Willingness of pediatric researchers to justify and separate "pediatric" studies

Pediatric neurologists have so far most openly challenged the children-are-therapeutic-orphans and the children-are-not-small-adults mantras [34–37]. Other clinicians continue justifying separate "pediatric" studies, including representatives of the Paediatric Antiretroviral Working Group (PAWG) [38], of pediatric oncology, of organizations that investigate Juvenile Idiopathic Arthritis (JIA), and others. A good indicator of a conflict of interest is where representatives of "pediatric" clinical research networks or organizations publish side-by-side with representatives of the regulatory authorities to praise pediatric legislation [14,38–43].

The EMA approach

In 2013, the EMA attempted to define extrapolation as "Extending information and conclusions available from studies in one or more subgroups of the patient population (source population), or in related conditions or with related medicinal products, to make inferences for another subgroup of the population (target population), or condition or product, thus reducing the need to generate additional information (types of studies, design modifications, number of patients required) to reach conclusions for the target population, or condition or medicinal product. ... Extrapolation from adults to children is a typical example but extrapolation may be applied in many other areas: e.g. (1) between population subsets, based on age (down and up age subsets), growth, maturation, sex, pregnancy, co-morbidities, impaired organ function, ethnic intrinsic and extrinsic factors; (2) between disease subtypes or stages, different diseases, symptoms; (3) between medicines, within and between classes; (4) from animal studies to humans; (5) from healthy volunteers to patients" [44].

In 2015, the EMA published a document that expanded the list of diseases classified as "pediatric" to liver cancer, renal cancer, Parkinson's disease, amyotrophic lateral sclerosis (ALS), and Huntington chorea [45]. On a formal level, this document appears to be scientific. It uses medical language and gives many references. But its content is not scientific it all. Diseases that occasionally occur also in patients before the 18th birthday are not automatically "pediatric."

The EMA's attempted definition of extrapolation shows that this term has multiple facets.

Firstly, the term "extrapolation" in the context of "pediatric drug development" is flawed. Young patients mature until their body is mature and hence can and should be treated with medicines in doses appropriate for an adult body. Also the bodies of school children do not differ from adult bodies as much as neonates differ from adults. Practitioners had from the beginning of pediatrics and from the beginning of available modern effective drugs known that many of their smaller patients need smaller doses. They used formulas such as Young's rule and Clark's rule in the US [3], or the British National Formulary (BNF) for Children (BNF-C) in the United Kingdom. The BNF-C is a good example of an approach based on common sense and clinical concerns without regulatory blur. Produced jointly by the British Medical Association, the Royal Pharmaceutical Society of Great Britain, the Royal College of Paediatrics and Child Health and the Neonatal and Paediatric Pharmacists Group, the BNF-C guides physicians, pharmacists and nurses on the use of drugs in young patients [46]. Dosing tables or formulas exist(ed) in many other countries in the respective local language, e.g. the "Pädiatrische Dosistabellen" in German [47].

The other side of the term "extrapolation" in is that it has gradually allowed some science and common sense slip into "pediatric drug development". To determine suitable doses for younger patients based on existing data of older patients is reasonable and necessary in clinical treatment and clinical development. But within "pediatric drug development", extrapolation also became strongly linked to separate "pediatric" approval of drugs, the demand for separate "pediatric" labels, and the thought that "off-label" use of drugs in "children" should be reduced as far as possible. Over the past decades, scientific approaches to predict the needed doses in younger patients based on adult data plus the ability for modeling and simulation have evolved.

Discussion

Most overviews of extrapolation in the context of "pediatric drug development" contain phrases that emphasize its place in the framework of drug approval, without differentiating between the physiological and the administrative and/or legal status of the patients. "Children deserve medical therapies that have been properly evaluated for safety and efficacy and formulated or otherwise designed specifically to meet their needs" [48]. "Therapeutic tragedies in pediatric patients contributed to formulation of the legal requirement that new medications had to be carefully studied before they could be approved for interstate sale" [14]. "The main benefit of modeling and simulation for pediatric medicines is that it enables the use of all the available information to make decisions and optimize the conduct and analysis of clinical trials in children because there are limited opportunities to collect data in children" [49]. While the methodology to extrapolate pharmacodynamics (PD) and PK from older to younger patients (or from old to very old patients in medicine for the elderly) is in itself neutral and scientific. But the justifications of extrapolation and its related techniques claim clinical concern for "children" as if separate pediatric labels would advance the healthcare of young patients on their own. PK/PD, physiology-based PK (PBPK), M&S, extrapolation, and many other techniques have strong scientific facets, but are also used in a context that supports separate "pediatric" regulatory drug approval [50–53], a contradiction in itself. Dose finding makes the more sense the younger the concerned children are, and the less sense the more their body is already mature.

A systematic review of 92 drugs FDA-approved in adults and adolescents and found that 87 (94.5%) had identical adolescent and adult dosing. In five drugs the recommended doses differed in adults and adolescents. The dosing for ribavirin-peginterferon α-2a for hepatitis is 180 μg/week was in adults, and 180 μg/1.73 m^2 $\times$ body surface area (BSA)/week in adolescents. As most adolescents have a BSA of <1.73 m^2, they would receive less than the adult dose. Paliperidone for schizophrenia has an adult dose range of 3 to 12 mg/d, and a "pediatric" dose range of 3 to 6 mg/day in patients <51 kg, and 3 to 12 mg/day in patients >51 kg. Fluocinolone for atopic dermatitis is to be applied thrice daily for adults, and twice daily for "children", without specific adolescent information, and "pediatric" dosing encompassing all patients $\geq$2years. Candesartan and valsartan for hypertension in patients 6 to 16 years old have lower starting dose ranges in "children" than in adults [54]. These data confirm simply that adolescents have already a mature body. Even in the five drugs where different doses are recommended, the differences are rather limited. Why not conclude that obviously separate dose finding in adolescents is not necessary?

Fig. 6.3.1 shows a fictitious warning for the transition from administrative childhood to administrative adulthood for patients treated with paliperidone. This warning is freely invented. Strictly logically, it would correspond to the different dosing recommendations for "children" and adults. However, the FDA and drug manufacturers are certainly aware that such a warning would not only arouse laughter and derision, but would certainly result in parents' and patients' becoming suspicious. A practitioner that has to prescribe ribavirin-peginterferon α-2a, paliperidone, fluocinolone, candesartan or valsartan in adolescents has to decide a reasonable dosing. Dose changes at a birthday would only undermine the trust of his patients and of their parents.

When clinicians were asked to analyze the "pediatric" clinical studies performed in partial onset seizures (POS)-type epilepsy for brivaracetam, they concluded that antiepileptic drugs that are effective in adults were also effective in young patients down to the age of two years. They even emphasized that for

URGENT WARNING

Paliperidone is approved for schizophrenia both in adults and children, but with different recommended doses. The FDA's upper age limit for pediatric use is the 17th birthday. Patients on paliperidone and their parents are urgently requested to make an appoint with their medical practitioner to re-adjust the patient's dose of paliperidone at his/her 17th birthday.

FIGURE 6.3.1 Ficticious warning paliperidone.

patients below the lower age range (<2 years) there were not enough data [35,36]. Other pediatric neurologists went further and asked the heretical question if regarding antiepileptic drugs for POS-type epilepsy children can be regarded as small adults [37]. Why did Momper et al. not come to the same overall conclusion [54]? Another study analyzed "pediatric" dose finding in molecularly targeted anticancer agents and found that the established doses corresponded largely to FDA-recommended adult doses [55]. Why did only pediatric neurologists dare to doubt the children-are-not-small-adults and the children-are-therapeutic-orphans mantras? Momper et al. are FDA employees who cannot challenge key assumptions of their employer [54]. At least Paoletti et al. conclude that, except in the case of a narrow therapeutic index and dose-activity relationship, current dose-finding trials in "children" appear to be suboptimal for drug development [55]. However, they do not challenge the administrative definition of "children."

In 2014, the FDA issued a guidance for industry, intended to assist companies in planning to conduct clinical studies in "pediatric populations." Effectiveness, safety, or dose-finding studies in pediatric patients involve gathering clinical pharmacology information, such as information regarding a product's pharmacokinetics and pharmacodynamics pertaining to dose selection and individualization [56]. This guidance explains the principles of pharmacodynamics, pharmacokinetics, pharmacogenetics and is based on the ICH definition of age groups within the "pediatric population", without addressing the difference between physiological maturation and administrative classification into age groups. It also contains a "Pediatric Study Planning & Extrapolation Algorithm" that had already been discussed in a previous publication as the "pediatric study decision tree" [57].

The EMA has addressed the concept of extrapolation since 2006, when it mentioned the need for extrapolation, accepting that it is often unrealistic to expect full efficacy and safety studies in "pediatric" patients. Pharmacokinetic (PK) data may be used to extrapolate efficacy and/or safety from data obtained in adults or in pediatric age groups other than the age groups applied for [58]. In the following the EMA published several follow-up documents [59–62], the last one for the, at present, "final" version [62].

During the last years, in an increasing number of disease areas full extrapolation of efficacy from adults to "children" has been accepted by the FDA, including POS, analgesia for opioids, nonsteroidal anti-inflammatory drugs (NSAIDs), acetaminophen, and local anesthetics from adults down to 2 years of age, gastroesophageal reflux disease (GERD) and hormonal contraception [48,57].

The FDA still demands PK, efficacy, and safety studies in <2-year-olds and in drugs with a new mode of action [15,16,48].

Infliximab, a monoclonal antibody (MAB) against TNFα was approved in the U.S. and the EU for several immune-mediated inflammatory diseases including plaque psoriasis in dermatology, rheumatoid arthritis, psoriatic arthritis and ankylosing spondylitis in rheumatology, and Crohn's Disease and ulcerative colitis in gastroenterology. Extrapolating efficacy from adults was discussed at an FDA Advisory Committee. It concluded that extrapolation of efficacy was appropriate for pediatric ulcerative colitis [48,63,64]. The EMA CMPH came to the same conclusion [65].

Extrapolation from adults for safety assessment in young patients is not accepted.

Regulators have agreed to waive efficacy studies in certain subgroups of children with JIA. Also for Crohn's Disease similarity between adults and children is now accepted. There is also global acceptance that partial extrapolation from adults in inflammatory bowel disease acceptable for "pediatric drug development" [48,66,67].

During its first decades, pediatric oncology emerged and evolved by using chemotherapy agents that had no specific "pediatric" approval [30]. In this period of time, pediatric oncology established a high societal respect. Participation in a clinical study was regarded as standard of care in the treatment of young patients with cancer. With the first US pediatric legislation, the FDA started to reward numerous "pediatric" cancer studies with individual chemotherapy agents that had already shown efficacy in clinical treatment as part of combination therapies [4,18,31]. These studies were performed in heavily pretreated patients that had in these days no more chance for a survival. It would have been better to let them die in peace instead of giving patients and their parents wrong hope and prolongating their misery. In justifying the pemetrexed written request, the FDA claimed that participation in a clinical study was standard of care treatment for pediatric cancer [29]. But in this context the study justification was misleading. Study participation in pediatric oncology was only standard of care in studies with therapeutic intent, not in medically senseless studies that aimed at labels for individual chemotherapy agents whose efficacy in combination treatment was already well known since decades.

Tyrosine kinase inhibitors (TKIs) were the first targeted agents in oncology. Imatinib was first approved for newly diagnosed Philadelphia chromosome positive chronic myeloid leukemia (Ph+ CML) in adults, then for relapsed or refractory (R/R) Philadelphia chromosome positive acute lymphoblastic leukemia (Ph+ ALL). The efficacy of imatinib in young patients with CML was similar to that in adults, forming the basis for FDA approval also in "pediatric patients" with Ph+ CML and Ph+ ALL in 2011 [68].

The recent approval by US and EU regulators of nusinersen for the treatment of infants with spinal muscular atrophy is an example for a disease without relevant adult reference population [69,70]. Adults can be affected by spinal muscular atrophy, a diagnosis in infancy is the most severe clinical phenotype and is universally fatal [71].

The FDA has started to increasingly accept "extrapolation" from adults into the "pediatric population" [48,57].

Conclusions

Looking back into all the studies the FDA requested for pain, for POS epilepsy, for inflammatory diseases, for gastrointestinal reflux disease and for hormonal contraception, and for other pharmaceuticals, we can state two fundamentals. Firstly, many "pediatric" studies requested by the FDA in the past were questionable, medically and scientifically unnecessary, unethical and in breach of the declaration of Helsinki. This should not be swept under the carpet, but should be clearly stated. Secondly, to a relevant degree the FDA is already moving toward a direction with a rather simple principle: drugs work largely in the same way in "children" and adults. With few exceptions, the EMA has remained much more dogmatic, continues demanding PIP after PIP, although the EMA itself is aware that for most PIP-demanded "pediatric" studies there are not enough patients on this planet. Many PIP-demanded "pediatric" studies cannot recruit sufficient patients. This has been discussed in several critical papers [4,31,32], but is even admitted in a paper co-authored by an EMA employee [72].

Separate regulatory "pediatric" studies and separate "pediatric" drug approval are to a large degree superfluous. Where young patients need lower doses, this can and should be stated in the label. The on-label/off-label framework was successfully introduced to protect the population against toxic substances sold as medicines. Its imposture on the administratively defined "pediatric population has not been successful in advancing medical and pharmaceutical treatment of young patients."

The concept of extrapolation allows a limited portion of science and common sense into handling the approval of effective drugs in young patients. Many techniques used in extrapolation are useful and have the potential to at least reduce the number of patients that are abused in questionable "pediatric" studies. However, the term itself is also misleading. Earlier or later, FDA and EMA will have to revise the flawed concept of "pediatric drug development."

References

[1] FDA 1994. Specific requirements on content and format of labeling for human prescription drugs; revision of "pediatric use" subsection in the labeling; final rule. Available from: https://www.govinfo.gov/content/pkg/FR-1994-12-13/html/94-30238.htm.

[2] Colón AR. Nurturing childen. A history of pediatrics. Westport, CT: Greenwood Press; 1999.

[3] Kearns GL, Abdel-Rahman SM, Alander SW, Blowey DL, Leeder JS, Kauffman RE. Developmental pharmacology - drug disposition, action, and therapy in infants and children. N Engl J Med 2003;349(12):1157–67. Available from: https://pdfs.semanticscholar.org/55f8/1745303e9aaec7f4cb85f0b5921eec14a9c0.pdf.

[4] Rose K, Neubauer D, Grant-Kels JM. Rational use of medicine in children – the conflict of interests story. A review Rambam Maimonides Med J 2019;10(3):e0018. Available from: https://doi.org/10.5041/RMMJ.10371Review. Available from: https://www.rmmj.org.il/userimages/928/2/PublishFiles/953Article.pdf.

[5] Burns LE, Hodgman JE, Cass AB. Fatal circulatory collapse in premature infants receiving chloramphenicol. N Engl 1 Med 1959;261:1318–21.

[6] Silverman WA, Andersen DH, Blanc WA, Crozier DN. A difference in mortality rate and incidence of kernicterus among premature infants allotted to two prophylactic antibacterial regimens. Pediatrics 1956;18:614.

[7] AAP 1995. Guidelines for the ethical conduct of studies to evaluate drugs in pediatric populations, committee on drugs. Am Acad Pediatrics, Pediatrics 1995;95(2):286–94.

[8] Kritzer HM. Propensity to sue in England and the United States of America: blaming and claiming in tort cases. J Law Soc 1991;18(4):400–27.

[9] Lochlann Jain SS. Injury: the politics of product design and safety law in the United States. Princeton, NJ, USA: Princeton University Press; 2006.

[10] McGovern F. Punitive damages and class actions. Lousiana Law Rev 2010;70:435–62. Available from: https://scholarship.law.duke.edu/cgi/viewcontent.cgi?article=2762&context=faculty_scholarship.

[11] Bal BS. An introduction to medical malpractice in the United States. Clin Orthop Relat Res 2009;467(2):339–47. Available from: https://www.ncbi.nlm.nih.gov/pmc/articles/PMC2628513/.

[12] Kass JS, Rose RV. Medical malpractice reform: historical approaches, alternative models, and communication and resolution programs. AMA J Ethics 2016;18(3):299–310. Available from: https://journalofethics.ama-assn.org/sites/journalofethics.ama-assn.org/files/2019-12/pfor6-1603.pdf.

[13] Christensen ML, Helms RA, Chesney RW. Is pediatric labelling really necessary? Pediatrics 1999;104(3 Pt 2):593–7.

[14] Ward RM, Benjamin Jr DK, Davis JM, et al. The need for pediatric drug development. J Pediatr 2018;192:13–21.

[15] Berde CB, Walco GA, Krane EJ, et al. Pediatric analgesic clinical trial designs, measures, and extrapolation: report of an FDA scientific workshop. Pediatrics 2012;129(2):354–64.

[16] Hertz S. 2016. Analgesic developments for pediatric patients. Available from: https://www.fda.gov/downloads/AdvisoryCommittees/CommitteesMeetingMaterials/PediatricAdvisoryCommittee/UCM495096.pdf.

[17] Varley CK. Treating depression in children and adolescents: what options now? CNS Drugs 2006;20(1):1–13.

[18] Gören JL. Antidepressants use in pediatric populations. Expert Opin Drug Saf 2008;7(3):223–5.

[19] Ten leading causes of death by age group, United States – 2018. Available from: https://www.cdc.gov/injury/images/lc-charts/leading_causes_of_death_by_age_group_2018_1100w850h.jpg.

[20] Whittington CJ, Kendall T, Fonagy P, et al. Selective serotonin reuptake inhibitors in childhood depression: systematic review of published versus unpublished data. Lancet 2004;363(9418):1341–5.

[21] Rennie D. Trial registration. A great idea switches from ignored to irresistible. JAMA 2004;292(11):1359–62.

[22] Dickersin K, Rennie D. The evolution of trial registries and their use to assess the clinical trial enterprise. JAMA 2012;307(17).

[23] Kagle A. (undated). Driven to settle: Eliot Spitzer v. GlaxoSmithKline and undisclosed clinical trials data regarding paxil. Available from: https://web.law.columbia.edu/sites/default/files/microsites/career-services/Driven%20to%20Settle.pdf.

[24] Wikipedia Study 329. Available from: https://en.wikipedia.org/wiki/Study_329.

[25] www.clinicaltrials.gov.

[26] https://en.wikipedia.org/wiki/ClinicalTrials.gov.

[27] Christensen ML, Franklin BE, Momper JD, Reed MD. Pediatric drug development programs for type 2 diabetes: a review. J Clin Pharmacol 2015;55:731–8.

[28] Auvin S, French J, Dlugos D, et al. Novel study design to assess the efficacy and tolerability of antiseizure medications for focal-onset seizures in infants and young children: a consensus document from the regulatory task force and the pediatric commission of the International League against Epilepsy (ILAE), in collaboration with the Pediatric Epilepsy Research Consortium (PERC). Epilepsia Open 2019;4(4):537–43. Available from: https://doi.org/10.1002/epi4.12356 eCollection 2019 Dec.

[29] FDA 2001. Pemetrexed original pediatric written request. Available from: https://www.fda.gov/media/80043/download.

[30] Adamson PC. Improving the outcome for children with cancer: development of targeted new agents. CA Cancer J Clin 2015;65(3):212–20. Available from: https://www.ncbi.nlm.nih.gov/pmc/articles/PMC4629487/pdf/nihms733413.pdf.

[31] Rose K, Grant-Kels JM. Pediatric melanoma – the whole (conflicts of interest) story. Int J Womens Dermatol 2018;5(2):110–15. Available from: https://doi.org/10.1016/j.ijwd.2018.10.020. Available from: https://www.ncbi.nlm.nih.gov/pmc/articles/PMC6451736/pdf/main.pdf.

[32] Rose K, Grant-Kels JM. The meanings of "pediatric drug development". A review. Ther Innov Regul Sci 2019;53(6):767–74.

[33] FDA 2014. Ipilimumab written request. Available from: https://www.fda.gov/media/106997/download.

[34] Rose K, Neubauer D, Grant-Kels JM. Ethical issues in pediatric regulatory studies involving placebo treatment. J Pediatr Epilepsy 2020; (in press).

[35] Pellock JM, Carman WJ, Thyagarajan V, Daniels T, Morris DL, D'Cruz O. Efficacy of antiepileptic drugs in adults predicts efficacy in children: a systematic review. Neurology 2012;79(14):1482–9. Available from: https://www.ncbi.nlm.nih.gov/pmc/articles/PMC4098824/pdf/zn11482.pdf.

[36] Pellock JM, et al. Extrapolating evidence of antiepileptic drug efficacy in adults to children ≥2 years of age with focal seizures: the case for disease similarity. Epilepsia 2017;58(10):1686–96. Available from: https://onlinelibrary.wiley.com/doi/epdf/10.1111/epi.13859.

[37] Wadsworth I, Jaki T, Sills GJ, et al. Clinical drug development in epilepsy revisited: a proposal for a new paradigm streamlined using extrapolation. CNS Drugs 2016;30(11):1011–17. Available from: https://www.ncbi.nlm.nih.gov/pmc/articles/PMC5078157/pdf/40263_2016_Article_383.pdf.

[38] Penazzato M, Gnanashanmugam D, Rojo P, et al. Optimizing research to speed up availability of pediatric antiretroviral drugs and formulations. Clin Infect Dis 2017;64(11):1597–603.

[39] Kelly LE, Davies EH, Saint-Raymond A, et al. Important issues in the justification of a control treatment in paediatric drug trials. Arch Dis Child 2016.

[40] van Riet-Nales DA, Römkens EG, Saint-Raymond A, Kozarewicz P, Schobben AF, Egberts TC, et al. Oral medicines for children in the European paediatric investigation plans. PLoS One 2014;9(6):e98348.

[41] Herold R, Saint-Raymond A, Norga K. Too few medicines for children with cancer. JAMA Pediatr 2014;168(6):583.

[42] Ruperto N, Vesely R, Saint-Raymond A, et al. Impact of the European paediatric legislation in paediatric rheumatology: past, present and future. Ann Rheum Dis 2013;72(12):1893–6.

[43] Ruperto N, Eichler I, Herold R, et al. A European network of paediatric research at the European Medicines Agency (Enpr-EMA). Arch Dis Child 2012;97(3):185–8.
[44] EMA 2013. Concept paper on extrapolation of efficacy and safety in medicine development. Available from: https://www.ema.europa.eu/en/documents/scientific-guideline/concept-paper-extrapolation-efficacy-safety-medicine-development_en.pdf.
[45] EMA 2015. European medicines agency decisionCW/0001/2015 of 23 July 2015 on class waivers. Available from: https://www.ema.europa.eu/en/documents/other/european-medicines-agency-decision-cw-0001-2015-23-july-2015-class-waivers-accordance-regulation-ec_en.pdf.
[46] British National Formulary (BNF) for Children (BNF-C). Pharmaceutical Press, London, UK, many editions.
[47] Linse L., Pädiatrische Dosistabellen. Dosierung kinderärztlich verordneter Arzneimittel. Wissenschaftliche Verlagsgesellschaft, Stuttgart, Germany, many editions.
[48] Barrett JS, Bishai R, Bucci-Rechtweg C, et al. Challenges and opportunities in the development of medical therapies for pediatric populations and the role of extrapolation. Clin Pharmacol Ther 2018;103(3):419–33.
[49] Manolis E, Eldirdiry Osman T, Herold R, et al. Role of modeling and simulation in pediatric investigation plans. Paediatr Anaesth 2011;21(3):214–21.
[50] Yellepeddi V, Rower J, Liu X, et al. State-of-the-art review on physiologically based pharmacokinetic modeling in pediatric drug development. Clin Pharmacokinet 2019; 58(1):1–13.
[51] Sage DP, Kulczar C, Roth W, et al. Persistent pharmacokinetic challenges to pediatric drug development. Front Genet 2014;5:281.
[52] Villiger A, Stillhart C, Parrott N, et al. Using physiologically based pharmacokinetic (PBPK) modelling to gain insights into the effect of physiological factors on oral absorption in paediatric populations. AAPS J 2016;18(4):933–47.
[53] Templeton IE, Jones NS, Musib L, et al. Pediatric dose selection and utility of PBPK in determining dose. AAPS J 2018;20(2):31.
[54] Momper JD, Mulugeta Y, Green DJ, et al. Adolescent dosing and labeling since the food and drug administration amendments act of 2007. JAMA Pediatr 2013;167(10):926–32.
[55] Paoletti X, Geoerger B, Doz F, et al. A comparative analysis of paediatric dose-finding trials of molecularly targeted agent with adults' trials. Eur J Cancer 2013;49(10): 2392–402.
[56] FDA 2014. General clinical pharmacology considerations for pediatric studies for drugs and biological products. Available from: https://www.fda.gov/media/90358/download.
[57] Dunne J, Rodriguez WJ, Murphy MD, et al. Extrapolation of adult data and other data in pediatric drug-development programs. Pediatrics 2011;128(5):e1242–9.
[58] EMA 2006. Guideline on the role of pharmacokinetics in the development of medicinal products in the pediatric population. Available from: https://www.ema.europa.eu/en/documents/scientific-guideline/guideline-role-pharmacokinetics-development-medicinal-products-paediatric-population_en.pdf.
[59] EMA 2016. Reflection paper on extrapolation of efficacy and safety in pediatric medicine development. Available from: https://www.ema.europa.eu/en/documents/regulatory-procedural-guideline/draft-reflection-paper-extrapolation-efficacy-safety-paediatric-medicine-development-first-version_en.pdf.
[60] EMA 2017. Reflection paper on the use of extrapolation in the development of medicines for paediatrics. Available from: https://www.ema.europa.eu/en/documents/scientific-guideline/draft-reflection-paper-use-extrapolation-development-medicines-paediatrics-revision-1_en.pdf.

[61] EMA 2018. Overview of comments received on 'Reflection paper on the use of extrapolation in the development of medicines for paediatrics' (EMA/189724/2018). Available from: https://www.ema.europa.eu/en/documents/scientific-guideline/overview-comments-received-reflection-paper-use-extrapolation-development-medicines-paediatrics-ema/189724/2018-revision-1_en.pdf.

[62] EMA 2018. Reflection paper on the use of extrapolation in the development of medicines for paediatrics. Final. Available from: https://www.ema.europa.eu/en/documents/scientific-guideline/adopted-reflection-paper-use-extrapolation-development-medicines-paediatrics-revision-1_en.pdf.

[63] Hyams J, Damaraju L, Blank M, et al. Induction and maintenance therapy with infliximab for children with moderate to severe ulcerative colitis. Clin Gastroenterol Hepatol 2012;10(4):391–9 e1.

[64] FDA 2016. Ulcerative colitis: clinical trial endpoints: guidance for industry: https://www.fda.gov/downloads/Drugs/GuidanceComplianceRegulatoryInformation/Guidances/UCM515143.pdf.

[65] EMA 2016. Guideline on the development of new medicinal products for the treatment of Crohn's disease: Available from: http://www.ema.europa.eu/docs/en_GB/document_library/Scientific_guideline/2016/07/WC500211430.pdf.

[66] Vesely R., EMA, 2016. Extrapolation workshop: extrapolation of dosing, efficacy and safety of biologics in JIA, IBD and psoriasis. EMA history. Available from: http://www.ema.europa.eu/docs/en_GB/document_library/Presentation/2016/05/WC500207583.pdf.

[67] Vesely R. PReS13-SPK-1182: six years of eu paediatric regulation - what was achieved for paediatric rheumatology. Vesely Pediatric Rheumatol 2013;11(Suppl 2):I15. Available from: https://ped-rheum.biomedcentral.com/track/pdf/10.1186/1546-0096-11-S2-I15.

[68] Cohen MH, Williams G, Johnson JR, et al. Approval summary for imatinib mesylate capsules in the treatment of chronic myelogenous leukemia. Clin Cancer Res 2002;8(5):935–42. Available from: https://clincancerres.aacrjournals.org/content/8/5/935.full-text.pdf.

[69] EMA 2017 EPAR Spinraza. Available from: http://www.ema.europa.eu/ema/index.jsp?curl=pages/medicines/human/medicines/004312/human_med_002119.jsp&mid = WC0b01ac058001d124.

[70] FDA 2016 Spinraza (nusinersen) prescribing information. Available from: https://www.accessdata.fda.gov/drugsatfda_docs/label/2016/209531lbl.pdf.

[71] Butchbach ME. Copy number variations in the survival motor neuron genes: implications for spinal muscular atrophy and other neurodegenerative diseases. Front Mol Biosci 2016;3:7. Available from: https://www.ncbi.nlm.nih.gov/pmc/articles/PMC4785180/pdf/fmolb-03-00007.pdf.

[72] Hwang T.J. et al. Delays in completion and results reporting of clinical trials under the paediatric regulation in the European Union: a cohort study. Available from: https://journals.plos.org/plosmedicine/article?id=10.1371/journal.pmed.1002520.

Subchapter 6.4

Daily deceit in "pediatric" studies

Daily deceit in "pediatric" studies

Both the FDA and the EMA require for approval in the "pediatric" population additional, separate "pediatric" clinical (and other) studies, justified by the concept that they are not small adults and "therapeutic orphans" [1]. "Children" are defined chronologically by being younger than 17 years of age by the FDA [2], and as younger than 18 years by the EU [1]. The FDA does not have the authority to mandate "pediatric" studies in orphan diseases, but can for such diseases nevertheless reward "pediatric" studies financially by patent extensions. The EU has no such restrictions in its pediatric regulation [1]. In the EU, companies must commit to separate "pediatric" studies in detailed "pediatric investigation plans" (PIPs). It takes one year to negotiate a PIP with the EMA. The weak point of all FDA/EMA-rewarded/mandated "pediatric" studies is that minors are *legally* still "children," when this is *bodily* and *physiologically* no longer the case; also younger children do not remain as vulnerable as newborns until they are officially adult. Newborns are vulnerable, but they mature. The older children get, the more their body grows. Medicines treat the body, not the legal status. Adolescents are *bodily* no longer "children" from the end of puberty on [3–8].

The regulatory authorities have massively increased the number of "pediatric" studies first through voluntary financial rewards in the US, followed by mandatory studies in the US as well, and then through mandatory requirements in PIPs in the EU. These "pediatric" studies are performed worldwide [9–13]. In the explanations given to parents and patients in the framework of individual clinical studies, in justifications of these studies by the regulatory authorities on their websites and in medical journals, in "pediatric" reports of the regulatory authorities, and in publications of such studies in medical journals, many "factoids," misleading, and openly untrue claims are made to an extent that this amounts to systematic deceit. Until now, fraud in clinical research is mostly discussed when individual researchers secretly falsify research results or freely invent nonexistent patients and publish about them, in the hope not to get caught [14,15]. Fraud in healthcare committed by individuals or organizations often has direct criminal financial intentions [16]. Here, we discuss a completely different, new and "modern" type of deceit. Patients, parents and the public are given misleading explanations and justifications of "pediatric" studies. Distorting and misleading terms are used. The existing high trust toward the state and scientific authority in general is used to give these "pediatric" studies the appearance of truly scientific research. A new form of deceit in the 21st century.

This is neither an evil conspiration of a few malignant individuals or of a secret organization. It began with observed toxicities in preterm newborns in the 1950s, i.e., at a point of time when modern drug development was at its very beginning [17]. It became a movement called "pediatric drug development" to which several textbooks were dedicated [18,19]. When the FDA published in 2001 a first report, there was still honest belief that performing "pediatric" clinical studies leading to "pediatric" labels would significantly and measurably improve pediatric healthcare: "The absence of pediatric testing and labeling may also expose pediatric patients to ineffective treatment through underdosing, or may deny pediatric patients therapeutic advances because physicians choose to prescribe existing, less effective medications in the face of insufficient pediatric information about a new medication. ... The incentives provided by the newly authorized pediatric exclusivity should lead to significant advances in pediatric medicine. Superior drug treatment information is expected to permit quicker recoveries from childhood illnesses, with fewer attendant hospital stays, physician visits and parental work days lost" [20]. These expected results were clear *clinical* and *measurable* expectations. In its next report, the FDA has dropped such measurable expectations and replaced reports about achievements by describing regulatory activism [21].

The following ten points give a compressed overview, showing that there are no isolated errors, but systematic deceit. To what degree the main players act deliberately or in self-deceit is a more philosophical question and thus has only secondary relevance.

1. Responding to criminal medical experiments in the concentration camps of the German Nazi Third Reich, the World Medical Association (WMA) issued in 1964 a declaration on the ethical principles for medical research in humans: the Declaration of Helsinki [22]. It is continuously developed further and expanded. It has no direct legal force, but is recognized worldwide as the key document that sets out the ethical foundations of human research. The Declaration of Helsinki clearly states that medical research should help to further understand causes, development and effects of diseases and improve their prevention, detection and treatment [22]. In no place does the Declaration of Helsinki allow the repetition of proof-of-efficacy studies in humans before they reach their 17th or 18th birthday for purely regulatory reasons.
2. Since young people are not allowed to consent to study participation on their own before they become legally of age, they must be informed about the respective trial together with their parents or their legal guardians. The parents must document their "informed consent" in writing,

and young patients old enough to understand the basics of a clinical study are expected to document their assent as well [23]. Parents and young patients are given written information that explains the key elements of the study ("informed consent form"). The justifications for separate regulatory "pediatric" studies are outlined in a way to make laypersons think that the respective study makes medical sense. EMA PIPs require separate studies in "children" aged 1 to 17 or 2 to 17 years, or separate studies for different age groups of minor patients, e.g., one study in 12 to 17 years old, and another one in 6 to 11 years old patients. As soon as the underlying assumption is challenged that young people are not physically mature before their 18th birthday, the justifications for the "pediatric" studies collapse like a house of cards. It amounts to systematic deception of parents, patients, and the public. This is not criminal fraud. The goal of this deception is not to trigger direct payments by the parents, but to get parents' consent and young patients' assent for participation in a "pediatric" study.

3. For the doctors who conduct the informed consent discussion, the need to convince parents and young patients means that every single conversation is characterized by a fine line between still acceptable white lies and open deceit. Decades ago the internal maturation of the human body, including the maturation of liver enzymes during the first days and weeks of life, the fast maturation of the kidneys during the same period of time, and further aspects of the infant's maturation began to be recognized [24–26]. In these days, the mantra emerged that everything is different in "children". Today we know a lot more in detail. The children-are-not-small-adults mantra is getting more and more fragile. The US regulatory agency FDA has renounced separate "pediatric" studies in adolescents from 12 years of age in cancer, leukemia, and other malignancies [27]. It has approved crisaborole, a nonsteroidal topical against atopic dermatitis, based on pivotal studies in patients 2–79 years old [28]. It accepts "extrapolation" of efficacy in antiepilepsy drugs targeting the most frequent type of epilepsy, partial-onset seizures (POS), down to the age of 2 years [29]. Thus, in a wide array of individual clinical areas the FDA accepts that separate "pediatric" efficacy studies are no longer justified, while in other areas it still sticks to the children-are-therapeutic-orphans mantra [30]. With the exception of POS epilepsy down to the age of four years [31], the EMA continues to demand a complete separate clinical development program in "children" [2–8], triggering studies that recruit on every continent of this planet with the exception of Antarctica [11–13]. Some of the medical doctors involved in these studies may still believe the children-are-therapeutic-orphans mantra, which emerged decades ago in an exaggerated reaction to the first findings of developmental pharmacology, but skepticism is growing. Two "pediatric" melanoma studies had to be discontinued

because doctors no longer saw any point in denying young patients standard-of-care therapy, i.e., combining two drugs, while the EMA-demanded "pediatric" studies only offered one drug (one study was also FDA-rewarded) [32,33]. These two studies did not have therapeutic intentions.

4. Many committed pediatricians want the respective drug to be approved in minors as well. For this, the authorities insist on separate "pediatric" studies. Openly criticizing regulatory authorities is not part of the daily job of individual doctors or other involved healthcare professionals. They discuss such issues maybe with colleagues at conferences to the extent they dare, and at the workplace only as far as open discussion is allowed or even encouraged. Overall, they come to terms with the two realities in which they live. Everyone is familiar with arranging himself with contradicting expectations and demands, including medical doctors and other healthcare professionals that have to handle questionable or senseless rules at the place of work. You pretend to follow all instructions. Depending on your personal character, you follow these instructions to the letter, or you are more flexible.
5. In the treatment of young persons, a set of rules has developed in which science, common sense and official rules diverge. Two "pediatric" melanoma studies were abandoned, but a serious intellectual brainstorming of these events has not yet occurred. Many senseless and harmful "pediatric" studies continue today: in minors with depression [34], juvenile idiopathic arthritis, hay fever [35], inflammatory skin diseases [36], cystic fibrosis [37], multiple sclerosis [38], epilepsy [39], and cancer [7,8,11–13]. Many more examples are given in this book.
6. In the "pediatric" studies, the regulatory authorities have set up an apparently consistent pseudo-scientific framework that repeatedly justifies separate "pediatric drug development" [10,40–42]. But this framework does not withstand critical questions about its intellectual foundations. Why are the regulatory authorities so much focused on senseless and even harmful alleged "pediatric" studies? At the EU agency EMA, it is a fascinating mixture of dogmatism, pedantic schoolmasterly behavior, demonstration of power, pomposity, and missionary zeal. As an English-speaking institution, the EMA is rather insulated from the reality in the EU where the majority of citizens speak other languages. Critical voices may – perhaps - be able to come through many years too late, maybe best exemplified by the continued demand for separate proof-of-efficacy studies in POS epilepsy in children aged 3–4 years [31], where the FDA now accepts that they are unnecessary [29]. In malignant diseases, the EMA has not changed its attitude at all. To the contrary, it has recently declared diseases that occasionally occur also in minors to be "pediatric" for which it demands since 2018 separate "pediatric" studies, including liver cancer, renal cancer, Parkinson's

disease, amyotrophic lateral sclerosis (ALS), and Huntington chorea. This decision was made in 2015, but due to legal reasons it is in force from 2018 on only [43]. EMA employees seriously claim in scientific publications that they have no conflict of interest [41]. They do not profit financially immediately from these "pediatric" studies. But their employment depends on the justification and enforcement of "pediatric" studies. They get appreciation from working at the central EU medical regulatory authority, the EMA. The EMA is primarily not respected for its scientific work, but more because it has the power to approve or reject new drugs and the power to mandate clinical studies from pharmaceutical companies. Furthermore, it has the power to invite clinical specialists to special meetings for consultation. It has created a network of pediatric research, serving academic clinicians' continuous need for funds [44]. Clinical "pediatric" studies are performed by academic pediatric researchers. Pharmaceutical companies must pay them, or they are declared non-compliant regarding PIPs they had to commit to.

7. An official EMA document, available on the internet, seriously claims that off-label use of drugs in "children" is always dangerous [45]. But the entire discipline of pediatrics, including the treatment of childhood cancer [46], neonatology [47], and further sub-disciplines, emerged successfully in their first decades "off-label" long before the term "off-label" even existed [48], and, incidentally, long before the EMA was established in 1995.
8. Parents expect doctors to be honest. But the justifications for most "pediatric" studies are misleading and not based on science. Parents and readers of publications that justify separate "pediatric" studies have to decipher the language in which the particular study is justified to see that the informed consent procedure deceives parents and young patients for each and every "pediatric" study. It is a different kind of deceit, unlike the openly criminal falsification of data or the free invention of nonexistent patients by individual researchers. It is harder to get to the bottom unless you are prepared. It is a systematic deceit involving authorities, researchers, commercial contract research companies and the pharmaceutical industry that partially profits from these studies, and partially is forced to commit to them and to sponsor them. The main role here is not malice, and not criminal behavior by individual fraudsters, but rather the acceptance of a flawed concept that has the official seal of approval. The material interests involved here are indirect. Industry pays for "pediatric" studies that are conducted by research institutions and commercial clinical research organizations (CROs), with resulting careers in academic research, regulatory, industry, or commercial clinical research operations. A new challenge of the 21st century.
9. Apart from the deception of parents and young patients in the informed consent information, the pseudoscientific justifications for published

studies contain other elements of deception. Alleged scientific questions are claimed to have been addressed by the respective published study. This claim is made toward the scientific community. Where an authority offered to prolong a patent in exchange for a "pediatric" study, the disease is characterized in the academic publication as a "pediatric" disease, even if this is not the case. This occurred for example in an international study on nasopharyngeal carcinoma (cancer of the nose and the windpipe) [49]. But nasopharyngeal carcinoma occurs in persons of all ages [50]. In the publication, nasopharyngeal carcinoma is described as a disease occurring "in children and adolescents" [49]. But nasopharyngeal is not a "pediatric" disease. In the mentioned study, the patients were up to 21 years old. Patients 21 years old are definitely no longer children. But the FDA had offered a patent extension. All main players profited, with the exception of the patients.

10. The EMA five- and ten-year reports on EU child legislation list many alleged achievements [51]. Upon a closer look, these "achievements" are trickery. For all drugs for which a separate child approval has been achieved, the report claims that the respective drug is now "available" for "children." This is untrue. All drugs were and are available without separate "pediatric" approval upon prescription by medical doctors. In addition, the demand for separate "pediatric" studies has the consequence that most drugs are approved for young people much later than for adults. The claimed "pediatric" population includes adolescents that legally are still children, but no longer bodily. Medicine treats the physical patient, not his legal status.

References

[1] Hirschfeld S, Saint-Raymond A. Pediatric regulatory initiatives. Handb Exp Pharmacol 2011;205:245–68 556.

[2] Hirschfeld S. History of pediatric labeling. Available from: https://www.slideserve.com/marlin/history-of-pediatric-labeling.

[3] Khan L. Puberty: onset and progression. Pediatr Ann 2019;48(4):e141–5.

[4] Abreu AP, Kaiser UB. Pubertal development and regulation. Lancet Diabetes Endocrinol 2016;4(3):254–64.

[5] Snyder CK. Puberty: an overview for pediatric nurses. J Pediatr Nurs 2016;31(6):757–9.

[6] Wood CL, Lane LC, Cheetham T. Puberty: normal physiology (brief overview). Best Pract Res Clin Endocrinol Metab 2019;33(3):101265.

[7] Rose K. The challenges of pediatric drug development. Curr Ther Res Clin Exp 2019. Available from: https://doi.org/10.1016/j.curtheres.2019.01.007.

[8] Rose K, Grant-Kels JM. The meanings of "pediatric drug development". A review. Ther Innov Regul Sci 2019;53(6):767–74.

[9] Dunne J, Murphy MD, Rodriguez WJ. The globalization of pediatric clinical trials. Pediatrics 2012;130(6):e1583–91.

[10] EMA 2017: 10-year report to the European Commission. Available from: https://ec.europa.eu/health/sites/health/files/files/paediatrics/2016_pc_report_2017/ema_10_year_report_for_consultation.pdf.

[11] Rose K, Grant-Kels JM. Questionable international pediatric studies in the United States and Russia triggered by regulatory authorities. Asian J Res Med Pharm Sci 2018;3(3). Available from: http://www.journalrepository.org/media/journals/AJRIMPS_63/2018/Apr/Rose332018AJRIMPS40776.pdf.

[12] Rose K, Grant-Kels JM. Questionable industry-sponsored pediatric studies in China triggered by United States of America (US) and European Union (EU) regulatory authorities. SF Pharma J 2018;1:1. Available from: https://www.scifedpublishers.com/open-access/questionable-industry-sponsored-pediatric-studies-in-china-triggeredby-united-states-of-america-us-and-european-union-eu-regulatoryauthorities.pdf.

[13] Rose K, Neubauer D, Grant-Kels JM. Rational use of medicine in children – the conflict of interests story. A review Rambam Maimonides Med J 2019;10(3):e0018. Available from: https://doi.org/10.5041/RMMJ.10371Review. Available from: https://www.rmmj.org.il/userimages/928/2/PublishFiles/953Article.pdf.

[14] Bhutta ZA, Crane J. Should research fraud be a crime? BMJ 2014;349:g4532.

[15] Byrne J. We need to talk about systematic fraud. Nature 2019;566(7742):9.

[16] Thornton D, Brinkhuis M, Amrit C, Aly R. Categorizing and describing the types of fraud in healthcare. Procedia Computer Sci 2015;64:713–20. Available from: https://reader.elsevier.com/reader/sd/pii/S1877050915027295?token = F3CB1240220CAB1510AAEEEBEC55A43D4BE935109AD3EB6944152D0B1EAEDC5078A123E7F01911C0B382036FF3D38ADB.

[17] Guidelines for the ethical conduct of studies to evaluate drugs in pediatric populations, committee on drugs. American academy of pediatrics, pediatrics 1995;95(2):286–94.

[18] Mulberg AE, Murphy MD, Dunne J, Mathis LL, editors. Pediatric drug development: concepts and applica-tions. 2nd ed. Chichester: John Wiley & Sons, Ltd; 2013.

[19] Rose K, van den Anker JN, editors. Guide to paediatric drug development and clinical research. Basel: Karger; 2010.

[20] FDA 2001. The pediatric exclusivity provision. January 2001. Status report to congress. Available from: https://www.fda.gov/downloads/Drugs/DevelopmentApprovalProcess/DevelopmentResources/UCM049915.pdf.

[21] FDA 2016. Best pharmaceuticals for children act and pediatric research equity act. Status report to congress. Available from: www.fda.gov/downloads/ScienceResearch/SpecialTopics/PediatricTherapeuticsResearch/UCM509815.pdf.

[22] World Medical Association (WMA) Declaration of Helsinki – Ethical principles for medical research involving human subjects. Adopted by the 18th WMA general assembly, Helsinki, Finland, June 1964, and amended by the 64th WMA general assembly, Fortaleza, Brazil, October 2013. Available from: https://www.wma.net/policies-post/wma-declaration-of-helsinki-ethical-principles-for-medical-research-involving-human-subjects/.

[23] De Lourdes Levy M, Larcher V, Kurz R, et al. Informed consent/assent in children. Statement of the ethics working group of the confederation of European specialists in paediatrics (CESP). Eur J Pediatr 2003;162(9):629–33.

[24] Kearns GL, Abdel-Rahman SM, Alander SW, et al. Developmental pharmacology - drug disposition, action, and therapy in infants and children. N Engl J Med 2003;349(12):1157–67.

[25] Blumer JL. Developmental pharmacology: past, present and future. Acta Paediatr Jpn 1996;38(6):555–61.

[26] Crane E, Tutag Lehr V, Mathew M, Aranda JV. Developmental pharmacology and therapeutics. In: Buonocore G, Bracci R, Weindling M, editors. Neonatology. Milan, Italy: Springer Publishers; 2012. p. 364–9. chapter 52.

[27] FDA 2019. Considerations for the inclusion of adolescent patients in adult oncology clinical trials. Guidance for industry. Available from: https://www.fda.gov/media/113499/download.

[28] FDA 2016. Crisaborole label. Available from: https://www.accessdata.fda.gov/drugsatfda_docs/label/2016/207695s000lbl.pdf.

[29] FDA 2019. Drugs for treatment of partial onset seizures: full extrapolation of efficacy from adults to pediatric patients 2 years of age and older. Guidance for industry. Available from: https://www.fda.gov/media/130449/download.

[30] Sun H, Temeck JW, Chambers W, Perkins G, Bonnel R, Murphy D. Extrapolation of efficacy in pediatric drug development and evidence-based medicine: progress and lessons learned. Ther Innov Regul Sci 2017;2017:1–7. Available from: https://www.ncbi.nlm.nih.gov/pmc/articles/PMC5587157/pdf/nihms901908.pdf.

[31] EMA 2018. Guideline on clinical investigation of medicinal products in the treatment of epileptic disorders. Available from: https://www.ema.europa.eu/en/documents/scientific-guideline/draft-guideline-clinical-investigation-medicinal-products-treatment-epileptic-disorders-revision-3_en.pdf.

[32] Rose K, Grant-Kels JM. Pediatric melanoma – the whole (conflicts of interest) story. Int J Womens Dermatol 2018;5(2):110–15. Available from: 10.1016/j.ijwd.2018.10.020. Available from: https://www.ncbi.nlm.nih.gov/pmc/articles/PMC6451736/pdf/main.pdf.

[33] Geoerger B, Bergeron C, Gore L, et al. Phase II study of ipilimumab in adolescents with unresectable stage III or IV malignant melanoma. Eur J Cancer 2017;86:358–63.

[34] Rose K, Neubauer D, Grant-Kels JM. Too many avoidable suicides occur worldwide in young patients. A review. Rambam Maimonides Med J 2019. Available from: https://www.rmmj.org.il/userimages/965/1/PublishFiles/977OnlineFirst.pdf.

[35] Rose K, Kopp MV. Pediatric investigation plans for specific immunotherapy: questionable contributions to childhood health. Pediatr Allergy Immunol 2015;26(8):695–701.

[36] Rose K, Happle R. The impact of regulation on pediatric psoriasis drug approvals: the challenge of the European Union (EU) pediatric investigation plans. Pediatr Dermatol 2017;34(3):e154–9.

[37] Rose K, Spigarelli MG. Cystic fibrosis treatment: a paradigm for new pediatric medicines, globalization of drug development and the role of the European medicines agency. Children 2015;2:108–30. Available from: https://www.mdpi.com/2227-9067/2/1/108.

[38] Rose K, Neubauer D, Grant-Kels JM. Ethical issues in pediatric regulatory studies involving placebo treatment. J Pediatr Epilepsy 2020; (in press).

[39] Rose K, Mueller T. Children with multiple sclerosis should not become therapeutic hostages. Ther Adv Neurol Disord 2016;9(5):389–95. Available from: https://www.ncbi.nlm.nih.gov/pmc/articles/PMC4994785/pdf/10.1177_1756285616656592.pdf.

[40] Rocchi F, et al. 2011. The European paediatric legislation: benefits and perspectives. Available from: https://www.ncbi.nlm.nih.gov/pmc/articles/PMC2933611/pdf/1824-7288-36-56.pdf.

[41] Tomasi PA, Egger GF, Pallidis C, et al. Enabling development of paediatric medicines in Europe: 10 years of the EU paediatric regulation. Pediatr Drugs 2017;19:505–13.

[42] Ward RM, Benjamin Jr DK, Davis JM, et al. The need for pediatric drug development. J Pediatr 2018;192:13–21.

[43] EMA 2015. EMA/PDCO summary report on the review of the list of granted class waivers. Available from: https://www.ema.europa.eu/en/documents/other/ema/pdco-summary-report-review-list-granted-class-waivers_en.pdf.

[44] European Network of Pediatric Research at the EMA (Enpr-EMA). Available from: http://enprema.ema.europa.eu/enprema/.

[45] EMA 2004. Evidence of harm from off-label or unlicensed medicines in children. Available from: http://www.ema.europa.eu/docs/en_GB/document_library/Other/2009/10/WC500004021.pdf.

[46] Adamson PC. Improving the outcome for children with cancer: development of targeted new agents. CA Cancer J Clin 2015;65(3):212–20.

[47] Philip AG. The evolution of neonatology. Pediatr Res 2005;58(4):799–815.

[48] Plate V. The impact of off-label, compassionate and unlicensed use on health care laws in preselected countries. Available from: http://hss.ulb.uni-bonn.de/2009/1936/1936.pdf.

[49] Casanova M, Enis Özyar E, Patte C, et al. International randomized phase 2 study on the addition of docetaxel to the combination of cisplatin and 5-fluorouracil in the induction treatment for nasopharyngeal carcinoma in children and adolescents. Cancer Chemother Pharmacol 2016;77(2):289–98.

[50] Brennan B. Nasopharyngeal carcinoma. Orphanet J Rare Dis 2006;1:23 Review.

[51] EMA 10-year Report to the European Commission. General report on the experience acquired as a result of the application of the paediatric regulation. Available from: https://ec.europa.eu/health/sites/health/files/files/paediatrics/2016_pc_report_2017/ema_10_year_report_for_consultation.pdf.

Subchapter 6.5

Myths in today's medical world and "pediatric" studies

Introduction

In the justification of "pediatric drug development" several myths and misunderstandings are repeated so often that we address them separately. Gut feelings, myths, and convictions play a large role in our life. Specifically in times and areas where we *feel* insecure we tend to cling to feelings and myths that we hope are right. Evidence-based medicine is such a myth as far as it overestimates the weight of formal clinical trials methodology and underweighs medical thinking and down-to-earth assessments of the worth of modern medicines in our world that has become increasingly complex.

Only medicines that are labeled for "children" are safe in "children"

"Off-label use doubles the frequency of adverse drug reactions, which are sometimes life-threatening" [1]. This statement refers to two further papers. One reported a prospective study in UK pediatric wards that classified administered drugs for on-label or off-label and recorded adverse drug reactions (ADRs). The incidence of ADRs was comparable to other studies, but more ADRs occurred in the intensive care unit. A high risk of ADRs was associated where many drugs were given to respective patients in the intensive care unit. Roughly half the ADRs occurred with opiates. This paper simply confirms that complex clinical challenges are more difficult to handle than simple situations [2]. Another study analyzed prescriptions of office-based pediatricians in France. Half the ADRs occurred in infants, half in children, none in adolescents. More ADRs were observed in indications not covered by the respective label, but the authors conclude: "the risk of ADRs could be acceptable if the therapeutic benefit is largely greater" [3]. Thus, the papers referred to do not support the claim of a double frequency of ADRs in off-label use. The three quoted papers were written in a period where separate "pediatric" studies were seen with much enthusiasm. This enthusiasm has calmed down, but the intellectual core of the myth that only drugs with a separate "pediatric" label are safe still needs to be challenged.

Labels for the "pediatric" population cover a population that physiologically ranges from preterm, extremely immature and vulnerable newborns over term newborns to school age children and adolescents. *Bodily*, only some of the administratively defined "pediatric" population (US before the 17th, EU before the 18th birthday) are still children. The problem is not that pediatric labels are missing, but that the definition of "pediatric" is wrong. Puberty is a slow process. During puberty the body becomes mature [4–8]. However, administratively and legally the respective person is still minor and a "child."

Physicians without solid experience should not prescribe any drug to any seriously ill patients of any age. The grain of truth in the pediatric warnings was that in the 1940s/1950s much less was known than today about newborns' different absorption, distribution, metabolism, and excretion (ADME) as compared to adults [9]. Developmental pharmacology stepwise elucidated this. But there is a fundamental difference between justified warnings of toxicities in infants [10], and exaggerated warnings that "children" of all ages need separate studies [11–13]. These warning extrapolate the real and serious risk of toxicities in very young humans into an alleged danger of drugs into the entire "pediatric" population, defined by the administrative age limit of the 17th (FDA) or the 18th birthday (EU) [14–20]. Half a century ago, when the entire process of drug development was new and still relatively few effective drugs existed, the medical world was unaware of the internal maturation of the organs responsible for ADME and of the consequences of this maturation for drug treatment in very young patients. This unawareness should not be confused with a lack of pediatric labels.

For pharmaceutical companies, the market of pediatric diseases is too small

There is broad belief in the clinical world that for pediatric diseases the market is too small for commercial drug development. This opinion has been expressed specifically for pediatric oncology [21], and is expressed in general terms in the preamble to the EU pediatric regulation: "Market forces alone have proven insufficient to stimulate adequate research into, and the development and authorization of, medicinal products for the paediatric population" [13]. But longevity of the entire population in developed countries has increased, child mortality has decreased, and more and more breakthrough medications are developed for diseases that often predominantly affect young patients. These include effective drugs against recurrent or relapsed lymphoblastic leukemia [22,23], against cystic fibrosis [24,25], against sickle cell anemia [26–28], and many more. They have been developed through the forces of the market and despite "pediatric" legislation.

The more resources we invest into pediatric research, the better the outcome

There is the belief that the more we invest into something the better the outcome. But reality is more complex. On the market, there is always an abundance of offers that promise the blue from the sky if you buy this or that product. Pediatric drug development is a good example. Billions have been invested into "pediatric" clinical studies. In the majority of cases, these studies were unnecessary and questionable, others "only" massively exaggerated. The money for these studies was virtually thrown out of the window. In many further cases, effective treatment was withheld from young patients, in form of placebo, or comparison to "standard of care" or outdated treatment. All main players in this theater speak of "better medicines for children," of improving healthcare for children, and similar claims. But young persons have not profited from these studies. However, they have advanced careers in academia, regulatory authorities, pharmaceutical industry and commercial clinical research operations.

Common sense and evidence-based medicine

In reaction to the thalidomide disaster, the US based in 1962 drug approval by the FDA on proof of safety and efficacy in clinical studies [29,30]. The term "evidence-based medicine" was introduced into the medical literature in 1991 and became a movement from the early 1990s on. It aimed at enabling front-line clinicians in assessing the credibility of research evidence, understanding the results of clinical studies, and determining how best to apply the results of such studies to their everyday practice. In the following, treatment guidelines published in journal articles and associated textbooks led to evidence-based medicine becoming increasingly integrated into medical curricula worldwide [31,32]. Since the early 1990s, the frequency of articles that in their headline contain the terms "evidence-based medicine," "guidance," or "guideline" has increased almost exponentially [33]. The Cochrane Collaboration played a key role in promoting the methodology of systematic reviews [31,33–36].

But clinical studies and reviews produce evidence about *average* results for heterogeneous groups of patients [37]. The number of effective drugs has almost exponentially increased since the 1960s. The currently available guidelines can without doubt be helpful in clinical practice. However, reviews and guidelines cannot predict if a given therapeutic decision will help the patient at a given point in his clinical course [37]. At the end, the physician has to make decisions of complex clinical situation where he cannot follow guidelines blindly.

The term "evidence-based medicine" does not want to see the world behind studies and their publications. Clinical studies are not produced by academic researchers in an interest-free zone. Most are financed by pharmaceutical companies that want to bring their product to the market. Nothing is wrong with this. Wrong is the illusion that the resulting publications are pure science. The framework of controlled studies has continuously improved. Today, no study can be published unless is has been listed in a publicly accessible registry before the study has started. Without www.clinicaltrials.gov, this book would have been impossible. Evidence-based medicine has strongly contributed to better drugs. But it is also an illusion. There is no interest-free zone. All we can do is to balance different interests without blindly trusting anybody.

A meanwhile famous paper criticizes apparently seriously the lack of double-blind randomized clinical studies to prove that parachutes work at all [38]. It describes in rather stilted medical terminology the use of parachutes to prevent death and major injuries when persons fall down from high heights. It mentions the "military industrial complex" that has earned billions of dollars with parachutes; medical doctors' alleged obsession "with disease and power, who will not be satisfied until they control every aspect of our lives (Journal of Social Science, pick a volume)" and conclude that in the end there are only two options: accept that, "under exceptional circumstances, common sense might be applied when considering the potential risks and benefits of interventions"; or "continue our quest for the holy grail of exclusively evidence-based interventions" and stop using parachutes outside of a properly conducted trial. At the end of the paper, they express the belief that those who advocate evidence-based medicine and criticize interventions that lack an evidence base will not hesitate to demonstrate their commitment by volunteering for a double-blind, randomized, placebo-controlled, crossover trial. This paper mocks brilliantly the exaggerated beliefs in evidence-based medicine and the illusion of a holy grail it has produced.

"Pediatric drug development" is probably the clinical area where an exaggerated emphasis on the methodology of clinical studies has resulted in the largest systematic blind spot. All FDA- and EMA-demanded "pediatric" studies conform formally, methodologically and statistically to the rules and regulations of clinical studies and evidence-based medicine. But so far, the Cochran movement has not fundamentally criticized "pediatric drug development" and all the "pediatric" regulatory studies that seem to be methodologically correct but lack the most crucial characteristic any clinical study should have: they lack scientific and medical sense. There is no medical sense in performing separate placebo-controlled studies in children and adolescents with drugs whose efficacy in humans has already been proven.

The key message of Drs. Smith and Pell is to use common sense in assessing the value of a given study, not to only look at formal criteria of the study methodology [38]. A follow-up paper on the lack of clinical studies about parachutes' capability to prevent death and trauma does not reflect this key message. Instead, it reports that for jumping off a nonflying airplane it does not make a difference if you carry a parachute or a backpack [39].

Chapter 2 of the pediatric standard textbook *Rudolph's Pediatrics* addresses "Decision making. Use of evidence-based medicine" [40]. It lists key questions to be asked when the results of a specific study are considered for translation into a therapeutic decision. All listed questions are formal. The one key question that should be asked first is missing: did the respective study make sense? We do not need separate studies to show that insulin, painkillers, antibiotics, or antiepileptic drugs work also in minors. We need to know how to dose them, we need to be aware of specific toxicities, and of their interaction with other drugs. Too many questionable studies have been rewarded and continue to be rewarded by the FDA, were mandated or continue to be mandated by the FDA, or are demanded by the EMA [14–20].

Without "pediatric" labels, drugs can be denied third-party reimbursement

Lack of "pediatric" labels can result in denial of third-party reimbursement [41]. But this is not a valid argument to advocate for separate "pediatric" studies and separate "pediatric" labels. The entire discipline of pediatric oncology emerged off-label [42], long before the term "off-label" emerged in 1988 [43]. The declaration of Helsinki demands that clinical studies should always aim at improving therapy, diagnosis or understanding of diseases [44]. To achieve this, studies must be based on medical sense and science. That without "pediatric" labels reimbursement institutions can refuse payment for treatment is not a valid justification for separate "pediatric" studies. If young patients are excluded by drug labels from reasonable clinical treatment, the problem is with the labels. A similar argument is that off-label use might result in denial of malpractice insurance coverage [41]. Regulatory authorities do not have the right to tell the physician what to prescribe and what not. If a physician refuses to prescribe a medication whose use is well-established in clinical practice, he can even be sued for medical negligence and malpractice because he did not prescribe this medication [29]. Again, labels that arbitrarily exclude young patients from reasonable treatment are the problem, not the lack of clinical studies.

The administrative side of medicine has become stronger and stronger over the past decades. So far, it has been overlooked that also administrations and administrative institutions have a life of their own and can develop hidden interests that did not exist when these institutions were established. We do not see the results of such new conflicts of interest on a superficial glance. Those parents who increasingly refuse to let their children participate in medically questionable clinical studies [45] *feel* that something is wrong, and make the right decision. Here we try to give a rational justification to these correct feelings.

Conclusions

Myths play a more important role in medicine, in evidence-based medicine, and in our entire daily life than we like to admit. They can for a while obfuscate, but not forever. Sooner or later, it is necessary to address them and to demystify them.

References

[1] Seyberth H. Problems of prescription drug use in children. Dtsch Arztebl Int 2009;106(3):23–4. Available from: https://www.aerzteblatt.de/pdf.asp?id = 63003.

[2] Turner S, Nunn AJ, Fielding K, Choonara I. Adverse drug reactions to unlicensed and off-label drugs on paediatric wards: a prospective study. Acta Paediatr 1999;88:965–8.

[3] Horen B, Montastruc JL, Lapeyre-Mestre M. Adverse drug reactions and off-label drug use in paediatric outpatients. Br J Clin Pharmacol 2002;54:665–70.

[4] Cheng HL, Harris SR, Sritharan M, et al. The tempo of puberty and its relationship to adolescent health and wellbeing: a systematic review. Acta Paediatr 2019.

[5] Khan L. Puberty: onset and progression. Pediatr Ann 2019;48(4):e141–5.

[6] Abreu AP, Kaiser UB. Pubertal development and regulation. Lancet Diabetes Endocrinol 2016;4(3):254–64.

[7] Snyder CK. Puberty: an overview for pediatric nurses. J Pediatr Nurs 2016;31(6):757–9.

[8] Wood CL, Lane LC, Cheetham T. Puberty: normal physiology (brief overview). Best Pract Res Clin Endocrinol Metab 2019;33(3):101265.

[9] Kearns GL, Abdel-Rahman SM, Alander SW, Blowey DL, Leeder JS, Kauffman RE. Developmental pharmacology drug disposition, action, and therapy in infants and children. N Engl J Med 2003;349(12):1157–67. Available from: https://pdfs.semanticscholar.org/55f8/1745303e9aaec7f4cb85f0b5921eec14a9c0.pdf.

[10] Shirkey H. Therapeutic orphans. J Pediatr 1968;72(1):119–20. Available from: https://pdfs.semanticscholar.org/f1cb/acdbac19fa56236b919fb7799eaacaa10c77.pdf.

[11] AAP 1995. Guidelines for the ethical conduct of studies to evaluate drugs in pediatric populations, committee on drugs. Am Acad Pediatrics, Pediatrics 1995;95(2):286–94.

[12] Shaddy RE, Denne SC, Committee on Drugs and Committee on Pediatric Research. Clinical report—guidelines for the ethical conduct of studies to evaluate drugs in pediatric populations. Pediatrics 2010;125(4):850–60. Available from: https://pediatrics.aappublications.org/content/pediatrics/125/4/850.full.pdf.

[13] Regulation (EC) No 1901/2006 of the European parliament and of the council of 12 December 2006 on medicinal products for paediatric use and amending regulation (EEC) No 1768/92, Directive 2001/20/EC, Directive 2001/83/EC and Regulation (EC) No 726/2004. Available from: http://ec.europa.eu/health/files/eudralex/vol-1/reg_2006_1901/reg_2006_1901_en.pdf.

[14] Rose K, Neubauer D, Grant-Kels JM. Rational use of medicine in children—the conflict of interests story. A review Rambam Maimonides Med J 2019;10(3):e0018. Available from: https://doi.org/10.5041/RMMJ.10371Review. Available from: https://www.rmmj.org.il/userimages/928/2/PublishFiles/953Article.pdf.

[15] Rose K, Grant-Kels JM. Pediatric melanoma—the whole (conflicts of interest) story. Int J Womens Dermatol 2018;5(2):110–15. Available from: 10.1016/j.ijwd.2018.10.020. Available from: https://www.ncbi.nlm.nih.gov/pmc/articles/PMC6451736/pdf/main.pdf.

[16] Rose K, Grant-Kels JM. The meanings of "pediatric drug development". A review. Ther Innov Regul Sci 2019;53(6):767–74.

[17] Rose K, Neubauer D, Grant-Kels JM. Ethical issues in pediatric regulatory studies involving placebo treatment. J Pediatr Epilepsy 2020; (in press).

[18] Rose K. The challenges of pediatric drug development. Curr Ther Res Clin Exp 2019. Available from: https://doi.org/10.1016/j.curtheres.2019.01.007.

[19] Rose K, Neubauer D, Grant-Kels JM. Ethical issues in pediatric regulatory studies involving placebo treatment J Pediatr Epilepsy 2020;eFirst. Available from: https://doi.org/10.1055/s-0040-1712147.

[20] Rose K, Grant-Kels JM. Pediatric melanoma—the whole (conflicts of interest) story. Int J Womens Dermatol 2018;5(2):110–15. Available from: https://doi.org/10.1016/j.ijwd.2018.10.020. Available from: https://www.ncbi.nlm.nih.gov/pmc/articles/PMC6451736/pdf/main.pdf.

[21] Boklan J. Little patients, losing patients: pediatric cancer drug development. Mol Cancer Ther 2006;5(8):1905–8. Available from: http://mct.aacrjournals.org/content/5/8/1905.full-text.pdf.

[22] Maude SL, Laetsch TW, Buechner J, et al. Tisagenlecleucel in children and young adults with B-cell lymphoblastic leukemia. N Engl J Med 2018;378:439–48.

[23] FDA 2017. Tisagenlecleucel label Available from: https://www.fda.gov/files/vaccines%2C%20blood%20%26%20biologics/published/Package-Insert---KYMRIAH.pdf.

[24] FDA 2017. Kalydeco® (ivacaftor) label. Available from: https://www.accessdata.fda.gov/drugsatfda_docs/label/2017/203188s019lbl.pdf.

[25] FDA 2019. Trikafta label. Available from: https://www.accessdata.fda.gov/drugsatfda_docs/label/2019/212273s000lbl.pdf.

[26] FDA 2019. Crizanlizumaba label. Available from: https://www.accessdata.fda.gov/drugsatfda_docs/label/2019/761128s000lbl.pdf.

[27] FDA 2017. L-glutamine label. Available from: https://www.accessdata.fda.gov/drugsatfda_docs/label/2017/208587s000lbl.pdf.

[28] FDA 2019. Voxelotor label. Available from: https://www.accessdata.fda.gov/drugsatfda_docs/label/2019/213137s000lbl.pdf.

[29] Janssen WM. A historical perspective on off-label medicine: from regulation, promotion, and the first amendment to the next frontiers First In: Levy MC, editor. USA Off-Label Communications. Washington, D.C.: Food and Drug Law Institute; 2008.

[30] Rägo L, Santo B. Drug regulation: history, present and future In: van Boxtel CJ, Santo B, Edwards IR, editors. Drug benefits and risks: international textbook of clinical pharmacology. revised 2nd edition Uppsala, Sweder: IOS Press & Uppsala Monitoring Centre; 2008. p. 65–77chapter 6. Available from: https://www.who.int/medicines/technical_briefing/tbs/Drug_Regulation_History_Present_Future.pdf.

[31] Djulbegovic B, Guyatt GH. Progress in evidence-based medicine: a quarter century on. Lancet 2017;390(10092):415–23.

[32] Sackett DL, Rosenberg WM, Gray JA, et al. Evidence based medicine: what it is and what it isn't. BMJ 1996;312(7023):71–2. Available from: https://www.ncbi.nlm.nih.gov/pmc/articles/PMC2349778/pdf/bmj00524-0009.pdf.

[33] Tebala GD. The emperor's new clothes: a critical appraisal of evidence-based medicine. Int J Med Sci 2018;15. Available from: https://www.medsci.org/v15p1397.pdf.

[34] Greenhalgh T, Howick J, Maskrey N. Evidence based medicine renaissance group Version 2 BMJ 2014;348:g3725.

[35] Cochrane Youtube Available from: https://www.youtube.com/channel/UCV85pBXQRwdv5LTgGt_Xt4g.

[36] Wikipedia: Cochrane Available from: https://en.wikipedia.org/wiki/Cochrane_(organisation).

[37] Horwitz RI, Hayes-Conroy A, Caricchio R, et al. From evidence based medicine to medicine based evidence. Am J Med 2017;130(11):1246–50.

[38] Smith GC, Pell JP. Parachute use to prevent death and major trauma related to gravitational challenge: systematic review of randomized controlled trials. BMJ 2003;237(7427):1459–61. Available from: https://www.ncbi.nlm.nih.gov/pmc/articles/PMC300808/pdf/32701459.pdf.

[39] Yeh RW, Valsdottir LR, Yeh MW, et al. Parachute use to prevent death and major trauma when jumping from aircraft: randomized controlled trial. BMJ 2018;363:k5094. Available from: https://www.bmj.com/content/bmj/363/bmj.k5094.full.pdf.

[40] Nagappan S, Roberts KB. Pediatric decision making: use of evidence-based medicine. In: Rudolph CD, et al., editors. Rudolph's pediatrics. New York: McGraw-Hill; 2011. p. 3–4. chapter 2.

[41] Wilson JT. An update on the therapeutic orphan. Pediatrics 1999;104(3 Pt 2):585–90. Available from: https://pediatrics.aappublications.org/content/pediatrics/104/Supplement_3/585.full.pdf.

[42] Adamson PC. Improving the outcome for children with cancer: development of targeted new agents. CA Cancer J Clin 2015;65(3):212–20.

[43] Plate V. The impact of off-label, compassionate and unlicensed use on health care laws in preselected countries. Available from: http://hss.ulb.uni-bonn.de/2009/1936/1936.pdf.

[44] World Medical Association (WMA) Declaration of Helsinki—ethical principles for medical research involving human subjects. Adopted by the 18th WMA general assembly, Helsinki, Finland, June 1964, and amended by the 64th WMA general assembly, Fortaleza, Brazil, October 2013. Available from: https://www.wma.net/policies-post/wma-declaration-of-helsinki-ethical-principles-for-medical-research-involving-human-subjects/.

[45] Waubant E, Banwell B, Wassmer E, Sormani MP, Amato MP, Hintzen R, et al. Clinical trials of disease-modifying agents in pediatric MS: opportunities, challenges, and recommendations from the IPMSSG. Neurology 2019.

Chapter 7

Juvenile animal studies

Introduction

Before a new drug is given for the first time to humans, it must already have gone through a series of preclinical testing that aim to find out how the compound is absorbed, distributed, metabolized, and excreted in animals to establish a safe first dose in humans and to detect characteristics of the new compound that might later cause problems once it has gone through clinical testing and is broadly used as a medicine. There are two types of preclinical testing: in vitro, i.e., in test tubes, and in vivo, i.e., with living animals, mostly rats and mice, but sometimes also rabbits, dogs, or monkeys [1]. For both types of testing, there are detailed guidelines on national and international level [2]. All tests must conform to the rules of "Good Laboratory Practice" (GLP), which includes detailed documentation [1]. The studies in living animals include administration of very high doses relative to later clinical therapeutic doses to trigger adverse events and to see potential toxicities. Preclinical testing is part of the scientific discipline of toxicology, which is sometimes defined as the science that deals with poisons and their effect or as the scientific study of the characteristics and effect of poisons. A more inclusive definition of toxicology is "the study of symptoms, mechanisms, treatment, and detection of poisoning, especially the poisoning of people" [3]. The relevance and the complexity of toxicology is reflected in the number of handbooks and the number of editions, respectively [3–5]. Companies that develop drugs have either an own department of toxicology or outsource most of the toxicological work to nonclinical contract research organizations. Most colleagues in the clinical development department in pharmaceutical companies have usually little to do with their counterparts in the toxicology ("tox") department, unless suddenly tumors or other nasty surprises occur in tested animals and the development of a promising new compound is interrupted temporarily or is definitely abandoned [3].

Within the US and the EU pediatric legislation, juvenile animal studies (JAS) within the framework of toxicology studies have become part of the safety evaluation in the development of new drugs [6,7]. National and international guidelines have been developed [8–10]. "The conduct of additional nonclinical investigations should be undertaken only when previous nonclinical and human data are judged to be insufficient to support pediatric studies.

Considering the Patient in Pediatric Drug Development. DOI: https://doi.org/10.1016/B978-0-12-823888-2.00008-9

A juvenile animal study is designed to address safety concerns that cannot be adequately addressed in other nonclinical studies or pediatric clinical trials, including potential long-term safety effects." [10]

What is the value of animal studies to predict toxicities in humans?

Animal studies were introduced as a requirement for drug development as part of the US Federal Food, Drug, and Cosmetic Act in 1938 [11,12]. The underlying assumption of all nonclinical and animal studies is that they can help to avoid later fatal disasters. "The nonclinical safety studies, although usually limited at the beginning of clinical development, should be adequate to characterize potential adverse effects that might occur under the conditions of the clinical trial to be supported. "[13] The largest such disaster in drug development was thalidomide, which lead to the malformation of tens of thousands of babies by an apparently harmless tranquilizer pill [14–16].

The value of animal studies in predicting future adverse effects is being increasingly challenged, as they might be based on scientifically flawed assumptions [17]. One of the reasons that they continue until now might be that it that they convey the feeling that "something" is done. Several times, toxicities occurred in humans after animal studies had declared the respective compounds "safe," including a cytokine storm in a phase 1 study of the anti-CD28 monoclonal antibody TGN1412 [18,19], and other comparable tragedies [17]. Furthermore, when animal studies falsely identify a compound as unsafe, it is mostly abandoned from further development. Undoubtedly many potentially beneficial medicines that have failed animal testing have been lost to patients; the magnitude of this type of error is unknown. Furthermore, many highly beneficial drugs would have failed animal testing and would never have been brought to the market, but they were developed before animal testing was required, including penicillin, which is fatal to guinea pigs; paracetamol, which is toxic in dogs and cats; and aspirin, which triggers embryo toxicity in rats and rhesus monkeys [17,20]. An analysis of the most comprehensive quantitative database of publicly available animal toxicity studies yet compiled concluded that the results from these studies, specifically rat, mouse, and rabbit models, are highly inconsistent predictors of toxic effects in humans, and are little better than what would result merely by chance, or tossing a coin, in providing a basis for deciding whether a compound should proceed to testing in humans [21]. If no one single species can add evidential weight in this regard to any other species, then how can any nonhuman species be expected to add evidential weight to what is likely to happen in humans? This is not something that can be fixed by improving the rigor of the animal tests [22,23], although there are also exponents that think such a fixing is possible [24].

The justification of juvenile animal studies

JAS are justified with the same arguments that also justify the entire movement of "pediatric drug development." The FDA guidance for industry on non-clinical safety evaluation of pediatric drug products [8] refers to the statement of the American Academy of Pediatrics (AAP) that addresses the lack of "pediatric" labels [25]. Both documents address uncritically the term "children" as defined by the FDA in 1979: persons younger than 17 years [26,27]. The same line of argumentation is documented in the justification of JAS by the EMA: "The main aim of non-clinical studies to support the development of medicinal products to be used in pediatric patients is to obtain information on the potentially different safety profiles from those seen in adults. Juvenile animal studies can be used to investigate findings that cannot be adequately, ethically, and safely assessed in pediatric clinical trials" [9]. Many of the FDA/EMA-rewarded/demanded "pediatric" studies are not pediatric at all, as they define "children" administratively, and not by the bodily status. Others are massively exaggerated. The truly challenging time window in human development are the first weeks after birth, specifically in preterm newborns [28]. Children do not remain as immature and vulnerable as preterm newborns or term newborns until they become administratively adult. The entire movement of "pediatric drug development" extrapolated the existing challenges of drug toxicities in preterm newborns and newborns into the entire "pediatric" population that is not defined by physiological criteria, but by the administrative age limit of the 17th (FDA) or the 18th birthday (EU) [29–33].

The overviews that characterize the field of JAS uncritically accept the chronological definition of "children" by an administrative age limit [7,10,34–40]. In other words: the official justifications for JAS are scientifically as robust as the general justification of "pediatric drug development," i.e., as robust as a house of cards.

While overviews provided by active or retired representatives of regulatory authorities justify and take as granted the general concept of "pediatric drug development" and the resulting additional demand for JAS, in overviews that also include representatives of commercial drug development, there is only one overarching common conclusion: at present, JAS have become an integrated part of the drug development process that pharmaceutical companies have to deal with [6,7,10,34–41]. However, there is also broad agreement that the medical and scientific sense of these studies has not been proven.

One recent review openly challenges the value of JAS in oncology. It analyzed the starting doses, maximal tolerated doses, dose limiting toxicities, and toxicities of phase 1 pediatric clinical trials for 25 molecularly targeted anticancer agents and 4 biologics, and showed that safe administration to pediatric oncology patients could have been done based only on adult doses and safety profiles without any knowledge of the findings in JAS. The authors conclude that abandoning routinely conducting JAS for most molecularly targeted oncology drugs would expedite testing in young oncology patients and allow precious drug development resources wasted for JAS to be applied to other promising projects [42]. The authors do not address the fundamentally weak point of the justification of "pediatric" studies that many "pediatric" studies are not performed in "children," but in bodily mature young persons, a fact that at least the FDA has meanwhile accepted for modern anticancer drugs [43].

Discussion and conclusions

In comparison to the "pediatric" clinical studies in young patients, JAS have the advantage that at least they do not harm young patients by withholding effective treatment at all in placebo comparison, by comparison to outdated treatment, or by exposing young patients to exaggerated studies where dose-finding could be done in much smaller and much less expense studies in a therapeutic, "opportunistic "setting [29–33]. JAS cost much less compared to the high costs of clinical studies in humans. Thus, there is the temptation for the team that negotiates an "initial pediatric study plan" (iPSP) with the FDA or a "pediatric investigation plan" (PIP) with the EMA to offer FDA or EMA at least "something" to be done in the area of "pediatric drug development." As long as the power of the "moral imperative" to perform "pediatric" clinical studies is not broken by a serious debate of the flaws of this concept [25], JAS offer a token that can be used in the negotiation procedure. Although probably all of them are medically and clinically senseless, they cost much less and do not harm young human patients. Large companies can afford such a negotiation style.

We might compare JAS with the longevity of taxes once they have been established. In 1902, the German emperor Wilhelm II introduced a sparkling wine tax in order to finance, among other things, his war fleet. This tax is still in place today and amounts to €1.02 per bottle [44]. We could also compare JAS with the fact that there is nothing as permanent as the tendency of "temporary" government programs to continue without end [45]. The academic discussion about the lack of value of JAS will probably run in circles until "pediatric drug development" is critically discussed in its entirety in the public and until parent advocacy groups participate in such a discussion. Once such a discussion has started to stir the public opinion, the lack of sense of additional JAS should be included.

References

[1] FDA 2018. Step 2: Preclinical Research. <https://www.fda.gov/patients/drug-development-process/step-2-preclinical-research>.

[2] ICH preclinical safety guidenlines ICH S 1 through ICH S 12, <https://www.ich.org/page/safety-guidelines>.

[3] Lodola A, Stadler J. Pharmaceutical toxicology in practice: a guide to non-clinical development. Hoboken, NJ, USA: Wiley; 2011.

[4] Klaassen CD. Casarett & Doull's toxicology: the basic science of poisons. Ninth edition New York, NY, USA: McGraw Hill; 2019.

[5] Murray L, Daly F, Little M, Cadogan M, editors. Toxicology Handbook. second edition Chatswood NSW, Australia: Churchill Livingston, Elsevier; 2011.

[6] Baldrick P. Juvenile animal testing: assessing need and use in the drug product label. Ther Innov Regul Sci 2018;52(5):641–8.

[7] Soellner L, Olejniczak K. The need for juvenile animal studies – A critical review. Regul Toxicol Pharmacol 2013;65(1):87–99.

[8] FDA 2006. Guidance for Industry. Nonclinical safety evaluation of pediatric drug products, CDER, 2006. <https://www.fda.gov/media/119658/download>.

[9] EMA 2008. Guideline on the need for non-clinical testing in juvenile animals of pharmaceuticals for paediatric indications. Ref. EMEA/CHMP/ https://www.ema.europa.eu/en/documents/scientific-guideline/guideline-need-non-clinical-testing-juvenile-animals-pharmaceuticals-paediatric-indications_en.pdf.

[10] International Council For Harmonisation Of Technical Requirements For Pharmaceuticals For Human Use (ICH) 2020. ICH Harmonized Guideline. Nonclinical Safety Testing In Support Of Development Of Paediatric Pharmaceuticals S11. <https://database.ich.org/sites/default/files/S11_Step4_FinalGuideline_2020_0310.pdf>.

[11] Hajar R. Animal testing and medicine Heart Views 2011;12(1):42Jan-Mar. Available from: https://www.ncbi.nlm.nih.gov/pmc/articles/PMC3123518/.

[12] Jacobs AC, Hatfield KP. History of chronic toxicity and animal carcinogenicity studies for pharmaceuticals. Vet Pathol 2013;50(2):324–33 <https://journals.sagepub.com/doi/pdf/10.1177/0300985812450727>.

[13] ICH 2009. ICH Harmonised Tripartite Guideline M3(R2), nonclinical safety studies for the conduct of human clinical trials and marketing authorization or pharmaceuticals, M3 (R2), 2009. <https://database.ich.org/sites/default/files/M3_R2__Guideline.pdf>.

[14] Vargesson N. Thalidomide-induced teratogenesis: history and mechanisms. Birth Defects Res C Embryo Today 2015;105(2):140–56 <https://www.ncbi.nlm.nih.gov/pmc/articles/PMC4737249/>.

[15] Ridings JE. The thalidomide disaster, lessons from the past. Methods Mol Biol 2013;947:575–86.

[16] Thomann KD. Die Contergan-Katastrophe. DÄ 2007;104(41):A2778–82 <https://www.aerzteblatt.de/pdf.asp?id = 57224>.

[17] Van Norman GA. Limitations of animal studies for predicting toxicity in clinical trials. Is it time to rethink our current approach? JACC Basic Transl Sci 2019;4(7):845–54 <https://reader.elsevier.com/reader/sd/pii/S2452302X1930316X?token = 1617DBA9119DF789D489530BD836D626CA51FE8916D795F36E1F5EBD777ECE302AF10155A8C00DE6B2518B71201D0A36>.

[18] Suntharalingam G, Perry MR, Ward S, et al. Cytokine storm in a phase 1 trial of the anti-CD28 monoclonal antibody TGN1412. N Engl J Med 2006;355(10):1018–28. Available from: https://www.nejm.org/doi/pdf/10.1056/NEJMoa063842?articleTools = true.

[19] Attarwala H. TGN1412: from discovery to disaster. J Young Pharm 2010;2(3):332–6.

[20] Van Norman GA. Limitations of animal studies for predicting toxicity in clinical trials. Part 2: potential alternatives to the use of animals in preclinical trials. JACC Basic Transl Sci 2020;5(4):387–97 <https://reader.elsevier.com/reader/sd/pii/S2452302X20301261?token = 12679F4264042DD2551E276394996BD86CECE9488DA8BBEBF6E304C710692B0B1B8AF7525B65F1ABEAE71F1FD8402E7E>.

[21] Bailey J, Thew M, Balls M. An analysis of the use of animal models in predicting human toxicology and drug safety. Altern Lab Anim 2014;42:189–99.

[22] Bailey J, Thew M, Balls M. Predicting human drug toxicity and safety via animal tests: can any one species predict drug toxicity in any other, and do monkeys help? Altern Lab Anim 2015;43:393–403.

[23] Balls M, Bailey J, Combes RD. How viable are alternatives to animal testing in determining the toxicities of therapeutic drugs? Expert Opin Drug Metab Toxicol 2019;15(12):985–7.

[24] Everitt JI. The future of preclinical animal models in pharmaceutical discovery and development: a need to bring in cerebro to the in vivo discussions. Toxicol Pathol 2015;43(1):70–7.

[25] AAP. Guidelines for the ethical conduct of studies to evaluate drugs in pediatric populations, committee on drugs 1995 Am Acad Pediatrics, Pediatrics 1995;95(2):286–94.

[26] Hirschfeld S. History of Pediatric Labeling. <https://www.slideserve.com/marlin/history-of-pediatric-labeling>.

[27] Hirschfeld S, Saint-Raymond A. Pediatric regulatory initiatives. Handb Exp Pharmacol 2011;205:245–68 556.

[28] Kearns GL, Abdel-Rahman SM, Alander SW, Blowey DL, Leeder JS, Kauffman RE. Developmental pharmacology - drug disposition, action, and therapy in infants and children. N Engl J Med 2003;349(12):1157–67 <https://pdfs.semanticscholar.org/55f8/1745303e9aaec7f4cb85f0b5921eec14a9c0.pdf>.

[29] Rose K, Neubauer D, Grant-Kels JM. Rational use of medicine in children – the conflict of interests story. A review. Rambam Maimonides Med J 2019;10(3):e0018. Available from: https://doi.org/10.5041/RMMJ.10371 Review <https://www.rmmj.org.il/userimages/928/2/PublishFiles/953Article.pdf>.

[30] Rose K, Grant-Kels JM. The meanings of "pediatric drug development". A review. Ther Innov Regul Sci 2019;53(6):767–74.

[31] Rose K. The challenges of pediatric drug development. Curr Ther Res Clin Exp 2019 <https://doi.org/10.1016/j.curtheres.2019.01.007>.

[32] Rose K, Neubauer D, Grant-Kels JM. Ethical issues in pediatric regulatory studies involving placebo treatment. J Pediatr Epilepsy 2020; eFirst <https://doi.org/10.1055/s-0040-1712147>.

[33] Rose K, Grant-Kels JM. Pediatric melanoma – the whole (conflicts of interest) story. Int J Womens Dermatol 2018;5(2):110–15. Available from: https://doi.org/10.1016/j.ijwd.2018.10.020 <https://www.ncbi.nlm.nih.gov/pmc/articles/PMC6451736/pdf/main.pdf>.

[34] Duarte DM. Use of juvenile animal studies to support oncology medicine development in children. Reprod Toxicol 2015;56:97–104.

[35] Carleer J, Karres J. Juvenile animal studies and pediatric drug development: a European regulatory perspective. Birth Defects Res B Dev Reprod Toxicol 2011;92(4):254–60.

[36] Silva-Lima B, Due Theilade-Thomsen M, Carleer J, et al. Juvenile animal studies for the development of paediatric medicines: a description and conclusions from a European Medicines Agency workshop on juvenile animal testing for nonclinical assessors. Birth Defects Res B Dev Reprod Toxicol 2010;89(6):467–73.

[37] Barrow PC, Schmitt G. Juvenile Nonclinical Safety Studies in Support of Pediatric Drug Development. Methods Mol Biol 2017;1641:25–67.

[38] Tassinari MS, Benson K, Elayan I, et al. Juvenile animal studies and pediatric drug development retrospective review: use in regulatory decisions and labeling. Birth Defects Res B Dev Reprod Toxicol 2011;92(4):261–5.

[39] Fisher Jr JE, Ravindran A, Elayan I. CDER experience with juvenile animal studies for CNS drugs. Int J Toxicol 2019;38(2):88–95 <https://journals.sagepub.com/doi/pdf/10.1177/1091581818824313>.

[40] EMA 2017. Results of juvenile animal studies (JAS) and impact on anti-cancer medicine development and use in childrenProject report. <https://www.ema.europa.eu/en/documents/scientific-guideline/results-juvenile-animal-studies-jas-impact-anti-cancer-medicine-development-use-children_en.pdf>.

[41] Schmitt G, Ridings J, De Schaepdrijver L, et al. Nonclinical safety considerations for the development of pediatric-first. Drugs: An Ind View Ther Innov Regul Sci 2016;50(5):632–8.

[42] Visalli T, Bower N, Kokate T, et al. Lack of value of juvenile animal toxicity studies for supporting the safety of pediatric oncology phase I trials. Regul Toxicol Pharmacol 2018;96:167–77.

[43] FDA 2019. Considerations for the Inclusion of Adolescent Patients in Adult Oncology Clinical Trials. Guidance for Industry. https://www.fda.gov/media/113499/download.

[44] Sparkling Wine (Winzersekt): not only for individualists. <https://www.germanwines.de/knowledge/wine-more/sparkling-sekt/>.

[45] The University of Chicago 2012. Milton Friedman in his own words. <https://mfidev.uchicago.edu/about/tribute/mfquotes.shtml>.

Chapter 8

Child-friendly formulations: tablets, quick-dissolving formulations, liquids, and more

Introduction

Children up to the age of roughly six years, and senior patients, specifically those with neurodegenerative diseases, cannot swallow tablets or pills. Drugs given to very young and very old patients must be given in another form, mostly as liquids or, increasingly, as a quick-dissolving (orodispersible) tablet, dispersing rapidly when put on the oral mucosa. Altogether, such formulations are called "pediatric" or "child-friendly" formulations. [1,2] There are also many healthy adults that have serious problems swallowing pills or tablets. Pediatric formulations available in the United States are generally liquids or powders for reconstitution. They require purified water and refrigeration, both of which are not guaranteed in the developing world or in developed countries in the case of natural disasters. Extemporaneous formulations are a common workaround for the lack of commercially available preparations, but there are challenges regarding lack of dose accuracy, stability, and consistency in preparation. [3]

Probably, the obligation to develop child-friendly formulations for all drugs is the most reasonable part of pediatric legislation. That babies, infants, and young children cannot chew from birth on, do not have teeth yet, and cannot process or digest solid food during their first years of life is well-known by anybody who has raised children. We associate with the terms "child" or "pediatric" mostly in this period of time when children still depend of specific food preparations by the parents, other family members, or servants; but the role of servants has declined in developed countries. In the context of child-friendly formulations the term "child" is used with the meaning of small, sweet, young, and vulnerable young humans. But in the overall term of "pediatric drug development," the two meanings of the term child are blurred. Eight- or ten-year-old school children no longer need child-friendly formulations of medicines, at least no more than adults that cannot swallow tablets. [4–8]

Considering the Patient in Pediatric Drug Development. DOI: https://doi.org/10.1016/B978-0-12-823888-2.00026-0

Before World War II, there was a lack of formulations suitable for persons than could not swallow pills or tablets. But there was also a lack of effective medicines in general. In these days, all pharmacists were trained as compounding pharmacists. Most drugs these days were not mass-produced. Instead, pharmacists had to prepare medications based on physicians' orders or prescriptions. In the 1930s, about three-quarters of all prescriptions in the US were compounded. The art and science of compounding was taught in all pharmacy schools as part of the pharmacy curriculum. Industrial production and emerging drug development have significantly changed the practice of pharmacy and the need for compounded medications. By the 1970s, less than 1% of prescriptions were still compounded. The focus for pharmacists shifted to dispensing and advising patients. [9] Provision of compounded pediatric formulations was, for a period of time, the last large area where the arts of compounding by the pharmacist still used to play a major role. [10]

The EU pediatric regulation and child-friendly formulations

When companies develop new drugs, today part of this development is the submission of a pediatric investigation plan (PIP) to the EU EMA. This PIP has to "propose" preclinical safety studies in young animals, "pediatric" clinical studies, and the development of child-friendly formulations. "Propose" is in quotation marks because if the EMA is not satisfied with the "proposed" studies, it will reject the entire PIP and the approval of the drug is blocked in the EU. "Pediatric" clinical studies must consider all patients aged from birth to 17 years old; these clinical studies are partially truly pediatric studies, partially studies in young persons that bodily are no longer children, but they are still "children" administratively, while their body is already mature.

The European Paediatric Formulation Initiative (EuPFI) was established in 2007 in parallel to the enacting of the EU pediatric regulation, [11,12] which in turn had been triggered by the enacting of the first US pediatric laws since 1997. [4–8,13] While for many years usually new drugs reached the market only in solid forms, the pediatric laws have forced companies increasingly to provide new drugs also in liquid or other formulations that can be administered to rather young patients, and hence also to seniors. [2,3]

In young children, one major reason the child rejects a given medication is because it is not yet able to override the reflex of spitting out anything that does not taste well. Adults know that medicine often does not taste well, and often they even expect a bad taste. [1,2] An essential part of formulation development is taste masking.

The EMA published in 2006 a "Reflection paper on the formulations of choice of children," in 2013 a "Guideline on pharmaceutical development of medicines for pediatric use," and furthermore give an overview of "pediatric" formulation requirements. [14–16] The EMA documents address the challenges of pediatric formulations in young and very young children. The terms "formulations of choice of children" and "pharmaceutical development of medicines for pediatric use" are both misleading, as they only cover a limited part of the administratively defined "pediatric population." [4–8] So far, overviews over "pediatric formulations" have not yet addressed this misleading use of the terms "pediatric" and "child/children." [1,3,10,11,17–20] There are several textbooks on pediatric formulations and pediatric dosings. [21–23] As these address pediatric healthcare professionals that only see young patients, for these books and the involved healthcare professionals this blur does not play a major role. But even a medical textbook from 2014 that addresses pediatric formulations within the framework of drug development did not address this blur. [2]

Excipients

Drug treatment depends not only on the drug substance itself, but also on ingredients forming medicines (excipients). The choice and the composition of excipients are crucial factors to be considered in developing child-friendly formulations. Excipient safely and commonly used in adults' therapy could be harmful for small and very small children. Alcohol or propylene glycol cause neurotoxicity; furthermore, some preservatives may lead to allergic reactions. Another questionable issue is the utilization of parabens in young children. The most common polymers used for obtaining modified release (MR) formulations are cellulose derivatives utilized as coating polymers, taste-masking agents, or a microparticles matrix. Ethylcellulose as a biocompatible and gastro resistant polymer is used for preparing sustained-release sirup with hydrocodone and chlorpheniramine indicated for children above six years of age. Ethylcellulose in aqueous suspension form was also used for formulating modified-release microspheres with mirabegron by a spray-drying technique to obtain sustained-release suspensions. Most cellulose derivatives are generally recognized as safe (GRAS) for use in pharmacotherapy of young patients. [24] However, for most excipients used in pediatric formulations, safety data are still limited. The EMA guidelines demand to assess the safety profile of excipients, so the presented data must be actualized, related to the age group, and relevant to the maximum daily exposure uptake. [3,25,26]

Major advances in child-friendly formulations and future trends

New techniques include multiparticulate modified-release solid dosage forms, minitablets, tablets that dissolve immediately in the oral mucosa (orodispersible formulations), [3,25] orally disintegrating mini tablets, [26] and three-dimensional (3D) printing. [25] Pharmaceutical use of 3D printing has increased over the past years to develop oral dosage forms with MR. The main idea in using 3D printing revolves around the aim to develop pharmaceuticals to meet personalization needs also of young patients. 3D printing was utilized to create a multiactive solid dosage form with five different drugs within the same capsule with two separate release profiles, called Polypill, which would be especially useful for patients who must take several drugs several times a day. The culmination of 3D printing applications in oral dosage forms was the FDA approval in 2015 of 3D printed levetiracetam (spritam) tablets for oral suspension, the first 3D-printed FDA-approved drug as a prescription adjunctive therapy for treating patients with epilepsy from the age of four years old (or more than 20 kg). The technology enables immediate disintegration of the drug with a sip of water, making it easy to administer, even in high doses. ZipDose technology creates a porous formulation using a 3D process that binds powders without compression. [25]

Negotiations about which excipients are safe for younger patients is one of the key negotiations between drug developer and regulatory authorities in "pediatric" drug development. [2]

Conflicts of interest

Although the demand for pediatric formulations is the only area within "pediatric drug development" that has contributed and continues to contribute to better healthcare for very young and very old patients, it is not free of conflicts of interest. In reviews by representatives of EuPFI and in other overviews over pediatric formulations the overarching concept of "pediatric drug development" is presented as an overall positive concept. [1,11,12,25,26]

A paper discussing the situation of pediatric healthcare in Canada on the background of pediatric formulation issues asks for the Canadian federal government to "support paediatric drug trials." [10] Representatives of the UK regulatory authority should no longer be allowed to present PIP case studies as if these were academically acceptable development plans. [11] Pharmaceutical companies are forced to submit PIPs under the threat of nonapproval of their new drugs in the EU. [4–8] EuPFI is supported by a number of pharmaceutical companies. [12] For academic pharmaceutical researchers, these funds are welcome to support their research activities, but these funds are not neutral.

Challenges during development

As the development of pediatric formulations with optimized properties for the market is often challenging, preliminary "enabling" formulations are often used in early pediatric studies prior to the introduction of final market formulations in the confirmatory study or studies. Supportive clinical studies on the bioavailability of the final market formulation as compared to the preliminary enabling formulation may be required to bridge from adult and/or enabling formulations to the final pediatric formulation. [3,27]

Discussion and conclusion

As far as young and very young children are concerned, the demand to develop child-friendly or pediatric formulations is the only part of the EU pediatric regulation that has contributed to improved child healthcare. That in the past for many drugs no child-friendly formulations were commercially available was a challenge to all parents, pediatricians, healthcare professionals, and specifically pharmacists, resulting in the necessary assignment of vast resources to in-house compounding. Such compounding, however, had often the challenge of lack of stability data. Nevertheless, most discussions and presentations on the advances in pharmaceutical formulation development are presented in a way that shows that the presenters are unaware of the blur between the US and EU pediatric legislation in using the terms "child" and "pediatric." [3,10,11,17–20,25] It would be desirable for the EuPFI to assume for future meetings a more neutral position also towards the EMA. [28]

References

[1] Hanning SM, Lopez FL, Wong IC, et al. Patient centric formulations for paediatrics and geriatrics: similarities and differences. Int J Pharm 2016;512(2):355–9. Available from: 10.1016/j.ijpharm.2016.03.017.

[2] Bar-Shalom D, Rose K. Pediatric formulations – A roadmap. New York, USA: AAPS Press & Springer; 2014. Free download of introduction ("preface"), sample pages, and tables of contents. Available from: https://www.springer.com/gp/book/9781489980106.

[3] Zajicek A, Fossler MJ, Barrett JS, et al. A report from the pediatric formulations task force: perspectives on the state of child-friendly oral dosage forms. AAPS J 2013;15 (4):1072–81.

[4] Rose K, Neubauer D, Grant-Kels JM. Rational use of medicine in children – the conflict of interests story. A review Rambam Maimonides Med J 2019;10(3):e0018 Review. Available from: 10.5041/RMMJ.10371; https://wwwrmmj.org.il/userimages/928/2/PublishFiles/953Article.pdf.

[5] Rose K, Grant-Kels JM. Pediatric melanoma – the whole (conflicts of interest) story. Int J Womens Dermatol 2018;5(2):110–15. Available from: 10.1016/j.ijwd.2018.10.020; https://wwwncbi.nlm.nih.gov/pmc/articles/PMC6451736/pdf/main.pdf.

[6] Rose K, Grant-Kels JM. The meanings of "pediatric drug development" A Review Ther Innov Regul Sci 2019;53(6):767–74.

[7] Rose K. The challenges of pediatric drug development. Curr Ther Res Clin Exp 2019. Available from: https://doi.org/10.1016/j.curtheres.2019.01.007.

[8] Rose K, Neubauer D, Grant-Kels JM. Ethical issues in pediatric regulatory studies involving placebo treatment J Pediatr Epilepsy 2020;eFirst. Available from: https://doi.org/10.1055/s-0040-1712147.

[9] McElhiney LF. Compounding for children: the compounding pharmacist. In: Bar-Shalom D, Rose K, editors. Pediatric Formulations – A Roadmap. New York, USA: AAPS Press & Springer; 2014. p. 329–34. chapter 22.

[10] McLaughlin T, Jong G, Gilpin A, et al. Pharmacare in Canada: the paediatric perspective. Paediatr Child Health 2020;25(2):113–24. Available from: 10.1093/pch/pxz176.

[11] Salunke S, Tuleu C. Formulating better medicines for children-still too far to walk. Int J Pharm 2016;511(2):1124–6.
[12] European Paediatric Formulation Initiative (*EuPFI*) www.eupfi.org.
[13] Hirschfeld S, Saint-Raymond A. Pediatric regulatory initiatives. Handb Exp Pharmacol 2011;205:245–68.
[14] EMA 2006. Reflection paper on the formulations of choice of children. https://www.ema.europa.eu/en/documents/scientific-guideline/reflection-paper-formulations-choice-paediatric-population_en.pdf.
[15] EMA 2013. Guideline on pharmaceutical development of medicines for paediatric use. https://www.ema.europa.eu/en/documents/scientific-guideline/guideline-pharmaceutical-development-medicines-paediatric-use_en.pdf.
[16] EMA 2020. Paediatric formulations. https://www.ema.europa.eu/en/human-regulatory/research-development/paediatric-medicines/paediatric-investigation-plans/paediatric-formulations.
[17] Salunke S, Liu F, Batchelor H, et al. European paediatric formulation initiative (EuPFI)-formulating ideas for better medicines for children. AAPS PharmSciTech 2017;18(2):257–62. Available from: 10.1208/s12249-016-0584-1 Epub 2016 Jul 15.
[18] Salunke S, Tuleu C. Formulating better medicines for children-collaborate to innovate. Int J Pharm 2018;536(2):487–9. Available from: 10.1016/j.ijpharm.2017.08.009.
[19] Ivanovska V, Rademaker CMA, van Dijk L, et al. Pediatric formulations: a review of challenges and progress. Pediatrics 2014;134(2):361–72.
[20] Hepburn CM, Gilpin A, Autmizguine J, et al. Improving paediatric medications: a prescription for Canadian children and youth. Paediatr Child Health 2019;24(5):333–9.
[21] Jew RK, Soo-hoo W, Erush SC. Extemporaneous formulations for pediatric, geriatric, and special needs patients. 2nd edition Bethesda, MD, USA: American Society of Health-System Pharmacists; 2010.
[22] Nahat M.C., Pai V.B. (Editors). Pediatric drug formulations. Cincinatti, OH, USA, 2014.
[23] Taketomo C.K., Hodding J.H., Kraus D.M. Lexi-comp's pediatric dosage handbook with international trade names index: including neonatal dosing, drug administration, and extemporaneous preparations. Hudson, OH, USA, 2010, 17th ed.
[24] FDA 2019. Generally recognized as safe (GRAS). https://www.fda.gov/food/food-ingredients-packaging/generally-recognized-safe-gras.
[25] Trofimiuk M, Wasilewska K, Winnicka K. How to modify drug release in paediatric dosage forms? Novel technologies and modern approaches with regard to children's population. Int J Mol Sci 2019;20(13):3200. Available from: https://www.mdpi.com/1422-0067/20/13/3200.
[26] Comoglu T, Ozyilmaz ED. Orally disintegrating tablets and orally disintegrating mini tablets - novel dosage forms for pediatric use. Pharm Dev Technol 2019;24(7):902–14.
[27] Ricci BM. Bridging studies in support of oral pediatric formulation development. Int J Pharm 2013;457(1):323–6.
[28] EuPFI 2020. EuPFI 2020 virtual conference http://www.eupfi.org/upcoming-conference/12th-eupfi-conference-virtual/

Chapter 9

What do young patients really need?

Introduction

This book has led the reader through many clinical areas where clinical specialists, representatives of regulatory authorities and of pharmaceutical companies declare that too few "pediatric" studies had been performed in the past, that too many "children" are treated off-label, and that off-label treatment put "children" in danger. The only clinical area that truly deals day and night exclusively with children is neonatology. But neonatology emerged like pediatric oncology decades before the term "off-label" was used a first time [1]. Both pediatric oncology and neonatology were pioneering disciplines in the beginning. Both emerged independently from the influence of regulatory authorities. While pediatric oncology had at the beginning the advantage that its most relevant drugs, chemotherapeutic agents, were already used and FDA-approved since many years in adult cancer types [2], neonatology had other initial conditions. In early neonatology, the availability of antibiotics was crucial, as was the availability of thermoregulation, oxygen, incubators, and other mechanical tools [3–5].

Pediatric legislation

That the FDA tried to catch up with pediatric oncology, neonatology, and many other clinical pediatric subspecialties was not the result of sudden, independent tragedies in many individual pediatric areas, respectively, but resulted from the adoption of the children-are-therapeutic-orphans concept that became a mantra [6–9]. It was partially imposed by the FDA and partially adopted by leading representatives of many clinical subdisciplines who thought and hoped that finally they had found a powerful institution that would be able to promote their respective discipline and/or subdiscipline. Stepwise, the regulatory logic of "pediatric drug development" has also invaded leading representatives of pharmaceutical industry [10–14].

The only ones that did not profit from the sudden maelstrom of "pediatric" studies were the young patients themselves. The quality of pediatric healthcare has constantly improved during the last century. Primarily not

Considering the Patient in Pediatric Drug Development. DOI: https://doi.org/10.1016/B978-0-12-823888-2.00023-5

through better information in drug labels, but because better drugs were developed, because physicians and healthcare professionals developed a more collaborative attitude toward parents, because better guidelines were written, because the dosing in young patients became better defined, because pediatric formulations for very young patients became mandatory, and because the training and qualification of physicians and other healthcare professionals improved constantly.

Most drugs work in the same way in old, young, and very young children, such as vaccines and antiinfectives against bacteria, viruses, and fungi. Some diseases require a certain level of maturity of the body, such as multiple sclerosis, depression, or other psychiatric diseases. Babies cry a lot, but they are not depressive. Other diseases can begin at birth or even already in utero, such as epilepsy. Some diseases are much rarer in young patients, such as hypertension, which mostly develops in later age when the arteries become more rigid. However, pediatric hypertension exists [15,16]. Often, but not always, it is connected with obesity. However, antihypertensive drugs do not change their mode of action with the patient's 17th or 18th birthday.

Clinical studies to prove safety and efficacy of new drugs became the basis of drug approval with the efficacy amendment of 1962 to the Federal Food, Drug, and Cosmetic Act [17]. This was a very successful step in drug development and has become a principle that today is recognized and in force worldwide [18].

The adoption of the children-are-therapeutic-orphans concept and its becoming law in the US had led to a unprecedented increase of pediatric clinical studies since 1997 [19]. However, as shown in the preceding chapters, most of these studies lack medical, clinical, and scientific sense. They repeat proof of efficacy in young patients. In some areas, drugs have not been approved in "children." This is probably in all such areas due to the artificial definition of the inclusion criteria into the "pediatric" studies that usually included many young patients that were bodily already mature. Where "pediatric" studies compare to no treatment at all by placebo [9,20] or to outdated treatment, they harm young patients [21]. The EU pediatric regulation has amplified the demand for "pediatric" studies into areas where the FDA has no authority to mandate "pediatric" studies, exaggerating the "pediatric" demands in its "pediatric investigation plans" (PIPs) to a degree that finally led to the detection of the lack of sense of the entire "pediatric drug development" movement [6–9,21–23].

Reasonable studies

When the bodies of young people become mature, they need corresponding doses [6–9,21–24]. When they are still young and small but are no longer babies, they need smaller doses than adults. To find out these doses, we do not need separate approval of drugs in "children" and separate multicenter international regulatory dose-finding studies. Today's techniques of clinical pharmacology such as modeling and simulation, physiology-based pharmacokinetics (PK) and pharmacodynamics (PD), and more allow calculation of future doses. To confirm these doses, "opportunistic" studies in small studies in a few centers are sufficient [25,26]. If there are safety concerns, registries are much better to detect adverse events as registries cover a much higher number of patients than can be covered in regulatory "pediatric" studies.

Entire generations of pediatric researchers have been taught in their training about the holy grail of "evidence-based medicine" [27–30]. The debate on how to return to common sense will take time. Potential risks of new drugs and potential benefits need to be balanced. The moment clinical details are discussed, things become more complicated than one would think in the beginning.

The debate how to proceed will hopefully be controversial and candid. Hopefully, patient advocacy groups and parents will join the overdue discussion.

Conclusions

Industrial drug development started a bit more than half a century ago. It helped to trigger the emergence of entire new clinical disciplines and subdisciplines, including neonatology, developmental pharmacology, and pediatric oncology. Once it is broadly recognized that strong conflicts of interest have driven many of the main protagonists of "pediatric drug development" [31], a constructive debate will be possible.

Separate approval of drugs in adults and "children," defined by an administrative age limit, was and is a historical mistake that needs to be corrected. Companies should perform reasonable studies combined in adults and young patients as far as this is possible. Drugs should be approved for human beings. If there are specific safety concerns, this could and should be put into the label. Where there are safety concerns that need to be investigated, registries should be organized. Mistakes such as the warnings against the use of antidepressants in young patients or the nonapproval of antidiabetic drugs in "children" by the FDA need to be corrected [6–9,32]. Exaggerated demands for studies in juvenile animals need to be downsized, as well as exaggerated regulatory demands for pediatric formulations.

Drug development is historically still comparatively young. The entire medical disaster described in this book can be seen a "pediatric" disease of drug development in general. It resulted from learning about absorption, distribution, metabolism, and excretion of food and drug in very young humans and was in the years and decades thereafter exposed to systematic exaggerations that were partially based on hidden conflicts of interest. In the interest of scientific honesty and to restore public trust in science and authorities, this will need to be addressed candidly. Independent academic centers will have to reanalyze the data collected in this book. Furthermore, there are many more clinical areas that need further in-depth analysis.

The described "pediatric" disease of drug development will not kill the patient. Drug development needs to become mature. One of the many challenges in drug development is the constant criticism that commercial drug development is greedy. Commerce in its entirety is greedy. We live in this world, and we have to find mechanisms and ways to prevent damage by too much greed.

Steps toward maturity in drug development will help patients, advance healthcare, and boost the economy. We live in a free society. It is good that candid criticism is no longer answered by the threat of torture and death on the stake.

References

[1] Plate V. The impact of off-label, compassionate and unlicensed use on health care laws in preselected countries. <http://hss.ulb.uni-bonn.de/2009/1936/1936.pdf>.

[2] Adamson PC. Improving the outcome for children with cancer: development of targeted new agents. CA Cancer J Clin 2015;65(3):212–20.

[3] Jorgensen AM. Born in the USA – The history of neonatology in the United States: a century of caring. <http://images.abbottnutrition.com/ANHI/MEDIA/Nurse%20Currents%20NICU%20History%20June%202010.pdf>.

[4] Philip AG. The evolution of neonatology. Pediatr Res 2005;58(4):799–815. <https://www.nature.com/articles/pr2005743.pdf?origin = ppub>.

[5] Vidyasagar D. "Half a century of evolution of neonatology: a witness's story": Dr. K.C. Chaudhuri lifetime achievement award oration delivered at AIIMS, New Delhi on 7th September 2014. Indian J Pediatr 2015;82(12):1117–25. Available from: https://doi.org/10.1007/s12098-015-1838-8.

[6] Rose K, Neubauer D, Grant-Kels JM. Rational use of medicine in children – The conflict of interests story. A review. Rambam Maimonides Med J 2019;10(3):e0018 Review. Available from: https://doi.org/10.5041/RMMJ.10371. <https://www.rmmj.org.il/userimages/928/2/PublishFiles/953Article.pdf>.

[7] Rose K, Grant-Kels JM. The meanings of "pediatric drug development" A Review Ther Innov Regul Sci 2019;53(6):767–74.

[8] Rose K. The challenges of pediatric drug development. Curr Ther Res Clin Exp 2019. Available from: https://doi.org/10.1016/j.curtheres.2019.01.007.

[9] Rose K, Neubauer D, Grant-Kels JM. Ethical issues in pediatric regulatory studies involving placebo treatment. J Pediatr Epilepsy 2020. <https://www.researchgate.net/publication/342200539_Ethical_Issues_in_Pediatric_Regulatory_Studies_Involving_Placebo_Treatment>.

[10] Severin T, Corriol-Rohou S, Bucci-Rechtweg C, et al. How is the pharmaceutical industry structured to optimize pediatric drug development? Existing pediatric structure models and proposed recommendations for structural enhancement. Ther Innov Regul Sci 2020. Available from: https://doi.org/10.1007/s43441-020-00116-4.

[11] Barrett JS, Bishai R, Bucci-Rechtweg C, et al. Challenges and opportunities in the development of medical therapies for pediatric populations and the role of extrapolation. Clin Pharmacol Ther 2018;103(3):419–33. Available from: https://doi.org/10.1002/cpt.1000 Epub 2018 Jan 31.

[12] Mulberg AE, Bucci-Rechtweg C, Giuliano J, et al. Regulatory strategies for rare diseases under current global regulatory statutes: a discussion with stakeholders. Orphanet J Rare Dis 2019;14(1):36. <https://ojrd.biomedcentral.com/track/pdf/10.1186/s13023-019-1017-5>.

[13] Bucci-Rechtweg CM, Ward RM. Tiny and forgotten: A call for focused neonatal policy reform. Ther Innov Regul Sci 2019;53(5):615–17.

[14] McCune S, Portman R. Innovation and opportunities in pediatric therapeutic development. Ther Innov Regul Sci 2019;53(5):564–6.

[15] Guzman-Limon M, Samules J. Pediatric hypertension. Diagnosis, evaluation, and treatment. Pediatr Clin North Am 2019;66(1):45–57.

[16] Taylor-Zapata P, Baker-Smith CM, Burckart G, et al. Research gaps in primary pediatric hypertension. Pediatrics 2019;143(5):e20183517. <https://www.ncbi.nlm.nih.gov/pmc/articles/PMC6564054/pdf/PEDS_20183517.pdf>.

[17] Janssen WM. A historical perspective on off-label medicine: from regulation, promotion, and the first amendment to the next frontiers. Food and Drug Law Institute, Levy MC (Editor). First Washington, D.C., USA *Off-Label Communications* (2008).

[18] Rägo L, Santo B. Drug regulation: history, present and future. In: van Boxtel CJ, Santo B, Edwards IR, editors. Drug Benefits and Risks: International Textbook of Clinical Pharmacology, Revised. 2nd edition Uppsala, Sweder: IOS Press & Uppsala Monitoring Centre; 2008. p. 65–77. chapter 6. <https://www.who.int/medicines/technical_briefing/tbs/Drug_Regulation_History_Present_Future.pdf>.

[19] Hirschfeld S, Saint-Raymond A. Pediatric regulatory initiatives. Handb Exp Pharmacol 2011;205:245–68.

[20] Waubant E, Banwell B, Wassmer E, Sormani MP, Amato MP, Hintzen R, et al. Clinical trials of disease-modifying agents in pediatric MS: opportunities, challenges, and recommendations from the IPMSSG. Neurology. 2019.

[21] Rose K, Grant-Kels JM. Pediatric melanoma – the whole (conflicts of interest) story. Int J Womens Dermatol 2018;5(2):110–15. Available from: https://doi.org/10.1016/j.ijwd.2018.10.020. <https://www.ncbi.nlm.nih.gov/pmc/articles/PMC6451736/pdf/main.pdf>.

[22] Rose K, Grant-Kels JM. Questionable international pediatric studies in the United States and Russia triggered by regulatory authorities. Asian J Res Med Pharm Sci 2018;3(3). <http://www.journalrepository.org/media/journals/AJRIMPS_63/2018/Apr/Rose332018AJRIMPS40776.pdf>.

[23] Rose K, Grant-Kels JM. Questionable industry-sponsored pediatric studies in China triggered by United States of America (US) and European Union (EU) regulatory authorities. SF Pharma J 2018;1:1. <https://www.scifedpublishers.com/open-access/questionable-industry-sponsored-pediatric-studies-in-china-triggeredby-united-states-of-america-us-and-european-union-eu-regulatoryauthorities.pdf>.

[24] Momper JD, Mulugeta Y, Green DJ, et al. Adolescent dosing and labeling since the food and drug administration amendments Act of 2007. JAMA Pediatr 2013;167(10):926–32.

[25] Gonzalez D, Melloni C, Yogev R, et al. Use of opportunistic clinical data and a population pharmacokinetic model to support dosing of clindamycin for premature infants to adolescents. Clin Pharmacol Ther 2014;96(4):429–37.

[26] Laughon MM, Benjamin DK. Mechanisms to provide safe and effective drugs for children. Pediatrics. 2014;134(2):e562–3.

[27] Sackett DL, Rosenberg WM, Gray JA, et al. Evidence based medicine: what it is and what it isn't. BMJ 1996;312(7023):71–2. <https://www.ncbi.nlm.nih.gov/pmc/articles/PMC2349778/pdf/bmj00524-0009.pdf>.

[28] Tebala GD. The emperor's new clothes: a critical appraisal of evidence-based medicine. Int J Med Sci 2018;15. <https://www.medsci.org/v15p1397.pdf>.

[29] Greenhalgh T, Howick J, Maskrey N. Evidence based medicine renaissance group. Version 2. BMJ. 2014;348:g3725.

[30] Djulbegovic B, Guyatt GH. Progress in evidence-based medicine: a quarter century on. Lancet. 2017;390(10092):415–23.

[31] Ward RM, Benjamin Jr DK, Davis JM, Gorman RL, Kauffman R, Kearns GL, et al. The need for pediatric drug development. J Pediatr 2018;192:13–21.

[32] Rose K, Neubauer D, Grant-Kels JM. Too many avoidable suicides occur worldwide in young patients. A review. Rambam Maimonides Med J 2019. <https://www.rmmj.org.il/userimages/965/1/PublishFiles/977OnlineFirst.pdf>.

Index

Note: Page numbers followed by "*f*" and "*t*" refer to figures and tables, respectively.

D

E

Kolibri 360 GmbH
Ferdinand-Jühlke-Straße 7
99095 Erfurt, Deutschland
produktsicherheit@kolibri360.de